Tragedy

The most profound question to be asked of a civilization is in what form it experiences its tragedies.

George Lukács

Tragedy

VISION AND FORM

SECOND EDITION

Robert W. Corrigan

THE UNIVERSITY OF WISCONSIN—MILWAUKEE

1817

HARPER & ROW, PUBLISHERS, New York
Cambridge, Hagerstown, Philadelphia, San Francisco,
London, Mexico City, São Paulo, Sydney

Sponsoring Editor: Phillip Leininger
Project Editor: Jo-Ann Goldfarb
Production Manager: Marion A. Palen
Compositor: TriStar Graphics
Printer & Binder: Halliday Lithograph Corporation
Cover: Irving Bogen

Tragedy: Vision and Form, Second Edition

Library of Congress Cataloging in Publication Data

Corrigan, Robert Willoughby, 1927–   ed.
   Tragedy, vision and form.

   Bibliography: p.
   1. Tragedy—Collected works.   2. Tragic, The—
Collected works.   I. Title.
PN1892.C58   1981   809.2′512   80–20313
ISBN 0–06–041371–9

For Robert Bechtold Heilman, whose warm and humane scholarship has deepened our understanding of the dramatic forms.

Contents

IX
SOME CLASSICS OF TRAGIC THEORY

Preface

The first edition of this book was published over fifteen years ago (1965). During the subsequent years it had a satisfying, if albeit modest, success. It became a standard reference work in libraries, a volume frequently used by teachers, scholars, and (much to my pleasure) theatre practitioners, and it was almost always mentioned in bibliographies and footnotes as the most ample and wide-ranging collection of essays on tragedy. But, more important, for more than a decade it was a regularly used textbook in countless college courses. As I went about the country, I would invariably meet people who had used the "tragedy anthology" (or its counterpart on comedy) when they were in school.

Thus I was overjoyed when Harper & Row asked me to do a second edition. This would give me an opportunity to reassess the book's contents, to incorporate changes that had been suggested to me over the years, to add some of the important new essays on tragedy that had been written since the first edition appeared, and to revise and expand my introduction to the earlier edition. The problem: what to leave out? The first cuts were easy—no author would be represented by more than one essay. Next, I realized that the section on "The Language of Tragedy" in the original edition was a bit forced and did not work very well, so I decided to eliminate it. Then, there were three essays which I admire very much but which did not seem appropriate or absolutely necessary, so I have omitted them. Finally, there were a number of essays that had either become so readily available or for any number of reasons could not be used in a new edition that they eliminated themselves. However, before commenting on their replacements, let me say a word about the book's organization.

Except for omitting the section on "The Language of Tragedy," I am still satisfied with the organizational plan of the first edition and have repeated it. The nine remaining sections into which I have divided the book probably do not need much explaining. The first five are concerned with the nature of the tragic spirit and the elements of the tragic form, as well as with our response to it. The last four groups cannot be related in this way. The essays on melodrama may be the most important ones in this book because each of them focuses in a different but equally meaningful way on those ideas which most often confuse our thinking about tragedy. There has been precious little written on this subject, and most of what has is not very helpful. The section entitled "The Climates of Tragedy" is particularly concerned with the problems facing the writer of tragedy in our time, and Section VIII is included to reveal how the great tragedies of the past have been reevaluated by the critics of today. Finally, I have included excerpts from four of the great classics of tragic theory both for practical purposes and to provide a comparison to more recent works.

Now, a word about the new material. One of the most obvious weaknesses of the original edition was the absence of essays that approached the subject of tragedy from a Marxist point of view. This has been corrected by including Georg Lukács' classic essay challenging more traditional approaches to tragedy and Raymond Williams' essay on Brecht's attempts to avoid the tragic. A second gap had to be filled. During the years since the book was first published, some of the most important work in dramatic criticism (indeed, all literary criticism) has been done by the French structuralists. Their work on tragedy has been especially illuminating, so I have added selections by Lucien Goldmann and Roland Barthes as examples of this significant new approach to the subject. I have included Lionel Abel's brilliant essay because it is a persuasive challenge to my own point of view, and hence the point of view that governed many of the other choices I made about what should be included in the book. Since the first edition was published, Walter Kerr has written one of the most important books on tragedy and comedy. His views are particularly useful because, as the current dean of American drama critics, his discussion of tragedy has been shaped and tested within the context of current and ongoing theatre practices. The essays by Joyce Carol Oates, Harvey Birenbaum, and Michael Goldman (who I think is one of the most interesting people writing on drama today) are selections from significant new books which have been published in recent years. Finally, I am delighted to include Harold Rosenberg's little known essay on Oedipus and Hamlet. Rosenberg had one of the great critical intelligences of our century, and although he is better known as an art critic (he was for years the art critic of the *New Yorker* magazine), his writing on the drama was imbued with the same kind of critical power.

Finally, I must thank the authors and permission editors of the various publishers with whom I have corresponded. Each of them was most cooperative. Thanks also to Phillip Leininger, the senior editor at Harper & Row who shepherded every step of this new edition, and to my always dependable and cheerful secretary, Margaret Rotter. In the first edition, I acknowledged my gratitude to and admiration for the late John Gassner by dedicating the book to him. Since no one understood the vital and evanescent nature of the theatre better than John, I am sure he would agree that this edition should be dedicated to one who has carried on his work since his death.

Robert W. Corrigan

Introduction

Tragedy and the Tragic Spirit

I. Mystery and the Forms of Drama

The theatre's long history confirms the fact that the stage is a realm of spirits, demons, and primordial gods, of wild fantasy and transcendental aspiration. It is a place of foreboding darkness and brightest light. It is a world of fear and loss and also one of triumph and joyous fulfillment. To enter this world is to enter the realm of mystery.

It is precisely because the theatre does make manifest the other world of mystery that it has always had such a powerful hold upon our imagination. Ultimately, the central concern of all human beings has been to deal with the mysteries of life, with those aspects of the numinous which haunt our experience. While the nature and definition of the numinous may differ from culture to culture and may change from age to age because our experience proves that what was thought to be mysterious need not be so, nonetheless there are certain abiding mysteries in human life which we can never totally understand or explain in rational terms no matter how hard we might try to do so. Life continually mocks the efforts of our intelligence to fathom it fully, and hence its mysteries never cease to haunt our imagination. And it is just because they do haunt us that we inevitably use our imagination in an effort to find some way of dealing with them. We create imaginative constructs which will explain the mysterious in the hopes that by doing so we will be endowed with the power to control it.

One of the most remarkable characteristics of the human imagination is the fact that whenever we confront an unfamiliar situation or enter into an unfamiliar setting or milieu, we invariably perceive it as having a theatrical quality, and we tend to react to it in theatrical terms. When we travel in foreign countries and observe, what is to us, alien behavior, it is almost like watching a play. Even in societies with customs more attuned to our own, we experience the same thing. Whenever we feel that we are outsiders, all unfamiliar customs and behavior will appear to us as theatrical. We are spectators at a play.

But what happens when circumstances make it impossible for us to remain outside the action? That whether we like it or not, we have to give up our spectator role and become a participant. Again, we perceive both ourselves and our behavior in theatrical terms. We become actors; we imitate what we believe is expected behavior as a way of making it our own. Acting is a means of mastering an alien reality. Moreover, we are aware of the many roles—roles which have no sense of innate or necessary consistency—which we play as an actor plays roles. The point is, that the more we think about it, the more aware we become of how

1

much of life is perceived, experienced, and judged in theatrical terms. We are always conscious of the fact that there is a theatricality in all human action.

This explains why one of the oldest metaphors to express the fundamental nature of human experience is voiced by the melancholy Jacques in the well known lines from Shakespeare's *As You Like It:*

> All the world's a stage,
> And all the men and women merely players.

From the beginnings of history and in every known culture, the idea that we play our lives out as if on stage cast in a divinely authored script before an audience of our fellow human beings has been a dominant image of man's view of himself. Even in markedly secular ages, such as our own, the theatrical metaphor has had a persisting power.

The reasons for this are numerous. To begin with, no matter how boldly each of us may assert that "I am the master of my fate; I am the captain of my soul," we are nonetheless haunted by a nagging sense that there are unseen, undefined, or unknowable forces which shape our lives; that there is a script of someone else's making which directs what happens to us. We feel this because no matter how deeply involved we may be in our ordinary, everyday lives we are always aware that somehow our experience is unreal, or at least it could be closer to reality. We are conscious of the fact that no matter how close to other people we may be, we really do not know them; in fact, we feel we can never really know ourselves. This leads us to wonder if there may not be another world that is as valid (or even more valid) than the world we commonly accept as real. Primitive man believed that there was another world—a world of the Gods—which was more real than his. Plato insisted that what we experienced as real was, in fact, only a shadow of a reality which could never be fully known. In the Middle Ages, life was viewed as part of God's grand design which man could never comprehend and would only be revealed to him at Judgment Day. According to Hindu thought, man and the world are but images in God's dream; and consequently, man's sense of reality is nothing but an illusion (*Maya*). The fairy tales of our childhood invariably begin by referring to an earlier time ("Once upon a time") when the Gods walked the earth which was more real than all subsequent history. Even in our rationalistic scientific age, much of our daily experience strikes us as illusory, and we are increasingly conscious of the existence of other realities.

However, thinking this way makes us feel uncomfortable; and while we can acknowledge the theatrical nature of much of our everyday lives, it provokes negative responses within us as well. For example, it is a commonplace observation that people tend to describe, and often judge, everyday experience in terms of the arts. We refer to landscapes as "poetic," or an individual's struggle with adversity as "epic," a beautiful body as "statuesque," graceful movements as "balletic," a woman's beauty as "lyric," a powerful image as "graphic," any kind of happy blending together of diverse elements as "symphonic," and so on. Invariably epithets from the arts tend to have positive and praiseworthy connotations. But just think of those that come from the theatre-related arts! When life experience is described as "theatrical," "operatic," "melodramatic," or "stagey," the connotation is invariably hostile and reveals our feelings that somehow that experience is insincere or inauthentic and therefore not to be trusted. Certainly, when we use such terms or phrases as "acting," "putting on an act," "playing up to," "making a scene," "making a spectacle of oneself," or "playing to the gallery" we are usually indicating some form of disapproval. The pejorative tone of these expressions reveals a deep-seated prejudice against the theatre. Why is this?

On the conscious level it is probably due to the fact that while we can see a certain validity to the idea that life is experienced in theatrical terms, we nonetheless reject it. Ultimately we abhor the thought that we are helpless puppets performing in a play over which we have no control. We really believe that we can and do make choices which alter the direction of our lives. We know that we do have an effect on the lives of other people that cannot be predetermined. While we acknowledge our many different roles in life, we believe there is a unifying consciousness which binds all of those roles together in a meaningful way—that role playing in life is not the same thing as what actors do in the theatre. In short, no matter how apt the idea that "all the world's a stage" may seem, we reject it as an adequate expression of how our life really is. In a sense this is true, but it isn't the whole story. If it were, the theatrical metaphor would have lost its power long ago, and certainly there would be no reason for theatrical terms to have such negative connotations or be indications of such a negative response.

There is probably a deeper and largely unconscious reason for our strongly held prejudice against the theatre, and it has the same roots as those impulses which make the theatre not only attractive but even necessary to our lives. Most of us, most of the time, have of necessity to go about with the business of living without giving too much thought to life's mysteries. There's the house to clean, the job to do, the children to get to school, the car and house to pay for. We haven't time for mysteries. Like the women of Canterbury in T. S. Eliot's play, *Murder in the Cathedral*, we go on "living and partly living" with "our private terrors, our particular shadows, our secret fears." But there is something about those private terrors, particular shadows, and secret fears: they have a way of creeping into our consciousness no matter how busy we are carrying out our mundane daily tasks. They always keep coming back to haunt us. We are all aware of the many ways in which we attempt to escape or to be distracted from their disturbing presence—work, drugs, alcohol, shopping, indiscriminate sex, etc.—and we sometimes try to deal with them in more creative and constructive ways such as entering into some form of psychiatric therapy or sincerely embracing a religious belief.

However, because it is just these terrors, shadows, and fears that are the unique subject matter of the theatre, human beings throughout history have found themselves turning to the theatre as one of the most satisfactory ways of confronting them. But this confrontation is as fearful as it is necessary. It is precisely because the theatre's chief function is to make present mystery, make manifest the unknown or the inexplicable, that it evokes such ambivalent responses within us. And the complexity of these responses is compounded by the very nature of the theatrical medium itself. Unlike the other arts which communicate through inanimate or abstract means (or some combination of the two), the theatre does so primarily through living human beings. Human beings as actors who confront and present mystery at the same time; human beings who are more and less than human; human beings whose feelings and responses are real and not real. Just as we go to the theatre as a way of confronting and dealing with those mysteries that haunt us, so the theatre deals with them in ways that

are haunting. There is something strange and almost ghostly about the whole experience and this accounts for the contradictoriness of our responses to everything related to the theatre. It is this quality of ghostliness which prompts our
fears even as it fulfills our needs. This ambivalence—this combination of attraction and apprehension—is at the heart of our response to the theatrical event.

Thus it is that whenever we go to the theatre, we enter into a situation
where those anxieties provoked by our never resolved confrontations with separation, loss and strangeness come back to haunt us. It is for this reason that the
theatre is often referred to as a realm of mystery. It is a place where those ghosts
which we carry with us all of our lives are made present in such a way that we
can experience them as if directly without having to fear the consequences of
that confrontation. The "as if" is important. Our experience of most events taking place on the stage—even in the frothiest comedy—would at best be anxious-
making, and in most instances would be too difficult to bear if we were dealing
with them directly. But we do not. We are always conscious of the fact that
what's going on only appears to be real. It is all an illusion; it is a representation
of reality, not reality itself; it is make believe. In fact, one of the most interesting
characteristics of theatre is the way it continually draws our attention to its essential theatricality. (The play within the play is a good example.) We tend to
forget that the word "illusion" is derived from the Latin word "to mock." One
of the reasons we experience theatre without directly experiencing fear, pain, or
anxiety is due to the fact that it is always mocking the unreality of its own nature. The theatre can speak the unspeakable and show that which should not be
shown because we are never allowed to forget that we are watching a play with
players playing.

Mention of the "as if" leads us to a discussion of one of the most interesting
yet most frequently misunderstood concepts of theatre: imitation. In his very important book, *Play, Dreams and Imitation in Childhood,* which has shaped so
much of our thinking about developmental psychology in the twentieth century,
the French psychologist Jean Piaget presents overwhelming evidence that we
tend to imitate those things which cause the most ambivalent emotions within
us. His central thesis is that the source of all imitation (and subsequently of all
play and playing) resides in those deeply rooted fears which are derived from
the "ghost reaction" of our infancy when we first became conscious of otherness
and which creates that condition of uncertainty of the self that haunts us for the
rest of our lives. Anthropologists and historians of religion (particularly Claude
Lévi-Strauss and Mircea Eliade) confirm that this pattern of behavior has always
and everywhere been operative and applies as much to the tribes of primitive
cultures—both past and present—as it does to the civilizations of modern man.
Like the infant or the members of a primitive tribe, we imitate the unknown
and the strange as a way of handling the fears which, because of their very
strangeness, they evoke. The rhythm of imitation is fear and aggressive response
and the working out of the rhythm is directly related to others, to spirits, to
ghosts. We imitate the unknown as a way of mastering and gaining dominance
over it. We give form to and identify with our secret terrors in the belief that by
accommodating ourselves to them we will gain control over them by assimilating
them to ourselves. (One of the basic premises of Bruno Bettelheim's fascinating
book, *The Uses of Enchantment,* is that the frightening figures in the fairy tales
of our childhood serve a very similar function in our development to maturity.)

Imitation, then, is the process by which we confront and transform our fear of the strange and unknown by becoming at one with it. And it is no accident that imitation is the essential process of the theatre. Every play is an imitation of an action which makes manifest a mystery, and the presentation of the play transforms the ghost by making it present and thus confrontable. The special power of the theatrical metaphor is that it is capable of dealing with those mysteries which are the central concern of all human beings and which never cease to haunt our imaginations. And it does so in human—not abstract—terms through the living presence of the actor, who is both a real person and at the same time a fictional character. This explains why we are so attracted to the theatre and why we are so fearful of it too. It also explains why each of the forms of drama is in some essential way ultimately concerned with dealing mediately with some aspect of the numinous or mysterious in human experience. This is as true of comedy as it is of tragedy, farce as it is of melodrama, or tragicomedy as it is of any of the various mutations of dramatic form enumerated by Polonius in the "Players' Scene" of *Hamlet*.

But having made this generalization, we must at once acknowledge that our experience of theatre—no matter how limited it may be—tells us that not only do plays take different forms, but the mysteries they manifest can be significantly different as well. Both *Oedipus the King* and *The Importance of Being Earnest* are foundling stories and hence are concerned with identity; but no one would ever confuse the two plays or what they are about. The governing spirit of each of them is so different that we can easily distinguish that not only is one a tragedy and the other a comedy, but they are centrally concerned with quite different aspects of experience. Similarly, while both *Antigone* and Webster's *The Duchess of Malfi* deal with great suffering, we perceive that they do so in ways that make them different in kind and not degree. The mysteries of life can be viewed from a number of perspectives, and throughout history certain dominant forms or types of drama have established themselves as ways that the theatre has given expression to them. Perhaps the best known and most highly regarded of these forms is tragedy.

II. Tragedy and the Tragic Spirit

Everything in nature is . . . . tragic in its fate.
GEORGE SANTAYANA

The facts of tragedy have haunted the spirit of every man in all ages, and for this reason the subject of tragedy has usually interested those who feel the need for a more intelligent awareness of themselves and the world in which they live. This has always been true, but never more so than it is today, when we feel that our lives are perched precariously on the brink of continual disaster. The number of books and articles on tragedy and the tragic written in the past forty years is overwhelming, and the very fact of their existence indicates that the conditions of our world have forced our imaginations to dwell once again on the facts of suffering, failure, and death.

Until World War II, "tragedy" was a dirty word in public parlance (we destroyed its power by indiscriminately using it to describe any kind of painful experience), and in academic circles it had become an honorific term reeking with a musty nostalgia for past ages of glory. It was argued that tragedy, the great flower of aristocratic societies, was dead and that all attempts to revive it in a democratic and egalitarian age were doomed to failure. Even the mighty Ibsen seemed small when placed next to Aeschylus, Sophocles, and Euripides, or Marlowe, Shakespeare, Corneille, and Racine. So said the professors. On the surface the students agreed, and they read their Sophocles with dutiful respect, but they really liked O'Neill, no matter how tin his ear was supposed to have been. In fact, it is now clear that tragedy hadn't died at all, it had just gone underground for a couple of centuries. Dostoevsky, Nietzsche, and Kierkegaard had told us so, but most people were not convinced. Dunkirk, Belsen, and Hiroshima changed all this, and once again tragedy has taken its place as an accepted part of our lives.

Looking back, it is easy to see how and why the subversion of tragedy occurred. After the Restoration and on into the eighteenth century, England had a new deal in politics and religion; the emerging middle-class economy was burgeoning and creating a new prosperity; a growing confidence in the methods of empirical science tended to dispel personal doubts; and the bright flame of the Enlightenment cast its light on all that had been dark and mysterious. Man may have been "Born but to die, and reasoning but to err," but as Pope went on, there *was* a plan, for those who would but look:

> All nature is but Art, unknown to thee;
> All Chance, Direction, which thou canst not see;
> All Discord, Harmony not understood;
> All partial evil, universal Good . . .

On the Continent, the romanticism of Rousseau and his followers had a similar effect on popular attitudes about tragedy. The Curse of Adam was a social blight, not an innate quality of man. Individual man was born good and was then corrupted by his society. But society could be changed, and it was the duty of all men of goodwill to work for its improvement. In reducing Evil to evils, catastrophe was institutionalized and therefore made remediable. Thus, by insisting that human suffering and failure are not so much the result of our essentially divided nature as the effects of impersonal and external social forces, Rousseauian romanticism tended to dissolve tragic guilt—although it was also largely responsible for creating the psychology of victimization.

The nineteenth century was more or less officially the century of progress, and tragedy was given little place in either official life or official art. The "Cult of Life" emerged victorious (in theory at least), and the tragic view of life was seen as the great enemy which had to be suppressed at all costs. Victorianism, with its sturdy morality, its conservatism, its willingness to compromise, and its ability to assimilate alien views into its unique brand of optimism, was riding high on the crest of a wave of material expansion and unthought-of prosperity. The voices of doubt and dissent were there, of course, but they were seldom heard. And in America we were too busy getting the land settled to worry much about aesthetic abstractions like tragedy.

At the turn of the present century, rumblings from the underground and occasional eruptions could be heard. The theatre, especially, had begun to change. We see it first in the later plays of Ibsen, such as *The Master Builder*, and in Strindberg's *Miss Julie* and his post-inferno plays; it rises to a frenzy in the works of the German Expressionists. Even a Fabian optimist like Shaw, who for so long had an answer for everything, began to come up with the most improbable solutions to the question of "What's to be done?" And as the final curtain descends with Saint Joan crying out, "O God that madest this beautiful earth, when will it be ready to receive thy saints? How long, O Lord, how long?" we know that the answer is "Never!" So we pass through the era of Maxwell Anderson and Clifford Odets and enter the Age of the Bomb. All the debates about the common man being tragic (invariably any discussion of tragedy will sooner than later evoke the question: "Is *Death of a Salesman* a tragedy?") are ample, if not always eloquent, testimony that tragedy is once more a central concern of many thoughtful people.

But as soon as we acknowledge the renewed possibility of tragedy, we invariably exclaim: "Where is it?" People turn feverishly to the giants of the past or to Aristotle's *Poetics* and bemoan the fact that while our world may certainly be tragic, it is not very hospitable to the nobility and grandeur that we tend to associate with tragedy as a dramatic form. In our lament we reveal that for all of our interest in the subject, we really do not understand it very well. We reveal the commonplace assumption that there is in Western culture a persisting "idea of tragedy" that can be defined in terms of certain formal or structural characteristics. The history of the Western theatre documents the fact that nothing could be further from the truth.

Going all the way back to the time of Aristotle, there has been a tendency to discuss tragedy in terms of form. That is, we tend to describe, define, and judge tragedy in terms of certain formal or structural characteristics which we assert must pertain to all tragedies, as if a tragedy were a sonnet or a sonata, a symphony or a Chinese landscape scroll. This is particularly true of those who use Aristotle's *Poetics* as a prescriptive guide book to the study of tragedy. Such an approach to tragedy—or any of the other forms of drama—could not be more wrong. It cannot begin to be a fruitful approach when dealing with the broad diversity of the modern theatre; nor is it helpful as a way of studying Elizabethan tragedy (consider how different the plays of Marlowe, Jonson, and Shakespeare are—not to mention the large number of lesser known playwrights); it won't work for the Greek theatre which we think of as being so homogeneous in nature that we tend to refer to all the tragedians writing in the Fifth Century B.C. as "the Greeks." The approach breaks down even when it is applied to the plays of any one of the Greek tragedians. (Think of how different Sophocles' *Antigone*, *Electra*, *Oedipus the King*, and *Oedipus at Colonus* are in form!) For the Greeks any play that was based on the legends of the historical aristocracy and performed at the festivals of Dionysus was a tragedy (literally "a goat song"). But this tells us very little about Greek drama and next to nothing about tragedy. If we look at the thirty-three extant plays of Aeschylus (525–456 B.C.), Sophocles (496–406 B.C.), and Euripides (485–406 B.C.) what do we find? Aeschylus wrote in the trilogy form (three directly related plays performed as a single unit), while Sophocles and Euripides did not. The Chorus played a central role in Aeschylean and Sophoclean drama, but in the plays of Euripides it often seems to be a useless and oftentimes awkward appendage. If we believe *Oedipus the King* to be a tragedy (for Aristotle it was the model tragedy) then by its terms Aeschylus' *Oresteia* is a divine comedy, Euripides' *Alcestis* is a domestic comedy, his *Helen* a soap opera, and his *Trojan Women* a melodrama. We tend to think of death as a decisive event in tragedy, yet in the majority of the classical Greek plays it is not central and often it does not occur at all. Still all of these plays were called tragedies. The issue of defining drama in terms of form and/or structure gets even more confusing if we start comparing and contrasting its manifestations in different periods of history or in different countries and cultures. There is no way we can relate *Hamlet* to *Antigone* or Ibsen's *Ghosts* to Euripides' *Medea* in terms of form. If they share something in common—and they do—it is something other than form. Therefore, if we want to deal with all of those plays we tend to think of as tragedies in a meaningful way, we must resist falling victim to what I have called the "formalistic fallacy in the study of dramatic genres." That is, we must avoid the kind of thinking about drama which assumes that tragedy of all ages has certain formal and structural characteristics in common.

From the outset we must make a distinction between "tragedy," which is a constantly changing dramatic form that makes manifest and communicates the experience of tragedy and the feelings it arouses, and "the tragic," which is a particular way of looking at experience that has persisted more or less unchanged in the Western world from the time of Homer to the present. When we talk about tragedy, we are in the realm of aesthetics; when we discuss the nature of the tragic, we are in the realm of existence. In short, the difference between the two is the difference between art and life. This does not mean they are not related, at times they may seem inseparable; but the distinction is real.

"Everything in nature is . . . tragic in its fate." The tragic writer of all ages has always been chiefly concerned with the fate of man, and we think of Aeschylus, Sophocles, Euripides, Shakespeare, Racine, Ibsen, and O'Neill as tragedians because their plays—although greatly different in form—give expression to the tragic nature of the human condition. The fate of each of us is that we are doomed to failure and defeat; we are born to die. The absurdist playwright, Arthur Adamov (1908–1970), described this fate quite pessimistically when he said in an interview shortly before he committed suicide:

> The destinies of all human beings are of equal futility. The refusal to live and the joyful acceptance of life both lead, by the same path, to inevitable failure, total destruction.

Scott Fitzgerald expressed the same idea somewhat more tenderly when he wrote to his daughter:

> Not one person in 10,000 finds time to form what, for lack of a better phrase, I might call the wise and tragic sense of life. By this I mean, the sense that life is essentially a cheat and its conditions are those of defeat.

This view has been formulated in many different ways, but the distinguishing characteristic of the tragic view of life is based upon the awareness that the central fact of the human condition is that we always fall short. The fact that, no matter how hard we try, our wills, our physical strength, our capacity to love, our imagination will ultimately fail us. The fact that our lives are defined by contradiction and paradox and that our experience of it defies all of our attempts to order and control it by rational means. The fact that to live is to accept the realization that life is violent and self-defeating, unjust and unfair, and at every turn marked by compromise. Finally, the fact that to live is to face the absurd contradiction that life is most fully affirmed by death. All writers of tragedy view life as a doomed struggle with necessity, or what the Greeks referred to as *Ananke*.

Necessity is not some kind of social disease that those who would change the world can ignore, soften, or legislate out of existence. Necessity is the embodiment of life's smallness, absurdity, and fragility; it is the acknowledgment of the limitation and mortality of all human experience. Man's struggle with necessity has been expressed in many forms and in varying contexts throughout history, but it is the constant of tragic drama and, insofar as they can be related, it is the bond that links each of those writers whom we refer to as tragedians.

The tragic view of life, then, begins by insisting that we accept the inevitable doom of our fate, and this fact is the mainspring of all tragic drama. However, our experience of tragedy tells us that it is more than this. The great tragedies of history also—and with equally compelling force—celebrate the fact that, while a man may have to learn to face and accept the reality of necessity, he also has an overpowering need to give a meaning to his fate. If man's fate, no matter how frightening, has no meaning, then why struggle? "If," as Kierkegaard wrote in *Fear and Trembling*, ". . . there were no eternal consciousness in a man, if at the foundation of all there lay only a wildly seething power which writhing with obscene passions produced everything that is great and everything that is insignificant, if a bottomless void never satiated lay hidden beneath all—what then would life be but despair?" But, like Prospero in Shakespeare's *The Tempest*, we tend to trust that our ending is not despair, and our experience with tragic drama is sufficient testimony to our capacity to give meaning to our fate.

The spirit of tragedy, then, is not quietistic; it is a grappling spirit. The nature and terms of the struggle vary in direct relationship to the individual dramatist's belief in the meaning of the struggle. It may take the form of a fierce pursuit of a finite goal as it does in so many of Ibsen's plays, or it may entail an almost suicidal aspiration toward the infinite as it does in the tragedies of Christopher Marlowe or Pierre Corneille. In every great tragedy we sense the validity of a meaningful struggle and the real possibility of it. Thus, tragic characters may win or lose; or more precisely, they win in the losing and lose in the winning. But it is the struggle itself that is the source of the dramatic significance, and it is out of this struggle with necessity that heroism is born.

When we think of tragic heroes, we usually think first of their great nobility of spirit. Oedipus, Faustus, Lear, or Solness may be right or wrong; they may suffer and be destroyed; but the emotional depth and intellectual capacity each of them brings to his suffering condition stamps him with the mark of greatness. We admire the hero because he resists the forces of fate.

Here, again, Aristotle—or at least the usual interpretation of the *Poetics*—has misled us. Aristotle called that characteristic of human will which dares to stand up against the universe and struggle with necessity *hubris*, or "overweening pride." In Aristotle's view such pride was the cause of the hero's suffering and ultimate destruction. Given the Greek philosopher's admiration for moderation in all its forms, one can understand why he interpreted the essential quality of the hero's character in this way. However, such an interpretation is refuted not only by the long history of tragic drama but more importantly by the responses of audiences as they experienced that drama. For tragedy reveals that *hubris* is that quality in a man which defies the *status quo* of being human; it is the protest against the limitations of being a human being. It cannot be considered as a character defect; it is an integral part of human nature. It is a necessary element of every feeling and thinking being.

Perhaps the history of the whole human race can be telescoped into this one tragic contradiction: man demands freedom, but he wills to submit. Only the tragic hero refuses to make such a compromise. Antigone is doomed not because she has "a tragic flaw" (what Aristotle called *hamartia*) but because she refuses to accept a ready-made fate. She wants her own fate—not the one the gods have chosen for her, not Creon's, not even that dictated by traditional beliefs. Antigone's tragic condition is that she, like all human beings, will ultimately fail. In her determination to honor her brother Polyneices, she chooses what is fated and so accepts the responsibility for her fate. The magnificence of this declaration of responsibility makes her heroic. Her fate is hers and no one else's.

Or let us take an even more obvious example. Assume that you, like Oedipus, are the crown prince of the city of Corinth and while at a party you overheard a conversation in which people said that the King and Queen are not your real parents. Understandably, this information gnaws on you and finally you go to the Oracle at Delphi (the source of all truth) to find out if this is, in fact, true. The Oracle answers your question by telling you that you will murder your father and marry your mother. That is your fate. So what do you do? Go back to Corinth and say to yourself, "Isn't it too bad that I have such a horrible fate? Oh, well, what will be, will be." No, Oedipus didn't say that. Nor would any hero. In effect, he said "I won't have it! If that's my fate I will fight it, I will change it." We know that Oedipus, in trying to escape his fate—something that tragedy continually confirms we never can succeed in accomplishing—insured its realization. But in refusing to passively accept it, he not only triggered a chain of events which lead to heroism, even more significantly he made his fate *his* fate. He made his fate his own; he earned his fate; he made it his fate and his alone. If Antigone or Oedipus have a flaw it should not be thought of as a sin or a prideful assertion of egotism, but rather as the human response to the limitations of our tragic condition.

Our most distinguishing characteristic as human beings is our self-criticizing intelligence. It is the source of our greatness, but it is also the cause of our most profound grief. It creates the occasions for tragedy in one of two ways: either when our reflective thought challenges the authenticity of our impulses, or when our impulses rebel against those threats to their fulfillment which our reason would erect to maintain itself. Nietzsche described this as the conflict between the Dionysian and the Apollonian, but whether we describe this conflict as one between freedom and domination, Eros and Thanatos, autonomy and constraint, gratification and repression, or genuine progress and eternal return, it makes little difference, for it is from the conflict of these two natures in each of us that the tragic experience emerges.

The ambiguity of all tragedy consists of the fact that our doomed need to die is the only means of regaining the spontaneity that life loses under the alienating, repressive systems created by the intelligence. This is the curse of Adam. He paid the price of death for an increase in intelligence. His curse dramatizes the connection between death and culture: the same rational process that strengthens man's chances to live also creates the conditions that make death inevitable and even attractive. The great tragedies reenact the necessity and the meaninglessness of this death drama; they show man's ultimate and inevitable alienation, but they also reveal that man's rational faculty is the cause of this condition. Tragedy, in short, shows why heroes are born, but it also depicts the bankruptcy of intelligence as a measure that one must take in a vain effort to escape the final estrangement. This explains why the action of tragedy seems creative and destructive at the same time, why the spirit of tragedy is the spirit of achievement. It is an end (usually death) and it is a fulfillment, a complete realization filled with a heightened sense of life.

It is the paradoxical nature of this confrontation with fate which leads the hero into what Karl Jaspers has called "boundary situations," those areas of experience where man is shown at the limits of his sovereignty. "Here," as Richard B. Sewall puts it in his The *Vision of Tragedy*, "with all the protective coverings stripped off, the hero faces as if no man had ever faced it before the existential question—Job's question, 'What is man?' or Lear's 'Is man no more than this?' " At this frontier, the hero with faith and those generalizations derived from his experience attempts to map his universe. What happens finally in tragedy is a failure of maps: in the tragic situation, man finds himself in a primitive country that he had believed his forefathers had tamed, civilized, and charted, only to discover they had not. Or the landscape has been distorted by an earthquake; or the map is simply inaccurate, or it does not go far enough, or it has gotten worn at the edges. But in tragedy, even if the maps fail the exploration goes on. This explains why tragedy has always had such a great hold on the human imagination: it brings us into direct touch with the naked landscape of the spirit.

However, to move into an area where the maps have failed is to throw man back upon himself, and the central fact about each of us is the dividedness of our natures. Tragedy is not about death; death is a fact of life, it is our companion whether we can acknowledge it or not. Tragedy is about our inevitable failure in everything we would aspire to because we can never be consistently whole; it is about the fact that the source of our failures resides within us and is not due to the operation of some external force. Indeed, the real key to the understanding of tragedy lies in recognizing that all tragedy has its roots in human struggles and springs from the basic dividedness of man's nature. (It is significant that the Greek word for "division" or "dividedness" is the same as the name of the Greek goddess of fate: Moira.) All drama is built upon catastrophe (literally, a shift in direction)—any event which overturns the previously existing order or system of things. As such, catastrophe itself lacks moral meanings; it is equally capable of producing joy and happiness or sadness and grief, depending on the context in which it occurs. The most important characteristic of tragedy—the one distinguishing it from all other dramatic forms, especially melodrama—is that all significant "catastrophic" events are caused by the inner dividedness of the protagonist and not by some external force. *King Lear* and *The Duchess of Malfi* have many things in common, but because Lear is clearly brought low by the dividedness of his own nature while the Duchess, in spite of her inner conflicts, is ultimately destroyed by forces not of her own making and over which she has never had any control, we consider Shakespeare's play a tragedy and Webster's a melodrama. A similar distinction can be found in classical Greek drama: certainly there is as much suffering in *The Trojan Women* as in *Oedipus the King*— probably more. But because the King of Thebes is responsible for his own suffering in a way that the victimized women of Troy are not, we correctly believe that the difference between the two dramas is one of kind and not degree. This distinction is important, because if the catastrophes of experience are considered to be the result of an external force—whether it be a divinity, a power of nature, or some societal pressure—then the individual is ultimately not responsible for them, no matter how much he might suffer because of them. Tragedy cannot exist if the protagonist does not eventually come to recognize that he is morally responsible for his deeds and that his acts are the direct offspring of choices he has made. Robert B. Heilman, in his important book *Tragedy and Melodrama: Versions of Experience*, argues that the tragic character is one in whom is incorporated "the dividedness of a humanity whose values, because they naturally elude the confines of formal logic, create an apparently insoluble situation." These divisions may and do take many forms, but they always present alternatives and demand that man must choose between them. And choice implies consciousness, for alternatives are not really alternatives if they do not in some way live in the hero's consciousness. Thus division is not only the occasion of self-knowledge, it is the very material of self-knowing. And self-knowledge derived from the irreconcilable conflicts within us is the very stuff of tragedy.

Tragedy begins by moving the hero into the destructive element. The playwright then presses these "boundary situations" to their fullest yield. In the midst of "the blight man was born for," the tragic dramatist demands of his hero what Hamlet demanded of himself: "How to be!" In the boundary situation what happens? What qualities does a man reveal? Through suffering what does he learn? Learn, not about the gods or the universe, for they are simply "given"; but, what does he learn about himself? The tragic dramatist carries the action to the uttermost limits. He explores the farthest reaches of human possibility. He knows that if we are not conscious of our contradictions, we will experience them as our fate.

Man's tragic condition is that he is doomed by Fate to defeat because of the dividedness of his nature. The affirmation of tragedy is that it celebrates a kind of victory of man's spirit over his fate. He has made his fate his own! This mortal encounter between the tragic and tragedy—between life and form—is the chief source of tension and turbulence in what we call tragic drama. In the ambiguity of that tension, death in some form usually triumphs, but heroism is born out of that mortal struggle, and its spirit lives on long after the corpse has been interred. It is an ambiguity which insists that the ultimate assertion of identity is finally to obliterate our identity. In one of his few, but always important essays on the theatre, the critic Harold Rosenberg put it this way:

> The assumption of tragedy is that in actual experience it is impossible to win, except by way of destruction itself—and winning through being destroyed is not a rational risk but a transcendental hypothesis.

This is another way of saying that tragedy celebrates one of the deepest and darkest of life's mysteries.

Such is the turbulence of the tragic. If we are to rescue the plays which celebrate these abiding conflicts from the dusty repositories where most masterpieces of culture are usually stored, we must find ways to rediscover that tension of struggle which is inevitable when men try vainly but nobly to impose a meaning on their own lives and on the world around them. If we are to succeed in this, we must recognize that the constant in tragedy is the tragic view of life or the tragic spirit: that sense that life is "essentially a cheat and its conditions are those of defeat." This spirit can and does manifest itself in many ways—both in drama and in life—but it is always there as a backdrop to man's fate, and tragedy is that dramatic form which both celebrates and protests against this condition.

And this is the chief reason for this book. The fact that tragedy is being taught in more and more of our colleges and schools is a sign of our cultural maturity. But this growth brings with it a new responsibility: what ideas will be transmitted in the process? This is not just an academic quibble. A failure to understand what tragedy is about can have important and undesirable consequences for our grasp of reality; confusion in this subject may result in our losing touch with certain ideas that are an indispensable means of contemplating and understanding and experiencing the human catastrophes that surround us everywhere. This volume is an attempt to bring together a number of essays which deal with such catastrophes of body and spirit with clarity and compassion.

I
THE TRAGIC VIEW
OF LIFE

On the Tragic*

Max Scheler

In the following we will speak of no particular art in which the tragic is portrayed. It is impossible to arrive at the phenomenon of the tragic through the art product alone, although the results of examining its extant forms might be most fruitful in discovering what it really is. The tragic is rather an essential element of the universe itself. The material made use of by the art product and the tragedian must contain beforehand the dark strain of this element. To determine what makes a tragedy genuine we must first have as precise a notion as possible of the phenomenon.

It is doubtful whether the tragic is essentially an esthetic phenomenon. We are speaking of life and history in general without placing ourselves in any particular esthetic circumstance, no matter how unusually full of tragic events and circumstances. The question of how the tragic works on our emotions or of how we come to "enjoy" the tragic in some art form we are purposely avoiding. These things can not tell us what the tragic is. The usual "psychological" method of observation, proceeding from the investigation of the experiences of one observing a tragic incident to its "objective understanding," tries to discover and describe the evocations of these experiences. Such a method avoids the issue rather than clarifies it.[1] It tells us only what the tragic does, not what it is. The tragic is above all a property which we observe in events, fortunes, characters, and the like, and which actually exists in them. We might say that it is given off by them like a heavy breath, or seems like an obscure glimmering that surrounds them. In it a specific feature of the world's makeup appears before us, and not a condition of our own ego, nor its emotions, nor its experience of compassion and fear. What goes on in the observer of the tragic as he feels this heavy breath and sees this shimmering darkness that encircles the head of the "tragic hero" is not related to his ability to understand this phenomenon by using his own symbolical way of looking at this feature in the world's makeup. There are people who are blind, or half blind, to the tragic—like Raphael, Goethe, and Maeterlinck.[2] One must know what the tragic is to depict this experience. Moreover, the experience is historically far more variable than the tragic itself. A tragedy of Aeschylus arouses entirely different emotions today than in his time, although the tragic is just as perceptible to both ages.

The mental processes of understanding the tragic, the inner perception of

* Max Scheler, "On the Tragic," Bernard Stambler, tr., *Cross Currents*, Vol. IV (1954), pp. 178–191.
[1] Even the famous definition of Aristotle: The tragic is that which arouses pity and fear.
[2] Cf. Maeterlinck's *La Sagesse et la Destinée*.

how it is brought to us, are to be distinguished from what one experiences in observing the tragic. This is not the same as the "experience" theory of the tragic. It has nothing to do with depicting the way it works on us psychologically. However, the former places the problem close to the essence of the tragic and its essential manifestations. Consequently, it should not be disregarded.

How then should we proceed? Should we indiscriminately gather together examples of the tragic, selecting those events that impress men as being such, and then ask what they possess in common? This would be a method of induction that would lend itself well to experimental support. Yet this would bring us only to the observation of our own ego when the tragic works upon us. What right have we to trust men when they call something tragic? A plurality of opinion does not help here. Without knowledge of what the tragic is, must we be forced to decide between the opinions that have weight and those which do not? But even taking this for granted, we would still have to justify ourselves. We would have a confused mass that we would call tragic. What would the common element be that would justify this judgment of ours? Nothing more than the fact that they are all called tragic.

All induction would presuppose that one knows beforehand what the essence of the tragic is, and not just what events are tragic. Our method of procedure will be different. The few examples and statements of others that may be given are not to serve as the basis for abstracting by induction a concept of the tragic. They will rather give us some rough draft in which to see the basic use of the word and the phenomenon expressed therein, without taking into account who uses the word and to what intent. They will provide the basis for seeing in what experience this phenomenon comes to its given state. We do not assume that the examples are facts in which the tragic adheres as a property. They are only something which will contain the basic manifestations of the tragic. They will provide us with the opportunity of searching out these manifestations and finally of arriving at the tragic itself. It is not a question here of proofs but of indications or signs.

One should also guard against treating the tragic as a phenomenon with its own metaphysical, religious, and otherwise speculative interpretations. The tragic is not the result of an interpretation of the world and the important events of the world. It is a fixed and powerful impression that certain things make and one which can itself be subjected to many different interpretations. Theories like that which Maeterlinck proposes, basically the theory of every Rationalism and Pantheism, are totally wrong. According to these theories the tragic is the result of a false and unstable interpretation of the world. The tragic is attributed to the ways of thinking in uncivilized times with uncontrolled emotions. Or it is a sort of sudden bewilderment in the face of the defects of the world against which one knows of no help, or—what is the simple consequence of this as stated by Maeterlinck—no helper is at hand, no helper to put the matter in order. They obscure rather than clarify the essence of the tragic; their own outlook and times prevent them from seeing it. We, however, reason that these interpretations of the world are wrong because they have no place for the undeniable fact of the tragic and that any age which does not perceive it is insignificant.

Metaphysical interpretations of the tragic are most interesting. But the phenomenon itself is taken for granted by them. Certain metaphysicians like Eduard von Hartmann make God Himself the tragic hero. Others think the tragic lies only on the surface of things and that underneath all tragedies lies an imperceptible harmony, into which they are finally resolved. But to know where the tragic has its source, whether in the basic structure of existence or in human passions and unrest, is to know already what the tragic is.

Every interpretation fails before the inflexibility of reality which reduces it to silence.

This question of the tragic is only one example of the importance of contrasting the changing whims of the times with the facts of reality.

The Tragic and Values

All that can be called tragic is contained within the realm of values and their relationships.

In a universe free of values, such as that constructed by mechanical physics, there are no tragedies.

Only where there is high and low, nobleman and peasant, is there anything like a tragic event.

The tragic is not a value like beautiful, ugly, good, or bad. The tragic appears in objects only through the interplay of their inherent values.

It is always founded on values or connected with values. To repeat, it is found only in that realm where there are objects of value and where these work in one way or another on each other.

Serenity, sadness, grandeur, and earnestness can be classified among the more tranquil values. The tragic is absent here. It appears in the realm of changing values and circumstances. Something must happen for it to appear. There must be a period of time in which something is lost or destroyed.

In empty space—Schiller notwithstanding—dwells much sublimity, but not the tragic. In a spaceless world the tragic might be possible, but never in a timeless world. In its basic connotations the tragic always implies a determined effectiveness in doing and in suffering. The tragic "character" remains such only as long as he has the necessary dispositions for tragic acting and suffering. Even a situation calling for opposition of forces or their reconciliation is only tragic as long as it contains this effectiveness. If the tragic is to appear, however, this effectiveness must take on a definite direction, a direction toward the annihilation of a positive value in a determined hierarchy. The strength which annihilates it must possess this value itself.

To belong to the category of the tragic some values must be destroyed. With regard to man it does not have to be his existence or his life. But at least something of his must be destroyed—a plan, a desire, a power, a possession, a faith. The destruction as such is not tragic. It is rather the course that an object of lower or equal positive values, never of higher values, is able to force upon it. We can hardly call it tragic for a good man to defeat and bring about the downfall of an evil man, nor for a nobleman to do the same to a peasant. Moral approval precludes a tragic impression here. This much is certain. It is also certain that it must be an object of high positive value that destroys a value. (Values such as the honest with respect to the wicked, the good with regard to the bad, and the beautiful compared to the ugly, are here called positive. All values have this opposition and duality, even excluding their degree of "higher" and "lower.") The tragic is apparent only where the strength to destroy a higher positive value proceeds from an object possessing this positive value. The manifestation is, moreover, purest and clearest where objects of equally high value appear to undermine and ruin each other. Those tragedies most effectively portray the tragic phenomenon in which, not only is every one in the right, but where each person and power in the struggle presents an equally superior right, or appears to fulfill an equally superior duty. If an object of higher positive value, let us take for example a good, just man, is overpowered by some insignificant evil object, the tragic is at once senseless and irrational. In place of arousing tragic pity, it arouses painful indignation. Tragic pity can never fall completely into the depths of pain and disgust, but must maintain some semblance of coolness and calmness.

The tragic is first of all a struggle that is occasioned in an object of high positive value, i.e., of a high moral nature, generally treating of the family, marriage, or the state. The tragic is a "conflict" which takes place between the positive value and the very object which possesses it. The great art of the tragedian is to set each value of the conflicting elements in its fullest light, to develop completely the intrinsic rights of each party.

On the Tragic and Grief

It is true that in some way all tragic events are sad, but in a very definite sense. This is precisely what fate is, an event surrounded by this quality of sadness.[3] On the other hand it arouses sorrow in the feelings of men. It makes the soul sad.

Not all sad persons are tragic characters, however. Every death is sad and makes those left behind sad as well, but assuredly not every death is tragic. Let us disregard for a moment that type of grief that is produced in us independently of any perception of values, almost as if caused by a "neutral" feeling. We would rather consider the "grieved over something." The nature of a certain event arouses our sentiments and produces this feeling in us. It should not appear to be caused by our individual wishes or aims, but only by the worth of the object. The tragic grief has a double characteristic, one rooted in itself, the other in its subject.

This kind of grief is free from all indignation, anger, reproach, and that accompanying the desire "if it had only been otherwise." It is a calm, quiet fullness; a special kind of peace and composure is characteristic of it.

The atmosphere of tragic grief will be absent if we are aroused to do something about it. Once the event has been completed and brought to its climax, any indication of a compromise or of some chance to avert the catastrophe makes tragic grief impossible.

Tragic grief contains a definite composure. It is thus distinguished from all specifically personal griefs, those which come from a personal experience of being "sad about something." It comes to us from the outside through the soul; it is occasioned by events that are "tragic." The tragedies of Aeschylus show especially well how to awaken this atmosphere of grief in its utmost purity.

We will now point out the twofold characteristic feature of the tragic which causes this atmosphere. One is the very nature of the world's makeup; every individual sad event is thus determined. The other is based on the appearance of an uncompromising inevitability of the destruction of a value, a species of destruction which every tragedy must contain.

[3] That the quality of the sad is definitely not a "feeling," nor a so-called "empathic feeling," cf. the essay, "Idole der Selbsterkenntnis."

In every genuine tragedy we see more than just the tragic event. We see over and above it the permanent factors, associations, and powers which are in the very makeup of the world. It is these which make such a thing possible.[4] In every tragic event we are directly confronted with a definite condition of the world's makeup without deliberation or any sort of "interpretation." This confronts us in the event itself; it does not result from what it does to the things which brought it about. It is only momentarily connected with the event and is independent of the elements that make it up. It is present in the form of a slight presentiment.

Every objective grief like that of a tragic event has its own depth. (I take the word here in a transferred meaning like the "depth" of a room.) It has its own immensity, too, which distinguishes it from a very limited, determined event. The depth is brought about by the fact that its subject is twofold. One is the element of the event that has been seen by us. The other is that point in the world's makeup that is exemplified by the event and of which the event is but an example. Grief seems to pour out from the event into unlimited space. It is not a universal, abstract world-makeup that would be the same in all tragic events. It is rather a definite, individual element of the world's construction. The remote subject of the tragic is always the world itself, the world taken as a whole which makes such a thing possible. This "world" itself seems to be the object immersed in sorrow. In the foreground of this darkness of sorrow we see the specific event and fate standing out all the more clearly.

The element in the world's makeup which produces these situations seems to do so without any warning. In producing them it ignores the peculiarities of the causes of the event and even its normal effects. It is this which causes the second essential element of the tragic, its inevitability.

We will clarify this later. Right now we are interested in the peculiar atmosphere which it lends to the tragedy.

There is a whole category of feelings and affections that can be connected with the destroying of a value. Their essence is in being "preventable," even if in a particular case they may or may not have been prevented. It doesn't matter what these feelings might be—dread, fear, anger, horror, or the like; they all have in general the characteristic of "excitement." Thinking about the possibility of its turning out otherwise, or even better, causes this excitement. In men it is more frequently caused by the thought, "If so and so had only acted differently." This excitement is able to take hold of a man only because he is a practical being and, as it were, the potential actor in any event.

It softens when the inevitability is seen as an impossibility. The grief does not cease to be what it is, but it assumes the character of the feelings of dissatisfaction, excitement, and pain. These are taken in the same narrow sense as the physical feelings of fear, horror, and the like.

Tragic grief is pure, without physical arousement. In a certain sense even a feeling of "contentment" is joined with it.

There is no desire to do away with the event which led to the destruction of some value. This is abolished by seeing its inevitability.

We see that the tragic seems to have its ultimate roots in the essential makeup of the world itself. It is this which clears away all sense of culpability or responsibility. When we see this in the nature of the event a certain reconciliation

[4] We mean "such a thing" in the sense of "a so-constituted value."

takes place. It is a species of reconciliation which fills us with peace and rest and with resignation. This resignation banishes the weakness and pain that would come from contemplating a better-made world.

Thus the specific sadness of the tragic is really an objective character of the event itself. It is independent of the individual circumstances of the beholder. It is free from the feelings provoked by excitement, indignation, blame, and the like. It has a depth and immensity. It is not accompanied by physical feelings or by what can be called real pain. It has a definite resignation, contentment, and a species of reconciliation with the existence which it chances to have.

The Tragic Knot

We asserted previously that in the tragic a struggle takes place between two objects possessing high positive value and that one of them must be overcome. There is one case where this is fulfilled to the highest degree. It happens when the objects are not different events, persons, or things, but coincide in one event, person, or thing; even better, in one and the same quality, power, or ability.

It would be most tragic if the same power which has brought either itself or another object to a very high positive value becomes its destroyer—especially if this takes place in the very act of its achievement.

If we are observing a certain action which is realizing a high value, and then see in that same action that it is working towards the undermining of the very existence of the being it is helping, we receive the most complete and the clearest of tragic impressions.

The same tragic impression occurs when a special courage or boldness which permits a man to accomplish an heroic deed undermines him because it exposes him to a danger that a moderately prudent man would avoid—"If only I were prudent enough I would not be called Tell." Another example is the man with high ideals towards a spiritual goal who permits them to become shipwrecked on the little things of life. Everyone according to Madame de Staël's dictum has the mistakes of his virtue: the same traits of character which permitted a man to do his best have brought him to catastrophe.

We don't have to talk only of human beings here. An art gallery can be destroyed by the very fire that was kindled to preserve the picture. The event has a sharp tragic character. The flight of Icarus is tragic. The very wax which glued his wings to him melts in the same degree as he flies toward the sun.

The use of the phrase, "the tragic knot," is a pertinent metaphor. It illustrates the inner entanglement between the creation of a value and the destruction of a value as they take place in the unity of the tragic action and the tragic event.

Something else can be deduced from the aforesaid. It is not the relationship between values that constitutes the "stage" for the tragic event, nor is it the connection of causal events which it contains. It is rather a special reference of the value relationships to the causal relationships. It is an essential characteristic of our world—and thus of every world—that the course of the causal events disregards completely the value of things. The exigencies of values as they develop toward a unity or as they unfold themselves toward their ideal fulfillment is not taken into account by the causal series. The simple fact that the sun shines on the good and bad alike makes tragedy possible. At times it may happen that the causal relationships simultaneously coincide with an increase of the values. This is accepted as only accidental. It is not occasioned by intrinsic determination. Nor is it occasioned by a consideration of what the values need to reach their fulfillment or that the causality is at hand to produce them.

Without this basic condition there can be no tragedy.

There would be no tragedy in a world which operated on an established system of laws whereby each thing had the powers and capabilities commensurate with its values, and whereby its activity was directed only towards the exigencies of developing or unifying these values. Tragedy would likewise be impossible in a world operating on a system of laws whereby the powers would be directed against the exigencies of these values, purposely opposing them. The tragic would thrive in a satanic world as well as in a divine—a fact that Schopenhauer forgot in his discussion of the tragic.

We see the tragic only when in one glance we embrace both the causality of things and the exigencies of their immanent values. In this unified glance the mind tries to synthetize the conditions in which it finds these values so as to arrive at the unity it is trying to achieve. Then it follows the course of events in their causal sequence. The result is a clear insight into the independence of these two things. It is here that we may see the formal "background" of all tragedies.

Obviously, it is not in the mere knowledge of this circumstance that the tragic exists. The tragic comes into sight only when this independence of the two elements becomes embodied in a concrete event.

What has just been said casts new light on our definition. For never is our insight so clear and so concentrated as when we see that the same action may in some places produce a high value and in others—quite indifferently—destroy this value.

Here then—where we are able to see the unity of an action at a single glance and not by discursive connection, limb by limb—here is a circumstance known previously only by concept which has now come tangibly within our grasp.

What do we mean when we say that in the tragic the destruction of value is "necessary"? Surely not the destruction of causality in general!

Is the question then one of "causal" necessity or is it likely to be one of quite another kind of necessity? Here one might begin to discriminate and say that it is indeed causal necessity but of a particular kind, that is, "inner necessity," and consequently a necessity which depends not on influences breaking in from the outer world but rather on the eternal nature of things and men. Only as such can things and men undergo the tragic fate. Actually this concept of the tragic— widely held though it may be—is not borne out by the facts.

When a man who seems destined for a certain fate, either by congenital disease or by any sort of natural predisposition, is brought low the first time that external circumstance has a chance to work upon him—such an event does not seem tragic to us even if the highest values inhered in him, values independent of this natural predisposition. Thus Ibsen, with all his artistic genius, has not succeeded in making of Oswald, in *Ghosts*, a tragic figure, since the worm of destruction gnawing at Oswald is the result of a disease he has inherited from his father. We miss here something that belongs to the essence of the tragic hero: that the evil which drives the hero to his downfall pertains to those against whom the struggle is being waged, and also that such a struggle be actually waged.

Both these requirements are missing in *Ghosts*. Nor is the tragic hero to be found in him who immediately surrenders to the inimical, and who at the first dismissive word, immediately abnegates and resigns himself. The "necessity" of which we are now speaking must rather be of such a kind as to take its course even after the performance of all the "free" actions that may be tried in an attempt at flight. When we see the catastrophe opposed by all free efforts of will and means, and can still trace its irruption as "necessary"; when we can even trace, through the turmoil and anguish of this struggle to avert the catastrophe, a species of transcendent necessity: then and then only do we have an example before us of tragic "necessity."

Tragic necessity is not the necessity of the course of nature, a necessity which lies beneath freedom and the power of the will and which may be conceived as the free essence which permits the best linking of events in nature. Rather is tragic necessity of such a kind that it lies *above* freedom: it is to be found only in the conclusion of free acts or of "free causes" in the total sphere of causality, in which may be found even "unfree causes," that is, those which are the results of prior causes.

Wherever men are presented as "milieu-defined," as completely determined by "relationships," as in the naturalist "drama," we have a much less likely source of the tragic than in the drama which gives us the impression that consciously free choices are clearly and conclusively driving the events of the play to its catastrophe. Consequently neither naturalism and determinism on the one hand nor the rationalistic thesis of a "freedom of the human will" limited only by the chances of nature can provide a comprehension of the tragic, or anything more than the beginning of such comprehension. Both these views of the world have no place for the tragic since they make no provision for essential necessity reaching out above the qualities of nature and free choice.

There is still another reason why it is inadequate to define as "inner" that species of necessity we are here discussing. Immanent cause is that which in a thing or in a person exists as latent predisposition, or capacity, or skill, which functions at the inception of true relationships to other things or situations or persons. Wherever we encounter a strictly defined predisposition to the decline of value we must recognize an absence of the true development, of the veridical renewal, of the inner historicity which is needed for the tragic event: in such a situation the catastrophe itself would be predictable if we had a firm and exact picture of the character. The tragic however contains this paradox that when we behold the destruction of value it seems completely "necessary" and at the same time completely "unpredictable." Though the catastrophe may come closer and closer, driven by all the contributory factors (whether free or not), and each new event is visibly pregnant with danger, yet there must still remain one moment when everything—even by ideal calculation—could still turn out quite differently: whereupon from all this complexity is brought forth a deed which resolves these lurking factors into the unity of one species of reality by a means not rationally predictable.

The seemingly "propitious turn of events" just before the catastrophe, which so many tragic poets have been fond of, is a special means to exclude from the audience even the slightest appearance of "predictability." Even the increase of tension, which every tragedy must arouse, would not be possible if the catastrophe did not seem to us to be well founded from the beginning in the latent inner qualities of the characters and their relationships. It is *concrete* causality, which has nothing to do with "natural law," which governs tragic events as it also governs the irreversible motions of the constellations in their consummation of causality—that species of causality which is rightly called the truly "historical." For this we must return to the assertion of Schopenhauer that tragedy never exhibits true "character development" but only "character revelation," revelation of what was previously latent as disposition and character.

Even the tragic transformation of a character, the alteration of disposition and mentality, the essential and latent diversion from the previous course of life—even this transformation is seldom either the catastrophe itself or even an important part of it. A specifically tragic phenomenon is to be seen in the interruption—even in the midst of external victories—of a course of life directed towards certain values as goals. Tragic necessity is to be seen above all in the essence and essential relations of the inevitability and inescapability of things founded in society.

Even these negative definitions indicate that the species of "necessity" we have been talking about becomes apparent only when every conceivable kind of skill seems to be brought into play to halt the destruction of value and to preserve the value in question. Consequently two species of value-destruction are essentially untragic: first, those instances which are tinged with guilt because someone has failed in a duty definitely assigned to him; second, those instances which might have been avoided by the use of available techniques and means. In general, then, the quality of the tragic is lacking when the question "Who is guilty?" has a clear and definite answer.

Only where no such answer can be given does the stuff of tragedy begin to appear. We may use the term "tragic" only when we feel that everyone concerned in the story has hearkened to the demands of his duty with the utmost of his capabilities, and yet the disaster has had to occur. The tragic consists—at least in human tragedies—not simply in the absence of "guilt" but rather in the fact that the guiltiness can not be localized. Wherever we can substitute, in place of a man who plays a role in the unfolding of a catastrophe, another man who is like the first but morally better—that is, one who has a finer sympathy for moral opportunities as well as a greater energy of the moral will—to the extent that we can perform such substitution the growth of a feeling of tragedy is stunted by the amount of blame we can pin on the responsible person.

In such an instance "necessity" is missing as a quality of the tragic phenomena. Consider, for example, the death of Christ; suppose we were able to have the idea that his death, instead of being an essential relationship between His divine purity and the profaneness and opposition of an obdurate "world," had been brought about by the particular moral laxity of Pontius Pilate, or by the wickedness of an individual named Judas, or by the inimical deeds of the Jews. If we were then able to imagine Jesus of Nazareth surrounded not by these men but by a group morally "better," or if we could place him in a different historical context where he would come to higher recognition and repute—if we could do these things the impression of the tragic would vanish.

The death of Jesus is tragic only when it is presented—everywhere and forever—as the consistent adherence to the higher duty of all the parties concerned.

An execution, for example, can never have a tragic culmination. The tragic appears when the idea itself of "justice" appears as leading to the destruction of higher value. An execution, if it is unavoidable, awakens deep sympathy; if it were avoidable it might arouse deep anger or irritation, but never tragic sympathy.[5]

If it is true that a disaster becomes tragic only when everyone has done his duty and, in the usual sense of the word, no one has incurred "guilt," it becomes part of the essence of tragic conflict that this conflict be guiltless and unavoidable even before judges who approach the ideal in wisdom and virtue. The tragic misdeed is even definable as that which silences all possible moral and legal powers of judgment; and, on the other hand, every conflict is essentially untragic when by moral and legal lights it is seen to be obvious and simple. Every essential confusion of the bounds of right and wrong, of good and evil, in the unity of action; every maze of threads, of motives, of views, of duties, so presented as to seem to lead equally well to a judgment of "right" or "wrong"; every complication which is not based on necessary moral and legal wisdom but which instead produces from the circumstances alone an absolute confusion of our moral and legal powers of judgment—every such complication pertains to the subjective side of tragic feeling and thereby transposes us completely from the realm of possible "right" and "wrong," from possible "accusation" and "indignation." "Tragic guilt" is of a kind for which no one can be blamed and for which no conceivable "judge" can be found.

Out of this error of our moral judgments, out of this pardonable search for a subject upon whom to pin this "guilt," a guilt which appears to us as such with crystal clarity—only out of this appears that specific tragic grief and tragic sympathy of which we have been speaking, along with its unique peace and reconciliation of the emotions. Now too the shifting of that which is to be feared to the cosmos itself appears as the essence of the reconciliation of the individual men and wills with the culminating deeds and events in which they have been taking part.

In this way, tragic guilt becomes something other than definable "right" and "wrong," or than "obeying obligation" or "defying obligation."

But individual men have quite different microcosms of values, dependent on the extent of their actual moral awareness and even on the extent of their possible moral awareness. Only on these bases can be measured their possible "duties" and areas of duty—quite independently of all the peculiarities of their empirical real situations. If every individual does his "duty," to the extent that he does this he behaves *morally;* not otherwise can he do something of equal *value* or *be* in any way of equal value. How deep his gaze thereby penetrates into the macrocosm of moral value, which contains the entire extent of the realm of possible good and evil, and how deep a hold he takes within this macrocosm, are in no way to be decided by the extent to which each individual dutifully produces the "best" of the realm of values with which he has been endowed. It is not duty and the performance of it that "ennoble"—as the Kantian, short-sighted ethic puts it—but rather "noblesse oblige": this is the original nobility of man, which establishes for him quite varied arrays of possible duties—duties which stand in varied relationships to the moral world and are variously "significant" for it.

---

[5] It is for this reason that Aeschylus, in his *Eumenides,* furnishes the judges of the Areopagus with both black and white marbles to indicate the guilt or innocence of Orestes.

It makes a difference whether the man doing his duty is a grocer or a noble king; the first one in a vague way obeys a few moral value-distinctions, doing his "duty" with a couple of poor concepts of choice, while the other, living in the fullness of manifold human and other moral relationships, with a finely articulated and higher realm of moral value-distinctions before his eyes, does his "duty" while he demonstrates the highest value given to him, and in will and deed realizes this value. The latter man in this action must conduct himself as occasionally opposed to duty, while the man blind to value blandly performs *his* "duty." If we were now to say that in a true tragic presentation everyone must do his "duty," or at least that it would be prudent so to do, and that—even if everyone has done his duty—the destruction of value and the consequent lessening of the total moral value of the world must nevertheless take place, we would thereby still not know how to exclude this quite different dimension of the moral value-distinction of the individual and of his being taking part in the tragedy. It is rather a quite different species of the tragic which, in this dimension of being, bruises "noble" individuals against the strongly articulated "duties" of the mob. And it appears to be a particular melancholy-ironic glory of this kind of tragedy that the noble individual should accept a moral guilt that his companions do not accept. To the extent that the noble person can more easily become "guilty" than the ignoble—in accord with his richer and higher realm of duties—he is susceptible to a moral "risk" which ever bears with it something potentially tragic, as this risk simultaneously praises and blames his noble nature. The Prometheus of technic, who stole fire from Zeus, is a tragic figure; but even more tragic are the moral Prometheuses in whose eyes a moral world comes with the brilliance of lightning, a moral world that never previously existed. . . . While they are realizing values and acquiring duties which the vulgar do not yet know how to see as value or to feel as duty, the vulgar are themselves only doing their "duty" while the noble see as "evil" what may still be "good" for the vulgar. Here is one instance of the tragic "fall" for the "noble," in that his every eventual moral disapproval of the vulgar must necessarily remain silent—to the extent that only through "good consciences" can his sacred "duty" be accomplished.

We can now penetrate more deeply into "tragic guilt" if we are careful to remain clear on the matter of what, in such a case, is the completion of the duty of the noble. Let it be a proposition here—with no attempt at proof—that moral "good" is the relation by which we realize or tend to realize in a given action that a preference indicates a more highly conceived value.[6] To prefer the higher value is always equivalent to depreciating the lower value, that is, to discontinue the realization of this lower value. However, all "moral norms," i.e., all imperative rules of a general type, are only exercises in what to will and what to do, as suggested by the average levelling of values in any given epoch resulting from the "situations" which are typical of and regularly recurring in this epoch; still, even this levelling of values provides "higher" values which must be realized. Every material rule of morality contains the presuppositions of the particular positive world of good appropriate to its level of civilization. What happens then when the "noble" man perceives a value which is higher than the average, a value which is generally trodden under in the levelling of values, and accomplishes his advance in the moral cosmos of value, an advance that the vulgar are not yet

[6] Cf. my book, *Der Formalismus in der Ethik und die materiale Werkethik*, vol. I, Niemeyer, Halle, 1914.

ready to grasp? In such a case it must be obvious to him that what appears "good" and "dutiful" according to the ruling morality now becomes wicked and evil—and by the same token becomes for him "opposed to duty." And this realization is not avoidable but rather—to use a term of Kant's—a "necessary perception" (*"notwendiger Schein"*). And since everything that can be generally a "moral law"—even to the most complete codification and strongly logical presentation of these laws—inevitably exhibits the positive material world of values of the "time," the "time" itself being determined by the prevailing system of value-levelling—such a man must violate the prevailing moral precept and also violate everything in the moral world that comes into the orbit of such precepts. He must necessarily appear "guilty" even before the fairest judge, when he is in fact guiltless and is so seen by God alone. That this is so is not an irregularity but rather part of the essence of all moral development. Here I mean to point out the root of that necessary and "guiltless guilt," which has hitherto been expressed in this paradoxical form only with a feeling for the justice of it. What is essential here is the necessity of the deception into which the most just moralist must blunder when confronted with the "tragic hero." Although the tragic hero with moral awareness[7] is obviously essentially the opposite of a sinner, he can not be distinguished from a sinner by the age in which he lives. Only to the extent that his newly experienced value becomes established and becomes the prevailing "morality" can he be seen and known—and then only in historical retrospect— as a moral hero. And so there are no present tragedies—there are only tragedies of the past. The tragic man necessarily goes his way in his "present" quiet and speechless. He strides unrecognized through the mob; he may even be there considered a sinner. The error of an instance which separates genius from sinner is here not an accidental but a necessary error. Here, in this tragic fate of the moral genius we can perhaps grasp, in a single species and fashion, the nerve of fate, the complete unpredictability of moral development in man. And even in the absolutely inevitable "fate" and the related absolute loneliness of the moral genius we can see a moment of the type of the tragic, as it may have happened to Jesus in Gethsemane. Here likewise appears the total fate of the world as it appears compressed into the experience of one man, as though in this moment he were standing alone and yet in the "middle," in the center of all the forces that animate the universe. His experience is as though whole epochs of history occurred in him, yet with no one else being aware of his experience—as though everything lay unified in his hand. And perhaps through this something more may become clear: the tragic hero of this kind is not guilty of his guilt, but rather it "happens" to him: this justifiable circumlocution repeats a very characteristic moment of "tragic guilt." That is: that the "guilt" comes to him and not he to the guilt! . . ."*Ihr fuhrt ins Leben ihn hinein.* . . ."

Nevertheless this "fall" into guilt does not mean that the tragic hero, either through immoderate passion or through stress and a drive in one direction, is so moved that this drive becomes the central point of his ego and his will consequently is impelled in this same direction. This is also the case in the usual moral guiltiness—at least in great measure; and quantities cannot here serve as a basis for differentiation. Even in the midst of the most powerful stresses the will which "follows" such a direction remains a new action, an action not entirely determined by this stress! The tragic guilt into which the hero "falls" is much more

---

[7] We are speaking here only of this kind and not of the tragic hero in general.

accurately characterized by calling it a "guilty" doing or renunciation of doing which darkens the areas of his possible choices and so makes a certain kind of guilt unavoidable, since the choice of the "best" meaning is necessarily in error.

Moral or "guilty guilt" is based on the act of choice; tragic or unguilty guilt is rather based on the sphere of choice! The act of choice is consequently for the tragic hero free of guilt—just the reverse of what obtains in moral guilt, in which the sphere of choice also entails objectively guiltless possibilities, and only the guilt of the act is important. And so the tragic hero "becomes guilty" while doing a guiltless thing.

The consequence of what has been said is the absurdity of the schoolmasters' theory that a moral guiltiness is to be sought in tragedies, and that the tragic poet instead of being a respectable performer of a tragic phenomenon is made into a moral judge over his heroes, whom he punishes for their deeds while at the same time he animates them to perform those deeds. Only total blindness for the phenomenon of tragedy could hatch out this silliest of all theories.

But we should also fall into error if we should try to make the correct concept of tragic guilt serve as the complete definition of the tragic phenomenon. However, since from its earliest presentations the tragic has been a universal phenomenon, not one specifically human or limited to static will, such a definition is self-destructive. However, note this: where a "tragic guilt" is actually portrayed—and it is not the deed of the hero which brings the guilt upon him or is involved in the "catastrophe," nor is his downfall the bearer of the tragic phenomenon, but rather the "guilt of error" itself, and consequently the fact that purity of will falls into guilt—here is the very bearer and root of the tragic.

In this way it is tragic that Othello falls into the guilt of having to kill his beloved, and that guiltless Desdemona should be killed by her beloved who loves her. In his own words, "For, in my sense, 'tis happiness to die," the death of Othello is not punishment for his deed, which as "punishment" must terminate a conscious evil; rather is it deliverance. Tragic guilt is therefore not a condition of the tragic phenomenon—which would indeed be a *circulus in demonstrando*, if the guilt had to be not any sort of "guilt" but only "tragic" guilt—but it is a species of the tragic itself, and to the extent that we are here dealing with moral value, it is therefore a species of absolute value—so to speak, the culminating point of the tragic. Neither death nor any other mischance but only his "fall into guilt" constitutes the tragic fate of the hero.

Tragedy and the
Tragic Vision*

Murray Krieger

> If there were no eternal consciousness in a man, if at the foundation
> of all there lay only a wildly seething power which writhing with
> obscure passions produced everything that is great and everything
> that is insignificant, if a bottomless void never satiated lay hidden
> beneath all—what then would life be but despair?
>
> —Søren Kierkegaard, *Fear and Trembling*

Now of course the tragic is not the only vision projected by our serious literature
and philosophy, nor is it necessarily the profoundest vision. But it is surely the
most spectacular, and the most expressive of the crisis-mentality of our time.
Consequently, it has won for those works obsessed with it the excited attention of
our most stimulating critical minds. Perhaps in their excitement over the individual work they have neglected to define in general terms what the vision is—
which is probably as it ought to be with the practicing critic. In any case there
does not seem to be a systematic effort to say what is meant by the phrase and
what, given this meaning, it has meant to recent writing.

It must be granted that, as with all terms of this kind, any meaning imposed
upon it must be an arbitrary one that may or may not command agreement. But,
agreed upon or not, it is valuable critically as it throws a consistently clear albeit
diffuse light upon a broad enough and deep enough area in our literature. I propose here to create for the term a tentative definition that I have found most illuminating of modern literature and the modern mind, and in the balance of this
volume to use it to conduct exploratory operations on a certain few novels of the
last hundred or so years in order to demonstrate its incisive powers. Since I have
some idea about where I shall come out, I must admit that my explorations will
have all too much direction to them and that consequently they will somewhat
mislead us about the total reality of the works in the interest of showing the
widespread relevance of my definition. By way of defense I can plead only that
the definition was empirical in its origin and that it followed my probings into
the individual novels rather than the other way round; in other words, that the
meaning I am trying to create for the term is one that in my reading of these
novels I feel that I have discovered.

* Murray Krieger, "Tragedy and the Tragic Vision," from *The Tragic Vision* (Holt, Rinehart and
Winston, 1960), pp. 1–21. Copyright © 1960 by Murray Krieger. Reprinted by permission of Holt,
Rinehart, and Winston Publishers. [The footnotes for this selection have been renumbered.]

It is surely needless to add that the act of enclosing a number of literary works within the limits of a given definition hardly passes any judgment upon works on either side of the boundary. For a work not to qualify as an example of the tragic vision is hardly a mark against it. Indeed, in the eyes of many, it may be quite the contrary. Of course, the meaning I want to establish for the tragic vision—indeed, any that would be worth very much—will be far more restrictive than the general lay usage of "tragedy" or "the tragic," which somehow broadens out to synonymity with catastrophe, the sorrowful, that which stems from or leads to "pessimism." But how, if we limit ourselves to technical literary definition, can we find for the tragic any meaning beyond that of Aristotle? The answer is, by moving from formalistic aesthetics to what I would term "thematics."

Thus it becomes necessary first to determine the extent to which we want the meaning of "the tragic vision" entangled with that of "tragedy," surely a term well enough defined in our critical tradition. The most obvious difference I would mark between the two is also a crucial one: "tragedy" refers to an object's literary form, "the tragic vision" to a subject's psychology, his view and version of reality. It is more than a difference between two extant approaches to the tragic. Rather, the second has usurped the very possibility of the first after having been born side by side with it. Perhaps it would be more accurate to say that the tragic vision was born *inside* tragedy, as a part of it: as a possession of the tragic hero, the vision was a reflection in the realm of thematics of the fully fashioned aesthetic totality which was tragedy. But fearful and even demoniac in its revelations, the vision needed the ultimate soothing power of the aesthetic form which contained it—of tragedy itself—in order to preserve for the world a sanity which the vision itself denied.

It is for these reasons that the reader who as a modern is obsessed with notions of the tragic ought in a way to find himself disappointed on turning for the first time to Aristotle's celebrated definition in the *Poetics*. We have been so accustomed to doing this treatise deference—and rightfully so from a formalistic point of view—that we can no longer approach it freshly and feel the letdown that should be ours as we glance over its superficial formal prescriptions that are to pass as a description of so sacred and reverenced a literary genre. All this about magnitude and completeness and catharsis—are these to do justice to the profound complex of metaphysical and psychological forces which the tragic unleashes? Or so, at least, we ought as moderns to say superciliously. But probably we should have expected no more than this from the *Poetics*. Perhaps it was not for the Greek theoretical consciousness—even in as late a representative as Aristotle—to be as self-consciously aware of the disturbing implications of the tragic mentality as it was of the formal requirements which transcended, or rather absorbed, this mentality and restored order to the universe threatened by it.

The cathartic principle itself, in maintaining that pity and fear are not merely to be aroused but to be purged, is evidence of the need in tragedy to have dissonance exploded, leaving only the serenity of harmony behind. As has often been noted, the peace of cosmic reconciliation is most explicitly insisted upon in the concluding portion of the *Oresteia*—the sublime *Eumenides*—or in the magnificent end of Oedipus' story at *Colonus*. Here is the restorative spirit of superhuman purgation at its most refined. Even in the less exceptional tragedies which do not conclude in such thorough and profound tranquillity—in those, that is, which end more "tragically" in the lay sense—there is often the touch of transcendent grace which saves the cosmos for us in the midst of the ir-revocable devastation of human resources. It may, on rare and splendid occa-sions, be the pure shining thing of *Lear;* it may more often be little more than the matter-of-fact re-establishment of political order—an order, however, that reflects and is sanctioned by the cosmic order—which may be one of the reasons that it is so helpful to have tragedy concern itself with the fortunes of ruling princes.

But even if there were none of these, so long as tragedy remained a defined literary form, the fearsome chaotic necessities of the tragic vision would have to surrender finally to the higher unity which contained them. It is perhaps in this sense that we can speak of the formally sustained literary work ultimately com-ing to terms with itself. And from the standpoint of the audience—or at least the trained and sophisticated audience—even if there were no thematic ele-ments of release for the passions aroused by the tragic performers, the disciplin-ing and restricting demands upon aesthetic contemplation made by the rounded aesthetic whole would effect the catharsis demanded by Aristotle. The purging of dangerously aroused emotions, following as it does upon the satisfaction, the soothing grace, bestowed upon wayward materials by aesthetic completeness, uses form to overcome the threat of these materials and, consequently, these emotions. This roundedness, this completeness, carrying "aesthetic distance" with it as it brings us the assurances of form, presents us its formal order as a to-ken, a security—something given in hand—to guarantee the cosmic order be-yond the turbulence it has conquered. Thus it is that the cathartic principle *is* ultimately a purely formalistic one, even as tragedy, despite its foreboding rum-blings, can remain a force for affirmation through its formal powers alone. Thus it is too that in the *Poetics* Aristotle rightly limits himself to formal consider-ations, leaving to later and less solvent generations the thematic implications of the vision which, so long as it is aesthetically framed in tragedy, is denied in its very assertion.

It is finally Hegel who, after many centuries during which no radically new approaches are made to tragedy—or at least none that are relevant to my inter-ests here—takes up the task of explaining tragedy and catharsis in the thematic terms that Aristotle could afford to take for granted. Although it must be con-ceded that Hegel's analysis is clearly indebted to his metaphysic and his general philosophic method and although he does not concern himself with purely for-mal considerations, it is just this notion of reconciliation, of a final uniting or re-uniting, that he emphasizes as the conclusive power of tragedy.[1] His insistence on the absoluteness, the wholeness, the indivisibility of what A. C. Bradley trans-lates as "the ethical substance" is clue to Hegel's attempt to create a metaphysi-cal equivalent for the unity of the Greek world—the unity which, translated into form, allowed tragedy to overcome the heretical defiance of its hero.

For Hegel the *hamartia* that defines the tragic hero always arises from his exclusive identification with a single moral claim, a claim which, however just within its own sphere, is, from the view of a total morality—that is, the ethical substance—merely partial, a too-assertive particular. Thus the hero's vision is

[1] For Hegel on tragedy, see his *The Philosophy of Fine Art*, trans. F. P. B. Osmaston (London, 1920), I, 272–313; II, 213–215; IV, 295–303, 308–326, 330–342. A. C. Bradley's is of course a brilliantly suc-cinct and, by now, a classical summary of the Hegelian view ("Hegel's Theory of Tragedy," *Oxford Lectures on Poetry* [London, 1909], pp. 69–95).

necessarily destructive of the unity of the moral world, threatening with its mon-omaniac tendencies to produce an anarchy of unsupported metonymic leaps. And in defense of its absolute claims, the ethical substance must justly assert its oneness by ensuring the defeat of the hero whose nature it is, "at once his great-ness and his doom, that he knows no shrinking or half heartedness, but identifies himself wholly with the power that moves him, and will admit the justification of no other power."[2]

But this assertion of the ultimate unity of the moral order is what for Hegel leaves Greek tragedy with a final affirmation that transcends the carnage, "an aspect of reconciliation" that authoritatively seals the moral universe for even the most harshly devastated of its sacrificial victims, the bearers of the tragic vi-sion. Here is a significant attempt to account thematically for the catharsis prin-ciple, to bring tragedy—for all its deadly turbulence—to the very threshold of a Wordsworthian "tranquil restoration." And who is to say that this restoration is not part of what may seem to be implied by the Aristotelian concept of *dénoue-ment*—a falling action which does not usually stop with the hero's final destruc-tion but leads to a quiet beyond the grave: to a resettling of things in acceptance of this destruction?

Of course it is this final inhibition of the tragic vision, this imposition of for-mal and moral order upon that which threatens it, that allows these dramas to be properly called classical in the best sense. And when the embracing frame is lost, the romantic tragic vision bursts forth unencumbered—often in merely melo-dramatic splendor—in no longer reconcilable defiance of traditional aesthetic as well as ethical order. Thus it may seem that Hegel, in assuming the virtues of the Greek world to be those of his own philosophic construct, is hardly representa-tive of the self-conscious modernism that has dominated the last century and a half of our psychological history; the modernism that is characterized by frag-mentation rather than by the ever-uniting synthesis which Hegel tried valiantly, if vainly, to impose upon it as its salvation. Can his or can any all-resolving "ethi-cal substance" have validity for us as an absolute and claim our allegiance ac-cordingly? Can it now claim the all-commanding universality that justly, though ruthlessly, imposes itself on the subversive tragic hero in its midst? Or is the trag-ic hero, as modern, fulfilling a proper human function and even a proper human obligation in standing with his integrity as an individual outside the universal? Which is another way of suggesting that whatever universals we may be left with do not deserve the obedience of the most daring of us. Hegel created a sys-tem whose universals, like those of the Greek world or even of the Elizabethan world as we find it reflected in Shakespeare, have a metaphysical sanction; whose social and political institutions have a cosmic sanction. How accurate an account is this of the shabby, Babbitt-like arbitrary things that must—if any-thing does—pass with our world as universals, given our secularized, hand-to-mouth versions of the claims of religion, of politics, of social morality? Surely the absolute is not to be found immanently within such as these. Justice, then, has passed from the universal to the rebellious individual; accordingly, our appropri-ate spokesman on matters relating the individual to the universal and the abso-lute is not the anachronistic system builder, Hegel, but that heterodox and unprofessional wrecker of the Hegelian universe, Søren Kierkegaard.

[2] Bradley, p. 72.

Faith is precisely this paradox, that the individual as the particular is higher than the universal, is justified over against it, is not subordinate but superior—yet in such a way, be it observed, that it is the particular individual who, after he has been subordinated as the particular to the universal, now through the universal becomes the individual who as the particular is superior to the universal, for the fact that the individual as the particular stands in an absolute relation to the absolute.[3]

At what is for Kierkegaard the most crucial moment of man's existence—the moment of the leap to faith—the absolute is attainable only through the individual, the particular, the purely personal. It is denied to the universal. Here, unhappily enough perhaps, is the answer of modernism's "isolato" to the Hegelian attempt to restore the union of men within a congenial universe that sanctioned, indeed commanded, and fixed its divine blessing upon, this union. For Kierkegaard, the ultimate act—the act of faith—cannot be mediated, since only universals can mediate. Consequently, the paradox of faith is "inaccessible to thought" and cannot be verbally communicated, both thought and language—like reason, on which they largely depend—necessarily expressing universals. Further, it is the inaccessibility of faith to mediation that makes the Abraham who intended to sacrifice Isaac either a murderer or a "true knight of faith"—in my terminology, either a tragic visionary[4] or a religious visionary—but *not* the sacrificer of his individual self to the universal expressed in moral law. The latter individual would be the highest form of ethical man but, for Kierkegaard, something less than either visionary. And Kierkegaard's Abraham, whichever visionary he may be, repudiates the universal. Thus the "immediacy" of either the tragic or the religious vision eliminates the universal as a possible resting place for the errant, as a possible justification of what he has so privately dared to will. And we can never be sure which of the two visions he carries. Indeed, now beyond reason, how can he himself claim certainty? For the religious vision would be too easy for Kierkegaard if one could *know* its authenticity.

The categories which Kierkegaard can help us impose provide our insecure world with alternatives to the way of Greek tragedy as it is interpreted by Nietzsche as well as by Hegel. While Nietzsche is, like Kierkegaard, an unhappy epitome of modern man, an alienated creature who is close to being himself a tragic visionary, he is like Hegel in wistfully finding and admiring in early tragedy the elements of reconciliation that give order to elements of chaotic conflict. Nietzsche sees united in tragedy the Apollonian and Dionysian motives, appropriately named by him for their respective gods: the one the dreamlike, sublime, and gracefully measured order of the light principle, in the highest sense the civilizing principle; the other the primordial, orgiastic release of the natural principle—the "underground" reality probably related to Jung's "racial unconscious" or to Freud's "id"—the barbarizing principle.[5] Nietzsche sees these motives as akin to the forces represented by the creative and yet restrained Olympians and

[3] *Fear and Trembling,* by Søren Kierkegaard, trans. Walter Lowrie (Princeton, N.J.: Princeton University Press, 1941), p. 82.
[4] In light of the shriveling of the tragic concept in the modern world and the reduction of a total view to the psychology of the protagonist, I believe that this protagonist is now more appropriately designated "tragic visionary" than he is "tragic hero."
[5] For this entire discussion, see "The Birth of Tragedy," trans. C. P. Fadiman, *The Philosophy of Nietzsche* (New York: Modern Library, n.d.), especially pp. 951–969, 992–1017.

by the chaos-producing Titans, except, of course, that instead of the unreconcilable warfare between Olympians and Titans there is in Greek culture a perfect blending of the Apollonian and the Dionysian.

> The Greek knew and felt the terror and horror of existence. That he might endure this terror at all, he had to interpose between himself and life the radiant dreambirth of the Olympians. . . . out of the original Titan thearchy of terror the Olympian thearchy of joy gradually evolved through the Apollonian impulse towards beauty. . . . How else could this people, so sensitive, so vehement in its desires, so singularly constituted for *suffering*, how could they have endured existence, if it had not been revealed to them in their gods, surrounded with a higher glory?

Thus the Apollonian can so transform Dionysian terror "that lamentation itself becomes a song of praise."

Here is another thematic rendering of the principle of catharsis. But in order to make the formula work properly, both motives have to be maintained and maintained in equal strength. The Dionysian must be there for the Apollonian to transform, so that Apollonian radiance can retain its brilliance only by continually illuminating the Dionysian abyss. But it is an abyss which must not be denied, indeed must be acknowledged for what it is. Without the Dionysian, the Apollonian would seem to reflect a shallow, unearned optimism, a misreading of life that leaves the inescapable terror out of it. Thus Nietzsche can scorn the bland interpretations of "the serious and significant idea of Greek cheerfulness": "no matter where we turn at the present time we encounter the false notion that this cheerfulness results from a state of unendangered comfort." For the Apollonian cannot sustain itself in isolation; it can exist only in counterposition to the Dionysian. Otherwise it becomes perverted—as Nietzsche tells us it was perverted through Euripides—into the merely "Socratic," that moralistic denier of the Dionysian and consequently the destroyer of tragedy.

But what if we should find the Dionysian without the Apollonian? Here we would have life unalleviated, endlessly and unendurably dangerous, finally destructive and self-destructive—in short, the demoniacal. In effect it would be like tragedy without that moment in which the play comes round and the cosmos is saved and returned to us intact. It would be, in other words, the tragic vision wandering free of its capacious home in tragedy. The therapy produced by catharsis, which allowed the subversive elements to be healthily exposed and aesthetically overcome, would no longer be available. And the alienated members, now unchallenged, would be free to turn inward upon themselves to nourish their indignation in the dark underground. Nietzsche himself has told us:

> The tradition is undisputed that Greek tragedy in its earliest form had for its sole theme the sufferings of Dionysus, and that for a long time the only stage-hero was simply Dionysus himself . . . until Euripides, Dionysus never once ceased to be the tragic hero . . . in fact all the celebrated figures of the Greek Stage—Prometheus, Oedipus, etc.—are but masks of this original hero, Dionysus.

But picture a world into which Dionysus cannot be reabsorbed by way of the Apollonian with its final assertion of Greek "cheerfulness" and aesthetic form, a world in which the Apollonian and Dionysian—long since torn asunder—must live in a lasting separation that causes each to pervert its nature, the Apollonian becoming the superficial worship of happiness and the Dionysian the abandoned worship of demonism. Our modern tragic vision is the Dionysian vision still, except that the visionary is now utterly lost, since there is no cosmic order to allow a return to the world for him who has dared stray beyond.

The Kierkegaardian spirit would rather characterize the tragic vision as "despair," perhaps finally much the same thing. It is despair which for Kierkegaard is both the most wretched and the most hopeful stage of man's sub-Christian existence. With some interpolation and considerable simplification on my part, the phenomenological pattern one may draw from Kierkegaard for the tragic visionary may be seen as something like the following sketch.[6] A man lives his day-to-day existence below the religious level, either "aesthetically," as an amoral or submoral hedonist, or "ethically," by easily subscribing, consciously or unconsciously, but for the most part automatically, to that hierarchy of moral values which enables him comfortably to function. If he is a self-conscious moralist, he is concerned with the discovery of order in apparent disorder; concerned, that is, with universal principles, but principles that are discoverable in and referable to the world of human relations.

While the ethical level is certainly an advance over the mindless complacency in the midst of an unperceived chaos found on Kierkegaard's "aesthetic"[7] level, nevertheless this ethical level, because it sees values—and the order constructed in terms of values—as immanent rather than as transcendent, must itself remain pragmatic in its dictates for action. The orderly and abstract principles, bounded by the uses of this world and resting on rationality, much resist the paradox or absurdity which for Kierkegaard characterizes the immediacy and subjectivity of Christian consciousness. Thus finally common-sense pragmatism must inhere in the ethical level.[8] And our ethical man, assuming the validity of his abstract and universal principles inasmuch as they are conducive to order, can make decisions cleanly, can act in accordance with these principles—as if they were the absolute—since they blink the possible existence of a true moral

---

[6] In the interest of accuracy it must be acknowledged that Kierkegaard himself explicitly defines what he calls the tragic hero very differently from the way I am attributing to his view here. In *Fear and Trembling* he specifically claims that "the tragic hero still remains within the ethical." He sees the tragic hero as allowing himself to be embraced by the universal, his most cherished interests to be sacrificed to it. Perhaps here, as in so many other instances, Kierkegaard finds himself borrowing from the very Hegelianism he is bent on destroying. I believe that, as part of his dissatisfaction with the aesthetic in general, he never took this matter of the tragic as seriously as he might have taken it, that he never realized the revolutionary treatment of it that is promised by his other philosophic claims. It is thus, I hope, in the Kierkegaardian spirit, that I use Kierkegaard to support my own claims about the tragic though they run counter to his own occasional declarations.

[7] Whenever I use this term in the very special way of Kierkegaard I shall set it in quotation marks. Where it appears without them, it is being used in its common sense that pertains primarily to works of art and to our proper and limited responses to them as art.

[8] It is here, in his insistence that religion has dimensions beyond morality, that Kierkegaard strikes at the roots of that naturalistic humanism which would identify the two. Of course one may claim that Kierkegaard rather overdoes their separation since for him, it seems, the one (religion) can begin only where the other (morality) leaves off. I must, however, make it clear that, whenever speaking here of Kierkegaard's concept of religion, I mean only his version of Christianity. It must be conceded that in many places he refers to a pre-Christian, almost naturalistic religion, one in which the absolute is still immanent in the universal and which, consequently, still falls within the ethical. But if this stoical kind of religion can produce "the knight of infinite resignation," in its security it of course cannot begin to reach toward "the true knight of faith," who is rather a product of the loneliness and daring, the absurdity and subjectivity of Christian consciousness. It is only his notion of Christianity—defiant as it is of the ethical—to which Kierkegaard attributes absolute value, so that, to simplify matters, I have felt justified in speaking of it informally as his notion of religion in general, to the neglect of his other, inferior kind of religion.

dilemma characterized by endless ambiguity. This is the farthest reach of Hegelian man.

But our man can undergo a cosmic "shock": he can one day, to use Kafka's metaphor, wake up and find himself irrevocably arrested "without having done anything wrong." Or an Ahab, living until then by the proper laws of seamanship, can one day lose his leg to the leviathan; a Lord Jim, living until then by a schoolboy's code of honor, can one day be paralyzed into inaction and be made to play the coward's role. Melville's Pierre, having dedicated himself at all costs to absolute righteousness, can discover in his righteousness a lust that has led to incest; Conrad's Kurtz, having dedicated himself through altruism to a missionary zeal, can discover in his zeal a worship of self and of gold that has led to blood sacrifice. Perhaps this shattering seizure is precisely what ethical man has had coming for assuming, as fallible individual, his identification with an ethical absolute. For the ethical is, by definition, the universal. And, however well meaning, the individual may very well be doomed to pervert the absolute he claims to represent, since he comes to it as individual and particular, and thus as unsanctioned.

In any case, with the shock our man is jarred loose. For "aesthetic" man the oblivious evasions of hedonic existence will of course no longer do. And ethical man, confronted by a moral contradiction which resists the elimination of either pole as well as the synthesis of both, finds suddenly that the neatly ordered and easily enacted worldly rights and wrongs of his ethical assumptions are utterly inadequate to the data of his moral experience. Unless he yields to "infinite resignation" by blindly, if courageously, sacrificing himself to the implacable demands of ethical absoluteness—thus at all costs still remaining Hegelian man[9]— he must deny its authority forever. And then, hopelessly adrift from his or any other moorings, he can float into will-lessness and thus abdicate from tragic heroism, or he can surge toward the demoniac. If his rebellion has rendered him unfit for society and its necessary universals—its laws—it is because, at whatever price, he has seen beyond them. If his end, as tragic, must be condemned even as it is pitied by the trim categories of worldly morality, he may, prideful as he is, take further pride in the fact that he has defiantly looked upon those insoluble cosmic antinomies which have dictated his fall.

Someone like Conrad's Marlow, however—the sensible even if sensitive man—must, at whatever cost to his pride and his vision, finally rest in the ethical level, however sympathetic he may be to those who have renounced it to move into the realm of the tragic. Who is to say whether it is out of a "failure of nerve" or out of a special strength flowing from a profoundly tranquil vision, hardly known to us since the Greeks, that he has resisted the unmitigated tragic? It depends, very likely, on whether our view is Kierkegaard's or that of a less austere, less Protestant authority; on whether ours is the tragic vision or the classic vision.

On the other hand, our excommunicated ethical man, realizing the complete futility of human existence, cannot find a relationship with anything beyond it. His permanent forsaking of the universal seems to forbid it. This, the essence of the tragic vision, is "the sickness unto death," despair. It is the stage

---

[9] This is in effect Kierkegaard's own definition of the tragic hero. He allows him to go no further; and this admission on my part indicates how far beyond him I have without authorization moved using his tools.

induced by the shock; the stage which, beyond the "aesthetic" and the ethical, yet falls short of Kierkegaard's version of the Christian. An advance over the first two, it is yet much more treacherous and, if one remains in it continually, far more miserable. If one can attain a break-through—a bravely irrational one unmediated by universals—he can reach the glories of transcendence; if he fails, he must live in the contemplation of nothingness. Or, to put it more specifically, at best he can become a Kierkegaard, if we grant that Kierkegaard ever, or for very long, accomplished the leap of faith; if not, he must remain in the torments of the Zarathustrian Nietzsche or of a more consistent Heidegger who constantly and unblinkingly dares to encounter the nothingness that has capriciously hurled him into momentary existence. But he can never again rest in the self-deceptions of our John Deweys: those of our insistent naturalists who, for all the hardheadedness of their religious disbelief, are yet naively optimistic believers in a structured social morality and in social progress. These are, from the Kierkegaardian standpoint, the men of little heart; those who, evading the atheist's existential obligation to confront nothingness and its frighteningly empty consequences, construct elaborate rational structures based on nothing else: who whistle in the dark as if all were light.

One may prefer to say that it represents a supreme act of human courage to create meaningful communal structures of value on a substructure of acknowledged nothingness. Perhaps, as humanists say, man's creating God *is* a more sublime act than God's creating man. Perhaps. But the honest existentialist—anxious to confront his ontological status—would see the naturalist's structure in the void as an evasive act of bravado, not a closing act of bravery.

In the Kierkegaardian universe, then, there are two authentic visions—those I have termed the tragic and the religious—that can be earned through crisis by being forged in what Dostoevsky spoke of as the "great furnace of doubt." The other I have referred to is in this sense an illusory one. For the cheerfully naturalistic vision, which, pampering its security, denies itself nothing despite the fearsome implications of its own metaphysical denials, which existentially shirks the void it must rationally insist upon, is a precrisis vision, an illusion of ethical man demanded by his comfort, but one the stricken man can no longer afford. Like Kurtz, the tragic visionary may at the critical moment search within and find himself "hollow at the core," but only because he has suddenly been seized from without by the hollowness of his moral universe, whose structure and meaning have until then sustained him. What the shock reveals to its victim— the existential absurdity of the moral life—explodes the meaning of the moral life, its immanent god and ground. And there can be no post-crisis meaning and god except in defiance of reason, in acknowledgment of the impossibly paradoxical nature of moral existence. But this is to go beyond the despair that defines the tragic visionary and to make the leap to the transcendent subjectivity of the only kind of religious vision that the Kierkegaardian Protestant world leaves to the stricken.[10]

---

[10] Although this issue may not seem germane to a discussion of the tragic vision, it is worth adding— in order to expose another favorite illusion of our naturalistic and anti-existential tradition—that the religious vision described here cannot in fairness be reduced to any so-called "failure of nerve." This phrase the Kierkegaardian would reserve for the ethical man who flees the impact of the shock, for the naturalist himself. The shock may indeed cause our nerves to quake, but they fail only with the failure of our inner strength to manage, from the depths of despair, the awesome leap that makes "the true knight of faith"—no easy accomplishment and hardly a soothing one. The earned religious

On the other hand, the tragic visionary, in taking the alternative of defiance and seizing upon nothingness, is alone bold enough to take the existential consequences of his godlessness; and he takes them with pride, the very *hybris* that, in its sinfulness, moved him to godlessness rather than to transcendence. But he does not, like the naturalist, try to play both sides of the street to earn the prize of an ungrounded something: a world philosophically negated which is somehow made to yield the existential ease that would come if there were a meaning and purpose to be grasped. Sick of his precrisis delusion, the tragic visionary is God's angry man who will take only the real thing. He will refuse any longer to fool himself with the comfortable communal halfway houses of good works as a substitute for the absolute dedication of a religious faith which his inherited skepticism, issuing its curse, has denied him.

Of course, from a less severely Protestant point of view, other "authentic" visions would be sanctioned. One that concerned me earlier is what I called the classic vision, a vision that is of the world without being crass, that is universal and conducive to order without optimistically thinning moral reality as the superficially ethical man would. This vision is the all-embracing one of an older world and an older order. It is what I have tried to talk about in discussing the formal and thematic triumph of tragedy over the errant tragic vision it contained within it. It is as if the security of the older order wanted to test the profundity of its assurances, its capacity to account for the whole of human experience, and thus bred within itself the tragic vision as its *agent provocateur*. And by having the rebellion incarnate in the tragic visionary finally succumb to a higher order which absorbs but never denies the "destructive element," by purifying itself through the cathartic principle, tragedy is asserting the argument a fortiori for the affirmation of its humanistic and yet superhumanistic values. Consequently, it can witness all that befalls its hero without sharing in his disavowal of the meaning of our moral life; without denying, with him, the sensibleness of the universe and of life despite the explosive terrors they can hold in store.

But human possibilities, reduced as they are by disintegrations within the world that produced a Kierkegaard as its spokesman, no longer can reach to so inclusive a vision. If the only appeal to universals, to order, is pre-religious as well as pre-tragic, then the path of the religious visionary is as solitary as the tragic visionary's. And the ethical once shattered, there is no higher return to community—although, of course, for the less daring there may always be a retreat. The tragic vision remains what it was, but it can no longer be made through tragedy to yield to an order and a shared religious vision. The ultimately absorbent power of tragedy, symbolic of the earned affirmation of universals, is gone, with the result that the solitary visionary is left unchallenged, except by

vision must not be cheapened. It is a vision that runs quite counter to that implied by the Philistine claim that there were "no atheists on Bataan." No matter how devout the final protestations of these doomed souls, these protestations were all simply too comforting in their urgency, from the Kierkegaardian point of view, to have a claim to religious authenticity. Thus Kierkegaard comments on people who want to make an easy, escapist thing of faith:

... these caricatures of faith are part and parcel of life's wretchedness, and the infinite resignation has already consigned them to infinite contempt. ... They would suck worldly wisdom out of the paradox. Perhaps one or another may succeed in that, for our age is not willing to stop with faith, with its miracle of turning water into wine, it goes further, it turns wine into water. (*Fear and Trembling*, p. 50.)

the threats of uncomprehending and unsympathizing destruction at the hands of aroused ethical righteousness, the arm of social practicality. This is hardly the all-deserving antagonist the tragic vision once had, nor is it one that can command a satisfying aesthetic completeness any more than it can a moral-religious unity. Instead, in the Kierkegaardian universe, we now find for the aware and authentic existent an unresolvable disjunctive: either the way of nothingness or the way of transcendence, but both equally the way of utter solitude. The universals which must damn him have been left behind.

It is perhaps for these reasons that recent literature expressing an earned religious vision is hard to come by. For this kind of religious vision is primarily characterized by the fact that it cannot be shared. Equally subjective, the tragic as the demoniac vision can at least be dramatized by being contrasted to the ethical with which it is at war and which, in defense of society, must seek to punish it—for good reasons and for bad. We can be shown the ambiguous nature of the values at stake in this struggle: the need for the insights provided by the tragic to advance our understanding beyond the unaccommodating caution of social necessity as institutionalized in the ethical; and yet the need to strike out at the visionary, to cling to the props society provides, at whatever cost to insight, since, man being a social animal, his struggle through daily drudgeries is a crucial and ordering activity that must not be threatened.

To sustain a balance and, consequently, an aesthetic tension between these antagonists, the author must resist identifying himself too thoroughly either with the tragic visionary or with the representative of the ethical. If he becomes one with his ethical man, he must dismiss the tragic realm too summarily, without granting its power—however costly—of revealing the full density of moral experience and the shallowness of the reasonable order it has been forced to cast off. And he must sell the vision short as vision, however quick he is to see it as tragic, or anyway as doomed, if not as at worst merely execrable or at best pathetic. Or if, on the other hand, the author becomes one with his tragic visionary, he so cuts himself off from man's communal need that, in surrendering to moral chaos, he surrenders also the only possibility left him to impose aesthetic form. Further, he shows himself to be too sure of the vision to acknowledge it as really tragic, however quick he is—in contrast to our too ethical author—to grant its value as a vision. Only within the balance, and the mutual qualifications it provides, can the vision be maintained both as tragic and as a vision worthy of our concern and our wonder. Thus, at the one extreme, in *Heart of Darkness*, for example, Conrad, through his alter ego Marlow, rejects Kurtz—indeed is utterly offended by the man—only in continual acknowledgment that his rebellion against decency, however odious, renders him in some way superior even to Marlow. And, at the other extreme, close as Gide comes to embracing the reckless passions of his hero in *The Immoralist*, the classical artist in him maintains enough distance to reveal to us honestly, and even with some condemnation, their destructive and self-destructive consequences.

Even with the ethical and the tragic held in such balance, however, the ethical may seem finally to be treated superciliously and even as at least half blind to what really is going on. And since the tragic is from the ethical standpoint so dangerously evil, there would seem to be a need for some level beyond the ethical from which the tragic visionary would be judged absolutely—a level which would include his insight and with it soar beyond a parochial pragmatism, but one which would have passed beyond the rage of rebellion to a final, perhaps other worldly affirmation. But this is to call once again for what we no longer have—for the transformations that only tragedy can perform. For how are we now to distinguish outwardly between the religious and the tragic, between the angelic and the demoniac, when both equally transgress the ethical and the universal? As Kierkegaard in such brilliant detail asks, how shall we tell the Abraham among us from the self-deceived, maddened infanticide? To stop short of the religious insight is of course to rest in demonism; yet to leap to the religious vision, itself a perilous undertaking, is not to deny the temporal and, of course, the dramatic validity of the tragic. In neither instance is a retreat to the ethical possible. And the balance of necessities between the tragic and the ethical must continue as the primary mode of dramatic conflict, with the inherent weaknesses of each—the moral failing of the one and the visionary failing of the other—poised against each other to create the unresolvable tension that must now replace tragedy's more sublime catharsis as the principle of aesthetic control.

By now I hope I have clarified the sense in which I have been speaking of the unrelieved tragic vision as a modern vision, which is to claim also that it is a Protestant vision and, in an obvious sense, a romantic vision. Further, in its seizing upon the particular and its denial of any totality it is an heretical vision; and in its defiance of all rational moral order it is a demoniac vision. Finally, in a very special sense it is a casuistic vision; and it is this characteristic, perhaps, that makes it especially accessible to literary portrayal. The tragic vision, a product of crisis and of shock, is an expression of man only in an extreme situation, never in a normal or routine one. Literature dealing with it frequently dwells on the exceptional man; and when it does choose a normal man it does so only to convert him, by way of the extremity he lives through, into the exceptional man. The tragic vision is, by my definition, a vision of extreme cases, a distillate of the rebellion, the godlessness which, once induced by crisis, purifies itself by rejecting all palliatives. And the tragic visionary, by the stark austerity of his ontological position and of his dramatic position in the fable, is the extremist who—despite his rich intermingling with the stuff of experience—finds himself transformed from character to parable.

The literary obsession with extremity, with the exceptional, may represent an attempt at realism ultimately more sincere and more authentic than the cultivation of the norm, of what Lionel Trilling celebrates as "the common routine." If one wishes to assume the Kierkegaardian version of the human predicament, he will insist that it does and that at all times it has represented the only authentic attempt at realism. Even without Kierkegaardian psychoanalysis, however, we must admit that, at least in our time, driven as it is by crises and "arrests" and blind as it is to the healing power and saving grace of tragedy, the tragic has come, however unfortunately, to loom as a necessary vision and—or so it seems to the sadder of us—as one that can be neither reduced nor absorbed. Or is it, perhaps, that the Kierkegaardian version is right and that our world has itself become the tragic visionary, in its unbelief using self-destructive crises to force itself finally to confront the absurdities of earthly reality—those which have always been there lurking beneath for the visionary who would dare give up all to read them? Which is to ask, fearfully and even unwillingly, whether we have not been beguiled by aesthetic satisfactions and whether the utterly stripped tragic vision may not after all be less illusory than the fullness which shines through tragedy.

The Tragic Vision
Twenty Years After*

Murray Krieger

It is now just twenty years since *The Kenyon Review* published my essay, "Tragedy and the Tragic Vision," which two years later became the crucial opening chapter of my book, *The Tragic Vision*, and then had its life renewed in several subsequent anthologies. I think it is useful—at least for me—to look with hindsight at the full significance, together with the limits, of what I was doing then, and at the way in which it turned out to relate to developments in criticism since that time.

What stands out was my attempt then to carve out a place for the dark, underground, private vision we think of as tragic outside the soothing, containing form of tragedy; in other words, to create a thematic genre—characterized even to the end more by tension than by resolution—which expresses the rebelliousness and disbelief of a Protestant anti-ethic such as has dominated our great and most moving fictions since the early 19th Century. In other words, the secession of the radically subjective tragic vision from the ultimate radiant fullness of tragedy as a transcendent literary form was seen as a reflection of the Kierkegaardian secession of the individual, as absolute particular, from the claims of the ethical universal. And a number of our most distinguished modernist works were then viewed (the more clearly, I hope) within the perspective permitted by this generic model.

What we were left with was not simply a new thematic claim to a form created in the teeth of unyielding tensions rather than a form riding the crest of resolution, but also an historical claim that such a form was representative of our existential plight. So the studies in the book were to trace the tug-of-war between the character's (that is, the represented "tragic existent's") pull toward chaos and the literary work's pull toward a transcending and containing order, especially since the work is no longer a properly licensed tragedy (properly licensed, that is, by a society with transcending universals sufficiently authorized to make them stick) and since all ethical universals have come to be seen as fraudulent impositions sponsored by social complacency. The work, in other words, tries to exercise formal containment of its materials in order to permit them to be apprehended by our form-receiving categories of sense and mind, though those materials—let loose in the now uncontained protagonist—seem in their chaotic nature to be committed to tearing apart all forms, including that of this very work. There is in such a work a constantly self-undoing crisis, an ongoing con-

* "*The Tragic Vision* Twenty Years After" by Murray Krieger from *Poetic Presence and Illusion: Essays in Critical History and Theory* (Johns Hopkins University Press, 1979).

flict within an aesthetic (that is, a sensuously perceived) whole which seeks to define itself by its power to contain thematic elements even as they threaten its
permanent fracture.

So the work, supervising the tension between ethical universals it cannot believe in and the demoniacal particularity it cannot permit to wander unleashed,
constantly is both repairing and undoing itself, both a seamless unity and coming
apart at the seams. It alternately and simultaneously both maintains and subverts
its authenticity as vision and as the object of a single act of our attention seeking
to hold itself together. But what the work of the tragic vision undermines most of
all is the attempt of our aesthetic habit to see it as tragedy itself in its wholeness.
As a consequence, it is denied—or rather denies to itself—the over-arching formal reassurances, indeed the absolution, which the cosmic security of tragedy
used to provide for *its* materials, forever giving itself the last word as it gathers
them up, however shattered we thought they were, lying about the stage.

In retrospect, it now seems to me that, by my defining the literature of the
tragic vision as that which demolished the metaphysical substructure on which
the cosmic assurance of tragedy rested, I was anticipating the deconstructionist
critical temperament which was soon to follow. We have seen the transcendent
security provided by the cosmic form, which masquerades as the aesthetic form
of tragedy, now reduced to the psychological dimensions of the character who
dismantles that form. It is a reduction of ontological absolutes to society's shabby
universals sanctioned only by its crassest motives of self-preservation and, in the
protagonist himself, a reduction from hero to outcast madman, wallowing in
self-aggrandizement. As I viewed his disruptive actions—and the vision that
flowed from them—what was deconstructed was both the ontological and the
aesthetic, both the structure of the world and the structure of the work. I sought
to rehearse a reality sponsored by the disbelief which emerges from the Nietzschean temper and gives rise to a literature of the thematic underworld; and
legions of Nietzschean disbelievers have come along since then, echoing this literature, but with sharpened deconstructionist tendencies, invariably "finding"
just those tendencies in the objects of their discourse. And these objects, whether
they are newly created ones or representations of older ones, take on a self-consciousness, a self-deconstruction, which forces them to find themselves at odds
with themselves, repeopling their self-disrupted worlds as they go along.

The Tragic Vision, then, was an extreme statement about the radical transformations which tragic materials had undergone in the modern world; and I
balanced the reckless embrace of extremity a decade later in *The Classic Vision*,
a "retreat from extremity," although the latter is not our concern here. What
does remain methodologically interesting to me now about *The Tragic Vision*—
although I'm not sure how conscious I was of it or how formative a notion it was
if I *was* conscious of it—is the extent to which I depended on the role of the narrator's voice to establish distance from the tragic existent's and to try at once to
carry the tension and to relieve it. The voice was usually one of sanity, yet of absolute interest in the protagonist stopping just short of obsession or even identity
with him; but most of all the voice betrayed the tension generated by the collision between sanity and commitment to a mad surrogate. The paradoxical combination of ethical distance and existential empathy in the narrator's relation to
the protagonist sustained the strained balance between the level of vision and the
level of existence. I now suspect that I was less than fully aware of these separa-
tions as I notice that only in the new Preface to the two-volume paperback re-

print, *Visions of Extremity in Modern Literature* (1973), did I explicitly seek to retract the ambiguity in my use of the phrase "tragic visionary" in the earlier volume in order to distinguish the tragic-existent protagonist from the tragic-visionary narrator.

I am consequently able to see now the probable reason for my dealing exclusively with the novel in *The Tragic Vision*, that is, for my insistence that the tragic vision required the giving up not only of tragedy as a form but also of drama as a genre. And it had, I think, nothing to do with the questionable commonplace that successful dramatic tragedy is a thing long ago departed from us. What I sought in prose fiction must have been the extra dimension created by the narrator's dialogistic voice, the dimension of a reflexive self-consciousness which permitted the novel to display a breakdown of the brilliantly and objectively controlled form of old tragedy. But of the novel of the tragic vision, one could say, here was a work wilfully out of control and kept that way by a narrator conscious of his role and of the finally irreconcilable conflict between him and his materials—most of all, between him and his mad creature, or creature-as-surrogate. Here is our narrator-companion, a voice unfit for tragedy in that he is less than tragedy would allow, telling us about *his* companion, an agent unfit for tragedy in that he is more than tragedy would allow to be untamed by its transcendent (and dramatic) form. And it must have been my instinctive judgment that this narrative voice, which was our existential alternative, but also—and more importantly—our visionary absolute (if nothingness can achieve absolute status), was not simply a newer, novelistic version of the dramatic Chorus; rather that in its role as fictive creator it was a deconstructionist God, who saw chaos and said—not that it was good—but that it *was* and that he could *tell* it, find a word for it, without making it into order.

I now believe that I was very likely wrong to exclude drama from the tragic vision just as I excluded the healing aspects of tragedy from it. But even as I utter this judgment, I suspect that it may well be the product of what has happened to the theater—or, to be more accurate and more modest, what has happened to my sense of the theater—since my original conception of the tragic vision. My guess now is that I saw the novel then as a potential deconstruction of the drama—just the sort needed to reduce tragedy to tragic vision. This is to say that I singled out for value those recent manifestations in the novel which self-consciously played upon the reflexivity that is built into its narrative point of view: the ruminations of Ishmael confronted by his Ahab, of Marlow confronted by his Kurtz or his Lord Jim, of Zeitblom confronted by his Leverkühn, to name a few. And in these auto-dialogues-without-resolution I thought I found the unending tension which was to replace catharsis as the dominant moving power in a literature—and in a world—too late for tragedy.

But I am now aware of developments, in our time, in the writing for the theater and in the production (as well as the criticism) of older as well as newer plays (which, in effect, turn them all into newer plays), developments which use the peculiar devices available to drama in order to emphasize the self-conscious reflexivity which has always been locked in its form. Writers, critics, and directors have been breaking through the long-sustained veil of objective dramatic presentation, a veil naively held before would-be writers and would-be readers of what was presumably written within the terms of such strictures. I now understand that it was naive of me unconsciously to have accepted such a notion of drama as a prerequisite for the construction of tragedy, so that my deconstruction of tragedy into tragic vision called for an implied deconstruction of drama into novel. For what I now see clearly is that the drama, more than any other genre, has self-consciousness and reflexivity built into its very presentational nature. There it stands before us—with its actor-impersonators and their make-believe pseudo-actions, its masks and masquerades—the very stuff of mutually complicitous illusion, as commentators since Dr. Johnson have been constantly reminding us and as playwrights from the dawn of dramatic works in the West have been saying to those of us who would try to read them that way. For any play which would exploit its *merely* mimetic character and for any producer who would approach his theater with an insistence on such exploitation, the drama—as would-be imitation of *reality*—is swallowed up into its radical of presentation, its reality deconstructed, if not altogether dissolved.

So it may well be that, as the novel developed into a self-consciously aesthetic form, it learned to manipulate its narrative nature—that which differentiated it from drama—as a way of getting beyond drama and giving itself a special role in the development of self-consciousness in the 19th Century, hardly a strong period for the drama, which was for the most part still stuck in archaic conceptions about itself. The novel had shown, in those moments when it restricted itself to the objective presentation of dialogue with stage directions, that it could try to catch up to the naive conception of drama; but in its more developed moments (at least those which critics like me look for and find to be more developed) the novel showed it could move beyond such a conception by freeing itself to break its apparent form, to fragment it into reflections produced by an endless set of mirrors. In its turn the drama, once it rejected a naive conception of itself, could move forward toward where the novel had gone, and even beyond, because the full consciousness of the ambiguous realities represented by the drama creates such mirrorizing effects as the primary element of its aesthetic definition. The self-conscious construction of drama *as* drama is a deconstructive act. In increasing numbers playwrights, directors, and critics have been telling us so.

It may well be that what even I have at last learned can be traced, not to this mythical historical race and rivalry which I have suggested between the novel and the drama—with one catching up with and passing the other, only to be caught up with and passed in turn—but to the crucial recent influence upon our awareness of what the film is capable of, with both the drama and the novel racing to keep up with the many new dimensions which, thanks to the film, they can now envision and which, they instinctively know, can be envisioned by their audiences as well. The film lies between the two and is accessible to both: it apparently shares its radical presentation with the drama as a physical, living representation before its audience (a natural rather than an arbitrary sign, an 18th-Century aesthetician would say), but it can explode time and space and image with a freedom that the novel can share in kind although it cannot approach it in degree. And the recent theater has frequently tried to borrow for itself this breakaway power of the film, though it has had to struggle with its own traditional nature to do so. Surely, as we look at developments in both fiction and the theater from our vantage point today, we must see the self-conscious indulgence in multiple realities through eyes which have watched such indulgence reach the extravagant degree it has in the recent history of film.

Whatever the cause, it is surely the case that the deconstructive impulse now maintains itself at a highly self-conscious level both in the dramas written in the last several decades and in the older dramas produced as new ones during that period. And any notion of a reduced tragic vision, built as mine was on the dismantling of the total form which was tragedy, would have to include within its range the fruits of both the recent revolution in playwriting and the equally revolutionary concepts governing every facet of recent dramatic production. I will leave to the many among us who can speak with authority of such recent developments in the theater the expert discussion of examples of plays and productions; and I will be prepared to change my mind if such examples do not substantiate my impression. For as of now I am convinced that these revolutions thoroughly reconstitute our dramatic canon, both which plays we include and how we newly construct (and deconstruct) even the most venerable of our automatic inclusions.

Our new perception may well lead us to worry about whether, so far—at least—as we can conceive, there is left standing anything so transcendently full in its unquestioned construction as we had thought tragedy to be, or whether all has dwindled into the tortuous reflections and re-reflections of the tragic vision. Behind the promise of healing which the illusionary veil of tragedy seemed to offer, the raw edges of the tragic vision lie waiting to break through, once our self-consciousness—sponsored by the reflexivity of the presentation—is roused. Or is it that the tragic by this point so overlaps the ironic vision that the two in effect become the same? With full tragedy now beyond the reach of our vision—even in the case of those venerable old, but now remote, plays that went by that name—perhaps the adjective "tragic" is itself no longer deserved and should wither away, like the state in the mythical version of communism. The total indulgence of reflexivity and self-consciousness, the collapsing of literature and all our literary realities by way of that absurdity we call "life," these must lead us to the threshold of the ironic and the absurd. It may indeed be history's irony for the tragic vision, having reduced tragedy to itself, now itself to be reduced to no more than the ironic, although—in the light of the world around us—it will have to be enough.

The Vision
of Tragedy*

Richard B. Sewall

LEAR   Why, thou wert better in thy grave than to answer with thy
uncovered body this extremity of the skies. Is man no more than
this? Consider him well. Thou owest the worm no silk, the beast no
hide, the sheep no wool, the cat no perfume. Ha! here's three on 's
are sophisticated; thou art the thing itself. Unaccommodated man is
no more but such a poor, bare, forked animal as thou art.

—*King Lear*

When at the end of the *Symposium* Socrates insisted to his friends Aristophanes
and Agathon that "the genius of comedy is the same as the genius of tragedy,
and that the writer of tragedy ought to be a writer of comedy also," the friends,
says Plato, were "compelled to assent, being sleepy, and not quite understanding
his meaning." It had been a long night, with much wine, and the friends might
well have agreed to almost anything. But whether they would have agreed under different circumstances, and just what Socrates' arguments were, are other
questions. One would like to know precisely what he said. Or perhaps the affair
was a bit of a paradox spun out for his own amusement. For it seems clear—at
least it is the thesis of this book—that the genius of tragedy is not the same as the
genius of comedy. As for Socrates' notion that every writer ought to be able to do
both, there can be no objection. Some few have done both. What he had in
mind, perhaps, was the undeniable truth that the highest comedy gains its power
from its sense of tragic possibility, and the profoundest tragedy presents a full if
fleeting vision, through the temporary disorder, of an ordered universe to which
comedy is witness. Without a sense of the tragic, comedy loses heart; it becomes
brittle, it has animation but no life. Without a recognition of the truths of comedy, tragedy becomes bleak and intolerable.

But since the Greeks first wrote what they called tragedies and comedies,
and Aristotle in the *Poetics* formulated some principles about them, writers have
been conscious of the two modes—each with its own demands—as engaging
them in different undertakings, involving them in different worlds. They have
gauged their predilections and capacities against the demands of each and have
deliberately chosen one or the other, or some calculated mixture. They have of-

* Richard B. Sewall, "The Vision of Tragedy," from *The Vision of Tragedy* (Yale University Press,
1959), pp. 1–8. [Footnotes for this selection have been omitted.]

ten been explicit about it. Shakespeare announced his plays as "tragedies" or "comedies," or, when he chose, mixed the modes with the recklessness of Polonius. Marlowe spoke his intention when in the prologue to *Tamburlaine* he asked his audience to view his hero in "the tragic glass." Ben Jonson ventured into tragedy in his own scholarly, methodical way, boasting to have discharged (in *Sejanus*) all the crucial "offices of a *Tragic* writer," which he got from Aristotle. Milton's choice of the tragic form to express his final mood was deliberate and especially significant in relation to the tragic undertones of *Paradise Lost*. Artists are free—but free to choose their own sort of bondage. It is they and not so much the critics who have worked to maintain the integrity of the forms. Their conscious, explicit choices show that in their eyes the forms are real and different and not merely an academic conspiracy. The phenomenon is a powerful example of the fruitful interaction of tradition and individual talent.

Tragedy, traditionally the most exalted of the forms, has exerted on artists of many generations, not only Greek and Elizabethan, a compelling influence. Its effect on the individual talent has sometimes been noble and often disastrous. It requires an independent, radical vision whose lack is as fatal as the lack of a sense of ultimate harmony is in comedy. Sophocles and Euripides, though building on Aeschylus' original insights and to this extent acting in imitation of him, used the form he had established to express their own individual and radical visions. The Elizabethans, whose nervous and independent force worked creatively on whatever form they chose, expanded and improvised to suit their own expressive needs. Since then, as writers not so vitally equipped have attempted to write tragedy, the sense of strain and artificiality is frequent.

The French at their best (Racine, for instance) embodied the true tragic vision in a finely disciplined form; but their next best shows how precarious is the balance between creation and imitation. Milton's vision in the masterful *Samson Agonistes* has been called only "spasmodically tragic." In lesser artists, who approached tragedy too analytically or (it would seem) for its prestige, the strain is painfully obvious. The English theater after the Restoration produced plays called tragedies which are informed, rather, by the moral or "heroic" vision. The romantic poets, great admirers though they were of the Greeks and the Elizabethans, showed how far their world actually was from the world of *Oedipus* and *Lear* (which Shelley described as "the deepest and sublimest of the tragic compositions") when they ventured into tragedy. Shelley's preface to *The Cenci* is an earnest little treatise on tragedy; but he tried the form only once. As his wife wrote, "the bent of his mind went the other way." So did Byron's and Tennyson's, although they both wrote what they called tragedies. Goethe was perhaps wisest when he said "the mere attempt to write tragedy might be my undoing."

In the nineteenth century certain of the novelists had the surest sense of the thing itself. Genuine and vital strains of Greek and Hebraic tragic traditions, intensified by the tragic insights of Christianity, appear impressively, for instance, in Hawthorne, Melville, and Dostoevski. Hawthorne, whose sense of kinship with Greek and Elizabethan tragedy he more than once indicated, invested Hester Prynne with some of the hard outlines of Antigone's character and with much of the passion and color of an Elizabethan. Melville shaped Ahab as "a mighty pageant figure, fit for noble tragedies" and had him chase his "Job's whale" to the far quarters of the globe. Both novels show clearly that their authors were sensitive to the problem of making the tragic vision real to nineteenth-century democratic America. Dostoevski opened up a vast new tragic area by his own peculiar synthesis of the basic insights of all the traditions. Ibsen and O'Neill, Conrad, Kafka, and Faulkner (to name only a few) have each in their own way explored the area which he plotted out. Whether they have written "tragedies" is not at present the point, but they seem closer to the tragic spirit than the Romantic and Victorian imitators.

But how can it be said that a novel by Kafka or Faulkner is more truly tragic than *The Cenci?* What is the "true" tragic spirit, the thing itself? Is it right to say that writers choose the form, or does the form in some subtle way choose them? Shelley chose the form—his wife tells how the idea of writing a tragedy had haunted him long before he encountered the story of *The Cenci*—but, quite clearly, he himself was not chosen. Shakespeare's tragedies are grouped in a period of his life when, as far as we can tell biographically, the "bent of his mind" seems to have been that way. Goethe never felt chosen. He realized that the tragic sense of the world and of man's destiny was not his, and he stayed away. There was nothing that he could not have mastered technically; indeed, Shelley showed how far a near-perfect executive form could be from the thing itself. But tragedy demands qualities of vision which neither of them had.

In general, the tragic vision is not a systematic view of life. It admits wide variations and degree. It is a sum of insights, intuitions, feelings, to which the words "vision" or "view" or "sense of life," however inadequate, are most readily applicable. The tragic sense of life, as Unamuno describes it, is a subphilosophy, or a prephilosophy, "more or less formulated, more or less conscious." It reaches deep down into the temperament, "not so much flowing from ideas as determining them." It is an attitude toward life with which some individuals seem to be endowed to high degree, others less, but which is latent in every man and may be evoked by experience. Unamuno finds it characteristic of some nations and not others. Horace Walpole's epigram, "this world is a comedy to those who think, a tragedy to those who feel," has only relative truth, but it is significant in showing how readily the terms become metaphors to describe a view of life, a cast of thought or temperament.

The tragic vision is in its first phase primal, or primitive, in that it calls up out of the depths the first (and last) of all questions, the question of existence: What does it mean to be? It recalls the original terror, harking back to a world that antedates the conceptions of philosophy, the consolations of the later religions, and whatever constructions the human mind has devised to persuade itself that its universe is secure. It recalls the original un-reason, the terror of the irrational. It sees man as questioner, naked, unaccommodated, alone, facing mysterious, demonic forces in his own nature and outside, and the irreducible facts of suffering and death. Thus it is not for those who cannot live with unsolved questions or unresolved doubts, whose bent of mind would reduce the fact of evil into something else or resolve it into some larger whole. Though no one is exempt from moments of tragic doubt or insight, the vision of life peculiar to the mystic, the pious, the propagandist, the confirmed optimist or pessimist—or the confirmed anything—is not tragic.

Nor is the tragic vision for those who, though admitting unsolved questions and the reality of guilt, anxiety, and suffering, would become quietist and do nothing. Mere sensitivity is not enough. The tragic vision impels the man of action to fight against his destiny, kick against the pricks, and state his case before God or his fellows. It impels the artist, in his fictions, toward what Jaspers calls "boundary-situations," man at the limits of his sovereignty—Job on the ash-heap, Prometheus on the crag, Oedipus in his moment of self-discovery, Lear on the heath, Ahab on his lonely quarter-deck. Here, with all the protective covering stripped off, the hero faces as if no man had ever faced it before the existential question—Job's question, "What is man?" or Lear's "Is man no more than this?" The writing of a tragedy is the artist's way of taking action, of defying destiny, and this is why in the great tragedies there is a sense of the artist's own involvement, an immediacy not so true of the forms, like satire and comedy, where the artist's position seems more detached.

The findings of the anthropologists about the origins of tragedy are not irrelevant here. Even though they cannot be verified historically, they seem psychologically true. The religious ritual out of which it is thought tragedy grew—the dance of mourning in the fall festival at the death of the old year or (as some think) the ritual sacrifice of propitiation—was in itself an action, a response to a condition, a kind of answer to the question of existence. It was an answer in terms of gesture and action rather than language, and represents, perhaps, man's first attempt to deal creatively with pain and fear. Any action at all was better than nothing. It was not until later, when man graduated from the condition of pain and fear to the condition of suffering—which is the condition of pain and fear contemplated and spiritualized—that the response was verbalized in some kind of art form, a dirge or lament. Even in the most sophisticated of forms, literary tragedy, the element of gesture and action is strong, but it is the contemplated and individual response to suffering rather than the instinctive and tribal. Unamuno's fine anecdote about Solon shows elements of both—the primitive response by gesture (weeping) and the comment from the depths of an anguished spirit. "Why do you weep for the death of your son," the skeptic asked Solon, "when it avails nothing?" "I weep," replied Solon, "precisely because it avails nothing."

It is this sense of ancient evil, of "the blight man was born for," of the permanence and the mystery of human suffering, that is basic to the tragic sense of life. It informs all literature of a somber cast—the dirge, the lament, the melancholy lyric or song, the folk ballad of betrayal and death. It colors many scenes in the great epics and hovers about the best comedy as an imminent possibility. The tragedies of the tradition, from Aeschylus to Dostoevski, say this about it: that by most men it must be learned—and learned through direct, immediate experience: that is, through suffering. So universal is this testimony that it can be taken as one of the constants of tragedy, and the starting point. All men must learn to feel what wretches feel. In the lives of many writers of tragedy there is abundant evidence of deep autobiographic meaning in this recurrent theme, a fact of relevance to the sense of innerness and involvement that tragedy possesses above other forms.

Pressing out from this initial phase of the tragic vision, the artist's action or response takes him beyond the lament or the melancholy lyric toward an increasingly complicated dialectic as he contemplates the thrust and counterthrust of man against destiny. Here his cause is one with the philosophers and theologians, the difference being that the artist's dialectic is not of ideas in the abstract but of ideas in action, ideas as lived. His dialectic is not so much with words as with lives, and his focus is not so much man thinking as man acting, man "on the way." Where the philosophers and moralists would generalize an experience, find unity in multiplicity, and reduce experience to viable categories and prescriptions, the tragic artist explores each experience directly, *de novo,* for whatever it may reveal about man's capacities and possibilities. He presses the "boundary-situation" for its total yield. Whatever he finds man capable of, in action and under extremest pressure, is to him the truth, whether it be abject and miserable or sublime and redeeming. This truth constitutes the "discovery" of tragedy.

Historically, literary tragedy has always appeared at the mature period of a culture, not at its beginning. Although it retains the primitive sense of terror at what Joyce called "the secret cause" of suffering, it is in another sense highly sophisticated. It puts to the test of action all the formulations of philosophy and religion. In the three major western cultures—Hebrew, Greek, and Christian— there have come times (our present era may be one of them) when for reasons internal and external, spiritual and sociological, the questions of ultimate justice and human destiny seem suddenly to have been jarred loose again. Often these critical periods, or "moments," come after a long period of relative stability, when a dominant myth or religious orthodoxy or philosophic view has provided a coherent and sustaining way of life. Suddenly the original terror looms close and the old formulations cannot dispel it. The conflict between man and his destiny assumes once more the ultimate magnitude. It appears to be not a matter of accident, a temporary and limited disturbance, but an essential change in the face of the universe. The whole of society is involved, and the stake is survival. Thus the sense of despair in the early chapters of Job's complaint, the sense of doom in Greek tragedy, Gloucester's fears in the first act of *Lear,* and the sense of disintegration in *The Brothers Karamazov.*

In such periods, and in such moods, artists confront the existential question all over again. They ask, like the elderly trader in Conrad's *Lord Jim,* "How to be?" and embody their answers, ambiguous and tentative, in their "boundary-situations." Each age has different tensions and terrors, but they open on the same abyss. If each new artist's primary source must be the data of his own experience and observation, he just as surely learns from his fellow artists who have stared into the same depths. What they came up with, the statement of their fictions, constitutes the tradition—a total evaluation expressed in a literary form. As the tradition guides the new vision, the vision tests it, alters its focus and direction or expands its compass. Direction and focus may change, but the vision is constant.

Is There a Tragic Sense of Life?*

Lionel Abel

For Merry Abel, 1940-1964, In Memoriam

Our Estimate of Writers with the "Tragic Sense"

We set a particular value on those writers of plays—sometimes of novels—who give expression to what has been called the "tragic sense of life." Do we over-value them? The truth is, I think, that we value them in a very special way, for we see demonstrated in their works the possibility of viewing life other than with optimism or pessimism. And for ourselves, when we reflect, the only possible choice lies with one or the other of these extremes, so that it is not only the art of the writer of tragedy we admire, but some special insight, which we feel that we can achieve only through his intervention, and which he—for that is our assumption—enjoys by some peculiar privilege of rare wisdom or intelligence, or some yet more mysterious endowment. He seems more *philosophic* than other writers of equal art or scope, so that by a kind of tacit consent philosophers have honored authors of tragedy as the most *philosophical* of writers. In this estimate of the writer of tragedy I think there is a misunderstanding of his very special achievement, hence also a misunderstanding of what he achieves, namely, tragedy. If we can correctly think out what we are right to admire the author of tragedy for, we may correct some wrong notions of what tragedy is.

Our Dissatisfaction with Optimism and Pessimism

Now it should be clear why optimism as an attitude toward life cannot satisfy us. It should be clear, too, that our dissatisfaction with it is mainly *intellectual*. For we are quite naturally optimistic insofar as we are active beings, living in time and planning the future which our very life structure requires us to think of as being capable of yielding to our purposes. But when we reflect, when we re-member "things said and done long years ago," and also the things we did not say or do, as well as those said and done by others, we realize—we have to—that there are a great many negative facts. Only a few of these, and there are a great many of them, would be enough to invalidate any optimistic hypothesis that the world as it is can be truthfully described as *good*. Instances of such negative facts may be remote or local: the unjust sentence passed on Socrates, or the fact raised by André Malraux at a congress of Soviet writers during the thirties of a man run over by a trolley car.[1] Such negative facts are able to render void all optimistic *generalizations* about the world, just as a few tiny facts which remain obdurate to explanation are sufficient to refute a whole scientific theory accounting for a multitude of others. So those who live by optimistic beliefs are like bad scientists, clinging, despite the evidence, to refuted theories.

But what about the negative facts? Do they at least justify pessimism? Not as a hypothesis, not as a generalized view. For the negative facts comprise merely one set of facts, and the world is such that no one set of facts is able to speak for it. We know that having heard one set out, we must listen to very different facts. Alas for the heartbreak of the defeated and the dead: if we do not straightway share their fate, we are forced to think of something else.

The Russian thinker Chestov—I will not call him a philosopher—repeated again and again in his writings that the injustice done to Socrates was a fact he could not endure. He thought, too, that a fact of this sort should make us suspicious of any facts we ordinarily think of as positive. But even if the positive facts were far fewer than the negative they could still not justify our electing for pessimism. (For Schopenhauer a preponderance of negative facts did justify pessimism; his argument lacks subtlety.) The positive facts remain, and they prevent us from resolving without artificiality in favor of a pessimistic view. A very few positive facts can make pessimism unacceptable. This is illustrated, I think, in the biblical story of Abraham's debate with God when the Lord was intent on destroying the wicked cities of Sodom and Gomorrah. Abraham argued that if there were even ten good men in those cities, the Lord's proposed action would be unjust. And God finally conceded Abraham to be the better philosopher, admitting that if there were even fewer than ten good men in Sodom and Gomorrah, His pessimisim about the two cities would be unjustified, notwithstanding all the wicked in them.

That the positive facts stand in the way of a resolve for pessimism is not in any sense an argument for being optimistic. Far from it! It is a sad fact indeed that sadness will bring us closer than lightness of spirit to the heart of things.

What argues for optimism is that it is required by our life structure. If we plan to be optimistic, then at least we are not contradicting ourselves; but if we plan to be pessimistic—and since we live in time, to be pessimistic means to plan to be pessimistic—then we are contradicting ourselves; we are placing our trust in the view that things will be untrustworthy; we are reasoning that Failure cannot fail, and so, in a sense, can be depended on. Then too, except in cases of present or permanent distress, optimism is natural and spontaneous, while pessimism is inevitably theatrical. Life requires optimism; but optimism leaves out of account and quite disregards pain, frustration and death; such disregard is, of course, intellectually shallow. So we are back with our dilemma: we can be optimists or pessimists; but can we *want* to be either?

The Tragic Sense

The remedy is a fantastic one: it is a vision of the irremediable. We go to the theatre to see a tragedy. We see human action in the clearest light the mind can cast

[1] The reply made to Malraux was that the Soviet authorities would see to it that accidents of that sort decreased annually. The argument of the Soviet writers was for optimism, to them obligatory; the greater relative safety of future generations would more than make up for the absolute harm which had befallen one individual.

on it, and behold, we see the human person at his best. We do not disregard pain
or frustration or death; in fact we give them our whole attention, and they do
not make us pessimistic, they give us joy. As Aristotle said, we are relieved of
pity and terror, the very emotions pessimism would yield to and optimism would
avoid. We see life tragically; we have for the duration of the play at least and
perhaps for some time afterward the tragic sense. Would that it were more lasting!

Can we make it so? Can we not make permanent the view of life we enjoyed in the theatre and in recollection afterward for however short a time? Can
we not acquire or develop a sense of life such as the playwright himself must
have had? Of course, we cannot be Sophocles, Shakespeare, or Racine. The question then is: can the tragic sense be acquired without the special genius of the
writer of tragedy, and if so, how?

Why We Cannot Acquire the Tragic Sense

Suppose, though, for I think this true, that what we call the tragic sense does not
form part of the playwright's genius and does not involve superior capacities of
mind; then it must be the result of experience. Of what experience? The answer
to this question is obvious; we should have thought of it immediately: the experience which leads to the tragic sense of life is the experience of tragedy; it is by
undergoing tragedy that one arrives at the tragic sense. Or rather, the word "arrives" is misleading here, for one does not acquire or develop the tragic sense; it
is not realized but imposed; one never possesses it, one has to be possessed by it.

We cannot add the tragic sense to our present sense of life, be that present
sense optimistic or pessimistic. And without our present sense we have neither
terms nor criteria with which to decide whether the tragic sense is worth what it
will cost us. And from this it follows that no reason can ever be given for recom-
mending the tragic sense, however good or great a thing the tragic sense may be.

Herbert J. Muller, in a recent book, *The Spirit of Tragedy*, has had the te-
merity to urge on us the acquisition of the tragic sense for reasons which he himself does not deny are frankly utilitarian. He writes: "We might not continue to
get along as a free, open society without more of the tragic sense of life." I think
the error he has fallen into is expressed in his use of the word "more." If we had
some of the tragic sense of life then perhaps we could get still *more* of it, but it
would not be the drastic thing it is if that were the way it could be come by. The
prospect we would face, if we had not just "more" of the tragic sense but enough
of it to have it, would be one of all or nothing.

So we cannot urge the tragic sense on ourselves or on others. To try to attain
it or to recommend it is comical and self-refuting, tragedy being real only when
unavoidable. There would be no such things as tragedy if a tragic fate could be
rationally chosen.

The Writer of Tragedy and the Philosopher

But what about the writer of tragedy? Must he not possess the tragic sense of life
since he is able to make it available to us at least for the time we spend under his
spell? Is there not reason for thinking that the writer of tragedy must have a
more permanent relation to the tragic view than those who receive it from him?
Does he have a special philosophy, a tragic philosophy if you please, permanent-

ly his, and which through his art he is able to share with us in some small measure? Now I do not think the writer of tragedy has to have any view of life drastically different from our own.

Supposing he were a philosopher, what difference would that make? He could not by means of philosophy resolve the question of optimism or pessimism, which we who are not philosophers face. For philosophers are also either optimistic or pessimistic. (Some philosophies are neutral, but this last attitude is finally comprised under pessimism. Neutrality to life really means pessimism about it.)

When the vision of a writer of tragedy is stated philosophically, it is always converted (I submit, necessarily) into a form of optimism or of pessimism. I shall give two examples. The first is taken from Matthew Arnold's famous poem *Dover Beach*. Arnold, looking out at the sea from Dover Beach and hearing in the cadence of the waves the "eternal note of sadness," thinks of Sophocles:

> Sophocles long ago
> Heard it on the Aegean, and it brought
> Into his mind the turbid ebb and flow
> Of human misery;

And the image of Sophocles hearing the note of "human misery" leads Arnold to this pessimistic declaration:

> Ah, love, let us be true
> To one another! for the world, which seems
> To lie before us like a land of dreams,
>
> So various, so beautiful, so new,
> Hath really neither joy, nor love, nor light,
> Nor certitude, nor peace, nor help for pain;

The view of life expressed here is not one that I, or any one else, could derive from seeing a performance of *Oedipus Rex, Oedipus at Colonus,* or *Antigone.* Perhaps Sophocles had such thoughts when he looked at the Aegean, but these are not the thoughts we think when witnessing his tragedies. And from the reports about Sophocles by his contemporaries, we are scarcely justified in calling to mind an individual contemplating human misery. The tragic poet was said to have been charming, gracious, genial, and with no better opinions about politics or life than other cultivated Athenians.

The wonderful Spanish writer and thinker Miguel de Unamuno, who is actually responsible for the phrase "the tragic sense of life," trying to state this "tragic sense" as a philosophical attitude, converts it, I think, into a refined and pleasing, though somber, form of optimism. Unamuno's tragic sense is even a misnomer; there is little tragic about it, for he is not urging us to set something above life; rather what he does urge us to set above life is nothing other than life, immortal life, the immortality of the soul, on which immortality he asks us to gamble the existence we are certain of. That this violently optimistic Christianity should attract us with its death-splashed Spanish cloak is due, of course, to our obscure recognition, even if we have not thought the matter through, that optimism presented simply as optimism would offer us only what we are well acquainted and dissatisfied with.

A novel and, I think, quite wrong view that thought, even philosophic thought, can have and has had a tragic cast is presented by Lucien Goldmann in his much-praised book on Pascal and Racine, *Le Dieu Cadré*. According to Goldmann there are certain philosophers whose thought can be characterized as tragic. He cites as instances Pascal and Kant. Why is their thought tragic? Because, says Goldmann, it expresses the conflict in them between alternatives and exclusive world views, the world view of mathematical science and the world view of revealed religion. But surely no character on the stage would be convincing in the tragic hero's part if his torment were due to nothing more drastic than his inability to choose between or mediate conflicting views. In fact, Kant and Pascal did both. What I mean is this: Kant opted for religion in his metaphysics and for science in his epistemology. And I think Pascal did the same in his distinction between *l'esprit géométrique* and *l'esprit de finesse*.

I submit that it is not through any particular philosophy that the tragic writer is able to give expression to his tragic sense of life, although this tragic sense does have for us, the audience, a virtue which has been called philosophic. Then is it by art alone that the writer of tragedy affects as he does?

The very great probability is, I suggest, that the writer of tragedy is no more endowed with a tragic sense of life than are we to whom he makes it available. By which I mean that he, too, in his regular experience of life, is condemned to the same unsatisfactory choice between optimism and pessimism that we are, and that only in the act of writing a tragedy, only by making the tragic view available to us, is he himself enabled to envisage life in such terms. His creation then is a communion with us, in the experiencing of a view of things which we could not have without him, but which he in turn can only have insofar as he is capable of extending it to us.

Why could we not have the tragic sense without the *written* tragedy? Let us consider this point from a somewhat different angle. There is something we could have without the help of art, and which many people may confuse with the tragic sense, namely the feeling of a *pessimism that is justified*. This is all we can get from the lesser masters of the art of tragedy, from Euripides, Webster, and Tourneur at their best, and from Shakespeare in his unsuccessful tragedies such as *Troilus and Cressida*, *Coriolanus*, *Timon of Athens* and *King Lear*. Moreover, this justified pessimism appears at times even in the greatest works but it is not this which makes them tragic. When Richard in Shakespeare's *Richard II* complains of the vulnerability of kings,

> . . . for within the hollow crown
> That rounds the mortal temples of a king
> Keeps Death his court; and there the antic sits . . .
> Allowing him a breath, a little scene . . .
> . . . and humour'd thus,
> Comes at the last, and with a little pin
> Bores through his castle wall, and farewell king!

he gives expression to a pessimism which in view of his situation he is certainly justified in feeling. And the greatness of the verse penetrates Richard's feeling completely; what he says seems all the more inevitable because said in lines of such power. Who can be secure if the best protected of men, the king, is not? It is to be noted that a negative fact, in this instance death, armed with so mean and trivial an instrument as a pin, is seen as rendering meaningless the highest state a man can aspire to, that of a kingliness. Later in the play Richard will say:

> ... nor any man that but man is
> With nothing shall be pleas'd till he be eas'd
> With being nothing.

The feeling expressed here of life's meaninglessness we may all have felt, indeed must have felt, at some time or other and with some measure of poetry, too, for such feelings provide a verbal talent all by themselves. We would not need the art of tragedy to acquaint us with such a judgment of life nor even with the necessity to pronounce it consummately.

A judgment of life similar in its pessimism to Richard's and equally justified is uttered by Macbeth:

> Life's but a walking shadow, a poor player,
> That struts and frets his hour upon the stage
> And then is heard no more. It is a tale
> Told by an idiot, full of sound and fury,
> Signifying nothing.

This judgment, too, we could form for ourselves without either the experience of tragedy or Shakespeare's art. But what we could not get without actual or invented tragedy is the experience of resolution when nothing can follow from resolve, a resolution beyond optimism or pessimism, hope or despair. This we get from Macbeth's great words:

> Though Birnam Wood be come to Dunsinane,
> And thou opposed, being of no woman born,
> Yet will I try the last.

Richard's speech about the death of kings is a protest against the weakness and impotence of the most highly placed. Macbeth's lines of resolution express a much more complicated feeling, one in which are allied, to use Heidegger's phrase, "utter impotence and super power." Richard's lines about the death of kings, justifying pessimism, point to the negative fact of death which renders optimistic notions of life invalid even for a king. Macbeth's lines of resolution refer to no negative facts at all, not to anything common in human experience, not even to the common experience of kings, but exclusively to the withdrawal of their aid from him by those metaphysical beings, the witches, who had for a time supported him. Macbeth's lines are thrilling; Richard's are merely sad. What has to be explained is why Macbeth's lines thrill us, and why he had to pass through the experience of tragedy in order to be able to utter them. The weakness of Richard is evident, so is Macbeth's. But whence comes Macbeth's power?

What Is Tragedy?

In tragedy it is not the negative facts, rendering optimism invalid, which finally cause misfortune. Such negative facts as commonly threaten all of us are even converted by the mechanism of tragedy into positive goods. Blindness is an evil; yet Oedipus deliberately blinds himself; death we would think is to be avoided at all costs; yet Antigone elects to die and denies her sister, Ismene, the same privilege. Ajax, when told that if he spends the day in his tent he will be allowed to live, deliberately leaves his tent and falls on his sword. In the tragic universe the negative facts of experience are finally unimportant. What might lead us in ordinary life to be pessimistic is never the cause of tragedy.

What is the cause then of tragedy? It is the opposition, as Hegel affirmed, of two conflicting goods. Tragedy is never caused by what is unambiguously evil. It is the sheerly positive in conflict with the sheerly positive that destroys the tragic protagonist. In the Greek world it was the collision of the values of the family with those of the state. Those contrary values, as Aeschylus and Sophocles understood them, could not be held to with equal fidelity in any superior experience of life. The superior man would inevitably violate the one or the other.[2] Perhaps it may be said that while this may have been true of the ancient Greek world, it was not true of the Shakespearean world. For in what sense can the witches who incite Macbeth to kill Duncan be called sheerly positive? In what sense can they be called representatives of the good? Are they not the expression of unmitigated evil?

If they were, *Macbeth* would not be a tragedy. It would be a melodrama, and Macbeth's story would merely be that of a villain defeated. But once again, in what sense can the witches be said to represent the good? In this sense: the witches in *Macbeth* are the only dramatic expression of the metaphysical. Duncan, the reigning king, is presented as kingly, just, morally right. But Macbeth and Banquo are the characters in the play who have direct contact with the representatives of the metaphysical, that is to say, the witches. Now in *Macbeth* the metaphysical does not coincide with the moral, but is at odds with it; yet both are to be valued. Since the justification for kingship was finally metaphysical—the Elizabethans believed in the divine right of kings as opposed to any merely moral right to kingship—how could an immoral deed of murder to attain kingship, when metaphysical forces, in this case, the witches, seemed to support that deed, be thought of as evil? And, in fact, we never feel Macbeth is evil. We think of him as suffering, suffering because he has violated moral values he cannot deny, in support of values neither he nor Shakespeare's age thought criticizable in moral terms. As in the Greek tragedies, we have in *Macbeth* good pitted against good, and the protagonist is the victim of their collision. What is dreadful then is never the mere negative facts ordinary experience fears. It is the good which is dreaded and has to be dreaded. Soren Kierkegaard, peculiarly sensitive to these matters, summed up what, I think, can be called the experience of tragedy when he said in his acute analysis of dread that it is fundamentally dread of the good.

What Has the Writer of Tragedy Seen?

So the tragic writer has to have seen some collision of good with good in order to have been able to arrange the events he describes into a tragedy. Was he predis-

---

[2] It may be asked: why is a collision of values different from a collision of world views? But a collision of views, even if we call them world views, takes place within *consciousness* and not within the *world*. Values such as the family and the state are not merely values; they are valued realities. I should like to point out here that one of the most interesting insights of Martin Heidegger—much more interesting than his remarks about anguish and guilt, which have become part of current twaddle—is his judgment that world views imply the absence of a world rather than a world's enduring presence. Tragedy takes place in a world, not in a consciousness which is uncertain as to what the world is.

posed to see some such collision of good with good? Not, I should say, if it were not there to be seen, even if only he saw it. For can we want to see what is is undesirable to see? Some of us may out of ambition or perversity, but not the writer of a proper tragedy. He sees what it is undesirable to see without desiring to see it. This is one of the things we admire him for. To be sure, there are others. But in any case, what must be understood here is that the object of his vision was given by his age or epoch and not created by him alone. The collision of good with good which he witnessed had then to be given him along with others to see: his part was to take what he saw, and what others may have seen, and fashion it into art.

Thus the tragic view, properly understood, means to have seen the necessity for tragedy, to have recognized it rather than to have created it. That the tragic vision results from a direct act of seeing, and not from the holding of any particular view, or from any predilection for interpreting reality tragically, is something we must understand in order to evaluate that vision and judge it for its true worth. Just as in the tragedy he is going to write, the dramatist will set forth a sequence of events whose connections are necessary, so he himself can only be stirred to set forth such a sequence of events by the sight of a fatality that was thrust upon his view and which was necessarily, not accidentally, there before him.

Once again: what did he see? A collision of good with good. Is it desirable that such a collision come within our view? Not in life. No. Nobody can genuinely say that he wants to see a tragedy enacted anywhere but on the stage. For it is a misfortune to a society or to a culture if its main values contradict one another. On the other hand, tragedy, that art which expresses the collision and not the harmony of such values, is in itself a positive aesthetic good. But this good, this aesthetic good, is achieved through an appropriate description of the ultimate in human misfortune: that man's values should contradict rather than support one another.

Once Again "The Tragic Thinker"

Perhaps it is right to say of the writer of tragedy that his thought, since it had to be equal to what he saw—what he saw was tragedy—is a kind of "tragic thinking." But this can only mean that the writer of tragedy has not permitted any philosophy or ideology to impede or obstruct his vision. But what about those thinkers who have been called "tragic," as for instance Pascal? As I indicated before, I think the term "tragic" when used to designate the thought of anyone not the writer of a tragedy is always wrongly used. Nonetheless, there are in Pascal's *Pensées* many dramatic characterizations of experience which give us a kind of thrill comparable to the kind we get from tragedy. My contention is that in the case of such *Pensées*, Pascal has merely created an abstract replica of the kind of collision of values we find embodied with ever so much more concreteness in tragic poetry. Here is one of the most famous of Pascal's thoughts:

> Man is but a reed, the feeblest of Nature's growths, but he is a thinking reed. There is no need for the whole universe to take up arms to crush him; a breath, a drop of water, may prove fatal. But were the universe to kill him, he would still be more noble than his slayers; for man knows that he is crushed, but the universe does not know that it crushes him.

I think what we have here is an imitation in conceptual terms of the kind of event set forth in a real tragedy. It is to be noted that Pascal begins by saying men can be destroyed by a drop of water or a breath; but he chooses not to continue the thought that men can be destroyed by such small means. The drop of water, the breath, are tiny facts: acting negatively, they would be of no interest in tragedy. So in Pascal's thought they are expanded—in possibility, of course—into the universe. From the breath, the drop of water, Pascal goes to the whole universe, which he imagines in the act of overwhelming a man. Even then, says Pascal, the man would be nobler than his slayer. But, in any case, the slayer would be noble, being the universe. Insofar as Pascal's thought here may strike one as tragic, I should say that the event he has described was modeled on that structure of events always present in a true tragedy. For he who is destroyed in a true tragedy is always destroyed by something of worth. The drop of water, the breath, may be thought of, as I said before, as tiny facts behaving negatively but which Pascal had finally to forget about and obscure from his view in order to make a true judgment of man's nobility in misfortune.

What We Should Admire the Writer of Tragedy For

Let us turn from the "tragic thinker" to the writer of tragedy. Why do we admire him? Not for his philosophy, for he has none. If he does hold to one in his personal life, this is not pertinent to his achievement or to our judgment of it. Nor are we required to think of him as a master of experience, as wiser or more deeply human than ourselves. Let us admire him for his art; we should recognize, though, that what he gives us goes far beyond what art generally or regularly gives. And let us admire him for his luck, too, at having been given by his age the opportunity to see in his mind's eye certain paradigm instances of human adversity. Does not Pushkin say that the day after the flooding of Petrograd, "Khostov, poet, favorite of the heavens, already sang in verses never to die the griefs of Neva's shores?"[3]

Moreover, the effort the writer of tragedy makes has to be immense. He has seen the collision of the main values of his age or culture; he has seen the nonmeaning of meanings. Now the mind naturally seeks for meanings; the writer of tragedy has to deny and reverse this process in the very movement with which he yields to it.

His interest is, of course, an aesthetic one. May I speak for just one moment from a professional point of view? When you have written a play you are faced with this problem: what does this play mean? If it is meaningless, it is uninteresting. Suppose it does have a meaning, though. This is scarcely better. Have you not then reduced the action in your play to the illustration of an idea? Now illustrative art is scarcely better for many of us today than is meaningless art. Here the idea of tragedy exerts its fascination. For it is the kind of idea that attains to its truth only when represented in the work itself: the play, the tragedy. We are much more clear about what tragedy is when we see a tragedy enacted than when we try to reason about tragedy.

And let us not forget that what the writer of tragedy gives, he himself gets in the very act of giving: communion with us in a privileged view of human ad-

---

[3] From Pushkin's poem *The Bronze Horseman* in Edmund Wilson's translation.

versity. We admire him then for what he makes us see, a world where the highest values collide and in which we know we could not live. We recognize this when the curtain comes down and we do not know where to go. We have to become optimists or pessimists again in order to think of going home.

II
CHARACTERISTICS
OF THE TRAGIC

Basic Characteristics of the Tragic*

Karl Jaspers

The tragic looms before us as an event that shows the terrifying aspects of existence, but an existence that is still human. It reveals its entanglement with the uncharted background of man's humanity. Paradoxically, however, when man faces the tragic, he liberates himself from it. This is one way of obtaining purification and redemption.

Breakdown and failure reveal the true nature of things. In failure, life's reality is not lost; on the contrary, here it makes itself wholly and decisively felt. *There is no tragedy without transcendence.* Even defiance unto death in a hopeless battle against gods and fate is an act of transcending: it is a movement toward man's proper essence, which he comes to know as his own in the presence of his doom.

Where awareness of the tragic has become fundamental to man's awareness of reality, we speak of tragic readiness.[1] But we must distinguish between awareness of the transitoriness of things and genuine awareness of the tragic.

When he thinks of transitoriness, man views the actual events leading up to death, as well as the ephemeral character of all life, as parts of the natural cycle of growth, decay, and renewed growth. He recognizes himself as within nature and identifies himself with it. Here man comes upon a secret that makes him tremble. What is the soul which, independent of the flux of time, knows itself to be immortal, although aware of the finiteness of its worldly existence, aware that it is doomed to pass away in death? Yet, neither this fact of mortality nor this secret of the soul can rightly be termed tragic.

Genuine awareness of the tragic, on the contrary, is more than mere contemplation of suffering and death, flux and extinction. If these things are to become tragic, man must act. It is only then, through his own actions, that man enters into the tragic involvement that inevitably must destroy him. What will be ruined here is not merely man's life as concrete existence, but every concrete embodiment of whatever perfection he sought. Man's mind fails and breaks down in the very wealth of its potentialities. Every one of these potentialities, as it becomes fulfilled, provokes and reaps disaster.

A yearning for deliverance has always gone hand in hand with the knowl-

---

* Karl Jaspers, "Basic Characteristics of the Tragic," from *Tragedy Is Not Enough* (Beacon Press, 1952), pp 41–56. Copyright © 1952 by Beacon Press. Reprinted by permission of Beacon Press. [Translator's minor footnotes for this selection have been omitted and those remaining are renumbered.]

[1] *Tragische Haltung.* This is the inner attitude of composure in the face of tragedy; it resembles Hamlet's "the readiness is all."

edge of the tragic. When man encounters the hard fact of tragedy, he faces an inexorable limit. At this limit, he finds no guarantee of general salvation. Rather, it is in acting out his own personality, in realizing his selfhood even unto death, that he finds redemption and deliverance.

He may find this deliverance through his sheer strength to bear the unknown without question, and to endure it with unshakable defiance. This, however, is the mere seed of deliverance, its barest possible form. Or he may find deliverance by opening his eyes to the nature of the tragic process which, brought to light, can purify the mind. Finally, deliverance may already have preceded contemplation of the tragic process in the case where some faith has, from the outset, led life onto the road to salvation. Then, tragedy appears as overcome from the beginning as man transcends to the unseen, to God, the background of all backgrounds.

Ways of Interpreting Tragic Knowledge

The meaning of those tragedies that lie before us as the work of poets cannot possibly be reduced to a single formula. These works represent man's labor dealing with his knowledge of the tragic. Situations, events, social forces, religious beliefs, and types of character are the means through which man expresses the tragic.

Every one of the great poems has a meaning which cannot be exhausted by interpretation. They offer no more than directions for interpretation to pursue. Where complete rational interpretation is possible, poetry becomes superfluous—indeed, there has never been truly poetic creation from the very beginning. Where interpretation can make some elements stand out clearly, it heightens their accessibility precisely by virtue of a profound vision that is uncharted, that is not exhaustible by any analysis or interpretation.

In all poems the intellectual construction of the poet asserts itself. In proportion, however, as the thought emerges as such without being made incarnate in dramatic figures, poetry grows weaker. To that degree, then, the work is generated not by the power of tragic vision but by philosophical preference. This is not to say that thoughts in tragic poetry may not have crucial philosophical significance.

Now that we have reviewed tragic knowledge as a whole, our interpretation must give more searching answers to three problems:

1. What do the objective aspects of the tragic look like? What is the pattern of tragic existence and of a tragic course of events? How is it conceived in thought? Our interpretation of tragic subjects in poetry will yield the answer.

2. How do the subjective aspects of the tragic work themselves out? How does the tragic enter into consciousness? How is tragic knowledge achieved and, through it, deliverance and redemption?

3. What is the meaning of any fundamental interpretation of the tragic?

The Tragic as Subject of Poetry

Without trying to define the tragic, we visualize the stark immediacy of tragic events as they have achieved form and expression in poetry.

Our interpretation must hold fast to the content of the poet's original vision, to what already has been expressed and interpreted in his work. Interpretation adds to this vision the meaning which is or might be implied in it, whether or not the poet had explicitly thought of it.

In poetry, tragic consciousness gives body to its own thought: it is only through the tragic mood that we can sense tension and disaster in events affecting us directly or in the world as a whole. Tragedy shows up in battle, in victory and in defeat, in guilt. It is the measure of man's greatness in breakdown and failure. Tragedy reveals itself in man's unconditional will to truth. There it stands revealed as the ultimate disharmony of existence.

The Tragic Atmosphere

Life and death, the cycle of blossoming and withering away, the fact of transitoriness, do not yet establish in themselves any tragic atmosphere. The onlooker can calmly contemplate this process in which he is himself included and by which he is sheltered. The tragic atmosphere arises as the strange and sinister fate to which we have been abandoned. There is something alien that threatens us, something we cannot escape. Wherever we go, whatever we see, whatever we hear, there is something in the air which will destroy us, no matter what we do or wish.

This mood occurs in Indic drama as the vision of a world which is the setting of our life, a setting in which we have been abandoned without any protection. Thus, in *Kausika's Wrath:*

> The whole world seems a carrion-ground,
> A plain of corpses slain by Siva's servant, Time.
> The firmament at dusk seems red
> With blood of victims executed.
> Like embers of a pyre
> The feeble sun-disk glows; stars above
> Seem but a boneyard in the sky;
> And, like a skull bleached white,
> Glares the pale moon . . .

Moods of horror dominate some works of Brueghel and Hieronymus Bosch, as well as Dante's *Inferno.* But this mood is nothing more than foreground. We must look for something deeper, but we cannot find it without first passing through these terrors.

The tragic atmosphere in Greek drama is not the mood of all nature. Rather it is related to particular events, particular human figures, perhaps as the tension that grips everything even prior to any specific deed or occurrence, the tension that warns of doom, though no one yet knows what form the doom will take. Aeschylus' *Agamemnon* gives us an example, and one of singular magnificence.

The tragic mood assumes the many shapes of so-called pessimism and its various pictures of this world, whether in Buddhism or in Christianity, in Schopenhauer or in Nietzsche, in the *Edda* or in the *Nibelungenlied.*

Battle and Collision

Truth and reality split apart. In consequence of this split, men must support each other in community, and they must battle in collision. Tragic knowledge sees those battles which are unavoidable. The question for the tragic poet is precisely this: Who is battling whom, and what is really colliding with what?

Immediately, the battle which has found poetic expression is the battle of men against men, or of man against himself. Incompatible needs, duties, motives, and qualities of character are locked in combat. Psychological and sociological analysis seems to make these battles understandable in terms of fact. But the poet sees farther and deeper. It is his task to render tragic knowledge visible, and all these limited realities serve him merely as raw material. Through this raw material he points out what is truly at issue in this conflict. The conflict is now understood according to the interpretations of the antagonists, or of the poet and, through him, the spectator. These interpretations of the battle are themselves realities. For significance so uncovered has always generated the strongest motive power. This significance emerges in the plot of the tragedy.

Such interpretations, when embodied in the work of art itself, are either immanent or transcendent. Tragedy may be immanent, as in a battle between the individual and the universal, or as in a battle of different ways of life that succeed each other in history; or it may be transcendent, as in a battle between men and gods, or as in a battle between the gods themselves.

The Individual and the Universal

The individual is opposed to universal laws, norms, necessities: untragically, he represents mere willfulness opposing the law; tragically, he represents the genuine exception which, though opposing the law, yet has truth on his side.

General principles are concentrated in the forces of society, in social stratification, rules and offices. Hence society may give rise to tragedy. On the other hand, general principles may be concentrated in human character as an imperative of eternal laws which run counter to the drives and the personality of the individual. Hence there are also tragedies that arise from character.

Commonly, tragic works based on such interpretations are poetically weak. Human drives which are entirely concrete, and general rules which are entirely abstract, can meet in conflicts that may be rationally developed. But they do not take visible shape as compelling visions of the depths of existence. The very transparency of these alternatives exhausts the problem. Where there is no sense of the infinite vastness of what is beyond our grasp, all we finally succeed in conveying is misery—not tragedy. This is the peculiar predicament of modern tragedy since the Enlightenment.

The Clash of Ways of Life

A comprehensive philosophy of history should interpret the changes in man's condition as a meaningful succession of historical ways of life; in every epoch these ways of life account for the general situation and the prevailing patterns of action and thought. They do not replace each other suddenly. The old is still alive while the new unfolds itself. The mighty breakthrough of the new is bound at first to fail against the staying power and coherence of the old way of life not yet exhausted. Transition is the zone of tragedy.

According to Hegel, the great heroes of history are tragic figures in this sense. They embody the new idea, purely and uncompromisingly. They arise in sunlike splendor. Their real significance goes unnoticed at first, until the old way of life senses its danger and gathers all its forces to destroy the new in the form of its outstanding representative. Whether Socrates or Julius Caesar, the first victorious protagonist of the new principle becomes, at the same time, the victim at the border of two eras. The old is justified in asserting itself, for it still functions; it is still alive and proves itself through its rich and elaborate traditional patterns of life, even though the seed of decay has already begun its fatal germination. The new is justified also, but it is not yet protected by an established social order and culture. For the time being it is still functioning in a vacuum. But it is only the hero, the first great figure of the new way of life, whom the old, in a last frantic rally of all its forces, can destroy. Subsequent breakthroughs, now untragic, will succeed. Plato and Augustus Caesar are brilliantly triumphant; they realize the vision; they mold men through their works; they shape the future. But they live with their gaze fixed upon the first hero who was the victim.

This interpretation represents a particular philosophy of history. It sets out to speculate only about what is immanent in this world, but proceeds to assign substance and personality to historic units which actually cannot be verified. It ends by endowing historical patterns with quasi-demonic self-direction.

Men Against Gods

The battle takes place between the single individual and the "powers," between man and demons, between man and the gods. These powers are elusive. They escape man if he would grasp or just understand them. They are both there and not there. The same god is helpful and vicious.

Man does not know. Unknowingly and unconsciously he falls prey to the very powers that he wanted to escape.

Man rebels against the gods, as Hippolytus, the chaste youth in the service of Artemis, revolted against Aphrodite. He is overcome in battle with the unconquerable one.

Gods Against One Another

The battle is a collision of the powers, of the gods themselves: man is only a pawn in these terrible games, or their scene, or their medium; but man's greatness consists precisely in his act of becoming such a medium. By this act, he becomes imbued with a soul and identical with the powers.

In the *Antigone* of Sophocles, the hidden gods of chthonic or political origin are basically such powers locked in mutual combat. But in Aeschylus' *Eumenides* the battles of the gods are quite manifest and in the foreground, determining the needs of men. In the *Prometheus* such battles are represented even without man's entering upon the scene.

Tragic world views always contain evidence of struggles. But is struggle tragic in and for itself? Or if not, what makes it tragic? To decide this question, we must explore further aspects of the tragic world view.

Victory and Defeat

Who or what conquers in tragedy? Men and the powers are colliding. The outcome suggests decision in favor of the conqueror: the losers are wrong. But this is not true. Rather, we discover the following aspects of the tragic:

1. Victory is not his who triumphs but his who fails in defeat. In suffering failure, the loser conquers. The apparent victor is in truth inferior; his victory is fleeting and hollow.

2. *What conquers is the universal,* the world order, the moral order, the universal laws of life, the timeless—but the very recognition of such universality implies its rejection: the nature of the universal is such that it must crush this human greatness which opposes it.

3. *In reality nothing conquers.* Instead, everything becomes questionable, the hero as well as the universal. Compared with the *transcendent,* all is finite and relative, and therefore deserves to be destroyed, the particular as well as the universal, the exception as well as the rule. Both the exceptional man and the sublime order have their own limits, beyond which they break down. What conquers in tragedy is the transcendent—or rather even this does not conquer, for it makes itself felt only through the whole situation. It neither dominates nor submits; it simply exists.

4. In victory and in defeat, in the very process of achieving a solution, a new historical order is born, transitory in its turn. Its significance applies first to the particular knowledge of the tragic from which it arose. The rank of a tragic poet is then determined by the content which he draws from victory and defeat, and from their resolution.

Guilt

Tragedy becomes self-conscious by understanding the fate of its characters as the consequence of guilt, and as the inner working out of guilt itself. Destruction is the atonement of guilt.

To be sure, the world is full of guiltless destruction. Hidden evil destroys without being seen; it acts without being heard; no worldly authority so much as hears about it, any more than when someone was being tortured to death in the dungeon of a castle. Men die as martyrs without being martyrs, in so far as no one is present to bear witness or to learn of their martyrdom. Every day some defenseless creatures are being tortured and destroyed on this earth. Ivan Karamazov flies into a mad rage at the thought of the children killed for mere pleasure by the warring Turks. But this whole heartrending, gruesome reality is not tragic, in so far as disaster is not the atonement of a guilt and is unconnected with the meaning of this life.

The question of guilt, however, is not limited to the actions and lives of individual men. Rather, it refers to humanity as a whole, of which every one of us is a part. Where are we to look for the guilt that is responsible for all this undeserved disaster? Where is the power that makes the innocent miserable?

Wherever men saw this question clearly, they conceived of the idea of complicity in guilt. All men are jointly committed and jointly liable. Their common origin and their common goal account for this. A token of this, though not an explanation, is that we feel shaken and perplexed at the following thought, which seems absurd to our limited understanding: I am responsible for all the evil that is perpetrated in the world, unless I have done what I could to prevent it, even to the extent of sacrificing my life. I am guilty because I am alive and can continue to live while this is happening. Thus criminal complicity takes hold of everyone for everything that happens.

We must therefore speak of guilt in the wider sense of a guilt of human existence as such, and of guilt in the narrower sense of responsibility for any particular action. Where our own guilt is not limited to certain specific wrongdoings but, in a deeper sense, is found in the very nature of human existence, there the idea of guilt becomes truly inclusive. Tragic knowledge, therefore, distinguishes these two kinds of guilt:

First: Existence is guilt. Guilt in the larger sense is identical with existence as such. The idea, already found in Anaximander, recurs in Calderón, although in a different sense—that man's greatest guilt is to have been born.

This is revealed also in the fact that my very existence causes misery. Indian thought has an image for this: with every step, with every breath, I destroy living beings. Whether I act or not, merely by existing I infringe upon the existence of others. Passive or active, I incur the guilt of existence.

A particular life is guilty through its origin. True, I did not desire this world nor my particular existence in it. But I am guilty against my will, simply because it is I myself who have this origin. My descent from guilty ancestors causes my own guilt.

Antigone is born contrary to the law as the daughter of Oedipus and his own mother. The curse of her descent is active within her. But her very exclusion from the norm of legitimate descent accounts for her singular depth and human feeling: she possesses the surest and most unshakable knowledge of the divine law. She dies because she is greater than the others, because her exceptional case embodies truth. And she dies gladly. Death to her means release; all along her road of action she is at one with herself.

A particular character is guilty because of what he is.[2] Character is itself a form of destiny—in so far as I detach myself from my own character and turn to look upon it.

What baseness there is in me, what desires to do evil, what unregenerate pride there is in my perversity—all this I myself have neither wanted nor created. Yet I am guilty of all this. And my guilt begets my destiny, whether I die unwillingly and unredeemed, or whether I am destroyed in trying to transcend my base nature by summoning up a deeper resource of my being—a resource which enables me to reject what I was, even though I cannot become what I long to be.

Second: Action is guilt. Guilt in the narrower sense is found in any distinct action I carry out freely in the sense that it need not occur and could also occur differently.

Guilty action may consist in flouting the law; it is personal arbitrariness consciously opposing the universal for no other reason than its own arbitrariness. It is the consequence of culpable ignorance, of half-conscious transpositions and concealments of motives. Nothing else is involved in such wilfulness beyond the misery of meanness and evil.

The situation is different when tragic knowledge recognizes the guilt of an action. Truthful and morally necessary action, although springing from the foundation of freedom, may entail failure. Man cannot escape his guilt through right and truthful conduct: guilt itself seems incurred guiltlessly. Man takes this

[2] This was the "Orphic" view of Rohde and Nietzsche, now generally abandoned on the basis of new manuscript evidence brought forward by Diels. See, e.g., Jaeger, *Theology,* pp. 34 ff.

guilt upon himself. He does not try to evade it. He stands by his guilt, not out of personal stubbornness, but for the sake of the very truth, which is destined for failure in his necessary sacrifice.[3]

Man's Greatness in Failure

Tragic knowledge cannot be extended and deepened without seeing in man the quality of greatness over and above his atonement of guilt.

That man is not God is the cause of his smallness and undoing. But that he can carry his human possibilities to their extreme and can be undone by them with his eyes open—that is his greatness.

What we essentially learn from tragic knowledge, therefore, is what makes man suffer and what makes him fail, what he takes upon himself in the face of which realities, and in what manner or form he sacrifices his existence.

The tragic hero—man heightened and intensified—is man himself in good and evil, fulfilling himself in goodness and canceling out his own identity in evil.[4] In each case his existence is shipwrecked by the consistency with which he meets some unconditional demand, real or supposed.

His resistance, stubbornness, and pride drive him into the "greatness" of evil. His endurance, his dauntlessness, his love, raise him up into the good. Always he grows in stature through the experience of life at its limits. The poet sees in him the bearer of something that reaches beyond individual existence, the bearer of a power, a principle, a character, a demon.

Tragedy depicts a man in his greatness beyond good and evil. The poet's view resembles that of Plato: "Or do you suppose that great crimes and unmixed wickedness spring from a slight nature and not from a vigorous one . . . while a weak nature will never be the cause of anything great, either for good or for evil?" It is from the most gifted type of man that "these spring who do the greatest harm to communities and individuals, and the greatest good . . . but a small nature never does anything great for a man or a city."[5]

---

[3] *Schuld des Soseins*. This is guilt, not of existence, origin, or action, but arising from the stubbornness and meanness in one's character.
[4] *Im Bösen, sich vernichtigend*. This implies both physical and spiritual self-destruction.
[5] Plato, *Republic*, VI, 491 e, 495 b. Shorey translation (Loeb Classical Library).

The Tragic Mask*

George Santayana

Masks are arrested expressions and admirable echoes of feeling, at once faithful, discreet, and superlative. Living things in contact with the air must acquire a cuticle, and it is not urged against cuticles that they are not hearts; yet some philosophers seem to be angry with images for not being things, and with words for not being feelings. Words and images are like shells, no less integral parts of nature than are the substances they cover, but better addressed to the eye and more open to observation. I would not say that substance exists for the sake of appearance, or faces for the sake of masks, or the passions for the sake of poetry and virtue. Nothing arises in nature for the sake of anything else; all these phases and products are involved equally in the round of existence, and it would be sheer wilfulness to praise the germinal phase on the ground that it is vital, and to denounce the explicit phase on the ground that it is dead and sterile. We might as justly despise the seed for being merely instrumental, and glorify the full-blown flower, or the conventions of art, as the highest achievement and fruition of life. Substance is fluid, and, since it cannot exist without some form, is always ready to exchange one form for another; but sometimes it falls into a settled rhythm or recognizable vortex, which we call a nature, and which sustains an interesting form for a season. These sustained forms are enshrined in memory and worshipped in moral philosophy, which often assigns to them a power to create and to reassert themselves which their precarious status is very far from justifying. But they are all in all to the mind: art and happiness lie in pouring and repouring the molten metal of existence through some such tenable mould.

Masks are accordingly glorious things; we are instinctively as proud of designing and wearing them as we are of inventing and using words. The blackest tragedy is festive; the most pessimistic philosophy is an enthusiastic triumph of thought. The life which such expressions seem to arrest or to caricature would be incomplete without them; indeed, it would be blind and abortive. It is no interruption to experience to master experience, as tragedy aspires to do; nor is it an interruption to sink into its episodes and render them consummate, which is the trick of comedy. On the contrary, without such playful pauses and reflective interludes our round of motions and sensations would be deprived of that intellectual dignity which relieves it and renders it morally endurable—the dignity of knowing what we are doing, even if it be foolish in itself, and with what probable issue. Tragedy, the knowledge of death, raises us to that height. In fancy

* George Santayana, "The Tragic Mask," in *Soliloquies in England and Later Soliloquies* (Charles Scribner's Sons, 1922), pp. 131–135. Reprinted with the permission of Charles Scribner's Sons.

73

and for a moment it brings our mortal wills into harmony with our destiny, with the wages of existence, and with the silence beyond. These discoveries of reason have fixed the expression of the tragic mask, half horror and half sublimity. Such is the countenance of man when turned towards death and eternity and looking beyond all his endeavours at the Gorgon face of the truth. This is not to say that it is less human, or less legitimate, to look in other directions and to make other faces. But whether the visage we assume be a joyful or a sad one, in adopting and emphasizing it we define our sovereign temper. Henceforth, so long as we continue under the spell of this self-knowledge, we do not merely live but act; we compose and play our chosen character, we wear the buskin of deliberation, we defend and idealize our passions, we encourage ourselves eloquently to be what we are, devoted or scornful or careless or austere; we soliloquize (before an imaginary audience) and we wrap ourselves gracefully in the mantle of our in-alienable part. So draped, we solicit applause and expect to die amid a universal hush. We profess to live up to the fine sentiments we have uttered, as we try to believe in the religion we profess. The greater our difficulties the greater our zeal. Under our published principles and plighted language we must assiduously hide all the inequalities of our moods and conduct, and this without hypocrisy, since our deliberate character is more truly ourself than is the flux of our invol-untary dreams. The portrait we paint in this way and exhibit as our true person may well be in the grand manner, with column and curtain and distant land-scape and finger pointing to the terrestrial globe or to the Yorick-skull of philos-ophy; but if this style is native to us and our art is vital, the more it transmutes its model the deeper and truer art it will be. The severe bust of an archaic sculp-ture, scarcely humanizing the block, will express a spirit far more justly than the man's dull morning looks or casual grimaces. Every one who is sure of his mind, or proud of his office, or anxious about his duty assumes a tragic mask. He de-putes it to be himself and transfers to it almost all his vanity. While still alive and subject, like all existing things, to the undermining flux of his own substance, he has crystallized his soul into an idea, and more in pride than in sorrow he has of-fered up his life on the altar of the Muses. Self-knowledge, like any art or sci-ence, renders its subject-matter in a new medium, the medium of ideas, in which it loses its old dimensions and its old pace. Our animal habits are transmuted by conscience into loyalties and duties, and we become "persons" or masks. Art, truth, and death turn everything to marble.

That life should be able to reach such expression in the realm of eternal form is a sublime and wonderful privilege, but it is tragic, and for that reason distasteful to the animal in man. A mask is not responsive; you must not speak to it as to a living person, you must not kiss it. If you do, you will find the cold thing repulsive and ghastly. It is only a husk, empty, eyeless, brittle, and glazed. The more comic its expression the more horrible it will prove, being that of a corpse. The animal in man responds to things according to their substance, ed-ible, helpful, or plastic; his only joy is to push his way victoriously through the material world, till a death stops him which he never thought of and, in a sense, never experiences. He is not in the least interested in picturing what he is or what he will have been; he is intent only on what is happening to him now or may happen to him next. But when the passions see themselves in the mirror of reflection, what they behold is a tragic mask. This is the escutcheon of human nature, in which its experience is emblazoned. In so far as men are men at all, or men of honour, they militate under this standard and are true to their colours.

Whatever refuses to be idealized in this way, they are obliged to disown and commit to instant oblivion. It will never do for a mind merely to live through its passions or its perceptions; it must discern recognizable objects, in which to centre its experience and its desires; it must choose names and signs for them, and these names and symbols, if they are to perform their function in memory and intercourse, must be tightly conventional. What could be more unseemly than a fault in grammar, or in many a case more laughable and disconcerting? Yet any solecism, if it were once stereotyped and made definitely significant, would become an idiom: it would become a good verbal mask. What is not covered in this way by some abiding symbol can never be recovered; the dark flood of existence carries it down bodily. Only in some word or conventional image can the secret of one moment be flashed to another moment; and even when there is no one ready to receive the message, or able to decipher it, at least the poet in his soliloquy has uttered his mind and raised his monument in his own eyes; and in expressing his life he has found it.

The Metaphysics
of Tragedy*

Georg Lukács

Nature makes a man from a child, and a chicken from an egg;
God makes the man before the child and the chicken before the egg.
—Meister Eckehart: *The Sermon of the Noble Soul*

1

A drama is a play about man and his fate—a play in which God is the spectator.
He is a spectator and no more; his words and gestures never mingle with the
words and gestures of the players. His eyes rest upon them: that is all. "Whoever
sees God, dies," Ibsen wrote once; "but can he who has been seen by God continue to live?"

Intelligent men who love life are aware of this incompatibility, and they
have some unkind things to say about drama. Their clear hostility does greater
justice to the nature of drama than the apologies of its timorous defenders. The
enemies of drama say that it is a falsification of reality; it makes reality cruder
than it is. Not only does it—even in Shakespeare—take away the richness and
fulness of reality, not only do the brutal events of drama always just choose between life and death, cheating reality of its exquisite psychological subtleties: the
principal reproach is that drama creates a vacuum between human beings. In
drama, there is only one person who speaks (his technique being a perfect reflection of his innermost nature) while the other merely answers. But the one begins
and the other ends, and the quiet, imperceptible flux of their relationship with
one another, which real life alone can really bring to life, become lifeless and
rigid in the harsh process of the dramatic description. What these critics say is
full of the most profound truth. But rash defenders of drama come forward and
invoke Shakespeare's richness, the restless shimmering of naturalistic dialogue,
the blurring of all the contours of fate in Maeterlinck's destiny plays. They are
rash defenders indeed, for what they have to propose in defence of the drama is
only a compromise—a compromise between life and dramatic form.

Life is an anarchy of light and dark: nothing is ever completely fulfilled in
life, nothing ever quite ends; new, confusing voices always mingle with the chorus of those that have been heard before. Everything flows, everything merges
into another thing, and the mixture is uncontrolled and impure; everything is

* Georg Lukács, "The Metaphysics of Tragedy," *Soul and Form*, Translated by Anna Bostock (The
MIT Press, Cambridge, Mass., 1974), pp. 152–174. Copyright © 1971 The Merlin Press LTD., London. Reprinted by permission from The Merlin Press.

destroyed, everything is smashed, nothing ever flowers into real life. To live is to live something through to the end: but *life* means that nothing is ever fully and completely lived through to the end. Life is the most unreal and unliving of all conceivable existences; one can describe it only negatively—by saying that something always happens to disturb and interrupt the flow. Schelling wrote: "We say a thing 'lasts' because its existence is not in conformity with its nature."

Real life is always unreal, always impossible, in the midst of empirical life. Suddenly there is a gleam, a lightning that illumines the banal paths of empirical life: something disturbing and seductive, dangerous and surprising; the accident, the giant moment, the miracle; an enrichment and a confusion. It cannot last; no one would be able to bear it, no one could live at such heights—at the height of their own life and their own ultimate possibilities. One has to fall back into numbness. One has to deny life in order to live.

What men love about life is its atmospheric quality, its uncertainty, forever swinging this way and that, like a pendulum—but one that never swings out as far as it can go. They love the great uncertainty of life which is like a monotonous, reassuring lullaby. But the miracle is what determines and is determined: it bursts incalculably into life, accidentally and out of context, and ruthlessly turns life into a clear, an unambiguous equation—which it then resolves. Men hate and fear the unambiguous. Their weakness and cowardice make them welcome any obstacle that is imposed from the outside, any barrier that is put in their way. Unimaginable, eternally unreachable Gardens of Eden for idle dreams bloom for them behind every rock face whose sheerness they can never conquer. Life for them is longing and hoping, and what fate puts out of their reach is turned cheaply and easily into inner riches of the soul. Men never know life at the point where all the streams of life converge. Where nothing is fulfilled, everything is possible. But the miracle is fulfilment. It snatches from life all its deceptive veils, woven of gleaming moments and infinitely varied moods. Drawn in hard and ruthless outline, the soul stands naked before the face of life.

Only the miracle, however, has reality before the face of God. For God there is no relativity, no transition, no nuance. His glance robs every event of all that is temporal and local about it. Before God, there is no difference between seeming and substance, appearance and idea, event and destiny. The question of value and reality loses all its meaning: before the face of God, value creates reality and does not have to be dreamed or imagined as reality. This is why every true tragedy is a mystery play. Its real, central meaning is a revelation of God before the face of God. The god of nature and destiny, who is always speechless and always unredeemed, brings forth the voice of the god who slumbers inside man, the voice which, in life, has fallen silent; the immanent god awakens the transcendental god into life. "Because, without a creature, God cannot desire to have effect or movement, he desires to have effect and movement in and with the creature," says the little book of the perfect life; and Hebbel speaks of "God's inability to conduct a monologue".

By contrast, the gods of reality, of history, are obstinate and rash. The power and beauty of pure revelation do not satisfy their ambition. They want not only to be the spectators of the fulfilment of revelation, but also to direct and accomplish that fulfilment. Their hands tug wilfully at the enigmatic yet obvious tangle of the threads of fate and, by entangling them still more, achieve a perfect yet meaningless orderliness. They walk on to the stage and their appearance reduces man to a puppet, destiny to providence; that which, in tragedy, is a grave event becomes, in life, a gratuitous gift of redemption. God must leave the stage, but must yet remain a spectator; that is the historical possibility of tragic epochs. And because nature and fate have never been so terrifyingly soulless as they are today, because men's souls have never walked in such utter loneliness upon deserted paths, because of all this we may again hope for the coming of tragedy—once all the dancing shadows of a friendly order, which our cowardly dreams have cast upon nature to allow us a false sense of security, have entirely disappeared. "Only when we have become completely godless," says Paul Ernst, "shall we have tragedy once more." Think of Shakespeare's Macbeth, whose soul could not bear the gravity of the necessary way to the necessary goal. Witches still dance and sing round him at the crossroads of fate, and awaited miracles proclaim to him that the day of the ultimate fulfilment has come. The wild chaos which surrounds him, which is re-created by all his actions, which entangles his will, is truly chaotic only to the blind eyes of his longing, and only as chaotic as his own frenzy must be to his own soul. In reality both are a judgement of god: the same hands of the same providence guide both. Deceptively, they raise him to the heights, deluding his longing with fulfilments; deceptively they place every victory in his hands; everything he does succeeds, until everything has been fulfilled—and then everything is snatched from him all at once. Outside and inside are still one in Macbeth: the same hand guides the destiny and the soul. Drama, here, is still a judgement of God, and every stroke of the sword is still part of the divine plan of providence. Or take Ibsen's Jarl, who in his dreams was always a king and who could not be a king except in his dreams. What he hopes to obtain from the struggle of different forces is a judgement of God, a verdict upon the ultimate truth. But the world round him goes on its way, untouched by such questions or answers. All things have become dumb, and laurels or defeats are awarded indifferently at the end of the struggle. Never again will God's judgement be clearly heard in the workings of destiny. It was God's voice that gave life to the whole; but then that life had to go on by itself, alone, and the judging voice fell silent forever. This is why Jarl can be victorious where Macbeth was defeated; he is the victim doomed to perish, and as victor he is even more defeated than he would be as loser. The tones of tragic truth ring out pure and clear: the miracle of life, the destiny of tragedy is merely what reveals souls. Too alien from one another to be enemies, the two face one another—that which reveals and that which is revealed, the revelation and its object. What is revealed is alien to that which has occasioned its revelation—higher, and coming from a different world. The soul, having become Self, measures its whole previous existence with a stranger's eye. It finds that previous existence incomprehensible, inessential and lifeless; it can only dream that once it was different, for this new way of being *is* being. It was but idle accident that dictated the dreams, and but the accidental ringing of a distant bell that brought awakening in the morning.

Naked souls conduct a dialogue here with naked destinies. Both have been stripped of everything that is not of their innermost essence; all the relationships of life have been suppressed so that the relationship with destiny may be created; everything atmospheric between men and objects has vanished, in order that nothing should exist between them but the clear, harsh mountain air of ultimate questions and ultimate anwers. There, at the point to which the miracle of accident has raised a man and his life, tragedy begins: and this is why he is forever banished from the world of tragedy. For he can no longer put into that life the hazardous and enriching things he puts into ordinary life. Tragedy can extend in only one direction: upwards. It begins at the moment when enigmatic forces have distilled the essence from a man, have forced him to become essential; and the progress of tragedy consists in his essential, true nature becoming more and more manifest. A life that excludes accident is flat and sterile, an endless plain without any elevations; the logic of such a life is the logic of cheap security, of passive refusal before everything new, of dull repose in the lap of dry common sense. But tragedy needs no further accident; it has incorporated accident into its world forever, so that it is always and everywhere present in it.

The question of the possibility of tragedy is the question of meaning and essence. It is the question whether everything that is there, *is*—just because, simply because, it is there. Are there not degrees and gradations of being? Is "being" a property of all things, or is it a value-judgement passed upon things, a distinction and differentiation between them?

This, then, is the paradox of drama and tragedy: how can essence come alive? How can it become the sensual, immediate, the only real, the truly "being" thing? Drama alone creates—"gives form to"—real human beings, but just because of this it must, of necessity, deprive them of living existence. Their life is made up of words and gestures, but every word they speak and every gesture they make is more than gesture or word; all the manifestations of their life are mere cyphers for their ultimate relationships, their life merely a pale allegory of their own platonic ideas. Their existence can have no reality except the reality of the soul, the reality of lived experience and faith. "Lived experience" is latent in every event of life as a threatening abyss, the door to the judgement chamber: its connection with the Idea—of which it is merely the outward manifestation—is no more than the conceivable possibility of such a connection in the midst of the chaotic coincidences of real life. And faith affirms this connection and transforms its eternally unprovable possibility into the *a priori* basis for the whole of existence.

Such existence knows no space or time; all its events are outside the scope of logical explanation, just as the souls of its men are outside the scope of psychology. Let me be more precise: the time and space of tragedy have no perspective that might modify or mitigate them, and neither the outward nor the inner reasons for action and suffering in tragedy ever affect their essence. Everything counts in tragedy, and everything has equal force and weight. There is in tragedy a threshold of life-possibility, of the ability to be aroused into life; everything that is on the right side of this threshold, everything that can live, is always present, and everything is present in equal measure. For a character in tragedy, to be there at all—to exist—is to be perfect. Medieval philosophy had a clear and unambiguous way of expressing this. It said that *ens perfectissimum* was also *ens realissimum;* the more perfect a thing is, the more it *is;* the more a thing corresponds to its idea, the greater is its being. But how does one experience one's idea, and one's identification with that same idea, in real life? (For tragedy is the most real life that is.) In lived life, this is not a question of epistemology (as it is in philosophy), but the painfully and immediately experienced reality of the great moments.

The essence of these great moments is the pure experience of self. In ordinary life we experience ourselves only peripherally—that is, we experience our motives and our relationships. Our life ordinarily has no real necessity, but only the necessity of being empirically present, of being entangled by a thousand threads in a thousand accidental bonds and relationships. But the basis of the whole network of necessities is accidental and meaningless; everything that is, could just as well be otherwise, and the only thing that seems really necessary is the past, simply because nothing more can be done to change it. But is even the past really necessary? Can the accidental flow of time, the arbitrary displacement of one's arbitrary point of view vis-à-vis one's lived experience, change the essential nature of that experience? Can it make something necessary and essential out of the accidental? Can it transform the periphery into the centre? It often seems that it can, but that is only an illusion. Only our momentary and accidental knowledge makes something rounded and changeless of the past. The smallest modification of that knowledge, such as any accident may occasion, sheds new light upon the "unchangeable" past, and suddenly, in that new light, everything acquires a different meaning and actually becomes different. Ibsen only *seems* to be a disciple of the Greeks, continuing in the tradition of the drama of Oedipus. The real meaning of his analytical dramas is that there is nothing unchangeable about the past—that the past, too, is flowing, shimmering and changeable, constantly transformed into something different by new insights.

The great moments of life, too, bring new insights, but these only seem to belong to the series of continual, eternal re-evaluations. In reality they are an end and a beginning, giving men a new memory, a new ethic and a new justice. Many things disappear which before appeared to be the very cornerstones of life, while small, barely perceptible things become the new supports of life. A man can no longer walk along the paths where he used to walk, nor can his eyes find any direction in them; yet now he easily climbs pathless mountain peaks and strides confidently over bottomless marshes. A deep forgetfulness and a clairvoyance of the memory overpower the soul; the blinding light of the new insight illuminates its centre, and everything that belongs to the centre blossoms into life. This sense of necessity is not the result of the inescapable workings of causality; it is without cause, it leaps across all the causes of empirical life. Being-necessary now means being intimately bound up with the essence; it needs no other reason, and the memory retains only this one necessary thing and simply forgets the rest. This alone, then, is the defendant before the judgement and the self-judgement of the soul. Everything else is forgotten, all the whys and wherefores; this alone is weighed upon the scales. The judgement is a cruelly harsh one, without mercy or reprieve; sentence is passed ruthlessly upon even the smallest fault, the faintest suggestion of a betrayal of the essence. Anyone whose sketchiest, long-forgotten gesture implies that he may once have fallen short of his own essence is excluded from the circle of real men. No richness or grandeur of the soul's gifts can alter this judgement, and a whole life filled with glorious deeds counts as nothing before it. But it forgets, with radiant clemency, any sin of ordinary life which has not encroached upon the centre; even to speak of forgiveness is to exaggerate, for the judge's eye simply passes over such sins without noticing them.

Such a moment is a beginning and an end. Nothing can succeed it or follow upon it, nothing can connect it with ordinary life. It is a moment; it does not signify life, it *is* life—a different life opposed to and exclusive of ordinary life. This is the metaphysical reason for the concentration of drama in time, of the condition of unity of time. It is born of the desire to come as close as possible to the timelessness of this moment which yet is the whole of life. (Unity of place is the natural symbol of such sudden standing still in the midst of the continual change of ordinary life, and is therefore a technically necessary condition of dramatic form-giving.) Tragedy is only a moment: that is the meaning of the unity of time: and the technical paradox contained in trying to give temporal duration to a moment which, by its very nature, is without such duration, springs from the inadequacy of expressing a mystical experience in terms of human language. "How can one give form to what is without image, or prove what is without evidence?" asks Suso. Tragic drama has to express the becoming-timeless of time. To fulfil all the conditions of unity is actually to unite the past, the present and the future. Not only is their empirically real sequence disturbed and destroyed by turning the present into something secondary and unreal, the past into a threat, the future into a familiar experience (although perhaps an unconscious one); even the way in which these moments follow one upon the other is no longer a sequence in time. In terms of time, such drama is completely and rigidly static. Its moments exist in parallel rather than in series; it no longer lies within the plane of temporal experience. Unity of time is a paradoxical notion in any case; any attempt to limit time or to make it circular—and this is the only way to achieve unity of time—contradicts the very nature of time. (One need only think of the inner rigidity of the circular movement in Nietzsche's theory of recurrence.) But drama interrupts the eternal flow of time not only at its beginning and its end, bending the two poles towards each other and melting them together; it carries out this same stylization at every instant of the drama; every moment is a symbol, a reduced-scale image of the whole, distinguishable from it only by its size. To fit these moments together must therefore be a matter of fitting them *into* one another, not *after* one another. The French classicists looked for rational reasons to explain their true insight in this matter, and by formulating the mystical unity in a rationalistic way, they reduced the profound paradox to something trivial and arbitrary. They made of this supra- and extra-temporal unity a unity *within* time, of the mystical unity a mechanical one. Lessing—although there is much one could disagree with him about, precisely on this issue—was right to feel that Shakespeare came essentially closer to the Greeks than their apparent successors; but he, like the French, offered explanations which were superficial, rationalistic, and therefore false.

The tragic experience, then, is a beginning and an end at the same time. Everyone at such a moment is newly born, yet has been dead for a long time; and everyone's life stands before the Last Judgement. Any "development" of a character in drama is merely apparent; it consists of the experiencing of such a moment, of the character being raised into the world of tragedy inside whose periphery, until then, only his shadow could enter. It is this character's becoming-man, his awakening from a confused dream. It always happens suddenly and all at once; the preparatory part is there only for the spectator's sake, it prepares the spectator's soul for the leap of the great transformation. The tragic character's soul ignores everything preparatory, and everything changes in a flash, everything suddenly becomes essential when the fateful word is spoken at last. Likewise, the tragic character's composure (or serenity or rapture) in the face of death is heroic only in appearance, only in the ordinary language of psychology. The dying heroes of tragedy—as a young dramatist once put it—are dead a long time before they actually die.

The reality of such a world can have nothing in common with that of temporal existence. Realism is bound to destroy all the form-creating and life-maintaining values of tragic drama. We have already listed all the reasons for it. Drama is bound to become trivial if its lifelikeness conceals that which is dramatically real. And lifelikeness fitted into a genuinely dramatic structure becomes superfluous and is ignored by the senses. The inner style of drama is realistic within the mediaeval, scholastic meaning of the word, but this excludes all modern realism.

Dramatic tragedy is the form of the high points of existence, its ultimate goals and ultimate limits. Here the mystical-tragical experience of essentiality becomes separate from the essential experience of mysticism. The peak of existence, experienced in mystical ecstasy, disappears in the cloudy sky of the Unity of the All; the intensification of life which results from such ecstasy makes the person who experiences it merge into all things, and all things into each other. The real existence of the mystic begins only when all differentiation has vanished forever; the miracle which his world has created must destroy all forms, for his reality—the essence—exists only behind the forms, disguised and concealed by them. The miracle of tragedy is a form-creating one; its essence is selfhood, just as exclusively as, in mysticism, the essence is self-oblivion. The mystical experience is to suffer the All, the tragic one is to create the All. In mysticism, it is beyond all explanation how a self can absorb everything into itself, how, in a state of melting flux, it can destroy everything distinctive about itself and the whole world and yet retain a self to experience this cancellation of the self. In tragedy, the opposite is just as inexplicable. The self stresses its selfhood with an all-exclusive, all-destroying force, but this extreme affirmation imparts a steely hardness and autonomous life to everything it encounters and—arriving at the ultimate peak of pure selfhood—finally cancels itself out. The final tension of selfhood overleaps everything that is merely individual. Its force elevates all things to the status of destiny, but its great struggle with the self-created destiny makes of it something supra-personal, a symbol of some ultimate fate-relationship. In this way the mystical and the tragic modes of experiencing life touch and supplement one another and mutually exclude one another. Both mysteriously combine life and death, autonomous selfhood and the total dissolving of the self in a higher being. Surrender is the mystic's way, struggle the tragic man's; the one, at the end of his road, is absorbed into the All, the other shattered against the All. From being at one with all things, the former leaps across into the deeply personal world of his ecstasies; the latter loses his selfhood at the moment of its truest exaltation. Who can tell where is the throne of life, where that of death? They are the poles which ordinary life melts together and mutually weakens, for only thus—bereft of strength and scarcely recognizable—can ordinary life bear either life or death. Each, separately, means death—the ultimate frontier. But their relationship to one another is that of fraternal enemies: each represents the sole real victory over the other.

The wisdom of the tragic miracle is the wisdom of frontiers. A miracle is always unambiguous, but everything unambiguous divides and points in two directions. Every ending is always an arrival and a cessation, an affirmation and a denial all at once; every climax is a peak and frontier, the point of intersection between life and death. The tragic life is, of all possible lives, the one most exclusively of this world. That is why its frontier always merges into death. Real, ordinary life never reaches the frontier; it knows death only as something frightening, threatening, meaningless, something that suddenly arrests the flow of life. Mysticism overleaps the frontier and thus robs death of any value as reality. But for tragedy, death—the frontier as such—is an always immanent reality, inseparably connected with every tragic event. The reason for this is not only that the ethic of tragedy must have as its categorical imperative the continuance unto death of everything that has begun; nor is it only that the psychology of tragedy is a science of death-moments, of conscious last moments when the soul has already given up the broad richness of existence and clings only to what is most deeply and intimately its own. Quite apart from these and many other negative reasons, death is also—in a purely positive and life-affirming sense—the immanent reality of tragedy. The experiencing of the frontier between life and death is the awakening of the soul to consciousness or self-consciousness—the soul becomes conscious of itself because it is thus limited, and only because and in so far as it is limited. This is the question posed at the end of one of Paul Ernst's tragedies:

> Can I still want when there is nothing that I cannot do
> And others are no more than puppets on my strings?
> ... Can a god win glory for himself?

and the answer to the question is this:

> There must be limits to what we can achieve
> Or else the world we live in is a lifeless desert.
> We only live by what is not attainable.

"Can a god win glory for himself?" Put more generally still, the question might run: Can a god live? Does not perfection cancel out being? Is not pantheism, as Schopenhauer said, just a polite form of atheism? Could it be said that the various forms of God's becoming man, God's dependence on the ways and means of the human form, are a symbolic expression of this feeling—the feeling that, in order to come alive, even God must forsake his formless perfection?

The double meaning of the frontier is that it is simultaneously a fulfilment and a failure. In a confused way this is the metaphysical background to ordinary life, the simple recognition that a possibility can become a reality only when all other possibilities have been eliminated. Here, however, the primal possibility of a soul becomes the only reality; the contrast between it and other souls is not only that between something realized and something merely possible, but that between the real and the unreal, between the necessarily thought and the unthinkable and absurd. This is why tragedy is the awakening of the soul. The recognition of the frontier extracts the soul's essential nature, lets everything else fall away, but gives to this essential nature the existence of an inner and only necessity. The frontier is only outwardly a limiting and possibility-destroying principle. For the awakened soul it is the recognition of that which is truly its own. Everything human is possible, but only if one has an abstractly absolute idea of man. Tragedy is the becoming-real of the concrete, essential nature of man. Tragedy gives a firm and sure answer to the most delicate question of platonism: the question whether individual things can have idea or essence. Tragedy's answer puts the question the other way round: only that which is individual, only something whose individuality is carried to the uttermost limit, is adequate to its idea—i.e. is really existent. That which is general, that which encompasses all things yet has not colour of form of its own, is too weak in its universality, too empty in its unity, ever to become real. It is too existent to have real being; its identity is a tautology; the idea is adequate only to itself. Thus tragedy's answer to Plato's verdict is to transcend platonism.

The deepest longing of human existence is the metaphysical root of tragedy: the longing of man for selfhood, the longing to transform the narrow peak of his existence into a wide plain with the path of his life winding across it, and his meaning into a daily reality. The tragic experience, dramatic tragedy, is the most perfect, the only perfect fulfilment of this longing. But every longing fulfilled is a longing destroyed. Tragedy sprang from longing, and therefore its form must exclude any expression of longing. Before tragedy entered life, it became a fulfilment and therefore abandoned the state of longing. That is the reason for the failure of modern tragedy. It wanted to introduce the *a priori* of tragedy into tragedy itself, it wanted to turn a cause into an active principle; but it succeeded only in intensifying its lyricism until it became a kind of soft-centred brutality. It never crossed the threshold of dramatic tragedy. Its atmospheric, yearning, indefinite, tremulous dialogues possess lyrical value but are entirely outside dramatic tragedy. Its poetry is the becoming-poetic of ordinary life, that is to say only the intensification of ordinary life and not its transformation into dramatic life. Such stylization is opposed to dramatic stylization, not only by its method but also in its aim. Its psychology emphasizes that which is momentary and transient in human souls; its ethic is one of understanding all and forgiving all. It tones down, softens and prettifies people in a poetic manner. That is why the public today are always complaining about the harshness and coldness of the dialogue of any tragic playwright; yet this harshness and coldness is only an expression of the playwright's contempt for the puny transports with which everything tragic has to be surrounded nowadays because those who deny the tragic ethic are too cowardly to deny tragedy itself, and those who affirm it are too weak to bear it in its undisguised majesty. Nor does the intellectualization of the dialogue, confined to a clearly conscious mirroring of the sense of destiny, mean coldness: it means human authenticity and inner truth in this particular sphere of life. In tragic drama, to simplify the characters and events is not a form of poverty but a form of richness given by the very nature of the genre. People occur in such drama only when the encounters between them have acquired the status of destiny, and moments of destiny are the only ones depicted. The inner truth of such moments thus becomes an intelligible outward truth, and the concentrated, formula-like expression of this truth in the dialogue reflects not cold intellectualization but the lyrical maturity of the character's own sense of destiny. Here, and only here, the dramatic and the lyrical cease to be mutually opposing principles; here lyricism is the true drama carried to its highest peak.

2

Brunhild is the first success granted to Paul Ernst as a writer of tragedies. As a theoretician, he foresaw it long ago; he felt obliged, as a matter of deepest principle, to reject even the finest works created today or in the recent past, and he tried to explain this in terms of the very essence of drama. And so, in one or two of his theoretical studies, he worked right through to that essence—to absolute drama, if we are to use his own terminology. But his theories were for him simply means to an end, to be justified retrospectively by the attainment of that end in practice. *Brunhild* is his first real action, the first steel cast without any dross, a work that has faults but no flaws.

It is Ernst's first "Greek" drama—the first resolute departure from the path along which great German drama has travelled since the days of Schiller and

Kleist: the path whose goal was to marry Sophocles with Shakespeare. The German dramatists' titanic struggle for a modern-classical dramatic style sprang from their reluctance to make the sacrifice which Greek drama demands. They sought—and Ernst's early tragedies are attempts in the same direction—a simple monumentality equivalent to that of the Greeks, but without forfeiting the Shakespearean multiplicity of colours and events. Such attempts were bound to fail, because they had to accommodate two ways of giving form to relationships, the way of drama and the way of life—two ways which are mutually exclusive because the one must inevitably inhibit or even destroy the working of the other. Ernst has found the strength to make the great sacrifice—the sacrifice of all outward richness of life for the sake of achieving an inner richness, the sacrifice of all sensual beauty for the sake of thrusting through to the deeper, non-sensual beauty of the ultimate sense of life, the sacrifice of all material content so that the pure soul-content of pure form may be revealed. His is the *tragédie classique* reborn: he deepens and interiorizes the aims of Corneille, Racine and Alfieri. It is a genuine return to the eternally great model for all drama that seeks the soul of form—the *Oedipus* of Sophocles.

Everything here, as in the *Oedipus*, is reduced to the maximum economy and intensity. A courtyard between castle and church is the only setting; only the two pairs of lovers and Hagen are allowed upon the stage, and the time allotted for the unfolding of destiny is the span of one brief day.

The play begins at dawn after the wedding night, and the sun has not yet set when Siegfried is carried home dead from the hunt and, when Brunhild has committed suicide, they are burned together upon the funeral pile, separated from each other only by Siegfried's sword. This concentration of events is not merely outward. In the inner relationships of the play, in the intimate contacts between the characters, their loves and hates, their ascents and falls, in their words which mirror their inner lives, there is not a trace of superfluity or ornamentation for its own sake—but only destiny and necessity. The gestures and words of the characters are, by their deepest nature, Greek—indeed, being more consciously stylized, perhaps more Greek than those in many ancient tragedies. The consciousness of the dialectic of their destiny is perhaps still clearer and more penetrating than in Hebbel, and their expression—as in Hebbel and in the Greeks—is an epigrammatically pointed and concise fitting together of the essentials. But just as in Hebbel and in the Greeks—just as in any genuine tragedy—this rationalizing, which we might call mystical rationalism, never banalizes the inexpressible quality of destiny. For it is not will, and still less reason, that is responsible for the tragic entanglement of men and deeds. The fact that these are noble men and women of great and penetrating intellect, men and women who recognize their destiny and salute it in respectful silence, cannot make any difference to the workings of destiny but only deepens its mysterious and inexplicable quality.

This tragedy is a mystery play about sacred and profane love. The one kind of love is limpidly clear, it points forward and upward, it is necessity itself; the other is confusion and eternal darkness, aimless, planless and pathless. *Brunhild* is a mystery play about love among superior and inferior human beings, about love equal and unequal, about love which elevates and love which debases. Gunther as king and hero has been spoilt for tragedy, and Ernst does not attempt to rescue him; indeed, he sacrifices Kriemhild as well. They are the inferior pair of lovers, beings with lower instincts, who do not seek equality in love, beings who must never hope to create anything in their own likeness but must always fear it, beings for whom the mere existence of others striding more freely towards goals invisible to them is a dread and a reproach; beings who want to be happy but who practise vengeance and fear it. Siegfried and Brunhild are the other kind.

It is a mystery play about greatness, happiness . . . and about the frontiers. About that greatness which seeks itself and finds happiness and, in the warm darkness of happiness, longs once more for itself, and eventually reaches the frontiers and finds tragedy and death. About happiness which longs for greatness, yet can only pull greatness down to its own level; which can make the path of greatness longer and harder, yet can never stop greatness in its tracks, and has to stay behind, empty and alone. Greatness wants perfection—it is bound to want it—and perfection is tragedy, the final end, the falling silent of every note. Tragedy as the privilege of greatness: Brunhild and Siegfried are burned upon the same funeral pile, but Gunther and Kriemhild remain alive. Tragedy as universal law, as the final goal which yet is but a beginning in the eternal circle of all things.

> For we are like the green earth that waits for snow
> And like snow that waits for the thaw.

But man is conscious of his fate, and so his fate means more to him than the crest of a wave that is bound to sink into the trough and, later to become a crest once more, a game repeated over and over again for all eternity. Man is conscious of his fate, and calls this consciousness "guilt." And by feeling that everything that had to happen to him is of his own making, he draws firm contours round everything inside himself which accidentally happens to enter the flowing circumference of his accidental life-complex. He makes a necessity of it; he creates frontiers round himself; he creates himself. Seen from the outside, there is no guilt, there can be no guilt; every man sees every other's guilt as an accident of fate, as something which the slightest, faintest breath of wind might have caused to be otherwise. Through guilt, a man says "Yes" to everything that has happened to him; by feeling it to be his own action and his own guilt, he conquers it and forms his life, setting his tragedy—which has sprung from his guilt—as the frontier between his life and the All. Greater men draw such frontiers round larger parts of their lives than lesser men do; they leave nothing outside that once belonged to their lives. And that is why tragedy is their privilege. For the lesser kind there is happiness and unhappiness and revenge, because they always feel it is the others who are guilty. For them, everything comes only from the outside, their life can merge nothing into itself: they are untragic and their life is without form. But for one of the higher kind, the guilt of another— even if it destroys him—is always only fate. Herein is the deep mystery of guilt and entanglement and fate.

All this is built into the sheer architecture of a rigid, transitionless dichotomy. A thousand threads of fate connect the two greater human beings with the two lesser ones, yet not one of these threads constitutes a real link. So ruthlessly sharp is this inner division within the couples that the play might perhaps have disintegrated had Ernst not bridged the gap by a wide arch which connects the opposite sides, even if it emphasizes still more strongly the breadth of the abyss which lies between them. This connecting arch is Hagen. He represents the higher being as servant, with his servanthood as his greatness and his frontier; the man who has all the greatness and all the guilty awareness of fate inside him, yet around whom frontiers have been drawn by something outside and far beyond his own self. This man is not yet tragic—however harsh the blows which fate may deal him—because his "must," for all its interiority, still comes from the outside; yet he is capable of experiencing events as his own—in other words, as fate. His frontiers are drawn both on the outside and on the inside; and so the firmly delimited, formed quality of his life places him above the two lesser beings, and yet he stands below the two higher ones because he is, after all, their vassal—their highest vassal, the nearest to their throne—but no more than that, because his frontiers limit him, too, because his possibilities of conquering life are predetermined for him and not by him.

The crystalline transparency of the words conveys most strikingly the mysterious, unfathomable quality of the work. Just as their clarity cannot reveal the workings of fate, so the lucid consciousness with which they say everything that is essential about each character cannot, after all, bring the characters closer to one another or make them understand one another. Each word is a Janus' head; the one who says it sees always only one side, the one who hears it sees the other, and there is no possibility of the two coming closer together; each word that could serve as a bridge needs a bridge in turn. And, in the same way, the actions of the characters are not a sure sign of anything: the good man commits the evil deed, and, often, the other way about; longing conceals the true path, duty destroys the strongest bond of love. And so, at the end, each stands alone, for there is no communion in the face of fate.

3

Such a simplifying of dramatic conditions, however, entails grave sacrifices. The historical element of the play (by which we mean everything that is colourful and unrepeatable about it) is, after all, much more than just an impediment to strict stylization. The playwright's sensual, artistic pleasure in imagining the rich world outside is not his only motive for introducing this "historical" element. The relationship between history and tragedy is one of the deepest paradoxes of dramatic form. Aristotle was the first to express it by saying that drama is more philosophical than history. But does not drama, by thus becoming "more philosophical," lose its own very special essentiality? Surely its deepest meaning, the pure immanence of its laws, the perfect concealment of ideas within facts, the perfect disappearance of ideas behind facts—surely all these are put at risk by its becoming "more philosophical than history"? The point at issue is not the unity of idea and reality, but an involved, confused, indistinguishable convolution of the two. When we feel that something is "historical," then hazard and necessity, accidental happenings and timeless laws, causes and effects lose their absoluteness and become no more than possible points of view vis-à-vis facts which may modify such notions but can never completely absorb them. Being-history is a completely pure form of being; one might say it is Being as such. Something is because it is, and as it is. It is strong and great and beautiful simply because it is incomparable and incompatible with any *a priori* imposed by an order-creating rationality.

Yet there *is* an order concealed in the world of history, a composition in the confusion of its irregular lines. It is the undefinable order of a carpet or a dance; to interpret its meaning seems impossible, but it is still less possible to give up trying to interpret it. It is as though the whole fabric of fanciful lines were waiting for a single word that is always at the tip of our tongues, yet one which has never yet been spoken by anyone. History appears as a profound symbol of fate—of the regular accidentality of fate, its arbitrariness and tyranny which, in the last analysis, is always just. Tragedy's fight for history is a great war of conquest against life, an attempt to find the meaning of history (which is immeasurably far from ordinary life) in life, to extract the meaning of history from life as the true, concealed sense of life. A sense of history is always the most living necessity; the form in which it occurs is the force of gravity of mere happening, the irresistible force within the flow of things. It is the necessity of everything being connected with everything else, the value-denying necessity; there is no difference between small and great, meaningful and meaningless, primary and secondary. What is, had to be. Each moment follows the one before, unaffected by aim or purpose.

The paradox of historical drama is the combining of both these necessities: the one which flows without cause from the inside, and the other which flows meaninglessly outside; its goal is the becoming-form, the mutul intensification of two principles which appear to be fundamentally exclusive of one another. The further the two are from each other, the more profound tragedy seems to become. For they touch one another only when carried to an extreme; they delimit and strenghten each other by their categorical opposition to one another. This is why a playwright is attracted precisely by the historical element of a story, not by the general meaning which can be read into it. Here, he thinks, he can find the ultimate symbol of human limitation, pure constraint upon pure will, the clear, unambiguous resistance of matter to creative, form-imposing will. The unselective power of that which exists just because it exists ruthlessly separates the action from the intention, and drives the man who intends an action to execute it with a purity which defiles the inner purity of the intention and separates the action from its aim. The idea which lay hidden in the action or life-situation is revealed, destroying the real idea that lay timeless and uncreated within it, the one which alone could have elevated it to essential being. The power of what merely "is" destroys what it "should be." The young Hebbel wrote in his diary: "A good Pope is always a bad Christian."

This is the meaning of Paul Ernst's historical tragedies—the experience of his heroes, Demetrius and Nabis, Hildebrand and the Emperor Henry. Before these men meet one another, everything that is lofty and noble in them lies unseparated within their souls, just as all the possibilities for good and evil lies unseparated in every action which expresses them. But their meeting separates everything within a single instant. These men experience the only real disappointment there is: the disappointment of complete fulfilment. I do not mean the fear that reality will destroy their illusions, that fear which makes Romantics flee from life and its actions; the men in such plays live in the world of tragedy, not of ordinary life. I am speaking of the disillusionment of fulfilment: the disillusionment which follows action, which was inherent in past actions and will follow again upon new ones. Such men do not wearily abandon the struggle. The inner innocence which makes them reach out of everything—greatness and goodness, power and freedom, the way and the goal—reveals a disproportion between longing and fulfilment which is not the disproportion between idea and reality, but between different ideas. The noble man is always chosen for kingship. Everything in him strives towards that end. But kingship and the idea of kingship do not allow of nobility; the highest goals, the innermost essence of kingship demands something different—harshness and wickedness, ingratitude and compromise. The royal soul wants to fulfil the ultimate value of its personality in a royal life, for everywhere else it is confined and constrained; yet the throne makes the same demands upon all, and just because the royal soul is nobly conscious of duty, it is forced to do things which are alien and repulsive to it. Thus it is that Demetrius and Nabis stand face to face, the victorious rebel who is a king's son and the mortally wounded usurper. The young king strides impetuously into the hall where his own father's defeated murderer awaits him; but the dying man has only to utter a few words full of harsh wisdom, and a different Demetrius steps over his dead body to ascend the throne. Nabis has not spoken to the man who has defeated him, but to the heir who is to inherit his kingdom; he has spoken the words of a man disappointed in the deepest recesses of his soul, a man who wanted to do good, "the good that is not hard to understand," yet oceans of blood had to flow and his soul had to wither inside him in order that he might become a king such as his sense of duty and the age in which he lived required. And Nabis' corpse has scarcely grown cold before a new Nabis is seated upon his throne, broken, forsaken by joy, forced to be cruel, alone and friendless: Demetrius, the young king with the pure and hopeful soul, surrounded by a host of devoted friends, Demetrius who heard Nabis speak those words.

In the snow-filled castle courtyard at Canossa, where Gregory and Henry meet for the first and last time, victory and defeat are still more difficult to disentangle. The Pope and the Emperor, who already in the first four acts of their lives had been each other's destiny, now meet at last. God has given the Pope a gentle soul and a happiness-desiring, happiness-bestowing one to the Emperor, but the great struggle between them has crushed everything human, everything specific to themselves, in them both. Hildebrand has had to become harsh and cruel; he has not only had to discard all ordinary happiness, but also to sacrifice and betray the poor whom he once saw it as his mission to help. He has had to do this in order to receive into his hands the power of creating God's kingdom. He has had to become a sinner and to appear a saint, and the path of redeeming, alleviating repentance, open to all other men, is closed to him; his soul will go down into hell to eternal damnation. All his sacrifices are in vain. The adulterer whom he has excommunicated, the Emperor who stands in the way of his plans, now kneels before him feigning contrition like the clever statesman that he is, and he, the unredeemed, must break his only weapon with his own hands by withdrawing the excommunication. The emperor has won, but the radiant man who reached out for happiness with gleaming hands, who effortlessly gave and received happiness, Henry the man, is dead. Gregory leaves Canossa bowed and beaten; Henry will enter Rome as the victor.

> I rose a different man from when I knelt.
> He must curse God because he wanted what was right;
> I have done wrong, yet I bless God.
> He goes to die, I am already dead:
> His death is death, but mine is life.

Henry has won, Gregory is beaten. But did the Emperor win? And was the Pope defeated? The march on Rome has become possible, Gregory will be deposed, but did not the king of the world, the lord of all the world's glories, kneel as a penitent before a priest? Did not the Emperor bow before the Pope? And will not the priests, whom Gregory has deprived forever of all human semblance and capacity for happiness, always stand henceforth as judges over every mortal? Did not Henry forget the Emperor when he won, and Gregory forget the Pope when, lamenting, he broke his sword?

This necessity—perhaps the truest and certainly the most real of all—nevertheless has something humiliating about it. The heroes who await death here as their redemption from life are not only broken but defiled and estranged from their own selves. The heroes of tragedy always die happy, already alive in their death; but here death is not the absolute exaltation of life, the direct extension of a life lived in the right direction, but only an escape from oppression, from the impurity of the real world—a return of the soul from an alien life itself. The hero, it is true, does not feel any remorse on account of his deeds or of their vanity, and he does not return to the naïvely beautiful dreams he used to dream before he came into contact with reality. He knows that all the struggles, all the humiliations, are necessary for his life, for his becoming-manifest, for his only possible redemption. And yet this only possible redemption is not the true one, and that is the deepest disappointment of his soul. The frontiers which historical happenings draw round his soul, the frontiers to which history drives his soul, are not its true, specific frontiers—they are common to all men to whom these things might happen, to all those who might breathe the same air. The development which is granted or thrust upon the heroes of these tragedies always has about its nature something deeply alien to them. They become essential indeed, and their souls, relieved of the oppression of ordinary reality, breathe deeply and happily; but an alien being becomes real within them when the final forces are released. Death is the return, the first and only attainment of their own essence. The great struggle is only a roundabout way of getting there. History, through its irrational reality, forces pure universality upon men; it does not allow a man to express his own idea, which at other levels is just as irrational: the contact between them produces something alien to both—to wit, universality.

Historical necessity is, after all, the nearest to life of all necessities. But also the furthest from life. The realization of the idea which is possible here is only a roundabout way of achieving its essential realization. (The sad triviality of real life is here reproduced at the highest possible level.) But the whole life of the whole man is also a roundabout way of reaching other, higher goals; his deepest personal longing and his struggle to attain what he longs for are merely the blind tools of a dumb and alien taskmaster. Only very few become conscious of this; Pope Gregory knows it at a few ecstatic moments of his life:

> My body is a stone
> which a boy's hand threw into the lake
> My "I" is the force which draws circle upon circle on the water
> when the stone has long lain slumbering at the bottom.

Neither side of historical necessity lends itself to dramatic form-giving; the one is too high for it, the other too low, and yet their indissoluble and inseparable unity is the only true nature of history. It is at this point that the technical paradoxes of historical tragedy spring from the metaphysical paradox of the relationship between tragic man and historical existence: the paradox of inner distance between the spectator and the characters, the paradox between the characters' different degrees of life and life-intensity, the clash between the symbolic and the lifelike in the characters and events of historical drama. The historical view of life does not allow of any abstraction of place or time or the other principles of individuation: the essential part of men and events is inseparably bound up with the apparently secondary and accidental; the characters of historical drama must "live" and the events portrayed must show all the colourful variegation of real life. This is why Shakespeare's plays, although anti-historical at the core, could—on account of their immense richness and life-likeness—be seen as the greatest examples of historical drama, and indeed had to be seen as such. Shakespeare unconsciously represents the empirical element in history, and he does it with unequalled power and unparalleled richness. But the ultimate meaning of history, wherein it goes beyond everything personal, is so abstract that in order to represent it we would have to out-Hellenize everything we know of Greek drama. The paradoxical dream of synthesizing Sophocles with Shakespeare sprang from the wish to create a historical drama.

Any attempt at such a synthesis must, however, introduce a certain duality into the characters of the drama. Where the heroes are concerned, a solution of the problem is conceivable—the dualism we speak of could simply become their central experience; the flaw could be placed at the centre of the work and in that way, perhaps, be transcended after all. No one has yet succeeded in doing this, yet that does not prove that the problem is insoluble. But the impossibility of artistically creating a historical-dramatic destiny (i.e. one in which the historical element is really important and not just an accidental expression of a purely and timelessly human conflict) is crucial as a matter of principle, too. The human beings in whom destiny becomes form are split into two fundamentally different parts: the ordinary human being standing in the midst of real life is turned suddenly, in a single instant, into a symbol, the vector of a supra-personal, historical necessity. And since this becoming-symbol does not grow from the innermost recesses of the soul but is carried by alien forces to other alien forces, and the human personality is only an accidental connecting link, only a bridge for the progress of a destiny which is a stranger to it, it must irreparably destroy the unity of the character. The motives at work in the characters are alien from them and raise them into a sphere where they are bound to lose all their humanity. But if this impersonal element has been given form in drama, then the character must, during the not-yet or no-longer symbolical part of his life, float incorporeally among the living; he should be seen differently from everything round him, and yet should form a single, indivisible world with his environment. Gerhart Hauptmann always chooses to create individual human beings, and must therefore renounce the higher necessity of the historical—that which should be the true meaning of his plays. Paul Ernst's goal is the precise opposite. But when his Kallirhoë, the bride of Demetrius, is suddenly transformed by her own recognition of an historical necessity from a living and loving creature into the mere executor of that necessity, such concretization of something purely abstract has an almost grotesque effect; the purely symbolic figures in *Canossa* (the old peasant most particularly) are unsatisfactory, and in the *Gold* tragedy this tendency is carried to baroque proportions.

Form is the highest judge of life: the tragedy which finds expression in history is not completely pure tragedy, and no dramatic technique can wholly disguise this metaphysical dissonance; insoluble technical problems are bound to spring up at every point of the drama. Form is the only pure revelation of purest experience, but just for that reason it will always stubbornly refuse to be imposed on anything that is oppressive or unclear.

4

Form is the highest judge of life. Form-giving is a judging force, an ethic; there is a value-judgement in everything that has been given form. Every kind of form-giving, every literary form, is a step in the hierarchy of life-possibilities: the all-decisive word has been spoken about a man and his fate when the decision is taken as to the form which his life-manifestations can assume and which the highest moments of his life demand.

The most profound verdict which tragedy pronounces, then, is an inscription over its gate. Just as the inscription over Dante's gates of hell tells all who enter to abandon hope, so this inscription eternally refuses entrance to all who are too weak or too lowly to dwell in the kingdom of tragedy. In vain has our democratic age claimed an equal right for all to be tragic; all attempts to open this kingdom of heaven to the poor in spirit has proved fruitless. And those democrats who are consistent about their demand for equal rights for all men have always disputed tragedy's right to existence.

In *Brunhild* Paul Ernst wrote his mystery play about tragic men and women. *Ninon de l'Enclos* is its counterpart—a play about untragic people. In the former he gave form to human beings as he most fervently desired them to be; in the latter he gave life to figures essentially most alien to him. But the man who wrote the latter play, too, is a writer of tragedy and therefore he had to carry it to an extreme—to the point of tragedy; only, at the moment of the ultimate decision, his heroine slips out of the tentacles of tragedy, consciously refuses everything noble and fatal that had previously hung like a halo about her head, and rushes back into ordinary life, which has been waiting eagerly to receive her. Her motto is carved upon this final moment: it defines her value and at the same time her limitation. As a result of the struggle for freedom which she has fought against herself, she has become strong enough to be able to breathe the air of tragedy, to live within the periphery of tragedy. But, like all human beings of her particular kind, she lacks the final consecration of life. She is the highest of an inferior species: this is the verdict which the dramatic form passes upon the value of her life. She wanted to attain the highest for herself, and has attained it—the highest, which is freedom; but her freedom is simply liberation from all bonds, not, in the last analysis, a freedom organically born out of her innermost self, identical with the highest necessity—not the completion of her life. Her freedom is the freedom of harlots. She has freed herself from every strong interior bond—from man and child, fidelity and great love. She has made heavy sacrifices for this liberation, accepting many smaller, humiliating bonds, such as love that is sold or given away for the sake of a passing whim may create in a woman's life. She has suffered greatly from her loss and has borne with pride the trials imposed upon her by her self-appointed fate—but still it has only been an easing of her life, an escape from its heaviest necessities. Such self-liberation of a woman is not the fulfilment of her essential necessity as is the real self-liberation of a tragic man, and the conclusion of the play raises a question which Ernst the theoretician had foreseen long before: can a woman be tragic in herself and not in relation to the man of her life? Can freedom become a real value in a woman's life?

The core of Paul Ernst's life's work is the ethic of poetic literature, just as that of Friedrich Hebbel's was the psychology of poetic literature. Because, for both, form has become the goal of life, a categorical imperative of greatness and self-perfection, Ernst is always thought of as a cold formalist and Hebbel as a metaphysician of pathology. But whereas the fate of Hebbel's heroes is the tragically impotent struggle of real men for the perfect humanity of men who live in formal works of art—in other words, the profoundly problematic, psychologically experienced high moments of empirical living—Ernst places this perfect and rounded higher world as a warning, a call to action, a light and a goal upon the path of men, but is not concerned with their actual becoming-real. The validity and strength of an ethic does not depend on whether or not the ethic is applied. Therefore only a form which has been purified until it has become ethical can, without becoming blind and poverty-stricken as a result of it, forget the existence of everything problematic and banish it forever from its realm.

1910

Pragmatism and the Tragic Sense of Life*

Sidney Hook

I

"What, if anything, has philosophy to tell us about the human condition, about the fate of man and his works?" This question in all its changes I have heard repeatedly on three major continents. It is asked mostly by philosophical laymen—by students and teachers and men of letters in search of a center, or at least a shelter, in a world become dark and insecure because of the shadows of totalitarianism and war. It is asked at interdisciplinary conferences; and by academic administrators in search of projects to recommend to foundations, projects which, to use an expression in wide use, "are not merely of technical philosophical concern."

The question: What saving message do philosophers bring their fellowmen? I have heard asked even by professional philosophers agonizing over the fact that they have a subject but no apparent subject-matter. It was heard at the XIIth International Congress of Philosophy at Venice—and there the Soviet philosophers undertook to answer it. It is raised periodically by voices in this country and in our own association as a protest against analytic philosophy. It was the central theme of the Third East-West Philosophers' Conference where for six weeks forty older and almost as many younger philosophers tried to discover what bearing philosophy had on social practice. At one point we were told to imagine that we had the ear of the statesmen of the world, and were challenged to give them counsel on how to put the world's affair in order. No one recalled Plato's experience at Syracuse or reflected upon the fact that as far as we can judge the only request Aristotle made of Alexander, when he had *his* ear, was that he send back fresh biological specimens from Asia. Indeed, it is not likely that with his views about the essential superiority of the Greeks to the rest of mankind that Aristotle would have given his blessings to Alexander's enlightened, if premature, attempt to establish a world culture or that he would even have been sympathetic to the purpose of the East-West Philosopher's Conference.

This question, with which I begin, is certainly a large one and may be deemed an appropriate theme for discussion in conjunction with John Dewey's centenary year.

* Sidney Hook, "Pragmatism and the Tragic Sense of Life," from the Proceedings and Addresses of the American Philosophical Association, October, 1960, pp. 5–26.

94

II

For some time now philosophers have been disputing with each other about what philosophy should or should not be. They would be better occupied, it seems to me, doing each what he thinks philosophically worth while instead of objecting either to linguistic analysis or metaphysical speculation, as the case may be. The issue is not one of proper definition or even whether philosophy is a science or a body of knowledge of comparable objectivity, but rather whether it is worth doing, whether there is sufficient illumination and fun in pursuing certain themes, ignored by others, to justify continuing to do so. After all no one really believes that only science is a self-justifying enterprise. But since the subject has become moot and since there has developed a wide concern about what, if anything, philosophy has to say of general human concern, some remarks about it are in order.

As some of you are aware, I have for many years concerned myself with problems of social and political and legal philosophy, with "problems of men" as authentic as any of those recognized by thinkers who would reform modern philosophy. But I find myself increasingly out of sympathy with those who have impugned the whole philosophical enterprise because of its failure to serve as a beacon to mankind in distress. When I ask myself why I feel uncomfortable and at odds with those who attack philosophers because they have nothing of immediate, practical moment to say, I find that my conception of philosophy although stated sometimes in words similar to theirs, differs in important ways. Put most succinctly, although I believe that philosophy is a *quest* for wisdom, many of those who cite this phrase, too, speak and act as if they already had it. The difference may be only of nuance and emphasis but it has a profound bearing on one's conception of the appropriate role of the philosopher in the culture of his time. It is the difference between being a moralist and being a moralizer. The moralizer may be called "the shouting moralist," of whom Santayana somewhere says that he "no doubt has his place but not in philosophy." It is a difference, on the one hand, between *analyzing* specific and basic social problems and conflicts, and *clarifying* the issues in dispute with all the tools at one's command—and, on the other, *proclaiming* solutions and programs on the basis of antecedent commitments which one shares with some faction of his fellowmen. It is the difference between approaching problems of human experience in terms of one's vocation as a philosopher, which is to do intellectual justice to the varied and conflicting interests present or discovered, and one's vocation as a citizen limited by specific duties he must fulfill. It is the difference between intellectual concern which may or may not lead to programs of action and commitment to programs of action which by their very nature estops self-critical thought.

In the course of its history philosophy has been many things. But its distinctive concern at all times *has* been the quest for wisdom. Otherwise there would be no point in including thinkers like Descartes or Leibnitz in the history of philosophy in addition to the history of science or mathematics. What distinguishes the philosopher as a moralist from the philosopher as a mathematician, logician or natural scientist, and from the ordinary man as a philosopher, is his sustained reflective pursuit of wisdom. This means two things. The systematic study of the knowledge which is relevant to wisdom: and the analysis of the commitments we assume and rule out when knowledge is related to policy. All of us know that wisdom and knowledge are not the same thing but we sometimes mistakenly speak as if they are opposed. A man may have knowledge of many things and not be wise but a wise man cannot be ignorant of the things he is wise about. He must have knowledge of the nature and career of values in human experience; knowledge of the nature and history of the situations in which they develop and conflict; knowledge of the minds and emotions of the carriers of value; knowledge of the consequences of actions taken or proposed. The wise man is not one who merely recites moral principles and applies a ready-made schedule of moral obligations to the problems and perplexities of value conflict. He is one who on the basis of what he already knows, or believes he knows, makes fresh inquiry into the situations which define alternatives and exact their costs. "Only the conventional and the fanatical," observes Dewey, "are always immediately sure of right and wrong in conduct." This means that a philosopher must earn his title to be wise not by right of philosophical tradition or philology but by the hard work of acquiring relevant knowledge and by hard thinking about it.

Here lie important tasks for the philosopher. To be wise he must immerse himself in the actual subject matters (not necessarily experiences) out of which life's problems arise. To be wise about economic affairs he must study economics, to be wise about problems of law he must study law, to be wise about politics he must study history, sociology and other disciplines. To be wise about war and peace he must study military technology and the theory and practice of communism including its strategic exploitation of peace movements to disarm the free world. Indeed, these subjects are so interrelated that to be wise about any one of them he must study them all. And I might add, in view of some current writing, to be wise about education it is not enough merely to rebaptize the ends of the good life as ends of a good education, too, as if without operational application to concrete historical situations, they had any but a peripheral bearing on the great, current problems of education. One must study social history, the psychology of learning, the methods and techniques of pedagogy to achieve educational wisdom. To enumerate the ends of the good life is not enough. Nor is a primer on logical analysis which can serve as an introduction to the study of *any* subject, a primer to a philosophy of education.

All of these problems are of tremendous complexity because of the number of independent variables they contain, because they rarely permit of controlled experiment, and because the community must sometimes act upon them in desperate urgency before the analysis is complete. This should make for humility among philosophers even as they bring to the study of these problems the methodological sophistication, the arts and skills of analysis which are the hallmarks of their profession. This is what *I* mean by "the problems of men." It is philosophy not as a quest for salvation but as a pursuit of understanding of great cultural issues and their possible upshot. It does not start from a complete stock of philosophical wisdom which it dispenses to others with hortatory fervor but with an initial sense of concern to meet the challenge of the great unresolved problems of our time, offering analysis of these problems which will win the respect of the specialist and yet command the attention of everyman, e.g. how to preserve peace *and* freedom, achieve adequate and meaningful vocations for all, design patterns of creative leisure, effect desegregation if possible without coercion, establish a welfare state and a spirit of enterprise, preserve national security and the right to dissent. It is philosophy as *normative* social inquiry. And it is *not* social reform. How could philosophy be identified with social reform in view of the existence of many esteemed philosophers from Aristotle to Santayana whose judgments of wisdom were conservative, hostile to social reform? Such identification would be comparable to defining a physicist as one who was committed to a specific hypothesis in physics.

At this point my inner ear senses unspoken murmurs of surprise. "Surely," some of you must be saying, "this constitutes a repudiation of John Dewey's conception of philosophy, for, after all, does not Dewey call upon philosophers as philosophers to do precisely what is being urged they should not do? Does not Dewey call upon philosophers to play the role of social reformers?" My answer is: "Not as I understand him and not as he is to be understood in the light of all he has written."

Here is not the place to provide the documentation. I content myself merely with saying that Dewey has a very *complex* conception of philosophy. Philosophy is indeed concerned primarily with what I call normative problems of social inquiry. But its function is also to provide leading, speculative ideas in science—natural and social. And a third function is to weave together certain families of ideas into a philosophical synthesis. "There is a kind of music of ideas," he says, "which appeals, apart from any question of verification, to the mind of thinkers!" Nor is this all. The philosopher must bring some perspective or vision to bear upon the world which is related to issues of value and hence makes the analysis of normative problems of social inquiry more sensitive. "Philosophies," declares Dewey, "are different ways of construing life. . . ."

There is more, then, than problems of normative social inquiry which falls within the province of the philosopher's concern. There is the illuminating perspective in which they are seen which is metaphysics. "If philosophy be criticism," Dewey asks in *Experience and Nature*, "what is to be said of the relation of philosophy to metaphysics?" His answer briefly is that metaphysics is a description of those gross features of the world which constitute the backdrop of the theatre of human activity against which men play out their lives. The conduct of life and the analysis of its problems, however indirectly, will reflect what we believe to be the generic features of human experience in the world. In this sense, as ultimately related to the human scene and the adventure of human life, but not to ontology, metaphysics is "a ground map of the province of criticism establishing base lines to be employed in more intricate triangulations."

This brings me finally to my theme of the tragic sense of life as a feature of human experience which provides an illuminating perspective upon the analysis of man's problems. The juxtaposition of the expressions "pragmatism" and "the tragic sense of life" may appear bewildering to those who understand pragmatism as a narrow theory of meaning and "the tragic sense of life" as the hysterical lament that man is not immortal—the theme song of Unamuno's book of that title. To speak of pragmatism and the tragic sense of life is somewhat like speaking of "The Buddhism of John Dewey" or "The Dewey Nobody Knows."

I am not aware that Dewey ever used the phrase "the tragic sense of life" but I know that growing up in the shadow of the Civil War, he felt what I shall describe by it and that it is implied in his account of moral experience. At any rate nothing of moment depends upon whether the view is actually Dewey's or Hegel's or William James' or Nicolai Hartmann's in all of whom it can be found. I take the responsibility of the interpretation and its application. It is a perspective which seems to me to illumine the pragmatic view that problems of normative social inquiry—morals in the broad sense—are the primary—not exclusive—subject matter of philosophy, and that reason or scientific intelligence can and should be used to resolve them.

By the tragic sense of life I do not understand merely sensitivity to the presence of evil or suffering in the world although all tragic situations to some degree involve one or the other. And since I have mentioned Buddha I should like to say that the presence of the evils in the world which led Buddha to surrender his Kingdom in order to seek salvation for himself and mankind are not to me the realities fundamental to the tragic sense of life. There were three things in Buddha's experience, reflection upon which led him to a renunciation of his princely lot and a quest for liberation from desire and incarnate existence—sickness, old age and death. One can very well understand why in the world in which he lived and for many centuries thereafter until our own, these phenomena loomed so large in the overpopulated and poverty-stricken areas of Asia. Nonetheless if we are to distinguish between the sense of the *pitiful* and the sense of the *tragic*—sickness, old age and even many forms of death, despite their numbing effect upon human sensibility, are not necessarily to be classified as tragic.

First, given the rapidly expanding horizons of knowledge in our age, there is nothing in the nature of things which requires that the sick, any more than the poor, must always be with us. If scientific medicine develops at the same pace in the next few hundred years as it has in the last century, it is not shallow optimism to anticipate that the most serious forms of sickness will disappear and not be replaced by others. Even where sickness is present it may be the occasion of tragedy but by itself is not an illustration of it. In relation to the forces of nature man's lot may appear pitiful. The tragic is a moral phenomenon.

What is true of sickness is true of old age. The aged arouse our compassion because of their feebleness and fragility—and the multiplicity of their aches and pains. When these are absent—and this, too, is a concern of scientific medicine—there is a chance for serenity, wisdom and beauty of spirit to manifest themselves. There is sometimes a grandeur and stateliness about an old tree which aged persons do not possess because the processes of physical degeneration, and the consequent weakening of the vital powers, make man pitiful. There is no tragedy in growing old biologically but only sorrow; the element of the tragic enters in the defeat of plans or hopes, in the realization that in much grief there is not much wisdom, and that we cannot count merely upon the passage of time alone to diminish our stupidities and cruelties.

But what of death—Buddha's third appalling discovery—preoccupation with which has become so fashionable today among some European existentialist philosophers that their philosophy seems to be more a meditation upon death than upon life? Is not death the ultimate source of whatever is tragic in life? I cannot bring myself to think so. Nor can I convince myself that its nature and significance in life waited to be discovered by Kierkegaard and Heidegger and their modern disciples.

It is the reflective attitude towards death not the popular attitude or the one displayed by those in its last agonies, which throws light on its nature and place in life. The attitude exhibited by Socrates in facing it seems wiser than that expressed by the contemnors of the rational life who not content with talking about what they find when they look into themselves inflate it into a universal trait of the human psyche. So Tolstoy who is quoted by existentialist writers, writes: "If a man has learned to think, no matter what he may think about, he is always thinking of his own death. All philosophers are like that. And what truth can there be, if there is death?" Logically, of course, this makes no more sense than the even more extreme statement of Sartre that "if we must die then our life has no meaning," which to those who solve some problems in life and therefore find some meaning, might be taken as a premise in a new short proof of human immortality. All this it seems to me expresses little more than a fear of death and a craving for immortality. It is a commonplace observation, however, that most human beings who desire immortality desire not unending life but unending youth or other desirable qualities which life makes possible. The fable of Juno and her lover in which Juno petitions the Gods to take back the gift of eternal life they had conferred upon a mortal indicates that the Greeks knew that a life without end could be a dubious blessing. In this respect the Hellenes were wiser than the Hebrews whose God drives Adam from Paradise after he had eaten of the fruit of the tree of knowledge to prevent him from eating of the fruit of the tree of eternal life. Agony over death strikes me as one of the unloveliest features of the intellectual life of our philosophic times—and certainly unworthy of any philosophy which conceives itself as a quest for wisdom. It has never been clear to me why those who are nauseated by life, not by this or that kind of life but any kind of life, should be so fearful of death.

Wisdom is knowledge of the uses of life and death. The uses of life are to be found in the consummatory experiences of vision and delight, of love, understanding, art, friendship and creative activity. That is why in a contingent world of finite men, vulnerable to powers they cannot control which sometimes robs them of the possibility of any justifying consummations, death has its uses, too. For it gives us some assurance that no evil or suffering lasts forever. To anyone aware of the multitude of infamies and injustices which men have endured, of the broken bodies and tortured minds of the victims of these cruelties, of the multiple dimensions of pain in which millions live on mattress graves or with minds shrouded in darkness, death must sometimes appear as a beneficent release, not an inconsolable affliction. It washes the earth clean of what cannot be cleansed in any other way. Not all the bright promises of a future free of these stains of horror can redeem by one iota the lot of those who will not live to see the dawn of the new day.

It is nobler to exist and struggle in a world in which there is always a vital option to live or die. The fear of death, the desire to survive at any cost or price in human degradation, has been the greatest ally of tyranny, past and present. "There are times," says Woodbridge, "when a man ought to be more afraid of living than dying." And we may add, there are situations in which because of the conditions of survival, the worst thing we can know of anyone is that he has survived. We have known such times and situations. They may come again.

Even in a world in which all injustices, cruelties and physical anguish have disappeared, the possibility of withdrawing from it makes the world insofar forth a better and a freer world. So long as we retain possession of our faculties, our decision to remain in the world indicates a participating responsibility on our part for those events within it which our continuance affects. If human beings were unable to die they would to that extent be unfree. Man shares a *conatus sui esse persevare* with everything else in the world or at least with all other sentient beings. But just because he can on rational grounds give up his being, choose not to be, he differentiates himself most strikingly from his fellow creatures in nature. I conclude therefore that death as such is not a tragic phenomenon and that its presence does not make the world and our experience within it tragic. It would be truer to call tragic a world in which men wanted to die but couldn't.

What, then, do I mean by the tragic sense of life and what is its relevance to pragmatism? I mean by the tragic sense a very simple thing which is rooted in the very nature of the moral experience and the phenomenon of moral choice. Every genuine experience of moral doubt and perplexity in which we ask: "What should I do?" takes place in a situation where good conflicts with good. If we already know what is evil the moral inquiry is over, or it never really begins. "The worse or evil," says Dewey, "is the rejected good" but until we reject it, the situation is one in which apparent good opposes apparent good. "All the serious perplexities of life come back to the genuine difficulty of forming a judgment as to the values of a situation: they come back to a conflict of goods." No matter how we resolve the opposition some good will be sacrificed, some interest, whose immediate craving for satisfaction may be every whit as intense and authentic as its fellows, will be modified, frustrated or even suppressed. Where the goods involved are of a relatively low order, like decisions about what to eat, where to live, where to go, the choice is unimportant except to the mind of a child. There are small tragedies as there are small deaths. At any level the conflict of values must become momentous to oneself or others to convey adequately the tragic quality. Where the choice is between goods that are complex in structure and consequential for the future, the tragic quality of the moral dilemma emerges more clearly. And when it involves basic choices of love, friendship, vocations, the quality becomes poignant. The very nature of the self as expressed in habits, dispositions and character is to some extent altered by these decisions. If, as Hobbes observes, "Hell is truth seen too late," all of us must live in it. No matter how justified in smug retrospect our moral decisions seem to have been, only the unimaginative will fail to see the possible selves we have sacrificed to become what we are. Grant that all regrets are vain, that any other choice would have been equally or more regretted, the selves we might have been are eloquent witnesses of values we failed to enjoy. If we have played it safe and made our existence apparently secure, the fascinating experience of a life of adventure and experience can never be ours, and every thought of a good fight missed will be accompanied by a pang. It is a poor spirit William James reminds us who does not sense the chagrin of the tardy Crillon, who arriving when the battle is over is greeted by Henry IV with the words: "Hang yourself, brave Crillon! We fought at Arques, and you were not there!" On the other hand, if we have scorned to put down our roots, hugged our liberty tightly to ourselves by refusing to give hostages to fortune, become crusaders or martyrs for lost causes, we have thrust from ourselves the warmth of sustained affection, and the comforting regularities which can best heal the bruised spirit.

There is a conflict not only between the good and the good but between the good and the right where the good is a generic term for all the values in a situation and the right for all the obligations. The *concepts* of good and right are irreducible to each other in ordinary use. We are often convinced we must fulfill a certain duty even when we are far from convinced to the same degree that the action or the rule it exemplifies will achieve the greatest good. The "good" is related to the reflective satisfaction of an interest: "the right" to the fulfillment of a binding demand or rule of the community. There is no moral problem when in doing the right thing we can see that it *also* leads to the greatest good or when striving for the greatest good conforms to our sense of what is right. But the acute ethical problems arise when in the pursuit of the good we do things which appear not to be right, as e.g., when in order to avoid the dangers of war a nation repudiates its treaty obligations or when in order to win a war non-combatants are punished who are in no way responsible for the actions of others. They also arise when in doing what is right our actions result in evil consequences, as e.g., when a dangerous criminal, set free on a legal technicality, kills again or when the refusal to surrender to the unjust claims of an aggressor results in wholesale slaughter. Many have been the attempts made to escape the antinomies between the right and the good by defining the good as the object of right or the right merely as the means to the good. All have failed. To act upon the right no matter what its consequences for human weal or woe seems inhuman, at times insane. The thirst for righteousness has too often been an angry thirst satisfied if at all by long draughts of blood. On the other hand, the attempt to do good by *any* means no matter how unjust, is subhuman and usually irrational.

As compared to traditional ethical doctrines, ideal utilitarianism reaches farthest in our quest for an adequate ethics but in the end it, too, must be rejected. And it was the pragmatist and pluralist, William James, long before Pritchard and Ross, who indicated why in the famous question he asked: "If the hypothesis were offered us of a world in which Messrs. Fourier's and Bellamy's and Morris' Utopia should all be outdone, and millions be kept permanently happy on the one simple condition that a certain lost soul on the far off edge of things should lead a life of lonely torture, what except a specifical and independent sort of emotion can it be which would make us immediately feel . . . how hideous a thing would be its enjoyment when deliberately accepted as the fruit of such a bargain?" The situation is unaltered if we recognize that there are other goods besides happiness and that justice is itself a good, because in that case the conflict breaks out again between good and good. In this connection I would venture the statement that it is the failure to see the radical pluralism in the nature of the goods which are reckoned in the consequences of an action which accounts both for Moore's view that it is self-evident that it can *never* be right knowingly to approve an action that would make the world as a whole worse than some alternative action and for Kant's view that there are some duties that it would *always* be right to perform, even if the consequences of the action resulted in a worse world or in no world at all. No specific rule can be laid down as absolutely binding in advance either way. Nothing can take the place of intelligence; the better or the lesser evil in each situation can be best defined as the object of reflective choice. Even the decision in the stock illustration of the text-books whether to execute an innocent man or turn him over to be tortured in order to save the community from destruction—would depend upon a complex of circumstances. It is perfectly conceivable that an unjust act will sometimes produce the greater good or the lesser evil. It is sometimes necessary to burn down a house to save a village. Although when applied to human beings the logic seems damnable, few are prepared to take the position of Kant in those agonizing moral predicaments that are not uncommon in history, especially the history of oppressed minority peoples, in which the survival of the group can be purchased only at the price of the pain, degradation and death of the innocent. No matter how we choose, we must either betray the ideal of the greater good or the ideal of right or justice. In this lies the agony of the choice.

Many have been the attempts to escape the guilt of that choice. I cite one from the past. During the Middle Ages, Maimonides writing on the Laws of the Torah to guide his people discusses what a community is to do when it is beset by enemies who demand the life of one man with the threat to kill all if he be not turned over to them: Maimonides teaches that they are to refuse to turn over any man even if all must die in consequence, except if their enemies call out the name of a specific person. I had heard this teaching defended on the ground that if the community itself had to make the decision who was to die, it would be taking the guilt of an innocent man's death upon itself, which is impermissible. But if the enemy names the man, then he can be turned over because the guilt and sin fall now on *their* heads. By this miserable evasion it was thought that the tragic choice could be avoided. But it turns out that Maimonides has been misread. What Maimonides really taught is that only if the name of the person who has been called out is of one already under the death sentence for his crimes should he be surrendered. But never an innocent man. "Never," however, is a long time. It is problematic whether the Jews would have survived if they had always abided by Maimonides' injunction.

If anything, human beings are more readily inclined to sacrifice the right to the good than the good to the right especially in revolutionary situations which have developed because of grievances too long unmet. It can easily be shown that it was Lenin's conception of Communist ethics which implicitly defined the right action as consisting in doing *anything*—literally anything that would bring victory in the class struggle—which explains the transformation of a whole generation of idealists into hangmen. In fact the health of the revolution whether in the times of Robespierre or Castro never really requires the holocaust of victims offered up to it. But no revolution including our own has ever been achieved without injustice to someone. However the conflict between the principles of right and the values of good be theoretically resolved, in every concrete situation it leads to some abridgement of principle or some diminution of value.

The most dramatic of all moral conflicts is not between good and good, or between good and right, but between right and right. This in its starkest form is the theme of Sophoclean tragedy but the primary locus of the tragic situation is not in a play but in life, in law, and in history. Innocence in personal matters consists in overlooking the conflict of moral duties and obligations. Innocence in political matters, the characteristic of ritualistic liberalism, consists in failing to see the conflicts of rights in our Bill of Rights and the necessity of their intelligent adjustment. In our own country we have witnessed again and again the antinomy of rights revealed in divided loyalties, in the conflict between allegiance to the laws of the state and allegiance to what is called divine law or natural law or the dictates of conscience. On the international scene it is expressed in the conflict of incompatible national claims, each with *some* measure of justification, as in the Israeli-Arab impasse.

One of the noteworthy features of moral intuitionism as illustrated in the doctrines of Ross is this recognition that *prima facie* duties conflict and that every important moral act exhibits at the same time characteristics which tend to make it both *prima facie* right and *prima facie* wrong so that although we may claim certainty about these *prima facie* duties, any particular moral judgment or action is at best only probable or contingent. As Ross says, "There is therefore much truth in the description of the right act as a fortunate act." From this the conclusion to be drawn, it seems to me, is that the most important *prima facie* duty of all in a situation requiring moral decision is that of *conscientiousness*, or reflective assessment of all the relevant factors involved, and the searching exploration of our own hearts to determine what we sincerely want, whether we really wish to do what is right in a situation or to get our own scheming way come what may. As much if not more evil results from confusion of our purposes and ignorance of our motives than from ruthless and clear-eyed resolve to ignore everyone's interests but one's own. This emphasis on the importance of reflective inquiry into the features of the situation which bear on the rightness of an action seems to me to be more important than Ross' conception or interpretation of the intuitive apprehension of our *prima facie* duties. It is easier to doubt that we have this faculty of infallible intuition than that our intelligence has the power to discover our conflicts and mediate between them.

Irony is compounded with tragedy in the fact that many of the rights we presently enjoy we owe to our ancestors who in the process of winning them for us deprived others of their rights. In some regions of the world the very ground on which people stand was expropriated by force and fraud from others by their ancestors. Yet as a rule it would be a new injustice to seek to redress the original injustice by depriving those of their possessions who hold present title to them. Every just demand for reparations against an aggressor country is an unjust demand on the descendants of its citizens who as infants were not responsible for the deeds of aggression. That is why history is the arena of the profoundest moral conflicts in which some legitimate right has always been sacrificed, sometimes on the altars of the God of War.

The Christian and especially the Buddhist ethics of purity which seeks to transcend this conflict and avoid guilt by refusal to violate anyone's right in such situations, can only do so by withdrawing from the plane of the ethical altogether. This may succeed in God's eyes but not in man's. The Buddhist saint or any other who out of respect for the right to life of man or beast refuses ever to use force, or to kill, even when this is the only method, as it sometimes is, that will save multitudes from suffering and death, makes himself responsible for the greater evil, all the more so because he claims to be acting out of compassion. He cannot avoid guilt whether we regard him as more than man or less than man. No more than we does he escape the tragic decision.

There are three generic approaches to the tragic conflicts of life. The first approach is that of history. The second is that of love. The third is that of creative intelligence in quest for ways of mediation which I call here the pragmatic.

The approach of history is best typified by Hegel precisely because he tries to put a gloss of reason over the terrible events which constitute so much of the historical process. Its upshot is woefully inept to its intent. It suggests not only that whatever cause wins and *however* it wins, is more just than the cause which is defeated, but that the loser is the more wicked and not merely the weaker. Further, it calls into question the very fact of tragic conflict from which it so perceptively starts. No one has seen more profoundly into the nature of the tragic situation than Hegel and its stark clash of equally legitimate rights. But his solution, expressed in Schiller's dictum *Die Weltgeschichte ist das Weltgericht*, as Hegel develops it, makes the philosophy of history a theodicy. It thereby vulgarizes tragedy. For it attempts to console man with a dialectical proof that his agony and defeat are not really evils but necessary elements in the goodness of the whole. The position is essentially religious. No monotheistic religion which conceives of God as both omnipotent and benevolent, no metaphysics which asserts that the world is rational, necessary and good has any room for genuine tragedy.

The approach of love is incomplete and ambiguous. It is incomplete because if love is more than a feeling of diffused sympathy but is expressed in action no *man* can love everyone or identify himself with every interest. Empirically love has produced as much disunity as unity in the world—not only in Troy but in Jerusalem. Injustice is often born of love, not only of self-love but of love of some rather than others. Love is not only incomplete but ambiguous. There are various kinds of love and the actions to which they lead may be incompatible. An order of distinction is required. A man's love for his family must be discriminatory: his love of mankind not. He cannot love both in the same way without denying one or the other. The quality of love is altered with the range of its generalization. In one sense love always shows a bias which reinforces some conflicting interest; in another it gives all conflicting values its blessing without indicating any specific mode of action by which conflict can be mediated. Love may enable a person to live with the burden of guilt which he assumes when he sacrifices one right to another. But it is no guide to social conflict as the last two thousand years have shown. Because the Lord loves man equally nothing follows logically about the equality of man before the Law. "The *Agape* quality of love," says Tillich, "sees man as God sees him." But what *man* can tell us how *God* sees man? "Agape," continues Tillich, "loves in everybody and through everybody love itself." Karl Barth speaks more simply and intelligibly, and with a basic brutality which is the clue to his crude neutralism, when he claims that such love has no bearing whatever for the organization of any human society.

Finally there is the method of creative intelligence. It, too, tries to make it possible for men to live with the tragic conflict of goods and rights and duties, to mediate not by arbitrary fiat but through informed and responsible decision. Whoever uses this method must find his way among all the conflicting claims. He must therefore give each one of them and the interests it represents tongue or voice. Every claimant therefore has a right to be heard. The hope is that as much as possible of each claim may be incorporated in some inclusive or shared interest which is accepted because the alternatives are less satisfactory. To this end we investigate every relevant feature about it, the conditions under which it emerged, its proximate causes and consequences, the costs of gratifying it, the available alternatives and *their* costs. Every mediation entails some sacrifice. The quest for the unique good of the situation, for what is to be done here and now, may point to what is better than anything else available but what it points to is also a lesser evil. It is a lesser evil whether found in a compromise or in moderating the demand of a just claim or in learning to live peacefully with one's differences on the same general principle which tells us that a divorce is better for all parties concerned than a murder. In every case the rules, the wisdom, the lessons of the past are to be applied but they have presumptive, not final, validity because they may be challenged by new presumptions. "The pragmatic import of the logic of individualized situations," says Dewey, "is to transfer the attention of theory from pre-occupation with general conceptions to the problem of developing effective methods of inquiry," and applying them. It is a logic which does not preach solutions but explores the suggestions which emerge from the analyses of problems. Its categorical imperative is to inquire, to reason together, to seek in every crisis the creative devices and inventions that will not only make life fuller and richer but tragedy bearable. William James makes essentially the same point as Dewey in the language of ideals. Since in the struggles between ideals "victory and defeat there must be, the victory to be philo-sophically prayed for is that of the more inclusive side—of the side which even in the hour of triumph will to some degree do *justice* to the ideals in which the vanquished interests lay. . . ." But prayer is not enough. He goes on: "*Invent some manner* of realizing your own ideals which will also satisfy the alien de-mands—that and that only is the path of peace." To which we must add, pro-vided there is a reciprocal will to peace in the matter. And even then, your own or the alien demands or both must be curtailed.

As you may have gathered by this time, I have been concerned to show that this pragmatic approach to the moral problem can not only be squared with the recognition of tragic conflicts, of troubles, minor and grave, which dog the life of man in a precarious world, but that it gets its chief justification from this rec-ognition. Intelligence may be optimistic when it deals with the control of things but the moral life by its very nature forbids the levity and superficiality which has often been attributed to the pragmatic approach by its unimaginative critics.

Indeed I make bold to claim that the pragmatic approach to tragedy is more serious, even more heroic, than any other approach because it doesn't re-sign itself to the bare fact of tragedy or take easy ways out at the price of truth. Where death does not result from the tragic situation, there are always conse-quences for continued living which it takes responsibly without yielding to de-spair. It does not conceive of tragedy as a pre-ordained doom, but as one in which the plot to some extent depends upon us, so that we become the creators of our own tragic history. We cannot then palm off altogether the tragic out-come upon the universe in the same way as we can with a natural disaster.

Contrast this attitude towards tragedy with the Hegelian fetishism of histo-ry which in the end is but the rationalization of cruelty. Contrast it with the Judaic-Christian conception which offers at the price of truth, the hope that the felicities of salvation will both explain and recompense human suffering. Con-trast it with the attitude of Unamuno whose hunger for immortality is so intense that he sees in intelligence or reason the chief enemy of life, both in time and eternity. For him the joy and delight of life is the conflict of value and value no matter what the cost. "The very essence of tragedy," he tells us, "is the combat of life with reason." And since the Inquisitor is concerned with the eternal life of his victim's soul, the potential victim must defend the Inquisitor's place in soci-ety and regard him as far superior to the merchant who merely ministers to his needs. "There is much more humanity in the Inquisitor," he says. Crazed by this thirst for the infinite, Unamuno glorifies war as the best means of spreading love and knowledge. He illustrates the dialectic of total absurdity and caprice in thought which often prepares the way for atrocity in life. Here is no quest for the better, for the extension of reasonable controls in life and society, for peace in action.

To be sure, Unamuno is so horrified by the flux of things in which all things are ultimately liquefied that he expresses pity for the very "star-strewn heavens" whose light will some day be quenched. But this cosmic sentimentality is dis-dainful of the vexatious, unheroic daily tasks of mediating differences, even of mitigating the consequences of irreconcilable conflicts, of devising ways to limit human suffering whose ubiquitous presence is the alleged cause of spiritual ag-ony.

No two thinkers seem so far removed from each other as Miguel de Una-muno and Bertrand Russell—and as philosophers they are indeed related as a foothill to a Himalayan peak. But this makes all the more significant the similarity of their attitude towards the arts of social control which require the extension of man's power over nature. For Russell, any philosophy, and particularly one like Dewey's, which interprets ideas as implicit guides to activity and behavior, and knowledge as dependent upon experimental reconstructive activity in the situation which provokes it, exhibits "the danger of what may be called cosmic impiety." It is an arrogant power-philosophy whose insolence towards the universe is hardly less objectionable when it stresses social power than individual power.

It is fortunate that Russell's attitude—in which he is not always consistent—towards scientific power and control of our natural environment has not prevailed, otherwise the whole of modern civilization including modern medicine would never have developed. The charge of megalomania against any view of knowledge just because it is not a pure spectator view is absurd. For the pragmatic view accepts the Spinozistic dictum that nature can be changed only by nature's means. The problem is to discover or devise these means. This cannot be intelligently done without experimental activity. According to Russell's own position, power itself is neither good nor bad but only the uses and ends of power. But since he also tells us that there is no such thing as a rational or irrational end, that intelligence or reason is helpless in determining what we should do with our power, one can argue with much better warrant that it is *his* view, *if acted upon*, that increases "the danger of vast social disaster" than the pragmatic view which believes that by changing nature and society, men can to some extent change themselves in the light of rationally determined ends. No humane person can read history without being moved more by man's failures to use the knowledge he has had to remove the evils and sufferings which were remedial than by his attempt to achieve too great a control or power over nature. It was not science which was responsible for the use of the atomic bomb. It was politics—a failure of politics to understand the true situation. The pitiful disparity at any particular time between what we know and don't know is sufficient to inspire a sense of humility in the most intellectually ambitious. But it is only in the most vulgarized sense of the term "pragmatism," a sense which Russell helped to popularize by flagrant misunderstandings, that the adequacy of a theory of knowledge, which regards activity or experiment as integral to the achievement of knowledge of fact, can be judged by its alleged social consequences.

I am more interested tonight in stating a position than establishing it. As I understand the pragmatic perspective on life, it is an attempt to make it possible for men to live in a world of inescapable tragedy,—a tragedy which flows from the conflict of moral ideals,—without lamentation, defiance or make-believe. According to this perspective even in the best of human worlds there will be tragedy—tragedy perhaps without bloodshed but certainly not without tears. It focuses its analysis on problems of normative social inquiry in order to reduce the costs of tragedy. Its view of man is therefore melioristic, not optimistic. Some philosophers belittle man by asking him to look at the immensities without: others belittle him by asking him to look at the perversities and selfishness within. Pragmatism denies nothing about the world or men which one truly finds in them but it sees in men something which is at once, to use the Sophoclean phrase, more wonderful and more terrible than anything else in the universe, viz., the power to make themselves and the world around them better or worse.

In this way pragmatic meliorism avoids the romantic pessimism of Russell's free man, shaking his fist in defiance of a malignant universe, and the grandiose optimism of Niebuhr's redeemed man with his delusions of a cosmic purpose which he knows is there but knows in a way in which neither he nor anyone else can possibly understand.

To the meliorist the recognition of the gamut of tragic possibilities is what feeds his desire to find some method of negotiating conflicts of value by intelligence rather than war, or brute force. But this is not as simple as it sounds. There is no substitute for intelligence. But intelligence may not be enough. It may not be enough because of limitations of our knowledge, because of the limited reach of our powers of control. It may not be enough because of the recalcitrance of will—not merely the recalcitrance of will to act upon goods already known and not in dispute, but because of unwillingness to find out what the maximizing good in the situation is. And although we are seeking to settle conflicts of value by the use of intelligence rather than by force, is it not true that sometimes intelligence requires the use of force?

Let us take this last question first. Faced by a momentous conflict of values in which some value must give way if the situation is to be resolved, the rational approach is to find some encompassing value on the basis of some shared interest. This, as we have seen, involves willingness to negotiate—to negotiate honestly. The grim fact, however, is that there is sometimes no desire to reason, no wish to negotiate except as a holding action to accumulate strategic power, nothing but the reliance of one party or the other upon brute force even when other alternatives may exist. In such cases the moral onus rests clearly upon those who invoke force. Their victory no more establishes their claim to be right than a vandal's destruction of a scientists' instruments of inquiry has any bearing on the validity of his assertions, evidence for or against which, could have been gathered by the instrument destroyed. The intelligent use of force to *prevent* or crush the use of force where a healthy democratic process, equitable laws and traditions and customs of freedom make it possible to vent differences in a rational and orderly way, is therefore justifiable even if on prudential grounds one may forego such action. This means that tolerance always has limits—it cannot tolerate what is itself actively intolerant.

There is a tendency in modern philosophical thought which, in rejecting too sweeping claims for the role of intelligence in human affairs, settles for too little even when it does not embrace a wholesale skepticism. Of course, a man may know what is right and not do it just as he may know what is true and not publicly assert it. In neither case is this a ground for maintaining that we cannot know what action is more justified than another or what assertion is more warranted than another. The *refusal* to follow a rational method, to give good reasons is one thing: the claim that there are different rational methods, different *kinds* of good reasons each with its own built-in modes of validity, is something else again—and to me unintelligible. To be sure, the acceptance of rational method is not enough. Men must have some non-rational element in common. Hume is on unquestionably solid ground in asserting that reason must always *serve* a human need, interest or passion. But his mistake outweighed his insight when he contended that rational method could only be a servant or slave of what it served and that needs, interests and passions could not be changed or transformed by the use of intelligence. In our flights into space if we encounter other sentient creatures capable of communicating with us, it is more likely that their logical and mathematical judgment will be the same as ours than their ethical judgments, because we can more readily conceive creatures of different needs than of different minds.

At any rate the world we live in is one in which men do not share all their needs and interests and yet it is one in which they have sufficient needs and interests in common to make possible their further extension, and to give intelligence a purchase, so to speak, in its inquiry.

The most difficult of all situations is one in which even the common use of methods of inquiry seems to lead to conclusions which are incompatible with each other although each is objectively justified. There is always an open possibility of ultimate disagreement no matter how far and long we pursue rational inquiry. We can conceive it happening. In such situations we must resign ourselves to living with our differences. Otherwise we must fight or surrender. But it is simply a non-sequitur to maintain that because no guarantee can be given that there will not be ultimate disagreement, penultimate agreements cannot be validly reached and justified.

In any case we cannot in advance determine the limits of reason or intelligence in *human* affairs. So long as we don't know where it lies, it is sensible to press on, at the same time devising the means to curb the effects of the refusal to reason when it manifests itself. Above all, we must avoid oversimplifying the choice of evils and encouraging the hope that to be unreasonable will pay dividends.

We are moving into another period of history in which freedom once more is being readied for sacrifice on the altars of survival. The Munichmen of the spirit are at work again. The stakes are now for the entire world. Our task as philosophers is not to heed partisan and excited calls for action, but rather to think through the problems of freedom and survival afresh. In a famous pronouncement two years ago Bertrand Russell declared that if the Kremlin refused to accept reasonable proposals of disarmament, the West should disarm unilaterally "even if it means the horrors of Communist domination." Although he no longer believes this, there are many others who do. I know that common sense is at a discount in philosophy but in ethics it should not be lightly disregarded. A position like this obviously can have only one effect, viz., to encourage the intransigence of those who wish to destroy the free world without which there cannot be a free philosophy. You cannot negotiate successfully by proclaiming in advance that you will capitulate if the other side persists in being unreasonable. Our alternatives are not limited to surrender and extinction of freedom, on the one hand, and war and the danger of human extermination on the other. There are other alternatives to be explored—all tragic in their costs but not equally extreme. The very willingness, if necessary, to go down fighting in defence of freedom may be the greatest force for peace when facing an opponent who makes a fetish of historical survival. On pragmatic grounds, the willingness to act on a position like Kant's *fiat justitia, pereat mundus* may sometimes—I repeat—sometimes—be the best way of preserving a just and free world—just as the best way of saving one's life is sometimes to be prepared to lose it. The uneasy peace we currently enjoy as a result of "the balance of terror" is tragic. But it may turn out that it is less so than any feasible alternative today. If it endures long enough and it becomes clear to the enemies of freedom that they cannot themselves survive war, they may accept the moral equivalents of war in the making. The pragmatic program is always to find moral equivalents for the expression of natural impulses which threaten the structure of our values.

I have perhaps overstressed the sense of the tragic in human life in an effort to compensate for the distortions to which pragmatism has been subject. There is more in life than the sense of the tragic. There is laughter and joy and the sustaining discipline of work. There are other dimensions of experience besides the moral. There is art and science and religion. There are other uses for intelligence besides the resolution of human difficulties. There is intellectual play and adventure. But until men become Gods—which will never be—they will live with the sense of the tragic in their hearts as they go in quest for wisdom. Pragmatism, as I interpret it, is the theory and practice of enlarging human freedom in a precarious and tragic world by the arts of intelligent social control. It may be a lost cause. I do not know of a better one. And it may not be lost if we can summon the courage and intelligence to support our faith in freedom—and enjoy the blessings of a little luck.

III
THE FORM
OF TRAGEDY

The Tragic Rhythm*

Susanne Langer

As comedy presents the vital rhythm of self-preservation, tragedy exhibits that of self-consummation.

The lilting advance of the eternal life process, indefinitely maintained or temporarily lost and restored, is the great general vital pattern that we exemplify from day to day. But creatures that are destined, sooner or later, to die—that is, all individuals that do not pass alive into new generations, like jellyfish and algae—hold the balance of life only precariously, in the frame of a total movement that is quite different; the movement from birth to death. Unlike the simple metabolic process, the deathward advance of their individual lives has a series of stations that are not repeated; growth, maturity, decline. That is the tragic rhythm.

Tragedy is a cadential form. Its crisis is always the turn toward an absolute close. This form reflects the basic structure of personal life, and therewith of feeling when life is viewed as a whole. It is that attitude—"the tragic sense of life," as Unamuno called it—that is objectified and brought before our eyes in tragedy. But in drama it is not presented as Unamuno presents it, namely by an intellectual realization of impending death which we are constitutionally unable to accept and therefore counter with an irrational belief in our personal immortality, in "immortalizing" rites and supernatural grace.[1] Irrationalism is not insight, but despair, a direct recognition of instincts, needs, and therewithal of one's mental impotence. A "belief" that defies intellectual convictions is a frantically defended lie. That defense may constitute a great tragic theme, but it is not itself a poetic expression of "the tragic sense of life"; it is actual, pathetic expression, springing from an emotional conflict.

Tragedy dramatizes human life as potentiality and fulfillment. Its virtual future, or Destiny, is therefore quite different from that created in comedy. Comic Destiny is Fortune—what the world will bring, and the man will take or miss, encounter or escape; tragic Destiny is what the man brings, and the world will demand of him. That is his Fate.

*Susanne Langer, "The Tragic Rhythm," from *Feeling and Form* (Charles Scribner's Sons, 1953), pp. 351–366. Used by permission of Charles Scribner's Sons. Copyright 1953, Charles Scribner's Sons.
[1] See his *The Tragic Sense of Life, passim.* Unamuno's feelings are strong and natural; his aphorisms are often poetic and memorable. With his philosophical assertions, however, one cannot take issue, because he prides himself on being inconsistent, on the ground that "life is irrational," "truth is not logical," etc. Consistency of statements he regards as a mark of their falsity. Like some exasperating ladies, who claim "a woman's right to be inconsistent," he cannot, therefore, be worsted in argument, but—also like them—he cannot be taken seriously.

What he brings is his potentiality: his mental, moral and even physical powers, his powers to act and suffer. Tragic action is the realization of all his possibilities, which he unfolds and exhausts in the course of the drama. His human nature is his Fate. Destiny conceived as Fate is, therefore, not capricious, like Fortune, but is predetermined. Outward events are merely the occasions for its realization.

"His human nature," however, does not refer to his *generally* human character; I do not mean to say that a tragic hero is to be regarded as primarily a symbol for mankind. What the poet creates is a personality; and the more individual and powerful that personality is, the more extraordinary and overwhelming will be the action. Since the protagonist is the chief agent, his relation to the action is obvious; and since the course of the action is the "fable" or "plot" of the play, it is also obvious that creating the characters is not something apart from building the plot, but is an integral portion of it. The agents are prime elements in the action; but the action is the play itself, and artistic elements are always for the sake of the whole. That was, I think, what prompted Aristotle to say: "Tragedy is essentially an imitation[2] not of persons but of action and life, of happiness and misery. All human happiness or misery takes the form of action; the end for which we live is a certain kind of activity, not a quality. Character gives us qualities, but it is in our actions—what we do—that we are happy or the reverse. In a play accordingly they do not act in order to portray the Characters; they include the Characters for the sake of the action. So that it is the action in it, i.e. its Fable or Plot, that is the end and purpose of the tragedy; and the end is everywhere the chief thing."[3] This "end" is the work as such. The protagonist and all characters that support him are introduced that we may see the fulfillment of his Fate, which is simply the complete realization of his individual "human nature."

The idea of personal Fate was mythically conceived long before the relation of life history to character was discursively understood. The mythical tradition of Greece treated the fate of its "heroes"—the personalities springing from certain great, highly individualized families—as a mysterious power inherent in the world rather than in the man and his ancestry; it was conceived as a private incubus bestowed on him at birth by a vengeful deity, or even through a curse pronounced by a human being. Sometimes no such specific cause of his peculiar destiny is given at all; but an oracle foretells what he is bound to do. It is interesting to note that this conception of Fate usually centers in the mysterious predictability of acts someone is to perform. The occasions of the acts are not foretold; the world will provide them.

For the development of tragedy, such determination of the overt acts without circumstances and motives furnished an ideal starting point, for it constrained the poets to invent characters whose actions would issue naturally in the required fateful deeds. The oracular prophecy, then, became an intensifying symbol of the necessity that was really given with the agent's personality; the "fable" being just one possible way the world might elicit his complete self-realization in endeavor and error and discovery, passion and punishment, to the limit of his powers. The prime example of this passage from the mythical idea of

---

[2] "Imitation" is used by Aristotle in much the same sense in which I use "semblance." I have avoided his word because it stresses similitude to actuality rather than abstraction from actuality.
[3] *De Poetica*, chap. 6, II (1450a), translation by W. R. Roberts.

Fate to the dramatic creation of Fate as the protagonist's natural, personal destiny is, of course, the *Oedipus Tyrannus* of Sophocles. With that tremendous piece of self-assertion, self-divination and self-exhaustion, the "Great Tradition" of tragedy was born in Europe.

There is another mythical conception of Fate that is not a forerunner of tragedy, but possibly of some kinds of comedy: that is the idea of Fate as the will of supernatural powers, perhaps long decreed, perhaps spontaneous and arbitrary. It is the "Fate" of the true fatalist, who takes no great care of his life because he deems it entirely in the hand of Allah (or some other God), who will slay or spare at his pleasure no matter what one does. That is quite a different notion from the "oracular" Fate of Greek mythology; the will of a god who gives and takes away, casts down or raises up, for inscrutable reasons of his own, is Kismet, and that is really a myth of Fortune.[4] Kismet is what a person encounters, not what he is. Both conceptions often exist side by side. The Scotsman who has to "dree his weird" believes nonetheless that his fortunes from moment to moment are in the hands of Providence. Macbeth's Weird Sisters were perfectly acceptable to a Christian audience. Even in the ancient lore of our fairy tales, the Sleeping Beauty is destined to prick herself—that is, she has a personal destiny. In Greek tradition, on the other hand, where the notion of "oracular Fate" was so generally entertained that the Oracle was a public institution, Fate as the momentary decree of a ruling Power is represented in the myth of the Norns, who spin the threads of human lives and cut them where they list; the Three Fates are as despotic and capricious as Allah, and what they spin is, really, Kismet.

Tragedy can arise and flourish only where people are aware of individual life as an end in itself, and as a measure of other things. In tribal cultures where the individual is still so closely linked with his family that not only society but even he himself regards his existence as a communal value, which may be sacrificed at any time for communal ends, the development of personality is not a consciously appreciated life pattern. Similarly, where men believe that Karma, or the tally of their deeds, may be held over for recompense or expiation in another earthly life, their current incarnation cannot be seen as a self-sufficient whole in which their entire potentialities are to be realized. Therefore genuine tragedy—drama exhibiting "the tragic rhythm of action," as Professor Fergusson has called it[5]—is a specialized form of art, with problems and devices of its own.

The word "rhythm," which I have used freely with respect to drama, may seem a question-begging word, borrowed from the realm of physiology—where indeed the basic vital functions are generally rhythmic—and carried over somewhat glibly to the realm of conscious acts, which, for the most part—and certainly the most interesting part—are not repetitive. But it is precisely the *rhythm* of dramatic action that makes drama "a poetry of the theater," and not an imitation (in the usual, not the Aristotelian sense) or make-believe of practical life. As Hebbel said, "In the hand of the poet, Becoming must always be a passage from *form* to *form* [von *Gestalt* zu *Gestalt*], it must never appear, like amorphous

---

[4] Cf. N. N. Martinovitch, *The Turkish Theatre*, p. 36: "According to Islamic speculation, man has almost no influence on the development of his own fate. Allah is sovereign, doing as he likes and accounting to no one. And the screen of the haial [the comic shadow theater] is the dramatization of this speculative concept of the world."

[5] In *The Idea of a Theater*, especially p. 18.

clay, chaotic and confused in our sight, but must seem somehow like a perfected thing."[6] The analysis and definition of rhythmic structure, given in Chapter 8 with reference to musical forms,[7] may be applied without distortion or strain to the organization of elements in any play that achieves "living" form.

A dramatic act is a commitment. It creates a situation in which the agent or agents must necessarily make a further move; that is, it motivates a subsequent act (or acts). The situation, which is the completion of a given act, is already the impetus to another—as, in running, the footfall that catches our weight at the end of one bound already sends us forward to land on the other foot. The bounds need not be alike, but proportional, which means that the impetus of any specially great leap must have been prepared and gathered somewhere, and any sudden diminution be balanced by some motion that carries off the driving force. Dramatic acts are analogously connected with each other so that each one directly or indirectly motivates what follows it.[8] In this way a genuine rhythm of action is set up, which is not simple like that of a physical repetitive process (e.g. running, breathing), but more often intricate, even deceptive, and, of course, not given primarily to one particular sense, but to the imagination through whatever sense we employ to perceive and evaluate action; the same general rhythm of action appears in a play whether we read it or hear it read, enact it ourselves or see it performed. That rhythm is the "commanding form" of the play; it springs from the poet's original conception of the "fable," and dictates the major divisions of the work, the light or heavy style of its presentation, the intensity of the highest feeling and most violent act, the great or small number of characters, and the degrees of their development. The total action is a cumulative form; and because it is constructed by a rhythmic treatment of its elements, it appears to *grow* from its beginnings. That is the playwright's creation of "organic form."

The tragic rhythm, which is the pattern of a life that grows, flourishes, and declines, is abstracted by being transferred from that natural activity to the sphere of a characteristically human action, where it is exemplified in mental and emotional growth, maturation, and the final relinquishment of power. In that relinquishment lies the hero's true "heroism"—the vision of life as accomplished, that is, life in its entirety, the sense of fulfillment that lifts him above his defeat.

A remarkable expression of this idea of tragedy may be found in the same book from which I borrowed, a few paragraphs above, the phrase, "the tragic rhythm of action." Speaking of Hamlet, Professor Fergusson observes: "In Act V . . . he feels that his role, all but the very last episode, has been played. . . . He is content, now, to let the fated end come as it will. . . . One could say that he feels the poetic rightness of his own death. . . .

"However one may interpret it, when his death comes it 'feels right,' the only possible end for the play. . . . We are certainly intended to feel that Hamlet, however darkly and uncertainly he worked, had discerned the way to be obedient to his deepest values, and accomplished some sort of purgatorial progress for himself and Denmark."[9]

---

[6] Friedrich Hebbel, *Tagebücher*, collected in Bernhard Münz's *Hebbel als Denker* (1913). See p. 182.
[7] See pp. 126–129 [*of Feeling and Form*].
[8] An act may be said to motivate further acts indirectly if it does so through a total situation it helps to create; the small acts of psychological import that merely create personality are of this sort.
[9] *Op. cit.*, pp. 132–133. "To be obedient to his deepest values" is nothing else than to realize his own potentialities, fulfill his true destiny.

"The second scene of Act V," the critique continues, "with the duel between Hamlet and Laertes, shows the denouements of all the intrigues in the play. . . . But these events, which literally end the narratives in the play, and bring Claudius' regime to its temporal end, tell us nothing new but the fact: that the sentence, which fate or providence pronounced long since, has now been executed. It is the pageantry, the ceremonial mummery, in short the virtual character of this last scene which makes us feel it as the final epiphany. . . . "[10]

Tragic drama is so designed that the protagonist grows mentally, emotionally, or morally, by the demand of the action, which he himself initiated, to the complete exhaustion of his powers, the limit of his possible development. He spends himself in the course of the one dramatic action. This is, of course, a tremendous foreshortening of life; instead of undergoing the physical and psychical, many-sided, long process of an actual biography, the tragic hero lives and matures in some particular respect; his entire being is concentrated in one aim, one passion, one conflict and ultimate defeat. For this reason the prime agent of tragedy is heroic; his character, the unfolding situation, the scene, even though ostensibly familiar and humble, are all exaggerated, charged with more feeling than comparable actualities would possess.[11] This intensification is necessary to achieve and sustain the "form in suspense" that is even more important in tragic drama than in comic, because the comic denouement, not marking an absolute close, needs only to restore a balance, but the tragic ending must recapitulate the whole action to be a visible fulfillment of a destiny that was implicit in the beginning. This device, which may be called "dramatic exaggeration," is reminiscent of "epic exaggeration," and may have been adopted quite unconsciously with the epic themes of ancient tragedy. But that does not mean that it is an accidental factor, a purely historical legacy from an older poetic tradition; inherited conventions do not maintain themselves long in any art unless they serve its own purposes. They may have their old *raison d'être* in new art forms, or take on entirely new functions, but as sheer trappings—traditional requirements—they would be discarded by the first genius who found no use for them.

Drama is not psychology, nor (though the critical literature tends to make it seem so) is it moral philosophy. It offers no discourse on the hero's or heroine's native endowments, to let us estimate at any stage in the action how near they must be to exhaustion. The action itself must reveal the limit of the protagonist's powers and mark the end of his self-realization. And so, indeed, it does: the turning point of the play is the situation he cannot resolve, where he makes his "tragic error" or exhibits his "tragic weakness." He is led by his own action and its repercussions in the world to respond with more and more competence, more and more daring to a constantly gathering challenge; so his character "grows," i.e. he unfolds his will and knowledge and passion, as the situation grows. His career is not change of personality, but maturation. When he reaches his limit of mental and emotional development, the crisis occurs; then comes the defeat, either by death or, as in many modern tragedies, by hopelessness that is the equivalent of death, a "death of the soul," that ends the career.

It has been reiterated so often that the hero of tragedy is a strong man with

---

[10] *Op. cit.*, p. 138.
[11] As Robert Edmond Jones has put it: "Great drama does not deal with cautious people. Its heroes are tyrants, outcasts, wanderers. From Prometheus, the first of them all, the thief who stole the divine fire from heaven, these protagonists are all passionate, excessive, violent, terrible. 'Doom eager,' the Icelandic saga calls them." *The Dramatic Imagination*, p. 42.

one weakness, a good man with one fault, that a whole ethics of tragedy has grown up around the significance of that single flaw. Chapters upon chapters—even books—have been written on the required mixture of good and evil in his character, to make him command pity and yet make his downfall not repugnant to "our moral sense." Critics and philosophers, from Aristotle to Croce, have written about the spectator's acceptance of the hero's fate as a recognition of the moral order he has defied or ignored, the triumph of justice the hero himself is supposed to accept in his final "conciliation" or "epiphany." The restoration of the great moral order through suffering is looked upon as the Fate he has to fulfill. He must be imperfect to break the moral law, but fundamentally good, i.e. striving for perfection, in order to achieve his moral salvation in sacrifice, renunciation, death.

All this concern with the philosophical and ethical significance of the hero's sufferings, however, leads away from the *artistic* significance of the play, to discursive ideas about life, character, and the world. At once we are faced with the usual dilemma of the critic who sees art as a representation of actual life, and an art form as a *Weltanschauung*: not every work of the genre can really be said to express the *Weltanschauung* that is supposed to characterize it, nor to give us the same general picture of the world, such as the "moral order" in which justice is inevitably done or the amoral "cosmic order" in which man is a plaything of forces beyond his control. Then the critic may come to the despairing conclusion that the genre cannot be defined, but is really just a name that changes its essential meaning from age to age. No less an authority than Ashley Thorndike decided that tragedy is really indefinable; one can trace the historical evolution of each conception, but not the defining attribute that runs through them all and brings them justly under one name. The only features that he found common to all tragedies were representation of "painful and destructive actions," and "criticism of life."[12] Either of these could, of course, occur in other art forms, too. A. C. Bradley, in his excellent *Shakespearean Tragedy*, points out that Shakespeare did not, like the Greek tragedians, postulate a superhuman power determining men's actions and accidents, nor a special Nemesis, invoked by past crimes, belonging to certain families or persons; he claims, in fact, to find no representation of Fate in Shakespeare.[13] Even justice, he holds, is not illustrated there, because the disasters men bring upon themselves are not proportioned to their sins; but something one might call a "moral order," an order not of right and wrong, but at least of good and evil. Accident plays its part, but in the main the agents ride for the fall they take.[14] Edgar Stoll, exactly to the contrary, maintains that the action in Shakespeare's tragedies "does not at bottom develop out

[12] "Any precise and exact definition is sure to lack in comprehensiveness and veracity . . . We seem forced to reject the possibility of any exact limitation for the dramatic species, to include as tragedies all plays presenting painful or destructive actions, to accept the leading elements of a literary tradition derived from the Greeks as indicating the common bonds between such plays in the past, but to admit that this tradition, while still powerful, is variable, uncertain, and unauthoritative." (*Tragedy*, p. 12.) At the end of the book he sets up, as the only common standard, "an unselfish, a social, a moral inquiry into life." (p. 376.)

[13] In a footnote on p. 30 he writes: "I have raised no objection to the use of the idea of fate, because it occurs so often both in conversation and in books about Shakespeare's tragedies that I must suppose it to be natural to many readers. Yet I doubt whether it would be so if Greek tragedy had never been written; and I must in candour confess that to me it does not often occur while I am reading, or when I have just read, a tragedy of Shakespeare."

[14] The discussion of justice (Lecture I, "The Substance of Tragedy," p. 5) is noteworthy especially for his recognition of the *irrelevance of the concept* to dramatic art.

of character."[15] One could go on almost indefinitely in citing examples of contradiction or exception to the various standards of tragic action, especially the fatalistic standard.

The fallacy which leads to this crisscross of interpretations and opinions is the familiar one of confusing what the poet creates with what he represents. It is the fallacy of looking, not for the artistic function of everything he represents and the way he represents it, but for something that his representations are supposed to illustrate or suggest—something that belongs to life, not the play. If, then, tragedy is called an image of Fate, it is expected to illustrate the workings of Fate. But that is not necessary; it may just as well illustrate the workings of villainy, neurosis, faith, social justice, or anything else the poet finds usable to motivate a large, integral action. The myth of Fate often used in Greek tragedies was an obvious motif, as in later plays romantic love defying circumstance, or the vast consequences of a transgression. But one should not expect a major art form to be bound to a single motif, no matter in how many variations or even disguises; to reduce the many themes that may be found in tragedy, from Aeschylus to O'Neill, all to "the workings of Fate," and the many *Weltenschauungen* that may be read out of (or into) it to so many recognitions of a supernatural order, a moral order, or a pure causal order, leads only to endless sleuthing after deeper meanings, symbolic substitutions, and far-reaching implications that no playgoer could possibly infer, so they would be useless in the theater.

Fate in tragedy is the created form, the virtual future as an accomplished whole. It is not the expression of a belief at all. Macbeth's fate is the structure of his tragedy, not an instance of how things happen in the world. That virtual future has the form of a completely individualized, and therefore mortal, life—a measured life, to be exhausted in a small span of time. But growth, efflorescence, and exhaustion—the prototype of Fate—is not what the play is about; it is only what the movement of the action is like. The play is about somebody's desires, acts, conflict, and defeat; however his acts are motivated, however his deeds undo him, the total action is his dramatic fate. Tragic action has the rhythm of natural life and death, but it does not refer to or illustrate them; it abstracts their dynamic form, and imprints it on entirely different matters, in a different time span—the whole self-realization may take place in days or hours instead of decades of biological consummation—so the "tragic rhythm" stands clear of any natural occasion, and becomes a perceptible form.

The kind of art theory that measures the value of drama by the way it represents life, or by the poet's implied beliefs about life, not only leads criticism away from poetry into philosophy, religion, or social science, but also causes people to think of the protagonist as an ordinary fellow man whom they are to approve or condemn and, in either case, pity. This attitude, which is undoubtedly derived—whether rightly or mistakenly—from Aristotle, has given rise to the many moral demands on the hero's character: he must be admirable but not perfect, must command the spectators' sympathy even if he incurs their censure; they must feel his fate as their own, etc.[16]

---

[15] *Shakespeare and Other Masters*, p. 31.
[16] Thorndike regarded tragedy as the highest art form, because, as he put it, "it brings home to us the images of our own sorrows, and chastens the spirit through the outpouring of our sympathies, even our horror and despair, for the misfortune of our fellows." (*Op. cit.*, p. 19.) Shortly before, he conceded that it might also give us—among other pleasures—"aesthetic delight in a masterpiece." (p. 17.)

In truth, I believe, the hero of tragedy must *interest* us all the time, but not as a person of our own acquaintance. His tragic error, crime, or other flaw is not introduced for moral reasons, but for structural purposes: it marks his limit of power. His potentialities appear on stage only as successful acts; as soon as his avowed or otherwise obvious intentions fail, or his acts recoil on him and bring him pain, his power has reached its height, he is at the end of his career. In this, of course, drama is utterly different from life. The moral failure in drama is not a normal incident, something to be lived down, presumably neither the doer's first transgression nor his last; the act that constitutes the protagonist's tragic error or guilt is the highwater mark of his life, and now the tide recedes. His "imperfection" is an artistic element: that is why a single flaw will do.

All persistent practices in art have a creative function. They may serve several ends, but the chief one is the shaping of the work. This holds not only for character traits which make a dramatic personage credible or sympathetic, but also for another much-discussed device in drama—so-called "comic relief," the introduction of trivial or humorous interludes in midst of serious, ominous, tragic action. The term "comic relief" indicates the supposed purpose of that practice: to give the audience a respite from too much emotional tension, let them have entertainment as well as "pity and fear." Here again traditional criticism rests too confidently, I think, on Aristotle's observations, which—after all—were not the insights of a playwright, but the reflections of a scientifically inclined man interested in psychology. Aristotle considered the comic interlude as a concession to human weakness; and "comic relief" has been its name ever since.

The humorous interludes in tragedy are merely moments when the comic spirit rises to the point of hilarity. Such moments may result from all sorts of poetic exigencies; the famous drunken porter in *Macbeth* makes a macabre contrast to the situation behind the door he beats upon, and is obviously introduced to heighten rather than relieve the tense secrecy of the murder.

But the most important fact about these famous touches of "comic relief" is that they always occur in plays which have a vein of comedy throughout, kept for the most part below the level of laughter. This vein may be tapped for special effects, even for a whole scene, to slow and subdue the action or to heighten it with grotesque reflection. In those heroic tragedies that are lowered by the incursion of farce, and not structurally affected by its omission, there is no integral, implicit comedy—no everyday life—in the "world" of the play, to which the clowning naturally belongs and from which it may be derived without disorganization of the whole.[17] In *Macbeth* (and, indeed, all Shakespearean plays) there is a large, social, everyday life of soldiers, grooms, gossips, courtiers and commoners, that provides an essentially comic substructure for the heroic action. Most of the time this lower stratum is subdued, giving an impression of realism without any obvious byplay; but this realism carries the fundamental comic rhythm from which grotesque interludes may arise with perfect dramatic logic.

The fact that the two great rhythms, comic and tragic, are radically distinct does not mean that they are each other's opposites, or even incompatible forms.

---

[17] Thorndike points out that *Tamburlane* is of this genre: "Originally," he says, "the play contained comic scenes, omitted in the published form and evidently of no value in structure or conception." (*Op cit.*, p. 90.)
See also J. B. Moore, *The Comic and the Realistic in English Drama.*

Tragedy can rest squarely on a comic substructure, and yet be pure tragedy.[18] This is natural enough, for life—from which all felt rhythms spring—contains both, in every mortal organism. Society is continuous though its members, even the strongest and fairest, live out their lives and die, and even while each individual fulfills the tragic pattern it participates also in the comic continuity.[19] The poet's task is, of course, not to copy life, but to organize and articulate a symbol for the "sense of life"; and in the symbol one rhythm always governs the dynamic form, though another may go through the whole piece in a contrapuntal fashion. The master of this practice is Shakespeare.

Did the stark individual Fate of the purest Greek tragedy rule out, by its intense deathward movement, the comic feeling of the eternally full and undulating stream of life? Or was the richness that the comic-tragic counterpoint creates in other poetic traditions supplied to Aeschylus and Sophocles by the choric dance which framed and embellished the play? The satyr play at the end of the long, tragic presentation may well have been necessary, to assure its truth to the structure of subjective reality by an exuberant celebration of life.

There is yet another factor in drama that is commonly, and I think mistakenly, treated as a concession to popular taste: the use of spectacle, pageantry, brilliant show. Many critics apparently believe that a playwright makes provision for spectacular effects quite apart from his own poetic judgment and intent, simply to lure the audience into the theater. Thorndike, in fact, asserts that the use of spectacle bespeaks "the double purpose, hardly separable from the drama and particularly manifest in the Elizabethan dramatists, the two desires, to please their audiences and to create literature."[20] Brander Matthews said bluntly that not only theater, but all art whatever is "show business," whatever it may be besides.[21]

Art, and especially dramatic art, is full of compromises, for one possible effect is usually bought at the expense of another; not all ideas and devices that occur to the poet are co-possible. Every decision involves a rejection. And furthermore, the stage, the available funds, the capabilities of the actors, may all have to be considered. But no artist can make concessions to what he considers bad taste without ruining his work. He simply cannot think as an artist and accept inexpressive forms or admit an element that has no organic function in the whole. If, therefore, he wishes to present spectacular scenes, he must start with an idea that demands spectacular presentation.

Every play has its intended audience, and in that audience there is one preeminent member: the author. If the play is intended for, say, an Elizabethan audience, that honorary member will be an Elizabethan theater-goer, sharing the best Elizabethan taste, and sometimes setting its fashion. Our dramatic critics write as though the poets of the past were all present-day people making conces-

---

[18] A striking example is J. M. Barrie's little tragedy dating from the first World War, *The Old Lady Shows her Medals*. Despite the consistently comic treatment one expects the inevitable (and wordless) last scene.

[19] There is also a genre known as "tragicomedy" (the Germans call it *Schauspiel*, distinguishing it from both *Lustspiel* and *Trauerspiel*), which is a comic pattern playing with the tragic; its plot-structure is *averted tragedy*, temporizing with the sense of fate, which usually inspires a tragic diction, little or no exuberance (humor), and often falls into melodrama. A study of its few artistic successes, and their precise relations to pure comedy and pure tragedy, might raise interesting problems.

[20] *Op. cit.*, p. 98.

[21] *A Book About the Theater*, pp. 8–9. Cf. *supra*, p. 320.

sions to interests that have long spent themselves. But the poets who provided stage spectacles had spectacular ideas, and worked with them until their expressive possibilities were exhausted.

The element of pure show has an important function in dramatic art, for it tends to raise feeling, whatever the feeling is. It does this even in actual life: a splendid hall, an ornate table arrangement, a company in full dress, make a feast seem bigger and the gathering more illustrious than a plain table in a cafeteria, refectory, or gymnasium, with the guests in street dress. A splendid funeral, passing in procession behind chanting priests, is more solemn than a drab one, though perhaps no one at the spectacular service feels more sad than at the colorless one. In the theater, the element of show is a means of heightening the atmosphere, whether of gaiety or terror or woe; so it is, first of all, a ready auxiliary.

But in tragedy it has a more specialized and essential function, too. Tragedy, which expresses the consciousness of life and death, must make life seem worth while, rich, beautiful, to make death awesome. The splendid exaggerations of the stage serve tragic feeling by heightening the lure of the world. The beautiful world, as well as the emotional tone of the action, is magnified by the element of spectacle—by lighting and color, setting and grouping, music, dance, "excursions and alarums." Some playwrights avail themselves freely of this help; others dispense with it almost entirely (never quite; the theater is spectacular at any time), because they have other poetic means of giving virtual life the glory that death takes away, or despair—the "death of the soul"—corrupts.

Spectacle is a powerful ingredient in several arts. Consider what playing fountains can do for a courtyard or a square, and how a ceremonial procession brings the interior of a cathedral to visible life! Architectural design may be marvelously altered by a supplement of fortuitous spectacle. The Galata bridge over the Golden Horn in the middle of Istanbul, with thousands of people and vehicles passing over it, coming from steep hillsides on either hand, looks as though it were hung from the mosque-crowned heights above; without the pageantry of its teeming cosmopolitan traffic it shrinks to a flat thoroughfare across the river, between its actual bridgeheads. An esplanade without the movement of water below it would be utterly unimpressive; flooded with moonlight, which picks out the surface movement of the water, or standing immovable against a towering surf, it may become veritably an architect's dream.

But pure show, not assimilated to any art, does not constitute a "work." Acrobatics, tennis playing, some beautiful occupational rhythms such as hauling nets, swinging hammers, or the evolutions of boats in a race, are fascinating, aesthetically thrilling, so they hold the spectator in a joyful trance; but they are not art. For a work of art, this trance is only one requisite. Spectacle, however beautiful, is always an *element* in art. It may well be a major element, as it was in Noverre's ballets, and in the court masques, but even these largely spectacular products are rated as "works" because they had something else that motivated the display: an imaginative core, a "commanding form." A circus could be a work of art if it had some central feeling and some primary, unfailing illusion. As it is, the circus sometimes contains genuine little "works"—a riding act that is really an equestrian dance, a piece of clowning that rises to genuine comedy. But on the whole the circus is a "show," not a work of art, though it is a work of skill, planning and fitting, and sometimes copes with problems that arise also in the arts. What it lacks is the first requisite for art—a conception of feeling, something to express.

Because a dramatic work has such a core, everything in it is poesis. It is, therefore, neither a hybrid product pieced together at the demand of many interests, nor a synthesis of all the arts—not even of a more modest "several." It may have use for paint and plaster, wood and brick, but not for painting, sculpture, or architecture; it has use for music, but not for even a fragment of a concert program; it may require dancing, but such dancing is not self-contained—it intensifies a scene, often abstracts a quintessence of its feeling, the image of sheer powers arising as a secondary illusion in the midst of the virtual history.

Drama is a great form, which not only invites expression of elemental human feeling, but also permits a degree of articulation, complexity, detail within detail, in short: organic development, that smaller poetic forms cannot exhibit without confusion. To say that such works express "a concept of feeling" is misleading unless one bears in mind that it is the whole life of feeling—call it "felt life," "subjectivity," "direct experience," or what you will—which finds its articulate expression in art, and, I believe, only in art. So great and fully elaborated a form as (say) a Shakespearean tragedy may formulate the characteristic mode of perception and response, sensibility and emotion and their sympathetic overtones, that constitutes a whole personality. Here we see the process of art expression "writ large," as Plato would say; for the smallest work does the same thing as the greatest, on its own scale: it reveals the patterns of possible sentience, vitality, and mentality, objectifying our subjective being—the most intimate "Reality" that we know. This function, and not the recording of contemporary scenes, politics, or even moral attitudes, is what relates art to life; and the big unfolding of feeling in the organic, personal pattern of a human life, rising, growing, accomplishing destiny and meeting doom—that is tragedy.

The Mythos of Autumn: Tragedy*

Northrop Frye

Thanks as usual to Aristotle, the theory of tragedy is in considerably better shape than the other three *mythoi*, and we can deal with it more briefly, as the ground is more familiar. Without tragedy, all literary fictions might be plausibly explained as expressions of emotional attachments, whether of wish-fulfilment or of repugnance: the tragic fiction guarantees, so to speak, a disinterested quality in literary experience. It is largely through the tragedies of Greek culture that the sense of the authentic natural basis of human character comes into literature. In romance the characters are still largely dream-characters; in satire they tend to be caricatures; in comedy their actions are twisted to fit the demands of a happy ending. In full tragedy the main characters are emancipated from dream, an emancipation which is at the same time a restriction, because the order of nature is present. However thickly strewn a tragedy may be with ghosts, portents, witches, or oracles, we know that the tragic hero cannot simply rub a lamp and summon a genie to get him out of his trouble.

Like comedy, tragedy is best and most easily studied in drama, but it is not confined to drama, nor to actions that end in disaster. Plays that are usually called or classified with tragedies end in serenity, like *Cymbeline*, or even joy, like *Alcestis* or Racine's *Esther*, or in an ambiguous mood that is hard to define, like *Philoctetes*. On the other hand, while a predominantly sombre mood forms part of the unity of the tragic structure, concentrating on mood does not intensify the tragic effect: if it did, *Titus Andronicus* might well be the most powerful of Shakespeare's tragedies. The source of tragic effect must be sought, as Aristotle pointed out, in the tragic *mythos* or plot-structure.

It is a commonplace of criticism that comedy tends to deal with characters in a social group, whereas tragedy is more concentrated on a single individual. We have given reasons in the first essay for thinking that the typical tragic hero is somewhere between the divine and the "all too human." This must be true even of dying gods: Prometheus, being a god, cannot die, but he suffers for his sympathy with the "dying ones" (*brotoi*) or "mortal" men, and even suffering has something subdivine about it. The tragic hero is very great as compared with us, but there is something else, something on the side of him opposite the audience, compared to which he is small. This something else may be called God,

* Northrop Frye, "The Mythos of Autumn: Tragedy," from *The Anatomy of Criticism: Four Essays* (copyright © 1957 by Princeton Unviersity Press; Princeton Paperback, 1971), pp. 206–223. Reprinted by permission of Princeton University Press.

gods, fate, accident, fortune, necessity, circumstance, or any combination of these, but whatever it is the tragic hero is our mediator with it.

The tragic hero is typically on top of the wheel of fortune, halfway between human society on the ground and the something greater in the sky. Prometheus, Adam, and Christ hang between heaven and earth, between a world of paradisal freedom and a world of bondage. Tragic heroes are so much the highest points in their human landscape that they seem the inevitable conductors of the power about them, great trees more likely to be struck by lightning than a clump of grass. Conductors may of course be instruments as well as victims of the divine lightning: Milton's Samson destroys the Philistine temple with himself, and Hamlet nearly exterminates the Danish court in his own fall. Something of Nietzsche's mountain-top air of transvaluation clings to the tragic hero: his thoughts are not ours any more than his deeds, even if, like Faustus, he is dragged off to hell for having them. Whatever eloquence or affability he may have, an inscrutable reserve lies behind it. Even sinister heroes—Tamburlaine, Macbeth, Creon—retain this reserve, and we are reminded that men will die loyally for a wicked or cruel man, but not for an amiable backslapper. Those who attract most devotion from others are those who are best able to suggest in their manner that they have no need of it, and from the urbanity of Hamlet to the sullen ferocity of Ajax, tragic heroes are wrapped in the mystery of their communion with that something beyond which we can see only through them, and which is the source of their strength and their fate alike. In the phrase which so fascinated Yeats, the tragic hero leaves his servants to do his "living" for him, and the center of tragedy is in the hero's isolation, not in a villain's betrayal, even when the villain is, as he often is, a part of the hero himself.

As for the something beyond, its names are variable but the form in which it manifests itself is fairly constant. Whether the context is Greek, Christian, or undefined, tragedy seems to lead up to an epiphany of law, of that which is and must be. It can hardly be an accident that the two great developments of tragic drama, in fifth-century Athens and in seventeenth-century Europe, were contemporary with the rise of Ionian and of Renaissance science. In such a world-view nature is seen as an impersonal process which human law imitates as best it can, and this direct relation of man and natural law is in the foreground. The sense in Greek tragedy that fate is stronger than the gods really implies that the gods exist primarily to ratify the order of nature, and that if any personality, even a divine one, possesses a genuine power of veto over law, it is most unlikely that he will want to exercise it. In Christianity much the same is true of the personality of Christ in relation to the inscrutable decrees of the Father. Similarly the tragic process in Shakespeare is natural in the sense that it simply happens, whatever its cause, explanation, or relationships. Characters may grope about for conceptions of gods that kill us for their sport, or for a divinity that shapes our ends, but the action of tragedy will not abide our questions, a fact often transferred to the personality of Shakespeare.

In its most elementary form, the vision of law (*dike*) operates as *lex talionis* or revenge. The hero provokes enmity, or inherits a situation of enmity, and the return of the avenger constitutes the catastrophe. The revenge-tragedy is a simple tragic structure, and like most simple structures can be a very powerful one, often retained as a central theme even in the most complex tragedies. Here the original act provoking the revenge sets up an antithetical or counterbalancing movement, and the completion of the movement resolves the tragedy. This happens so often that we may almost characterize the total *mythos* of tragedy as binary, in contrast to the three part saturnalia movement of comedy.

We notice however the frequency of the device of making the revenge come from another world, through gods or ghosts or oracles. This device expands the conceptions of both nature and law beyond the limits of the obvious and tangible. It does not thereby transcend those conceptions, as it is still natural law that is manifested by the tragic action. Here we see the tragic hero as disturbing a balance in nature, nature being conceived as an order stretching over the two kingdoms of the visible and the invisible, a balance which sooner or later *must* right itself. The righting of the balance is what the Greeks called *nemesis*: again, the agent or instrument of *nemesis* may be human vengeance, ghostly vengeance, divine vengeance, divine justice, accident, fate or the logic of events, but the essential thing is that *nemesis* happens, and happens impersonally, unaffected, as *Oedipus Tyrannus* illustrates, by the moral quality of human motivation involved. In the *Oresteia* we are led from a series of revenge-movements into a final vision of natural law, a universal compact in which moral law is included and which the gods, in the person of the goddess of wisdom, endorse. Here *nemesis* like its counterpart the Mosaic law in Christianity, is not abolished but fulfilled: it is developed from a mechanical or arbitrary sense of restored order, represented by the Furies, to the rational sense of it expounded by Athene. The appearance of Athene does not turn the *Oresteia* into a comedy, but clarifies its tragic vision.

There are two reductive formulas which have often been used to explain tragedy. Neither is quite good enough, but each is almost good enough, and as they are contradictory, they must represent extreme or limiting views of tragedy. One of these is the theory that all tragedy exhibits the omnipotence of an external fate. And, of course, the overwhelming majority of tragedies do leave us with a sense of the supremacy of impersonal power and of the limitation of human effort. But the fatalistic reduction of tragedy confuses the tragic condition with the tragic process: fate, in a tragedy, normally becomes external to the hero only *after* the tragic process has been set going. The Greek *ananke* or *moria* is in its normal, or pre-tragic, form the internal balancing condition of life. It appears as external or antithetical necessity only after it has been violated as a condition of life, just as justice is the internal condition of an honest man, but the external antagonist of the criminal. Homer uses a profoundly significant phrase for the theory of tragedy when he has Zeus speak of Aegisthus as going *hyper moron, beyond* fate.

The fatalistic reduction of tragedy does not distinguish tragedy from irony, and it is again significant that we speak of the irony of fate rather than of its tragedy. Irony does not need an exceptional central figure: as a rule, the dingier the hero the sharper the irony, when irony alone is aimed at. It is the admixture of heroism that gives tragedy its characteristic splendor and exhilaration. The tragic hero has normally had an extraordinary, often a nearly divine, destiny almost within his grasp, and the glory of that original vision never quite fades out of tragedy. The rhetoric of tragedy requires the noblest diction that the greatest poets can produce, and while catastrophe is the normal end of tragedy, this is balanced by an equally significant original greatness, a paradise lost.

The other reductive theory of tragedy is that the act which sets the tragic process going must be primarily a violation of *moral* law, whether human or divine; in short, that Aristotle's hamartia or "flaw" must have an essential connection with sin or wrongdoing. Again it is true that the great majority of tragic heroes do possess hybris, a proud, passionate, obsessed or soaring mind which brings about a morally intelligible downfall. Such hybris is the normal precipitating agent of catastrophe, just as in comedy the cause of the happy ending is usually some act of humility, represented by a slave or by a heroine meanly disguised. In Aristotle the hamartia of the tragic hero is associated with Aristotle's ethical conception of *proairesis*, or free choice of an end, and Aristotle certainly does tend to think of tragedy as morally, almost physically, intelligible. It has already been suggested, however, that the conception of catharsis, which is central to Aristotle's view of tragedy, is inconsistent with moral reductions of it. Pity and terror are moral feelings, and they are relevant but not attached to the tragic situation. Shakespeare is particularly fond of planting moral lightning-rods on both sides of his heroes to deflect the pity and terror: we have mentioned Othello flanked by Iago and Desdemona, but Hamlet is flanked by Claudius and Ophelia, Lear by his daughters, and even Macbeth by Lady Macbeth and Duncan. In all these tragedies there is a sense of some far-reaching mystery of which this morally intelligible process is only a part. The hero's act has thrown a switch in a larger machine than his own life, or even his own society.

All theories of tragedy as morally explicable sooner or later run into the question: is an innocent sufferer in tragedy (i.e., poetically innocent), Iphigeneia, Cordelia, Socrates in Plato's *Apology*, Christ in the Passion, not a tragic figure? It is not very convincing to try to provide crucial moral flaws for such characters. Cordelia shows a high spirit, perhaps a touch of wilfulness, in refusing to flatter her father, and Cordelia gets hanged. Joan of Arc in Schiller has a moment of tenderness for an English soldier, and Joan is burned alive, or would have been if Schiller had not decided to sacrifice the facts to save the face of his moral theory. Here we are getting away from tragedy, and close to a kind of insane cautionary tale, like Mrs. Pipchin's little boy who was gored to death by a bull for asking inconvenient questions. Tragedy, in short, seems to elude the antithesis of moral responsibility and arbitrary fate, just as it eludes the antithesis of good and evil.

In the third book of *Paradise Lost*, Milton represents God as arguing that he made man "Sufficient to have stood, though free to fall." God knew that Adam would fall, but did not compel him to do so, and on that basis he disclaims legal responsibility. This argument is so bad that Milton, if he was trying to escape refutation, did well to ascribe it to God. Thought and act cannot be so separated: if God had foreknowledge he must have known in the instant of creating Adam that he was creating a being who would fall. Yet the passage is a most haunting and suggestive one nonetheless. For *Paradise Lost* is not simply an attempt to write one more tragedy, but to expound what Milton believed to be the archetypal myth of tragedy. Hence the passage is another example of existential projection: the real basis of the relation of Milton's God to Adam is the relation of the tragic poet to his hero. The tragic poet knows that his hero will be in a tragic situation, but he exerts all his power to avoid the sense of having manipulated that situation for his own purposes. He exhibits his hero to us as God exhibits Adam to the angels. If the hero was not sufficient to have stood, the mode is purely ironic; if he was not free to fall, the mode is purely romantic, the story of an invincible hero who will conquer all his antagonists as long as the story is about him. Now most theories of tragedy take one great tragedy as their norm: thus Aristotle's theory is largely founded on *Oedipus Tyrannus*, and Hegel's on

Antigone. In seeing the archetypal human tragedy in the story of Adam, Milton was, of course, in agreement with the whole Judaeo-Christian culture tradition, and perhaps arguments drawn from the story of Adam may have better luck in literary criticism than in subjects compelled to assume Adam's real existence, either as fact or as a merely legal fiction. Chaucer's monk, who clearly understood what he was doing, began with Lucifer and Adam, and we may be well advised to follow his example.

Adam, then, is in a heroic human situation: he is on top of the wheel of fortune, with the destiny of the gods almost within his reach. He forfeits that destiny in a way which suggests moral responsibility to some and a conspiracy of fate to others. What he does is to exchange a fortune of unlimited freedom for the fate involved in the consequences of the act of exchange, just as, for a man who deliberately jumps off a precipice, the law of gravitation acts as fate for the brief remainder of his life. The exchange is presented by Milton as itself a free act or *proairesis*, a use of freedom to lose freedom. And just as comedy often sets up an arbitrary law and then organizes the action to break or evade it, so tragedy presents the reverse theme of narrowing a comparatively free life into a process of causation. This happens to Macbeth when he accepts the logic of usurpation, to Hamlet when he accepts the logic of revenge, to Lear when he accepts the logic of abdication. The discovery or *anagnorisis* which comes at the end of the tragic plot is not simply the knowledge by the hero of what has happened to him—*Oedipus Tyrannus*, despite its reputation as a typical tragedy, is rather a special case in that regard—but the recognition of the determined shape of the life he has created for himself, with an implicit comparison with the uncreated potential life he has forsaken. The line of Milton dealing with the fall of the devils, "O how unlike the place from whence they fell!", referring as it does both to Virgil's *quantum mutatus ab illo* and Isaiah's "How art thou fallen from heaven, O Lucifer son of the morning," combines the Classical and the Christian archetypes of tragedy—for Satan, of course, like Adam, possessed an original glory. In Milton the complement to the vision of Adam on top of the wheel of fortune and falling into the world of the wheel is Christ standing on the pinnacle of the temple, urged by Satan to fall, and remaining motionless.

As soon as Adam falls, he enters his own created life, which is also the order of nature as we know it. The tragedy of Adam, therefore, resolves, like all other tragedies, in the manifestation of natural law. He enters a world in which existence is itself tragic, not existence modified by an act, deliberate or unconscious. Merely to exist is to disturb the balance of nature. Every natural man is a Hegelian thesis, and implies a reaction: every new birth provokes the return of an avenging death. This fact, in itself ironic and now called *Angst*, becomes tragic when a sense of a lost and originally higher destiny is added to it. Aristotle's hamartia, then, is a condition of being, not a cause of becoming: the reason why Milton ascribes his dubious argument to God is that he is so anxious to remove God from a predetermined causal sequence. On one side of the tragic hero is an opportunity for freedom, on the other the inevitable consequence of losing that freedom. These two sides of Adam's situation are represented in Milton by the speeches of Raphael and Michael respectively. Even with an innocent hero or martyr the same situation arises: in the Passion story it occurs in Christ's prayer in Gethsemane. Tragedy seems to move up to an *Augenblick* or crucial moment from which point the road to what might have been and the road to what will be can be simultaneously seen. Seen by the audience, that is: it cannot be seen by the hero if he is in a state of hybris, for in that case the crucial moment is for him a moment of dizziness, when the wheel of fortune begins its inevitable cyclical movement downward.

In Adam's situation there is a feeling, which in Christian tradition can be traced back at least to St. Augustine, that time *begins* with the fall; that the fall from liberty into the natural cycle also started the movement of time as we know it. In other tragedies too we can trace the feeling that *nemesis* is deeply involved with the movement of time, whether as the missing of a tide in the affairs of men, as a recognition that the time is out of joint, as a sense that time is the devourer of life, the mouth of hell at the previous moment, when the potential passes forever into the actual, or, in its ultimate horror, Macbeth's sense of it as simply one clock-tick after another. In comedy time plays a redeeming role: it uncovers and brings to light what is essential to the happy ending. The subtitle of Greene's *Pandosto,* the source of *The Winter's Tale,* is "*The Triumph of Time,*" and it well describes the nature of Shakespeare's action, where time is introduced as a chorus. But in tragedy the *cognitio* is normally the recognition of the inevitability of a causal sequence in time, and the forebodings and ironic anticipations surrounding it are based on a sense of cyclical return.

In irony, as distinct from tragedy, the wheel of time completely encloses the action, and there is no sense of an original contact with a relatively timeless world. In the Bible the tragic fall of Adam is followed by its historical repetition, the fall of Israel into Egyptian bondage, which is, so to speak, its ironic confirmation. As long as the Geoffrey version of British history was accepted, the fall of Troy was the corresponding event in the history of Britain, and, as the fall of Troy began with an idolatrous misapplication of an apple, there were even symbolic parallels. Shakespeare's most ironic play, *Troilus and Cressida,* presents in Ulysses the voice of worldly wisdom, expounding with great eloquence the two primary categories of the perspective of tragic irony in the fallen world, time and the hierarchic chain of being. The extraordinary treatment of the tragic vision of time by Nietzsche's Zarathustra, in which the heroic acceptance of cyclical return becomes a glumly cheerful acceptance of a cosmology of identical recurrence, marks the influence of an age of irony.

Anyone accustomed to think archetypally of literature will recognize in tragedy a mimesis of sacrifice. Tragedy is a paradoxical combination of a fearful sense of rightness (the hero must fall) and a pitying sense of wrongness (it is too bad that he falls). There is a similar paradox in the two elements of sacrifice. One of these is communion, the dividing of a heroic or divine body among a group which brings them into unity with, and as, that body. The other is propitiation, the sense that in spite of the communion the body really belongs to another, a greater, and a potentially wrathful power. The ritual analogies to tragedy are more obvious than the psychological ones, for it is irony, not tragedy, that represents the nightmare or anxiety-dream. But, just as the literary critic finds Freud most suggestive for the theory of comedy, and Jung for the theory of romance, so for the theory of tragedy one naturally looks to the psychology of the will to power, as expounded in Adler and Nietzsche. Here one finds a "Dionysiac" aggressive will, intoxicated by dreams of its own omnipotence, impinging upon an "Apollonian" sense of external and immovable order. As a mimesis of ritual, the tragic hero is not really killed or eaten, but the corresponding thing in art still takes place, a vision of death which draws the survivors into a new unity. As a mimesis of dream, the inscrutable tragic hero, like the proud and silent swan, becomes articulate at the point of death, and the audience, like the poet in *Kubla Khan*, revives his song within itself. With his fall, a greater world beyond which his gigantic spirit had blocked out becomes for an instant visible, but there is also a sense of the mystery and remoteness of that world.

If we are right in our suggestion that romance, tragedy, irony and comedy are all episodes in a total quest-myth, we can see how it is that comedy can contain a potential tragedy within itself. In myth, the hero is a god, and hence he does not die, but dies and rises again. The ritual pattern behind the catharsis of comedy is the resurrection that follows the death, the epiphany or manifestation of the risen hero. In Aristophanes the hero, who often goes through a point of ritual death, is treated as a risen god, hailed as a new Zeus, or given the quasi-divine honors of the Olympic victor. In New Comedy the new human body is both a hero and a social group. The Aeschylean trilogy proceeds to the comic satyr-play, which is said to have affinities with spring festivals. Christianity, too, sees tragedy as an episode in the divine comedy, the larger scheme of redemption and resurrection. The sense of tragedy as a prelude to comedy seems almost inseparable from anything explicitly Christian. The serenity of the final double chorus in the St. Matthew Passion would hardly be attainable if composer and audience did not know that there was more to the story. Nor would the death of Samson lead to "calm of mind, all passion spent," if Samson were not a prototype of the rising Christ, associated at the appropriate moment with the phoenix.

This is an example of the way in which myths explain the structural principles behind familiar literary facts, in this case the fact that to make a sombre action end happily is easy enough, and to reverse the procedure almost impossible. (Of course we have a natural dislike of seeing pleasant situations turn out disastrously, but if a poet is working on a solid structural basis, our natural likes and dislikes have nothing to do with the matter.) Even Shakespeare, who can do anything, never does quite this. The action of *King Lear*, which seems heading for some kind of serenity, is suddenly wrenched into agony by the hanging of Cordelia, providing a conclusion which the stage refused to act for over a century, but none of Shakespeare's tragedies impresses us as a comedy gone wrong—*Romeo and Juliet* has a suggestion of such a structure, but it is only a suggestion. Hence while of course a tragedy may contain a comic action, it contains it only episodically as a subordinate contrast or underplot.

The characterization of tragedy is very like that of comedy in reverse. The source of *nemesis,* whatever it is, is an *eiron,* and may appear in a great variety of agents, from wrathful gods to hypocritical villains. In comedy we noticed three main types of *eiron* characters: a benevolent withdrawing and returning figure, the tricky slave or vice, and the hero and heroine. We have the tragic counterpart to the withdrawn *eiron* in the god who decrees the tragic action, like Athene in *Ajax* or Aphrodite in *Hippolytus;* a Christian example is God the Father in *Paradise Lost.* He may also be a ghost, like Hamlet's father; or it may not be a person at all but simply an invisible force known only by its effects, like the death that quietly seizes on Tamburlaine when the time has come for him to die. Often, as in the revenge-tragedy, it is an event previous to the action of which the tragedy itself is the consequence.

A tragic counterpart to the vice or tricky slave may be discerned in the soothsayer or prophet who foresees the inevitable end, or more of it than the hero does, like Teiresias. A closer example is the Machiavellian villain of Elizabethan drama, who, like the vice in comedy, is a convenient catalyzer of the action because he requires the minimum of motivation, being a self-starting principle of malevolence. Like the comic vice, too, he is something of an *architectus* or projection of the author's will, in this case for a tragic conclusion. "I limned this night-piece," says Webster's Lodovico, "and it was my best." Iago dominates the action of *Othello* almost to the point of being a tragic counterpart to the black king or evil magician of romance. The affinities of the Machiavellian villain with the diabolical are naturally close, and he may be an actual devil like Mephistopheles, but the sense of awfulness belonging to an agent of catastrophe can also make him something more like the high priest of a sacrifice. There is a touch of this in Webster's Bosola. *King Lear* has a Machiavellian villain in Edmund, and Edmund is contrasted with Edgar. Edgar, with his bewildering variety of disguises, his appearance to blind or mad people in different roles, and his tendency to appear on the third sound of the trumpet and to come pat like the catastrophe of the old comedy, seems to be an experiment in a new type, a kind of tragic "virtue," if I may coin this word by analogy, a counterpart in the order of nature to a guardian angel or similar attendant in romance.

The tragic hero usually belongs of course to the *alazon* group, an impostor in the sense that he is self-deceived or made dizzy by hybris. In many tragedies he begins as a semi-divine figure, at least in his own eyes, and then an inexorable dialectic sets to work which separates the divine pretence from the human actuality. "They told me I was everything," says Lear: " 'tis a lie; I am not ague-proof." The tragic hero is usually vested with supreme authority, but is often in the more ambiguous position of a *tyrannos* whose rule depends on his own abilities, rather than a purely hereditary or *de jure* monarch (*basileus*) like Duncan. The latter is more directly a symbol of the original vision or birthright, and is often a somewhat pathetic victim, like Richard II, or even Agamemnon. Parental figures in tragedy have the same ambivalence that they have in all other forms.

We found in comedy that the term *bomolochos* or buffoon need not be restricted to farce, but could be extended to cover comic characters who are primarily entertainers, with the function of increasing or focussing the comic mood. The corresponding contrasting type in tragedy is the suppliant, the character, often female, who presents a picture of unmitigated helplessness and destitution. Such a figure is pathetic, and pathos, though it seems a gentler and more relaxed mood than tragedy, is even more terrifying. Its basis is the exclusion of an individual from a group, hence it attacks the deepest fear in ourselves that we possess—a fear much deeper than the relatively cosy and sociable bogey of hell. In the figure of the suppliant pity and terror are brought to the highest possible pitch of intensity, and the awful consequences of rejecting the suppliant for all concerned is a central theme of Greek tragedy. Suppliant figures are often women threatened with death or rape, or children, like Prince Arthur in *King John*. The fragility of Shakespeare's Ophelia marks an affinity with the suppliant type. Often, too, the suppliant is in the structurally tragic position of having lost a place of greatness: this is the position of Adam and Eve in the tenth book of *Paradise Lost*, of the Trojan women after the fall of Troy, of Oedipus in the Colonus play, and so on. A subordinate figure who plays the role of focussing the tragic mood is the messenger who regularly announces the catastrophe in Greek tragedy. In the final scene of comedy, when the author is usually trying to get all his characters on the stage at once, we often notice the introduction of a new character, generally a messenger bearing some missing piece of the *cognitio*, such as Jaques de Boys in *As You Like It* or the gentle astringer in *All's Well*, who represents the comic counterpart.

Finally, a tragic counterpart of the comic refuser of festivity may be discerned in a tragic type of plain dealer who may be simply the faithful friend of the hero, like Horatio in *Hamlet*, but is often an outspoken critic of the tragic action, like Kent in *King Lear* or Enobarbus in *Antony and Cleopatra*. Such a character is in the position of refusing, or at any rate resisting, the tragic movement toward catastrophe. Abdiel's role in the tragedy of Satan in *Paradise Lost* is similar. The familiar figures of Cassandra and Teiresias combine this role with that of the soothsayer. Such figures, when they occur in a tragedy without a chorus, are often called chorus characters, as they illustrate one of the essential functions of the tragic chorus. In comedy a society forms around the hero: in tragedy the chorus, however faithful, usually represents the society from which the hero is gradually isolated. Hence what it expresses is a social norm against which the hero's hybris may be measured. The chorus is not the voice of the hero's conscience by any means, but very seldom does it encourage him in his hybris or prompt him to disastrous action. The chorus or chorus character is, so to speak, the embryonic germ of comedy in tragedy, just as the refuser of festivity, the melancholy Jaques or Alceste, is a tragic germ in comedy.

In comedy the erotic and social affinities of the hero are combined and unified in the final scene; tragedy usually makes love and the social structure irreconcilable and contending forces, a conflict which reduces love to passion and social activity to a forbidding and imperative duty. Comedy is much concerned with integrating the family and adjusting the family to society as a whole; tragedy is much concerned with breaking up the family and opposing it to the rest of society. This gives us the tragic archetype of Antigone, of which the conflict of love and honor in Classical French drama, of *Neigung* and *Pflicht* in Schiller, of passion and authority in the Jacobeans, are all moralized simplifications. Again, just as the heroine of comedy often ties together the action, so it is obvious that the central female figure of a tragic action will often polarize the tragic conflict. Eve, Helen, Gertrude, and Emily in the *Knight's Tale* are some ready instances: the structural role of Briseis in the *Iliad* is similar. Comedy works out the proper relations of its characters and prevents heroes from marrying their sisters or mothers; tragedy presents the disaster of Oedipus or the incest of Siegmund. There is a great deal in tragedy about pride of race and birthright, but its general tendency is to isolate a ruling or noble family from the rest of society.

The phases of tragedy move from the heroic to the ironic, the first three corresponding to the first three phases of romance, the last three to the last three of irony. The first phase of tragedy is the one in which the central character is given the greatest possible dignity in contrast to the other characters, so that we get the perspective of a stag pulled down by wolves. The sources of dignity are courage and innocence, and in this phase the hero or heroine usually is innocent. This phase corresponds to the myth of the birth of the hero in romance, a theme which is occasionally incorporated into a tragic structure, as in Racine's *Athalie*. But owing to the unusual difficulty of making an interesting dramatic character out of an infant, the central and typical figure of this phase is the calumniated woman, often a mother the legitimacy of whose child is suspected. A whole series of tragedies based on a Griselda figure belong here, stretching from the Senecan *Octavia* to Hardy's Tess, and including the tragedy of Hermione in *The*

Winter's Tale. If we are to read *Alcestis* as a tragedy, we have to see it as a tragedy of this phase in which Alcestis is violated by Death and then has her fidelity vindicated by being restored to life. *Cymbeline* belongs here too: in this play the theme of the birth of the hero appears offstage, for Cymbeline was the king of Britain at the time of the birth of Christ, and the halcyon peace in which the play concludes has a suppressed reference to this.

An even clearer example, and certainly one of the greatest in English literature, is *The Duchess of Malfi*. The Duchess has the innocence of abundant life in a sick and melancholy society, where the fact that she has "youth and a little beauty" is precisely why she is hated. She reminds us too that one of the essential characteristics of innocence in the martyr is an unwillingness to die. When Bosola comes to murder her he makes elaborate attempts to put her half in love with easeful death and to suggest that death is really a deliverance. The attempt is motivated by a grimly controlled pity, and is roughly the equivalent of the vinegar sponge in the Passion. When the Duchess, her back to the wall, says "I am the Duchess of Malfi still," "still" having its full weight of "always," we understand how it is that even after her death her invisible presence continues to be the most vital character in the play. *The White Devil* is an ironic parody-treatment of the same phase.

The second phase corresponds to the youth of the romantic hero, and is in one way or another the tragedy of innocence in the sense of inexperience, usually involving young people. It may be simply the tragedy of a youthful life cut off, as in the stories of Iphigeneia and Jephthah's daughter, of Romeo and Juliet, or, in a more complex situation, in the bewildered mixture of idealism and priggishness that brings Hippolytus to disaster. The simplicity of Shaw's Joan and her lack of worldly wisdom place her here also. For us however the phase is dominated by the archetypal tragedy of the green and golden world, the loss of the innocence of Adam and Eve, who, no matter how heavy a doctrinal load they have to carry, will always remain dramatically in the position of children baffled by their first contact with an adult situation. In many tragedies of this type the central character survives, so that the action closes with some adjustment to a new and more mature experience. "Henceforth I learn that to obey is best," says Adam, as he and Eve go hand in hand out to the world before them. A less clear cut but similar resolution occurs when Philoctetes, whose serpent-wound reminds us a little of Adam, is taken off his island to enter the Trojan war. Ibsen's *Little Eyolf* is a tragedy of this phase, and with the same continuing conclusion, in which it is the older characters who are educated through the death of a child.

The third phase, corresponding to the central quest-theme of romance, is tragedy in which a strong emphasis is thrown on the success or completeness of the hero's achievement. The Passion belongs here, as do all tragedies in which the hero is in any way related to or a prototype of Christ, like *Samson Agonistes*. The paradox of victory within tragedy may be expressed by a double perspective in the action. Samson is a buffoon of a Philistine carnival and simultaneously a tragic hero to the Israelites, but the tragedy ends in triumph and the carnival in catastrophe. Much the same is true of the mocked Christ in the Passion. But just as the second phase often ends in anticipation of greater maturity, so this one is often a sequel to a previous tragic or heroic action, and comes at the end of a heroic life. One of the greatest dramatic examples is *Oedipus at Colonus*, where we find the usual binary form of a tragedy conditioned by a previous tragic act, ending this time not in a second disaster, but in a full rich serenity that goes far beyond a mere resignation to Fate. In narrative literature we may cite Beowulf's last fight with the dragon, the pendant to his Grendel quest. Shakespeare's *Henry V* is a successfully completed romantic quest made tragic by its implicit context: everybody knows that King Henry died almost immediately and that sixty years of unbroken disaster followed for England—at least, if anyone in Shakespeare's audience did not know that, his ignorance was certainly no fault of Shakespeare's.

The fourth phase is the typical fall of the hero through hybris and hamartia that we have already discussed. In this phase we cross the boundary line from innocence to experience, which is also the direction in which the hero falls. In the fifth phase the ironic element increases, the heroic decreases, and the characters look further away and in a smaller perspective. *Timon of Athens* impresses us as more ironic and less heroic than the better known tragedies, not simply because Timon is a more middle-class hero who has to buy what authority he has, but because the feeling that Timon's suicide has somehow failed to make a fully heroic *point* is very strong. Timon is oddly isolated from the final action, in which the breach between Alcibiades and the Athenians closes up over his head, in striking contrast with the conclusions of most of the other tragedies, where nobody is allowed to steal the show from the central character.

The ironic perspective in tragedy is attained by putting the characters in a state of lower freedom than the audience. For a Christian audience an Old Testament or pagan setting is ironic in this sense, as it shows its characters moving according to the conditions of a law, whether Jewish or natural, from which the audience has been, at least theoretically, redeemed. *Samson Agonistes*, though unique in English literature, presents a combination of Classical form and Hebrew subject-matter that the greatest contemporary tragedian, Racine, also reached at the end of his life in *Athalie* and *Esther*. Similarly the epilogue to Chaucer's *Troilus* puts a Courtly Love tragedy into its historical relation to "payens corsed olde rites." The events in Geoffrey of Monmouth's British history are supposed to be contemporary with those of the Old Testament, and the sense of life under the law is present everywhere in *King Lear*. The same structural principle accounts for the use of astrology and other fatalistic machinery connected with the turning wheels of fate or fortune. Romeo and Juliet are starcrossed, and Troilus loses Criseyde because every five hundred years Jupiter and Saturn meet the crescent moon in Cancer and claim another victim. The tragic action of the fifth phase presents for the most part the tragedy of lost direction and lack of knowledge, not unlike the second phase except that the context is the world of adult experience. *Oedipus Tyrannus* belongs here, and all tragedies and tragic episodes which suggest the existential projection of fatalism, and, like much of the Book of Job, seem to raise metaphysical or theological questions rather than social or moral ones.

Oedipus Tyrannus, however, is already moving into the sixth phase of tragedy, a world of shock and horror in which the central images are images of *sparagmos*, that is, cannibalism, mutilation, and torture. The specific reaction known as shock is appropriate to a situation of cruelty or outrage. (The secondary or false shock produced by the outrage done to some emotional attachment or fixation, as in the critical reception of *Jude the Obscure* or *Ulysses*, has no status in criticism, as false shock is a disguised resistance to the autonomy of culture.) Any tragedy may have one or more shocking scenes in it, but sixth-phase tragedy shocks as a whole, in its total effect. This phase is more common as a subordinate aspect of tragedy than as its main theme, as unqualified horror or despair makes a difficult cadence. *Prometheus Bound* is a tragedy of this phase, though this is partly an illusion due to its isolation from the trilogy to which it belongs. In such tragedies the hero is in too great agony or humiliation to gain the privilege of a heroic pose, hence it is usually easier to make him a villainous hero, like Marlowe's Barabas, although Faustus also belongs to the same phase. Seneca is fond of this phase, and bequeathed to the Elizabethans an interest in the gruesome, an effect which usually has some connection with mutilation, as when Ferdinand offers to shake hands with the Duchess of Malfi and gives her a dead man's hand. *Titus Andronicus* is an experiment in Senecan sixth-phase horror which makes a great deal of mutilation, and shows also a strong interest, from the opening scene on, in the sacrificial symbolism of tragedy.

At the end of this phase we reach a point of demonic epiphany, where we see or glimpse the undisplaced demonic vision, the vision of the *Inferno*. Its chief symbols, besides the prison and the madhouse, are the instruments of a torturing death, the cross under the sunset being the antithesis of the tower under the moon. A strong element of demonic ritual in public punishments and similar mob amusements is exploited by tragic and ironic myth. Breaking on the wheel becomes Lear's wheel of fire; bear-baiting is an image for Gloucester and Macbeth, and for the crucified Prometheus the humiliation of exposure, the horror of being watched, is a greater misery than the pain. *Derkou theama* (behold the spectacle; get your staring over with) is his bitterest cry. The inability of Milton's blind Samson to stare back is his greatest torment, and one which forces him to scream at Delilah, in one of the most terrible passages of all tragic drama, that he will tear her to pieces if she touches him.

The Concept
of Tragedy
and the "Science"
of Literature*

Lucien Goldmann

If we denote any attempt to understand reality as *science* or theoretical thought we must admit that a considerable discrepancy has appeared between what are normally known as "exact sciences"—mathematics, physics, chemistry—and the "human sciences". This discrepancy can be seen not only in the contrast in the scope and precision of the findings achieved in each of these domains, but also as far as the terminology is concerned. The terms habitually employed in the human sciences lack both *precision* and *functional capacity*, two essential properties if investigators are to agree, if not about their theories and analyses, at least about the actual object of their study, about the nature of the truths they investigate and the ideas they advance. Besides, a similar discrepancy also exists within these human sciences—we need only compare the "science of literature" with the other branches of sociology and history—and at present the scientific study of literature is far more an aspiration than a reality.

There is nothing surprising, therefore, in my starting this study of Racine with the problem of language and definition. The collective consciousness, or the "common sense" of critics and spectators, has produced a statement which I am quite ready to accept, anyhow for the time being: *Racine is above all a tragic writer*. But in order to use this statement as my starting point it has to be given a precise meaning and this presupposes the definition of the terms *tragedy* and *tragic*.

Though most historians and critics agree to clasify a certain number of writers—Aeschylus, Sophocles, Euripides, Racine, and, partially, Shakespeare—as tragedians, they also refer to the "tragedies" of Rotrou, Quinault, Corneille and even Victor Hugo. They hardly ever ask themselves whether *all* the theatrical works of writers reputed to be *tragic* are really *tragedies*.

From the vast quantity of literature devoted to tragedy there emerges one hypothesis, formulated with greater or less clarity: an essential bond exists between the idea of tragedy and the idea of *destiny* or *fatality*. And there is no doubt that this can be applied to a whole series of works by Aeschylus, Sophocles and Shakespeare, as well as to Racine's *Phèdre*. Had this hypothesis, however unsatisfactory it might be, been taken more seriously it would no longer have been possible to speak of the "tragedies" of Quinault, Garnier or Corneille. A considerable advance would have been made in the knowledge and use of words, for, though the idea of *destiny*, regarded as an incomprehensible fatality

*Lucien Goldmann, *Racine*, translated by Alastair Hamilton (Rivers Press, 1972). Reprinted by permission of Rivers Press and Writers and Readers Publishing Cooperative, London.

dominating the hero's existence and acts, is valid for characters like Orestes, Oedipus, Macbeth or Phèdre, it obviously cannot be applied to Antigone, Andromaque, Junie or Titus. Rather than give up this idea, therefore, we should merely regard it as the characteristic of one form of tragic literature. What we still need to do is to find a definition capable of embracing the *two* forms of tragedy.

Another idea, implicit rather than explicit, which appears together with that of *destiny* in most works on tragedy, is the idea of the "serious play". But this is far too general to have any functional value. Besides, it includes the concept of *drama*, which is just as vague but which seems to have a different significance. I therefore suggest that we adopt, temporarily and for as long as it is practicable, a distinction which might be a first step towards the development of a precise and scientific terminology. I shall call a "tragedy" *any play in which the conflicts are necessarily insoluble*, and a "drama" *any play in which the conflicts either are solved* (at least on a moral level) *or fail to be solved because of the fortuitous intervention of a factor which, according to the laws governing the universe of the play, might not have operated.* . . .

Let us pause to consider the implications of my original hypothesis—that tragedy is defined by the necessarily insoluble nature of the conflicts which occur. To start with this means that, in every tragedy, there is an absolute primacy of morals over the actual state of affairs, of *what ought to be* over *what is*. It means that a tragedy is the representation of a universe dominated by a conflict of values and that every attempt to understand it on the basis of the characters' *psychology* is a misapprehension and is doomed to fail. Indeed, the conflicts between the various "egoisms", conflicts of interest or passion, are never *essentially* insoluble. It is always by *accident* that the passions of two particular individuals are not reciprocal, that Oreste loves Hermione, while Hermione loves Pyrrhus, who loves Andromaque. On the other hand it is an absolute *moral* duty for Andromaque to remain faithful to Hector and to do everything in her power to save the life of Astyanax. Similarly it is always by *accident* that one of the antagonists triumphs over the other in a conflict of interests or ambition, that Néron should get the better Agrippine and not vice-versa.

So all these characters are in themselves essentially *dramatic*, and if the plays where we encounter them are tragedies it is precisely because the unity and coherence of their universe only appears from the point of view of other characters who are entirely different, characters like Andromaque, Junie, Titus and Phèdre who are dominated by an *ethical* need, and whom we can call *tragic heroes*.

Yet it is not enough to characterise tragedy solely by the primacy of morality and the conflict of values, for the universe of *drama* is also frequently based on an ethical problem: take Corneille's plays and Racine's *dramatic* works, *Mithridate, Iphigénie* or *Athalie*. The tragic universe is one where values and their corresponding moral requirements are absolute, dominated by the category of *all or nothing*, without *the slightest notion of degree or compromise*. The tragic universe knows no nuance. It only knows right and wrong, reality and unreality, and contains neither graduality nor transition.

In tragedy an insuperable gulf separates the characters lacking value and reality (either because they live a compromise or because they are so obsessed by passion or ambition that they lack any form of consciousness) from the *real* tragic characters, who are aware of both their needs and their limitations and whose every act counts, independently of all motives and psychological explanations, with the same force and intensity.

Apart from historic hope and action, inaccessible to the tragic view, everyday life consists of unawareness, selfish ambition and blind passion, approximate and partial accomplishments and half-realized hopes. Its inhabitants either resign themselves to it or seek consolation in an inner life or in dreams. This is why everyday life remains a confused and ambiguous mixture without ever becoming a clear, univocal structure. This is also why it never reaches that extremely elevated threshold of consciousness and rigour required by the tragic universe whose law Pascal expressed when he said that all that is not fully valid with relation to the infinite, all that is not true and right, is equally valueless, false and wrong. We see why tragic conflicts are insoluble from the start. The need for *absolute* values, for the totality which rules the universe of every tragedy, is radically and irremediably opposed to a world dominated by compromise, relativity and the more or less.

Here, then, are three constituent elements of every tragedy: *an essentially insoluble conflict* resulting from the clash between a *world* which knows only relativity, compromise, the more or less, and a *universe* dominated by the need for *absolute values*, for *totality*, and governed by the law of *all or nothing*.

But who is it who demonstrates this need in the eyes of the world? Sometimes, or more precisely, in the tragedies "without peripeteia or recognition", it is the tragic hero himself: Andromaque, Junie or Titus. But these characters remain aware that they are conforming to an external need which surpasses them. And what of the tragedies of fatality "with peripeteia and recognition", as in the cases of Oedipus, Orestes or Phèdre? There is only one answer, and it brings us to the third and most important figure in the tragic universe: fatality, transcendency, God.

This last term is probably the most precise provided we realize that it does not mean the God of any specific religion. Tragedy is no more connected with Christianity than with the religion of the Greeks, although the Christian God, like the Greek gods, or those of any other religion, can have a tragic aspect. Consequently, Racine had no difficulty in transposing an almost unmodified version of Port-Royal's concept of Christianity into a pagan universe.

We have thus come to a fourth *essential* element of every tragedy: the existence of a figure who demands the realization of an absolute justice alien to any compromise and who observes the unfolding of the action. *Tragedy can be defined as a spectacle under the permanent observation of a deity.*

But we still have to specify the characteristics of the tragic God or gods whose most salient trait is primarily negative. The deity who rules the universe of tragedy is the very opposite of the providential God, for he never shows the hero which path he should follow in order to realize an authentic existence. Though he is *always present* this God remains a *hidden god,* a god who is *always absent*. This is the key to tragedy. The protagonists are perfectly capable of living both away from the deity, in the absence of God (all those who form the *world* do so), and in the presence of God and under his protection. The paradox of his continual presence and absence alone obstructs the "false consciousness" of an ignorant world as much as it does the certainty of the mystic. It makes life impossible.

In the words of the greatest tragic thinker in French literature the perpetual presence of the deity prevents men from "falling asleep", while his perpetual absence turns this sleeplessness into an agony (Pascal, *Pensées*, Edition Brunsch-vieg, fragment 553). Moreover, the absence, the hidden nature of the deity, can appear in the two different ways which constitute the two forms of tragedy. As in most Greek tragedies and in *Phèdre*, the gods can blind man; they can leave him a prey to evil, to the illusion of being able to live, although he has long entered the universe of their absolute and implacable justice, only at the last moment revealing to him his fault and its consequences. These are the avenging gods of the tragedy "with peripeteia and recognition", of the tragedy of destiny. Or they can give the hero from the outset that which, in the other type of tragedy, they only allow him at the end: the full awareness of the divine requirements and of the impossibility of satisfying them in this life. But they then become spectators. Under their observation Junie, Titus, Bérénice (at the end of the play) and (up to a point) Andromaque act as the heroes of tragedies "without peripeteia or recognition". They act as the heroes of tragedies of human greatness and *refusal*.

In both cases, however, the tragic God remains a hard and implacable God, a God whose sentence disregards any motive or explanation, a God who knows neither forgiveness nor meekness and who judges nothing but the *act* (whenever the act has touched the essence, from however great a distance and for however short a time) and not the man, his life, his intention. He is also a God who disregards the unessential world which is too unreal and transparent to detain his attention.

IV
THE TRAGIC HERO

The Evolution of the Tragic Hero*

George Boas

Let me say at the outset that I am not going to play that ancient game of trying to define the indefinable. Names of literary *genres* are but tags for works of art which have certain historical relations, but there is no more reason to believe that *Hamlet* and the *Eumenides* have a common essence than there is to insist that Louis Capet and Louis Philippe have a common essence, or that the Lever Building in New York and Lincoln's log cabin have a common essence. People have been trying for years to give satisfactory definitions of such terms as "tragedy," "comedy," "novel," even "poetry," and they have never succeeded. The reason for their failure is clear enough. Words have a history. When they are first used, it is likely that they are unambiguous, but as time goes on, they are applied to more and more different things. Even invented names, like *Kodak*, come to broaden their extension and at one time the Eastman Company had to run an advertisement announcing, "If it isn't an Eastman, it isn't a Kodak." This does not deny the obvious fact that probably everything can be found to have something in common, if only the character of being talked about. So all things made by man have a common trait—they are human artifacts. But the reason why we are interested in a play or a poem or a picture or building or musical composition is not its similarity to all other plays, poems, pictures, buildings, and musical compositions, for most of the time we do not even perceive that similarity. There must be thousands of Frenchmen, living and dead, who have enjoyed a performance of Racine's *Phèdre* without seeing its similarity to either Euripides's or Seneca's *Hippolytus*. Our interest in a work of art is to be sure intensified if we can locate it in the tradition to which it belongs, but one does not have to be a literary historian to be moved by a novel, poem, or play. Fortunately we are not all as yet Ph.D.'s, and it is devoutly to be hoped that we shall never all have that sad distinction. The history of ideas, like the history of taste, is a very important subject which illuminates obscure passages and thus makes it possible for us to understand works of art which seemed opaque at first sight. But at the same time it must be admitted that some works of art are dead, or so close to it that they can be kept alive only in an oxygen tent of footnotes and explanatory introductions. That this is so is a clear indication that the universality and eternality of great literature is an illusion, for even the greatest books require constant re-editing and thus re-interpretation. Homer, Lucretius, Dante, Shakespeare,

* George Boas, "The Evolution of the Tragic Hero," *The Carleton Drama Review*, Vol. I, No. 1 (1955–1956), pp. 5–21. [Footnotes in this selection have been renumbered.]

even Goethe would lie unopened on the dusty back shelves of libraries without the work of editors.

Lest I be thought to be too dictatorial, we shall consider for a moment the remaining Greek tragedies. We all know from reading Aristotle's *Poetics* what they are supposed to have in common, from their high seriousness to their cathartic effect on the baser emotions. To add another interpretation of what Aristotle actually said, or even of what he was trying to say, would be cruel and unusual punishment on a captive audience. I should prefer to rescue these dramatic poems from the Aristotelians, most of whom upon scrutiny turn out to be disciples of Horace or of St. Thomas Aquinas, and to look at them afresh. We have seven plays of Aeschylus, seven of Sophocles, and nineteen of Euripides. The total is but a small fraction not merely of all the tragedies written for the Theatre of Dionysus, but also of those written by our three authors. For Aeschylus wrote between eighty and ninety plays, Sophocles over one hundred and twenty, Euripides over ninety. We have less than ten percent of the plays of these three men to go on and we have no way of knowing how representative our remaining plays are or even if they are what modern taste would call the best of all that were written. Consequently it should always be borne in mind that any generalization made about Greek tragedy has to be based on a very imperfect sample.

Using this sample, we can make the following statements, for what they are worth. First, Greek tragedy was built around certain plots which were supposed to be historical. There is the plot of the returned hero who like Agamemnon comes back from the wars to find conditions at home something less than satisfactory. In his case he discovers his wife adulterously joined to her lover Aegisthus. Or there is the plot of the person who is the unwitting instrument of divine plans, like Oedipus and his daughters. Or there is the glorification of a recent historical event such as the victory of the Greeks over the Persians at Salamis; or the spectacular presentation of an ancient myth, such as that of the culture-hero Prometheus or of the daughters of Danaus. The one generalization which one can make about these plots, or subject-matters, is that they were all well known to the audience, much as the story of the Passion or the Fall of Man or the assassination of Lincoln would be to American audiences. Clearly in such cases the element of surprise was bound to be lacking. One could no more have Antigone decide for some reason or other not to bury Polyneices than one could have one of the Rover Boys appear in Ford's Theatre and knock the pistol out of Booth's hand just as he was about to shoot the President. We can not say that the hero does what he does because of Fate, or that the outcome is always determined by an oracle, or that the main character possesses a tragic flaw, or anything of that sort. But we can say that the audience could not be taken by surprise at the outcome. Today we are unaccustomed to his technique. We say that we prefer suspense, though musical audiences love to hear the same old pieces played over and over again and children are very exigent in their demand for accurate repetition of stories. We say that we do not approve of plays in which the *dénouement* can be seen as soon as the drama begins; we want it to be concealed. In fact, in some cases such as the short stories of O. Henry, we do not know until the last sentence what is going to happen. Apparently this demand was not characteristic of the Athenians.

In the second place, the very familiarity which the audience had with the plots made their development seem logical. There are Greek tragedies in which the hero or heroine tells the audience that he has to make a choice and that the result of the choice is already known to him. Thus even *Prometheus Bound*, which is almost like an oratorio, in that nothing takes place except the presentation of what Professor Kitto has called a situation, opens with the announcement of Prometheus's crime, the crime of having disobeyed the command of Zeus. And despite the taunts of Force, that one named *Forethought* should have known the consequence of his acts, Prometheus replies in his opening speech,

> Whatever comes,
> Stands clear before my vision. I can suffer
> Nothing that I foreknew not. I must bear
> All that is doomed, as best I may; well knowing
> None can do battle with Necessity.[1]

Similarly in *Antigone*, Sophocles has his heroine state clearly her course of action and her knowledge of what will happen if she pursues it. Sometimes, as in the Oedipus legend, the choice is only half-real, and consists in trying desperately to avoid the web which has been woven by the Fates and foretold by the oracle. But even here the hero knows what the oracle has said, though the sting of the tragedy is his inability to so choose as to refute the oracle, he makes every attempt to do so. This simply means that certain causes have certain effects and that when a causal series is initiated, nothing can be done to divert it from its natural course. Zeus alone is free; the world is governed by Necessity. It is only in a few plays, such as Euripides's *Orestes*, that there exists a hint of divine intervention in the affairs of men, for whereas in Homer the gods are always interfering in one way or another to protect their favorites—or defeat each other—in the tragic dramatists they seem to stay pretty well in the background. In *The Eumenides* of Aeschylus the final decision about the fate of Orestes is determined by a vote of Athena but it is interesting to observe that the struggle otherwise is an even one, though Apollo resorts to curious physiological theories to prove that murdering his mother was less evil than revenging his father.[2] Regardless of the theories, the causes of the Furies and that of Apollo are evenly balanced until the last moment. *Hippolytus* may similarly be interpreted as a symbolic statement of Olympian quarrels. But the rival claims of Artemis and Aphrodite are presented at the beginning and end of the play as prologue and epilogue. The goddesses themselves do not interfere in the action, for after all Aphrodite does not try—to say nothing of succeed—to change Hippolytus's mind; and Phaedra dies, in spite of her cult of the goddess, and so does Hippolytus in spite of his cult of her rival divinity. What happens is the logical outcome of a choice of conduct.

When I say "logical," I use the term loosely. The analogy between cause and effect and premise and conclusion is far from strict. There is no logic, it might be said, in any effect's following from any cause. It is no more logical that a man pay for his sins with death than it would be if he paid for them with prosperity. But when we are sufficiently habituated to seeing certain effects following certain causes, we attribute to the succession of events a kind of compulsive force, as if nothing else could possibly happen. The difference between causal

---

[1] All translations, unless otherwise indicated, are by F. L. Lucas, as published in his *Greek Drama for Everyman*, London (J. M. Dent and Sons, Ltd.), by permission of the translator and publisher.
[2] Orestes himself does this in Euripides.

and logical necessity may be hard to grasp but it is a real difference nevertheless. That is why it is worth pointing out.

This brings us to a third characteristic of the remaining Greek tragedies. Whether the heroes have to make a choice between two equally legitimate courses of action, as Hegel seemed to think, or not, they have to make a choice and the usual result of it is self-defeat. I say "usual" for here again the generalization will not hold up in all cases. In *The Persians* there is nothing to come out badly, no self-defeat possible except for the enemy. In *Prometheus Bound* we have but one part of a trilogy and do not really know what took place in the last part. But we have some reason to believe that after the liberation of the Titan things took a turn for the better, as far as he was concerned. This at any rate is the orthodox view. Readers of Hesiod will recall another version of the myth according to which little good came to mankind with the introduction of fire into their lives. And in fact there will always be dispute about just what "badly" means. A person's death may with some justice be thought of as self-defeat, especially if he is responsible for it. But on the other hand, in what sense of the word does *Antigone* come out badly or result in self-defeat, since the heroine herself chose to do what she did? Her death may even be called self-fulfillment, as it seems to be in Anouilh's version of the play. With the exception of a few plays, one can conclude that the tragedies usually ended with the death of the hero.

There is still another characteristic of the Greek tragedies which we must not overlook. I refer to the Chorus. The role of the Chorus has been as hotly disputed as everything else in this domain. I have even heard it suggested that it existed for comic relief. It behaves like a thermometer, rising and falling with the temperature of the scene. It shifts its point of view without rhyme or reason, seeming to say that everyone is right. And in fact in a logical universe everyone is right. In such a world right and wrong are eternal principles which in themselves are really unintelligible. They become the premises from which everyting flows. In the *Oresteia* revenge is of unquestioned importance, just as it seems to be in *Hamlet*. But so also is respect for a mother. The premises do not form a logical system at all but frequently are in contradiction with one another. Electra and her brother have only to decide whether the crime of leaving a father's murder unavenged is worse than that of matricide. That a person is more closely related to his father than to his mother, as Euripides makes Orestes argue, as if he had Aristotle's *De generatione animalium,* is the excuse for the matricide, though it naturally turns out to be a poor excuse. And the Chorus is not slow to point this out. If it had been a good excuse, there would have been no tragedy. Again, the constant harping on the privileges of royal blood presumably did not seem bizarre to the democratic Athenians; they accepted this apparently as an immutable principle. The various immutable principles are often presented to us by the Chorus as if it were important for the audience to know what the plays are really about. The laws are what matter, not the desires of individuals. That this principle was significant even outside the theatre appears in Plato's *Apology.* But there happens to be conflict between some of the laws themselves. I think that one sees this most clearly in *Antigone,* where the ethics of obedience comes head-on into collision with practical action. It would seem to me, though in this I am probably in the minority, that one of the main functions of the Chorus is to comment upon or to expound this philosophy, setting forth the poet's own ideas, or at least those ideas which he believes his public to share. Often the long choral passages are purely lyrical, like hymns; often they take the form of prayers.

There are passages in *Agamemnon* which might be lifted out of context and read as philosophical mediations. But these Theban elders, Corinthian matrons, Trojan women, Greek sailors, usually do nothing except comment. For instance, in the long narrative that follows the sentinel's opening speech in *Agamemnon* we find the Chorus saying,

> Zeus, whoever He may be
> By that name on Him I call
> (If 'tis thus He would be known),
> Though I weigh infinity,
> Naught my thought may grasp at all,
> Save Him alone,
> To lift away this load of pain
> Burdening my soul in vain . . .
>
> He hath shown man wisdom's ways,
> He hath made His ordinance plain
> Unto all—"By suffering learn!"
> Sleepless still, the sinner pays:
> Dark memories, drop by drop, return,
> Till stubborn hearts are schooled by pain.
> So the stern Gods give their grace,
> Holding in Heaven the helmsman's place.

This is surely more likely to be the opinion of Aeschylus than that of a group of senile Argives. At times, however, the Chorus acts simply as an audience for one of the characters, but an audience which presumably reacts as would be fit and proper for the public itself. It does not further the movement of the drama, but comments on it. It is as if the audience were brought upon the stage and made articulate. It is in these cases that the Chorus voices such conventional philosophy, though it is also possible that when, as is true of Euripides, the dramatist was unconventional in his philosophic and religious ideas, the Chorus was too. It appears to tell the real audience what to think or, if one prefer, it voices the opinions as well as the emotions of the dramatist. But whatever it does, it obviates the necessity of our modern dramatists for pretending that the stage is real life. No Athenian dramatist had to go to extremes of ingenuity which a man like Ibsen, to say nothing of Eugène Scribe, had to employ to tell the audience what it was supposed to know. He seems to have realized that he was presenting a play in a theatre, and not photographing scenes from real life, and hence if he wanted something conveyed to the audience, he could make the Chorus do it.

It should also be pointed out that the heroes of all Greek tragedies were either gods or princes. This was erected into a rule by Aristotle and transmitted to us by the Renaissance theorists. We see its observance both in the French imitators of Greek tragedy and in Shakespeare even when he had a non-Hellenic subject. The Marxists have much of this. To them it is evidence that the dramatists identified themselves with the ruling class, even though in Athens the ruling class was not a hereditary aristocracy. It should be noted that if the plots of these spectacles were to be taken from history, there would be no way of avoiding the use of princes as protagonists. Ancient history says next to nothing about the common people and even the most unpleasant characters come from the nobility—indeed sometimes from Olympus. For that matter, whoever has found a

permanent place in literature, identified by his name, and not merely as Second
Citizen or Nurse or Messenger, is bound to develop into a nobleman as tradition
grows. Even Ethan Allen—at least in Vermont—has turned into a sort of nobleman. People seem to prefer that their heroes have no vulgar streaks. But be that
as it may, the fact is established, and the theory grew out of it that noblemen
were tragic, common people comic.

But once again it must be said that the evil ones are as noble as the good
ones. Agamemnon may be the victim, but his assassins are just as princely as he
is; neither Orestes nor Pylades is less or more princely than their victims; and
both Eteocles and Polyneices are brothers. It is thus impossible to distribute moral qualities on what the Marxists would call a class-basis. On the contrary, since
the tragic situation is man against fate, man against law, man against the gods,
man against necessity, social rank must count for nothing and the best way of reducing it to nonentity is to put all the characters on the same social level. Moreover, the situations are such that only divine beings or men descended from divine beings could be caught in them. For the old stories, hallowed by tradition,
were reinterpreted morally and one might as well object to the princely character of Agamemnon and Oedipus as to the similar position of Abraham, Isaac, and
Jacob. There emerge in all cultures certain figures who for one reason or another
captivate the imagination of the people of that culture. These figures become
national heroes, symbols of virtue, friendship, courage, self-sacrifice, wisdom.
What is particularly interesting about these Greek heroes is their tragic fate. No
tragedy has survived in which Deucalion and Pyrrha are the main characters.
Nor have we anything resembling the Book of Job.

Finally, the distinction between villain and hero is impossible to draw in the
remaining Greek tragedies. It is true that Menelaus shows up pretty badly according to our standards in Euripides's *Andromache*. But that may be because
he stands for Sparta and the author's feelings about Sparta are clearly expounded
in Andromache's famous tirade against its inhabitants. But it is also true that
Menelaus is none too heroic in *Orestes* either. But compared with Iago or Lady
Macbeth, he is a mild villain indeed. It seems safe to conclude that in general the
conflict in Greek Tragedy is not between people so much as within individuals.
It is that element which probably has given them such power over the modern
mind. For even when an ancient hero is doomed by fate, as Oedipus was, to
commit a crime, one sees him in the struggle against the inevitable. The outcries
against the gods, which are so characteristic of the speeches in Euripides, though
Prometheus on his rock does not hesitate to give his frank opinion of Zeus, are
again evidence that the tragic hero is made to feel himself caught in a situation
over which he has little control but in which he must make some decision, however futile. But the unhappy outcome always emerges from his decision. He
must choose and cannot choose well.

The tragedy of *Antigone* is the stock example of this. To us this drama is a
drama of the conscientious objector. The girl is faced with the choice of obeying
the law of the state or the law of the gods. If she obeys one law, she must perforce violate the other. In essence this choice is not different from that which
faces Orestes and Electra, for they too have to choose between two apparently
equal crimes. It is clear in the case of Antigone that she is free to choose, as her
sister is too, at least as free as Adam and Eve were. But she is not free to avoid
committing a crime. Moreover, though Creon in this play is far from being sympathetic to the modern reader, he is not the villain in the sense that he makes her

violate the law of the state. He meets a tragic fate too and the second half of the play is given over to that. There is no condemnation of his decree in this play; he is the king and he has issued a law and the law must be obeyed. It is true that burial rites may not seem very important to some modern sceptics, though there are plenty of religious people who would be horrified if they are not observed. The point is, however, not what we think of the special circumstances of the decree; it is rather the greater conflict within a conscience. It is easy enough to say flatly that civil disobedience is always wrong, but people who say that overlook the possibility of the law itself being wrong. Suppose that Antigone was living in our own time; what analogue could we find for her dilemma? We might choose the conflict between the religious law which is said to hold life sacred—though neither church nor state has ever held all life sacred—and statute law which commands one to kill. If a religious girl were asked by her brother who was trying to evade the draft to shelter him from the police, what should she do? If the answer is that she should dash to the telephone and notify the police to come and get him, then why do we condemn those children in Germany who were said to have denounced their anti-Nazi parents and brothers to the Gestapo? I hope that none of you will ever be put in such a situation, but we are not too far from it when we are asked to denounce our friends for supposed subversive activities. I remember the case of a French father who refused to give up two American aviators to the Germans even though his refusal he knew meant the slaughter of his innocent fourteen year old son. He made his choice—on what grounds I do not know—but he made it. I also recall the pleas of people charged with being collaborators that their collaboration bought the lives of their compatriots. But for that matter, one has only to go back to the story of St. Mary the Egyptian who sold her chastity in order to cross the river into Jerusalem. That there is a conflict between God and Caesar is surely nothing new. We resolve the conflict, as we usually resolve such problems, by closing our eyes to it. But the conflict is there nevertheless, unless we deny the rights of one law or the other. As Sophocles makes Antigone say,

> It was not God that gave me such commandments,
> Nor Justice, consorts of the Lords of Death,
> That ever laid on men such laws as these.
> Nor did I hold that in your human edicts
> Lay power to override the laws of God,
> Unwritten yet unshaken—laws that live
> Not from to-day, nor yet from yesterday,
> But always—though none knows how first made known.

What I wish to emphasize in these words is not merely Antigone's choice, but the inevitable tragedy of it. Here there is no way out, no manner of reasoning to what one might call a happy ending. Her death is no solution and even if she had been snatched up to Heaven by some god and put among the stars, the conflict would not have been resolved. When then we say that in some Greek tragedies we have situations presented, that is what we mean. We have first to admit that there are some problems which are insoluble, conflicts which cannot be reconciled. To protest is to wail over the insolubility of the problem of squaring the circle or doubling the cube. But this is precisely what is expected, paradoxically enough, in a logical universe. Reason rests, as we have suggested, on unproved premises. We have to choose our premises; we do not demonstrate them. We may choose them because of revelation, authority, faith, tradition, common-sense, what you will. But when they are chosen, certain things follow from them and when they are translated into action, the resultant acts cannot be reversed or modified. Perhaps that is why Antigone rejects her sister's attempt to share her guilt. It is she, Antigone, whose life is part and parcel of the deed known as the burial of Polyneices, and the consequent civil disobedience. How much of this was accepted overtly by Sophocles, I shall not pretend to say, but that it is there is clear enough. The very improbability of the stories lends support to this view. For the only way to make them probable is to humanize the characters, as Euripides is supposed to have done, and by that very process to lessen the tragic effect.

One sees this at work in such a tragedy as *Andromache*. In Euripides this is ostensibly the story of a mother's attempt to frustrate plots against her child's life, of the rivalry between a wife and a concubine, of the hatred between two states, Sparta and Athens, in fact, a confusion of conflicts from which scarcely any clear and single conflict can be untangled. The simplicity of *Antigone* has gone for the very reason that Euripides is beginning to see people as people, with all their jealousies, cowardice, and self-assertion. To a Greek perhaps the situation was different. The characters were historical, the story well known. The individuals may have emerged from the poetry as each upholding some moral principle, but to us they seem to be more real, more flesh and blood, and for that reason less significant morally than Antigone, Ismene, and Creon. The most one can do to clarify what goes on is to read into Hermione a woman's jealousy of her rival, and into Menelaus a father's interest in giving his daughter satisfaction, however ignoble her desires might be. The trick which Menelaus plays on Andromache is simply a melodramatic incident which displays the Spartans' treachery and nothing more. Andromache is given a speech in which she proclaims that her choice lies between buying her life with her child's death or his with hers. She exclaims against the unfairness of the choice in that it was not she who chose to be the slave and concubine of Neoptolemus, but the fortunes of war which put her in that position. The conflict which set *Antigone* in motion was a choice between two profound moral claims on the individual's conscience. In *Andromache* the conflict is that between two people. The history of this plot through Seneca to Racine would be well worth analysis, but in the time we have, we shall simply leap to Racine.

In the French writer's *Andromaque*, the situation is frankly accepted as an erotic duel. It is the psychology of love as a violent passion which pulls the strings. Whereas in Euripides the man in the case, Neoptolemus, does not even appear on the scene, in Racine he not only appears but becomes the pivot on which everything turns. He is in love with Andromache who is really faithful to the memory of Hector but who is supposed by her rival Hermione to be in love with Pyrrhus, that is Neoptolemus. Everybody misunderstands everybody else's motives, with the result that Hermione, for the sole purpose of revenging herself on Pyrrhus, promises to marry Orestes who is in love with her, if he will kill Pyrrhus. And then when he has killed him, she bursts into a magnificent and, it must be confessed psychologically true, tirade telling him that he should have known that she was driven to the idea by jealousy and that he should not have taken her seriously.

Ah! falloit-il en croire une amante insensée?
Ne devois-tu pas lire au fond de ma pensée?
Et ne voyois-tu pas, dans mes emportements,
Que mon coeur démentoit ma bouche à tous moments?
Quand je l'aurois voulu, falloit-il y souscrire?
N'as-tu pas dû cent fois te le faire redire?

This sort of thing is probably more to our taste than Euripides's drama, for our drama has become the conflict of persons, not of moral claims. The mythological status of the characters in the classical tragedy, the crystallization of their histories through tradition, made it next to impossible for a dramatist to introduce innovations of this type into his plays. They fell into a pattern established as a ritual. By drawing their characters down from the skies, the modern dramatist turned them into something resembling human beings.

We see the transformation almost completed in Shakespeare. It may be possible to interpret the plots of Shakespeare's tragedies as moral struggles, but I confess to never having seen such an interpretation which made much sense. Given the chivalric notion of honor and the need of revenging a father's death, I suppose that one can rewrite *Hamlet*, if one wishes, in the light of that concept. But what is one to make of *King Lear*, of *Julius Caesar*, of *Othello?* In all these cases it is the individual's personal psychology which determines the issue. Though the jealousy of Hermione in *Andromaque* seems to me to be more plausible than that of Othello, in both cases the individuals are victims of their own states of mind. There is nothing either in the situation or in any law of nature which compels them to act as they do. Granting that monsters such as Othello and Iago can exist, and your generation has grown accustomed to the existence of even worse psychological monsters, the emotional impact of their lines rests on their realism, an appearance heightened by the poetry. Now one can trace the history of the idea of personal psychology from Aristotle down and find that step by step it moves in the direction of giving more and more individuality to the person. Aristotle's *Nichomachean Ethics*, for instance, like his *Politics*, is based on the assumption that all men are alike—rational animals—though they may differ in their accidental traits. His pupil Theophrastus in the opening of his famous *Characters* raises the question "why it is that, while all Greece lies under the same sky and all the Greeks are educated alike, it has befallen us to have characters so variously constituted." His answer is that men fall into certain types or characters: The Flatterer, the Complaisant Man, the Surly Man, the Arrogant Man, the Ironical Man, and so on. The idea was backed up by the Humoralist School of Medicine which taught that a man's temperament was determined by the predominance of one of the four humors, from which we get the Sanguine man, the Melancholy man, the Choleric man, and the Phlegmatic man. This idea and its derivatives prevailed for centuries. The Horatian principle of consistency of character was accepted all through the Renaissance and we see it in satirical form in Molière's comedies of the Miser, the Hypocrite, the Misanthrope, the Hypochondriac, and I imagine, though I do not know for certain, that it is behind the *commedia dell'arte* with its set of stock characters all behaving in a ritualistic manner. I sometimes wonder whether the composition of the nineteenth century repertory companies, with their juvenile leads, their heavies, their comic figures, so faithfully reproduced in the English novel of the same period, did not arise out of the same idea. At any rate it is not until we come to Proust with his theory of the *intermittances du coeur* that the notion of consistency of character finally disappears. But naturally when this happens, behaviour becomes less explicable rationally, and the absurdity of behaviour in such writers as Cocteau—or perhaps even Gide—and later Sartre and the other existentialists, is a natural outcome of this more realistic view of human conduct.

The result of all this for tragedy is that whereas the tragic writer still sees tragedy as self-defeat, each self acts in its own way, and no motive is too absurd to be a real motive, a motive not merely real, but taken seriously by both audience and author. We get a glimpse of this in some bits of medieval Christian legend, such as that of the Jongleur of Notre Dame, where the motive of the juggler saves him though what he actually does is trivial. Thus both self-defeat and self-salvation come from within the individual himself. Hamlet, Lear, Othello, and their companions all bring about their own destruction, though aided and abetted by external circumstances—if a wife and friend can be called external. The human problem gradually becomes that of conquering the environment and of asserting one's superiority to all those forces which might end in one's annihilation. The importance of self-preservation, in the psychological sense of that term, has grown since the rise of popular government and the industrialization of production. For the threats to personal independence have also grown. We may submit to these forces of annihilation or we may fight against them. In our own country we have those who preach conformity to the general rule of living and those who struggle to find some way of saving the individual who is forced to live in a system which is becoming more and more corporate. Thus on the one hand we have the prophets who preach *esprit de corps*, school spirit, being one of the gang, dressing, eating, talking, believing, fighting, playing exactly as everyone else does, in short, being perfectly normal. The press, the radio, the advertising geniuses, of all sorts, spend their energies in homogenizing society. On the other hand, from Emerson and Thoreau down to William James, we have had our prophets who preach self-reliance, leadership, primacy, originality. If the former establish societies and clubs for all purposes, the latter set up fellowships and prizes for outstanding services or accomplishments. How a youngster ever succeeds in understanding the situation escapes one of my generation. If he strives for primacy, then he is not one of the boys; if he becomes one of the boys, then he must abandon those interests which the boys do not share. Clearly, if what I say makes sense, our dramas will involve the individual going down to defeat by submitting to the group or going down to defeat by fighting against the group. The main difference between our tragedies and those of the seventeenth century will be that our heroes sometimes gladly accept the premises of their ultimate defeat.

The clearest case of this sort of tragedy is the famous play of Arthur Miller, *Death of a Salesman*. This play was called according to its publishers,—"a usually well-informed source—" "one of the finest dramas in the whole range of the American theatre"; "something to make strong men weep and think," though whether the connection is causal or not we are not told; "so simple, central and terrible that the run of playwrights would neither care nor dare to attempt it . . . touched with the tragic sense of life"; "a poignant, shattering and devastating drama"; a play which "has majesty, sweep and shattering dramatic impact"; a play "in which all is right and nothing is wrong." But if I continue, the very accumulation of praise will become too comic to be borne. Now all this is supposed to say that *Death of a Salesman* roused the critics, usually pretty *blasés*, to a high pitch of enthusiasm. But perhaps the most telling comment on this drama was that of Mr. John Mason Brown, duly reprinted by the Book-of-the-Month Club, "Mr. Miller's play is a tragedy modern and personal, not classic and heroic." It is indeed modern, not merely in the chronological sense, but also in the cultural sense and it is personal, in that a human being, not a cause or a moral issue, is the centre of the tragedy. But the tragedy itself consists in the hero's glad acceptance of the conditions of life which will lead to his own annihilation.

These conditions are the competitive activities of commercial life. A salesman is presented as a man who, whether he believes that what he sells is worth selling or not, must nevertheless consider it his mission in life to sell it. He is a man, as one of the characters says, "way out there in the blue, riding on a smile and a shoeshine." His life becomes invested with an aura of romance and one is given to understand that perhaps the very triviality of the enterprise is what gives it its inherent value. For it is a life which of course is instrumental to the making of money for someone else; but for the salesman himself, it, like virtue, is its own reward. Where so many of the Greek heroes bewail their fate which entangles them in a web of disaster, Willy Loman, the hero of this piece, voices no complaints whatsoever. He is like a knight errant pursuing a goal whose importance he never stops to consider. In fact, he himself does not even consider the money he earns his reward. If a fellow is impressive and well liked, that is enough. Mr. Miller makes this crystal clear, this pathetic yearning to be popular, to win friends and influence people. Here is one of his most poignant comments on the situation, the ability of the American commercial hero to idealize a sordid job. And the catastrophe seems to consist in Willy's final waking up to the bitter fact that the only person whom he impresses and by whom he is well liked is his wife, to whom he has been unfaithful. His sons have turned their back on his ideal, his neighbors and relatives see through him, his employer discharges him now that his usefulness as a salesman is over. The shoeshine has worn off, the smile has become a set grimace—he is out in the blue on nothing and for nothing.

In this play the individual's personality is no longer his own creation; it is the fiction of the society in which he lives and works. It is no longer Willy Loman who has made himself, but forces over which he presumably has no control have done this job of creating a self for him. We are not told why he chose this life—we find him in it and the intimation, if not the overt assertion, of the play is that he has no choice. Even his son, Biff, who tries to escape, seems unable to. It was not of course an oracle which foretold this, no malignant deity, but just as Oedipus was wrecked by Apollo's decree and forced to commit crimes which he was deliberately trying to avoid committing, so Willy Loman is presented as a man whose destiny was planned by beings remote from his wishes and ideas. One never knows how far an author means to extend the theme of his play and it may be unfair to Mr. Miller to say that this one is a comment on the totality of our civilization. But one rather imagines that the enthusiastic comments of the critics arose from their feeling that it was a picture typical of our "American way of life." Judging from the propaganda in the press and on the radio, there is reason to believe that the salesman is the typical American. "To sell" has become a verb whose object may now be not merely consumer goods in the literal sense of the word, but also ideas and people. One sells a religious creed, a philosophic theory, oneself. It would be hopelessly superficial to say that one makes the sale simply for the sake of the money which one receives in exchange. If that were true, there might be at least some common-sense in it. On the contrary, one sells an idea, one sells oneself for the sheer love of selling. This may have become the one mode of expressing our will to power which is left to us. We have reached the end of the dialectical road; or as the popular phrase has it, we have come full circle. For once again, we are faced with the possibility of tragedy in the sense in which *Antigone* is tragic. Whatever choice she makes will lead to defeat. If Willy Loman had refused to sell, he would have been a failure in the eyes of American society; if he chose to sell, as he did, he must also end a worn-out heap of protoplasm muttering the gibberish of ideals which have no realization.

The love of horror seems essential to the Western soul. The myths of Greece are full of it; the stories of martyrdom and self-immolation color the whole of Christian literature; when the intellectuals of Europe in the eighteenth century went rationalistic, they developed the Gothic novel, the passion for ruins, the interest in decay; the Romantic movement, as we find it in Hugo, Poe, and Hoffmann meandered through the same old ruined castles inhabited by ghosts and other monsters; the later nineteenth century and the twentieth developed the novel of crime and detection; and we are now faced with a new crop of horror in the work of the Existentialists. Meanwhile, the non-literary world does its best to satisfy our craving for horror by doing horrible things: wars on a scale never before dreamt of, weapons which may well exterminate the whole race, genocide, torture, political persecution and, as far as our own country is concerned, crime on a gigantic scale which seems to have become a sport, engaged in for its own sake. We live in a world of horror and in our spare moments we amuse ourselves by reading about it. At the same time, organized religion flourishes as it has never flourished before, charitable foundations give away millions to fight disease, crime, and ignorance and we delude ourselves into thinking that never has man enjoyed a higher standard of living. And if the height of our standard of living is measured by our ability to sit back in comfort with a bottle of Coca-Cola by our sides watching television make clear the venality of our legislators and the timidity of our leaders, then it is very high indeed. But what else can we expect of a society in which salesmanship is the goal of every man's ambition? The tragedy of Willy Loman may be ignoble as compared to that of Prometheus or Antigone; we might nevertheless pause and ask ourselves whether in essence it is not the tragedy of every one of us, whether we know it or not.

Heroes and the
Way of Compromise*

Henry A. Myers

In a brief and pointed imaginary conversation between Frederick the Great and the utopian pacifists of his own time, William James once epitomized the almost comic clash between the attitude of the hero and that of the extreme advocates of moderation. "'Dogs, would you live forever?' shouted Frederick the Great. 'Yes,' say our utopians, 'let us live forever, and raise our level gradually.'"

History in the making today offers to the student of human affairs another chapter, already half-written, in the ancient conflict between extremism and moderation. We are perhaps too close to our world to determine the prime cause, if indeed there be one only, of its division into warring camps. One clue, however, is to be found in the events leading up to World War II: the worship of half-truths which made some peoples seek the heroic life as a national ideal while others sought to live by compromise alone.

Frederick, in spite of his fierce scorn, must have been clever enough to see how much he owed to the moderate men of his own time, who served him as foils. Looking back on the events of the past thirty years, we can see that our own Fredericks owed much of their success in enthralling the spirit of great nations to the fortune which made them loom large against a pale background of peoples who seemed to have lost the courage to face the fact that a willingness to die is sometimes the price of a life worth the living. The hero is always dramatic; the moderate is colorless by contrast, and especially so when he loudly proclaims his revulsion from every form of the heroic spirit.

What happens to a world in which the lines are sharply drawn between extremists and moderate men? Part of the answer is already written. First, the extremist forces his way of life upon his fellows. In the pursuit of his goal, whatever it may be, life is a bright coin which he is willing, at any moment, to exchange for glorious death; he scorns those who believe that a long and peaceful life is the only reasonable goal. In dealing with him, moderate men discover that compromise is not true compromise, but appeasement. Those who make this discovery have a choice between two equally extreme courses of action. Either they may themselves take heroic measures against the fanatic who will not compromise or they may persist in the error of appeasement until it becomes nihil-

* Henry A. Myers, "Heroes and the Way of Compromise," from *Tragedy: A View of Life* (Cornell University Press, 1956). Originally appeared in Milton Konvitz and Arthur Murphy: *Essays in Political Theory*. Copyright © 1948 by Cornell University. Reprinted by permission of Cornell University Press.

ism, the denial of the heroic in life which men sometimes pay for by losing their freedom and even their lives.

Living witnesses to this process, all the great nations were committed during World War II to the heroic way of life. Each was determined to fight on to victory or to death. Some sincerely believed that the moderate way of compromise is the only true way for men and for nations; but first, before they could think of ideal procedures, there was a job to be done, someone to be blotted out, someone with whom compromise was impossible.

After World War II, what? Freed from the menace of some of the new Fredericks, the moderates will presumably go back to the business of raising their level gradually. For some time they will have a new respect for *some* heroes, for those who successfully led them against the would-be world conquerors; but this new respect may easily vanish in the inevitable reaction against "blood, sweat, and tears." Will our utopians increase the power and menace of the remaining Caesars by again insisting that the way of compromise is always the best way of life?

We cannot correct the past mistakes which brought Caesarism into our world. The generation which turned moderation itself into a new form of extremism by refusing to find a place in their scheme of things for the heroic human spirit has done its work. But it is never too late to bring the lessons of experience to bear upon the future. A better understanding of human nature may yet save us from repeating old mistakes.

II

Dramatic poetry is a wonderful storehouse of the lessons of experience and possibly the best source of information concerning heroes and the heroic spirit. By an apparent paradox of intellectual history, the doctrine of the Superman, which exalts intensity of experience, and the philosophy of moderation, which aims chiefly at a long and complete life, were both derived from a study of the tragic hero. In the *Poetics* Aristotle described the extremism of the tragic hero as an error, a failure to find the moderate way, which causes his downfall. In *The Birth of Tragedy* Nietzsche concluded that only as an aesthetic phenomenon is life eternally justified, a conclusion which he expanded in his later writings into the view that life is worth the living only for the Superman, only for the tragic hero who lives dangerously, who risks all to gain all, who touches the heights and depths of experience.

The Birth of Tragedy was Nietzsche's first book. In tragedy he discovered the apparent explanation of his youthful admiration for Richard Wagner's heroic music; from a study of tragedy he derived the conclusions that have strongly influenced so many movements in modern society, movements ranging in intensity from the violence and brutality of the Nazi party to the relatively mild "strenuous life" advocated by Theodore Roosevelt.

According to his own account, Nietzsche at first undertook his study of tragedy to answer a question which seemed more likely to interest the scholars and philologists among whom he moved than to unsettle the world of affairs. Did their interest in tragedy indicate that the Greeks were a pessimistic or decadent people? Nietzsche decided, on the contrary, that tragedy represents the highest degree of affirmation and acceptance of life. In the years which saw the production of the great Attic tragedies the Greeks were a strong people, capable of facing reality at its worst without flinching.

In seeking the answer to his question Nietzsche contracted a raging fever of hero worship. The question of Greek pessimism widened out in his mind into the more important question of whether life is worth living. Most spectators of a great tragedy leave with a sense of reconciliation, with the feeling that life, though terrible, is just. On this point Nietzsche made an important reservation. Life is worth living, he decided, only for the extremist, only for the hero who reaches the heights and depths of feelings. Upon completing his study of tragedy, the future prophet of the Superman was prepared with the outlines of his message. Do you wish to make life worth living? Then love your fate; live dangerously and on the heights; be an extremist, a hero, a superman.

Nietzsche was fascinated by the intensity of the hero's experience, but Aristotle was more deeply impressed by its brevity. The simple fact revealed by tragedy is that heroes always live dangerously and usually do not live long. A comparison of Aristotle's remarks on the tragic hero in the *Poetics* with his theory of the golden mean in the *Nichomachean Ethics* shows the important influence of his study of dramatic poetry on his doctrine of moderation. Since heroes usually do not live long, the extremism which brings about their end is an error of judgment, a tragic failure in conduct. It is an error and a failure because happiness is not to be found in intensity of feeling but only in full self-realization, which requires a long and complete life. "For one swallow does not make a summer, nor does one day; and so too one day, or a short time, does not make a man blessed and happy." Virtue is the very opposite of the error of the tragic hero; it lies in the habit of choosing a mean between extremes, in the moderation which usually secures length of life.

Individual temperament is probably the only explanation for the paradoxical manner in which Aristotle and Nietzsche drew opposite conclusions from the same evidence. Quite clearly, one placed the highest value on the duration and completeness of experience, and the other placed it on intensity. The tragic hero, whose experience is intense, narrow, and brief, is a failure in the eyes of Aristotle and the ideal man in the eyes of Nietzsche.

The opposition between the cult of hero worship, which leads to Caesarism, and the philosophy of moderation, when it is carried to the extreme of nihilism, turns on the question of which quality of experience—intensity or duration—is more desirable. Aristotle himself never carried his doctrine of moderation to the extreme of nihilism. At the risk of inconsistency, he admitted that the virtuous man will sometimes prefer a swallow to a summer: "It is true of the good man too that he does many acts for the sake of his friends and his country, and if necessary dies for them . . . since he would prefer a short period of intense pleasure to a long one of mild enjoyment, a twelve-month of noble life to many years of humdrum existence, and one great and noble action to many trivial ones." The whole truth about human nature, as an answer to this question, can be derived from the same evidence from which the contradictory half-truths of hero worship and nihilism have been derived.

III

The tragic hero has enough in common with other men to make his fate significant to them, and at the same time is unusual enough to excite and hold their interest. His difference, which is the secret of his dramatic interest, is his intensity, which is first manifest in his unyielding purpose. The first quality which distinguishes the hero is the will to do or die, the uncompromising spirit which makes him pay any price, even life itself, for his object. It is this quality which Wolfe at Quebec has in common with Marlowe's Tamburlaine, which Stonewall Jackson shares with Melville's Captain Ahab. In itself it is without moral significance, for the unyielding hero may be either a saint or a sinner in the eyes of the spectator. But unyielding character is the spring from which heroic and dramatic actions flow.

The hero's attitude toward life is that of Ahab toward the whale; not even the gods can swerve him from his purpose. "Over unsounded gorges, through the rifled hearts of mountains, under torrents' beds, unerringly I rush! Naught's an obstacle, naught's an angle to the iron way!" Such intensity demands concentration, and Ahab's purpose is centered on a single object, Moby Dick. "Ay, ay!" he cries, "and I'll chase him round Good Hope, and round the Horn, and round the Norway Maelstrom, and round perdition's flames before I give him up." And so it always is with heroes: each has his favorite phantom, always something specific, never an abstraction. The hero does not die for love, or for power, or for success, or for revenge: he dies for Juliet, or for Abbie, or for Rautendelein, or for Desdemona; he dies to be Duncan's successor or for "infinite riches in a little room"; he dies to climb the tower that he has built. The hero is indeed always a monomaniac to some extent, but he is different from his fellow men only in degree, not in kind, only in the intensity with which he pursues his object.

In life and in drama the heroic is marked by an uncompromising will; in both, moreover, the difference between the simplest and the greatest is that the greatest brings the widest range of feeling and the highest intellectual power to bear upon his inflexible purpose. Such is the difference between Grant in the Wilderness and Lincoln in the White House, between Tamburlaine and Hamlet. Grant's determination to fight it out on the line is as firm as Lincoln's will to carry through the war, but Lincoln adds to fundamental determination an intellectual power made manifest in his brooding on the meaning of events, as in the Gettysburg and Second Inaugural addresses, and a wide range of feeling which carries him into the hearts of all the actors in the national tragedy. His acts of kindness to delinquent soldiers, his concern for the point of view of his opponents, his letter to Mrs. Bixby—make more pointed, more heroic, more valuable his determination to save the Union. We rightly value the heroic according to its cost to the hero; and a Hamlet, to whom the cost is so great as to make him seem at times weak in will, displays a richer heroism in one moment of tortured struggle than can be found in all the thoughtless, insensate fury of a Tamburlaine.

IV

Such is the nature of the hero; what are its inevitable consequences? If we may trust the testimony of all serious drama, the outstanding consequence is that the hero lives intensely but not long. Life is the price we must all pay for experience; most of us dole it out in little sums over a long period of time; the hero gladly pays in a lump sum.

A more profoundly significant consequence is that the hero always gets what he wants—and always pays the full price. Oedipus finds the unknown murderer, at a cost; Wolfe takes Quebec, but falls in the moment of victory; Ahab throws the harpoon, and dies; Romeo comes back to Juliet, in death. The hero can have anything he wants, for a price; but not even a hero can get something for nothing.

Drama reveals these consequences in many ways—by showing that the hero falls as far as he rises or that he is brought down by the very forces which bring· him to the top. The great turn of the wheel of fortune which carries the hero to the extremes of joy and grief, often in one moment of dazzling intensity, is the dramatic symbol of the endless little ups and downs, the little sorrows and joys, of ordinary men. The hero's great moment contains within itself rise and fall, fortune and misfortune, triumph and disaster. As Ahab at last faces the white whale alone, he cries: "Oh, now I feel my topmost greatness lies in my topmost grief." Othello's fate is wonderfully balanced in the moment of his discovery of Desdemona's innocence. For him this discovery means sheer exaltation; and yet this exaltation must come to him balanced by the horror of his own crime. Joy and sorrow are balanced with a terrible nicety, that wonderful balance which Edgar in *King Lear* notes in speaking of the death of his father:

> his flaw'd heart,—
> Alack, too weak the conflict to support!—
> 'Twixt two extremes of passion, joy and grief,
> Burst smilingly.

All these qualities suit the hero to the purposes and necessities of dramatic poetry. Some attempts have been made to dispense with the hero in serious drama. Maeterlinck says in a famous essay on tragedy:

> I have grown to believe that an old man, seated in his armchair, waiting patiently, with his lamp beside him . . . I have grown to believe that he, motionless as he is, does yet live in reality a deeper, more human, and more universal life than the lover who strangles his mistress, the captain who conquers in battle, or "the husband who avenges his honor."

That the old man is as tragic as the hero, no one should question: he too has his moments; he too pays for what he gets. If it were not so, if he were not tragic in this sense, then the hero of tragic drama could have no universal significance. The trouble with the old man in the armchair is that he is tragic but not dramatic. His life has meaning but lacks every other dramatic quality; intensity, suspense, surprise, reversal, heightened diction, power to excite basic feelings—all are missing. When we think of the tragic in terms of the two-sided nature of feeling which is the basis of the common destiny of men, one man is as good an illustration as another, but only the intense hero makes drama possible, and makes it possible for it to end within two hours.

After we have looked at enough heroes, we can readily understand Aristotle's reaction to their way of life. He sees the hero for what he is, if the ultimate standard of conduct is length and completeness of life: a man not "eminently good and just, yet whose misfortune is brought about not by vice or depravity, but by some error or frailty." No doubt this tragic flaw is simply the essential nature of the hero—his extremism. No hero ever chose the golden mean in a critical moment; no hero would ever sacrifice his purpose or any part of the "iron way" to the dictates of the kind of reason and virtue which bring length of life.

V

Great drama itself is not an adverse criticism of the way of heroes. Only confirmed Aristotelians believe that it is. Through his hero the dramatist is enabled

to present the essence of life; and from the character of the hero and his fate we
may draw our own conclusions. One famous exception is Ibsen's *Brand*, which
was deliberately intended to be an attack on the heroic way of life. Brand, the
fanatic priest, demands of all those about him, of his family and of his parishion-
ers, the same heroic devotion to God and negation of the world which he himself
seeks to practice. These demands result ultimately in the ruin of his family, the
revolt of his flock, and his own death. But Ibsen is able to make the case neither
better nor worse for the hero than have all great tragedies. Particularly interesting about the play, however, is what Ibsen, as a great dramatist, thought about
the nature of the hero. This is revealed in two phrases, one positive, the other
negative. "All or nothing," says Brand again and again to his followers in demanding their devotion. And warning them ever and again of evil, he repeats:
"The devil is compromise."

From *Brand* we might conclude that Ibsen ascribed the woes of mankind to
the iron way of heroes. But in *Peer Gynt*, his poetic satire on the Norwegian
character, he wrote an even more impressive criticism of the way of compromise. The play was written out of the depths of Ibsen's indignation with Norway
for her failure to ally herself with Denmark in the Danish-Prussian war. Peer
Gynt is the opposite of Brand. "Enough," is his motto, not "all or nothing." His
method is to go around obstacles and to abandon projects, ideals, and objectives
when they seem to demand the ultimate risk. Since, in following this method, he
wanders over the face of the earth, he seems to have led a richer life than Brand,
who fights it out with the devil of compromise within the narrow confines of his
parish. In the end, however, Peer is revealed as one who stands for nothing, a
man without principles or character, a nonentity. Like the objects of Thoreau's
pity, he has frittered away his life in detail. One could say to him, as to the little
mouse who was granted his wish to have wings: "You're nothing but a nothing;
you're not a thing at all."

All drama reminds us that it is a serious mistake to underestimate the power
of the heroic or to assume that people see only the unpleasant consequences of
the way of heroes and none of its compensations. The reverse is more often true.
"Hero worship" is a familiar term, but there is no similar familiar term to denote
reverence for the moderate man. Great drama excites not only pity and terror,
but also awe and admiration, and other feelings that lie so deep that we cannot
easily name them. Most of the power of the dramatic to excite deep feeling rests
in the hero. In him we see ourselves on a larger scale, often ourselves as we
should like to be, for who would not like to be firmer of purpose, more intent intellectually, capable of deeper feeling? While we hunger for more of life, we
cannot resist the appeal of the hero's intensity. We necessarily have our moments
when Aristotle's golden mean seems to be indeed a kind of "golden meanness," a
doctrine for the half-hearted who shrink from the farther reaches of experience,
a prescription for a long life and a dull one, a guiding principle for a world of
old men dozing in armchairs.

VI

Powerful indeed is hero worship. If drama were possible only in the form of
tragic poetry, one might agree with Plato in ruling poets out of the ideal state.
Tragedy by itself is an incomplete picture of life; since it presents only heroes to
us, it needs comedy as an antidote to the unbridled hero worship which at times

it might otherwise cause. Comedy, which teaches us to know a fool when we see one, teaches us also that not any fool can be a hero. The ordinary man, taking his stand on a trivial issue in his efforts to ape the hero, succeeds in being merely sullen. Or if he is, like Nietzsche, a gentle and serious young scholar, an intuitive but humorless philologist, too long fed on a diet of tragic poetry and Wagnerian music, he goes forth as a prophet to trouble the world with dreams of life aesthetically justified by a race of tragic heroes and to bring himself to madness.

To go with Oedipus, we need the Dionysos of *The Frogs*; to go with Hamlet, we need Falstaff; to go with the Cid, we need Orgon. A main effect of *The Frogs* is to show what happens to Dionysos, a sturdy but moderate middle-class soul who sets out to play the part of Hercules, a hero. If the point sinks in, we think twice before aping the way of heroes. As for Falstaff—he is neither a hero nor a fool: he knows how his kind of person should behave on a battlefield; and so, without shame, he lies down to play dead until the heroes have done their work. Orgon *is* a fool, who would never escape the machinations of Tartuffe were it not for the intervention of the king's officer. His folly, which takes the form of worship of the extreme forms of piety, makes him an ideal dupe for a hypocrite.

We may thank the comic spirit for deflating the pseudoheroic in life, and enlist it always in our service against the triumph of the simplest kind of hero, who has intensity of purpose without a correspondingly great capacity for thought and feeling. Such heroes, who are always without humor themselves, flourish in the absence of laughter. Meredith long ago pointed out that the comic spirit is an enemy of the sentimental, of the puritanical, and of the bacchanalian: it is even more strongly the sworn foe of the pseudoheroic and of the kind of hero whose brutality is the result of a will unguided by thought and feeling.

VII

Between great science, which seeks to show us *nature as it is*, caring nothing for what *it should be*, and great poetry, which has always shown us *human nature as it is*, caring nothing for what the reader thinks *it should be*, there can be no quarrel. But science in its beginnings had to contend with the pretensions of poets in the realm of nature; and today men neglect the solid realities of poetry for the vaporings of rhapsodists, who rest their dreams of progress toward Utopia upon their faith in the ability of science to do the impossible. It pleases us to smile at the pretensions of the philosopher-poet, Heraclitus, who thought that a new sun is born each day in the heavens. We see the folly of trying to make poetry do the work of mathematics. But the rhapsodists of our world are not poets who seek to take over the province of science; rather they are the pseudo scientists, who either in ignorance of or in defiance of the storehouse of wisdom to be found in poetry, would persuade us that the changes which man has been able to effect in his environment foreshadow even more wonderful changes in human nature itself. We have much to learn from both science and poetry. Science has taught us that the same old sun rises daily; the ancient wisdom of poetry is that it shines, and will always shine, upon the same old race of men—upon moderate men, heroes, and fools alike.

On one point Nietzsche was truly inspired: he saw that there is no place in a culture for tragic poetry once men have convinced themselves that they can change the basic conditions of their lives. For tragic poetry steels us to face evil as an inevitable aspect of experience; and it has no place in our culture if we believe that science and technology can free us from evil. Tragic poetry teaches us that each man pursues his own specific good, and that all too often the desire of two or more men for the same object makes conflict a brute fact in human affairs. Of what use is tragic poetry if we are bemused by the Socratic dream of a universal good acceptable to all and sharable by all? Tragic poetry teaches us that fanatics who seek an absolute good for mankind bring down upon men, by an inevitable recoil, their deepest sufferings. Of what use is tragic poetry, if madmen, lusting for personal power, convince us that paradise on earth will be possible once we have submitted ourselves to their wills?

This is the ancient wisdom of poetry which history today confirms: human nature is unchanging, and heroes, fools, and moderate men are always with us. Each of us, indeed, may be fated to play all of these roles in turn, and sometimes more than one role at once. There is often a comic view of even the admirable hero: the Socrates of *The Clouds*, snub-nosed, bald, homely as a gargoyle, absent-minded and absurd in his reasoning, is based upon life, as is the Socrates of the Dialogues. The world has decided that Plato has given us the truer measure of the man, but we should not forget the other portrait. Such twin portraits are often possible. When Rostand sought to follow Hugo's injunction to create heroes who would exhibit the contrast of the sublime and grotesque to be found in life itself, he wrote *Cyrano de Bergerac*, calling it a "heroic comedy" in order to point out that the heroic and the comic can in unusual instances go hand in hand. Cyrano, who says that he seeks "to be always admirable in all things," is a hero to outdo the ordinary hero, who is extreme in one thing only. "Everything to excess," a principle that is fantastic yet heroic, guides Cyrano's every act. When he fights, he fights a hundred men; when he is generous, he gives away all his money; when he is witty, he composes a ballade while fighting a duel. Spectators are so carried away by a blend of laughter and admiration that at the end no one can say which symbol is truer to the man, the grotesque, huge nose which makes him comic in appearance or the heroic plume which he wears in his hat, carrying it in death still unsmirched.

VIII

Are all men likely ever to agree that either intensity or duration is the higher value in experience? Not until the past is a completely false guide to the future; not until tragic poetry is completely out of touch with human nature. Since we have no grounds on which to predict the coming of a new kind of man, except the say-so of those romantic utopians who mistake science for magic, we must continue to think in terms of men as they are. In a world in which the fanatical extremist is a hardy perennial, always to be reckoned with, we must fortify ourselves with wisdom for the moment when our turn may come to play, as best we can, the part of heroes.

Since most men prefer a long life even at the expense of stretches of dullness, the Aristotelian golden mean points to the sensible course for men and nations most of the time. But if only one issue in a lifetime compels the moderate man to take a heroic stand, that is the one moment that fixes his place in history as either a man or a nonentity.

The trick is to know the right time and the right issue. No rule is possible.

The simple hero is driven on by inflexible character. The fool mistakes the time and is merely sullen over trifles.

The moment when moderate men take a stand is always grave, but it is not a time for despair. All is not lost. What is lost is the delusion that men can live by compromise alone. This delusion is an empty and negative form of extremism. It is nihilism—the heroic negation of the heroic in life. If we were to follow it consistently, we should become zeroes and tempt others to take our places. The world of human nature abhors a vacuum. When some men shrink altogether from the heroic, others are tempted to use it in its worst form.

Finally, in order to act wisely we must free ourselves from the half-truths designed to prove that the justice of our individual fate depends upon our choice between moderation and heroic action. All universal meaning in tragic poetry depends upon our recognition that in respect to justice the fate of the tragic hero is the same as that of the moderate man. Nietzsche was wrong in assuming that life can be justified only by living intensely. On the other hand, it is the tender sentimentalist, never the hero himself, who shrinks from the grand reversals which turn life into drama and history; and Aristotle was right in recognizing the compensations of heroic deeds, even if that recognition does invalidate his general criticism of the tragic hero. The Ahabs and Lincolns, the Cordelias and Antigones, accept their fate because they know its inner reality, the exaltation which accompanies suffering or dying for principles. The death of the hero is an affirmation of the unalterable conditions of life, a memorable symbol for multitudes who show their own acceptance by living.

There is justice in life for both the hero and the moderate man. The very surface of events points to it. What the hero gains in intensity, he usually loses in duration. What the moderate man gains in duration, he usually loses in intensity. But there is a deeper reality which unites heroes and moderate men in a common destiny. Both are subject to the fixed conditions whereby sorrow is the price of joy. Through the two-sided nature of human feeling, with its poles of good and evil, each pays for what he gets. The hero takes all, gives all, in one grand moment. The moderate man pays a little, lives to doze in his chair, and pays a little more. The choice between intensity and duration cannot upset the just equation whereby men pay with their lives for experience.

The Christian Tragic Hero: Contrasting Captain Ahab's Doom and Its Classic Greek Prototype*

W. H. Auden

Moby Dick is at once an heroic epic like the *Iliad*, an heroic tragedy like the *Oresteia*, an heroic quest like the legend of the *Golden Fleece*, and an allegorical religious quest like *Pilgrim's Progress;* it is also a nineteenth century American novel. Even if it were not the great book it is, it would therefore be of unusual interest to the critic who would compare the values believed in and the attitudes held at different stages in Western civilization. I propose in this article to consider only one of them, the concept of the Tragic Hero in Greece and in Christendom. Most of the characteristics one observes in Melville's hero can also be seen in, say, the heroes of Shakespeare's tragedies, but Melville's choral asides make them more explicit in his own case.

To sum up in advance, the conclusions I shall try to demonstrate are these: first, Greek tragedy is the tragedy of necessity; i.e., the feeling aroused in the spectator is "What a pity it had to be this way"; Christian tragedy is the tragedy of possibility, "What a pity it was this way when it might have been otherwise"; secondly, the hubris which is the flaw in the Greek hero's character is the illusion of a man who knows himself strong and believes that nothing can shake that strength, while the corresponding Christian sin of Pride is the illusion of a man who knows himself weak but believes he can by his own efforts transcend that weakness and become strong.

In using the term Christian I am not trying to suggest that Melville or Shakespeare or any other author necessarily believed the Christian dogmas, but that their conception of man's nature is, historically, derived from them.

As an example of Greek tragedy let us take *Oedipus Rex*. As a young man, Oedipus learns from a prophecy that he is fated to murder his father and marry his mother. Believing that his foster parents are his real parents he leaves Carthage [*sic*]. He meets an old man on the road; they quarrel about who shall give way to the other, and Oedipus kills him. He comes to Thebes, saves it from a

* W. H. Auden, "The Christian Tragic Hero," from *The New York Times Book Review*, December 16, 1945, pp. 1, 21.

monster, and is rewarded by the hand of its Queen, Jocasta. Thebes is stricken with plague, and the Oracle declares the cause to be the undetected presence of a criminal. Oedipus undertakes an investigation and discovers that the criminal is himself. In expiation of his crime he puts out his eyes, and Jocasta hangs herself.

A modern reader, accustomed to the tragedy of possibility, instinctively asks, "Where and when did he make the wrong choice?" and as instinctively answers, "He should not have listened to the prophecy in the first place, or, having done so, then he should never have struck the old man or anyone else and should never have married Jocasta or anyone else." But such thoughts would never have occurred to Sophocles or his audience. Macbeth and Captain Ahab are wrong to listen to the prophecies about them, because they are equivocal, and each reads into his a possibility he is wrong to desire; the prophecy Oedipus hears is not only unequivocal but something he is right to wish to avoid. When he kills the old man he feels no guilt, neither is he expected to feel any, and when he marries Jocasta there is nothing the matter with the relation as such. It is only when it turns out that, as a matter of fact, the former was his father and the latter is his mother that guilt begins.

The tragedy is that what had to happen happened, and if one asks what was wrong with Oedipus, that such a terrible fate should be assigned to him, one can only say that it is a punishment for a hubris which was necessarily his before he learnt of the prophecy at all; i.e., had he not had such a character, the prophecy would never have been made.

Other Greek heroes are faced with the tragic choice between two evils: Agamemnon must either sacrifice his daughter or fail in his duty to the Greek Army; Antigone must be false either to her loyalty to her brother or to her loyalty to her city.

The tragic situation, of learning that one is a criminal or of being forced to become one, is not created by the flaw in the hero's character, but is sent him by the gods as a punishment for having such a flaw.

The pessimistic conclusion that underlies Greek tragedy seems to be this: that if one is a hero, i.e., an exceptional individual, one must be guilty of hubris and be punished by a tragic fate; the only alternative and not one a person can choose for himself is to be a member of the chorus, i.e., one of the average mass; to be both exceptional and good is impossible.

How does "Moby Dick" compare with this?

The hero, Captain Ahab, far from being exceptionally fortunate, is at the beginning, what in a Greek tragedy he could only be at the end, exceptionally unfortunate. He is already the victim of what the modern newspaper, which is Greek in this respect, would call a tragedy; a whale has bitten off his leg: What to the Greeks could only have been a punishment for sin is here a temptation to sin, an opportunity to choose; by making the wrong choice and continuing to make it, Ahab punishes himself. To say that a character is tempted means that it is confronted by possibility, that it is not a fixed state but a process of becoming: the possibilities are not infinite; i.e., Ahab cannot become Starbuck or Pip or Ishmael or anyone else except Ahab, but the possibilities are eternal; the past is irrevocable but always redeemable now.

Thus we can at every moment answer the question, "What should Ahab do now?" Before the story opens he has suffered and made his first wrong choice. He was not wrong to make Moby Dick into a symbol of all the inexplicable suf-

fering in the world; on the contrary, the capacity to see the universal in the particular is the mark of human greatness, and it is only Flask, the Philistine trim-
mer, who says, "A whale is only a whale"; he was wrong, however, to insist on
his own explanation, that the motive behind the whale's act and behind all suffering is personal malevolence. Once he has done so, he can still be saved, but he
has made his salvation a much harder task, for he is now required to forgive the
whale personally, in contrast, for instance, to Captain Boomer, who, like Ahab,
has been deprived of a limb by Moby Dick, but in his pragmatic English way explains the whale's ferocity as mere clumsiness which is easier to forgive than
malice.

In Greek tragedy are two kinds of characters, the exceptional hero and the
average chorus, and neither can become the other; in Christian tragedy there is
not only an infinite variety of possible characters, varying all the way from
Ahab, the captain, who defiantly insists on being absolutely unique, down to Pip,
the cabin boy, who is too afraid to claim even his own name, but overshadowing
them all is the possibility of each becoming both exceptional and good; this ultimate possibility for hero and chorus alike is stated in Father Mapple's sermon,
and it is to become a saint—i.e., the individual who of his own free will surrenders his will to the will of God. In this surrender he does not become a ventrilo-
quist's doll, for the God who acts through him can only do so by his consent;
there always remain two wills, and the saint, therefore (unlike the late Greek
conception of the undramatic Sage who is good by necessity because he knows),
never ceases to be tempted to obey his own desires.

Of this possibility Ahab's career is at every point a negative parody.

The saint does not ask to be one, he is called to become one, and assents to
the call. The outward sign that Ahab is so called, is the suffering which is suddenly intruded into his life. What he is called to become, we do not, of course,
know for certain—all we know for certain is that he rejected it—but we can
guess that he was called to give up hunting whales—i.e., the normal cannibalistic
life of this world, a life which is permitted, for instance, to Queequeg (who,
though sinless, is not a saint, but the innocent man before the fall) but no longer
to Ahab once he has been made uniquely conscious of the suffering it inflicts. Of
the others, less is required: of Starbuck that he face evil instead of superstitiously
avoiding it, of Stubb that he face his fears instead of whistling in the dark; but of
Ahab alone is required, because he alone has the necessary heroic passion, to become a real and not a merely respectable Quaker.

Ahab is not deaf; he hears the call and refuses it with all the passion with
which he might have accepted it; like the saint he wills one thing—to kill Moby
Dick. For this he leaves his wife and child; for this his first act in the book is to
throw away his pipe, his last physical addiction, his last relation with the element
of earth; for this he destroys the ship's quadrant, its relation to the element of air
so that the Pequod can only know the universe through compass and line in
terms of the dualistic antagonism of fire and water.

The saint, knowing his will to be weak, may express his external resolve by a
temporal or bodily ritual act, but his vow and his act concern his own will alone.
Ahab attempts to use ritual as a magical means of compelling the wills of others,
as when he forces the crew to swear on their harpoons, and finally even to compel lifeless things, as when he baptizes a harpoon itself.

Just as the saint never ceases to be tempted to forsake his calling, so, vice
versa, Ahab is never free from the possibility of renouncing his refusal. Divine

grace offers itself, now in the nostalgic beauty of fine weather, now as Gabriel, the mad idolater of the whale, an unlovely reflection of himself, and finally, in its strongest and least disguised form, as the cry for help of a friend in distress when the Pequod meets the Rachel, and it is only after he has refused this last offer that his doom becomes necessary. Melville portrays this decisive change with great subtlety. For it is at this point that Ahab places the idiot Pip in his cabin and, in a grotesque parody of the saint as the servant of servants, takes for himself the humble position of lookout on the mast which is the negative image of the martyr's cross. Instead of gaining a martyr's crown, however, his hat, the badge of his authority, is snatched from his head by the Jovian eagle, and from this moment Fedallah, the slave, the projection of Ahab's will, seems suddenly to have taken charge of his creator, or rather his summoner. Fedallah is clearly intended by Melville, I think, to represent the demonic, i.e., that which (unlike Ahab, who is tempted by suffering) tempts itself and denies for the sake of denying, and about which, therefore, nothing historic can be said; we are only told his religion.

So Ahab, refusing life, goes unrepentant, like all of Shakespeare's tragic heroes, to the unnecessary death he has chosen, dragging with him all his companions, and the only survivor is, as in Greek tragedy, the Chorus, the spectator, Ishmael. But Ishmael is not, like the Greek Chorus, the eternal average man, for he isn't a character at all. To be a character one must will and act, and Ishmael has no will, only consciousness; he does not act, he only knows, and what he knows is good *and* evil, i.e., possibility. He cannot die because he has not yet begun to live, and he ends the book as a baby, reborn from the sea in Queequeg's coffin, thrust back into life as an orphan with his first choice still to make.

Tragedy and the Common Man*

Arthur Miller

In this age few tragedies are written. It has often been held that the lack is due to a paucity of heroes among us, or else that modern man has had the blood drawn out of his organs of belief by the skepticism of science, and the heroic attack on life cannot feed on an attitude of reserve and circumspection. For one reason or another, we are often held to be below tragedy—or tragedy above us. The inevitable conclusion is, of course, that the tragic mode is archaic, fit only for the very highly placed, the kings or the kingly, and where this admission is not made in so many words it is most often implied.

I believe that the common man is as apt a subject for tragedy in its highest sense as kings were. On the face of it this ought to be obvious in the light of modern psychiatry, which bases its analysis upon classic formulations, such as the Oedipus and Orestes complexes, for instance, which were enacted by royal beings, but which apply to everyone in similar emotional situations.

More simply, when the question of tragedy in art in not at issue, we never hesitate to attribute to the well-placed and the exalted the very same mental processes as the lowly. And finally, if the exaltation of tragic action were truly a property of the high-bred character alone, it is inconceivable that the mass of mankind should cherish tragedy above all other forms, let alone be capable of understanding it.

As a general rule, to which there may be exceptions unknown to me, I think the tragic feeling is evoked in us when we are in the presence of a character who is ready to lay down his life, if need be, to secure one thing—his sense of personal dignity. From Orestes to Hamlet, Medea to Macbeth, the underlying struggle is that of the individual attempting to gain his "rightful" position in his society.

Sometimes he is one who has been displaced from it, sometimes one who seeks to attain it for the first time, but the fateful wound from which the inevitable events spiral is the wound of indignity, and its dominant force is indignation. Tragedy, then, is the consequence of a man's total compulsion to evaluate himself justly.

In the sense of having been initiated by the hero himself, the tale always reveals what has been called his "tragic flaw," a failing that is not peculiar to grand or elevated characters. Nor is it necessarily a weakness. The flaw, or crack in the character, is really nothing—and need be nothing, but his inherent unwillingness to remain passive in the face of what he conceives to be a challenge to his dignity, his image of his rightful status. Only the passive, only those who accept their lot without active retaliation, are "flawless." Most of us are in that category.

But there are among us today, as there always have been, those who act against the scheme of things that degrades them, and in the process of action everything we have accepted out of fear or insensitivity or ignorance is shaken before us and examined, and from this total onslaught by an individual against the seemingly stable cosmos surrounding us—from this total examination of the "unchangeable" environment—comes the terror and the fear that is classically associated with tragedy.

More important, from this total questioning of what has previously been unquestioned, we learn. And such a process is not beyond the common man. In revolutions around the world, these past thirty years, he has demonstrated again and again this inner dynamic of all tragedy.

Insistence upon the rank of the tragic hero, or the so-called nobility of his character, is really but a clinging to the outward forms of tragedy. If rank or nobility of character was indispensable, then it would follow that the problems of those with rank were the particular problems of tragedy. But surely the right of one monarch to capture the domain from another no longer raises our passions, nor are our concepts of justice what they were to the mind of an Elizabethan king.

The quality in such plays that does shake us, however, derives from the underlying fear of being displaced, the disaster inherent in being torn away from our chosen image of what and who we are in this world. Among us today this fear is as strong, and perhaps stronger, than it ever was. In fact, it is the common man who knows this fear best.

Now, if it is true that tragedy is the consequence of a man's total compulsion to evaluate himself justly, his destruction in the attempt posits a wrong or an evil in his environment. And this is precisely the morality of tragedy and its lesson. The discovery of the moral law, which is what the enlightenment of tragedy consists of, is not the discovery of some abstract or metaphysical quantity.

The tragic right is a condition of life, a condition in which the human personality is able to flower and realize itself. The wrong is the condition which suppresses man, perverts the flowing out of his love and creative instinct. Tragedy enlightens—and it must, in that it points the heroic finger at the enemy of man's freedom. The thrust for freedom is the quality in tragedy which exalts. The revolutionary questioning of the stable environment is what terrifies. In no way is the common man debarred from such thoughts or such actions.

Seen in this light, our lack of tragedy may be partially accounted for by the turn which modern literature has taken toward the purely psychiatric view of life, or the purely sociological. If all our miseries, our indignities, are born and bred within our minds, then all action, let alone the heroic action, is obviously impossible.

And if society alone is responsible for the cramping of our lives, then the protagonist must needs be so pure and faultless as to force us to deny his validity as a character. From neither of these views can tragedy derive, simply because neither represents a balanced concept of life. Above all else, tragedy requires the finest appreciation by the writer of cause and effect.

No tragedy can therefore come about when its author fears to question absolutely everything, when he regards any institution, habit or custom as being either everlasting, immutable or inevitable. In the tragic view the need of man to wholly realize himself is the only fixed star, and whatever it is that hedges his nature and lowers it is ripe for attack and examination. Which is not to say that tragedy must preach revolution.

The Greeks could probe the very heavenly origin of their ways and return to confirm the rightness of laws. And Job could face God in anger, demanding his right and end in submission. But for a moment everything is in suspension, nothing is accepted, and in this stretching and tearing apart of the cosmos, in the very action of so doing, the character gains "size," the tragic stature which is spuriously attached to the royal or the highborn in our minds. The commonest of men may take on that stature to the extent of his willingness to throw all he has into the contest, the battle to secure his rightful place in his world.

There is a misconception of tragedy with which I have been struck in review after review, and in many conversations with writers and readers alike. It is the idea that tragedy is of necessity allied to pessimism. Even the dictionary says nothing more about the word than that it means a story with a sad or unhappy ending. This impression is so firmly fixed that I almost hesitate to claim that in truth tragedy implies more optimism in its author than does comedy, and that its final result ought to be the reinforcement of the onlooker's brightest opinions of the human animal.

For, if it is true to say that in essence the tragic hero is intent upon claiming his whole due as a personality, and if this struggle must be total and without reservation, then it automatically demonstrates the indestructible will of man to achieve his humanity.

The possibility of victory must be there in tragedy. Where pathos rules, where pathos is finally derived, a character has fought a battle he could not possibly have won. The pathetic is achieved when the protagonist is, by virtue of his witlessness, his insensitivity or the very air he gives off, incapable of grappling with a much superior force.

Pathos truly is the mode for the pessimist. But tragedy requires a nicer balance between what is possible and what is impossible. And it is curious, although edifying, that the plays we revere, century after century, are the tragedies. In them, and in them alone, lies the belief—optimistic, if you will, in the perfectibility of man.

It is time, I think, that we who are without kings, took up this bright thread of our history and followed it to the only place it can possible lead in our time—the heart and spirit of the average man.

V
THE EFFECTS
OF TRAGEDY

The Edge of Impossibility*

Joyce Carol Oates

We seek the absolute dream. We are forced back continually to an acquiescence in all that is hallucinatory and wasteful, to a rejection of all norms and gods and dreams of "tragedy" followed by the violent loss of self that signals the start of artistic effort: an appropriation by destruction, or an assimilation into the self of a reality that cannot be named. The art of tragedy grows out of a break between self and community, a sense of isolation. At its base is fear. If it is not always true that human life possesses value, it is at least true that some human life, or the abstract parody of human life as acted out by gods, has a profound and magical value, inexplicable. The drama begins only when a unique human reality asserts its passion against the totality of passion, "arranging the same materials in a unique pattern," risking loss of self in an attempt to realize self—there steps forward out of the world an Oedipus, an Antigone. The making of domestic landscapes into wilderness is the aspect of tragedy that always shocks us, for in our wholesome terror we cannot conceive of the justification of our lives calling forth a death of passion, an annihilation of passion—what are we except passion, and how are we to survive when this passion breaks its dikes and flows out into nature?

The hero at the center of tragedy exists so that we may witness, in his destruction, the reversal of our private lives. We adjust ourselves to the spectacle of an art form, we paralyze our skepticism in order to see beyond the artifice of print or stage, and we share in a mysterious dream the necessary loss of self, even as this self reads or watches, losing ourselves in the witnessing of someone's death so that, in our human world, this hero may be reborn. The tragic hero dies but is reborn eternally in our dreams; the crudity of our desire for an absolute—an absolute dream, an absolute key—is redeemed by the beauty that so often surrounds this dream. One can explain the dream but never its beauty.

The hero dies into our imaginations as we, helplessly, live out lives that are never works of art—even the helpless lives of "artists"!—and are never understood. Suffering is articulated in tragic literature, and so this literature is irresistible, a therapy of the soul. We witness in art the reversal of our commonplace loss of passion, our steady loss of consciousness that is never beautiful but only biological. Therefore our love for art, and our resentment of it. We consume ourselves into a present without horizon, and without value; the creations of our imagination consume themselves into a marvelous future, a universal future in

* Joyce Carol Oates, *The Edge of Impossibility: Tragic Forms in Literature* (The Vanguard Press, Inc., 1972). pp. 3–8. © 1972 by Joyce Carol Oates. Reprinted by permission of the publisher.

which we somehow share. The object of our fascination, in Husserl's words, *gives itself as having been there before reflection,* and we feel that the triumph over nothingness that art represents is assured of a future beyond even our ability to imagine. We acclaim the marvelous in ourselves.

Of the many contemporary critics who have written on tragedy, George Steiner and Lionel Abel are among the most provocative. Steiner's thesis, like that of Joseph Wood Krutch before him, is that tragedy is dead. We have heard this often, we will be hearing it often: "Tragedy is that form of art which requires the intolerable burden of God's presence. It is dead now because His shadow no longer falls upon us as it fell upon Agamemnon or Macbeth or Athalie." If it returns it will be in a new form, and Steiner implies that it will be a form perhaps unintelligible to the West. In his brief, strange book, *Metatheater,* Abel tries to solve the critical problem of the relationship between "tragedy" and less pure forms of drama by denying that tragedy is a natural Western art form at all. According to Abel, Shakespeare wrote no tragedies, with the possible exception of *Macbeth.* The dominant dramatic form is not tragedy but "metatheater"—the kind of drama that assumes the total subjectivity of the world and its metamorphosis, by way of a mysterious psychological process, into theater. Theater as *theater,* as self-conscious and ironic subjectivity—this is "metatheater."

What are we to make of such assumptions? Does the frequent appearance in dramatic literature of the world-as-stage and life-as-dream bring along with it the actual valuelessness of the contextual world? Where is history? Where is personal history? Certain critics are always convinced that an epoch creates art, but a great work always tells us that it is isolated, unique, accidental, and inexplicable—not even the possession of the creator himself—and that its true context is not history but dreams, ahistorical dreams. Like a personality, a work of art occurs once, and, re-experienced, is redefined; it has no "existence" at all. But to argue backward from this insight, to argue that the dreamlike quality of a work of art indicates a dreamlike, nihilistic culture beyond it, is irresponsible. If Hamlet represents the most developed figure of Western "metatheater," then he is a prince of nihilism and nothing more. According to Abel, "One cannot create tragedy without accepting some implacable values as true. Now, the Western imagination has, on the whole, been liberal and skeptical; it has tended to regard *all* implacable values as false." But from what ground does the play arise? What is its fundamental delusion? If the play is *Hamlet,* the hero's delusion is certainly not that he cannot locate truth, but rather that he cannot reject it powerfully enough; though appearances argue that all values are false, Hamlet's tragedy is that he cannot accept appearances. Out of his faith comes the tragedy.

Nothing can come from nothing, no energy from a bodiless spirit; thus, there can be no violence out of a sense of nothing, for violence is always an affirmation. Abel claims that the West has always been nihilistic in its imaginative literature, but how can such an assumption account for its very shape, the structural consummation of violent action? Art is built around violence, around death; at its base is fear. The absolute dream, if dreamed, must deal with death, and the only way toward death we understand is the way of violence. In the various works examined in this collection of essays, as well as in *Hamlet,* nihilism is overcome by the breaking-down of the dikes between human beings, the flowing forth of passion; Melville alone, with his essentially religious and superstitious imagination, can create a tragedy of "nihilism." In our ingenious theater of the absurd, and to some extent in Chekhov, the dramatic structure itself becomes equated with the sense of loss and inertia of the fictional characters, who are incapable of violence except as victims. And yet they perpetuate acts of violence, by being victims. Here human life is microscopic, imagined as magical and reductive to an instant in time, as in *Waiting for Godot:* "One day we were born, one day we'll die, the same day, the same second. . . . They give birth astride of a grave, the light gleams an instant, then it's night once more." In Beckett we have a true delight in boredom and in the boring of others, a powerful substitute for ancient types of aggression.

Parody is an act of aggression. Twentieth-century literature is never far from parody, sensing itself anticipated, overdone, exhausted. But its power lies in the authenticity of its anger, its parodistic instinct, the kind of art in which Mann's Adrian Leverkühn and Dostoevski's Ivan Karamazov excel: "the playing of forms out of which life has disappeared." If it is true, as George Steiner argues, that the death of God means the death of tragedy, then we need to ask what tragedy has dealt with all along—has it not been the limitations of the human world? What is negotiable, accessible, what can be given proper incantatory names, what is, in Nietzsche's phrasing, "thinkable"—this is the domestic landscape out of which the wilderness will be shaped. If communal belief in God has diminished so that, as writers, we can no longer presume upon it, then a redefinition of God in terms of the furthest reaches of man's hallucinations can provide us with a new basis for tragedy. The abyss will always open for us, though it begins as a pencil mark, the parody of a crack; the shapes of human beasts—centaurs and satyrs and their remarkable companions—will always be returning with nostalgia to our great cities.

The Psychology of Tragic Pleasure*

Roy Morrell

Mine is a hackneyed subject, and I should like to say at once that some obvious points which may appear heavily laboured in the first part of this paper, are included not in order to instruct, but to facilitate reference when I come to a psychoanalytical analogy at the end.

I have little room, in my theory, for the jargon of psychological pleasure terms such as Sadism and Masochism. The masochistic element in literature is familiar and it appears distinct from Tragedy. The Romantic mood which finds pleasure in "swooning to death" has, I know, been called tragic, but this is, I believe, a confusion. When Tragedy appears in nineteenth century literature, it seems alien and even shocking to the Romantic sensibility. The argument that the appeal of Tragedy is sadistic is likewise unconvincing: the critic argues—rightly, I think—that literature or drama which openly relishes cruelty repels those of us who are not sadists, yet those of us who are not sadists can find pleasure in Tragedy.

The argument in favour of sadism might, however, be pressed in a different way: it might be said that some "censorship" mechanism enables us to derive sadistic pleasure—those of us who deny that we are sadists—only from something not *too* sadistic, from something not recognizable as sadism. Psychologists do, in fact, extend the term sadism to include not only sexual violence or a relish in inflicting pain inexplicable except through some sexual analogy, but also a more general satisfaction in the discomfiture of others. At one time it seemed to me that tragic pleasure must be explicable in this way. Are not all but the best of men moved to envy the lot of their more energetic or more successful fellows? We may think we are unselfish, or good sportsmen, rejoicing in our friend's success, his windfall, his prize in the sweepstake—he bought only one ticket, lucky fellow, and we had bought ten—we may rejoice in his fat legacy. We cannot blame ourselves, we blame only him, when we quickly detect signs of "uppishness" in him; and we leave him to go his superior way. How quickly and virtuously, on the other hand, do we rally round with demonstrations of friendship and pity, refraining from the least mention of "poetic justice," should he lose his wealth as quickly as he acquired it. Nor is it entirely petty thus to wish for an assurance that Fate is not too unfair, that if she withholds from us her special favours, she does not deal us her worst blows. To see disaster befalling a great and fortunate person dwarfs our own worries and troubles, and makes them more

* Roy Morrell, "The Psychology of Tragic Pleasure," *Essays in Criticism*, Vol. VI, No. 1 (January, 1956), pp. 22–37.

easily bearable. Fate, great personages, disasters befalling them—these are the stuff of tragedy, and that pity should be seen as something related to envy, and therefore undesirable, perhaps indicates that Aristotle was thinking partly along these lines.

Reflection will show us, however, that any such theory is incomplete. It assumes a detachment on the part of the audience; it ignores the fact that most spectators and readers sympathize, or perhaps actually identify themselves with the hero. We may be more sophisticated than the schoolboy who forgets that Jim Hawkins is not himself, but we sympathize with Oedipus, Lear, Othello, Tess and Hugo actively enough to wish to avert the disasters which await them. In short, tragic pleasure does not arise through the gratification of a wish, but in a wish's frustration. This reminder should prevent our toying with psychological pleasure terms, masochism or sadism, dilute them as we may, or with any conception of "poetic justice." Tragedy does not "please" in this sense; it does not please our palate, nor awaken pleasurable anticipation. On the contrary, we resist Tragedy, and try to avert it. The pleasure arises only afterwards, and no small part of the pleasure is the discovery that we have the strength to face a world which is larger than the mere creation of our wishes.

There remain the anthropologists' data of the magical origins of Tragedy. We all know that pain, mutilation, sacrifice, ritual burial, once implied renewal, resurrection, the germination of the seed. But what have such things to do with us today? Having outgrown the magical view of the world, why have we not outgrown Tragedy? It is true that primitive impulses still move us unconsciously. Freud has shown that accidents, breakages and the like, are sometimes instinctive sacrifices, sops to Nemesis. We may not use the word *Hubris,* but we dislike and fear boasting; we touch wood, and hang up mistletoe; and in the same way the tragic experience, in which we suffer vicariously, may still be "good magic" and seem to appease the Fates.

The Fates indeed are merely projections of our anxieties, and if the Fates have gone, the anxieties remain. And it is in this way, I think, that we usually find the appeal of Tragedy defined today. If art is man's method of imposing a pattern on the disorderly material of life, Tragedy's function is to get under control life's most chaotic and difficult parts. Gilbert Murray said, "In its primitive form, drama was doing beforehand the thing you longed or dreaded to do; doing afterwards the thing that lived in your mind and could not be exorcised."

Modern warfare has shown that man has not outgrown this need for anticipating or exorcising. In Freud's account of war neuroses, he pointed out that the anxious individuals, whose imaginations pictured the horrors of battle in advance, were least liable to shell-shock. He also pointed out that recovery from shock was necessarily accompanied by dreams of the shocking experience. Attempts to cure the patient by diverting his mind always failed; his injured psyche was set on rehearsing and rehearsing the horror in daydreams and in sleep until gradually the experience was brought under control; and cures were accelerated not by removing the patients to the quiet of the country, trying to make them forget, but rather by reminding them of the battlefield, supplementing their imaginings by noises of bombardment and by additional shocks.

All this is well known, but it is interesting because, first, it suggests why surprise is unimportant in Tragedy. Indeed, as Mr. Lucas says, dramatic irony and suspense—with their hints of what is about to happen—far from detracting from the effect of tragedy only enhance the horror. We can, moreover, see a great tragedy again and again, without diminution of effect: it is, indeed, as if, within our own minds, Tragedy were never a performance, always a rehearsal. Second, Freudian psychology corroborates our previous impression that "Tragic Pleasure" is a phrase which can be used only with reserve, in inverted commas. We are not "pleased" by the destruction of the hero, any more than the soldier is "pleased" either by the shock which penetrates his illusions, or by the dreams by which he seeks to control or exorcise the terror. Pleasure there is indeed, but only afterwards, in the feeling of having gained control, partial or complete, over the chaotic experience.

In the book where Freud develops this theme—that certain human behaviour can be explained only by going, as the title puts it, "Beyond the Pleasure Principle," he analyses examples of play in children, where sometimes, by persistent repetition, the child's psyche obtains control over a painful experience. Freud then compares the psyche to a cell. He sees it as having a highly sensitive interior protected by a hard rind from the cruel shock-laden wind of the real world. Some objective reality may be absorbed into layers of the rind, and defences may be strengthened by marshalling energies from within to resist specific attacks—just as our soldier who was full of "horrible imaginings" before the battle, saved himself from shell-shock. Some adaptation is possible, but the psyche tries to "make do" with the simplest set of illusions which seems as if it might, with luck, work. Except that "work" is hardly the word: the psyche is essentially lazy, seeking to economize effort. Sooner or later, however, an unexpected disaster may break through these too simple defences, and the whole equilibrium of the psyche may be upset until the new experience has been absorbed and brought under control, and a more complex, a less dangerously sensitive, composition established.

There is nothing new in this: it is Gilbert Murray's theory of rehearsing and exorcising, in metaphor. But, as Freud explains, the metaphor of the cell economizing its energy in pursuit of a "pleasure principle" (its little labour-saving ideal home is really the home of the death instincts), but being forced to reorganize itself into more complex life—this metaphor refers these "unpleasure processes," of which the tragic experience is one, to the very principle of life itself. It is thus that the sperm forces the ovum to live, repeating in every individual the process by which organic life began. Whatever disturbances occurred during the cooling of the globe, one imagines life—not real life at first, but merely the potentiality of life—coming into being not once but many times, and fading out again, until some further disturbances intervened, enforcing a readjustment, a complication of the cell, the beginning of a cycle of life, before the simplicity of death could be reattained.

In this view, then, there are two sets of impulses, one set which can be termed "death instincts," which are innate; and the other set, reacting to disturbing stimulation from the outside, which enable the individual to adapt and to reorganize and to live more complexly—Tragedy exciting the second set. I am simplifying, perhaps; for instance I omit the possibility of innate disturbances which may complicate the life of the psyche by fifth-column activity within. With Freud's name on one's lips one is not likely to forget such impulses as complicated the life of Oedipus, for example. But on the whole I am not misrepresenting Freud, for in this book he does make mention—a single passing mention, but unambiguous—of Tragedy.

By "death instincts" Freud explains that he doesn't mean "suicide instincts." Death is not their immediate, only their ultimate aim; their immediate aim is the preservation of the established life-cycle to death, with the least possible interference or tension. Tragedy's preoccupation with death indicates no alliance with these "death instincts" but rather a desire to rid us of the numbing effect of its terror. But there are obvious reservations to be made here: in many tragedies we are reminded that death is not the worst that can happen to the hero, and I hope to show later that his death has, in addition, a special function to perform.

For the moment the essential function of Tragedy would appear to be the complicating and strengthening of the psyche by means of shocks from outside: not, of course, violent and disorganizing shocks, but mild, preventive, reorganizing ones. The participation in "tragic conflicts" may be a part of such reorganizing; though I am thinking of a toughening less crude than that which some German philosophers have thought desirable. Theoretically it would, I suppose, be possible to present a tragedy so horrible that there resulted a real shock—like shell-shock—from which the patient would have to be cured. In practice, however, we can usually protect ourselves by recalling, if we are forced, that what is happening on the stage is not "real." There is probably a level of tragedy, involving not too drastic a reorganization of the psyche, at which tragedy is most effective.

But when we come to define this level, and to consider the mechanism by which the tragic experience is conveyed to the audience, it seems to me that we are inevitably defining characteristics in the tragic hero. In Elizabethan tragedy, we are at once aware of the hero's position—Faustus's, Hamlet's, Clermont's, Othello's—a step or so ahead of his age. He develops fine sensibilities at heavy cost; he suffers and fails. The audience follow the hero's aspirations, his explorations in new realms of feeling; they face the possibility that such noble struggles will be thwarted by the insensibility and evil of the men around them, by the weight of the past, by blind chance. Despite the hero's defeat, however, the experience is, for the audience, a reorganization from the old life to the new fuller one; the cell is hindered in its easy acceptance of the old instinctive life cycle, and compelled to live more complexly. I believe a great tragedy always has this effect of bringing the consciousness to a threshold between the old and the new, although it may have other methods of doing this than by representing the hero as thus stepping to a threshold or beyond. Nor is the representation of such a hero alone sufficient: the nobility of Clermont is not enough, for instance, to make a great tragedy out of *The Revenge of Bussy D'Ambois*.

None the less, a great hero—one human enough for the audience's sympathy, and remarkable enough to lift their imaginations—is important. It is mainly through the hero's thoughts and feelings that we judge the truth of the world which the dramatist asks us to accept, its "values," its relevance to the possibilities of our own existence. I have already said we feel more than a detached sympathy for the hero; we feel more than "there, but for the grace of God, go I"; we identify ourselves, and go, with him. The extent of the identification varies in different members of the audience, and with different types of Tragedy. Some identification occurs even in Comedy; but the essence of comedy is that identification is partial and temporary and that we are continually dissociating ourselves in laughter. Stephen Haggard and Athene Seyler tell us in *The Craft of Comedy* that actors recognize this, keeping slightly "outside" the parts, self-dramatizing and slightly overcharacterizing, in comedy, but acting realistically and "straight," identifying themselves with their parts and trying to "live" them, empathizing—if I may use this word in a more limited sense than it is normally used in criticism—empathizing in the characters in a serious play. I used the word "realistically" inaccurately as a paraphrase of the actors' word "straight." In fact, too great a degree of realism with its reminders of the particular and commonplace can be distressing to the audience. If the audience too are to empathize in the hero, we should probably agree that a slightly stylized and remote production is more effective; indeed, this matter of "psychological distance" in drama has been explored by philosophers and critics.

My emphasis on the reality of the hero is unfashionable, and went out with Bradley. But although I am willing to defend this emphasis, I realise that the position has its dangers; particularly if adopted by actors. If an actor believes that a play exists for the sake of character, and for his acting of it, the result is frequently disastrous. Nothing repels an audience so much as finding that an actor, with a strong and perhaps highly mannered personality, has "got in" first. I am not arguing that personalities should dominate the play, least of all the personalities of actors. Such domination defeats the whole end of drama, which is not to give scope for actors or actresses (*pace* M Cocteau), nor to impress the audience, but to enable the audience to respond and react themselves. And they can only respond naturally and unselfconsciously if the actor has the tact to leave a little of the initiative to them, if he underacts a little, perhaps. And, needless to say, they can only respond if the whole play, the whole action, rings true. Only then can they also be convinced by the hero's part in it. I certainly do not believe that the play should be subordinated to character, none the less I do believe that for the full functioning—the purging—of Tragedy, our credulity, our four-dimensional acceptance, our ability to empathize in the tragic hero, or bovarize—as Huxley and others have called it—is always relevant. I need hardly distinguish here between bad bovarism and good: if we are tempted to identify ourselves with some hero of less intelligence and capacity for living than ourselves, it is probably to satisfy some dream of affluence or success; in short, to escape. Empathy in a character of a different kind, with a mind and soul larger than our own, requires effort and imagination, and, apart from any ordeal, any adjustment to the harsher realities which may be forced upon us by the tragic development of the plot, the greater awareness into which we are led tallies with the experience we derive from other great art.

Before considering whether this is the whole truth, I should like to recapitulate briefly and add to what I've said about the tragic hero. We have argued that whatever pleasure-principle factors enter, the distinctive appeal of Tragedy can only be explained by going "beyond the pleasure principle"; we suffer an ordeal, face life at its most difficult and complex, but derive pleasure in the new readiness and power we have gained thereby. To enable us to live more complexly and to persuade us that what we are getting is true to life—for it is important that we should not feel that the dramatist is either cheating us or sparing us, treating us as children who cannot be told the truth—we are invited to empathize in a hero of a certain type. We feel more deeply and subtly, act more courageously, more passionately, in him, and all the time with the conviction that it is true to life, a fuller life than our own. We may add that as drama has to work quickly, superficial superiorities, such as those of rank and fortune mentioned by classical critics, may predispose some of us to empathize, though modern class-conscious audiences may prefer other qualities. Whatever else the tragic hero is, however, he should not be dull: some conscientiously proletarian modern writers make a mistake, I think, when they solemnly present a drab little hero—unless they succeed in making out of him a twentieth-century Everyman. That may be as successful occasionally as the great character who lifts our imaginations, and it may invite our empathy no less.

Edith Sitwell has remarked that Tragedy always opens on a question, "Who?"—Who is the tragic hero? What is his significance? The answer is seldom given as explicitly as in the closing lines of *The Great God Brown:* the Police Captain, you may remember, has given Cybel a few minutes alone with the dying Brown to make him talk; he then comes in and asks, "Well, what's his name?" Cybel answers, "Man," and the Police Officer, his notebook open, asks "How d'yuh spell it?"

The spelling is not difficult: it is either "Everyman," ourselves, whose fate we must endure; or it is "Potential Man," whose powers of living it would be well for the species if we could assimilate.

Nothing of what I have said so far is new, and little, I hope, is controversial. But one point is unexplained: If Tragedy is, as I have described it, a vicarious ordeal, why is the unhappy ending essential? Why cannot the ordeal he provided by a serious and terrifying depiction of the sufferings of the hero, if he recovers from an almost mortal wound to live "happily ever after"? Death, as we know, is not essential. Oedipus lives on for a while; but in his despair, blood streaming from his eyesockets, he is a more terrible symbol of defeat than the hanged Jocasta. Defeat, the end of effective life, the end of hope for the hero—these are essential. His death, in fact, is convenient; but why?

It is true that the death of the hero is occasionally accompanied by the suggestion of a new start. Before the death of Henchard, some of our interest has been transferred to Elizabeth-Jane; Macbeth's death is followed by the coronation of Malcolm; there is even mention of the succession in *Hamlet;* but these are not "happy endings." Between the effect of *Hamlet* and that of *The Winter's Tale* there is a difference of kind not of degree: I know this difference depends not merely on the ending, but differences in the texture of the play throughout; and a key difference, in my view, is that in the Tragicomedy our sympathies are not centred to the same extent on a single person. In this, it seems to me there is a special propriety: that the audience should not be asked to empathize seriously and deeply in a hero who is going, not to die, but to live "happily ever after."

Still, there is this difference in texture and it would be fairer to compare the effect of *Villette* with that of *Jane Eyre*, or the two versions of a Shakespeare tragedy, before and after it had been doctored to "please" Restoration or eighteenth-century audiences. I don't think there can be serious doubt that, despite Aristotle's contrary opinion, the unhappy ending is indispensable for tragic effect, and the ordeal theory is incomplete. Indeed nothing would seem to fit the ordeal theory better than some modern crime fiction. Raymond Chandler does not spare his readers when he describes his hero being taught by some thug to mind his own business, but I have yet to encounter a critic who calls this literature tragic.

The effect of Tragedy is courage; not mere toughness, nor bravado, nor the will to display power, but simply calmness and readiness, the discovery that even in the harshest experiences there is, to quote Richards, "no difficulty"; the difficulty arises from the illusions and subterfuges by which we seek to dodge reality, and which we unconsciously fear are going to betray us.

But how does this change come about? How is it that for a time we are personally participating in the fears and difficulties of the hero, our need to dodge increased; and then that we are, almost suddenly sometimes, freed from these apprehensions, having achieved an impersonal objective attitude?

Freudian psychology helped us with a corroboration before, can it now provide us with an answer? We are again up against the difficulty of providing generalizations which are valid for all types of individuals—I recall a member of the Cambridge English Faculty who claimed that he had never experienced tragic catharsis: clearly my generalizations cannot include him. I put forward no chain of proof, tested at every link, only a kind of analogy which seems to me more plausible at some times than at others.

In pathological "fixations," when the psyche shrinks from developing into maturity, it often turns aside into a fantasy world comparable to the empathizing or bovarizing fantasies which we have been discussing. It is permissible to compare normal with pathological processes, for, as the example of Mme Bovary reminds us, no sharp line divides the two. It is a matter of better or of worse adjustment, and both possibilities are open to all of us.

At all events, with the conception of psychological fixation in mind, we can reframe our question thus, "Does Tragedy provide the individual in the audience with a means of expansion through empathy, through good 'bovarism,' and then, *but only in the destruction of the hero*, free the individual, break his empathy at the point where it is in danger of becoming a fixation, where his fantasies might otherwise usurp the energies required for real life?" If this question is framed correctly, we could say simply that the individual adjusts himself to real life because his fantasy life has died with the hero.

I do not know how general these fixation fantasies are, however, and I should like to establish an analogy between the tragic "empathy-ordeal-disaster" process and some more general fantasy process. But meanwhile one point is worth noting. Freud in dealing with fixations has concentrated mainly on infantile incest fantasies; the tragic function—of enabling one to grow and adjust oneself—might therefore be expressed as breaking free from a fixation, if one had no more to explain than *Oedipus Tyrannus*. But the main point hangs on Freud's reminder that an elaborate fantasy-living is *normal* in children. In their "endless imitation," they enter into fantasies, change them, discard them to meet the demands of real life, return to fantasy play at a moment's notice—they cease being soldiers or Red Indians and rush in to their real dinner, then rush out again to be pirates or shipwrecked mariners—doing safely, easily and normally what no adult can do without serious risk to his sanity. The explanation of this links up with what we said earlier about good and bad empathy: the whole principle of a child's life is growth, expansion; and his normal fantasies are informed inevitably with this expansion; they are, mainly, fantasies of growing up; and he is indeed growing minute by minute; except for the pathological case, the child with the infantile fixation, the child has no past, but only a future which he is constantly realizing. For the adult it is a different matter; every fantasy has the danger of becoming a fixation, a mental cancer growing inward when the normal expansive organic growth has slowed down, a step aside, a turn back to the past—unless, as we have suggested, the fantasy is of a special kind, derived from outside impact, demanding new effort, offering new opportunities of creative, imaginative, expansion.

But we are seeking in the realms of psychology for a more general type of fantasy, for comparison with tragic empathy. Is this not found in the artificially induced fantasy of the "transference," a part of the mechanism by which all psycho-therapeutic analysis was at one time attempted? An account of this mechanism is given in Jung's *Modern Man in Search of a Soul.* Jung describes the failure of Breuer's early therapeutic treatment, which Breuer with deliberate but, as it turned out, most unfortunate reference to Aristotle, called "Catharsis." Breuer's "Catharsis" was simply free confession aided by the probings of the physician, and Jung explains that it "consisted of putting the patient in touch with the hinterland of his mind." It failed because one of two kinds of fixation followed treatment and caused a relapse. In fact, though of course Breuer did not realize it at this stage, it did not purge effectively; the term "Catharsis'" had been usurped.

Breuer's treatment seemed to promise success; the patient always improved at first; but then one of two things happened: in some cases, to use Jung's words, "The patient goes away apparently cured—but he is now so fascinated by the hinterland of his own mind, that he continues to practice catharsis to himself at the expense of his adaptation to life. He is bound to the unconscious—to himself." In other cases, as is well known, the patient develops a sense of complete dependence on the physician, and collapses if the connection is severed. Both reactions are in the nature of fantasy-fixations: in the first case, the patient's fantasies are self-contained, they are fantasies about himself; in the second case a fantasy of child-parent dependence—the patient is the child; the physician the parent—is set up, and persists. In short, all Breuer had discovered or rediscovered was the relief and comfort of confession, and the helpless dependence which followed it.

Freud's system of analysis which superseded Breuer's made use of a similar relationship of dependence—the dependence of child-patient on father-confessor-physician—in the preliminary stages, but strove to break this "transference" later. This break was always regarded, of course, as indispensable for a cure; and, when properly successful, it effected something much more in the nature of a real catharsis. The important difference between Freud's analytical "transference" and Breuer's was that Freud's did not merely bring to light a few repressed thoughts and impulses from the "hinterland of the patient's mind," it strove also to bring the patient face to face with some terror, forced him to experience in his fantasy something which had been evaded in the past, something which provided a key to later conduct with its evasions and suppressions. Only if the psycho-analyst is able to lead the patient to a climax of resistance ending in painful temporary collapse, does this treatment end successfully and lead to the eventual readjustment of the patient. This process is different from that of Tragedy mainly in the fact that the patient is led back to a point where a wrong turning had been taken in his past development, where he takes the hurdle he had evaded then, and leaves his old self behind; whereas in tragedy, the individual is led forward. But there are points of comparison too: there is the initial fantasy, there is the postponed and resisted pain, eventually faced either in the death of the hero, or in what may be regarded as the death of the old incomplete self; there is also that oft-discussed, perhaps essential tragic element, "recognition," the "anagnorsis" of Aristotle, which is akin to, perhaps leads to, self-revelation.

I had hoped to explain Tragedy in terms of psycho-analysis and instead find myself expressing the analytical process in terms of tragedy. We can, however, add a few more bricks which seem to fit into the wall of this circular argument.

If the effect of tragedy depends, as I believe, upon the end, not merely upon any earlier ordeal; if, not indeed the death of the hero, but the end of what he stands for is essential to release the audience and enable them to adjust themselves to reality, if purgation depends not merely upon the intensity of the transference but indispensably also upon the way it is broken, then we might expect, as a result of empathizing in heroes who do not fail tragically, but instead live "happily ever afterwards," a pathological state of dependence similiar to the pathological condition of Breuer's patients. But this is not unlike Mme Bovary's state; and those people who, not making the mistake of Mme Bovary and attempting to live their day dreams, do none the less seek wish-fulfilment dreams in novels and films, are often called, with justice, film or fiction "addicts." Their first need after reading the average novel, or seeing the average film, seems to be to return to the cinema or the fiction library for another one. Whatever exciting or dangerous "ordeals" the addict has experienced vicariously, "purgation" is not one of them, and he attempts no adjustment but remains dependent on his fantasies. He could not continue to empathize in a person who is dead, but he is glad to do so in one who lives happily ever afterwards; and the more he gets from Hollywood or the bestseller-writer, the more dependent he becomes, upon his own fantasies, or upon the dispenser of them. I make the distinction because the tone of certain writers—talking down to the reader, flattering him, comforting him, encouraging his prejudices—has not escaped critical comment. It seems to me not impossible that a reader may get to the point of feeling that the favourite author knows him and his weaknesses and secrets so well that the author is almost in the reader's confidence; and as a sales device, ensuring the complete dependence of the reader upon the physician-confessor-guardian-parent of an author who continually dispenses absolution to the reader for not growing up, it is unrivalled.

Referring to *Hamlet* and *The Winter's Tale* earlier, I suggested that in a Tragicomedy there was a propriety in not inviting so deep and serious an empathy in the hero, as would be proper in Tragedy. The reason is implied in what I have just said: empathy does not break itself, and an author whose theme gives him no opportunity of breaking it, should not—if he intends to deal honestly with his public—invite it very deeply and intensely in the first place. Good Tragicomedy—and perhaps most of us would agree that Tragicomedy is not commonly entirely convincing—but the best Tragicomedy has some of the critical detachment of Comedy; or else it distributes the empathy amongst several characters.

Had I the time I should have liked to mention one or two other points. I think, for instance, that those moments to which Mr. Eliot has called attention, when the hero dramatizes himself and his lonely struggle against the Fates, find a place in my scheme. Such self-dramatization in real life is not amiable; we forgive it, in moments of exceptional stress, in those we know and love, but we take it as weakness. The heroes who do this kind of thing continually from the rise of the curtain on Act I are, as serious tragic heroes, intolerable. In great tragedy we forgive it, as we forgive it in ourselves and in our friends; but the dramatic effect lies in the fact that at such moments, when the audience know the limits of the hero's strength, the nearness of his end, and the hero too knows it, but is desperately hiding the knowledge from himself—at such moments our critical faculty is stirring to waken, and our empathy is, as it were, being worked loose.

I should also have liked to discuss those tragedies which the audience approaches quite detachedly, their critical sense awake throughout. In my view such Tragedies are a different species, and to regard them as the same leads only to confusion in theatrical production and in criticism.

But it is possible here to offer only a brief summary.

Tragedy is man's rehearsal of the harsher realities of life; by it the psyche's cell is forced out of its lethargy, its conservative instinctive life-cycle where it is only delusively secure, and it adapts itself to a more complex readiness for life.

The tragic hero is usually, as Aristotle said, uncommonly great and alive: only if he is great (but we mean by this not merely great in rank) does his downfall impress us with the insignificance of our own petty anxieties and mishaps; only if he is great—better than ourselves—does our attempt to share his experiences increase our own capacity for living. The place of the great hero is sometimes, however, successfully supplied by the figure of "Everyman" or by the representative not of all mankind but of a large group. Exceptionally our empathy may even be elicited by an idea, a "cause," with the success of which the fates of numerous individuals are bound up. This could be said not only of a few modern plays, but also of *Antigone*. Character, or some figure or idea in which the audience can identify themselves exactly as in a great character, is indispensable to tragedy; it must not dominate the action, but it is, despite Aristotle, as indispensable as action. In certain modern plays—*A Streetcar Named Desire*, *Lottie Dundass* and others—the action is adequate, the end is disastrous, but the persons are not tragic characters: their place is not in drama, but in a psychoanalyst's case-book; they are tawdry and second-rate persons with whom no audience can with advantage identify themselves, and their failure, whatever else it may be, is not tragic.

Finally, despite Aristotle, Mr. Lucas and others, the general seriousness of the theme is not enough: the action must end in disaster. More than a bare hint of the "rebirth" or renewal theme is dangerous. A production of *Macbeth*, for instance, which allowed all our sympathy for Macbeth to ebb before the desperate scenes in Acts IV and V, and encouraged us to identify ourselves and our interests in Malcolm, would transform the play into melodrama. But in the tragic end of the hero, and of the hopes we had in him, there is nothing defeatist; for only in his failure is some connection, some "transference" between us and our fantasy life in the play, broken, and our own energies set free.

The Celebration of Disaster*

Harvey Birenbaum

Come to the party. Tragedy is the celebration of disaster.

We sing that we are mortal, that life is right not merely in spite of death but because of it. Yesterday dies that today may be born. Each flash of the present lives at the expense of all time. The softness that makes us frail makes us tender. In our fear lies triumph. In our fury lies love. The grotesque and the sickening are reflexes of desire. The world of the stage—like the stage of the world—is littered with our dead surrounded by the dying. Life is impractical, unfeasible, inconceivable—yet the human animal will take more of it. So, in grim optimism, we congratulate each other: things couldn't be worse. I wish you joy of the worm.

We kill the king because he matters enough. Down with Hamlet, our love and self, and Lear, our dear miserable child-father. If our savior Oedipus is not destroyed, we will dance no more the holy dance of our drama. The king is our reality and we affirm dithyrambically that it is mortal. Death-bound, we will destroy as we are destroyed and commit the inevitable suicide. But we will go slow and savour the tears, which belong to us, and love one another in the abandon of sorrow.

We cannot know the meaning of tragedy without losing the knowledge of all that is familiar, stable, and safe, without following Faustus and Macbeth to the prospect of damnation. The mystery seduces us through strong fear, and so it should, for the mystery is our own. It leads toward the love of our own being, awkward and shameful, wrapped in the anguish of self-consciousness, but vibrant and full beyond measure.

The song will carry us if we surrender to it, without cautious thought or superior judgment ("As 'Well, well, we know,' or, 'We could and if we would'. . ."). You may abandon hope who enter here, and all the forms and shapes of sensible control. It is without thought and preparation, without beliefs, opinions or judgments that the feelings come clear and fully happen.

We proceed with our lives in our hands, and on this sacrifice we ourselves throw incense.

Characteristics of Tragedy

A tragedy is a play (in the broader sense of the word, an event) that conveys "the tragic sense of life." The tragic sense of life is a state of mind in which man's sit-

*Harvey Birenbaum, *Tragedy and Innocence* (San Jose State University 1977).

uation is experienced as "impossible": inherently self-destructive or dependent on terms that oppose it.

The tragic must be distinguished from the melodramatic and the didactic in esthetics, from the catastrophic in reality, and from the "merely pathetic" in both.

The tragic sense evokes a complex of feelings organically interrelated: shame, horror, disgust, grief, rage—and the sense of their encompassment. The tragic is always pathetic (arousing pathos) but the pathetic is not always tragic. In the *merely* pathetic there may be painful sorrow and despair but there is not the immersion in horror that in tragedy evokes a rage of protest, a resistance against the way things are that is one attribute of heroic integrity.

We often say that tragedy is what happens to one or more characters of the play, whom we call the tragic hero or heroes, but more properly tragedy is their condition. If we say it is their fate, then fate is simply the course through which their condition becomes clear to them. Tragedy, most importantly, is what the play communicates. The play is an instrument that functions to make the tragic statement; through their interaction the characters constitute the play and that statement. The characters function, however, not simply as individuals or as a representative society but as stylized bodies of consciousness. . . . Tragedy is about the feelings it arouses.

Nevertheless, it is often not enough to say that this play is a tragedy and that is not. Especially when we come to modern drama—from Ibsen on—at times we want to say, this play has a tragic quality, this tends toward the tragic, this is essentially tragic but not manifestly so and, of course, some of the most important modern works in the tragic mode lie outside drama altogether, such as novels by Faulkner and Hemingway. We should speak sometimes of quasi-tragedy, or "tragedy" in a looser sense, with no disparagement but only a sense of accurate vagueness. Many works partake of the real tragic quality in different ways and to different degrees without being fully immersed in it. They are not *not tragic* and can be distinguished from spurious tragedies that *are*.

In spite of your desire to be "fair," tragedy does take on evaluative force. The full tragic statement holds a special place in our consciousness, as an act of intense clarification that requires an honesty of perception and expression. Ordinarily we would insist that there is no goodness in any genre or mode of literature—better a brilliant farce than a mediocre "serious play"—yet a work that is capable of full tragic statement must be a great work. If it is not successful esthetically it is not really tragic. If it is tragic it achieves stature in spite of any incidental faults.

It is more meaningful to describe characteristics of tragedy than to attempt definition:

The subjective. Tragedy depicts life in the matrix of experience, as a process of feeling, thought, consciousness, interpreting behavior and action through their direct perception. It is about living not merely as a human being but as a human *self*—the universal unique, responsive and affective in a typical but personal way. Tragedy is therefore empirical, affirming knowledge only where it is learned firsthand, *im*-mediately—without the mediation of philosophical speculation or moral presupposition.

The definitive. First, tragedy speaks in absolutes, asserting or implying universal truths about man and the human condition. The tragic complex of feeling is communicated not merely for a character, on behalf of his isolated suffering, but *for the way life is*. These feelings may not be voiced explicitly within the work itself, by a character, but always they are at least implicit in the qualitative flow of experience. . . . Secondly, tragedy cuts through the vague, restrained and continually compromised conditions of ordinary life with a directness and purity of vision that sees the norm in intensity. It encounters evil as absolute evil, agony as absolute agony, and so forth. Its feelings are the epitome of feeling. Its darkness is utter black; its sense of horror disintegrates into nausea. . . . The generalization of tragedy is not, of course, the objective generalization of induction or consensus, yet it is more than a tentative, hypothetical assertion. It speaks mythically as though it voices all truth in order to chart one absolute dimension of truth. . . . Yet in another sense, no individual work *can* speak absolutely. The type is not the archetype and to reflect it always alters it. From epoch to epoch, from playwright to playwright, from play to play within one writer's canon, variations bring forth the theme, which cannot be stated otherwise. By being variations, they endow the statement with necessary individuality, immediacy and vitality—but they are variations on a theme and the theme is the essence.

The problematic. Tragic life is experienced as a predicament, one that rational or prescriptive interpretation cannot cope with. It is defined by contradiction, paradox, a sense of the trap, of life that must be lived under untenable conditions. Though life is impossible, it *will* be lived. Moreover, it *is* being lived in the perception that it cannot be lived. . . . The height of tragic knowledge is achieved through the depth of pain and degradation. Life is affirmed through the confrontation with death. Events that should breed pessimism glow with the optimistic warmth of rich emotion. . . . We see tragedy from the perspective of rational expectations, so we are puzzled, shocked and frustrated when the rational mind, confronting organic reality, turns back upon itself in paradox.

The violent. The mind both recoils from and protests against the strait-jacket of human limitation with a release of feeling that is at once self-assertive and destructive, destructive of both others and self, total reality. Twisted in the strait-jacket, the sensitivity of the mind releases the desire for life in violence, the extremity of which is death.

The existential. The mind experiences its absolute impotence in the face of discontinuity, the sense that the terms of existence do not hold together. The mind cannot move from life to death; the individual, unique in the universe, has no flow of contact with the social and conventional environment which presumes to define him. He is torn between: creative potentiality and the continuing norm of frustration; exuberance and the caution for survival; desire and the continually receding horizon of success; memory of past pleasure and realization of present pain; simple action and its eddies of consequence. Each of these sources of discontinuity leaves the self acutely aware of its own existence, alone absolutely.

The grotesque. At the heart of tragedy, revealed in at least a quick glance, is the disintegration of all decorum into gross ugliness. At once repellent and magnetic, the nightmare vision explores life's "negative space," penetrating the forbidden and the imprudent realms of experience, the indecorous, the frightening, the vicious. The bestial is human, the horrible is natural, chaos is visceral. The tragic hero does not die neatly on his sword, declaiming a proud farewell. Like Mark Antony, he is more likely to make a mess of it. The esthetic boundaries of the play, which set it off discreetly from the world, threaten to burst until they are revived on a new level in catharsis.

The restorative. The logic of tragedy is confrontation with reality, the only source of *value*. The movement is from an unstable, self-protective condition, through a process of attrition and suffering (ordeal, passion) to a poise of integration, where what has been actively feared is now actively embraced. A new continuity emerges from the experience of discontinuity itself, for the discontinuity is sensed as merely the self—withholding in fear and bewilderment. As the fear dissolves, the center holds its own as it could not do before. The vision of tragedy is eminently organic: ripeness is all.

Aristotle may have meant that tragedy purges us out of pity and fear through the process he called catharsis or he may have meant that it purges pity and fear of "dangerous" elements. We can use the word to mean what seems more tenable psychologically than either of these possibilities and more true to our actual experience. As we participate imaginatively in the tragic ordeal, we receive under the spell of projection what we ordinarily resist feeling through our identities. Masked, we go forth more securely ourselves, in a stylized life that has—in its heroic, or at least esthetic, elevation—both a specialness and a limited urgency. Catharsis, however, purges us not out of feelings but into them, and it leads us into our feelings in such a way, esthetically, that we are prepared to accept them and sense them provisionally in a state of poise. What is purged is our resistance, the anxiety or guilt which ordinarily devalues our experience, frustrating and obscuring it. Yet even such painful modern works as *Endgame* and *The Chairs* remain life-giving and we pay to see them. They restore us to the reality of our feelings, affirming our experience, no matter how negative the experience is in itself, if the feelings are honestly conveyed. We may remain terribly disturbed; we may leave the theater with more of a consciousness of pain that was only latent before, but we sense a legitimacy to the disturbance, perhaps even (in the courage of our negativism) with a certain satisfaction that overshoots the mark. . . . Catharsis is that factor which makes the spectacle of misery a positive experience.

"Tragedy" can be studied fruitfully as the history of a word, one that links a vaguely associated cluster of notions. We can study what the term has meant in different epochs or what it means to us now when we apply it to authors as distant from each other as Racine and Dostoyevsky. On the other hand, tragedy can be studied as a phenomenon, in both the ordinary and the philosophical sense, if we are willing to let the word serve to point towards that phenomenon. If we are willing to assume, also, that art is an adjunct to immediate reality and need not be treated with *too* much respect (and that criticism is a mere adjunct to art)—then we can study art for the life in it. We might also assume—a notion some readers may not deem academically legitimate—that there is a reality which can be known, a reality of common human experience. But we must risk the possibility that this reality is to be known not through philosophical speculation nor through consensus popular or elite nor through objective demonstration. It is to be known through the study of consciousness—subjectively though not impressionistically, personally though not privately, emotionally though not un-intellectually. The risk of error is obviously great, yet it is not the relativistic limitation of intellectual theory, asserting that every opinion has an absolute validity from its arbitrary viewpoint. The risk is the inevitable (tragic?) confusion and dimness of our own unconsciousness—but that is exactly what we are studying. If we wish to dive in, at any rate, the right direction will certainly be downward.

VI
TRAGEDY AND MELODRAMA

Melodrama*

Eric Bentley

The Bad Name of Melodrama

Some time ago I ran into a magazine article containing this comment on Joseph Conrad:

> One word comes before long to haunt the mind of any persistent reader of Conrad's stories—the word Melodrama. Why does he do it? What has he got against life? What is the purpose of all these feuds, assassinations, revealing plottings, these fearful disasters and betrayals. . . .

Not long afterwards I met with that passage again—quoted by a critic who proffers this answer to its queries: finding it difficult either to invent or report, Conrad has to derive his narratives from other narratives. "To such a temperament," writes our critic, " 'drama' is an alternative to dramatic life." And an example is provided. It has recently come to seem highly likely that the young Conrad tried to kill himself, and for what might be called prosaic reasons—"depression, bad health, and a financial mess." Instead of reporting the drab sequence of events, Conrad made out of it a melodrama of love and honor. The struggle within himself became in fiction a fight between two distinct persons.

The question why Conrad "does it" and what he "has got against life" are in greater need of explanation, surely, than his procedure. Only under the influence of a narrow and philistine Naturalism can we ask why an artist shows life at a remove and in some established genre. The transposition of an inner struggle to a duel between persons does not even need a convention to carry it; such changes are made nightly by everyone in his dreams. If one can make of one's tussles with suicidal wishes a drama of love and honor, one has given to private and chaotic material a public and recognizable form. One has made art out of fantasy and pain. One has found the link between emotion and civilized values. One has achieved universality.

All this, of course, would have been readily granted by our two critics but for the particular vehicle (form, convention) which Conrad chose: melodrama. It has a bad reputation—and that is the worst thing a word can have in the literary world just as it is the worst thing a man can have in the social world.

Where did this bad reputation come from? It is, I think, substantially the bad reputation of popular Victorian melodrama. Now it is unfair to judge anything by its weakest link, but it is not unfair to ask: how weak is its weakest link? What is the least that anyone would ask of a melodrama? As apt an answer as any is: a good cry. The contempt implied in terms like sob stuff and tear jerker is not more interesting than the very wide appeal of the thing despised.

An inquiry into melodrama—the appeal of melodrama—can legitimately start with a thought or two about tears.

In Praise of Self-Pity

What does it mean: to weep? Laughter has engaged the attention of many brains, among them some of the best. A brief search in book indexes and library catalogues calls attention to an extensive literature. Tears are a relatively unexplored ocean.

One reason why laughter has had a better press must be the obvious one: that laughter is (or is held to be) pleasant, whereas weeping is (or is held to be) unpleasant. Laughter is also something one gets a good mark for. What tired orator does not expatiate on the benefits of a sense of humor? To weep, on the other hand, is something that little boys are assiduously taught not to do. Women are greater realists: they will speak of having a good cry. The phrase points to perhaps the commonest function of tears: they are a mechanism for working off emotion—commonly, quite superficial emotion. But there are tears and tears. Crying your heart out is a matter of deep emotion. Then there are tears of joy. "Excess of sorrow laughs," says Blake, "excess of joy weeps." Shaw put it this way:

> Tears in adult life are the natural expression of happiness as laughter is at all ages the natural recognition of destruction, confusion, and ruin.

The tears shed by the audience at a Victorian melodrama come under the heading of a good cry. They might be called the poor man's catharsis, and as such have a better claim to be the main objective of popular melodrama than its notorious moral pretensions. Besides referring to superficial emotion, the phrase "having a good cry" implies feeling sorry for oneself. The pity is self-pity. But, for all its notorious demerits, self-pity has its uses. E. M. Forster even says it is the only thing that makes bearable the feeling of growing old—in other words, that it is a weapon in the struggle for existence. Self-pity is a very present help in time of trouble, and all times are times of trouble.

Once we have seen that our modern antagonism to self-pity and sentiment goes far beyond the rational objections that may be found to them, we realize that even the rational objections are in some measure mere rationalization. Attacks on false emotion often mask a fear of emotion as such. Ours is, after all, a thin-lipped, thin-blooded culture. Consider how, in the past half-century, the prestige of dry irony has risen, while that of surging emotion has fallen. This is a cultural climate in which a minor writer like Jules Laforgue can rate higher than a major one like Victor Hugo. Or think of our changed attitude to death. Would any age but this receive the death of admired persons "with quiet understatement"? We may think that Mr. Auden pours his heart out in his good poem on the death of Yeats, but just compare Mr. Auden's poem with the product of more old-fashioned culture, say, with Garcia Lorca's "Lament for the Death of Ignacio Mejias"! Would even Lorca's title be possible in English? Is lamenting something we can imagine ourselves doing? On the contrary we modernize the Greek tragedies by deleting all variants of "woe is me." If Christ and Alexander the Great came back to life, we would teach them to restrain their tears. . . .

Once I did see death done justice to. An Italian actor came on stage to announce the death of a colleague. He did indeed lament. He shook, he wept, he produced streams of passionate rhetoric, until the audience shook, and wept, and lamented with him. Now that is self-pity, certainly. One is not sorry for a corpse; one is sorry for oneself, deprived; and in the background is the fear of one's own death. But so much the better for self-pity. The experience was had, not refused.

The point has some importance for mental health. Modern psychiatry begins with those *Studies on Hysteria* in which Freud and Breuer try to explain what happens when emotional impressions are not allowed to wear themselves out. The shock of pain craves to be relieved and released by cries and writhings and tears. Good little boys who keep still and quiet under a rain of blows may pay for their stoicism twenty years later on a therapist's couch. Their resentments, instead of being worn away by a natural process, have been hoarded in the Unconscious.

If you have dismissed tears and loud lamentation from your daily life, you might check whether they are equally absent from your dreams at night. You may be no more sentimental than the next man, and yet find you have many dreams in which you weep profusely and at the same time disport yourself like an actor in the old melodrama: throwing yourself on your knees, raising your arms plaintively to heaven, and so forth. For you, in that case, grandiose self-pity is a fact of life. As it can only be copied by the use of grandiose style, the grandiosity of melodrama would seem to be a necessity.

Pity and Fear

I have been defending melodrama in its weakest link, for certainly self-pity is only valuable up to a point in life and only tolerable up to a point on the stage. Pity for the "hero" is the less impressive half of melodrama; the other and more impressive half is fear of the villain. Pity and fear: it was Aristotle in his *Poetics* who coupled them, and tried to give an account of the total effect of tragedy in these terms. It seems an oversimplification. In tragedy, most of us now feel, more is involved. Is more involved in melodrama? Is not working on the audience's capacity for pity and fear the alpha and omega of the melodramatist's job? In his *Rhetoric*, Aristotle explains that pity and fear have an organic relation to each other. An enemy or object of terror is presupposed in both cases. If it is we who are threatened, we feel fear for ourselves; if it is others who are threatened, we feel pity for them. One might wish to carry this analysis a little further in the light of the fact that most pity is self-pity. We are identified with those others who are threatened; the pity we feel for them is pity for ourselves; and by the same token we share their fears. We pity the hero of a melodrama because he is in a fearsome situation: we share his fears; and, pitying ourselves, we pretend that we pity him. To rehearse these facts is to put together the dramatic situation of the characteristic popular melodrama: goodness beset by badness, a hero beset by a villain, heroes and heroines beset by a wicked world.

Pity represents the weaker side of melodrama, fear the stronger. Perhaps the success of a melodramatist will always depend primarily upon his power to feel and project fear. Feeling it should be easy, for fear is the element we live in.

"We have nothing to fear but fear itself" is not a cheering slogan because fear itself is the most indestructible of obstacles. Therein lies the potential universality of melodrama.

Human fears are of two kinds. One belongs to the common-sense world: it is reasonable in the everyday sense to fear that one might slip on ice or that an airplane might crash. The other kind of fear—perhaps none too rationally—is called irrational. Savage superstitions, neurotic fantasies, and childhood imaginings spring to mind, and equally outside the bounds of common sense is the fear of God. Superstition and religion, neurosis and infantility are in the same boat.

Melodrama sometimes uses the "irrational" type of fear in such a direct form as that of Frankenstein's monster or Dracula. More often it lets irrational fear masquerade as the rational: we are given reasons to fear the villain, but the fear actually aroused goes beyond the reasons given. Talent in melodramatic writing is most readily seen in the writer's power to make his human villain seem superhuman, diabolical. Historically the villains in our tradition stem from the archvillain Lucifer, and a good deal of recent Shakespeare scholarship has been illustrating in detail the possible derivation of *Richard III* from the medieval Vice. The illustrations are nice to have; the principle was clear in advance. But where the villains stem from is relatively unimportant. What matters is whether a given writer can actually endow his villain with some of the original energy. We must catch a glimpse of hell flame, a whiff of the sulphur. This we do in even a comic work if the sense of horror is profound enough—as in Kleist's *The Broken Jug*. Among modern writers it must be admitted that the novelists—Melville or Emily Brontë—have been better diabolists than the playwrights. The stage villains, despite their reputation, have not been too monstrously evil. If their imprecations have seemed ludicrous, it is because the evil is not more than skin-deep. A villain shouldn't have to work too hard at villainy.

Because the drama tends to concentrate its vision in a few persons, it will tend to embody evil in a few villains, and often in a single one. This is not to say that it has no other resource. Melodramatic vision is paranoid: we are being persecuted, and we hold that all things, living and dead, are combining to persecute us. Or rather, nothing is dead. Even the landscape has come to life if only to assault us. Perhaps one might sense something of this vision behind Birnam Wood's coming to Dunsinane in *Macbeth*, even though the playwright provides soldiers to carry it. For Emily Brontë, at any rate, the Yorkshire moors and the Yorkshire weather are "the very devil"—just as much as her villain, Heathcliffe. Popular Victorian melodrama made extensive use of bad weather and dangerous landscape. High seas and deep chasms threaten to swallow our hero up. The very fact that I describe such events as "swallowing up" shows that a little of the animism rubs off, even on a critic.

It is amazing what the nineteenth-century stage could do in the presentation of raging seas, mountains, glaciers, frozen lakes, and the like, yet there were always much narrower limits than in a novel, and the playwright had to reinforce the hostility of landscape with other hostilities. "Melodramatic" artifices of plot come under this head, and particularly that notorious device: outrageous coincidence. It is often by virtue of this feature that melodrama is differentiated from tragedy, the argument being that the melodramatic procedure is too frivolous. Yet there are some particularly gross examples in the supreme tragedies, and, in general, outrageous coincidence, when not frivolously used, has no frivolous effect. It intensifies the effect of paranoia. It enlists circumstances in the enemy's ranks—as Strindberg did in real life when several little incidents conspired to deprive him of his absinthe on several successive occasions. It represents a projection of "irrational" fear.

Exaggeration

The long arm of coincidence is a freakish thing. Mention it and within a minute someone will use the word exaggeration. This brings us back both to the prejudice against melodrama and to the essence of melodrama itself. Like farce, this genre may be said, not to tumble into absurdity by accident, but to revel in it on purpose. To question the absurd in it is to challenge, not the conclusion, but the premise. In both genres, the writer enjoys a kind of *Narrenfreiheit*— the fool's exemption from common sense—and what he writes must be approached and judged accordingly.

We are accustomed to acknowledge only a slight degree of exaggeration, in the artistic reproduction of life—just enough, we tell ourselves, to sharpen an outline. The image in our minds is of portraits in which the painter renders the appearances much as we think we have seen them ourselves, though we permit him a ten per cent deviation because he's an artist. But suppose the deviation from common sense grows much greater? Is the picture necessarily getting worse all the time? No, but for exaggerations which are no longer slight but gross, we require another criterion. A difference of degree turns into a difference of kind. Of a melodramatist whom we disapprove, we must not say: "You have exaggerated too much," but: "You have exaggerated awkwardly, mechanically." We might even have to say: "You have exaggerated too little," for in an age of Naturalism a writer's courage sometimes fails him and he tries to pass off a tame duck as a beast of the jungle.

The exaggerations will be foolish only if they are empty of feeling. Intensity of feeling justifies formal exaggeration in art, just as intensity of feeling creates the "exaggerated" forms of childhood fantasies and adult dreams. It is as children and dreamers—one might melodramatically add: as neurotics and savages too—that we enjoy melodrama. Exaggeration of what? Of the facts as seen by the sophisticated, scientific, adult mind. The primitive, neurotic, childish mind does not exaggerate its own impressions.

What is a giant? A man, eighteen feet high. An exaggeration surely? Someone has multiplied by three. What is a giant? A grownup as seen by a baby. The baby is two feet high, the grownup, six. The ratio *is* one to three. There is no exaggeration.

There is a very fine French film, *Zero for Conduct*, in which school teachers are seen through children's eyes. They seemed enormous and distorted at times because the camera has been placed near their feet. People called the result stylization. The word suggests the sophisticated, the artificial, and the adult. What was done was naïve, natural, and infantile. The word "exaggeration" can be misleading.

There is something similar to say of the "grandiosity" of melodramatic acting. That we are all ham actors in our dreams means that melodramatic acting, with its large gestures and grimaces and its declamatory style of speech, is not an exaggeration of our dreams but a duplication of them. In that respect, *melodrama is the Naturalism of the dream life*. Nor is it only to our dreams that melodramatic acting corresponds. Civilization, as I have been saying, asks us to hide our feelings and even instructs us in the art of doing so. What feelings we cannot completely conceal we reduce to mere shadows of themselves. Hence the appositeness of the movie camera: it can see those minute movements of the features which is all that is left in civilized man of corporeal expression. When it enlarges them in close-ups ten or more feet high it is achieving the old melodramatic grandiosity in its own way and without the actors' assistance.

One of the principal emotions is Fear. What does it look like?

> The heart beats wildly ... there is a deathlike pallor; the breathing is labored; the wings of the nostrils are widely dilated; there is a gasping and convulsive motion of the lips, a tremor on the hollow cheek, a gulping and catching of the throat; the uncovered and protruding eyeballs are fixed on the object of terror; or they may roll restlessly from side to side. . . . The pupils are . . . enormously dilated. All the muscles of the body may become rigid or may be thrown into convulsive movements. The hands are alternately clenched and opened, often with a twitching movement. The arms may be protruded as if to avert some dreadful danger, or may be thrown wildly over the head.

What does Hatred look like?

> . . . intense frowning; eyes wide open; display of teeth; grinding teeth and contracting jaws; opened mouth with tongue advanced; clenched fists; threatening action of arms; stamping with the feet; deep inspirations—panting; growling and various cries; automatic repetition of one word or syllable; sudden weakness and trembling of voice . . . convulsion of lips and facial muscles, of limbs and trunk; acts of violence to one's self, as biting fists or nails; sardonic laughter; bright redness of face; sudden pallor of face; extreme dilation of nostrils; standing up of hair on head. . . .

Now someone might suppose I have been quoting descriptions of melodramatic acting. We today have certainly never thought of anyone but a stage villain grinding his teeth or giving vent to fiendish hate in a sardonic laugh. Actually, the first of these quotations is from Charles Darwin's book on the emotions, and the second is from an old Italian manual on the same subject. William James used to read both passages to his classes at Harvard, and they are preserved, where I myself found them, in his *Principles of Psychology*. If these are fair accounts of emotion, then melodrama is not so much exaggerated as uninhibited.

Language

Melodramatic dialogue has been the object of more mockery, perhaps, than even the plots and the characters and the acting. Naturally, vulgar melodrama is couched in vulgar rhetoric, but the joke against this rhetoric remains a poor one if the assumption is made, and it usually is, that plain, colloquial English should have been used, and not a heightened form of the language. An elevated rhetoric is a legitimate and indeed inexorable demand of melodrama. Ordinary conversation would be incongruous and anticlimactic.

In any case, the Victorian rhetoric that makes us smile was not a new thing, created by Victorian melodramatists: It was the lag-end—the rags and tatters, if you will—of something that had once been splendid. Few would call the dialogue of Victor Hugo's plays good tragic poetry. But it is good rhetoric, as is the dialogue of the German *Sturm und Drang* drama from which French Romantic drama derives. In England the postmedieval drama begins with the establishment of a melodramatic rhetoric in Marlowe's *Tamburlaine,* and melodramatic rhetoric subserved tragedy, or declined into bombast or banality, or merely served its natural purpose as the proper style of melodrama, until about 1850.

Almost exactly at that date we find the old melodramatic order confronting the new Naturalistic one in what should be a classic instance. Turgenev wrote a play about a woman and her stepdaughter both in love with the same man. This play—*A Month in the Country*—inaugurates the era of natural, unmelodramatic dialogue. Now the writing of *A Month in the Country* was possibly prompted by a play of Balzac's on the same theme, *The Stepmother,* in which some may be surprised to find the great "realist" still using the melodramatic method in general and the melodramatic rhetoric in particular. Turgenev's work ends with a quiet separation and an equally quiet departure by coach; Balzac's with poisonings, lifetime punishments, an appeal to God, and a hint of insanity:

STEPDAUGHTER   I have been told all. This woman is innocent of the crime she is accused of. Religion has made me realize that pardon cannot be obtained on high by those who do not leave it behind them here below. I took the key of her desk from Madame. I myself went in search of poison. I myself tore off this piece of paper to wrap it in; for I wanted to die.

STEPMOTHER   Oh! Pauline! take my life, take all I love . . . Oh! doctor, save her!

STEPDAUGHTER   Do you know why I come to pull you out of the abyss you are in? Because Ferdinand has just told me something which has brought me back from the tomb. He has such horror of being with you in life, that he is following me— me—into the grave, where we shall rest together, married by death.

STEPMOTHER   Ferdinand! . . . Ah! God Above! At what price am I saved?

FATHER   But, unhappy child, why are you dying? Am I not, have I ceased for one moment to be a good father? They say it is I who am guilty . . .

YOUNG MAN   Yes, General. And it is I alone who can solve the riddle for you, and make clear to you how you are guilty.

FATHER   You, Ferdinand, you to whom I offered my daughter, you who love her . . .

YOUNG MAN   My name is Ferdinand, Count of Marcandal, son of General Marcandal . . . you understand?

GENERAL   Ah! Son of a traitor, you could bring under my roof only death and treachery! . . . Defend yourself!

YOUNG MAN   Will you fight, General, against a dead man?
(*He falls.*)

STEPMOTHER   (*rushes to the Young Man with a cry*) Oh! (*She recoils before the father who advances toward his daughter; then she takes out a phial, but throws it away at once.*) Oh! No, I condemn myself to live for this poor old man! (*The father kneels beside his dead daughter.*) Doctor, what is he doing? . . . Could he be losing his reason? . . .

FATHER   (*stammering like a man who cannot find the words*) I . . . I . . . I . . .

DOCTOR   General, what are you doing?

GENERAL   I . . . I am trying to say a prayer for my daughter! . . .
(*The curtain falls.*)°

I have picked a passage from a great writer lest anyone be tempted to attribute the deficiencies of such writing to lack of talent. Another mistake would be to think that the advantage lies in every respect with Turgenev. In art, every advantage is also a disadvantage. The gentleness of muted strings and the majesty of the full orchestra cannot be presented concurrently. Turgenev and Chekhov achieved their special effects by foregoing others. Modern persons will tend to attribute Balzac's failure to the absurdity of the incidents: he piles on the agony till we smile. Yet this diagnosis cannot be correct—Shakespeare piles on as much agony and we do not smile. The failure is only one of a tired rhetoric that no longer gives to the events and situations sufficient support.

Zola and After

So, one could say, melodrama died with Balzac's generation, and Naturalism took its place in Turgenev's generation. As such generalizations go, it is not a bad one, but as such generalizations also go, it is misleading. What actually happened was both more curious and more complex. Naturalism did become the creed of the age. Its acceptance was indeed widespread, embracing most cultured people. It is a doctrine which I find present-day American students still regarding as the law of the Medes and Persians. The curious thing is that, while our age generally is dedicated to Naturalist principles, the outstanding writers of the age are forever protesting against them. The fact of the protest, and its frequency, proves the prevalence of the principles, right enough; but, going back over the record, it is amazing how *many* writers of how *many* different schools protested. It is even enlightening to learn what some of the champions of Naturalism actually did— and actually said.

Emile Zola, for instance, who is supposed to have killed melodrama and given birth to the Naturalistic philosophy. Hear him attack melodrama:

> I defy the romantics to put on a cloak and dagger drama; the medieval clanking of old iron, the secret doors, poisoned wines and all the rest of it would convince no one. Melodrama, that middle class offspring of the romantic drama, is even more dead and no one wants it any more. Its false sentimentality, its complications of stolen children, recovered documents, its brazen improbabilities, have all brought it into such scorn that our attempt to revive it would be greeted with laughter. . . .

Any wish one might feel to demonstrate the merit of plots about stolen children and recoverd documents is checked by the knowledge that Zola spoke under provocation of a thousand bad works of art. And note what, in this same preface to *Thérèse Raquin*, he proposes to replace bad melodrama with:

> I made the one dark room the setting for the play so that nothing should detract from its atmosphere and sense of fate. I chose ordinary, colorless, subsidiary characters to show the banality of every-day life behind the excruciating agonies of my chief protagonists. . . .

° I have translated this afresh because the only translation I could find was far more ponderous than the French. It renders "*coupable*" as "culpable," "*l'abîme où vous etes*" as "the abyss which had engulfed you," etc. I have left out a couple of speeches, and given the characters appellations calculated to help those who do not know the play.

"Banality," "colorlessness"—certainly these belong to the naturalistic conception as generally understood. But a "sense of fate"? "Excruciating agonies"? And the banality only a foil to these extremities? At this point, one remembers what had been the effect of removing "banalities" from the Victorian melodrama. It had been to reduce the spectator's anxiety by relieving him of contact with his own life. By such a reduction, melodrama was becoming ever more boring and silly. What Zola is really doing is recharging the battery of fear which had been allowed to run down. The substitution of a banal (that is, recognizable) milieu for a "romantic" (that is, unacceptable) milieu is to play on the spectator's anxieties. True, Zola regarded his view of environment as scientific, but in those days science was itself the supreme romance, and here we find him calling for a sense of fate—which is what his own depiction of environment, like Ibsen's and Strindberg's incidentally—bears witness to. Technically, Zola's accounts of the milieu differ from Melville's or Emily Brontë's. He goes through a certain rigmarole—or ritual—of sociobiology, but he arrives at similar results. He is melodramatic.

The most pointed and prolonged polemic ever conducted against melodrama is to be found in the works of Bernard Shaw, prefaces and plays alike. *The Devil's Disciple* is the obvious, crude example, but in the preface to *Saint Joan*, nearly thirty years later, Shaw is still hammering away at the same point and arguing that the merit of his new play lies in its avoidance of melodrama. Notably, he has changed the character of the historical Bishop Cauchon so that the latter will no longer remind anyone of a stage villain.

Now Shaw's Cauchon is certainly at some distance from the snarling, gloating, swaggering villain of vulgar melodrama, but, for all Shaw's propaganda against the idea of villains, is he not still a villain, and even a traditional one? It was scarcely a new idea to make the devil witty, genial, and sophisticated. Actors take to the role of Cauchon, just because, if they are experienced, they have played it many times before. One *may* smile and smile and be a villain: one often does.

If Shaw hated the morals of melodrama—the projection upon the world of our irresponsible narcissistic fantasies—he loved its manners. Maybe any man only parodies what he is secretly fond of; maybe he is envious of the parodied author's powers; or maybe he thinks he could outdo him. In any case, Shaw did not rest content with parody. After firing salvos at melodrama, he went on to steal its ammunition. As well as illustrating the limitations of melodrama, *The Devil's Disciple* exemplifies its merits, and, in the critical writings of Shaw, though we do not find the *name* of melodrama held in honor, we find the melodramatic element honored under other names: such as opera.

Unlike most opera-goers of today, Shaw enjoyed opera as a form of theatre, rather than a kind of concert, and he entered enthusiastically into just those libretti which the twentieth century has decided are so much bosh—such as the libretti of *Rigoletto* and *Il Trovatore*. Nor is this enthusiasm extracurricular: Shaw's plays themselves call for the "exaggerated," sweeping movements of operatic (that is, melodramatic) performance. At one time Shaw had to stress and reiterate this point because his stage director, Granville-Barker, leaned toward the Naturalistic use of both voice and body. A photograph survives of Shaw showing Barker a little swordplay in *Androcles and the Lion*. On the picture Barker has achieved only a "small," nervous attitude, while Shaw is striking a flamboyant pose with his feet set wide apart and his sword held high in the air.

His advice to Barker about his own form of theatre in general—"Remember that it's Italian opera"—we can translate: "Play it as melodrama."

The furthest that Shaw's playwriting ever got from melodrama was, I suppose, the "pure dialogue" of the "Don Juan in Hell" scene from *Man and Superman*. The cast is made up of a hero, a heroine, a villain, and a clown, a drama quartet which is said to have become standard in the hands of the French playwright Pixerécourt a hundred years earlier. Pixerécourt is listed in the textbooks as the founder of popular melodrama.

Since *Man and Superman* (1903) we have had various modernist schools of drama and various individual departures or one-man schools. The result of action and reaction, they present themselves as battling factions of contrasting conviction, yet it is impossible to mention one innovator of the period who was not trying to reintroduce the melodramatic. German Expressionism can be interpreted as the search for a modern dress for melodrama, Brecht's Epic Theatre as an attempt to use melodrama as a vehicle for Marxist thought. Cocteau, Anouilh, and Giraudoux have put the Greek myths to melodramatic use. Of the three, the most concentratedly melodramatic is Cocteau, perhaps because fear of persecution is his strongest emotion; in his *Orpheus,* the maenads are the hostile world of all melodrama.

What of Eugene O'Neill? Some think he revived tragedy. Those who disagree have usually spoken only of a failure. But if he often failed to achieve tragedy, O'Neill succeeded as often in achieving melodrama.

What O'Neill's father had chiefly done for a living was play Edmond Dantès in the melodrama *Monte Crisco.* The young O'Neill was a rebel against Father and considered himself a rebel against *Monte Cristo.* It remains a question, though, whether the modern ideas he picked up in Greenwich Village are the backbone of his work or whether, like many rebels against Father, he was not really identified with Father. That the son of an actor should be a playwright is in itself interesting. It is as if the son wished to write the father's lines and "work" him like a marionette. However this may be, *Mourning Becomes Electra,* as it seems to many of us, fails where it is modern and intellectual, succeeds where it is Victorian melodrama.

It was the melodramatic touch that O'Neill brought to the American theatre already in the twenties, that Lillian Hellman and Clifford Odets brought to it in the thirties, and that Tennessee Williams and Arthur Miller brought in the late forties. In the nineteen fifties, one of the most striking new presences in world theatre was Eugène Ionesco. His play *The Lesson* is about a mild-seeming teacher who murders forty pupils a day. Ionesco uses Grand Guignol as a vehicle for a vision of modern life. The same is true of the leading younger playwright in the German-language area, Friedrich Dürrenmatt. . . .

But I would not like to spoil the point by pushing it too far. The phrase "revival of melodrama" is far from covering all that is alive in modern drama, nor would I wish to call every play *a melodrama* in which there are melodramatic elements. On the contrary, I shall later propose the label *tragi-comedy* for some plays whose melodramatic qualities have been noted here. And of course there is no reason why the same play should not be seen, now as a melodrama, now as a tragi-comedy, now as something else again, if thereby its inherent qualities are brought out. Reality in this field, as in others, is various and variable, and each perspective on it has some peculiar advantage.

The Quintessence of Drama

As modern persons we are willy-nilly under the spell of Naturalism. However often we tell ourselves the contrary, we relapse into assuming the normal and right thing to be a subdued tone, small human beings, a milieu minutely reproduced. Indeed a tremendous amount of energy goes into keeping up this illusion of the monotonous mediocrity of everyday life: otherwise how could the genteel tradition have survived the discoveries of modern physics and the atrocities of modern behavior? I am arguing, then, up to a point, that melodrama is actually more natural than Naturalism, corresponds to reality, not least to modern reality, more closely than Naturalism. Something has been gained when a person who has seen the world in monochrome and in miniature suddenly glimpses the lurid and the gigantic. His imagination has been reawakened.

The melodramatic vision is in one sense simply normal. It corresponds to an important aspect of reality. It is the spontaneous, uninhibited, way of seeing things. Naturalism is more sophisticated but Naturalism is not more natural. The dramatic sense is the melodramatic sense, as one can see from the play-acting of any child. Melodrama is not a special and marginal kind of drama, let alone an eccentric or decadent one; it is drama in its elemental form; it is the quintessence of drama. The impulse to write drama, is, in the first instance, the impulse to write melodrama, and, conversely, the young person who does not wish to write melodrama, does not write drama at all, but attempts a nondramatic genre, lyric, epic, or what not. It should be clear, then, why in treating melodrama, farce, tragedy, comedy, I have put melodrama first.

In this chapter I have tried to break down a prejudice against melodrama, just as in previous chapters I tried to break down prejudices against plot and prejudices against type characters—and, *mutatis mutandis*, for the same reasons. At the same time, there has been a negative side to this chapter's argument. I have used the words "childish," "neurotic," "primitive," even the words "narcissistic" and "paranoid," and in this summing-up I have had to insert saving clauses like "up to a point" and "in a sense."

In *The Interpretation of Dreams* Freud says that neurotics, like children, "exhibit on a magnified scale feelings of love and hatred for their parents." The remark needs interpreting. What, for instance, is a nonmagnified scale of feeling, and who exhibits that? Sigmund Freud, when hating a father who humiliated himself before antisemites? Anna Freud, when dedicating her life to continuing the work of Sigmund Freud? I mean the *argumentum ad hominem* kindly; and it could be aimed at anyone. What I am saying is that any nonmagnified feelings represent an ideal standard, and what we all have are the magnified feelings of the child, the neurotic, the savage. Such feelings of course form the basis of melodrama, and are the reason for its manifold magnifications.

Though melodramatic vision is not the worst, it is also not the best. It is good "up to a point," and the point is childhood, neuroticism, primitivity. Melodrama is human but it is not mature. It is imaginative but it is not intelligent. If again, for the sake of clarity, we take the most rudimentary form of melodrama, the popular Victorian variety, what do we find but the most crass of immature fantasies? The reality principle is flouted right and left, one is oneself the supreme reality, one's innocence is axiomatic, any interloper is a threat and a monster, the ending will be happy because one feels that it has to be. In an earlier chapter I said theatre corresponded to that phase of a child's life when he creates magic worlds. I mean that that is where theatre comes from, not necessarily where it remains. Melodrama belongs to this magical phase, the phase when thoughts seem omnipotent, when the distinction between *I want to* and *I can* is not clearly made, in short when the larger reality has not been given diplomatic recognition.

Am I speaking now of all melodrama or just of the vulgar melodrama of Victorian popular theatres? It is hard to draw such a line, as it is hard to draw a line between melodrama and tragedy. Rather than separate blocks, the reality seems to be a continuous scale with the crudest melodrama at one end and the highest tragedy at the other. In tragedy the reality principle is not flouted, one is not oneself the sole reality to be respected, one's guilt is axiomatic, other people may or may not be threats or monsters, the ending is usually unhappy.

Yet the idea of such a scale is misleading if it suggests that tragedy is utterly distinct from melodrama. There is a melodrama in every tragedy, just as there is a child in every adult. It is not tragedy, but Naturalism, that tries to exclude childish and melodramatic elements. William Archer, a Naturalist, defined melodrama as "illogical and sometimes irrational tragedy." The premise is clear: tragedy is logical and rational. Looking for everyday logic and reasonableness in tragedy, Archer remorselessly drew the conclusion that most of the tragedy of the past was inferior to the middle-class drawing-room drama of London around 1910. Had he been consistent he would even have included Shakespeare in the indictment.

But tragedy is not melodrama minus the madness. It is melodrama plus something.

Tragedy and Melodrama: Speculations on Generic Form[*]

Robert Bechtold Heilman

I

This essay grows out of my sense of a persistent confusion in the use of the word *tragedy*. As critics, of course, we know that we can never expect to agree on final definitions that will make possible a consistent criticism. But the discrepancies which we can never finally eliminate, even in professional usage, have got completely out of hand in popular usage. This fact is my starting point, and in this sense, literary criticism merges with social criticism. The word *tragedy* means not only plays of a certain kind but almost all kinds of painful experiences: an early death, an unexpected death by disease, a financial failure, a suicide, a murder, an automobile accident, a train accident, an airplane accident, a successful military movement by a hostile power, a sadistic act, a government error, almost any act of violence. I recall an accident in which a small plane, whose pilot had bailed out, crashed into a building; the newspaper I was then reading headlined the story, "Tragedy to Plane and Factory." This seemed to stretch the idea of tragedy pretty far. The strain was increased by the fact, which was soon revealed, that the factory was a cheese factory, for to many people cheese will not seem the likeliest of tragic materials.

What I want to explore is the possibility of finding distinctions among the host of disagreeable events lumped under the word *tragedy*. Note my word *explore*. Such criticism is not logical demonstration; it is at best a form of rhetoric. That is, it succeeds in so far as it persuades anyone else that it is useful. The most the critic can hope for is to be partially persuasive.

An experiment in making distinctions should justify itself. However, I want to note what seems to me to be an especial danger in that loose use of the word *tragedy* that penetrates our whole society. I do not think we can simply rest in our knowledge that we have wide areas of bad usage. We need to make some effort to counter bad usage. For when a word is a catchall for many meanings only loosely related, it loses character. It tends to be used only for simple or wholesale or lump meanings. In fact, we can propose it as a law of language that when one word gains several meanings, the inferior meaning will tend to force the superior

[*] Robert B. Heilman, "Tragedy and Melodrama," *The Texas Quarterly*, Summer, 1960, pp. 36–50.

meaning out of circulation: I mean that the rougher, more general, looser, or la-
zier meaning will win out over the more exact or precise or demanding meaning. This is Gresham's law of semantic currency. When *tragedy* means the whole
world of misfortune we cannot distinguish particular misfortunes in terms of
their cause, nature, and meaningfulness. We lack the words for this; what is
worse, we lack the concepts. What we do not distinguish, we do not understand;
I will go a step further and suggest that if experiences are not understood, there
is a sense in which they are not even experienced. This confusion extends beyond
verbal haziness and begins to interfere with fundamental clarity of mind and
therefore, I think, with sense of reality.

II

I believe that the word *tragedy* may suitably be applied to one form of catastrophic experience, and that this can be differentiated from all others. For a
start, we may use Aristotle's definition of the tragic hero as the good man who
gets into trouble through some error or shortcoming for which the standard term
has become the tragic flaw. This I take to be a central, irreducible truth about
tragic reality.

This assumption of mine has a number of consequences. The first is that the
tragic character is essentially a divided character, and I shall regularly use *divided*, *dividedness*, and *division* as key words. The idea of goodness and the idea of
the flaw suggest different incentives and different directions, a pulling apart,
though not of pathological intensity, within the personality. The division in the
hero may be of different sorts. In the first place, it may reflect the kind of division that seems inseparable from human community—from the fact that, in the
ordering of life, we maintain different imperatives that correspond to different
and perhaps irreconcilable needs. Hamlet and Orestes, those heroes so different
from each other in time and place and yet so incredibly alike in the trials that
visit them, cannot avenge their fathers, the victims of evil deeds, without themselves committing evil deeds. Antigone cannot be true to family duty and love,
and to religious obligation, without contravening civil law; and Creon—who in
some ways is really a better tragic hero than Antigone—cannot or at least does
not maintain civil order without punitive decrees that profoundly violate human
feelings and sense of justice. Yet none of these heroes could refrain from the
course that leads to guilt without feeling intolerably acquiescent in a public evil.

Such heroes and heroines, if I do not misread them, incorporate the dividedness of a humanity whose values, because they naturally elude the confines of
formal logic, create an apparently insoluble situation. In this situation the crucial
actions of heroes, though they are exacted by a powerful sense of moral obligation, nevertheless become infused with guilt. For these heroes the two counterimperatives have so much authority that no observer can say with assurance, "It
would be better if Hamlet or Antigone or Cordelia had done so and so." Nor
could a fully aware person, caught between injunctions that are apparently incompatible, come out of such situations without damage; he could be safe only
by canceling part of his awareness. This canceling would surely threaten the
common order more than the ambiguous act does. Suppose Hamlet had decided
that the ghostly exhortations that he heard were simply the product of tensions
within himself, that he was worrying too much, that his best step was to get ad-

justed to the existent order and to stop brooding about evils which he couldn't help anyway and which might well be only imaginary. Or that Orestes had decided that his father deserved his fate, or Cordelia that she might just as well follow her sisters in apple-polishing an eccentric elder. Maybe these would be safe courses, at least temporarily. But what diminished persons we would have, and what a shrunken sense of reality.

Of characters caught in the Hamlet and Orestes situation we may say that they are divided between "imperatives," that is, different injunctions, each with its own validity, but apparently irreconcilable. With another type of tragic hero the division may be said to be between "imperative" and "impulse," between the moral ordinance and the unruly passion, between mandate and desire, between law and lust. Tradition and community give an ordinance, but egotism drives one away from it. Macbeth seeks power through politics, Faustus through intellect; what makes them tragic, as ordinary power-grabbers are not, is that neither of them can ever, in yielding to impulse, force out of consciousness the imperatives that he runs against. Oedipus has the same division, but with a different alignment of forces: he wants to obey the imperative but is betrayed by the riotous impulse. Finally, there is a third representative tragic dividedness— the split between impulse and impulse, which I believe to be a characteristic situation in Ibsen. Rebecca West and Rosmersholm, for instance, are divided between what I will call the impulses of the old order and those of rationalist enlightenment, in a peculiarly modern tragic situation.

I have used the term *imperative* to denote the obligation of general validity, the discipline of self that cannot be rejected without penalty, whether it is felt as divine law or moral law or civil law, or, in a less codified but no less prescriptive way, as tradition or duty or honor. Imperative reflects a communal consciousness. By *impulse* I refer to the force that originates in or is rooted in or identified with the individual personality and is of an almost biological sort; though the specific feelings that impel the individual may be of the widest occurrence in humanity, they are felt as a need, or as a satisfaction, or as an aggrandizement of the individual, in almost a bodily way. Imperative tends toward the self-abnegatory, impulse toward the self-assertive. But I do not wish to labor this distinction. I have made it, and I have suggested three basic patterns of division, as a way of trying to make concrete the idea of dividedness in the tragic hero.

There are two other consequences of the idea of tragedy as the experience of the good man with the flaw. The first of these is that division means choice: there are alternatives, and man must select one or another. This idea is so familiar that I will limit myself to this bare statement of it. The second is that choice implies consciousness: alternatives are not really alternatives, at least in the dramatic substance, if they do not in some way, however indirectly or however tardily, live in the consciousness of the hero. The drama is a lesser one—it has less range—if the hero simply does not know what it is all about or never comes to know what it is all about. Willie Loman is a hero of such limited consciousness that, for many readers, he pushes *Death of a Salesman* into a lower order of excellence. Division, finally, is not only the occasion of self-awareness or self-knowledge, but the very material of self-knowing. It is the inconsistent and the contradictory that require the studious intelligence; the unified, the coherent, the harmonious dissolve the world of alternatives and render the customary strivings of self-understanding irrelevant.

III

To sum up: *tragedy* should be used only to describe the situation in which the divided human being faces basic conflicts, perhaps rationally insoluble, of obligations and passions; makes choices, for good or for evil; errs knowingly or involuntarily; accepts consequences; comes into a new, larger awareness; suffers or dies, yet with a larger wisdom.

Now this is quite different from popular or journalistic tragedy (here we come to the social dimension of the problem): young man drives fast, hits truck that drives out in front of him, and he and his fiancée are killed. This will almost invariably be called, "Tragedy on Highway 90," and for many people this is *all* of tragedy. The death-dealing truck might be a disease or a careless engineer or a defective airplane wing or an assailant; the essence of it is the shock of unprogrammed death. This is a rather long way from the tragic pattern that we are able to discern in the practice of the Greeks and Elizabethans and at least in the intuitions of some moderns. Even in the most skillful journalism we would hardly be able to get inside the victims and see them as divided between options or struggling in a cloudy dilemma of imperative and impulse; they do not choose but are chosen; something just happens to them; consequences are mechanical, not moral; and most of all they do not grow into that deeper understanding, of themselves and of their fate, which is the dramatic heart of the experience. For in that sudden death there is little to understand; consciousness is not sharpened but is bluntly ended.

To use the term *tragedy* indiscriminately for what Oedipus does and experiences and learns, and for what happens to a car driver through his own or someone else's carelessness, I submit, is not a casual slip of the tongue or a laughable folk error, but a real confusion that can have undesirable consequences for our grasp of reality. For by our Gresham's law of semantic currency, the cheaper meaning forces out the meaning of precise value. Tragedy comes to mean *only* accidents and sudden death or anachronistic death. As a result we tend to lose touch with certain ideas that are an indispensable means of contemplating human catastrophe: the idea that calamity may come from divisions within human nature and within the ordering of life. The idea that man may choose evil. The idea that potential evil within him may overcome him despite resolution or flight. The idea that brutal events may come out of the normal logic of character. The idea that man is never safe from himself. The idea that the knowledge of such ideas is essential to the salvation of the individual and to the health of institutions. All these ideas are implicitly discarded if the word *tragedy* conveys to us only such a thing as a smashup on Highway 90. And what do we put in place of what is lost? The idea that the worst that can happen to us is an unexpected shortening of life. The idea that this cutting short is the work of causes outside ourselves. The idea that we are innocent victims. This is a fantastic loss of tools of understanding and, implicitly, an unhealthy oversimplification of reality.

Here you may want to argue that in using such a phrase as "only unhappy accidents" I am minimizing the extent, the influence, and the force of such events. Not at all. I do not deny the reality of accidents, the pain and anguish they cause, or their power to move us either in daily experience or in literary representation. I do not suppose that we can eliminate unhappy accidents, ignore them, forget them, deny their power over our actions and feelings, or discontinue making literature of them. All I am troubled by is calling them "tragedy," which I am hoping to persuade you is no trivial error. I have the greatest respect for the rare news editor who, instead of announcing "Tragedy on Highway 90," will say "Accident on Highway 90: Two Dead." There is the crux of the matter: putting experience into the right category. Now, for the category of event which is so widely called "Tragedy on Highway 90" the proper term, I suggest, is *disaster*. It is a sufficiently capacious term to include all kinds of fatal accidents, the mortal illnesses that strike (we think) ahead of time, the destructive blows of a nature not yet quite tamed, and all the murderous violence that comes directly or by ricochet from the envious, the hostile, and the mad. Its very etymology makes *disaster* an appropriate term: it implies an undoing by action of the stars, and thus it is a fitting metaphor for all the unhappinesses that seem to come from without, to have no meaningful causes, and to let us feel guiltless. From now on, then, instead of speaking of the two meanings of *tragedy*—the meaning implied in the literary examples that remain always alive, and the contemporary journalistic meaning that pervades all our speech—I shall use the terms *tragedy* and *disaster* to denote these areas of experience that may always be theoretically distinguished.

However much they may be interwoven in the concrete event, tragedy and disaster are two fundamentally different structures of experience; to confuse them will involve errors of three kinds—intellectual, emotional, moral. The intellectual error I have already described or implied: it is to seek the causes of evil always outside ourselves, to whitewash ourselves, to be always without responsibility for calamities. The loose use of the word *tragedy* also leads us to a concomitant error of feeling. For if tragedy is simply what happens to us, we are all victims; victims must be pitied; and we can soon ooze into a rich morass of self-pity. Obviously we don't want to pity ourselves, if we are well people; but the universalization of the disaster principle sneaks pity in the back door. Sometimes we can pity ourselves simply by pitying others: Othello is a case in point. Or, in glorifying the man who pities, we may reveal a desire to cuddle up under that sympathetic wing. The word *compassionate* has become a cliché of book reviewing; in our time it is almost an ultimate term of praise for a writer. It has become embarrassing. Is *compassion* the word that comes to mind when we think of Shakespeare's treatment of Lear or Sophocles' portrayal of Oedipus? Is it not rather completeness of understanding, insight into human division, a full sense of both excellence and flaw? Compare the Christopher Fry character who says, "I'm still remembering/I can give pain, and that in itself is loss/Of liberty." When we shift from feeling sorry for pain received to fear of pain given, we move from the sense of disaster toward the tragic sense.

The third error in taking disaster for tragedy is the moral one of adopting a single-standard quantitative view of life. Disaster centers in death: we are getting less life than we have coming to us. It is not necessary to quarrel with a universal disinclination to die, especially ahead of what looks like sound scheduling; but as a matter of clarity we should observe that in our day the quest for longevity is both more extensive and more passionate than it has ever been before. This appears in our obsession with disaster, the most forceful reminder of mortality. Disaster is the realm of quantity of life; tragedy, of quality of life. The inevitable fear of disaster can grow until it eliminates all issues of quality. I do not complain about fear of death, which is a fact of life; my point is only that the ending of life is not the sole imperfection of life, and that to act as though it is, is not healthful.

IV

In disaster, what happens comes from without; in tragedy, from within. In disaster, we are victims; in tragedy, we make victims, of ourselves or others. In disaster, our moral quality is secondary; in tragedy, it is primary, the very source of action.

In literature, the problem is that of distinguishing between tragedy and what I will call, for the time being, the literature of disaster, which is often called tragedy. I regard the two forms as generically different, though they look alike because they both depict suffering. The literature of disaster comprises all those pages in which we record what has been done to us by fire, famine, the sword, and unjust men; in which our role is that of Job, plagued by our own kind, by machines, and by nature. In tragedy, as an art form, we contemplate our own errors; in the literature of disaster we mark the errors of others and the imperfections of circumstance. In tragedy we act; in the literature of disaster we are acted upon.

In the literature of disaster we find victims of situations that range from very simple to very complex. Though I want to avoid little catalogues that are too neat, I will suggest that we can identify several basic types of the victims that artists have discerned—the victims of nature, the victims of society, the victims of evil individuals, and those who are victims of themselves. This last, of course, sounds very much like tragedy, and the distinction will have to be clarified later.

Since I do not have space for analysis of plays, I will have to be like the Oriental geometrician who stated a theorem, drew an illustrative figure, and substituted, for the steps of demonstration leading to a formal conclusion, simply the word *Behold!* I use Synge's *Riders to the Sea* as an example of the literature of disaster dealing with the victim of nature; this play is generally called a tragedy, but its core is pathos; we remain serene observers, sympathetic, sharing the sadness of death, but never drawn into the experience of division and of self-knowledge, for there is none. The victim of society, a familiar figure in post-Romantic sensibility, appears archetypally in Dr. Stockmann in Ibsen's *Enemy of the People*—an embarrassingly simple picture of a noble reformer done in by a crass community. Our emotional involvement here hardly approaches the adult level. The drama of disaster that deals with the victim of society is managed somewhat more complexly in Friedrich Duerrenmatt's *The Visit* (1955). In this play the townspeople, to gain a vengeful woman's gift of a billion marks, informally sentence to death and execute one of the town's leading citizens, the original seducer of the woman who gives the billion marks. Like various dramas of disaster, *The Visit* has a powerful impact because it devotes itself exclusively to demonstrating the infinitude of human venality. It gains power at the expense of depth and complication; it simply excludes any other human characteristic but vengefulness and corruptibility. It denies the division which is at the heart of tragedy; and so, I submit, it not only narrows the aesthetic experience but reduces us to shocked spectators of a crime. This is one of the two representative risks of the literature of disaster: at the popular extreme it may entice us into a stereotyped situation, ready-made for emotional wear; or, as in *The Visit*, it may lock us out of a situation by making it so eccentric that to enter it would be suicide. That, too, is always a risk of expressionist drama, to which *The Visit* belongs: in such difficulties, as well as in other matters, we realize postrealist expressionism is very much like prerealist allegory.

The victim of the politically disordered society appears in *The Diary of*

Anne Frank. Here again is a drama of disaster that offers simple and easy emotional experience, pity for victims; only at one point does it approach tragedy—at the point at which Mr. Frank says, of the tensions among the hiding victims of the Nazis, "We don't need the Nazis to destroy us. We're destroying ourselves." The victim of the evil individual is found in one of the great dramas of disaster in English—Webster's *The Duchess of Malfi,* in which a charming and innocent woman is tortured and destroyed by her cruel brothers. She is not presented tragically; she does not, like great tragic heroes, "earn" her fate. Her honorable conduct simply happens to run afoul of the purposes of her vicious brothers. Lear, on the contrary, has made Goneril and Regan efficacious in the world; they are projections of a part of his own divided nature. Lear has made his world in a way that the Duchess has not. Webster presents the evil brothers as autonomous—like a flood or holocaust that destroys. This is not to deny the existence of autonomous evil; it is simply to say that it is not the world of tragedy.

Finally, in Gorki's *Lower Depths* and O'Neill's *The Iceman Cometh* (two works with extraordinary similarities of plot and structure), we find plays that are concerned with disaster of personality: that is, with that kind of collapse which makes the individual incapable of normal adult life. When we speak of the disaster of the self, however, we remember that the origin of the tragic situation is also within the self. At the risk of too epigrammatic a contrast we may say that the disaster of self has its origin in weakness, the tragedy of self in strength. In disaster, individuals are not up to traditional requirements; in tragedy, they are not held down by traditional requirements and eventually find themselves not up to the special rules they propose for themselves. One aesthetic leads to Mr. Zero, the other to Dr. Faustus; one character says, "Pity me," the other says, "I have sinned."

In *The Duchess of Malfi* Bosola sums up the action with the phrase "Oh this gloomy world." In *Riders to the Sea* Maurya says, ". . . there isn't anything else the sea can do to me." In *The Iceman Cometh* Larry Slade concludes, "By God, there's no hope! . . . Life is too much for me." "This gloomy world"—what is done to me—what is too much for me: this is the realm of disaster—of what happens to the victims of nature, of societal power or war, of weakness before the exigencies of life, of disillusionment, of corruption, of evil men. The realm of actual disaster that is the raw material of literary art is a large one. We do not underestimate the immediacy or anguish of that realm, or fail in sympathy with those injured or betrayed by such events, if we say, once again, that such fates are something other than tragic, and that the drama portraying such fates is not of the tragic order.

For many things that are terrible are not tragic.

V

The term *literature of disaster* which I have so far used is a cumbersome term and a limiting term. I propose, as my final point, that the literature of disaster is really a subdivision of a larger literary type. To that type I will give the term *melodrama.*

I am aware that to take *melodrama,* which in casual contemporary usage is a derogatory term designating popular machine-made entertainments, and to apply it to a wide range of literature that includes sober work and somber tones may seem capricious to the point of scandal. I hasten to deny caprice and to explain that I use melodrama as a neutral descriptive term. I use it because I believe that what we call "popular melodrama" has reduced to stereotypes and thus has trivialized the basic structural characteristics of a form that can be serious as well as silly.

Let us look first at the popular sense of *melodrama*. Its nature is suggested by phrases such as these: pursuit and capture, imprisonment and escape, false accusation, cold-blooded villain, innocence beleaguered, virtue triumphant, eternal fidelity, mysterious identity, lovers reconciled, fraudulence revealed, enemies foiled; the whole realm of adventure; the realm of mystery from the supernatural to the whodunit; the realm of vice and crime from horror to detection to reform. It is the world of shock and thrill, of what is regularly called "gripping" and "poignant." But it is rarely devoid of ideas, however flat and hackneyed these may be. In a century and a half its color has been variously revolutionary, democratic, patriotic, antitotalitarian, reformist (anti-gambling, slavery, drinking, dope addiction, etc.). The form is represented with delightful amplitude in an early example, Thomas Morton's *Speed the Plough* (1798), which, along with various popular comic effects, contains upper-class injustice, *nouveau riche* snobbery, poor man's integrity, a lover who almost gives up the poor girl for the rich one, bigamy, economic threats, secret grief, irrational enmity, mysterious identity, old villainy disclosed in a bloodcurdling confessional, a castle fire and a rescue, and garnishings of patriotic sentiment.

When we are still not free from totalitarianism it may seem blasphemous to suggest that Lillian Hellman's *Watch on the Rhine*, an anti-Nazi play of 1941, offers us, even if a little more sophisticatedly, the same fare as *Speed the Plough*. There is a simple villain-hero structure: we have no choice but to hate the Nazi sympathizer and love everyone else, and everyone else is mostly delightful Americans.

Speed the Plough and *Watch on the Rhine* both have the stock devices of entertainment popular in their day. But beneath the standardized appeals there is a basic plot form—the conflict of villains and heroes, of what we nowadays laughingly call good guys and bad guys. Yet such a pattern of action should not be dismissed as the especial property of the simple-minded. For however dull or trite or grotesque the actions of these good and bad competitors may be, the plots are simply a debased popular form of a stable central structure that appears in all times and in trivial and sober plays alike: in this structure, man is pitted against some force outside of himself—a compact enemy, a hostile group, a social pressure, a natural event, an accident, or a coincidence. This is one of the persistent fundamental structures of literature, whether it appear in a silly or meretricious form in a cinema or television thriller or be elaborated with dignity and power in *The Trojan Woman* or *Romeo and Juliet*. It draws upon permanent human attitudes, some perilous and some preserving, whether we disavow these when they become ludicrous in a Western or scarcely recognize them in some extraordinary struggle into which we have been drawn by artistic skill— the story of Annapurna, *Nigger of the Narcissus*, *War and Peace*, *Richard III*.

In the structure of melodrama, I suggest, man is essentially "whole"; this key word implies neither greatness nor moral perfection, but rather an absence of the kind of inner conflict that is so significant that it *must* claim our first attention. He is not troubled by motives that would distract him from the conflict outside himself. He may, in fact, be humanly incomplete; but his incompleteness is not the issue. In tragedy, man is divided; in melodrama, he has at least a quasi wholeness against besetting problems. In tragedy, the conflict is within man; in melodrama, it is between men, or between men and things.

We can find virtually "whole" or undivided characters in Ibsen's Dr. Stockmann, fighting community greed, and Lillian Hellman's Kurt Müller, fighting against Nazis. They are created by the same conception of character that appears in popular heroes pitted against cattle rustlers, holdup men, or racketeers. I say this not to disparage but to note the neutral fact of identity of character structure. If we rarely inspect the characters of heroes, we inspect those of victims even less. We find a virtually unified nature in Synge's Maurya, whose family is cut down by the sea; in the Franks, cut down by Nazi malice; in the Duchess of Malfi, cut down by her sadistic brothers. Villains are whole characters too—for instance, Duerrenmatt's citizenry that murders for money, and the Duchess of Malfi's murderous brothers. Even the wretched characters depicted by Gorki and O'Neill have a kind of wholeness: the wholeness of half-beings really cut off from any counterimpulses that would leave them split between retreat and participation. Wholeness, in other words, is a technical structure of character and personality; it is morally neutral; in goodness or badness, strength or weakness, the protagonist is in the main free from divergent impulses.

When we speak of the structure of a form we refer not only to its system of characterization and arrangements of characters but to its dynamics, or, in other terms, the structure of its action. We have seen how the popular thriller and the serious problem play, as we usually call it, are organized alike—on some variation of the villain-hero conflict. The final problem is to see how the drama of disaster also belongs to this pattern. In all these cases we have an essentially undivided protagonist facing an outer conflict. In this kind of situation only several types of outcome are possible—victory, or defeat, or perhaps a stalemate or compromise. Here is the *key* point. Disaster and the popular happy-ending play are not different formal entities but are simply the opposite extremes of the spectrum of melodrama: at one end, man, essentially whole, is beaten down by his antagonist; at the other, also essentially whole, he comes out on top. At the one end, man is victim; at the other, victor. The nature of the conflict is the same, the central structure is the same, but the artist chooses one point of view or another. He may see man vs. nature or political forces or society or other individuals, and he may see him as lost or as triumphant; there are scores of plays doing it one way or the other. The identifying mark of the melodramatic structure is not the particular outcome of the plot, but the conception of character and the alignment of forces. This identity we can always find beneath a considerable diversity of arrangements of action.

Finally, the melodramatic organization of experience has a psychological structure. It puts us into a certain posture which we find agreeable and that within limits has a certain utility. In most general terms, what it affords is the pleasure of experiencing wholeness—not the troubling, uneasy wholeness that exists when all the divergent elements of personality remain within the field of consciousness, or the rare integration of powers that may be earned by long discipline, but the sensation of wholeness that is created when one responds with a single impulse or potential and lets this function as a surrogate for the whole personality. In this quasi wholeness he is freed from the anguish of choice and from the pain of struggling with counterimpulses that inhibit and distort his single direct "action." If there is danger he is courageous; he is not distracted by fear, expediency, or the profit motive. Or he can be serene in adversity, unhampered by self-seeking, by impatience with the frailties of others, or by doubt about ends. Thus Kurt Müller in *Watch on the Rhine* and the stage version of Anne Frank's father: through them, melodrama affords a unity of desirable feeling—of the wisdom to bear troubles, of practical competence against evil. One is untroubled by psychic or physical fumbling, by indecisiveness, by weak muscles or strong counterimperatives. One is under the pleasant yoke of what I will call a mono-pathy: that single strong feeling that excludes all others and thus renders one whole. It may be a monopathy of hope or, for that matter, a monopathy of hope-lessness; a monopathy of contempt for the petty, discontent with destiny, indig-nation at evil doing, or castigation of the guilt of others. Even in defeat and di-saster, in being overwhelmed and victimized, I am convinced, the human being is able to find certain monopathic advantages.

Melodrama, in sum, includes the whole range of conflicts undergone by characters who are presented as undivided or at least without divisions of such magnitude that they *must* be at the dramatic center; hence melodrama includes a range of actions that extend from disaster to success, from defeat to victory, and a range of effects from the strongest conviction of frustration and failure that serious art can dramatize to the most frivolous assurance of triumph that a mass-circulation writer can confect. The issue here is not the reordering of the self, but the reordering of one's relations with others, with the world of people or things; not the knowledge of self, but the maintenance of self, in its assumption of wholeness, until conflicts are won or lost. There is a continuous spectrum of possibilities from the popular play in which the hostile force is always beatable to the drama of disaster in which the hostile force is unbeatable; at one extreme we view man in his strength, at the other, in his weakness. In structure of feeling the form is monopathic.

But the tragic hero is divided; he is in some way split between different forces or motives or values. His nature is dual or even multifold; the different elements are always present and dramatically operative; they are always realities that have to be reckoned with. In structure of feeling we may call tragedy "poly-pathic." The monopathic concentration may actually make melodrama in some ways more overwhelming, as in *The Duchess of Malfi*, where everything en-larges the sense of ruin; but tragedy, where impulses and options are double and multifold, where we are drawn now this way and now that, exacts a very much more complex and troubling awareness. One example: the spectacle of the aged Lear in the storm is overwhelming, too. But it cannot inspire simply a mono-pathic pity, since we do not forget that in a sense Lear has created this storm himself. Profound pity for the victim, yes, but also acknowledgment of the para-doxical presence of justice, and sense of irony—all are present in a disturbing po-lypathic experience.

In melodrama, man is seen in his strength or in his weakness; in tragedy, in both his strength and his weakness at once. In melodrama, he is victorious or he is defeated; in tragedy he experiences defeat in victory, or victory in defeat. In melodrama, man is simply guilty or simply innocent; in tragedy, his guilt and his innocence coexist. In melodrama, man's will is broken, or it conquers; in trage-dy, it is tempered in the suffering that comes with, or brings about, new knowl-edge.

The pathological extreme of the tragic condition is schizophrenia—where normal dividedness is magnified into the split that is illness. The pathological ex-treme of the melodramatic condition is paranoia—in one phase, the sense of a hostile "they" who will make one their victim, and, in another phase, the sense of one's own grandeur and, implicitly, of the downfall of others. Melodrama has affinities with politics; tragedy, with religion. Pragmatic politics appears as a competition for power between good and evil; our side is "good," and the other side, "evil." In the religious view of man is a sense of his dividedness, of the co-presence of counterimpulses always striving for dominance, of the fact that throughout his life he is a dual creature with equal possibilities of coming to salvation or damnation. Melodrama leans toward the timely, tragedy toward the timeless; on the one hand we have the world of protest and problem plays; on the other, the world of meditation and myth.

So much for the efforts to pile up distinctions between two basic sets of habits and attitudes. We have described melodrama as monopathic, presenting man in defeat or victory, in guilt or innocence; as having affiliations with politics and history, drawn to the topics that change with time. We have described tragedy as polypathic, showing man's victory in defeat, his mingling of guilt and innocence; as having affiliations with religion and myth, seeking the constants that transcend change. I have meant to suggest rather than to insist. It would not be helpful to make absolute, unvarying boundary lines; in life and literature, as they exist, there are not many instances of pure types. The literary work or the human personality *leans* in one direction or the other; it rarely *plunges* toward an extreme. But one cannot judge the individual work, or the person's way of confronting reality—one cannot say that here is a melodramatic style with some moments of the tragic or that here is a tragic cast of mind that includes something of the melodramatic—without first distinguishing the theoretical poles of attraction. The test of these theoretical constructions is their helpfulness in identifying actual literary structures or in understanding the strategies of spirit that men devise to face an imperfect world.

Aesthetic of Revolution: The Marxist Melodrama*

Wylie Sypher

The world of Dickens, we agree, is constructed upon a dualism of values that, aesthetically, are the values of melodrama: the good people and the bad, the proud and the humble, the hard and the soft, the simple and the devious, the rich and the poor. Edmund Wilson has remarked that the only complexity of which Dickens appears capable is to make one of his noxious characters wholesome or to turn one of his clowns into a serious person. The mechanism of the Dickens morality is the choice between extreme situations. The mechanism of the Dickens psychology is opposition and conversion—revolution within the psyche.

These Dickensian oppositions and conversions—the revolutionary choice between extremes—are, aesthetically, the mechanics of much of the art and thought of the 19th Century, which reaches its most determinate effects by means of polarities. The extremities of the 19th Century dilemma are inherent in the bourgeois situation. They are recognized by Dostoievsky's underground man, who observes, "Every day I keep discovering in myself elements of the most opposite order conceivable, and can feel them swarming within me." Thus the underground psyche, the psyche in the bourgeois world, behaves by revolutionary exclusions and leaps. Dostoievsky's sickness is, he confesses, his desperate situation between contradictory wills: "The more I have recognized what is good and what constitutes the great and the beautiful, the deeper I have plunged into the mire." This desperation is also the sickness of Baudelaire, who step by step descended to the hell of his own vices. The choice either/or in Kierkegaard or Dostoievsky is an archetypal pattern of 19th Century response. The same mechanism of either/or operates in the spasmodic decisions to which Browning and the Brontës drive their characters, in Schopenhauer's will to power and will to passivity, in Carlyle's heroic codes for master and slave, in Nietzsche's satanic inversion of philistine ideals, and especially in the romantic antithesis of matter and spirit, and the iron laws of science that banished a personal deity from the universe and named God a gaseous vertebrate. The choice offered the Victorians was descent from Adam or descent from ape. The weaker 19th Century minds hovered near compromise. The stronger became revolutionary. The alternatives were too unequivocal to be unified or reconciled within the sensibility. The imagination was pressed away from the neutrality of the world toward overstatement.

* Wylie Sypher, "Aesthetic of Revolution: The Marxist Melodrama," *The Kenyon Review*, Vol. X, No. 3 (Summer, 1948), pp. 431–444.

The art of Dickens is of the coarser 19th Century texture in which the polarities are animated by picturesque instances that have the vitality of overstatement. The assurance of Macaulay, liberal historian and social critic, overcharges his opinions until they have little relevance beyond their rhetorical effects, their "style." A great deal of the 19th Century has style in this sense, a grossness of manner apparent in Hugo or Browning's imagery (where a tulip is a bubble of blood and a kiss is fresh as dewdrops from a wilding rose) or the brassy equations of Macaulay's prose:

> This progress, having continued during many ages, became at length, about the middle of the eighteenth century, portentously rapid, and has proceeded, during the nineteenth, with accelerated velocity. In consequence partly of our geographical and partly of our moral position we have, during several generations, been exempt from evils which have elsewhere impeded the efforts and destroyed the fruits of industry. While every part of the Continent, from Moscow to Lisbon, has been the theatre of bloody and devastating wars, no hostile standard has been seen here but as a trophy. While revolutions have taken place all around us, our government has never once been subverted by violence.

The tension within this prose is the tension of extreme situations that we feel in the rhetoric of Newman, the infamies of Baudelaire, the hysteria of Carlyle, which is more grotesque, or the immoralism of Nietzsche, which is more lyrical. In Dickens the malaise is released by the prose-poem, the blank-verse interludes in the novels; in Browning the pitch is higher but less sustained. In Ruskin the surge of the prose lengthens to enormous tidal periods that lose, eventually, some of their energy in the decorative confusion of Pater's impressions and the loose ripple of Swinburne's metre.

The writers of the 19th Century have an eye for what Gertrude Stein called *the event*. Their narratives, even in the case of "realists" like Zola or George Eliot, culminate with symbolic acts or gestures. We do not forget the well-managed climax such as the putrescence of Nana's white flesh or the drowning of Maggie and Tom in the Floss, just as we do not forget the crises between Astarte and Manfred, Catherine and Heathcliff, Nora and Helmer, Roxane and Cyrano—variations upon the theme of beauty and the beast. Not in the beginning, but in the end, is the act, the gesture. The limit of the 19th Century imagination is the final expressive tableau, a stasis, a consummate act. The most casual arrangements in the painting of Degas and Manet are carefully arrested impressions having the air of rehearsal. The 19th Century drama was not performed within the legitimate theatre, but was diffused—adulterated—into prose fiction, history, philosophy, social criticism, music, and painting, which, in turn, were contaminated by "events." The event is not only drama. It is melodrama, too.

2.

The thesis that melodrama is a characteristic mode of 19th Century thought and art becomes clearer when we attempt to identify contrasting modalities in the 18th and 20th Centuries. Although the 18th Century played its own incidental melodrama, we may say that the characteristic mode of enlightened thought and art was the mental fiction—those abstract and summary concepts erected inside the mind and harmoniously adjusted to each other within the rationalized order of Nature. These mental fictions were the substructure of the distinctive 18th

Century performances in every direction: the rights of man, the literary rules, the state of nature, the deistic world order, the coherent Newtonian universe with its fictions of absolute space and absolute time, the perfectibility of mankind, the theoretical codes of the encyclopedists, the generalizations of the heroic couplet, the regularity of the sonata, the balances of Augustan and Georgian architecture, the precise articulations of the formal garden, the nobility of the savage, the simple economic motives of enlightened self-interest. All these modes of the 18th Century mind could enlist the emotions, and often did; yet their substratum was the purely intellectual construct, the beautiful and coherent simplification that was not dramatized because it stood detached, without opposition or polarity, as an absolute assumption or idea, and because it was not animated or mythologized. The 18th Century sensibility moved freely and remotely in the clear atmosphere of the mental fiction.

Also in contrast to the 19th Century melodrama, the authentic 20th Century modality has abandoned the "event" and the theatrical act. We bear with us a sense of the conditional, of interrelationships, that the 19th Century did not. We cannot isolate events. Our interpretation is less personal. We are more scientific and sceptical. For us the universe is denser—a continuum, in fact, without the vacuums and intermissions necessary to distinguish the individual events. Our recognition of complexities is so involved that we cannot with assurance locate an event in its isolated status; we cannot separate it from its antecedents and contexts. Our novels have fewer emphatic moments and are devoted to close interconnections, uninterrupted impressions, multiple approaches. As Whitehead has put it, the whole is part of every event, and every event occurs only within the structure of the whole. Thus an event is for us a hypothetical occasion. Indeed, we have so far abandoned the melodramatic view that we have often withdrawn to impersonal, abstract representation of our perceptions. The disintegrations of cubism suggest our pictorial view. By a determined analysis or "destruction" of the object we reduce it to a study of intimate and manifold relationships, a fragmentation within a continuum of forms until the definition of the "subject" remains equivocal. In narrative the disintegration began as early as Chekhov, and has continued within Proust, Joyce, Stein, and Woolf. Melodrama has become, for us, an inappropriate and incredible modality.

If we may generalize upon the modalities of vision within the different periods: in the Middle Ages there was a modality of correspondences between the seen and the unseen which made available a scheme of parallels, symbols, allegories, and equivalents; in the Renaissance there was a modality of humanism, a view of man as free agent in a material universe adaptable to the liberated will and investigative mind of Leonardo, Machiavelli, Montaigne, Shakespeare, and Milton; in the 18th Century there was a modality of the intellectual fiction, the secular absolute existing as an assumption at some uncertain removal from the actuality it presumably interpreted; in the 20th Century there is a modality of relationships, a sense of the interdependencies within a continuum, pressures of environment and context, and the difficulty of isolating the event or determining its meaning.

3.

And for the 19th Century the modality is melodrama, the oversimplification into polarities and oppositions that may be animated by emphatic instances. To the

19th Century mind the very iron laws of science operate with melodramatic fatalism—the pressure of population against subsistence, the dynamics of supply and demand and the wages fund, the struggle for existence in a nature red in tooth and claw, the unalterable majestic course of matter and force mythologized by Hardy and the biologist Haeckel, the brooding malign policies of Egdon Heath and the awesome tyranny of power in geology and physics, with men and generations of men sealed within the grim and dusty hills of the Mongolian desert.

All this is melodrama, not tragedy; and certainly not science. The view of the world as a diagram of polar forces encourages not only a melodramatic ethics (the strong and the weak, the hard and the soft, the good and the bad) but also emotive history and emotive science, which, as Huxley confidently assumed, can satisfy the spiritual longings of man. Having done with a personal God, the 19th Century could now displace the drama in its mind into the universe itself by means of the laws of geology, biology, energy, and, more immediately, economics. By a confusion of categories the inevitabilities of matter and motion and political economy assume a moral sanction, just as in melodrama chance assumes the tenor of poetic justice, just as the impersonal "naturalism" of Zola and Ibsen always moves toward moral conclusions. The world becomes a theatre of tensions between abstractions. Melodrama has become social, if not cosmic.

The choices of the 19th Century are arbitrarily conceived and arbitrarily offered: the bourgeois or the blond beast, the slave or the master, democracy or aristocracy, the soiled woman or the pure, progress or poverty, free will or necessity, the Virgin or the Dynamo, God or Nature, bureaucracy or laissez-faire, poetry or science, culture or anarchy. The very attempt at "Victorian compromise," and its ineffectiveness—even in John Stuart Mill's scrupulous and tenacious indecisions—indicate how liable the 19th Century sensibility was to shift toward extreme situations, how ready it was to perform a "leap," a psychic revolution. Therefore the aesthetic category of melodrama becomes a modality of the 19th Century mind, which emancipated itself only with difficulty from oversimplified premises, a fatalism theatrically effective, and a displacement of moral responses into the universe. The declamatory language, the violent and symbolic gestures, the animation of polar opposites to the point of caricature are evidence of a psychic crisis. The social art of Forain, for instance, is not tragic or scientific, but given to the emphatic gesture, the picturesque event. Melodrama cannot admit exceptions, for they would immediately involve the action too deeply within the context of actuality and trammel the gesture. The types must behave with a decorum of extremes; the resolution must be vividly schematic. The tensions must concentrate toward a last overwhelming tableau, a final stasis beyond which one must not think. The aesthetic values of melodrama are the values of crisis, the event accepted as consummation. Simply because its situation is so precarious, the 19th Century mind is disposed to revolution—psychic revolution, at least.

According to the materialistic dialectic we should hardly expect that Marxism could wholly liberate itself from the archetypal behavior of 19th Century thought, the fallacy of melodrama, the revolutionary fallacy. To the 19th Century psyche, revolution is consummation. After our "revisions" of the 19th Century modality we now understand that revolution is not drama; that there are only events within revolutions. But these events are not revolutions. Revolution is not consummation.

4.

Theoretically the Hegelian dialectic—thesis, antithesis, and synthesis—is not liable to the melodramatic fallacy of sharp oppositions, choices between polarities, schematic exclusions, sudden flights from the relative to the absolute, from the complex to the simplified. Yet the tensions within bourgeois society represented many romantic choices between extreme situations. Dialectical materialism was an opportunity to check these romantic adventures, modulate the oppositions, and offer new and more discriminating structures to the 19th Century mentality of crisis. Engels, writing upon Feuerbach, said that the world is a complex of processes without final solutions or eternal truths; one must not be imposed upon by the old metaphysical antitheses between true and false, good and bad, necessary and accidental. "One knows that these antitheses have only a relative validity." Philosophically, then, the Marxist dialectic successfully utilizes the Hegelian strategy to penetrate further into the neutral process of reality and to level the melodramatic accents within the theatre of history, where the episodes do not converge upon a climax but extend into a complicated and minute internal relevance.

The mentality of crisis, however, had its effect upon Marx not in the philosophical but in the aesthetic category. A deep paradox within *Capital* is caused by a transposition from philosophic to aesthetic structures. Philosophically the work is not melodrama; aesthetically it is. And the aesthetic transvaluation here proves of the greatest consequence: in spite of the discriminations of his essentially undramatic dialectic Marx has yielded to the almost irresistible aesthetic temptation to prefigure the revolution as drama. This aesthetic transvaluation from dialectic to theatre has unexpected ethical and economic results. The mentality of crisis has always been favorable to poetry and symbolic action. A great deal of 19th Century poetry was written in prose. The Victorian novel has recently been appraised as poetry—*Wuthering Heights*, for example. History by Carlyle is no less poetic, like the philosophy of Nietzsche. In this sense *Capital* is a dramatic poem, or possibly a dramatic epic. Its great economic themes are treated chorally, with all the strophic progress of the ode and the almost rhythmic stress of an ironic injustice committed against the masses. If we are not distracted by the superficial diffusion of the book, its elaborate and energetic logic and its accumulation of evidence, we see that its concealed structure is mythical.

Perhaps *Capital* is archetypal 19th Century melodrama because it is, like the *Manifesto*, directed toward the final revolutionary act. In the bourgeois epoch tensions have converged until class antagonisms are simplified—oversimplified according to the canon of the dialectic itself. The social drama is on that account more rapid, more violent, more schematic than ever. In Kenneth Burke's phrase, the Marxist grammar of motive requires a terminology of action. But the culmination of the class struggle is the revolutionary stasis. The movement of history has been foreshortened toward the scene when the expropriators are expropriated. The dialectic is no longer a philosophic tactic; it is a program and Marx is writing the last episodes. History is no longer process; it is gesture. Archetypal melodrama, erupting into the materialistic dialectic, throws into question the status of the act—the revolution—within the Marxist system. The aesthetic mechanism, the transposition to myth, the theatrical climax have abbreviated the dialectic and may have damaged it irreparably.

Capital foreshortens the historical process by a dramatic structure—the beginning, middle, and end of capitalism. The opening is a juxtaposition of polarities figuratively arranged, a mythical opposition of forces: the free laborer confronting the capitalist. "One thing is clear," notes Marx: "Nature does not produce on the one side owners of money or commodities, and on the other men possessing nothing but their own labor-power. This relation has no natural basis, neither is its social basis one that is common to all historical periods." Only after the extinction of the older forms of social production—the passing of the saturnian economic reign—does the buyer of labor meet the seller of labor in the bourgeois *mise en scène*, the free and open market with its unalterable code of enlightened selfishness, supply and demand, and the sanctions of the acquisitive ego to truck, barter, and exchange. This complication of the economic drama "can only take place under certain circumstances that centre in this, viz., that two very different kinds of commodity-possessors must come face to face and into contact; on the one hand, the owners of money, means of production, means of subsistence, who are eager to increase the sum of values they possess by buying other people's labor-power; on the other hand, free laborers, the sellers of their own labor-power, and therefore the sellers of labor." The historical drama—in contrast to the historical dialectic—opens with this social re-arrangement, a fall into original capitalist sin. "And this one historical condition comprises a world's history." Or rather not the process of world's history but fateful dramatic absolute contradiction into which the dialectic has simplified itself by pressure and counter-pressure.

As the tensions narrow between counter-pressures, the dialectic of history becomes less flexible; the events become decisive. Severe and absolute contradiction determines the approaching reversal. In this conflict the proletarian, not the capitalist, appears to exercise freedom of will, and the relentless, undeviating motive of the exploiter, more histrionically realized than ever before in society, evokes the antagonistic response of the exploited—class-consciousness. There is no "recognition" or "discovery" for the capitalist, only for the worker. This "algebra of revolution" develops through "tendencies working with iron necessity towards inevitable results." As in melodrama, the actors become dehumanized: "here individuals are dealt with only in so far as they are the personifications of economic categories, embodiments of particular class-relations and class-interests." The impulses of the capitalist are rigidly conditioned by the role he has assumed. "The restless never-ending process of profit-making alone is what he aims at. This boundless greed after riches, this passionate chase after exchange-value, is common to the capitalist and the miser; but while the miser is merely the capitalist gone mad, the capitalist is a rational miser." Behavior has become symbolic; the *dramatis personae* react with the decorum of caricature. We have Marx's own annotation that "the characters who appear on the economic stage are but the personifications of the economical relations that exist between them." Melodrama has been superimposed upon the historical process. On the stage of the world "our friend Moneybags" is, for a while, lucky enough to find a class that can be bought and sold.

Clearly the melodrama does not exhaust the dramatic possibilities. Our friend Moneybags belongs in the Marxist social comedy, those Dickensian interludes in *Capital* full of grotesques like "the celebrated sophist and sycophant Edmund Burke" and Jeremy Bentham, "that insipid, pedantic, leather-tongued oracle of the ordinary bourgeois intelligence." There is also the parson Townsend, a lively ominous caricature, who argues, "It seems to be a law of nature that the poor should be to a certain degree improvident that there may always be some to fulfil the most servile, the most sordid, and the most ignoble offices in the community. The stock of human happiness is thereby much increased, whilst the more delicate are not only relieved from drudgery but are left at liberty without interruption to pursue those callings which are suited to their various dispositions." The 19th Century drama is ambiguous. In Dickens cruelty is extended to grotesque comedy. In Goya caricature is extended to savage hatred. In Dostoievsky farce extends to pathos. *Capital* is melodrama, comedy of humors, parody, and satire.

The primitive accumulation of capital having been accomplished and the mythos or action having been arranged, the shock of the class war mounts through a series of crises that are, in effect, a continuation of the Malthusian incident sketched in 1798.

> The law, finally, that always equilibrates the relative surplus-population or industrial reserve army, to the extent and energy of accumulation, this law rivets the laborer to capital more firmly than the wedges of Vulcan did Prometheus to the rock. It establishes an accumulation of misery corresponding with accumulation of capital.

Social involvements progress by an intensely emotive dynamics with free play of sarcasm and a dialectic of temperament:

> After capital had taken centuries in extending the working day to its normal maximum limit, and then beyond this to the limit of the natural day of 12 hours, there followed on the birth of mechanism and modern industry in the last third of the 18th century a violent encroachment like that of an avalanche in its intensity and extent. All bounds of morals and nature, age and sex, day and night were broken down. Capital celebrated its orgies.

Surely Marx has stood the Hegelian dialectic back on its head again, transforming the world by the demiurgos of his dramatic sense; if the world is not idea, at least the dramatic illusion plays over history. Lately it was argued that the test of a writer's achievement is his ability to transform the world by displacing his imagination far afield until he incorporates into his vision larger and larger areas of experience. If this is so, Marx displaced his imagination farther afield than any social dramatist of the 19th Century. His myth is more comprehensive, more fully realized, more totally displaced than the myths of Hegel, Taine, or Comte.

A unity of action sustains this diffused myth. The capitalist production must be continually and progressively revolutionized to increase the productivity of labor and the amount of surplus value. Thus the lazarus-layer of the proletarian is depressed further toward the condition of misery. Meanwhile, by a fatalism as somber as the system of Hardy's universe, the enormous power of the factories begets a feverish output—then a glut of markets, a crisis, and a sequence of collapses. Presently the theatre widens to include the entire scene of imperialism opening upon colonial perspectives. As the working day lengthens, the conflict over "the last hour" sets in, together with new cycles of production for profit, not for use. The "natural" cycle of exchange—Commodity-Money-Commodity— becomes distorted into the capitalist cycle of exchange for money—Money- Commodity-Money. Simultaneously the absolute general law of capitalist accumulation has been concentrating wealth until, by a dramatic foreshadowing, the expropriation of the exploiters is ironically begun.

This expropriation is accomplished by the action of the immanent laws of capitalistic production itself, by the centralization of capital. One capitalist always kills many.

The drama accomplishes its reversal. With the assurance of poetic justice Marx observes that "capitalist production begets, with the inexorability of a law of Nature, its own integation. It is the negation of negation." Were statistics ever so illuminated in the glaring light of the social theatre as in the mighty chapters on The Working Day and Machinery And Modern Industry, with their strophic declamations? "Capital is dead labor, that vampire-like, only lives by sucking living labor, and lives the more, the more labor it sucks." The outcome of these terrible strains between exploiter and exploited cannot be in doubt. As soon as the capitalist has engaged in the fratricidal policy of killing fellow capitalists and has condemned the masses to a condition of *la misère*, "from that moment new forces and new passions spring up in the bosom of society; but the old social organization fetters them and keeps them down. It must be annihilated; it is annihilated." The revolution is a mythical act; the negation of negation is final justice. "Centralization of the means of production and socialization of labor at last reach a point where they become incompatible with their capitalist integument. This integument is burst asunder. The knell of capitalist private property sounds. The expropriators are expropriated." In the end is the act. Revolution is consummation. As Engels commented, what is essential "is a social *act*." The dialectic has attained its final tableau by dislocating philosophy and history into drama—one of the greatest 19th Century leaps. It is necessary, because of the oversimplification of forces, that melodrama should end with a stasis so conclusive that it appears arbitrary; it is so in the Dickensian novel. It was apparently difficult for Marx to think beyond this final violent expropriation; it has remained difficult to do so because the revolution is theatre, not dialectic. The dialectic has been transvalued to a symbolic act, an apocalypse. The Marxist problem is to pass beyond this theatrical stasis. Lenin's theory of the withering of the state, the lower and higher socialism, is a somewhat ineffective and hasty motion to descend from apocalypse to dialectic, from drama to the process of history. There is, according to Lenin, "no shadow of an attempt on Marx's part to conjure up a Utopia, to make idle guesses about that which cannot be known." The course by which humanity proceeds to the higher communism "we do not and cannot know."

In its origin *Capital* was melodramatic—the undertaking to reverse the contemporary movement toward idealism and to stand the Hegelian system right side up by displacing the Hegelian idea into the actual world. Either system terminates in stasis—in Marx's case the "universal crisis," the revolution to end all revolutions, the consummate revolution within *and without* the psyche. The displacement of the dialectic into the material world was, of course, the achievement to secure for *Capital* a relevance beyond that of other melodramas. The Marxist melodrama is, at the very least, *about something*.

5.

The inclusive and damaging irony is this: melodrama is a notoriously bourgeois aesthetic. Here the dialectic has operated with its least expected fatalism—the Marxist revolution against the bourgeoisie is in itself an alarming symptom of the bourgeois malady.

To define its choices the 20th Century has often looked backward, particularly to Stendhal, Kierkegaard, Nietzsche, Dostoievsky—and Marx. Their definitions were usually made by emphatic instances enlarged to symbolic dimensions in Stendhal's romantic experimental man, Kierkegaard's anxious man, Nietzsche's superman, Dostoievsky's underground man, and Marx's revolutionary man. Our dilemmas can readily be suggested by the polarities and exclusions of melodrama. Yet melodrama, especially in its revolutionary stasis, is an aesthetic fallacy.

VII
THE CLIMATES
OF TRAGEDY

The Tragic Fallacy*

Joseph Wood Krutch

Through the legacy of their art the great ages have transmitted to us a dim image of their glorious vitality. When we turn the pages of a Sophoclean or a Shakespearean tragedy we participate faintly in the experience which created it and we sometimes presumptuously say that we "understand" the spirit of these works. But the truth is that we see them, even at best and in the moments when our souls expand most nearly to their dimensions, through a glass darkly.

It is so much easier to appreciate than to create that an age too feeble to reach the heights achieved by the members of a preceding one can still see those heights towering above its impotence, and so it is that, when we perceive a Sophocles or a Shakespeare soaring in an air which we can never hope to breathe, we say that we can "appreciate" them. But what we mean is that we are just able to wonder, and we can never hope to participate in the glorious vision of human life out of which they were created—not even to the extent of those humbler persons for whom they were written; for while to us the triumphant voices come from far away and tell of a heroic world which no longer exists, to them they spoke of immediate realities and revealed the inner meaning of events amidst which they still lived.

When the life has entirely gone out of a work of art come down to us from the past, when we read it without any emotional comprehension whatsoever and can no longer even imagine why the people for whom it was intended found it absorbing and satisfying, then, of course, it has ceased to be a work of art at all and has dwindled into one of those deceptive "documents" from which we get a false sense of comprehending through the intellect things which cannot be comprehended at all except by means of kinship of feeling. And though all works from a past age have begun in this way to fade there are some, like the great Greek or Elizabethan tragedies, which are still halfway between the work of art and the document. They no longer can have for us the immediacy which they had for those to whom they originally belonged, but they have not yet eluded us entirely. We no longer live in the world which they represent, but we can half imagine it and we can measure the distance which we have moved away. We write no tragedies today, but we can still talk about the tragic spirit of which we would, perhaps, have no conception were it not for the works in question.

An age which could really "appreciate" Shakespeare or Sophocles would

* Joseph Wood Krutch, "The Tragic Fallacy," *The Modern Temper* (Harcourt, Brace and World, 1957), pp. 115–143. Copyright 1929 by Harcourt Brace Jovanovich, Inc.; renewed 1957 by Joseph Wood Krutch. Reprinted by permission of the publisher.

have something comparable to put beside them—something like them, not necessarily in form, or spirit, but at least in magnitude—some vision of life which
would be, however different, equally ample and passionate. But when we move
to put a modern masterpiece beside them, when we seek to compare them with,
let us say, a *Ghosts* or a *[The] Weavers*, we shrink as from the impulse to commit some folly and we feel as though we were about to superimpose Bowling
Green upon the Great Prairies in order to ascertain which is the larger. The
question, we see, is not primarily one of art but of the two worlds which two
minds inhabited. No increased powers of expression, no greater gift for words,
could have transformed Ibsen into Shakespeare. The materials out of which the
latter created his works—his conception of human dignity, his sense of the importance of human passions, his vision of the amplitude of human life—simply
did not and could not exist for Ibsen, as they did not and could not exist for his
contemporaries. God and Man and Nature had all somehow dwindled in the
course of the intervening centuries, not because the realistic creed of modern art
led us to seek out mean people, but because this meanness of human life was
somehow thrust upon us by the operation of that same process which led to the
development of realistic theories of art by which our vision could be justified.

Hence, though we still apply, sometimes, the adjective "tragic" to one or
another of those modern works of literature which describe human misery and
which end more sadly even than they begin, the term is a misnomer since it is
obvious that the works in question have nothing in common with the classical examples of the genre and produce in the reader a sense of depression which is the
exact opposite of that elation generated when the spirit of a Shakespeare rises
joyously superior to the outward calamities which he recounts and celebrates the
greatness of the human spirit whose travail he describes. Tragedies, in that only
sense of the word which has any distinctive meaning, are no longer written in either the dramatic or any other form and the fact is not to be accounted for in
any merely literary terms. It is not the result of any fashion in literature or of
any deliberation to write about human nature or character under different aspects, any more than it is of either any greater sensitiveness of feeling which
would make us shrink from the contemplation of the suffering of Medea or
Othello or of any greater optimism which would make us more likely to see life
in more cheerful terms. It is, on the contrary, the result of one of those enfeeble-
ments of the human spirit not unlike that described in the previous chapter of
this essay, and a further illustration of that gradual weakening of man's confidence in his ability to impose upon the phenomenon of life an interpretation acceptable to his desires which is the subject of the whole of the present discussion.

To explain that fact and to make clear how the creation of classical tragedy
did consist in the successful effort to impose such a satisfactory interpretation
will require, perhaps, the special section which follows, although the truth of the
fact that it does impose such an interpretation must be evident to any one who
has ever risen from the reading of *Oedipus* or *Lear* with that feeling of exulta-
tion which comes when we have been able, by rare good fortune, to enter into its
spirit as completely as it is possible for us of a remoter and emotionally enfeebled
age to enter it. Meanwhile one anticipatory remark may be ventured. If the
plays and the novels of today deal with littler people and less mighty emotions it
is not because we have become interested in commonplace souls and their ungla-
morous adventures but because we have come, willy-nilly, to see the soul of man
as commonplace and its emotions as mean.

II

Tragedy, said Aristotle, is the "imitation of noble actions," and though it is some twenty-five hundred years since the dictum was uttered there is only one respect in which we are inclined to modify it. To us "imitation" seems a rather naïve word to apply to that process by which observation is turned into art, and we seek one which would define or at least imply the nature of that interposition of the personality of the artist between the object and the beholder which constitutes his function and by means of which he transmits a modified version, rather than a mere imitation, of the thing which he has contemplated.

In the search for this word the estheticians of romanticism invented the term "expression" to describe the artistic purpose to which apparent imitation was subservient. Psychologists, on the other hand, feeling that the artistic process was primarily one by which reality is modified in such a way as to render it more acceptable to the desires of the artist, employed various terms in the effort to describe that distortion which the wish may produce in vision. And though many of the newer critics reject both romanticism and psychology, even they insist upon the fundamental fact that in art we are concerned, not with mere imitation, but with the imposition of some form upon the material which it would not have if it were merely copied as a camera copies.

Tragedy is not, then, as Aristotle said, the *imitation* of noble actions, for, indeed, no one knows what a *noble* action is or whether or not such a thing as nobility exists in nature apart from the mind of man. Certainly the action of Achilles in dragging the dead body of Hector around the walls of Troy and under the eyes of Andromache, who had begged to be allowed to give it decent burial, is not to us a noble action, though it was such to Homer, who made it the subject of a noble passage in a noble poem. Certainly, too, the same action might conceivably be made the subject of a tragedy and the subject of a farce, depending upon the way in which it was treated; so that to say that tragedy is the *imitation* of a *noble* action is to be guilty of assuming, first, that art and photography are the same, and, second, that there may be something inherently noble in an act as distinguished from the motives which prompted it or from the point of view from which it is regarded.

And yet, nevertheless, the idea of nobility is inseparable from the idea of tragedy, which cannot exist without it. If tragedy is not the imitation or even the modified representation of noble actions it is certainly a representation of actions *considered* as noble, and herein lies its essential nature, since no man can conceive it unless he is capable of believing in the greatness and importance of man. Its action is usually, if not always, calamitous, because it is only in calamity that the human spirit has the opportunity to reveal itself triumphant over the outward universe which fails to conquer it; but this calamity in tragedy is only a means to an end and the essential thing which distinguishes real tragedy from those distressing modern works sometimes called by its name is the fact that it is in the former alone that the artist has found himself capable of considering and of making us consider that his people and his actions have that amplitude and importance which make them noble. Tragedy arises then when, as in Periclean Greece or Elizabethan England, a people fully aware of the calamities of life is nevertheless serenely confident of the greatness of man, whose mighty passions and supreme fortitude are revealed when one of these calamities overtakes him.

To those who mistakenly think of it as something gloomy or depressing, who are incapable of recognizing the elation which its celebration of human greatness inspires, and who, therefore, confuse it with things merely miserable or pathetic, it must be a paradox that the happiest, most vigorous, and most confident ages which the world has ever known—the Periclean and the Elizabethan—should be exactly those which created and which most relished the mightiest tragedies; but the paradox is, of course, resolved by the fact that tragedy is essentially an expression, not of despair, but of the triumph over despair and of confidence in the value of human life. If Shakespeare himself ever had that "dark period" which his critics and biographers have imagined for him, it was at least no darkness like that bleak and arid despair which sometimes settles over modern spirits. In the midst of it he created both the elemental grandeur of Othello and the pensive majesty of Hamlet and, holding them up to his contemporaries, he said in the words of his own Miranda, "Oh, rare new world that hath *such* creatures in it."

All works of art which deserve their name have a happy end. This is indeed the thing which constitutes them art and through which they perform their function. Whatever the character of the events, fortunate or unfortunate, which they recount, they so mold or arrange or interpret them that we accept gladly the conclusion which they reach and would not have it otherwise. They may conduct us into the realm of pure fancy where wish and fact are identical and the world is remade exactly after the fashion of the heart's desire or they may yield some greater or less allegiance to fact; but they must always reconcile us in one way or another to the representation which they make and the distinctions between the genres are simply the distinctions between the means by which this reconciliation is effected.

Comedy laughs the minor mishaps of its characters away; drama solves all the difficulties which it allows to arise; and melodrama, separating good from evil by simple lines, distributes its rewards and punishments in accordance with the principles of a naïve justice which satisfies the simple souls of its audience, which are neither philosophical enough to question its primitive ethics nor critical enough to object to the way in which its neat events violate the laws of probability. Tragedy, the greatest and the most difficult of the arts, can adopt none of these methods; and yet it must reach its own happy end in its own way. Though its conclusions must be, by its premise, outwardly calamitous, though it must speak to those who know that the good man is cut off and that the fairest things are the first to perish, yet it must leave them, as *Othello* does, content that this is so. We must be and we are glad that Juliet dies and glad that Lear is turned out into the storm.

Milton set out, he said, to justify the ways of God to man, and his phrase, if it be interpreted broadly enough, may be taken as describing the function of all art, which must, in some way or other, make the life which it seems to represent satisfactory to those who see its reflection in the magic mirror, and it must gratify or at least reconcile the desires of the beholder, not necessarily, as the naïver exponents of Freudian psychology maintain, by gratifying individual and often eccentric wishes, but at least by satisfying the universally human desire to find in the world some justice, some meaning, or, at the very least, some recognizable order. Hence it is that every real tragedy, however tremendous it may be, is an affirmation of faith in life, a declaration that even if God is not in his Heaven, then at least Man is in his world.

We accept gladly the outward defeats which it describes for the sake of the inward victories which it reveals. Juliet died, but not before she had shown how great and resplendent a thing love could be; Othello plunged the dagger into his own breast, but not before he had revealed that greatness of soul which makes his death seem unimportant. Had he died in the instant when he struck the blow, had he perished still believing that the world was as completely black as he saw it before the innocence of Desdemona was revealed to him, then, for him at least, the world would have been merely damnable, but Shakespeare kept him alive along enough to allow him to learn his error and hence to die, not in despair, but in the full acceptance of the tragic reconciliation to life. Perhaps it would be pleasanter if men could believe what the child is taught—that the good are happy and that things turn out as they should—but it is far more important to be able to believe, as Shakespeare did, that however much things in the outward world may go awry, man has, nevertheless, splendors of his own and that, in a word, Love and Honor and Glory are not words but realities.

Thus for the great ages tragedy is not an expression of despair but the means by which they saved themselves from it. It is a profession of faith, and a sort of religion; a way of looking at life by virtue of which it is robbed of its pain. The sturdy soul of the tragic author seizes upon suffering and uses it only as a means by which joy may be wrung out of existence, but it is not to be forgotten that he is enabled to do so only because of his belief in the greatness of human nature and because, though he has lost the child's faith in life, he has not lost his far more important faith in human nature. A tragic writer does not have to believe in God, but he must believe in man.

And if, then, the Tragic Spirit is in reality the product of a religious faith in which, sometimes at least, faith in the greatness of God is replaced by faith in the greatness of man, it serves, of course, to perform the function of religion, to make life tolerable for those who participate in its beneficent illusion. It purges the souls of those who might otherwise despair and it makes endurable the realization that the events of the outward world do not correspond with the desires of the heart, and thus, in its own particular way, it does what all religions do, for it gives a rationality, a meaning, and a justification to the universe. But if it has the strength it has also the weakness of all faiths, since it may—nay, it must—be ultimately lost as reality, encroaching further and further into the realm of imagination, leaves less and less room in which that imagination can build its refuge.

III

It is, indeed, only at a certain stage in the development of the realistic intelligence of a people that the tragic faith can exist. A naïver people may have, as the ancient men of the north had, a body of legends which are essentially tragic, or it may have only (and need only) its happy and childlike mythology which arrives inevitably at its happy end, where the only ones who suffer "deserve" to do so and in which, therefore, life is represented as directly and easily acceptable. A too sophisticated society on the other hand—one which, like ours, has outgrown not merely the simple optimism of the child but also that vigorous, one might almost say adolescent, faith in the nobility of man which marks a Sophocles or a Shakespeare, has neither fairy tales to assure it that all is always right in the end nor tragedies to make it believe that it rises superior in soul to the outward calamities which befall it.

Distrusting its thought, despising its passions, realizing its impotent unimportance in the universe, it can tell itself no stories except those which make it still more acutely aware of its trivial miseries. When its heroes (sad misnomer for the pitiful creatures who people contemporary fiction) are struck down it is not, like Oedipus, by the gods that they are struck but only, like Oswald Alving, by syphilis, for they know that the gods, even if they existed, would not trouble with them, and they cannot attribute to themselves in art an importance in which they do not believe. Their so-called tragedies do not and cannot end with one of those splendid calamities which in Shakespeare seem to reverberate through the universe, because they cannot believe that the universe trembles when their love is, like Romeo's, cut off or when the place where they (small as they are) have gathered up their trivial treasure is, like Othello's sanctuary, defiled. Instead, mean misery piles on mean misery, petty misfortune follows petty misfortune, and despair becomes intolerable because it is no longer even significant or important.

Ibsen once made one of his characters say that he did not read much because he found reading "irrelevant," and the adjective was brilliantly chosen because it held implications even beyond those of which Ibsen was consciously aware. What is it that made the classics irrelevant to him and to us? Is it not just exactly those to him impossible premises which make tragedy what it is, those assumptions that the soul of man is great, that the universe (together with whatever gods may be) concerns itself with him and that he is, in a word, noble? Ibsen turned to village politics for exactly the same reason that his contemporaries and his successors have, each in his own way, sought out some aspect of the common man and his common life—because, that is to say, here was at least something small enough for him to be able to believe.

Bearing this fact in mind, let us compare a modern "tragedy" with one of the great works of a happy age, not in order to judge of their relative technical merits but in order to determine to what extent the former deserves its name by achieving a tragic solution capable of purging the soul or of reconciling the emotions to the life which it pictures. And in order to make the comparison as fruitful as possible let us choose *Hamlet* on the one hand and on the other a play like *Ghosts* which was not only written by perhaps the most powerful as well as the most typical of modern writers but which is, in addition, the one of his works which seems most nearly to escape that triviality which cannot be entirely escaped by any one who feels, as all contemporary minds do, that man is relatively trivial.

In *Hamlet* a prince ("in understanding, how like a god!") has thrust upon him from the unseen world a duty to redress a wrong which concerns not merely him, his mother, and his uncle, but the moral order of the universe. Erasing all trivial fond records from his mind, abandoning at once both his studies and his romance because it has been his good fortune to be called upon to take part in an action of cosmic importance, he plunges (at first) not into action but into thought, weighing the claims which are made upon him and contemplating the grandiose complexities of the universe. And when the time comes at last for him to die he dies, not as a failure, but as a success. Not only has the universe regained the balance which had been upset by what *seemed* the monstrous crime of the guilty pair ("there is nothing either good nor ill but thinking makes it so"), but in the process by which that readjustment is made a mighty mind has been given the opportunity, first to contemplate the magnificent scheme of which it is a part, and then to demonstrate the greatness of its spirit by playing a role in the grand style which it called for. We do not need to despair in *such* a world if it has *such* creatures in it.

Turn now to *Ghosts*—look upon this picture and upon that. A young man has inherited syphilis from his father. Struck by a to him mysterious malady he returns to his northern village, learns the hopeless truth about himself, and persuades his mother to poison him. The incidents prove, perhaps, that pastors should not endeavor to keep a husband and wife together unless they know what they are doing. But what a world is this in which a great writer can deduce nothing more than that from his greatest work and how are we to be purged or reconciled when we see it acted? Not only is the failure utter, but it is trivial and meaningless as well.

Yet the journey from Elsinore to Skien is precisely the journey which the human spirit has made, exchanging in the process princes for invalids and gods for disease. We say, as Ibsen would say, that the problems of Oswald Alving are more "relevant" to our life than the problems of Hamlet, that the play in which he appears is more "real" than the other more glamorous one, but it is exactly because we find it so that we are condemned. We can believe in Oswald but we cannot believe in Hamlet, and a light has gone out in the universe. Shakespeare justifies the ways of God to man, but in Ibsen there is no such happy end and with him tragedy, so called, has become merely an expression of our despair at finding that such justification is no longer possible.

Modern critics have sometimes been puzzled to account for the fact that the concern of ancient tragedy is almost exclusively with kings and courts. They have been tempted to accuse even Aristotle of a certain naïveté in assuming (as he seems to assume) that the "nobility" of which he speaks as necessary to a tragedy implies a nobility of rank as well as of soul, and they have sometimes regretted that Shakespeare did not devote himself more than he did to the serious consideration of those common woes of the common man which subsequent writers have exploited with increasing pertinacity. Yet the tendency to lay the scene of a tragedy at the court of a king is not the result of any arbitrary convention but of the fact that the tragic writers believed easily in greatness just as we believe easily in meanness. To Shakespeare, robes and crowns and jewels are the garments most appropriate to man because they are the fitting outward manifestation of his inward majesty, but to us they seem absurd because the man who bears them has, in our estimation, so pitifully shrunk. We do not write about kings because we do not believe that any man is worthy to be one and we do not write about courts because hovels seem to us to be dwellings more appropriate to the creatures who inhabit them. Any modern attempt to dress characters in robes ends only by making us aware of a comic incongruity and any modern attempt to furnish them with a language resplendent like Shakespeare's ends only in bombast.

True tragedy capable of performing its function and of purging the soul by reconciling man to his woes can exist only by virtue of a certain pathetic fallacy far more inclusive than that to which the name is commonly given. The romantics, feeble descendants of the tragic writers to whom they are linked by their effort to see life and nature in grandiose terms, loved to imagine that the sea or the sky had a way of according itself with their moods, of storming when they stormed and smiling when they smiled. But the tragic spirit sustains itself by an assumption much more far-reaching and no more justified. Man as it sees him lives in a world which he may not dominate but which is always aware of him.

Occupying the exact center of a universe which would have no meaning except for him and being so little below the angels that, if he believes in God, he has no hesitation in imagining Him formed as he is formed and crowned with a crown like that which he or one of his fellows wears, he assumes that each of his acts reverberates through the universe. His passions are important to him because he believes them important throughout all time and all space; the very fact that he can sin (no modern can) means that this universe is watching his acts; and though he may perish, a God leans out from infinity to strike him down. And it is exactly because an Ibsen cannot think of man in any such terms as these that his persons have so shrunk and that his "tragedy" has lost that power which real tragedy always has of making that infinitely ambitious creature called man content to accept his misery if only he can be made to feel great enough and important enough. An Oswald is not a Hamlet chiefly because he has lost that tie with the natural and supernatural world which the latter had. No ghost will leave the other world to warn or encourage him, there is no virtue and no vice which he can possibly have which can be really important, and when he dies neither his death nor the manner of it will be, outside the circle of two or three people as unnecessary as himself, any more important than that of a rat behind the arras.

Perhaps we may dub the illusion upon which the tragic spirit is nourished the Tragic, as opposed to the Pathetic, Fallacy, but fallacy though it is, upon its existence depends not merely the writing of tragedy but the existence of that religious feeling of which tragedy is an expression and by means of which a people aware of the dissonances of life manages nevertheless to hear them as harmony. Without it neither man nor his passions can seem great enough or important enough to justify the sufferings which they entail, and literature, expressing the mood of a people, begins to despair where once it had exulted. Like the belief in love and like most of the other mighty illusions by means of which human life has been given a value, the Tragic Fallacy depends ultimately upon the assumption which man so readily makes that something outside his own being, some "spirit not himself"—be it God, Nature, or that still vaguer thing called a Moral Order—joins him in the emphasis which he places upon this or that and confirms him in his feeling that his passions and his opinions are important. When his instinctive faith in that correspondence between the outer and the inner world fades, his grasp upon the faith that sustained him fades also, and Love or Tragedy or what not ceases to be the reality which it was because he is never strong enough in his own insignificant self to stand alone in a universe which snubs him with its indifference.

In both the modern and the ancient worlds tragedy was dead long before writers were aware of the fact. Seneca wrote his frigid melodramas under the impression that he was following in the footsteps of Sophocles, and Dryden probably thought that his *All for Love* was an improvement upon Shakespeare, but in time we awoke to the fact that no amount of rhetorical bombast could conceal the fact that grandeur was not to be counterfeited when the belief in its possibility was dead, and turning from the hero to the common man, we inaugurated the era of realism. For us no choice remains except that between mere rhetoric and the frank consideration of our fellow men, who may be the highest of the anthropoids but who are certainly too far below the angels to imagine either that these angels can concern themselves with them or that they can catch any glimpse of even the soles of angelic feet. We can no longer tell tales of the fall of noble men because we do not believe that noble men exist. The best that we can achieve is pathos and the most that we can do is to feel sorry for ourselves. Man has put off his royal robes and it is only in sceptered pomp that tragedy can come sweeping by.

IV

Nietzsche was the last of the great philosophers to attempt a tragic justification of life. His central and famous dogma—"Life is good *because* it is painful"— sums up in a few words the desperate and almost meaningless paradox to which he was driven in his effort to reduce to rational terms the far more imaginative conception which is everywhere present but everywhere unanalyzed in a Sophocles or a Shakespeare and by means of which they rise triumphant over the manifold miseries of life. But the very fact that Nietzsche could not even attempt to state in any except intellectual terms an attitude which is primarily unintellectual and to which, indeed, intellectual analysis is inevitably fatal, is proof of the distance which he had been carried (by the rationalizing tendencies of the human mind) from the possibility of the tragic solution which he sought; and the confused, half insane violence of his work will reveal, by the contrast which it affords with the serenity of the tragic writers whom he admired, how great was his failure.

Fundamentally this failure was, moreover, conditioned by exactly the same thing which has conditioned the failure of all modern attempts to achieve what he attempted—by the fact, that is to say, that tragedy must have a hero if it is not to be merely an accusation against, instead of a justification of, the world in which it occurs. Tragedy is, as Aristotle said, an imitation of noble actions, and Nietzsche, for all his enthusiasm for the Greek tragic writers, was palsied by the universally modern incapacity to conceive man as noble. Out of this dilemma, out of his need to find a hero who could give to life as he saw it the only possible justification, was born the idea of the Superman; but the Superman is, after all, only a hypothetical being, destined to become what man actually was in the eyes of the great tragic writers—a creature (as Hamlet said) "how infinite in capacities, in understanding how like a god." Thus Nietzsche lived half in the past through his literary enthusiasms and half in the future through his grandiose dreams, but for all his professed determination to justify existence he was no more able than the rest of us to find the present acceptable. Life, he said in effect, is not a Tragedy now but perhaps it will be when the Ape-man has been transformed into a hero (the Übermensch), and trying to find that sufficient, he went mad.

He failed, as all moderns must fail when they attempt, like him, to embrace the tragic spirit as a religious faith, because the resurgence of that faith is not an intellectual but a vital phenomenon, something not achieved by taking thought but born, on the contrary, out of an instinctive confidence in life which is nearer to the animal's unquestioning allegiance to the scheme of nature than it is to that critical intelligence characteristic of a fully developed humanism. And like other faiths it is not to be recaptured merely by reaching an intellectual conviction that it would be desirable to do so.

Modern psychology has discovered (or at least strongly emphasized) the fact that under certain conditions desire produces belief, and having discovered also that the more primitive a given mentality the more completely are its opinions determined by its wishes, modern psychology has concluded that the best mind is that which most resists the tendency to believe a thing simply because it would be pleasant or advantageous to do so. But justified as this conclusion may be from the intellectual point of view, it fails to take into account the fact that in a universe as badly adapted as this one to human as distinguished from animal needs this ability to will a belief may bestow an enormous vital advantage as it did, for instance, in the case at present under discussion where it made possible for Shakespeare the compensations of a tragic faith completely inaccessible to Nietzsche. Pure intelligence, incapable of being influenced by desire and therefore also incapable of choosing one opinion rather than another simply because the one chosen is the more fruitful or beneficent, is doubtless a relatively perfect instrument for the pursuit of truth, but the question (likely, it would seem, to be answered in the negative) is simply whether or not the spirit of man can endure the literal and inhuman truth.

Certain ages and simple people have conceived of the action which passes upon the stage of the universe as of something in the nature of a Divine Comedy, as something, that is to say, which will reach its end with the words "and they lived happily ever after." Others, less naïve and therefore more aware of those maladjustments whose reality, at least so far as outward events are concerned, they could not escape, have imposed upon it another artistic form and called it a Divine Tragedy, accepting its catastrophe as we accept the catastrophe of an *Othello*, because of its grandeur. But a Tragedy, Divine or otherwise, must, it may again be repeated, have a hero, and from the universe as we see it both the Glory of God and the Glory of Man have departed. Our cosmos may be farcical or it may be pathetic but it has not the dignity of tragedy and we cannot accept it as such.

Yet our need for the consolations of tragedy has not passed with the passing of our ability to conceive it. Indeed, the dissonances which it was tragedy's function to resolve grow more insistent instead of diminishing. Our passions, our disappointments, and our sufferings remain important to us though important to nothing else and they thrust themselves upon us with an urgency which makes it impossible for us to dismiss them as the mere trivialities which, so our intellects tell us, they are. And yet, in the absence of tragic faith or the possibility of achieving it, we have no way in which we may succeed in giving them the dignity which would not only render them tolerable but transform them as they were transformed by the great ages into joys. The death of tragedy is, like the death of love, one of those emotional fatalities as the result of which the human as distinguished from the natural world grows more and more a desert.

Poetry, said Santayana in his famous phrase, is "religion which is no longer believed," but it depends, nevertheless, upon its power to revive in us a sort of temporary or provisional credence and the nearer it can come to producing an illusion of belief the greater is its power as poetry. Once the Tragic Spirit was a living faith and out of it tragedies were written. Today these great expressions of a great faith have declined, not merely into poetry, but into a kind of poetry whose premises are so far from any we can really accept that we can only partially and dimly grasp its meaning.

We read but we do not write tragedies. The tragic solution of the problem of existence, the reconciliation to life by means of the tragic spirit is, that is to say, now only a fiction surviving in art. When that art itself has become, as it probably will, completely meaningless, when we have ceased not only to write but to *read* tragic works, then it will be lost and in all real senses forgotten, since the devolution from Religion to Art to Document will be complete.

On Tragedy*

Kenneth Burke

Ambitious writers have selected the "death of tragedy" as an instance of science's destructive effect upon the highest poetry. Tragedy, they have observed, was developed out of a sense of theological or metaphysical stability; man was dignified; he had some direct or personal relationship with the forces of the cosmos; his problems were of vast importance in the universal scheme. But the "illusions" of tragedy are slain by the scientific point of view, which leaves us too humiliated for the noble, godlike posturings of tragedy, wherein man shares the "mystic participation" which M. Lévy-Bruhl attributes to the savage: that sense of the universe as being personally with him or against him. Tragedy is ruined, they say, when the "illusion" of man's personal connection with superhuman processes is lost, when he is looked upon as a mere species of animal that happens to inhabit a planet for a certain number of years between its birth and its extinction. This "death of tragedy" (and thus, the death of the very essence of poetry) is manifested already as an inability to write great tragedies—and in time it will even be manifested as an inability to appreciate the great tragedies already written. Such is, in essence, the position of those who hold to a fundamental opposition between poetry and science—and it has been stated with much fervour and fluency by Mr. Krutch in his volume *The Modern Temper*.

Mr. Krutch combines under his concept of tragedy both the tragic drama and the tragic spirit. Once a distinction is made between them, however, the issue may look less discouraging. The death of the tragic drama we should attribute to the crumbling of an ideology, as previously explained. The highly fluctuant nature of our thinking at the present time makes more naturally for the essayistic than the dramatic—and the death of tragedy is a natural corollary of this general situation. The question of "poetic illusions" need not enter.

In the matter of the tragic spirit, however, there seems to be no essential abatement at all. For if tragedy is a sense of man's intimate participation in processes beyond himself, we find that science has replaced the older metaphysical structure with an historical structure which gives the individual man ample grounds to feel such participation. What science has taken from us as a personal relationship to the will of Providence, it has regiven as a personal relationship to the slow, unwieldly movements of human society. It is to the greatest credit of Nietzsche that he made this readjustment so thoroughly, turning from the "tragic dignity" of theology to the "tragic dignity" of history, and showing that if there was something "poetic" in the sense of a stable metaphysical structure per-

* Kenneth Burke, "On Tragedy," *Counter-statement* (Hermes, 1953), pp. 252–255.

sonally concerned with the fate of man, there can be something equally "poetic" constructed out of the "illusion" or belief now current, the sense of the individual's place in an historical process. In another way the same readjustment was made by Pater in his Marius the Epicurean, where the "tragic fallacy" arises from our sense of Marius's close personal relationship to deep alterations in the mentality of peoples. Mr. Krutch himself, had he admitted a distinction between the tragic drama and the tragic spirit, would not have become involved, as he does in the task of disproving his own thesis at the close of his book. For having said that tragedy is dead, and that it is dead because the new scientific "truths" have destroyed the tragic "illusions," he ends: "Some small part of the tragic fallacy may be said indeed to be still valid for us, for if we cannot feel ourselves as great as Shakespeare did, if we no longer believe in either our infinite capacities or our importance in the universe, we know at least that we have discovered the trick which has been played upon us and that whatever else we may be we are no longer dupes." He will accept the full responsibilities of this "truth," though the "truth" deprive him of something so edifying, so necessary to the most wholesome human expansiveness, as tragedy: "If death for us and our kind is the inevitable result of our stubbornness, then we can only say, 'So be it.' Ours is a lost cause and there is no place for us in the natural universe, but we are not, for all that, sorry to be human. We should rather die as men than live as animals." He pictures those of his kind watching simpler men who, through having gone less far in their thinking, enjoy certain vital advantages (high among which is "tragic importance"). But though recognizing the advantages that lie with the simple, those of his kind will follow their thoughts even to disaster. Such are Mr. Krutch's obdurate conclusions.

Now, tragedy as a mechanism is based upon a calamitous persistence in one's ways. It is "nobler" when the persistence is due to a moral stability on the part of the hero than when it is due to a mere misunderstanding. What, then, if not the formula for tragedy is this position of Mr. Krutch? He will take a personal stand in relation to a *historic* process (the historic process being in this instance the loss of certain magical or theological or metaphysical "illusions" based upon "non-scientific" systems of causality)—and in this stand he will persist at all hazards. It is good to have a writer display so well the basic machinery for a modern tragedy in a book heralding the death of all tragedy.

Psychoanalysis and the Climate of Tragedy*

Stanley Edgar Hyman

Psychoanalysis and tragedy are not easy matters to discuss from a mere reading knowledge, with no experience either behind the footlights or on the couch. Yet if we take tragedy not as a subdivision of drama but as a larger complex of attitudes and actions found in many literary forms, and psychoanalysis as a cultural rather than a medical phenomenon, specialists have written little enough to our purpose, and the overlap between the two areas has been so inadequately discussed that a critic of literature may perhaps be pardoned for stepping in brashly where theater people and analysts hesitate to tread.

Tragedy as we know it had its first and greatest flowering in fifth-century Athens, in the plays of Aeschylus, Sophocles, and Euripides, and its fullest theoretical formulation in the *Poetics* of Aristotle. The forms of Attic tragedy, as Aristotle half knew from tradition, derived from the sacrificial rites of Dionysus, in which the god in bull or goat form was annually slain, dismembered, and resurrected. The plots of Attic tragedy came principally from Homer, and the bloody stories of incest and murder fit the ritual forms so well because the Homeric tales themselves, as Rhys Carpenter has shown most fully in *Folk Tale, Fiction and Saga in the Homeric Epics*, derive from similar rites far from Mount Olympus. Out of the *agon* or dramatic conflict between the god in human form and his antagonists evolved the ethical concepts of *hamartia* or shortcoming, the tragic flaw; and *hybris* or pride, the imperfect insight into man's true stature in relation to destiny and the gods. These defects motivated the action, and for the spectators, in Aristotle's formulation, the tragic action aroused pity and terror and symbolically purged them through catharsis. The moral ingredients of tragedy are thus: the flawed protagonist swollen with pride; *peripeteia*, the sudden pitiable and terrifying change in his fortunes; and a cathartic climax that Herbert Weisinger in *Tragedy and the Paradox of the Fortunate Fall*, borrowing the phrase from Isaiah, has called the "small moment," that desperate awaiting of the fateful outcome when all seems in doubt.

Buried in the Old Testament there are tragic dramas, particularly the very Greek story of Saul and his "bloody house" in the books of Samuel, but the later priestly theology has imposed its institutional conception of the sacrificial animal without blemish on the earlier *hybris* stories, and revised such obvious tragedies as Jonah and Job, the former into a curious redemptive comedy that concludes on the parable of the gourd, the latter with an ending that begs all its questions

*Stanley Edgar Hyman, "Psychoanalysis and the Climate of Tragedy," *Partisan Review*, Vol. XXIII, No. 2 (Spring, 1956), pp. 198–214.

and blandly returns all Job's earthly property twofold. On the basis of a theology where the only sins are disobeying God or worshiping rival gods, and the consequences of those are never in doubt, no agonistic form is possible, and the Judaic tradition has produced nothing like a tragic or dramatic literature.

Building on this tradition, Christianity too seems incompatible with a tragic literature, as Weisinger among others has shown. The great Christian drama of the Passion cannot be tragic because the perfection of Jesus eliminates *hybris* or any shortcoming, neither pity nor terror in Aristotle's sense is possible because of our inability to identify our own flawed human nature with the image of perfect goodness suffering absolute injustice, and the final victory is always certain. Drama with a human protagonist, insofar as it is Christian, cannot be tragic, since the issue has been settled once and for all by the victory of Jesus in His Incarnation, and His Atonement makes all subsequent private atonement unnecessary for the Christian,[1] who needs only some combination of Faith and Grace to participate in the antecedent act. Dante properly recognized this in identifying his great poetic drama as a divine comedy. When tragic possibility is reintroduced in Christian history it is invariably repudiated as heresy: the Manichean belief that the issue has not yet been finally settled, denying Incarnation its victory; or the Pelagian repudiation of Original Sin, obviating divine Atonement.

Nor have the great Oriental faiths produced anything we could properly call tragedy. Since their common sacrificial figure, as William Empson reminds us in *Some Versions of Pastoral*, is not the Western Dying God, typified by Jesus on the Cross, but an antithetical image of The Sincere Man at One With Nature, typified by the Buddha under the Bo tree, no Passion is possible, and there can be neither struggle nor victory. Lacking our characteristic Western philosophy of change, the great Oriental faiths seem to lock man in a permanent dualism, which does not become resolved in time, but has always been transcended in a higher unity pre-existent in the blinding moment of eternity.

I would submit that the great tragic literature of the modern world has escaped divine comedy by being only nominally Christian, and in fact deeply heretic at key points. Shakespeare may be Christian in *Measure for Measure* and *The Tempest*, but *Lear* and *Macbeth*, *Othello* and *Hamlet* are Christian only in their insistence on the radical imperfectibility of man. They exist in a Manichean and Pelagian universe where the Incarnation has never happened and the Atonement consequently did not occur. In this universe proud man is locked in mortal struggle with the inner forces of evil, and must win through to some private redemption and true-seeing by means of his own suffering, with no otherworldly allies. The great tragic novels like *Karamazov* and *Moby-Dick* are similarly Manichean and Pelagian, with Jesus appearing in person in the first to hear from the Grand Inquisitor the failure of His Incarnation, and Ahab in the second, striking through the mask of the Christian Atonement and finding his own sacrificial atonement, that of a Pelagian man-god, in the consubstantial mystery of immolation with the great whale.

The rise of rationalism, whether in its characteristic eighteenth-century

---

[1] I am leaving this statement in as a curiosity. I cannot imagine what came over me when I wrote it, since I know better and knew better then. Actually, Christian orthodoxy insists that Christ's Atonement makes atonement by the Christian necessary, and in fact Christ's Atonement is the event that makes later atonement possible. Christ, in short, is the Christian's representative, not his substitute. My 1956 statement is not far from the Antinomian heresy, that justification by Grace exempts from the moral law. [1963]

form as mechanical determinism or its characteristic nineteenth-century form as optimistic perfectibility, killed the tragic possibility that had coexisted with Christianity in pagan survival and Christian heresy. Francis Fergusson has defined the tragic rhythm of action in *The Idea of a Theater* as the movement from "Purpose" through "Passion" to "Perception" (acknowledging his debt to Kenneth Burke's *"poiema," "pathema," "mathema"*). Taking, as Aristotle did, Sophocles' *Oedipus Tyrannus* as the archetypal tragedy, Fergusson has discussed later dramatic literature as the hypertrophy of one or another phase of the tragic rhythm. In his terms, the rationalist world of mechanical determinism would permit no Purpose because we can have no free will or choice, no Passion because suffering becomes meaningless where we "understand" all and forgive all, and no Perception because no increase of self-knowledge could come from the discovery that everything has been externally caused. In the Victorian world of optimistic perfectibility (to return to our earlier terms) *hybris* can be dissipated by a bracing daily cold bath, *peripeteia* waits only on improvements in the social machinery, and what small moment of terror, doubt, or despair could survive the splendid teleological faith that the Heavenly City is at this moment having its building plots laid out on earth?

It is my belief that the writings of Sigmund Freud once again make a tragic view possible for the modern mind. Insofar as psychoanalysis is a branch of clinical psychology aimed at therapy, it is optimistic and meliorative (although Freud, in such statements as "Analysis Terminable and Interminable," was far more pessimistic about the difficulties and ultimate limits of cure in biological "rock-bottom" than the majority of his followers). Insofar as it is a philosophic view of man and a body of speculative insights that can be turned on every area of culture (that is, what Freud called "applied" psychoanalysis), it is gloomy, stoic, and essentially tragic. Its basic recognition is the radical imperfectibility of man, a concept it derives not from the Christian Fall, but from the Darwinian Descent. Freudian man is an imperfectible animal, and, as the biological punishment for having risen in the scale beyond the microorganism, a dying animal. The first protoplasm "had death within easy reach," Freud observes in *Beyond the Pleasure Principle*. For Freud, the aim of human existence is the reclamation of some cropland of ego from the "Zuyder Zee" of id, and the limited victory in this bitter struggle is achieved primarily through the traditional philosophic means of self-knowledge. Man's animal nature is to be controlled and channeled in the least harmful direction possible, not changed or abolished, and cure lies not in extirpating animality but in facing it and living with it.

Human life "is hard to endure," Freud says in *The Future of an Illusion*, but we must learn "to endure with resignation." "If you would endure life," he recommends in "Thoughts for the Times on War and Death," "be prepared for death." In such essays as "An Apology of *Raymond Sebond*" and "That to Philosophie, is to Learn How to Die," Montaigne confronted death as nobly and resolutely as Socrates in Plato's *Phaedo*, but without Socrates' eloquent faith in individual resurrection and the afterlife. Since many of us are not Socratics but skeptics, and our problem to adjust not to the dying animal that will be sloughed off to free some eternal spirit but to the dying animal that becomes putrid meat and nothing else, we might do well to eschew the easy consolations of religion and turn to whatever grimmer satisfactions exist in Freud's stubbornly materialist view. Here we can find not only an Original Sin—the Freudian myth of the expulsion from the Eden of the womb added to the Darwinian myth of the origin of death—in which the modern mind can believe, but some terrestrial hopes for redemption and the good life.

In terms of Greek tragedy, the Oedipus complex is another phrasing of *hybris* (of King Oedipus' own *hybris*, in fact), the child's swollen pride that he is a fitter mate for his mother than the tall stranger. Libido, the blind energy of sexual impulses, is equivalent to the ancient Greek "wild Ate," the daughter of Zeus and Strife, the wrath or madness that seizes the hero and moves him to senseless violence, destruction, or self-destruction. Sublimation is the small moment, the reintroduction of possibility, the birth of art and all human culture out of filth. Sublimation allows St. Francis to create a life of goodness out of an impulse to bestiality, or Bach to compose for an organ that is not the one with which psychoanalysis is preoccupied. Even the curative procedure of analysis itself, the transference, is a scapegoat mechanism, and Freud in his whole life and work is a sacrificial figure, almost a Dying God, even without the benefit of such probably apocryphal anecdotes as the one of Freud dashing out of his office shouting, "Why must I listen to such swinishness!"

If the human condition is ultimately animal, even swinish, man is nevertheless capable of moral action and sometimes of a life of sacrificial good, as Freud himself was. In terms of Ruth Benedict's somewhat oversimple dichotomy between shame cultures and guilt cultures, the Freudian neuroses are our own guilty or introjected equivalents for the public shame of wrong-doing in Attic tragedy, and they motivate an internal symbolic action like the redemptive ritual on the stage. For Freud, the choice is a newer dialectic statement of the old dualism, truly "beyond the pleasure principle": destroy others or turn the destruction inward. The ancient Zoroastrian divinities Ormuzd and Ahriman that Mani brought into Christianity are still locked in mortal combat in Freud's "exquisitely dualistic conception of the instinctive life," now called Eros the life instinct and Thanatos the death instinct. "The death instinct turns into the destructive instinct" when it is directed outward to the external world, Freud writes in "Why War?" and he concludes the grandest of his philosophic works, *Civilization and Its Discontents*, with the extremely moderate hope:

> Men have brought their powers of subduing the forces of nature to such a pitch that by using them they could now very easily exterminate one another to the last man. They know this—hence arises a great part of their current unrest, their dejection, their mood of apprehension. And now it may be expected that the other of the two "heavenly forces," eternal Eros, will put forth his strength so as to maintain himself alongside of his equally immortal adversary.

In essence, this prophetic statement, written as long ago as 1929, asks no more than the old horseplayer's reasonable prayer, "Lord, let me break even, I need the money."

If Freud produced a climate of opinion in which tragedy could again flourish, an important group of his followers in this country, the neo-Freudians or "revisionists," have done their best to dispel it as quickly as possible. In half a century of existence, psychoanalysis has raced through the whole religious cycle from revolutionary prophetic truth to smug Sunday sermon, and almost as soon as Freud's philosophy began to have an effect on our culture it was hushed up and denied in his name. The revisionists, principally the late Karen Horney, Erich Fromm, and the late Harry Stack Sullivan, along with a number of others of similar views, have put Freudian psychoanalysis into what Emerson called the "optative mood."

All began by publishing independently, but Horney and Fromm had had some contact in Berlin, where they had been influenced in varying degrees by Wilhelm Reich's "Freudo-Marxist" movement. Horney, who has written most extensively about the causes of her defection, has explained that she could not swallow either the views of feminine psychology Freud published in the *New Introductory Lectures* in 1933, or the death instinct, the former as a woman but the latter as a citizen. "Such an assumption," she writes of the death instinct in *New Ways in Psychoanalysis*, "paralyzes any effort to search in the specific cultural conditions for reasons which make for destructiveness. It must also paralyze efforts to change anything in these conditions. If man is inherently destructive and consequently unhappy, why strive for a better future?" In his more articulate strivings, befitting a social psychologist, Fromm found the gloomy fixities of biological instincts equally incompatible with hopes of improving the human condition by first making over society. Sullivan, from a very different background in clinical psychiatry, primarily with psychotics, came to similar conclusions. All three have influenced one another, first by their publications, later through direct discussion and a kind of uneasy collaboration. Their views and approaches, however, remain different enough so that one can choose to be a Horneyite, a Frommian, or a Sullivanite, and in some cases, like that of Clara Thompson, one can make several of these choices in succession.

The leading neo-Freudians, as well as their shifting followers, appear to be entirely sincere and dedicated psychoanalysts and psychiatrists, convinced by developments in the social sciences or by their own clinical experience that Freud was culture-bound, masculine-biased, cancer-morbid, or for some reason blind to what they can see. The result of their revisions has nevertheless, in my opinion, been not to improve or modernize psychoanalysis, but to abandon its key insights both as a science and as a philosophy. Their effect has been to re-repress whatever distasteful or tragic truths Freud dug out of his own unconscious or his patients', and to convert the familiar device of resistance into revisionist theory.

Freud always believed that "prudish America" would welcome his theories and water them down with equal enthusiasm, and his expectation has not been disappointed. The passion of Americans for constant reassurance that they live in the Garden of Eden (which Horney characteristically refers to as "the greater freedom from dogmatic beliefs which I found in this country") was in evidence as far back as 1912, when Jung wrote Freud from America that he was having great success in overcoming resistance to psychoanalysis by playing down sexuality, and Freud wrote back that he need not boast, since "the more he sacrificed of the hard-won truths of psychoanalysis, the less resistance he would encounter." Even predicting this American bowdlerization, however, Freud could hardly have imagined the extent to which it would be done in his name, in books worshipfully acknowledging his teaching or fulsomely dedicated to his memory. Paradoxically, with the aim of making psychoanalysis more scientific, the neo-Freudians have made it less so: where Freud was descriptive, they are hortatory; where he was the humble therapist, they are faith healers, inspirational preachers, be-glad-you're-neurotic Pollyannas.

The question of whether in fact Horney, Fromm, and Sullivan are Freudians or psychoanalysts at all seems to me of relatively minor importance, and is probably impossible to answer authoritatively anyway. In *The History of the Psychoanalytic Movement* in 1914, Freud reserved the right, as the founder of psychoanalysis, to say what it was and what it was not, but his various statements of the criteria involved shift disconcertingly. In the *History*, he calls the theory of "repression" in the unconscious the pillar on which the edifice rests, "really the most essential part of it," along with the empiric facts of "transference" and "resistance." "Every investigation which recognizes these two facts and makes them the starting-point of its work may call itself psychoanalysis," he writes, "even if it leads to other results than my own." Later in the book he describes the dream as "the shibboleth of psychoanalysis," and a few pages later declares that Jung's approach "no longer has the slightest claim to call itself psychoanalysis," apparently because it discards the sexual nature of the libido and the reality of the Oedipus complex. In other works, Freud makes the infantile sexual etiology of the neuroses the test of psychoanalysis, or remarks "a psychoanalytic, that is, genetic explanation."

If any investigation starting from the mechanisms of the unconscious may call itself psychoanalysis, the theories of Horney, Fromm, and Sullivan are probably psychoanalytic. They certainly recognize the existence of resistance and repression, and Horney even calls the concept of resistance "of paramount value for therapy." On the genesis of the neuroses from infantile sexuality, they are considerably less orthodox, since they recognize early sex frustrations as causative in some cases but insist that factors like "anxiety" or "the current life situation" are more relevant. They use the term "transference," but mean not a repetition of an infantile attachment, Freud's "cure through love," but, with Sullivan, a significant new sort of interpersonal relation, the first break in the patient's chain of "parataxic" distortions; or, with Horney, simply that human relationship of the patient's which is easiest to study, control, and explain to him. "As for the transference, it is altogether a curse," Freud wrote in a bleak letter to Pfister in 1910; it never occurred to him that he could solve the problem by a little Draconian redefinition.

If we take Freud's sexual concepts, so unattractive to Jung's American contacts in 1912, as basic, there is no likelihood of calling Horney, Fromm, and Sullivan Freudian psychoanalysts. I would take these basic concepts to be: *libido,* the volcanic sexual instinct; *id,* the caged beast of the unconscious ("a cauldron of seething excitement," Freud called it in a different metaphor); and the *Oedipus complex,* the destructive rivalry with one parent and attachment to the other. In varying degrees, the revisionists have denied all three or modified them out of recognition. For Horney, the libido concept is harmful nonsense suggesting discouraging limitations to therapy; the id is a "debatable doctrine" (what she keeps of Freud she calls "findings," what she rejects, "doctrines"); and the Oedipus complex does not exist in healthy adults, but is produced accidentally in neurotics, as Adler had suggested earlier, by parental sex-stimulation or parent-fostered anxiety. For Fromm, as for Jung, the sexual libido is simply an assumption "one does not share"; what Freud called id is largely eradicable drives produced by the culture; and the Oedipus complex is, Fromm agrees, the central phenomenon of psychology and the nucleus of all neuroses, but it is not a nasty sexual attraction to one parent and a murderous rivalry with the other, but merely a normal and healthy struggle against parental authority in the quest for freedom and independence. For Sullivan, sexual difficulties tend to be symptoms rather than causes, so that libido and id simply do not exist, and a variety of interesting interpersonal attachments take the place of the Oedipus complex.

The neo-Freudians insist on the importance of sociology and anthropology for knowledge of the ways in which the culture determines personality and character, or at least limits their possibilities. A good deal of their sociology, however, seems to be about as profound as Fromm's ingenious formulation "the most backward class, the lower middle class," and their anthropology is typified by Thompson's statement that Benedict has shown in the Kwakiutl or the Dobu "a whole society of psychically crippled and unproductive people," and that certain primitive cultures seem to be "predominantly destructive of man's best interests." If Fromm has read more modern anthropology than Freud, he has apparently been less affected by it, and cultural relativism has not laid a glove on him. In *The Sane Society*, Fromm equates all ethics with "Greco-Judaeo-Christian" ethics, a moral absolute, and remarks casually, "natural ethics, the Decalogue," with the engaging footnote: "Minus the first commandment, which bears on man's destiny and not on ethics."

The opportunity, vastly greater than Freud's, that the neo-Freudians have for acquiring some accurate information about the nature of man in society seems to have resulted only in cheerier illusions. Malinowski in *Sex and Repression in Savage Society* would appear to have confirmed the universality of the Oedipus complex by finding among his matriarchal Trobrianders an equivalent, the male child's rivalry with the culture's father surrogate, the mother's brother. The neo-Freudians have taken it instead to show that, in Horney's words, "the generation of such a complex depends on a whole set of factors operating in family life"; in other words, that all such unwholesome manifestations are socially produced and could be eliminated by social change. If Freud generalized a universal human psyche from an early practice consisting largely of neurotic Jewish middle-class women in turn-of-the-century Vienna, a reading of *The Golden Bough*, and his own self-analysis, all we can say is that the ingredients of that curious stew simmered down to more wisdom than all the resources of American industriousness have brought the neo-Freudians. Socrates sitting on a stone in the market place still knows more about the world than Alexander conquering it.

Ultimately, the differences of Horney, Fromm, and Sullivan with Freud reduce themselves to a contrasting view of human nature, to philosophic disagreement. The revisionists see man as fundamentally good, innocent, and unfallen; thus they inevitably have a different conception of human drives, relationships, and the aims of therapy. In Horney's view of the child frustration, sibling rivalry, the Oedipus complex, and similar factors are not ultimately determining; the important matters are "such parental attitudes as having real interest in a child, real respect for it, giving it real warmth," and "such qualities as reliability and sincerity." As for adults:

> It is so much easier for a woman to think that she is nasty to her husband because, unfortunately, she was born without a penis and envies him for having one than to think, for instance, that she has developed an attitude of righteousness and infallibility which makes it impossible to tolerate any questioning or disagreement. It is so much easier for a patient to think that nature has given her an unfair deal than to realize that she actually makes excessive demands on the environment and is furious whenever they are not complied with.

Horney cannot countenance the Freudian view because it would allow "no liking or disliking of people, no sympathy, no generosity, no feeling of justice, no devotion to a cause, which is not in the last analysis essentially determined by libidinal or destructive drives."

The aim of therapy is not Freud's modest relief from neurotic difficulties, but "true happiness," to which most patients, she says, had never even dared aspire. "The enjoyment of happiness is a faculty to be acquired from within," she adds, and the end of analysis for the patient is "to give him the courage to be himself," or in another formulation, "by rendering a person free from inner bondages make him free for the development of his best potentialities." Horney never doubts that when the patient has the courage to be himself it will be a good self, or that he has best potentialities to develop, because she shares Rousseau's faith that "the spontaneous individual self" is born free and good but is everywhere in environmental chains. Beneath everything there is some sort of ultimate, absolute "genuineness" in the personality, and it is this that gives her her faith, against Freud's "disbelief in human goodness and human growth," that "man has the capacity as well as the desires to develop his potentialities and become a decent human being."

Fromm charges that Freud may have been inspired in his theorizing by "an unsolved problem in the realtionship to his own mother," but nothing in Fromm's background has given him cause to doubt "the unconditioned love of the mother for her children *because they are her children*." The slogan of his "humanistic psychoanalysis" is "productive love," which enriches both parties and surpasseth understanding. Fromm's first book, *Escape From Freedom*, carries as its epigraph the unlovely Talmudic saying, "If I am not for myself, who will be for me?" His second book, inevitably entitled *Man for Himself*, explains how he got his key term ("Genuine love is rooted in productiveness and may properly be called, therefore, 'productive love' "). Since only a person genuinely capable of loving himself is capable of loving others, self-interest is a social good, as it was for Bernard Mandeville and Adam Smith. Fromm writes:

> The failure of modern culture lies not in its principle of individualism, not in the idea that moral virtue is the same as the pursuit of self-interest, but in the deterioration of the meaning of self-interest; not in the fact that people are *too much concerned with their self-interest*, but that they are *not concerned enough with the interest of their real self; not in the fact that they are too selfish, but that they do not love themselves.*

Even the superego in *The Sane Society* is loving and productive, "a voice which tells us to do our duty, and a voice which tells us to love and to forgive—others as well as ourselves."

The aim of therapy is naturally to free this true self for its true productive loving self-interest. "Mental health is characterized by the ability to love and to create," he writes, and "creation" as an ideal is defined rather broadly: "an ever-increasing number of people paint, do gardening, build their own boats or houses, indulge in any number of 'do it yourself' activities." As for the nature of man, "we look upon human nature as essentially historically conditioned," and Freud's Manichean dualism becomes the Christian certainty of victory for God's Party: "the forward-going life instinct is stronger and increases in relative strength the more it grows." We know that our redeemers live, even if they are only people in the French Communities of Work with "a resilient spirit of good will," "people who have said 'yes' to life"; not yet the truly "awakened ones" like "Ikhnaton, Moses, Kung Futse, Lao-tse, Buddha, Jesaja, Socrates, Jesus."

Sullivan's underlying philosophy seems essentially similar, although its expression is a good deal more rugged and considerably less inspirational. In *Conceptions of Modern Psychiatry*, Sullivan defines love as a "state of affectional
rapport," which has "great adaptive possibilities" and produces "a great increase
in the consensual validation of symbols." In *The Interpersonal Theory of Psychiatry*, he redefines it in even clammier terms:

> Intimacy is that type of situation involving two people which permits validations of
> all components of personal worth. Validation of personal worth requires a type of
> relationship which I call collaboration, by which I mean clearly formulated adjust-
> ments of one's behavior to the expressed needs of the other person in the pursuit of
> increasingly identical—that its, more and more nearly mutual satisfactions, and the
> maintenance of increasingly similar security operations.

For Sullivan, perhaps because so much of his clinical experience was with psychotics rather than neurotics, the aim of therapy is less ambitious: better interpersonal relations, better communication, and a positive direction toward goals
of collaboration and of mutual satisfaction and security. He is less impressed by
the miraculous "unique individual self" that will flower than Horney and
Fromm, and his vision of the nature of man is not so much Rousseau's uncor-
rupted innocent as a neutral network of interpersonal relations, as capable of
good, bad, or indifferent functioning as a telephone switchboard. How far it is
from a tragic vision we can see in such comments as: "When difficulties in the
sex life are presented by a patient as his reason for needing psychiatric help . . .
the patient's difficulty in living is best manifested by his very choice of this as his
peculiar problem."

Other neo-Freudians show similar optimism. Franz Alexander, the head of
the Chicago Psychoanalytic Institute, sponsors a shorter and more directed therapy, in line with his idea that the therapist is not dealing with the stubborn sexual libido, but with three basic human tendencies he has named: to recieve or
take, to retain, and to give or eliminate. Clara Thompson believes with Fromm
in "creative productive love," as a consequence of which she sees the aim of
therapy as "calm self-possession," the patient "free to develop his powers." Like
Horney, Fromm, and Sullivan, she simply cannot believe in the existence of evil.
Surely a child "in a perfectly benign environment" would not show "serious destructiveness," and any child warped by bad parents can be readily redeemed
"if a teacher, a Boy Scout leader or some other hero of childhood presents a consistently different attitude." Bruno Bettelheim, the principal of the Orthogenic
School at the University of Chicago, calls on psychoanalysis to emphasize "positive human emotions and motivations," and to interpret behavior in terms of
"inner freedom and human autonomy" and "man's inherent dignity." Beyond
these, there are Fay B. Karpf's "Dynamic Relationship Therapy," and what Patrick Mullahy, a Sullivanite trained in philosophy, describes as "the sense of adequacy, competence, and power which comes from self-respect and respect for
others—a rational feeling of power." An inch or two further, and we are lying
down in green pastures beside Norman Vincent Peale.

The question is not what degree of therapeutic success these doctrines give,
since the evidence suggests that any internally consistent system of interpretation accepted by the patient, from shamanism to the miraculous grottos of Zur-

ich, can cure,[2] but rather what happens to literature in a culture that has shaped them and is in turn somewhat shaped by them. If tragedy requires Freud's stoic winning through to the perception of harsh truth, and all the influence of our psychology goes directly against it, then perhaps we should be content with comedy or even farce. Unfortunately, the neo-Freudian doctrines could as readily be shown, I think, to be uncongenial to art of any sort. Comedy and farce, like dreams, are the disguised fulfillment of repressed wishes. As the dream is organized in reaction to the commanding injunctions of the superego, so the comic arts get their structuring from a similar ethical conflict, the opposition of accepted what-ought-to-be to what-is. In the cultural determinism of the interpersonalists, where whatever happens is no individual's fault, comedy is as impossible as tragedy.

Lionel Trilling, who has been uniquely distinguished among modern literary critics by his defense of Freudian orthodoxy against vulgarization and revision,[3] has remarked that one of the greatest contributions of psychoanalysis to literature is its image of the mind as a kind of poetry-making machine, so that it constitutes almost a science of tropes. Insofar as literary or artistic form and dream form are the products of similar devices, and operations analogous to condensation, displacement, and the rest shape the poem, Freud has given us one of the great critical tools for literary analysis. Where the revisionists deny genetic and dynamic factors and insist on "the current life situation," here, as on so many occasions, they repudiate insight and hobble art. Burke has written in *The Philosophy of Literary Form* that the poem consists of three aspects: dream, prayer, and chart. The neo-Freudian poem has for its dream, The validation of all components of personal worth; for its prayer, Help me to stop making excessive demands on the environment; for its chart, To thine own self-interest be true.

Perhaps a good measure of the fault lies in our country itself. In a paper, "Freud in America: Some Observations," read at the 1954 meeting of the American Psychological Association, Joseph Adelson discussed the resistance to Freud in terms of the deeply entrenched American idea of "the indefinite perfectibility of man" that Toqueville noted as early as 1835. Adelson writes:

> American feeling is animated by a zest for freedom; it cries out against constraint. While men may vary in what they achieve, their destinies are open and infinite. We may fall into error or failure, yet we do so, not because of an inner taint, but through circumstance; and circumstance, the American feels, can be rectified. Original sin, even in its most secular versions, has not attracted our thought. In changing the external, in modifying situations, men, we feel, can make and re-make themselves. It is in the idea of man's perfectibility and in the vision of a tractable world that Americans find their way to life's meaning. Throughout its history Amer-

[2] In *New Statesman* for January 7, 1956, Dr. H. J. Eysenck of the University of London printed some disconcerting figures on psychoanalytic cure, based on a review of the published material. Of neurotic patients treated by means of any kind of psychotherapy, approximately two out of three recover. Of neurotics who receive no therapy whatsoever, approximately two out of three recover. In other words, two out of three is apparently the percentage of spontaneous recovery. Since then, none of the letters in *New Statesman* taking issue with Dr. Eysenck's conclusions has challenged these figures.
[3] Since this was written, Trilling has published his 1955 Freud Anniversary Lecture, *Freud and the Crisis of Our Culture*, with its bold and brilliant vision of Freud's biological limitation as a sanctuary against the omnipotent tyranny of culture.

ican feeling has struggled against the concept of limitation and has been held by the attitudes of hope and optimismm.

Adelson summarizes Freud's contrary vision of human life, and adds:

> The American mood is substantially different. We experiment enthusiastically, trying this and that, all of our efforts informed by a vigorous faith in the endless plasticity of the human organism. It is my impression that we tend to disregard the dark and archaic components of the personality; at the very least we deprive them, rhetorically, of their vigor. Think of how Freud expressed the intensity of the instincts or of the superego—"oceanic," "surging," "raging." American psychology uses much blander adjectives. We tend to emphasize the ego's resources, its ability, somehow, to drive its way to health. In fact, the systems of Rogers, Horney, and Sullivan have in common the explicit assumption that the organism autonomously moves forward to growth. We incline to see the therapeutic task, then, as involving the strengthening of ego capacities. A friend of mine puts it this way: "We don't try to kill the weeds; we feed the clover and hope that *it* will kill the weeds."

If Freud, *in conjunction with* other intellectual and social forces, succeeded in denting this Emersonian optimism in the period between the two world wars, many of his most articulate followers have since labored to hammer it back into shape. No one can say that any given work of art is affected by any given body of ideas, but we must assume in general that ideas have consequences. It is instructive to note how many important contemporary writers have followed their earlier tragic work with later mellowings. Hemingway is a classic example. Where *The Sun Also Rises* and *A Farewell to Arms*, if not masterpieces, are authentically tragic, moving from Purpose through Passion to Perception; such later novels as *For Whom the Bell Tolls* and *Across the River and Into the Trees* are merely bathetic; and if Robert Jordan or Colonel Cantwell commits *hybris*, the author seems no longer aware of it. Where "The Undefeated" was a truly cathartic work of art, its recent rewriting as *The Old Man and the Sea* is almost a Frommian parody ("If I am not for myself, who will be for me?"). Faulkner has moved similarly from a fiction of ritual tragedy in *The Sound and the Fury* and *Light in August* to optimistic comedy or fairy tale, as have Steinbeck, Caldwell, and so many others. Such dissimilar poets as Frost and Eliot traveled the same route from earlier bleak stoicism to such later chatty affirmations as *A Masque of Mercy* and *The Confidential Clerk*. If on the whole our poets have been less affected than the novelists by the retreat from tragic insight, it is perhaps only that not many of them were ever there to begin with.

We would all enthusiastically welcome the psychoanalytic good society, where every psyche was well and whole, and no one had impulses that could not or should not be gratified. To the extent that a good part of our literature depends on our being deeply and irremediably sick, renouncing it would be a small price to pay for general psychic health, just as Hegel was prepared to slough off art as an inferior form of communion when the stage of perfect communion was realized. Even within our limited experience at present, we can see how our great literature depends on and is informed by the patterns of neurosis in our culture. To an unacculturated Cheyenne, King Lear would be simply an old man behaving very badly; to those gentle socialists the Mountain Arapesh, the whole disordered story of ungrateful children and rival claims to power and property would be meaningless. In real life, we are sure, Mr. and Mrs. Othello have no problem that a good marriage counselor couldn't clear up in ten minutes, and any of our clinics would give Iago some useful job around the grounds allowing him to work off his aggressions in some socially approved fashion.

Unfortunately, Mr. and Mrs. Othello do not exist in real life but in art, where their deadly misunderstanding is essential to our own well-being, and Iago is permanently out of the therapist's clutches. The psychoanalytic good society seems no nearer of achievement now than it did in Vienna in 1900, and to many of us it seems further off. Meanwhile all the Cheyenne are acculturated and apt to behave almost as badly as Lear, given similar provocation. If the Mountain Arapesh have not yet learned the joys of private property and early toilet training from our movies, they soon will, and one day they will all wear thin bow ties and know what bites sharper than the serpent's tooth. The trouble with the revisionist Freudians is not that they would give up art for the psychoanalytic good society, but that they pretend that it is already here, that we are well when we are in fact desperately ill, and they drive out art when it is almost the only honest doctor who will tell us the truth.

If Freud showed us that human life was nasty, brutish, and short, and had always been, he was only holding the mirror up to our own faces, saying what the great philosophers and the great tragic writers have always said. If we are serious, our reaction to this bitter truth is neither to evade it with one or another anodyne, nor to kill ourselves, but to set out humbly through the great tragic rhythm of pride and fall, so curiously alike in psychoanalysis and literature. At the end of this hard road we can see faintly beckoning that self-knowledge without which, we are assured on good authority, we live as meanly as the ants.

Tragedy and the American Climate of Opinion*

Orrin E. Klapp

America has always taken tragedy lightly. Too busy to stop the activity of their twenty-million-horse-power society, Americans ignore tragic motives that would have overshadowed the Middle Ages; and the world learns to regard assassination as a form of hysteria, and death as a neurosis, to be treated by a rest-cure. Three hideous political murders, that would have fattened the Eumenides with horror, have thrown scarely a shadow on the White House.

—Henry Adams

I

It has sometimes been remarked that Americans have a kind of armor against tragic experience. Courage, optimism, realism, the Pollyanna spirit—what should it be called? "Somehow missing from this land of plenty," says Norbert Wiener, is an awareness that "the world is not a pleasant little nest made for our protection, but a vast and largely hostile environment, in which we can achieve great things only by defying the gods; and that this defiance inevitably brings its own punishment."[1] We have our share of troubles, to be sure, but without the conviction that trouble is permanent and necessary; rather, it is an exceptional phenomenon that we must be good sports to face when it comes and work hard to eliminate as soon as possible. A poll would easily show that most Americans think of tragedy simply as fortuitous. Other typical attitudes support this general view: we should accentuate the positive and not dwell on the gloomy side, religion should make us happy,[2] stories should come out all right in the end. We are not, then (as Edith Hamilton said of the Greeks and Miguel Unamuno of the Spanish), a tragic people.

Probably this is why, though such plays are part of our cultural inheritance, they cannot be said to have much popular appeal. You could watch movies and television continuously for a month and not see a single example of tragedy,

* Orrin E. Klapp, "Tragedy and the American Climate of Opinion," *Centennial Review of Arts and Sciences*, 2 (Fall, 1958), pp. 396–413.
[1] *The Human Use of Human Beings* (New York: Houghton Mifflin, 1954), pp. 183–184.
[2] Paul Hutchinson, for instance, deplores the "cult of reassurance" that has so largely taken the place of the tragic conception of Christianity, in "Have We a 'New' Religion?," *Life*, April 11, 1955, pp. 138 ff. See also Reinhold Niebuhr, *Beyond Tragedy* (New York: Charles Scribner's Sons, 1955).

properly speaking.[3] One student of the mass mind, Leo Gurko, claims, however, that the success now and then of movies like *Hamlet* or Broadway plays like *A Streetcar Named Desire* is proof of a hunger for mature art in the general public.[4] I would like to believe it but would be more convinced by his argument if the evidence of demand were clearer in the popular media. How many movie stars may be called tragedians?

The lack of tragedy in America is the more curious when we consider that it is a *pleasure* we are missing. Those who may claim to understand it say that it is one of the keenest joys of the spirit to see a man plunge into a course of suffering from which he does not choose to escape. Edith Hamilton, indeed, states the paradox that "the greater the suffering, the more terrible the events, the more intense our pleasure." This joy has been described by Joseph Wood Krutch as an *elation* based on confidence in the greatness of man, from having watched him pass through mighty passions with supreme fortitude; and by Shelley as an exalted *calm* in which there is neither censure nor hatred but only knowledge and self-respect. If calm and elation are the products of tragedy, then why does it not rank with tranquillizing pills as a commodity on the American market? The same needs that favored the vogue of "peace of mind" books should make it a popular art form. It should be on a par with westerns and musical comedies. It should sell soap on the radio theatre. It should play a prominent part in American religion. But it clearly does none of these things. The explanation must be that the needs served by tragedy are different from those served by comfort; that the words like joy, calm, and elation are perhaps inadequate to convey to our minds what tragic satisfaction consists of—that the difficulty is semantic and ultimately cultural. We simply do not have a culture in which tragedy makes much sense.

Two main questions, then, emerge. First, what difference does it make, after all, whether or not Americans understand tragedy? The other requires an explanation: what are the elements of culture, or, as Kurt Lewin calls it, social climate, that stand in the way of the proper appreciation of this kind of art and its hero?

II

As to whether it makes any difference, there is an impressive number of thinkers like C. E. M. Joad, Reinhold Niebuhr, Paul Hutchinson, and J. W. Krutch, to name a few, who are concerned about the moral implications of the lack of tragedy. They see an improverishment of spirit inherent in the inability to see positive value in tragedy and its hero. Their concern, it need hardly be said, is not whether Americans will lose a pleasure, but whether they will sacrifice the hard-won maturity, wisdom, and religious understanding that seem somehow connected with the fate of the tragic hero. There is a political issue, too, best shown

[3] American movies, say Martha Wolfenstein and Nathan Leites, are shallow emotionally, however many great lovers and gunmen stalk the stage. Love is easily transferred and does not commit one to tragic consequences; crises take the form of external, not inner, conflict, in which winning is all-important and suffering is "pointless and unneccessary."—*Movies, A Psychological Study* (Glencoe, Illinois: Free Press, 1950), pp. 94–99, 295–301.
[4] Leo Gurko, *Heroes, Highbrows and the Popular Mind* (Indianapolis: Bobbs-Merrill, 1953), pp. 198, 302–304.

in novels like Huxley's *Brave New World* and Orwell's *Nineteen Eighty-Four;* that is, what kind of relation of man-to-man and state-to-man is implicit in an attitude lacking the tragic sense. Since tragedy is at the same time a check on pride and a testimony of human dignity, we may be fearful that without this perspective, leaders may act with too much assurance that they are right and with too little respect for the individuals under them.

It is to the underlying cultural and semantic problem, however, that I wish to give most attention here—to find out more about how and why the tragic hero is *misunderstood* in America. At the center of the problem, it seems to me, is the fact that the average American does not get the happiness—the sense of triumph, affirmation, and understanding—that experts say he should out of this kind of experience. So we may judge that he misinterprets it. And by looking at American culture and studying the reactions of audiences we may hope to see what it is that stands in the way of adequate understanding. My thesis is that there are three main reasons: (1) a stock of cultural images (social types) that displace or inhibit tragic perception; (2) an unfavorable climate of opinion and belief; and (3) an actual shrinkage that has occurred in the stature of the heroes being presented, making it easier to fail to see them as having the dignity necessary to be tragic.

On the score of competing cultural images, let us first look at some of the conceptions, the popular types, that stand in the way of tragic understanding. Because of their partial resemblance to the tragic figure, they may easily be assigned to any man who gets himself into serious trouble, and thus prevent people from seeing him in what may be called a deeper way. And because they are themselves appealing, they are interesting enough to steal the show from the tragic hero. One of these competing types is the *victim,* the sufferer of a disaster or wrong. While he gets plenty of sympathy, he is too innocent to be tragic: he lacks willful fault and inner conflict; he has not brought the trouble on himself; and so we feel only a melodramatic conflict between him and the villains or forces that have harmed him. The *soap opera heroine* suffers also, to be sure; but she also is melodramatic, rather like the victim, basically good, for whom in this case things work out well in the end. These features disqualify her as a tragic heroine. The *martyr,* too, suffers, but his is a willing and knowing sacrifice for a noble cause; he, too, is a melodramatic hero in conflict with villains; and on both counts he is too good, too "perfect," to be tragic. (On this reasoning, the death of Jesus is not a tragedy, strictly speaking,[5] nor is that of Joan of Arc, Nathan Hale, or any other noble soul who dies for a cause. They are simply too good in their crucial acts; they have not the flaws you find in an Othello, a Macbeth.) The *villain* suffers also; but he is not tragic because we are glad of what he gets, more or less; he is too bad to deserve much sympathy. When newspapers report that gangsters shoot one another, we are likely to say, not "tragic" but "so much the better." Yet many a man whom we write off as a villain might have been tragic if we had looked at him a little more closely. Still another figure competing with the tragic hero is the *daredevil,* who courts death and sometimes provides a mor-

---

[5] "Jesus is, superficially considered, a tragic figure; yet not really so. Christianity is a religion which transcends tragedy. Tears, with death, are swallowed up in victory. The cross is not tragic but the resolution of tragedy. . . . Christianity's view of history is tragic insofar as it recognizes evil as an inevitable concomitant of even the highest spiritual enterprises. It is beyond tragedy insafar as it does not regard evil as inherent in existence itself but as finally under the dominion of a good God."— Reinhold Niebuhr, *Beyond Tragedy* (New York: Charles Scribner's Sons, 1937, 1955), pp. 155, x–xi.

bid thrill at the curve of the racetrack. His smash-up is akin to disaster if it affects the audience, or to folly if the actor kills only himself. In the latter case, he is a fool, at a far pole from the tragic hero. Then there is the pathological *case*, a person who comes to ruin because of sickness or insanity. However horrible such an end may be, it has nothing of the essentially tragic, because, for one thing, it is not voluntary, and if we sympathize at all, it is as with a victim. Besides, if we see such a man as a crackpot or other kind of mental deviant, his abnormality works against tragic compassion; instead of sympathizing, more than likely we will be repelled. Finally, among all the other types competing with the tragic figure for popular interest and understanding must be mentioned the outright *fool*, who gets himself into absurd or disgraceful trouble; he suffers, to be sure, but usually receives more laughter than sympathy.[6]

With such a repertory of distracting types, it is small wonder that when a real tragic figure appears he is misunderstood. It is so easy to think of him in terms of these other types! How many times, for instance, has Hamlet been called a dreamer who couldn't make up his mind?—or psychoanalyzed to the point that he became a "case," and his tragic dignity disappeared into an Oedipus complex? Madame Bovary is strictly a tragic character, but many of us are tempted to classify her as either a very foolish or a very bad woman. Or, in the case of someone like Othello, we may lay all the blame on a villain who got him into trouble; we see him merely as a victim; and thus we deprive him of guilt and conflict. In other words, because we are used to thinking in terms like "villain," "fool," and other types with which our culture provides us, we easily miscast the tragic hero.

These misunderstandings may be of some help, however, in seeing, by contrast, what a tragic hero ought to be. He should be a complex figure, whose self-imposed punishment and conflict within challenge our compassion and understanding. He must (however foolish or wicked his course of action may superficially seem) keep his dignity and remain heroic. Any tendency to "write him off" as a fool, no-account, mental case, etc., is a sign of failure of understanding; so, also, is it to simplify him in the opposite way, to a point where he is all good, others are to blame, and he has no inner conflict.

If such are the miscastings likely to happen because of competing types in American culture, let us look at actual responses of audiences to tragedies, both in real life (news) and in art. By asking people what they think about a character and his fate, it is possible to analyze the main perceptual images and decide whether he is being understood or misunderstood, and in what ways.

First, an interpretation by a group of college students of news-stories of real life "tragedies," as they might be called in ordinary parlance. Two of these appeared on the same day in a local paper: one of a deserted husband who ran amok and killed his children; the other of a jealous ex-husband who dogged the life of his divorced wife, finally entered her apartment, and shot her, then himself. I discussed them with the group on the day they were reported. The interpretations were on the surface different. There was consensus that killer #1 was a poor fellow driven out of his mind by his wife's meanness; #2 was simply a villain and no sympathy was shown him. The main reason for this difference seems

[6] Viewed in terms of his social status, he is a ridiculed figure. See my "The Fool as a Social Type," *American Journal of Sociology*, LV (1949), 157–162; also Enid Welsford's excellent study, *The Fool, His Social and Literary History* (London, 1935).

to have been the way the news was reported. An interview in the papers had brought out #1's point of view, telling how his wife had wronged him, showing her, in other words, as the villain, him as the victim. There had been no such interview, however, with the dead #2; only the external features of the crime were reported; so he remained a villain though his crime was somewhat less serious in terms of numbers of people injured. Did killer #1 become tragic, then, in escaping from the villain's part? On the contrary, *neither* of the interpretations could properly be called tragic. It was simply a case of locating the villain. I cite these cases to show how hard it is to develop—one might say manufacture—such a complex viewpoint toward reality without a favorable culture and suitable art form to, as it were, blow up the experience to bigger than life-size.[7] All of the elements of a classic tragedy—a *Hercules Distracted*, an *Othello*—were there, no doubt, if one could only see them. But under the perceptual conditions of American culture, it is so much easier to see the simpler types of villain, victim, fool, and so on. In case #1 (which came closer to being tragic), sympathy had merely shunted from the victims to the killer (as a sick man, who became another victim), and hatred and blame had transferred to his wife. The basic melodramatic pattern remained.

But, you may say, it is too much to expect of any audience that they will see in raw facts—especially such as can be gotten from news reports—the elements of tragedy well enough to get the right feeling. The important question is, what do they see in an ideal drama, where the meaning and impact have been heightened by an artist?

I have, in fact, also discussed classic tragedies with adult groups after a recent reading. My experience has been (and I wonder how many teachers of literature will agree with me) that when people know it is a classic they are talking about, they make an effort to understand it according to the approved literary formulas, but, when the amenities are done, they usually get around to finding fault with the hero. There seems to be a need to blame him as a villain, or to escape involvement with him by calling him a fool, or to see him as a victim and put the blame on somebody else. This reaction is entirely consistent, as I see it, with my remarks about the armor that Americans have against tragic experience.

To find out more about this, especially the ways in which they were interpreting the hero and the extent to which alienation from him might be felt, I made a thematic analysis of responses to tragedy, asking 134 college students to choose a play or story with which they were familiar from a list of twenty well-known ones,[8] ranging from Sophocles' *Oedipus* to modern ones by O'Neill, Dreiser, Anderson, Williams, and Miller. Twenty-five of the students had seen the

---

[7] As Lord Chesterfield said, "Tragedy must be bigger than life, or it would not affect us." Behind this is the assumption that tragedy is not something that people just naturally grasp, but is a complex perception made possible by a set of cultural conditions and an invention—a device, an art form, for improving our perception of reality by enlarging certain aspects of it. So it is a contrived thing, unlikely to happen without the help of an artist. Since it is an invention, we do not expect a people to have tragedy, however hard their lot, unless they have borrowed or inherited it. This seems to accord with the fact that the distribution of tragedy is limited: the outlook of primitive peoples, judging by their tales and myths, is generally melodramatic; some advanced civilizations, such as India, are without the tragic sense; there have been only two great centers of tragic development, ancient Greece and Elizabethan England, both in the Western tradition.

[8] The heroes rated were: Willy Loman in *Death of a Salesman* by Arthur Miller, Blanche DuBois in *A Streetcar Named Desire* by Tennessee Williams, Romeo in *Romeo and Juliet*, Hamlet, Macbeth,

J. Arthur Rank production of *Romeo and Juliet* within a week and chose this for interpretation.

Let us look first at the side which is favorable to the appreciation of trage-dy. More than half said "a deeply significant and worthwhile experience" (61%); "symbolic of the experience of mankind" (53%). Somewhat less than half said "sympathize deeply with the hero" (43%); "a better-than-average person who displayed along with merits a serious fault or mistake" (44%). A third thought of the protagonist as "basically heroic" (30%); a fourth as "an admirable person" (25%). A fourth thought that the story had "a terrible but noble ending" (28%). Only a fifth thought the play demonstrated the "fortitude and dignity of the central character" (18%), and a sixth that it showed "the frailty of even strong or worthy people" (16%). These, of course, are not necessarily responses to tragedy as such, but they could be; they are [at] least oriented in that direction.

Much of this sympathy, however, is for that special kind of misunderstand-ing of tragedy that we have designated as martyrdom, for over a fourth saw the hero as "a kind of martyr for a social cause or value" (28%), and more sympathy is for the helpless victim, as shown below.

Many showed signs of missing the point and substituting an inadequate con-ception; for instance: "could have avoided trouble if he had used more sense" (53%) seems to imply that he is a fool and that the ending should have been hap-py (i.e., would have been but for his bungling). So does: "he brought it all on himself through mistakes or weaknesses" (40%). Throwing reproach on the hero tends to alienate the audience from him; he has spoilt the story as they expected it to work out. They leave him, so to speak, to stew in his own juice.

Very few, however, condemned him as an outright villain (7%). About half, on the contrary, "pitied him" (52%), as a "victim, helpless and not to blame for most of what happened" (45%). Some said "people took advantage of him or got him into trouble" (16%), or that he was "a good person injured by bad persons" (13%). These remarks excuse him, no doubt. But do they not do so by weakening him?

About one out of five were simply alienated by the story. It was: "some-thing that shouldn't have happened" (20%), a "gloomy and unpleasant story" (19%), "a pointless catastrophe" (12%); it "would have been better if it had end-ed more happily" (11%). Nineteen percent were indifferent to or repelled by the hero.

As you see, many of these responses appear to fall short of a tragic interpre-tation. Those who are alienated or see the story as just something that shouldn't have happened fall into this category. So also do those who weaken the hero till he is only a victim or a fool, since they rob him of dignity and free will. Less than half would grant that he was a better-than-average person, showing that in the eyes of many the tragedy endowed the sufferer with no special stature—that his manner of bearing misfortune was no better than that of anybody else. Those who melodramatized him as a martyr (about a third) generated sympathy at the

---

Mio in *Winterset* by Sherwood Anderson, Emperor Jones in *Emperor Jones* by Eugene O'Neill, Clyde Griffiths in *An American Tragedy* by Theodore Dreiser, Captain Ahab in *Moby Dick* by Her-man Melville, Mrs. Alving in *Ghosts* by Henrik Ibsen, Hedda Gabler in *Hedda Gabler* by Henrik Ib-sen, Raskolnikov in *Crime and Punishment* by Dostoyevski, Brutus in *Julius Caesar* by Shakespeare, King Lear, Antigone in *Antigone* by Sophocles, Orestes in *Electra* by Sophocles, Medea in *Medea* by Euripedes, and Phaedra in *Phaedra* by Racine.

expense of tragic insight, since, as we have seen, the martyr concept tends to exonerate a person for his trouble and throw the blame on villains.

More specifically, the main ways a tragic hero can be misinterpreted seem to be as: (1) a melodramatic good guy who for some inexplicable reason has failed, (2) a villain, (3) a fool, or (4) a passive and pathetic victim.

I feel this shows how in some ways we Americans have difficulty doing justice to the tragic character, especially to his complexity and dignity. Even if sympathetic, we are inclined to reduce him to a simpler or an inferior type (the martyr is simpler though not inferior). Sympathy (as for a victim or martyr) is no guarantee of tragic understanding; yet we may suspect that if it were not for the artist's working skillfully to build up sympathy, most tragedies would be villainies or follies of one kind or another.

Why does this reduction occur? Aside from the usual limitations of the human mind (such as ignorance and laziness), I think a theory of short-circuiting by cultural images is called for. That is, people respond to an event in terms of their stock of available images. They are likely to go to the image that is closest and easiest, among those which seem at all to fit the situation. We may grope for a name to call Medea, and fall back upon something like "villainess!" This amounts to a displacement of complex and delicate interpretations by simpler ideas. The ease of short-circuiting will depend on the prominence, range, and availability of character types in the culture; for example, whether art and drama have favored the building up of certain types more than others. The ratio of tragic to non-tragic stories in our culture should be expected to affect our ability to make such interpretations. Our interpretations should depend, also, on current conditions, such as whether a "crisis" mentality exists. Crises apparently favor villains, and it is generally recognized that melodrama is the enemy of tragedy. So a culture that favors melodrama (with its happy endings) works against tragedy. Something like this might also be said for comedy. That is, though its "relief" function in tragedy is recognized, too much slapstick in popular media probably creates an atmosphere in which people find it hard to make serious interpretations—they are looking for the fool, not for dignity.

After all, so much is wrong with the tragic hero! To the superficial view he is plainly a failure. Willy Loman kills himself. What satisfaction are people supposed to get out of that? A tragic hero is asked to perform the paradoxical feat of lifting the human spirit while plunging it into the most appalling catastrophes. And this is to be symbolized by a character who is full of weakness and conflict (compared with a folk hero like Sigurd or some of the more primitive dragonslayers). His very mistakes and flaws may alienate the audience to the point that they see him as a villain or fool. If he does not positively err, he may, like Hamlet with his hand suspended over the back of Claudius, be unable to deliver a fully satisfying blow. In any case, all that comes out of his downfall is a triumph obscurely implied.

Much depends, then, on a delicate set of conditions that would allow such a triumph to be perceived. Indeed, unless a culture were especially prepared to accept him, we might very well expect the tragic hero to be a total washout.

III

This brings our attention to the second main factor in American culture that makes it hard for the tragic hero to succeed: the climate of opinion, sometimes called the ethos. Some peoples seem to have an ethos that keeps them from seeing tragedy at all.[9] Ours is not so limiting as that, of course; but it does contain unfavorable perspectives or beliefs, three in particular that we shall try to analyze with the help of experts.[10]

One is the optimistic presumption that keeps us from appreciating the extent to which things—God, fate, history, nature—are not on our side. A vivid awareness of evil, says O'Connor, is essential to the idea of tragedy. Nietzsche said the same: "Banish evil, and it will go hard with the writers of tragedy." Now our age has managed to a great extent to banish evil by considering it not in the scheme of things. Characteristically, A. J. Cronin says, "If we think correctly and courageously, there is no misfortune inherent in human existence that we cannot turn to our ultimate advantage." Such a view is no doubt "healthy," but it is purely a presumption that the world is set up so that man can exploit it. Things should come out all right, says the optimistic presumption; but *this* did not come out all right; therefore something is wrong with it. So optimism must arm its hero with Excalibur, give him a horseshoe in his glove to guarantee success. One of these symbolic horseshoes in American life is the idea of progress. Another is the scientific optimism inherited from the eighteenth century. Another is the invincible belief in romantic marriage in spite of one failure out of three or four. A people used to the aspirin of optimism ask, quite reasonably, why should we experience pain in our dramas any more than in our dentist chairs? The best use they can make of tragic pain is didactic: a lesson about how to do better next time.

Optimism belongs, then, among the opiates that soften the awareness of evil and make life look like a set-up especially prepared for man. (Oddly, those who most often use the term "opiate," the Marxists, are themselves equally victims of this optimism, feeling that history is working out some kind of dialectic in favor of the society they want.) Other cultural opiates, not so prevalent in America, include: Puritanism, which tried to ostracize evil as the work of the Devil; fatalism, which takes all the responsibility for evil off man; other worldliness, which denies reality to material misfortunes; and the patriotic sentimentalization of death. It was the Romans, says Edith Hamilton, who thought it sweet to die for one's country; "the Greeks never said it was sweet to die for anything." Clearly, you can't have tragedy when such notions act as buffers to take the edge off the bitterest blows.

Equally unfavorable to the tragic hero is the naturalism which, developed as an artistic technique by European writers, has become an integral part of the American outlook. The American takes this view of things as normally as the medieval man did miracles and the Devil. Coming under a variety of names (mechanism, determinism, environmentalism, behaviorism, materialism, positivism, relativism, amoralism), it is essentially a picture of man submerged in an

[9] For example, the Zuni Indians, who have no place for struggle and extreme individualism, for heroes who, "fighting, fighting, fighting, die driven against the wall."—Ruth Benedict, *Patterns of Culture* (Penguin edition), p. 119. The Hindus lack tragedy because their ethos prevents them from seeing material misfortune as significant; nor is the individual important enough to them for tragedy to be meaningful.

[10] Especially Joseph Wood Krutch, *The Modern Temper* (New York, 1929). Besides Krutch's brilliant diagnosis, I have used others who have analyzed cultural conditions favorable and unfavorable to tragedy, notably William Van O'Connor, *Climates of Tragedy* (Baton Rouge, 1943), and Willard Farnham, *The Medieval Heritage of Elizabethan Tragedy* (Berkeley, 1936).

impersonal and subhuman nature. Naturalism is, of course, not just the realism of the naked eye but a scientific, largely materialistic and mechanical *interpretation* of human phenomena—a model. To be submerged in nature may mean such things as the following: all events have causes; the external causes of human acts are environment and heredity; morals are not metaphysical laws but natural parts of culture; man is not separated from other animals by a gulf, he is just the star performer in the zoo.

Such a view is bound to shape both the kinds of figures made by artists and the way they are interpreted. Stress on meaningless mechanism, external causation, may reduce a tragic hero to a beetle crushed under a rock. Studs Lonigan on a morgue slab is in some sense a symbol of the avalanche of naturalism over tragedy. So also is Clyde Griffiths, who, as depicted by Dreiser, is a puppet of circumstances. A mass of documentation is piled up to prove how social forces— home, education, deprivations, snubs, and denatured American ideals—move him toward his crime and to this extent lessen his freedom and responsibility. The pile-up of environmental forces also dulls the perception of evil, which (as O'Connor has shown) is essential for feeling tragedy. If I may try to explain this, it is because the evil of anything depends on two things: how important is he who suffers and how much of the trouble is due to the will of man. Reduce man either as sufferer or willing agent and it is impossible to have evil. This may lend significance to Krutch's observation that "the idea of nobility is inseparable from the idea of tragedy," and that "no man can conceive it unless he is capable of believing in the greatness and importance of man." What it seems to add up to, then, is that making nature more makes man less.

Yet, for all its threat, naturalism need not be fatal to a hero if, amid the mass of circumstances that seem to overwhelm him, he is allowed some loophole for noble choice. Thus Willy Loman in *Death of a Salesman* is a victim only to the extent that spurious American values—in this case the good-fellow ideal of success—have collapsed for him. But this victimization is not the last word; it becomes an *opportunity*, as Miller himself explains, for that burst of heroic determination in defeat which is the essence of tragedy. So by this play Miller claims that sordid life, for all its relentless pressures, need not be "below tragedy, as often asserted." The common man can take on such stature "to the extent of his willingness to throw all he has into the contest" to maintain his "chosen image" of what and who he is in the world.

A more serious blow to the hero's dignity and volition is to psychologize him, especially to analyze his conflicts in terms of psychopathology to a point where he is neither normal nor in control of what he does. The clinical character of many modern tragedies (such as those by O'Neill and Williams) is too obvious to need emphasis. Let me say only this: when a man becomes a "case," he ceases to be human to some extent. The disease occupies the foreground and, as it were, plays the part. Other writers have described this morbid effect as "converting art into an alienist's notebook," or an "obsession with filth" that obscures dignity. A possible result is disintegration of tragedy into mere horror and sensation.

If naturalism hurts tragedy, there is another element of the American ethos that gives little less than a *coup de grâce* to this kind of hero. It is the inability to make absolute commitments, called by David Riesman other-directedness (by moralists, opportunism). Anyone puzzled by the success of "brain-washing" on soldiers need not be so puzzled if he recognizes that many people today hold their beliefs conditionally, not absolutely. That is, their beliefs are inconsistent, come from all kinds of sources, and need to be upheld by agreement with others in the situation. Remove this condition of group support and there is no strong impulse to maintain them. Now a basic requirement of tragedy is to throw oneself completely into action, to "play the game through." Every great tragic figure has been true to his fault, so to speak. This is his tragic commitment. But the average American, while he may admire a martyr with a clear-cut cause of service, does not like to follow a course through to tragic consequences. He has too much common sense, for one thing. There is in him the spirit of the world, of compromise, of opportunism. He is proud of being flexible, able to start in a new direction when one line of action peters out. In other words, he is not obligated. "Die-hard" is his name for one who sticks too long to a cause. This is both a strength and a weakness. Putting it in terms of Riesman's character-types, a tragic actor must be *inner*-directed; it is commitment to something within and private that makes him tragic. The *other*-directed audience sees this "fault," sympathizes perhaps, but does not follow. For an other-directed person bases conduct on what others want him to do and therefore does not hold to a course of rather obstinate individuality. Theoretically, tragedy is impossible in an other-directed society. The tragic hero finds himself fighting alone—the crowd has deserted him. Now one who throws himself away on a lost cause, we well know, is a fool—so much for tragic dignity.

These ways of looking at things—optimism, naturalism, and other-directedness—seem to be the main elements of the American climate of opinion that stand in the way of the success of the tragic hero and help account for the unenthusiastic response of audiences to him. Bearing in mind the distracting types previously described, we see why it is so easy for him to be mis-cast and a misfit, and why he has such a hard time.

IV

There remains a fact about the hero himself that, regardless of what the climate of opinion and perceptual images may be, is bound to affect the way he is received. I mean that he is not the man he used to be. Partly as a result of the naturalism already described, the tendency among artists is to pick smaller men as subjects of tragedy. The standard of better-than-average, used in the Athenian and Elizabethan classics, has been abandoned. Comparing any fair sample of modern characters with those of earlier periods will show that there has been a decline in the stature of the tragic hero. The thing could be proven in feet and pounds, if need be; Krutch has demonstrated it convincingly by comparing people like Oswald Alving and Hamlet. This means that, regardless of social climate and cultural images, we have a harder time admiring the tragic hero today. He is such an ordinary person, his weaknesses and faults are so evident, that it is often hard to muster more than forgiveness for him. If we are to admire a Clyde Griffiths, a Blanche DuBois, an Emperor Jones, a Native Son, it must be all our own effort, so to speak; the artist has helped us but little—indeed, he may have so alienated us that we are unwilling to stay around for the funeral. Now (while this is entirely speculation), were tragic writers of today to choose clearly superior men as their subjects, we should have at least a favorable attitude toward them before the trouble started.

In short, the objective mediocrity of the modern hero combined with the unfavorable ethos and distracting cultural images make it very unlikely that an impression of grandeur will be produced when a man goes to pieces or blows his brains out before an American audience.

With such conditions working against the tragic hero, it is a wonder, indeed, that so many Americans do occasionally listen to his sombre lesson. While he cannot be said to be a popular type—and shows little signs of becoming one— he may serve by his presence to remind us, like an African mask in a modern living room, of insights that our ethos might otherwise hide. We test our perception on him, finding more often than not that he reflects themes of our own culture. Working like a prism, he scatters popular thought into its elements, showing its tendency to veer away from tragic insight to simpler modes of perception. But in so doing, he has utility for analyzing this thought. Enigma though he is—even if a fool in our eyes—he is, perhaps, capable of playing Touchstone for us.

VIII
THE CRITICISM
OF TRAGEDY

The Criticism of
Greek Tragedy*

William Arrowsmith

Unless I am mistaken, tragedy is also in deep need of some new perspectives in
the matter of its operative moral terms as well as in structure and plot. And particularly, I think, we need to question again the relevance of Aristotle on at least
two points—the so-called tragic flaw and the putative Aristotelian theory of
tragic structure, the structure that draws its sanction from the *Oedipus Rex* and
is reinforced by our modern preference for the organic. Aristotle is, I know, a
rough customer: he has of necessity immense authority, and one is never quite
sure whether one is talking about Aristotle or about something that has borrowed
the authority of his name. But I have never been able to satisfy myself that the
Poetics is the purely inductive treatise that scholars claim it is: again and again,
that is, what is inductive in the *Poetics* seems to me to be directed by what is not,
the pervasive notion of a purposive and rational universe and all that such a notion implies for tragedy and for the structure of tragedy. Thus for Aristotle a
tragic fall is grounded in a consistent and harmonious sense of a man's responsibility for his nature and his actions: when the hero falls, he falls for his own failure, and behind the rightness of his fall, working both pity and terror by the precise and relentless nature of its operations, stands the order which society and a
god-informed world impose upon the individual. What the law requires, the
world requires too, and so the Aristotelian play portrays, like an image of human
life, the individual torn and suffering between his nature and an objective
world-order.

   The tragic fall is, of course, in the common reading of Aristotle, based upon
the hero's possession of a tragic flaw; and whether as doctrine or habit, the attempt to find a tragic flaw in Greek plays seems to me a persistent stumbling-
block. If you really look at the *Oedipus*, for instance, it is immediately clear that
Oedipus' tragic flaw is hard to discover: one wants to know—if you begin with
the Aristotelian habit—just what in the hero's nature or his acts makes him suffer
as hideously as he does, and the obvious answers—his anger, his treatment of
Creon and Teiresias, his attempt to avoid his fate—are all unsatisfactory, or if
satisfactory, indict the gods that could afflict a man so grievously for such of-
fense. One recent critic of the play, an Aristotelian by conviction as well as habit,
recognized his dilemma immediately and proceeded to solve it by the suggestion
that Sophocles in this play has generalized *hamartia* into something like original
sin: Oedipus has no particular flaws but suffers in the very flaw of his humanity.

*William Arrowsmith, "The Criticism of Greek Tragedy" (Part III). *Tulane Drama Review*, Vol. III,
No. 3 (March 1959), pp. 50–57.

I suspect that very few classicists, whatever their religious color, will be happy with this theory, and I hope that even Aristotelians might object. But I use it to illustrate the kind of trouble that the expectation of a tragic flaw can create even in the treatment of a play which Aristotle regarded as the paradigm of his theories.

I cannot myself pretend to understand that mysterious play, but I wonder if we are perhaps not the better off for proceeding from the play rather than from Aristotle. Freed from our own *a prioris*, the experience of the play may at least propose itself in different terms. Thus it has always seemed to me that the single most pertinent fact of the *Oedipus* was not the hero's flaw, but his refusal to accept a ready-made fate: he wants his own fate, not the gods', and though his personal fate may be cut short by his doom, Oedipus at the close of the play insists upon distinguishing his own responsibility by blinding himself. It is the magnificence of his own declaration of responsibility that makes him so heroic: his fate is *his* and no one else's. His anger is anger, neither more nor less; it is not the source of his doom, but the irritant that he exhibits on the road to doom; and if he has a *hamartia*, it is not sin or flaw but the ungovernable tragic ignorance of all men; we do not know who we are nor who fathered us but go, blinded by life and hope, toward a wisdom bitter at the gates of hell. The cost of action is suffering, and heroism is the anguished acceptance of our own identities and natures, forged in action and pain in a world we never made. Whatever the final merits of this suggestion, it at least, I think, preserves the dignity of human passion in the play without violating in the name of a crude automatic justice the mysterious destiny that rules the play.

But crude or vulgar Aristotelianism has hurt all three dramatists, and Euripides in particular, and one of the most urgent tasks for the criticism of tragedy is the thorough re-examination of Euripidean structure; once we get Euripides straight, we may be in a position to see just where we have subtly distorted Aeschylus and Sophocles in the name of a misunderstood Aristotle. But here again, I think, criticism might best begin from the obvious—the long insistence of critics that Euripidean plays lack unity, fall into disparate actions or are merely episodes strung together. We start, that is, from the fact of dislocation and attempt to see whether dislocation might not be deliberate method rather than the hit-or-miss *ad hoc* work of a genius who consistently botched. What is immediately apparent if we start from this point is the real coherence of the plays so far as structure is concerned; what is most obvious in the *Heracles* or *Hecuba* is true also of the *Bacchae*, *Hippolytus* and *Medea*: all lack the kind of unity which the organic theory requires, all exhibit dislocation. If we ask why this is so, I think we find it mirrored by a curious doubleness in the action or in the given and created realities of the plays. Thus the *Heracles* shows two successive plateaus, the first a reality appropriate to legend and old convention, i.e. a world of mythical illusion, the second the full created tragic reality out of which heroism is born. If we look, say, at the *Orestes*, we discover a play which freely invents its own reality and then confronts the action so created with an epiphany of Apollo in which the whole motion of the play up to that point is flatly contradicted. We get a head-on collision, that is, between the action of the play and the traditionalizing impossible *deus ex machina*, and no attempt is made to modulate or explain these incompatible sequences. The same is true of the *Iphigeneia at Aulis*, and also, I think, of the *Medea* and *Electra*: their conclusions are simply at variance, as real events, from the whole tenor of the action. In the *Hippolytus* and *Bac-*

chae this doubleness is used in a different and less violent way: both plays dramatize the full incredibility of a traditional account of Olympian anthropomorphism—it is incredible that gods, real gods, should act as Dionysus and Aphrodite do. But once the familiar reality has been exposed and displaced, both plays proceed, in a symbolic manner, to hint at a deeper meaning and a different reality for these displaced gods. What I am trying to suggest is that again and again in Euripides, what makes the plays dislocated in structure is a deliberate juxtaposition of antithetical realities—the reality of the material which the play takes from legend and myth, and the new reality which the dramatist forces, as action, from his old material. We get the same kind of jar, that is, that our lives receive when they proceed upon inadequate conviction and are suddenly confronted with difficulty too great for the old conviction. But to my mind our understanding of Euripidean structure rests firmly upon our ability to understand the dramatic experience that bridges the two or even three plateaus of reality that most Euripidean plays exhibit. In the *Heracles*, for instance, we get between the two actions no *propter hoc* connection of the kind Aristotelians insist upon, and yet the connection seems to me, if not quite necessitous, at least valid with whatever validity the conversion of human experience possesses.

If heroism happens to arise from a fortuitous and accidental eruption of the irrational in the nature of things—as in the *Heracles* or the *Hippolytus*—the very fact that it is in the nature of things makes the eruption necessary or probable: we tend to disbar it only because our Aristotelian habits predispose us to a dramatic world like that of Sophocles, where the apparent irrationalities of experience are explained by a divine order we cannot comprehend. But as applied to Euripides, these habits and their corollary in a crude notion of the tragic flaw can only complicate chaos further. We need rather a theory of Euripidean structure which starts from dislocation and attempts to show the relation of this form to a world of moral disorder. Unless I am mistaken, such examination must also show the irrelevance of *propter hoc* structure to Euripides, whose sense of necessity in drama derives more from the motion of the human mind under stress and the patterns which men's convictions make when confronted by adventitious realities. A man's character may be his destiny, but for Euripides destiny is often dependent upon and defined by circumstances the hero never made, nor the gods either. Unless we can restore an understanding of the importance of the dramatist's assumed world for his form, Euripides must stand perpetually condemned or be explained with all the willful improbability of Verrall. At least the latest book on Euripidean structure—Gilbert Norwood's *Essays on Euripidean Drama*—makes the implicit claim that these dislocations of plot and internal inconsistencies in the plays are best explained as the work of fourth century redactors. This seems both unfortunate and unnecessary.

One final point. Nothing, I think, more effectively hinders our understanding of the experience of Greek tragedy than the inadequacy and crudity of meaning which critics and translators assign to the operative moral terms of Greek tragedy—*sōphia, hybris, anankeē, sōphrosunē, aristeia, timē, authadia* and the like. For in much criticism of tragedy these terms are used as though they possessed simple English equivalents, without, I think, adequate reference to the experience with which they were meant to cope. Alternatively, they are exposed to static definition without regard to the transformations which tragedy may force upon them as the hero moves from a situation of conventional morality and reality to an ordeal for which the traditional wisdom of the Chorus may be utterly inadequate. In such situations it is my conviction that the old moral terms are employed with a meaning so turbulent with fresh or restored experience that they are no longer the same terms, nor the hero to whom they apply the same man. *Timē*, for instance, is normally translated as *honor*, but its root meaning is price, or valuation, and in most tragedies where the concept is important—the *Antigone*, for instance—the word operates very much like the deep sense of our word "respect." Thus when Ismene claims that Antigone has not shown *timē* to her, and that Creon has not shown *timē* to Haemon, she means, not that she and Haemon have been dishonored, or insulted, but that they have not been respected: they have been disallowed the dignity of a fate and their dignity as individuals. They have, as it were, been priced all wrong, and this charge is, of course, central to the play, since Antigone claims to act for *philia* because she wished to give *timē* to Polyneices. What, the play seems to suggest, is the assertion of *philia* worth without *timē* too? And what is a *philia* which, in order to respect one person, shows disrespect to another, both equally claiming the rights of *philia*?

Or consider the word *sophia*, which we badly translate as "wisdom," as it gets into the *Bacchae*. Among other things, *sophia* means a knowledge and acceptance of one's nature and therefore of one's place in the scheme of things. It presupposes, that is, self-knowledge, and acceptance of those necessities that compose the limits of human fate. It also means the consequent refinement of feelings by which a man recognizes and respects the sufferings of others before necessity: it issues in compassion.[1] *Sophia* is further contrasted with its opposite, *amathia*, a deep, brutal, unteachable, ungovernable self-ignorance which breaks out in violence and cruelty. If the *sophos* is by definition susceptible to the feelings of civilized humanity, a compassion learned in fellow-suffering, the *amathēs* is callous and merciless, a barbarian by nature. But it is these meanings which crowd into the *Bacchae* and everywhere provide, through dramatic action and testing, the play's missing principle of order. For in the course of the action, through the very brutality which they use to support their claims to *sophia*, both Pentheus and Dionysus utterly expose their own *amathia*.

But more than the self-indictment of Pentheus or Dionysus is involved here. For Euripides has taken elaborate pains to show in Pentheus something more than the man who does not know the deep Dionysiac necessity of his own nature: he is also the proud iconoclastic innovator, the rebel at war with tradition, standing outside of the community's *nomos* [custom as law] and as *theomachos*, disdainful of any power above man. Ranged against him are Cadmus, Teiresias and the chorus, who all alike appeal to the massive tyranny of tradition and folk-belief, and constantly invoke as the sanction of society against the rebellious or anti-traditional man the words *sōphrosunē* and *dikē*. Thus in flat opposition to Pentheus' lonely arrogance of the "exceptional" (*perissos*) man, defying the community's *nomos* in the name of his own self-will, is set the chorus' tyrannous tradition: "Beyond the old beliefs, no thought, no act shall go (891-2)." We have, that is, a head-on collision between the forces which represent a brutally depraved conservative tradition and the arrogant exemplar of the ruthlessly anti-traditional mind. Both positions are alike in the cruel and bigoted violence with which they meet opposition, and the *sophia* and *sōphrosunē* and *dikē* which

---

[1] Cf. *Electra*, 11. 294–5, where Orestes states that pity (*to oiktos*) is never to be found among the *amatheis* but only among the *sophoi* i.e. compassion is a true component of "wisdom."

they both claim mock their pretensions and condemn their conduct. If the conduct of the chorus and Dionysus outrage our sympathies and finally enlist them on Pentheus' behalf, it is because, in the nature of things, the *amathia* of a man is less heinous than that of a god. But both are *amatheis*, Pentheus no less than the chorus, and the play as a whole employs them and their struggle as a bitter image of both Athens and Hellas terribly divided between the forces that, in Euripides' mind, more than anything else destroyed them: on the one side, the conservative and aristocratic tradition in its extreme corruption, disguising avarice for wealth and power with the fair professions of the traditional *aretai*, meeting all attempts at change or moderation with the tyranny of popular piety, and disclosing in its actions the callousness and refined cruelty of civilized barbarism; on the other side, the exceptional individual, selfish and egotistical, impatient of public welfare and tradition alike, opportunistic, demagogic and equally brutal in action. In saying this, I do not intend to dispute the obvious religious concerns of the *Bacchae*, but to stress what, to my knowledge, has not been emphasized, that the play is, like the *Heracles*, the *Electra* and the *Orestes*, a composite of discrete conversions, social and political as well as religious. And all of these concerns meet in the term *sophia* and its opposite, *amathia*, which at their widest enclose most of what we mean by "civilized" and "uncivilized," both morally and politically. Thus when Euripides has his chorus assert that *to sophon* is not the same as *sophia* he means that the pretensions and conventions and habits of civilization are by no means equivalent to civilized practices.

But in my opinion the same widening and deepening of the operative moral terms of Greek culture is to be found everywhere in tragedy—*philia* in *Antigone*, *sōphrosunē* in *Hippolytus*, *eugeneia* in *Heracles*, *aristeia* in *Orestes*, etc.—and it would be surprising if it were not so. But upon our sense of the play of the traditional or lazy meanings of these words and the definitions which the tragic action makes lies, I think, much of the turbulence now missing from the criticism of tragedy.

Let me close with a brief note on necessity, for necessity seems to me the crucial center of Greek tragedy, just as Greek tragedy seems to me unique in the firmness and sharpness with which it follows necessity into human action. In its basic aspect, necessity (*anankē*) is that set of unalterable, irreducible, unmanageable facts which we call the human condition. Call it destiny, call it fate, call it the gods, it hardly matters. Necessity is, first of all, death; but it is also old age, sleep, the reversal of fortune and the dance of life; it is thereby the fact of suffering as well as pleasure, for if we must dance and sleep, we also suffer, age and die. It is also sex, the great figure of amoral Aphrodite who moves in the sea, land and air and as an undeniable power in the bodies of men, compelling and destroying those who, like Hippolytus, refuse to accept her. Or it is Dionysus, the terrible ambiguous force of the *Bacchae*, "the force that through the green fuse drives the flower," and who destroys Pentheus who lacks the *sophia* that accepts him. It is the great god-sprung trap of the *Oedipus* and also the nature of Oedipus himself, that stubborn human courage of pride that drives him relentlessly into the trap. It is the necessity of political power which, in corruption, destroys Hecuba and Iphigeneia and Cassandra and Polyxena. It is the inherent hostility of blind chance, the incalculable daemonic malice which in the Euripidean *Heracles* calls out to the hero to die and tells him that there is no hope and no moral order in the world at all. Suspend necessity in the form of the play, and you get such charming, romantic plays as *Iphigeneia at Tauris* and the *Helen*.

Romantic, that is, because not tragic; and not tragic because necessity, the mainspring of tragedy, has been, for fun, for entertainment and experiment, removed. Where men are freed from the yoke of necessity, their lives cease to be tragic, and with the loss of suffering comes also the loss of dignity and *sophia*.

For it is in the *struggle* with necessity that heroism is born, and even the hero, if he is to retain his humanity, must accept necessity. Ripeness is all. And so we see Orestes discover purity and compassion in the face of a necessity that threatens to deform him as it has already deformed his father and mother and as it inevitably deforms the weak, the flawed, the average human nature. So too Antigone accepts her necessity, the consequence of her own act, humanity pushed to the extreme, and thereby comes again upon her humanity in the very act of acceptance and recognition of loss. So Oedipus by asserting his total utter responsibility for his own fate, wins the victory over a necessity that would have destroyed a lesser man. And so Heracles claims a moral dignity forever out of reach of the amoral powers that persecute him. There is a magnificence here in the power to rise, in the anguished acceptance that must always, in Greek tragedy, precede the winning of dignity. For it is here before necessity that old morality is unmade and then remade into a new thing. Thus Orestes, having discovered at least that compassion that made him hesitate, enables justice to be born. And so too at the close of the *Hippolytus* and *Bacchae* we see the suffering human survivors of the play discover, under the awful yoke of an intolerable necessity, the love and *compassion*, the shared suffering that makes men endure with love in a world which shrieks at them to die. Learn wisdom through suffering, says Aeschylus, and if we are loyal to the turbulence of Greek tragedy, we can see what he means. For, stripped to the bone, the essential *action* of the greatest of the Greek tragedies is an enactment of lives lived out under the double yoke of man's own nature and a world he did not make; the weaker fail or are deformed; the strong survive, and by surviving and enduring, liberate the dignity of significant suffering which gives man the crucial victory over his own fate.

The Riddles
of Oedipus*

Harold Rosenberg

The central intuition of Greek tragedy, as of psychoanalysis, is: there is one unique fact which each individual anxiously struggles to conceal from himself, and this is the very fact that is the root of his identity.

Kierkegaard describes a type of despair in which the self "wills desperately to be itself—with the exception, however, of one particular, with respect to which it wills despairingly not to be itself."

Action is heroic when, in addition to displaying courage, fidelity, etc., it involves an overcoming of this automatic will to ignorance, when it reverses the inner process that repels the one particular and forces the actor to embrace it.

Tragedy is the willful movement toward the hidden fact by which the hero is identified. The hero does not know what his action will disclose but he is impelled toward the disclosure. The curtain rises at the moment when the process of revelation begins. A messenger arrives, an encounter takes place. It is the same in *Oedipus Tyrannus, Macbeth, Hamlet, Othello, Crime and Punishment*. The first gesture begins to place the hero's apparent identity in question. Is he really a king, or a murdering parricide? Glamis, Cawdor or . . . ? Prince or clown? Hero or subman? *Hamlet* opens with "Who's there?" The first line of Macbeth after the witches' prelude is: "What bloody man is that?"

The hero is met with the Socratic demand: "Know thyself." In each instance, Man is also put into question—is *he* a king or a parricide, prince or clown? But the hero meets the demands of knowledge in terms of particular acts relating to himself, rather than by speculating about the human species. For the action is the point of the knowing, in that it partakes in creating, and makes itself responsible for, that which it brings to light. The tension of *Oedipus* arises from its hero's insistence on continuing the investigation as an aim to be fulfilled after its horrid findings have become as predictable as a result in mathematics. In action the disclosure of the self is an aspect of the self's coming into being—without the tragic or comic event of self-recognition, the self would not exist.

Hence the dramatic hero is always a hero of self-knowledge. Merely to dominate events without being taken by surprise by what one's acts unearth about oneself is to have missed the heroic. The history of mankind is filled with powerful personages empty of dramatic meaning.

Can the command, "Know thyself," be fulfilled through philosophy, or does it necessarily require action? The two riddles solved by Oedipus state what can be achieved by philosophy and what by action. First comes the riddle of the Sphinx, the "What-is-it-that . . . ?" riddle of philosophy. Then comes the riddle of Oedipus' individual being, the "Who-are-you . . . ?" riddle of tragedy.

The "What-is-it?" riddle put by the Sphinx of metaphysics could be solved by a generalization, and Oedipus slew this beast with the abstraction: Man. As Oedipus later boasted to Tiresias, he arrived at this reply through his own sagacity, not through divination; though perhaps he owed his genius for generalization to the fact that, having just slain his father, he thought of himself abstractly as Man rather than as a particular person—the deeper the crime one has to hide, the more abstract he tends to make himself.

At any rate, for his speculative triumph over the Sphinx, Oedipus was rewarded—given the kingdom of Thebes and its queen, and honored as a sage. He had run a deadly risk in going to meet the Sphinx. But it was a rational risk, in which one could win or lose. For the Sphinx slew only those who gave the *wrong* answer.

Existence, on the other hand, destroys those who give the right answer.

If philosophy could solve the problem of individual identity, the universal with which Oedipus replied to the Sphinx would have overpowered the evil design of the Fates. Since Oedipus knew what Man was, he should have been able to generalize his situation and to respond to it rationally, whatever it happened to be at the moment—one can imagine him explaining to his mother how absurd it would be to acknowledge personal guilt for the preordained. Had the slayer of the Sphinx mastered the secret of his own identity, or been able to liquidate his identity through philosophy, whatever he had done could be a step toward a happy ending, like the salvation of the Christian on his deathbed, or the restoration of the neurotic by psychoanalysis.

Solving the riddle of the Sphinx was, however, of no help to Oedipus—on the contrary, it led directly to his marriage with Jocasta. Philosophy, which at the beginning seemed so promising, not only failed Oedipus, it was responsible for his disaster. The riddle of the Sphinx led only to the second riddle, "Who are you?," which repeated the riddle of Man to Oedipus in terms of his own identity. This second riddle actually preexisted the first, since a man must be born before he is a man, and its content was the unique plot by which his existence was shaped: that he was doomed to slay his father and father children on his mother. In regard to this riddle philosophy was totally blind, and for arriving at the true answer to it Oedipus was destroyed.

The assumption of tragedy is that in actual life it is impossible to win, except by way of the destruction itself—and winning through being destroyed is not a rational risk but a transcendental hypothesis. Instead of the rewards that go to the abstract solver of problems, the payment for knowing oneself finitely, since it is a unique knowledge, and since it must be enacted in practice, is disgrace, banishment, death. Nations, classes also earn this tragic reward for stubbornly identifying themselves.

The hero suffers tragically for arriving at the right answer—in fact, only for the right answer. Through wrong answers Oedipus might have saved himself indefinitely, that is, until his false identity was destroyed by time. A wrong answer, one not leading to self-knowledge, may also bring misfortune, but the misery it causes, like that resulting from accident or lack of skill, is not tragic. The hero of a tragedy, however, cannot end with a wrong answer. For the tragedy begins in the revelation, when the possible wrong moves by which destiny can be averted have failed; and the tragedy moves forward in the knowing; its action belongs to the revelation, as the hero belongs to his ignorance, and is hence necessarily accurate. As his deeds displace his will, leaving him less and less choice, they become identical with his consciousness in its not-to-be-deflected hunter's interest in his own being—the plot is *not* an infernal trap or machine which he continues to resist; it reflects the interest of thought in his fate, that is to say, in his election; and the deeper he enters into that plot, the greater the ecstasy of his yielding to the truth it is bringing into being.

The second solution of Oedipus was not to be given all at once in a word; it had to achieve its reality in unfinished acts, partial disclosures, false scents that led in the right direction. This time Oedipus does not arrive at the answer through his cleverness or wisdom—indeed, he contributes to the dénouement only through the persistence of his mistakes. The answer comes to Oedipus through the predictions, recollections, anxieties and evasions of his entire world—shepherds, messengers, Jocasta and so on. And this time the answer is not "Man" but "I," like the biblical prophet's "Here I am."

Oedipus begins as a young philosopher and ends as an old hero—contrary to the progress of knowledge from the particular to the universal. And his tragic unveiling affects not his ideas but his energies—the demolition of his false identity opens up tremendous springs of vitality in him, though this increase in his forces is experienced as anguish. Unlike philosophical knowledge, which Socrates concluded is a readiness to die, tragic knowledge sweetens life beyond the need for consolation. Before his torment began, Oedipus was ready to die—with a philosopher's readiness. Why else would he have risked his life on the Sphinx's riddle? He was attracted to engimas, was possessed by a sense of the concealed fact—in short, was an amateur of the hidden. Like Plato's cave philosopher he was dazzled by the invisible, and his hold on reality was weak—all of which is another way of saying that he offered no great resistance to death. While he was a philosopher Oedipus let himself drift toward destruction, because his self was hidden from him. But when his tragedy has been fulfilled and he has attained the full horror of self-recognition, he does not kill himself. No, he demands to live, with a fury that still amazes us; and this desire for life grows ever stronger in his blind and hopeless exile, as his intimacy with himself increases. So that in Colonus, Oedipus is infinitely grander and more powerful than he was as King of Thebes, and his passion for life is so immense that it propels him into immortality.

What makes psychoanalysis the opposite of tragedy, both as a form of knowledge and in its effect on the psyche, is that the sufferer hands over to another—the analyst—the process of disclosing who he is, instead of struggling toward self-knowledge through action. He makes himself passive in the expectation of being shown to himself as an object. The unwrapping of his ego will, he believes, relieve the misery of his self-estrangement. Solving puzzles cannot, however, as Oedipus learned, constitute a path to identity but, at best, only to a theoretical conception of Man. Thus the "cure" of the psychoanalytical patient actually consists in emptying him of individuality and rendering him more abstract—for example, he is given his share in the universal Jocasta through under-standing how the Oedipus complex has affected him. The aboriginal fact by which he is identified is not brought to consciousness in a new enactment: in-stead, the fact has been dissolved mentally into the common formula. Because of its derivations from Greek mythology psychoanalysis believes it can open up the life-giving springs of tragic catharsis, but in practice the energizing fails to occur because of the inevitable abstractness of the psychoanalytical experience.

Those who speak of the tragedy of history conceive human collectivities as undergoing a process of identity-disclosure analogous to that of individuals. For Marx society is made up of several class identities in conflict with one another; each of these arrives at itself through a revolutionary enactment which trans-forms both its own existence and that of the historic whole in which it functions. Thus the Paris Commune, the first attempt of the proletariat to affirm itself as an independent collective entity, is termed a tragedy by Marx; while the attempt of French middle-class society to transcend itself through the false heroics of Louis Bonaparte is treated by Marx as a case of mistaken identities, hence a farce. That class identity is the central fact of contemporary social behavior is suggested by the incessant efforts of all modern societies, including those which have given the Marxist answer to the Sphinx (that is, Man, the worker), to con-ceal the class "I" in action under such substitute identities as Nation, Race, Party, Cult. For if the class identity is the true, active social persona of the world's laboring masses, it is by that fact the source of a slow, tragic undermin-ing of existing realities, and society, including the working class itself, cannot ex-perience the struggle of the new class to affirm itself without suffering the destructive consequences of solving the second riddle, that is, of discovering who this anonymous mass is. The moment the hidden name is called the wheels of tragedy begin to turn, the subjective being of each social class rises toward re-lentless self-expression, and the effort toward knowledge becomes a battle for survival.

The dramatic problem of the twentieth century is that of the relation be-tween collective identities active on the stage of history and the self of the indi-vidual as a more or less willing component of a mass. "I." If a social group is ac-tually a "being" which becomes engaged in the tragic process of self-knowledge regardless of the volition or intelligence of its individual members, the tradition-al concept of individual existence is put into question. History is *the* tragic spec-tacle—one in which everybody is at once a member of the cast and of a captive audience forced to become conscious of the unfolding of events. Yet the life in-terest of the individual remains his interest in knowing himself. Mass and indi-vidual actions are rival modes of self-knowledge that give rise to new dramatic forms.

"Know thyself" is the link between philosophy and drama, as "Suppress thyself" is the link between philosophy and science. In drama everything moves toward the repetition in consciousness of the unique identifying fact. First this fact is known to the Oracle, then to Oedipus in terms of mistaken identities and false moves, then it is realized through his action, then in his consciousness of his action, finally, in his transformation as the consequence of this consciousness and the reversal of his situation. The spiraling of events that establishes identity pro-vides the content of individual existence.

Scientific thinking moves in the opposite direction—toward experiences that can be duplicated experimentally and toward questions for which anyone can supply the right answer. The urge of the individual to self-repetition is in the view of science an atavism grounded in the blindness of self-love.

The problem of individual identity is the dilemma of philosophy. If philosophy attempts to deal with the single individual, it tends in the direction of action and beyond the border of generalization: it is forced to merge its thinking into art or into religion. If, on the other hand, philosophy excludes the individual in order to harmonize its methods with those of science, it cannot reach the individual except, as Kierkegaard points out, in a footnote; which means that philosophy replies to the question of "Who?" with an ethic of adjustment by which the individual is trimmed to fit the needs of some social or moral scheme without regard to what he might discover about himself as a unique being.

In Plato, "adjustment" is represented by the vision of harmony between the right and left horses of spirit. But despite Plato's so-called anti-tragic outlook, his ideal of rational self-curtailment is ironically contradicted by the dramatic image of Socrates, who embodies, fulfills and surpasses the theoretical presuppositions of virtue; who knows himself by "a species of madness," as well as by speculating about man; who grounds knowledge in recollection and the act of thinking in love; who, in a kind of exemplary self-temptation, lets loose and even encourages in himself the passions which are to be held in check; and who, by the manner of his death for "giving the right answer," demonstrates that the act of knowing must be completed tragically. It seems an essential presupposition of Plato's thought that philosophy tends toward the dramatic, that it develops its concepts through the conflicting notions of specific human beings, and that hence the dialogue, which is speculation within the mold of individual behavior and itself a mode of behavior, is the necessary form of philosophy. Through the dialogue and its actors, Plato attempts to overcome the dilemma of philosophy in the face of individual identity.

In the dialogue each speaker is a living hypothesis. He asserts himself and his ideas absolutely; but since his statements presuppose a listener, each statement actually begins: "Assuming that I am I and that humanity is like me, such and such is the case." It is impossible for a thinker in a dialogue to present himself as Philosophy. Kierkegaard argues that Socrates' very existence is hypothetical: "On this 'if' [of immortality] he risks his entire life, he has the courage to meet death, and he has with the passion of the infinite so determined the pattern of his life that it must be found acceptable—if there is an immortality."

When philosophy abandons the dialogue, when it becomes the voice of a single speaker, it cannot avoid asserting an absolute. By putting his name on the title page of his work, the philosopher declares that the "I" by which he is known is truly he, and that the truth known to this "I" can be the truth for all. Assuming that this claim is justified, the reader has become a tenant of the author's world, and this is the case even when the single, unhypothetical speaker is a purely instrumental thinker. The concealed teleology of instrumentalism, like that of any other non-dramatic philosophy, is that humanity is an instrumentalist in different degrees of perfection; so there is ideological effort in it to transform all men into Man.

It was clear to Kierkegaard that philosophy, when it does not voluntarily transcend itself in religion, ought to be many-voiced, that one should speak as oneself only with respect to the religious. Reasserting Plato's principle of philosophy as drama, he used pseudonyms for those of his works which were not sermons, and underlined the point by writing dialogues signed with pseudonyms. That Kierkegaard's disguises as an author were so thin indicates that he used them less to cover his identity before the public than as a sign that an author had to be another. In place of the self-suppression of the philosopher of knowledge for the sake of the universal, the philosopher of identity practices self-concealment as a token that he cannot speak for himself. He denies himself not in order to hide, but because his self *is* hidden; it is still to be arrived at, and the very aim of his thinking lies, as Kierkegaard says, in "becoming subjective," that is, himself.

But this becoming subjective is an activity that can be ended only by death: "The very point is that it should last for a whole life." Self-concealment represents the fact that at any given moment the thinker's identity has still to be attained. So the pseudonym is the signature of his faith, an avowal of the unknown and that it is always present. It is his means of affirming the other self both as a reality and as a possibility—but this affirmation is made negatively through declaring his visible, active self to be a disguise.

Hamlet, or What Shall I Become?
The Despair of Dramatic Philosophy

Considering the psuedonymous author of dramas and dialogues, a concealed philosopher holding back from the absolutes of religion and throwing forth fictions like a film projector, distributing himself into a cast of characters among whom he himself may not appear, one thinks at once of Hamlet instructing the players—how easy it is to act as an actor, so long as one does not have to act as oneself. But this thinker knows that direct affirmation of the self is impossible, since every form of action, even that of music or dance, is an estrangement.

Kierkegaard develops the incommunicability of the self, distinguishing this condition from the play acting of the modern snob of deep feeling. "Now he has even succeeded in obtaining town criers of inwardness, and a town crier of inwardness is quite a remarkable species of animal."

Since communication of the self is impossible except through approximation and hints, the philosopher of identity is driven to dramatic fiction. On the stage he can exchange his tentative self for a definite part, and thus desist from pursuing the unattainable "Who" by making himself over into a "That." On the stage, too, he can enact experimentally, and with reduced risk, the events by which he supposes himself to be identified, as Hamlet did in his play within the play, and thus approach the truth.

But while through drama the philosopher of self could keep the game going, he is drawn away from drama in the direction of religion, for drama leads him only to endless hypostatization, while through faith he may succeed in completing his actual self with the experience of God. For Kierkegaard, edifying works may be signed with one's own name.

Thus the pseudonymous philosopher, finding consciousness of his own identity to be beyond his capacities, is tempted to transform himself either into an actor or into a mystic; at the same time he is aware that to become either is to surrender, and that it is his obligation as a conscious individual to keep trying to realize the incommunicable in action. This mixture of desire for a role and fear of being trapped in a role constitutes the peculiar malady out of which arises modern action philosophy, with its dream of revolutionizing the metaphysical condition of man. Kierkegaard speaks of reading Hegel "in the light of action." But though for the action philosopher truth lies in doing, he retains his tie with philosophy in that he understands the aim of action to be the affirmation of identity in the consciousness and not merely the achievement of objective ends, as with the utilitarians. To discover the beginning of a self the actor must conceive his acts as experiments and keep his mind alert for clues as to which of these experiments might apply to him. In his dramatic laboratory any act is the potential originator of an identity more firmly defined than that of the author. One has only to move into the track of consequence and a life will be fatally structured. Here choice is the origin of existence, and the doer must be infinitely cautious.

Hence standing in the center of a vibrating field of possibility, the pseudonymous philosopher tends to refrain from action and suspend himself in the imaginary, that is, verbal action. Whatever he might do would be the deception of an actor; the worst self-deception would consist in favoring the actor whom he originally found masquerading in his image. All selves are equally justified; and "the self," said Kierkegaard, "despairingly wills to dispose of itself or to create itself, to make itself the self it wills to be, distinguishing in the concrete self what it will and will not accept." Kierkegaard could make himself into Don Juan or into Aesthete and be in accord with every word that each uttered. But to begin with himself was not even thinkable, except on the hypothesis of the religious or tragic "leap."

The dramatic philosopher's condition of suspension prior to the start of an action is, by the testimony of Hamlet and Kierkegaard, a condition of despair, the poetic despair of possibility without reality. No matter how passionate, how reasonable, how humanly sympathetic his behavior may be, it produces only momentary satisfaction, since it fails to bring him closer to self-realization. His good and his evil are as if performed for the benefit of an audience. Kierkegaard describes this despair of possibility:

> If the despairing self is active, it really is related to itself only as experimenting with whatsoever it be that it undertakes, however great it may be, however astonishing, however persistently carried out . . . in the last resort it lacks seriousness . . . every instant it can quite arbitrarily begin all over again, and however far a thought may be pursued, the whole action is within a hypothesis. It is so far from being true that the self succeeds more and more in becoming itself, that in fact it merely becomes more and more manifest that it is a hypothetical self.

The anguish of possibility is dramatized when the individual's situation is partly disclosed as a riddle which he can guess at, rather than as a set of circumstances prompting him to act. Hamlet learns how his father died, but this knowledge only multiplies his notions about himself. Similarly, a university professor discovers that his wife has been unfaithful to him, and this leads to his reinterpreting the facts in his memory to picture himself as a voyeur, or as a latent homosexual or as an intellectual sadist. Given his half-darkened situation, Hamlet experiments: he acts in order to bring about a disclosure, as if he were adding a chemical to a mixture, rather than to achieve a concrete result. His primary aim is to undermine the foundations of his life to date, in order to open the way to a new choice of roles; so that "quite arbitrarily," in Kierkegaard's phrase, he keeps questioning himself as if he were at a beginning. The reality of Hamlet as a character, in contrast to the usual order of dramatic fictions, is his desire for an aesthetic suspension, for the non-identity of his author. He stops for as long as he can in self-negation (Kierkegaard's "first movement of resignation").

Though Kierkegaard experienced the "renunciation of everything" after his love affair with Regina, he cannot be compared with Hamlet. Under the pressure of the plot the latter was forced to act; while Kierkegaard, suffering precisely from the absence of a "plot" in real life, remained a philosopher free to "make the movements" of resignation and faith, that is to say, to escape his situation by shadow actions of spirit. "Love," he says in *Fear and Trembling* about the lover resigned to the loss of his "princess," "became for him the expression for an eternal love, assumed a religious character, was transfigured into a love for the Eternal Being." This power of religion to do away with a fact does not exist in drama, where the hero is chained to his part; nor does it exist in the actual world, where the fact refuses really to be transfigured, as Kierkegaard so thoroughly explained in his psychological studies.

Kierkegaard accepted the Christian promise of salvation as *the* fact of human life, though he puts it to the extremest test of practice, from which it emerged as salvation "by virtue of the absurd." Salvation breaks across the Greek idea of tragedy and self-knowledge—in this vital respect, Christianity, like science, is the antagonist of drama, that is, of self-knowledge through action. To be saved means to have completed the partly disclosed self in the universality of God's commandments, to have moved away from the given condition of identity toward the "God-relation" in order to avoid pursuing the action to its conclusion. The Christian as Christian completes himself in the infinite; if he suffers it is because of the inadequacy of his faith. Thus a medieval Christian writer was quite logical when he wrote that Jesus could have forgiven the crime of Oedipus. In Christian thought the identifying fact is conceived as sin, which may be wiped away by divine mercy, as psychoanalysis wipes it away through steeping it in abstractions. Tragic action thus loses its function of concrete self-knowledge, and Oedipus appears not as a hero but as the victim of a meaningless arrangement of chance happenings. If individual identity is synonymous with sin, the only wisdom is to escape from senselessness and misery into an order of abstract ideas, that is, to renounce the second riddle of Oedipus.

Kierkegaard is the theoretician (as Dostoyevsky is the dramatist) of the despair of possibility without reality—that condition of modern man, who can no longer believe and who yet cannot acknowledge that he is a mere item in a system of abstract processes. Since he is not bound to anything given, he is capable of playing countless roles, but only as an actor, that is, with the consciousness that he has assumed a disguise. (If the disguise proves to be permanent, he will have trapped himself by his choice; if it is not permanent, he will have wasted his time in it and nullified a portion of his life.) The exchangeability of the fiction which he has become constitutes a degree of freedom never before attained by man in the mass. But it is the freedom to put on an act, for others and for oneself—the protagonist of Dostoyevsky's *A Raw Youth* is able to see himself simultaneously as a billionaire and as a St. Jerome in his cave.

The individual, however, is not content to be an actor. That there is no "I" that he will find at the bottom of his being is itself the "one particular" about which he continues to delude himself. It is his fixed belief in his ultimate identity that makes him a mimic of forms—and one who feels falsified by form. This is another way of saying that modern man is, ultimately, an aesthete—one whose highest ideal is not the good but a self constructed according to a model of "the most beautiful man," Socrates, for example, or Christ, or some revolutionist clothed in the glamour of the times.

Hamlet and
Our Problems*

Michael Goldman

Henry V, by virtue of his public role, is forced to be something of an actor—hence his apprenticeship at roleplaying in *Henry IV*. But every private man is an actor too—for our acts are often performances, in the sense that they strive either to express or conceal something that we think of as inside us, our true self. We are all actors, then, to a degree. But in the ordinary, professional sense of the word, what is an actor? An actor is a man who wants to play Hamlet. Playing the role of the Prince proves you are truly an actor and not a clown, an entertainer, a personality, a "type," or a movie star. It is the ultimate validation of an actor's professional status—and yet, curiously enough, it is far from being the hardest of acting tasks. Most men of the theater would probably accept Sir John Gielgud's characterization of the play as "audience-proof"; and certainly Macready's observation remains true today: a total failure in the role is rare.[1] Many other parts are harder to make a success of, and some—like King Lear—demand skills which the successful actor of Hamlet may not possess. But Hamlet strikes us as somehow unique in requiring and displaying the actor's art.

Why should this be so? One answer lies in the variety that Dr. Johnson recognized as a distinguishing excellence of the play. No other role offers so much action of so many different kinds. Hamlet is soldier, scholar, statesman, madman, fencer, critic, magnanimous prince, cunning revenger, aloof noble, witty ironist, man of the people, etc.; and he is regularly required to change from one role to another before our eyes or to maintain several—or a disarming mixture of several—at once. The play abounds in situations that require the principal actor to shift his mood or mode of action because of a change in audience. A number of examples result from Hamlet's having to deceive those around him, but there are many occasions when the shift does not come about as a result of the necessity for self-protection ("Horatio, or I do forget myself," the jokes with the gravedigger, his toying with Osric, the address to the players, the grand apology to Laertes). And there are intermediate stages where we cannot say with any precision whether Hamlet is "acting" or not. These are all occasions on which we are keenly aware of the actor's range and of the pleasures it can give us, of the dif-

[1] Rosamond Gilder, *John Gielgud's Hamlet* (New York, 1937), p. 50; *Macready's Reminiscences and Selections from His Diaries and Letters*, ed. Sir Frederick Pollock (New York, 1875), p. 37.

ferent things the man on the stage is able to do and do well, and of his skill in making something coherent out of this variety.

The problems involved here are in an important sense exemplary of all acting. For as Hamlet suggests in his speech to the players, there is a critical technical and aesthetic difficulty inherent in the variety available to any professional actor. Great acting demands "temperance," "smoothness," moderation, control—and variety tests this control to the full. Lear is required to do just one kind of thing for most of his play, a very momentous and demanding kind of thing to be sure, but his problem as an actor is to find sufficient variety (and reserves of energy) to get through the evening. Hamlet's problem, assuming he is competent to execute the incredibly many separate "bits" the play allows him, is to control them, to focus them, to find an overall conception in which each has its place, and to give a meaningful smoothness to his transitions. Hamlet is not urging any principle of simple realism when he reminds the actors that their art consists in holding the mirror up to nature. The actor's task is to interpret life:

> to show virtue her own feature, scorn her own image, and the very age and body of the time his form and pressure.　　　　　　　　　　　　　(*III, ii, 25—27*)

It is Prince Hamlet's task, too, and his problems are very similar to those of the actor who plays him.

Hamlet awakes in its audience a unique concern for the actor's art—and particularly for his interpretive skill, his ability to make satisfying sense out of all the actions he is called upon to perform. It is possible to ask of an actor who portrays King Lear, "How will he get through it?" and the "it"—what Lear undergoes—will be on our minds as much as Lear himself. But with Hamlet we ask as of no other play, "How will he act the part?"

We do not ask, "Will he make any sense of it?" In the theater at least *Hamlet* runs no risk of obscurity. Indeed one of the problems of Hamlet, and one reason why the role is both a supreme challenge and one in which it is very hard to fail utterly, is that even a crude, simplifying, singleminded interpretation—a making one kind of sense but not full sense of the role—can produce solid, effective theater.

Interpretation is one of the necessary questions of *Hamlet;* to an important extent it is something the play is "about." Like its chief character, *Hamlet* draws our attention to varieties of action and to the questions of interpretation they raise. Our experience of *Hamlet* in the theater is primarily an attempt to follow an action so various, intricate, and proliferating that it cries out for interpretation at every turn. The "problems" of the play point, finally, to the subtle means it employs for manipulating one of our most fundamental theatrical appetites: the desire for action that makes sense, especially for action that seems complete and resolved.

As an example, consider III, iii, where Hamlet comes upon the King at prayer. What does the audience see? Two great antagonists who have been maneuvering toward each other throughout the play are alone together at last. They do not look at each other. They do not act. In fact each is frozen in a posture that manifestly suggests an action he does not perform. We see a praying man and his armed opponent. Hamlet has brought his father's murderer to his knees. But the praying man is not praying and the man with the sword is not going to strike. The King, however, wants to pray, just as Hamlet wants to kill the King.

The moment we have waited for so patiently arrives and it is not what we meant at all. It is a scene of extraordinary and peculiar tension. The frozen action allows us to register simultaneously an intense impulse to action, an incompleted action, and no action—action whose meaning may be the opposite of what we see. Criticism of this scene has focused on the reasons Hamlet gives for not killing Claudius, but clearly any doubts we may have as to the significance of what Hamlet says at this point are only part of our response to this powerfully engaging stage image, only one of many uncertainties as to action and its interpretation that are being deployed in us. But "doubt" and "uncertainty" tend to suggest speculative states, reflective categories that might be applied to the play in retrospect. Though they are not inaccurate to describe part of our feeling in the theater, they obscure the major source of that feeling and hence its precise quality, which springs from the maneuvering of bodies on the stage and the rhythm of our response to the action as it unfolds.

To understand this more fully, an important technical device must be discussed. iii, iii is one of a number of places in *Hamlet*— particularly toward the middle of the play—where what might be called a "stop-action" technique is used, that is, where one or more players is stopped in mid-gesture and the action frozen in a variety of ways. As, for instance, when the First Player describes Pyrrhus stopping in the very act of killing Priam:

> for, lo! his sword,
> Which was declining on the milky head
> Of reverend Priam, seem'd i' th' air to stick.
> So, as a painted tyrant, Pyrrhus stood
> And, like a neutral to his will and matter,
> Did nothing.   *(II, ii, 499–504)*

It helps to visualize the Player performing in a style which marks him off as an "actor" from the other figures on stage, gesturing overemphatically, throwing himself into the part ("Look whe'er he has not turn'd his colour and has tears in's eyes"). We may expect that the player has suited the action to the word and frozen grandly.

The Player continues. Pyrrhus's gesture is started up again, but only after preparatory verbal fanfare that again draws attention to the stopped action:

> But, as we often see, against some storm,
> A silence in the heavens, the rack stand still,
> The bold winds speechless, and the orb below
> As hush as death, anon the dreadful thunder
> Doth rend the region; so, after Pyrrhus' pause,
> Aroused vengeance sets him new a-work;
> And never did the Cyclops' hammers fall
> On Mars his armour forg'd for proof eterne
> With less remorse than Pyrrhus' bleeding sword
> Now falls on Priam.   *(505–14)*

A few lines later Polonius stops him; he starts up once again, and immediately Hamlet interrupts! (It might be noted that Hamlet in giving the first few lines of the speech interrupts himself twice. The pattern of interruption contributes to the stop-action configuration, though there is probably little gesture or physical action to interrupt.)

Hamlet's soliloquy after the players leave turns on a violent self-interruption, as the Prince catches himself in the full flight of some great melodramatic gesture:

> . . . Bloody, bawdy villain!
> Remorseless, treacherous, lecherous, kindless villain!
> O, vengeance!
> Why, what an ass am I . . .   *(608–11)*

Again the shortened line ("O, vengeance!") orchestrates a stopped action.[2] Here, as at so many points in the play, we are made conscious of the fine line between genuine intensity and pose. Indeed, there is no line—and this is what the stop-action reveals. Hamlet's response is genuine in the sense that it is strongly felt, irresistible, and grows naturally and persuasively out of the situation. There is nothing in the preparation that suggests pretense, nor need there be. Hamlet is throwing himself into the role of revenger. But by interrupting himself at the height of his outburst, by freezing the pose, Hamlet draws our attention to his theatricality of gesture and language. At this moment, sincerity and "acting" are hard to tell apart—and one is not necessarily to be preferred to the other. In fact, Hamlet now is prompted by revulsion at his own playacting to use a much more elaborate piece of theatricality to catch the conscience of the King—the play within the play. The sudden break has allowed action to be revealed as acting, and has also involved us more deeply in doubt as to the ultimate direction or interpretation of any action.[3]

The stop-action tableaus play upon a question that recurs in various forms throughout *Hamlet:* when is an action not an action? It is raised of course in the "To be or not to be" soliloquy, where Hamlet—who has a moment ago appeared ready to catch the conscience of the King—now analyzes the conditions under which action loses its name or falls into non-being. Hamlet sees his situation as paradoxical—action results in not being. To be is not to act. And the question *when is an action not an action?* reappears in a dozen guises, as, for example, when is revenge not revenge? when is a madman not a madman? when is a mother not a mother? when is a funeral not a funeral? when is a suicide not a suicide? when is play in earnest?[4] If there is a "question of Hamlet" it is this. As

---

[2] The authenticity of this line has been questioned. But if Harold Jenkins is right, and it represents a playhouse interpolation, it still casts light on the way the speech was performed, and very likely on its intended effect. The actor felt the need or opportunity for marking the punctuation, for heightening the frozen posture with a posturing phrase. In any case, the stop-action is plain even without "O vengeance!" (See "Playhouse Interpolations in the Folio Text of *Hamlet,*" *Studies in Bibliography,* XIII [1960], 31–47.)

[3] Two or three other moments of stop-action deserve mention. The action of the play scene itself is stopped in a number of ways. The dumb show allows us to preview the murder of Gonzago in the slow-motion of pantomime, and later the performance is broken off sharply before the climax. The entrance of the Ghost in III, iv provides yet another example. Hamlet breaks off in the midst of his attack on the Queen to bend his eye on vacancy, and they are fixed in this tableau for several lines.

Robert Hapgood discusses a number of "arrested actions" in his "Hamlet Nearly Absurd: The Dramaturgy of Delay," *Tulane Drama Review* (Summer, 1965), pp. 132–45; several of his examples strike me as contributing to the effects described above. I should add, however, that Hapgood's understanding of these moments (which he treats primarily as instances of delay) seems to be very different from mine.

[4] Cf. Maynard Mack's superb essay, "The World of *Hamlet,*" *Yale Review,* 41 (1952), 513–14. My concern is less with the authenticity of "acts," as Professor Mack's is, than with the problems posed by our appetite for significant "action."

the role of Hamlet itself directs our attention to the problems of interpreting and making sense out of action, so the play is endlessly varying the motif of doubt as to the significance of action.

The famous problem of whether Hamlet is active or inactive may be understood as a misleading abstraction from this type of effect. The Prince may be described as either active or inactive because in *Hamlet* action is constantly losing its name. Though there is an endless variety of it, we are always aware—as in the stop-action sequences—of our appetite for a certain kind of completeness, a meaningfulness which we as members of the audience demand of action.

The critical approach that focuses on Hamlet's "inaction" typically concerns itself with his speculative capacities. But the familiar distinction that this interpretation turns on—between action and reason—is inappropriate to the play. Hamlet's Renaissance sense of human dignity unites reason and action in a single continuum. Man is a great piece of work because his capacity for both reason and action, for reason in action, is divine. Not only does reason exist to prompt us to action, it is only *used* when we act:

> Sure, He that made us with such large discourse,
> Looking before and after, gave us not
> That capability and god-like reason
> To fust in us unus'd.   *(IV, iv, 36–39)*

The actions that matter, of course, are the ones that make satisfying sense—full sense, not like Laertes' half-cocked rebellion, say, but like Hamlet's ultimate revenge. The importance of reason in action in *Hamlet*, of action that is meaningful in the face of difficult situations, may be seen if we compare three familiar speeches from the beginning, middle, and end of the play. The "To be or not to be" soliloquy where significant action is inhibited by the fear of death, is a paradoxical reversal of Hamlet's first soliloquy, in which he longs for death because he can no longer attribute significance to action ("How weary, stale, flat, and unprofitable, / Seems to me all the uses of this world"). But by the end of the play he sees a unifying meaning to all his actions; his life is now a "story" ("And in this harsh world draw thy breath in pain/To tell my story"). He is only afraid that death will keep it from being apparent to others.

Reason and action are not opposed in *Hamlet*, but for most of the play they fail to coalesce as either we or the characters would like them to. Without intelligible meaning, action is unsatisfying or disturbing, a fact exploited from the opening scene. We feel there not only doubt and interrogation but an immediate pressure to sort out the significances of a perculiarly tense and busy action. (Who's on duty here? Why does the wrong guard challenge? Why are they trying to get rid of Francisco? What does the ghost mean? Why are they on guard?) Our response is natural, as is that of the characters. Action and reason seek their meaning in each other, and nowhere more than in *Hamlet*. This may help to account for the special emphasis the play gives to the theme of speech (e.g. its concern with the way actors speak, the significant use of the word "discourse," the prominence of Osric, Hamlet's emphatic "say" at ɪɪ, ii, 596, where one would ordinarily expect "do")—for speech is a kind of intermediary step between willing significance and establishing it. It is neither reason nor action, but a reaching out of one toward the other. And it is exactly this effort that the action of *Hamlet* repeatedly highlights and foils.

Most of the characters are engaged in a continuing struggle to find out—

and interpret—what the others are doing or have done. Their efforts may be said to come to a head when Hamlet confronts the Queen. His address to the players has contained hints of the stress he will be under in this scene. In the very torrent, tempest, and whirlwind of his passion he will have to be careful, as the Ghost has warned him, not to o'erstep the modesty of nature. It is his toughest acting assignment so far, and when he comes to it he quite literally sets out to hold a mirror up to nature:

> Come, come, and sit you down. You shall not budge.
> You go not till I set you up a glass
> Where you may see the inmost part of you.
>
> *(III, iv 18-20)*

Again the difficult relations between action, acting, and the self come to the fore. Gertrude is a striking example of divorce between action and meaning. She has allowed herself to sleep with Claudius and become his queen largely by refusing to think about what she has been doing. She has followed her senses and blocked out the meaning of her actions. "What have I done?" is her revealing cry, and Hamlet proceeds to interpret for her (the italics are, of course, mine):

> HAMLET   Such an *act*
> That blurs the grace and blush of modesty
> ... O, such a *deed*
> As from the body of contraction plucks
> The very soul ...
> Yea, this solidity and compound mass,
> With tristful visage, as against the doom,
> Is thought sick at the *act*.
>   QUEEN   Ay me, what *act*,
> That roars so loud and thunders in the index?
>
> *(40-52)*

The fierce and disturbing intensity of their dialogue derives from Hamlet's insistence on the physical actuality of his mother's crime. He wants to make her *see*, to put action and meaning together, just as he has wanted to say what is in his heart and to act on his cue for revenge. But at the very moment Hamlet is trying to make the Queen interpret her own actions, a great tangle of misinterpretation forms around them. Polonius thinks Hamlet will kill the Queen. Hamlet thinks Polonius is the King. On two separate occasions and for different reasons, Gertrude thinks Hamlet is mad. To these we may add the Queen's "What have I done?" and our own curiosity as to why she doesn't see the Ghost. As so often in the play, an increasing pressure toward clarity has carried us into deeper uncertainty and doubt.

   To act significantly in these circumstances it is necessary to be an actor—to play a part and hence to use disguise, to be and not to be. One's inmost part may be that which passeth show, and any action may be such as a man might play, but some kind of playacting seems necessary to reveal what ordinary action keeps hidden. After the play-within-the-play Hamlet has announced, in rhetoric that reminds us of the theatricality of the revenger's occupation (" 'Tis now the very witching time of night ... Now could I drink hot blood") that he is ready for violent action—but with his mother he intends only to act the part, "I will speak daggers to her, but use none." Though his appearance will perfectly suit the reality within him, it will be only a pretense. He will act and not act, but the acting will be so effective that it will cause Polonius to cry out from behind the arras and result in a violence Hamlet did not (and did) intend. Hamlet has now been seen twice to attack the King and not to attack him, and he concludes the scene with his mother by saying goodnight five times before he leaves.

The play, then, is full of action, but the action is handled in such a way that our responses perform in effect an analysis of the feelings and appetites we attach to the very notion of action. We are regularly invited to complete an action—to consider what it means, to anticipate where it may lead—only to have our response blocked, distracted, or diverted, compromised in some way. The stop-action sequences; the early air of mystery; the multiple networks of doubt, deceit, and detection; the stress given to nuances and paradoxes of acting technique; the teasing verbal play with reason and action, saying and doing, being and not being, all contribute to this effect.[5]

Considered in this light, many matters which have provoked critical disagreement in the past may be recognized not as problems requiring solutions one way or the other, but as signs of the play's careful management of our response. The first act, for example, ends with Hamlet vowing vengeance and promising some secret course of action toward that end. In II, i, we learn that Hamlet has appeared to Ophelia in marvellous disarray, apparently mad. Is this part of his plan? The answer is that there are simply too many variables for us to be certain.

---

[5] There are a number of attractive minor examples of action losing its name. When the Ghost speaks up from the cellarage and Hamlet calls upon his friends to swear secrecy, the same action is repeated three or four times to the accompaniment of the Ghost's "Swear . . . Swear . . . Swear by his sword . . . Swear" [following Q₂]. The repetition tends to leach the solemnity out of the action, to blur its clarity in the very act of insisting on it—to detach the significant gesture from the felt significance.

Similarly, when Horatio brings his great news to Hamlet in the first act, they are so incapable of interpreting each other correctly they are forced to repeat themselves:

HAMLET	My father!—methinks I see my father
HORATIO	Oh, where, my lord?
HAMLET	In my mind's eye, Horatio. . . .
HORATIO	My lord, I think I saw him yesternight.
HAMLET	Saw? Who?
HORATIO	My lord, the King your father.
HAMLET	The King my father!

(ii, 184–91)

Actions are frequently repeated, allowing us to note the effect of different interpretations. Hamlet and the First Player recite the same speech; Claudius's treason is narrated by the Ghost, acted in dumb show and then again with words. Osric plays the fop and Hamlet imitates him. And there is a very funny and intricate variation on the theme of sincerity when Hamlet insists on welcoming Rosencrantz and Guildenstern *a second time* before welcoming the players. He insists that he must overact this second reception, so that when he acts less sincerely (he claims) for the players it will not falsify the meaning of his welcome to his old school friends:

GUILDENSTERN   There are the players.

HAMLET   Gentlemen, you are welcome to Elsinore. Your hands, come. The appurtenance of welcome is fashion and ceremony. Let me comply with you in the garb, lest my extent to the players, which, I tell you, must show fairly outward, should more appear like entertainment than yours. You are welcome.

(II, ii, 386–93)

He probably repeats his gestures of welcome two or three times during the speech.

When the Bristol Old Vic presented the play in New York, Hamlet actually appeared in this scene—out of Polonius's line of vision—and with a number of broad winks conveyed to Ophelia—and us—that he was just kidding; it was all part of the antic disposition. This is one way of clearing up the action, but it is not Shakespeare's way, which is not to clear it up. It is Hamlet's absence from the stage that gives the scene its significance. Shakespeare might have introduced him, could have rearranged existing material to do so. But without Hamlet we are forced to guess whether his charade was deliberately intended to mislead, or an expression of the anguish that is also developed in Act I. We only know for sure that Polonius's interpretation is wrong.

Shakespeare could also easily have allowed Hamlet to resolve another problem that has perplexed the critics: whether any significant delay occurs between Acts I and II. This is not simply a matter of the flexible time dimension of the Elizabethan stage. Shakespeare can be very explicit about linear time when it suits him. He can also deliberately follow an impossible sequence, as in *Othello*, and keep us from noticing—and he can simply be careless of time when it doesn't matter. But he does none of these things in this case. He does finally let us know that Hamlet has spent more time than he would have liked between I, v and II, i, but he allows us this information only at the very end of Act II. Thus, here—and elsewhere—the question of whether Hamlet delays unnecessarily is deliberately left opaque. There are good reasons for him to delay, but they are fed to us at the wrong time dramatically and in the wrong way for us to be confident that they are the right ones, or even to be sure the delay has been so egregious as at moments he claims it is.[6] The play of course does not permit us to fall into careful examination of these questions; they exist only as part of the pattern of interrupted action and blocked significance.

The pattern (like the Oedipal pattern) is designed to excite both our deepest interest and our deepest resistance. Unfortunately, because it is so original (and perhaps because it is disturbing) it has often provoked stupid "improvements." Since the "To be or not to be" soliloquy breaks the arc of feeling between Hamlet's appearance in II, ii and III, ii, many companies follow the mutilated First Quarto and place it in the midst of II, ii. It makes more "sense" that way, that is, it makes it easier to interpret Hamlet. For similar reasons, III, iii, which unexpectedly detours Hamlet into the King's closet, was for more than two centuries either omitted or substantially cut in most performances. But in both cases the break in our expectations, the resistance to interpretation, is vital.

Critics concerned with the problem of Hamlet's delay have long concentrated on the scene with Claudius and with reason. But the question to be asked here is not why does Hamlet delay, but why does the play delay—why are *we* delayed? There is more than a grain of truth in the facetious statement that Hamlet delays because there would be no play if he did not. Part of our response to the closet scene depends on our knowledge that the play cannot end here—and not merely because we have paid for an hour's more entertainment. As soon as Hamlet enters we know he will not kill the King. He cannot kill Claudius at prayer, not for theological reasons, sound as they may be, but for aesthetic ones. It is undramatic, too easy. The King's back is to him. There is no source of resis-

---

[6] "How all occasions do inform against me" (IV, iv, 32ff) gives us our strongest sense that Hamlet delays, and is the source for most critical speculation as to his reasons. But it should be observed that the soliloquy occurs at the only point in the play where Hamlet, under guard and on his way to England, has absolutely no opportunity for revenge.

tance. The play is going elsewhere. The action, we realize, would not satisfy us, though like Hamlet we have longed for it since the first act. If Shakespeare ever played with an audience, it is here: once again our desire for significant action is drawn upon in a way that also arouses our latent sense of how difficult this appetite is to satisfy.

When two such deeply opposed antagonists have been kept apart for so long by actions of such brilliance and complexity, we come to need an ending that will release all our pent-up energies. We need a spacious ending, a great clarifying release. And this is what we get in the splendid free-for-all that concludes the play, in which the King is hoist on both his petards, and Hamlet, after a display of athletic, military, and moral virtuosity, kills him in full possession of palpably damning evidence and is vindicated before a large audience. To the characters on stage the scene is confusion, an example of the futility of all efforts to force a significance on action, to grasp what Hamlet calls the invisible event. It is a tableau, finally, of "purposes mistook/Fall'n on the inventors' heads," but for us it is nothing of the sort. If an Elizabethan audience wanted to refer it to a theological principle they might see it as an example of the workings of Providence, but their rhythm of response to the action would be much the same as ours. All through the play we have been reminded, both explicitly and by the imagery and movement of the verse, of the pleasure that attends any great release of energy in ample and unambiguous action:

> . . . in grace whereof,
> No jocund health that Denmark drinks to-day,
> But the great cannon to the clouds shall tell,
> And the King's rouse the heavens shall bruit again,
> Re-speaking earthly thunder.   (*I, ii, 124–28*)

> But I will delve one yard below their mines,
> And blow them at the moon. O, 'tis most sweet,
> When in one line two crafts directly meet.
> (*III, iv, 208–210*)

> And let the kettle to the trumpets speak,
> The trumpet to the cannoneer without,
> The cannons to the heavens, the heaven to earth.
> (*V, ii, 286–88*)

Even when Claudius uses the opposite figure of a missile missing its target, he does it by way of another beautiful evocation of a sudden, sweeping, clearly aimed discharge

> Whose whisper o'er the world's diameter,
> As level as the cannon to his blank,
> Transports his poisoned shot, may miss our name,
> And hit the woundless air.   (*IV, i, 41–44*)

Now the final release comes in a scene which rarely fails to produce an overwhelming excitement and satisfaction.

Pressure toward a full physical clash onstage has begun at least as early as Hamlet's failure to kill the King at prayer, and progressed through his taunting of the King and escaping his guards, Laertes' abortive attack on Claudius, and Hamlet's inconclusive struggle with Laertes in the grave. We are also given the details of a wonderful fight at sea and the just deserts of Rosencrantz and Guildenstern (which is also the result of "a kind of fighting"). At last Hamlet is asked to "play" with Laertes, and the fencing match begins. It is an action whose significance keeps shifting: it means different things at different moments for the different players. And simultaneously we are aware of the gratifying opportunities it offers the actors. The court ceremony is elaborate. The fencing must be excellent. Nowhere is the Prince more various. The actors must show the difference between fencing in play and fighting in deadly earnest, with at least one intermediary stage between. But if the bystanders on the stage are confused by the results, we for once are not. All the significances are clear and we watch them explode into action. Every piece of inner villainy leaves its telltale outer mark and is repaid in fully emblematic action. ("The point envenom'd too!/ Then, venom, to thy work!") The purpose of playing is achieved; acting and being are one. In form and moving all is express and admirable.

The play ends with a final unambiguous discharge of energy. Fortinbras, who has a soldier's simple sense of what is appropriate, orders a peal of ordnance shot off. The air has been cleared. We have experienced, in this long heightening and ultimate fulfillment of our basic theatrical desires, the equivalent of Hamlet's tangled meditations on action and human worth. Hamlet has been concerned from the first with the good actor's root problem—sincerity. Any gesture is, after all, such as a man might play, but if this is the case how does one truthfully perform what is within him? In an earlier chapter I pointed out that Hamlet seems to be about eighteen at the play's beginning and thirty near its end. As a factual question the problem is of little importance, and there is nothing that absolutely contradicts the specific figure of thirty given by the gravedigger. But it is interesting that the two ages often mark a great change in a man's understanding of sincerity. At eighteen the imperative is not to live a lie. By thirty, one realizes how hard it is to be certain one isn't.

The problem of sincerity is of interest only in those for whom it is difficult. The obvious sincerity of Fortinbras, Laertes, and the First Player leave Hamlet irritated or envious. There is nothing within them that passes show. But to say "I have that within which passeth show," is really to challenge the whole enterprise of theater; it is to say I have a self which cannot be sounded in action, that any encounter I have with the world must merely be playacting in a derogatory sense. The crisis of young Hamlet's life comes when he is forced to act, forced by the Ghost to find a show that will be true to what is within him and to the world in which he finds himself. As with the actor who plays the role, the greatest strain falls on Hamlet's capacity for expressive coherence, for action that at each moment is true to the delicacy and difficulty of his entire situation. The tragic effect comes because we are made to feel that this achievement is possible for Hamlet only at the cost of great destruction.

A good way to see the nature of Prince Hamlet's difficulty in its relation to tragic emotion is to contrast his play with *Julius Caesar*, the tragedy immediately preceding it in composition. Prince Hamlet strikes us as an intellectual for much the same reasons Brutus does; we see them deliberating certain problems of action and attempting to formulate them in abstract terms. But Brutus's problem is that he would like to separate significance from the agents that produce significance. Though he cannot kill Caesar's spirit without killing Caesar, he tries to limit the significance of his act to the spiritual, to treat the "genius" as if it were independent of its "mortal instruments." Hamlet's problem, on the other hand, is to *attach* significance to action, to overcome his initial sense that all the uses of the world are flat and unprofitable, to fully unite action and reason, to find a revenge which is both internally and externally satisfying, an action that like all good acting holds the mirror up to nature.

But the achievement of clarity and full expressiveness in action is immensely difficult for Hamlet and immensely expensive. The destructive or demonic force that we are accustomed to encounter in tragedy seems in *Julius Caesar* to rise from the body of Caesar itself and is exemplified first in the blood that floods the stage and later in Caesar's ghost. The source of the energy that destroys Brutus, then, is the very element of the problem he has tried to overcome—Caesar's inescapable physicality, the mortal instruments that become genius only by virtue of their mortality. In the same way, Hamlet is finally destroyed and fulfilled by an action whose source is beyond his control. It is only when he has agreed not to force a significance upon his actions, not to look before and after but to let be, that he is swept to his revenge. The revenge kills him as it has also killed Gertrude, Ophelia, and Polonius. The destructive element turns out to be the very element in his situation which he has struggled in his mind to root out and overcome—whatever there is in the self that the mind cannot grasp and control in thought and adequately express in action.

We are thus brought back to the dubieties of the great central soliloquy. There are more things in heaven and earth than any man's philosophy can unravel. A taint of death lies not only in every action but in discourse of reason itself. Being and not being, playacting and sincerity, action and letting be, the pressure to clarity and the proliferation of doubt are inextricably intertwined in mortal experience. Shakespeare's tragic heroes are men who insist on the self-destruction proper to their genius; sooner or later they seek out that death which allows their capacities most fully to illuminate the world for the audience that watches them die. The destruction Hamlet seeks allows him to take as far as possible and to test to the full an impulse we all to some extent share, and to which the art of the theater is dedicated—through action to make sense of life.

Phèdre*

Roland Barthes

To name or not to name, that is the question. In *Phèdre* it is language's very being that is put on the stage: the profoundest of Racine's tragedies is also the most formal; for the tragic stake here is less the meaning of language than its manifestation, less Phaedra's love than her avowal. Or more exactly: to name Evil is to exhaust it entirely. Evil is a tautology, *Phèdre* a nominalist tragedy.[1]

From the outset, Phaedra knows she is guilty, and it is not her guilt that constitutes a problem, it is her silence:[2] that is where her freedom is. Phaedra breaks this silence three times: before Oenone (I,3), before Hippolytus (II,5), before Theseus (V,7). These three outbursts have a mounting gravity; from one to the next, Phaedra approaches an increasingly pure state of language. The first confession is still narcissistic, Oenone is merely her maternal double: Phaedra disburdens herself to herself, seeks her identity, makes her own history; her confession is an epic one. The second time, Phaedra binds herself magically to Hippolytus by a performance: she *represents* her love, her avowal is dramatic. The third time, she confesses publicly before the person who by his mere being has instituted the transgression; her confession is literal, purified of all theatre; her language is totally coincident with the fact, it is a *correction:* Phaedra can die, the tragedy is exhausted. We are dealing, then, with a silence tormented by the notion of its own destruction. Phaedra *is* her silence: to break this silence is to die, but also to die can only mean *having spoken.* Before the tragedy begins,

[1] *Quand tu sauras mon crime, et le sort qui m'accable,*
Je n'en mourrai pas moins, j'en mourrai plus coupable. (I,3)

When you learn what my crime is, and the fate that overwhelms me, I shall die not less, but more guilty.

—*Hippolyte? Grands Dieux!*
        —*C'est toi qui l'as nommé.* (I,3)

Hippolytus? O gods!
You are the one who spoke his name.

[2] *Phèdre, atteinte d'un mal qu'elle s'obstine à taire* ... (I,1)

Phaedra, stricken by a disease she refuses to name...

Phaedra already wants to die, but this death is suspended:[3] only speech will release this motionless death, restore to the world its movement.[4]

Phaedra, moreover, is not the only figure of secrecy; not only is her secret contagious, Hippolytus and Aricia also refusing to give any name to Phaedra's disease,[5] but further, Phaedra has a double who is also constrained by the terror of language: Hippolytus. For Hippolytus as for Phaedra, to love is to be guilty before that same Theseus who forbids his son to marry as a consequence of the vendettal law, and who never dies. Further, to love and to speak that love is, for Hippolytus, the same scandal; once again the guilt of the emotion is not distinguished from its nomination. Theramenes speaks to Hippolytus exactly as Oenone speaks to Phaedra.[6] Yet as Phaedra's double, Hippolytus represents a much more archaic state of mutism, he is a regressive double; for Hippolytus' constriction is one of essence,[7] Phaedra's is one of situation. Hippolytus' oral constraint is openly given as a sexual constraint: Hippolytus is mute *because* he is sterile; despite Racine's worldly precautions, Hippolytus is the rejection of sex, anti-Nature; his confidant, by his very curiosity, attests to the monstrous character of Hippolytus, whose virginity is a spectacle.[8] Doubtless Hippolytus' sterility is directed against the Father; it is a reproach to the Father for the anarchic profusion with which he squanders life.[9] But the Racinian world is an immediate

[3] *Une femme mourante et qui cherche à mourir* . . . (I,1)

A woman dying, and longing to die . . .

[4] *Et la mort, à mes yeux dérobant la clarté,*
Rend au jour, qu'ils souillaient, toute sa pureté. (V,7)

And death, darkening my eyes, restores all its brightness to the day they tainted.

[5] Hippolytus to Theseus:
. . . *Je devrais faire ici parler la vérité,*
Seigneur; mais je supprime un secret qui vous touche. (IV,2)

I should let truth speak for me here, my lord, but I pass over in silence a secret that concerns you alone.

Hippolytus to Aricia:
. . . *et que jamais une bouche si pure*
Ne s'ouvre pour conter cette horrible aventure. (V,1)

. . . lips so pure must never part to utter this horrible tale.

[6] Theramenes to Hippolytus:
Vous périssez d'un mal que vous dissimulez. (I,1)

You are dying of a disease you insist on concealing.

[7] Hippolytus' love for Aricia is a challenge to essence:
Maintenant je me cherche et ne me trouve plus. (II,2)

Now I seek and no longer find myself.

[8] *Et même, en le voyant, le bruit de sa fierté*
A redoublé pour lui ma curiosité. (II,1)

And even as I saw him, the rumor of his pride magnified twice over my curiosity about him.

[9] *Mais quand tu récitais des faits moins glorieux,*
Sa foi partout offerte et reçue en cent lieux . . .
Tu sais comme, à regret écoutant ces discours,
Je te pressais souvent d'en abréger le cours . . .
Et moi-même, à mon tour, je me verrais lié? (I,1)

But when you recounted his less glorious deeds, his faith pledged and accepted in a hundred places .

world. Hippolytus hates the flesh as a literal disease. Eros is contagious, one must disinfect oneself, avoid contact with the objects it has touched: Phaedra's mere glance at Hippolytus corrupts him,[10] his sword becomes loathsome once Phaedra has touched it.[11] Aricia, in this regard, is merely the homologue of Hippolytus: her vocation is sterility, not only by Theseus' decree,[12] but by her very being.[13]

Constriction is thus the form that accounts for shame, for guilt, and for sterility, and *Phèdre* is on all levels a tragedy of the imprisoned word, of life repressed. For speech is a substitute for life: to speak is to lose life, and all effusive behavior is experienced initially as a gesture of dilapidation: by the avowal, the flood of words released, it is the very principle of life that seems to be leaving the body; to speak is to spill oneself, that is, to castrate oneself, so that the tragedy is subject to the economy of an enormous avarice.[14] But at the same time, of course, this blocked speech is fascinated by its own expansion: it is at the moment Phaedra guards her silence most intensely that by a compensatory gesture she flings off the garments which envelop her and tries to reveal her nakedness.[15] We realize then that *Phèdre* is also a tragedy of accouchement. Oenone is truly the nurse, the midwife, who seeks to liberate Phaedra from her words at any price, who "delivers" language from the deep cavity in which it is confined. This intolerable confinement of the self, which is both mutism and sterility in the same impulse, is also, as we know, the essence of Hippolytus: Aricia will thus be Hippolytus' midwife as Oenone is Phaedra's; if Aricia is interested in Hippolytus, it is precisely in order to pierce him,[16] to make his words flow at last.

. . you know how reluctant I was to hear such things, how I often urged you to skip the recital . . . and now it is my turn to see myself corrupted.

[10] *Je ne puis sans horreur me regardez moi-même.* (II,6)

I cannot look at myself without horror.

[11] *Il suffit que ma main l'ait une fois touchée,*
Je l'ai rendue horrible à ses yeux inhumains;
Et ce fer malheureux profanerait ses mains. (III,1)

It is enough for my hand to touch his once, to make it horrible in his inhuman eyes; and this wretched sword would profane his hands.

[12] *Il défend de donner des neveux à ses frères,*
D'une tige coupable il craint un rejeton,
Il veut avec leur soeur ensevelir leur nom. (I,1)

He forbids her to bear children, nephews to her brothers, fearing a new branch of that guilty stock, and would bury the name with their sister.

[13] *Tu sais que de tout temps à l'amour opposée . . .* (II,1)

You know I have always opposed love . . .

[14] *J'ai pris la vie en haine . . .* (I,3)

I have taken a loathing to life . . .

[15] *Que ces vains ornements, que ces voiles me pèsent . . .* (I,3)

How these vain adornments, how these veils weigh me down!

[16] *Mais de faire fléchir un courage inflexible,*
De porter la douleur dans une âme sensible . . .
C'est là que je veux, c'est là ce qui m'irrite. (II,1)

But to bend an inflexible will, to awake pain in a sensitive soul . . . that is my desire, and what eludes me.

Further, in fantasy it is this midwife's role that Phaedra would play for Hippolytus; like her sister Ariadne, untangler of the Labyrinth, she wants to unravel the skein, reel off the thread, lead Hippolytus out of the cavern into daylight.[17]

Then what is it that makes speech so terrible? First of all, it is because it is an act that the word is so powerful. But chiefly it is because it is irreversible:[18] no speech can be taken back. Surrendered to the *logos*, time cannot be reversed, its creation is definitive. Thus by avoiding speech, one avoids action,[19] shifting the responsibility for it to others; and if one has begun to speak out of an "involuntary distraction," it is no use breaking off, one must go on to the end.[20] And Oenone's ruse consists not in *retracting* Phaedra's confession, in annulling it, which is impossible, but in *reversing* it: Phaedra will accuse Hippolytus of the very crime she herself is guilty of; speech will remain intact, simply transferred from one character to the other. For language is indestructible: the hidden divinity of *Phèdre* is neither Venus nor the Sun. It is that god "terrible to perjurers" whose temple stands at the gates of Troezen, surrounded by ancestral tombs, and before which Hippolytus will die. Theseus himself is the true victim of this god: though he has been able to *return* from the Underworld, to recover the irrecoverable, he is the one who speaks too soon. Semidivine, powerful enough to dominate the contradiction of death, he nonetheless cannot unsay what he had said: the gods send back the word he has uttered, in the form of a dragon that devours him in his son.

Of course, as the panic drama of defenestration, of opening, *Phèdre* employs an abundant thematics of concealment. Its central image is the Earth; Theseus, Hippolytus, Aricia and her brothers[21] are all descended from the Earth. Theseus is a strictly chthonian hero, a familiar of the underworld whose asphyxiating concavity his palace reproduces;[22] a labyrinthian hero, he has been able to

---

[17] *C'est moi, Prince, c'est moi, dont l'utile secours*
Vous eût du Labyrinthe enseigné les détours . . . (II,5)

I am the one, Prince, whose help would have taught you the way out of the Labyrinth's meanders . . .

[18] In *Phèdre*, a tragedy without marivaudage, words are never taken back: there are no "scenes."

[19] *La charmante Aricie a-t-elle su vous plaire?*
—Théramène, je pars, et vais chercher mon père. (I,1)

Can it be that the charming Aricia has won your heart?
—Theramenes, I am leaving, to seek my father.

[20] *Puisque j'ai commencé de rompre le silence,*
Madame, il faut poursuivre . . . (II,2)

Since I have begun to break the silence, lady, I must go on . . .

. . . Ah! cruel, tu m'as trop entendue . . . (II,5)

No, cruel Hippolytus, you have heard too much already . . .

[21] *Reste du sang d'un roi, noble fils de la Terre . . .* (II,1)

Last descendant of a king, noble son of the Earth . . .

. . . et la terre humectée
But à regret le sang des neveux d'Erechtée. (II,1)

And the drenched Earth reluctantly drank the blood of the nephews of Erechtheus.

[22] *Il me semble déjà que ces murs, que ces voûtes . . .* (III,3)

Already it seems as if these walls, these vaults . . .

triumph over the cavern, to pass back and forth between darkness and light, to know the unknowable and yet to return, while the site natural to Hippolytus is the shadowy forest, where he nourishes his own sterility.[23] Confronting this telluric bloc, Phaedra is divided: through her father, Minos, she participates in the order of the buried, of the deep; through her mother, Pasiphaë, she is descended from the Sun. Her principle is a troubled vacillation between these terms. She ceaselessly suppresses her secret, returns to the interior cavern, but ceaselessly, too, a force drives her to leave it, to expose herself, to join the Sun; and ceaselessly she testifies to the ambiguity of her nature: she fears the light, yet invokes it;[24] she thirsts for the day, yet taints it. In a word, her principle is the paradox of a *black light*,[25] that is, of a contradiction of essences.

Now this contradiction has, in *Phèdre*, an absolute form: the monster. At first, the monstrous threatens all the characters; they are all monsters to each other, and all monster-seekers as well.[26] But above all, it is a monster, this time a real one, which intervenes to resolve the tragedy. And this monster is the very *essence* of the monstrous—in other words, it epitomizes in its biological structure the fundamental paradox of *Phèdre*. It is the force that bursts out of the depths of the sea, it is what pounces upon the secret, breaks it open, ravishes it, tears it

---

[23] *Nourri dans les forêts il en a la rudesse.* (III,1)

He has the savagery of the forests where he was raised.

[24] *Vous haïssez le jour que vous veniez chercher.* (I,3)

You hate the very daylight you came to find.

[25] *Je voulais en mourant . . .*
. . . dérober au jour une flamme si noire. (I,3)

By dying, I sought to cleanse the day of a flame so black.

[26] Phaedra to Hippolytus:

Délivre l'univers d'un monstre qui t'irrite. (II,5)

Rid the world of a monster that pains you.

Aricia about Phaedra:

. . . Vos invincibles mains
Ont de monstres sans nombre affranchi les humains.
Mais tout n'est pas détruit, et vous en laissez vivre
Un . . . (V,3)

Your invincible hands have rid humanity of countless monsters, but not all are destroyed, you have left one alive . . .

Phaedra to Oenone:

. . . Va-t'en, monstre exécrable. (IV,6)

Leave me, you loathesome monster.

Hippolytus about himself:

Croit-on que dans ses flancs un monstre m'ait porté? (III,2)

Was I born from some monster's womb?

Phaedra about Hippolytus:

Je le vois comme un monstre effroyable à mes yeux. (III,3)

I regard him as a monster hideous to my sight.

apart, scatters and disperses it. To Hippolytus' principle of enclosure corresponds tragically—that is, ironically—his death by the dismemberment, the pulverization, broadly *extended* by the narrative, of a body hitherto essentially compact. Theramenes' narrative[27] constitutes, then, the critical point where the tragedy is resolved, that is, where the previous retention of all the characters is undone by a total catastrophe. So it is actually Hippolytus who is the exemplary character in *Phèdre* (though not the principal one); he is truly the propitiatory victim, in whom the secret and its explosion achieve their most gratuitous form. And in relation to this great mythic function of the broken secret, Phaedra herself is an impure character. Her secret, whose outcome is in a sense *tried out* twice, is finally released through an extended confession. In Phaedra, language recovers *in extremis* a positive function: she has time to die, there is finally an agreement between her language and her death, both have the same measure (whereas even the last word is stolen from Hippolytus). Like a sheet of water, a slow death creeps into her,[28] and like a sheet of water too, a pure, even language emerges from her; tragic time, that dreadful time which separates the spoken order from the real order, is purified, nature's unity is restored.

Phèdre thus proposes an identification of interiority with guilt; in *Phèdre* things are not hidden because they are culpable (that would be a prosaic view, Oenone's, for example, to whom Phaedra's transgression is merely contingent, linked to the life of Theseus); things are culpable from the very moment that they are hidden: the Racinian being does not release himself, and that is his sickness: nothing better attests the *formal* character[29] of the transgression than its explicit identification with a disease;[30] Phaedra's objective guilt (adultery, incest) is actually an artificial construction, intended to naturalize the suffering of the secret, to change form into content usefully. This inversion coincides with a more general movement, which establishes the entire Racinian edifice: Evil is terrible to the very degree that it is empty, man suffers from a *form*. This is what Racine expresses so well apropos of Phaedra when he says that for her, crime itself is a punishment.[31] Phaedra's entire effort consists in *fulfilling* her transgression, that is, in absolving God.

---

[27] There is a fine commentary on Theramenes' narrative by Leo Spitzer, in *Linguistics and Literary History*, Princeton University Press, 1948.

[28] *J'ai voulu . . .*
Par un chemin plus lent descendre chez les morts.
J'ai pris, j'ai fait couler dans mes brûlantes veines
Un poison . . . (V,7)

I sought to go down among the dead by a slower path, I have taken a poison that is flowing now through my burning veins . . .

[29] Claudel seems to have observed this *formal* character of Phaedra's disease when he says: "*Phèdre* is an atmosphere all to itself."

[30] *Phèdre, atteinte d'un mal qu'elle s'obstine à taire . . .* (I,i)

Phaedra, stricken by a disease she refuses to name . . .

[31] Preface, end of the first paragraph.

The Possibilities
and Perils of
Modern Tragedy*

John Gassner

I

A question that continues to agitate literary circles is whether it is possible to write tragedy in modern times and whether indeed it has been possible to produce tragedies at all ever since Ibsen's generation abandoned romanticism. The subject has become a veritable vested interest of academic criticism, but has also involved non-academic critics and creative writers. It has been impossible to declare a moratorium on the question because it thrusts itself into the foreground of discussions of the worth and pretensions of the modern theatre. Playwrights and critics who deplore the vogue of realism or the absence of poetry on the stage are especially inclined to make the impossibility of writing tragedy for the commerical theatre an article of faith. And it appears to be an absolute conviction on the part of some commentators that modern drama should be excluded from the aristocracy of letters altogether. Since tragedy is the most aristocratic of dramatic genres, it is a foregone conclusion of the literary mandarins that a tragic playwright cannot thrive in the theatre of the populace.

It is not the theatre, however, but the modern world that receives criticism's first and most devastating fire. How indeed should the exalted art of tragedy, which has traditionally dealt with the fate of singular individuals, flourish in the age of the common man? How should the grandeur of the tragic hero and the splendor of tragic vision survive in a world leveled down by democracy and cheapened by mass-production and mass-consumption, a world in which even emotions and ideas have been converted into commodities gaudily packaged for the buyer? At the same time, the leaders of this mandarin brand of criticism, many of whom have cherished ideals of classic or medieval unity, have been wont to observe that this world characterized by a distressing sameness is paradoxically a divided one. It is said to be incapable of providing the individual with a coherent view of himself and of his place in the universe. The same critics who disdain a world grown irrevocably common are apt to deplore the absence of communion in it. They regret the absence of tradition and belief in our mongrel culture. With no myth or cult to assure the continuity of time-honored values, with no religion to relate the individual unequivocally to the universe, with no fixity of class structure to bind men to their place, we presumably cannot have significant dramatic action: it cannot be significant because it cannot be

*John Gassner, "The Possibilities and Perils of Modern Tragedy," *Tulane Drama Review*, Vol. 1, No. 3 (June, 1957), pp. 3–14.

communally meaningful. The high concern with human fate that has characterized tragic art in past ages must therefore make way for considerations of temporary and local conflict between ant-men who are paradoxically common without being representative.

A commonplace realism, then, takes the place of the ideality to which the
art of tragedy aspires by historical example since the time of Aeschylus and by
critical prescript since the time of Aristotle. And it is a rare event indeed when
the language of the modern stage does not reflect the commonplace view of
mankind. The plot may pulsate with exciting events, as in the plays of O'Neill,
but the language limps behind the action and limits its tragic resonance. The inarticulateness so often postulated by realism as a result of its idolatry of verisimilitude dooms the characters to a level of consciousness too low to sustain an
impressive personality and a significant action. And that inarticulateness is itself
mainly a concomitant of the selection of low-grade personalities for dramatic
representation as well as of a low view of humanity. Rarely do the modern plays
assume or demonstrate that greatness of spirit we discover in an Antigone and
Oedipus or a Hamlet, Othello, and Lear. Henry James was surely correct when
he declared in one of his prefaces that "the agents in any drama are interesting
only in proportion as they feel their respective situations," and feeling communicates itself mainly through language. The prose of modern drama, often commonplace if not indeed barbarically colloquial, is both a symptom of the absence
of tragic art and a cause of its absence.

So runs the argument, which is fortified by the critics' dismal view of modern liberalism, which entertains nontragic premises in so far as it puts its trust in
rationalism, science, and sociology. When behavior is explained largely by heredity, instinct, and environment man is deprived of any genuine responsibility
for his actions that would make dramatic conflict humanistically relevant and
calamity morally significant. There can be no tragic heroes in the bleak commonwealth of conditioned animals. Nor is the individual given materially greater significance when he is treated as a psychological case history. His writhings
in the grip of a neurosis or psychosis may gratify our curiosity but not our moral
sense. He may be interesting as a specimen of morbidity, but his plight—his error and his suffering—will exalt neither the character nor spectator. A heroic
view of man, then, is the last thing that sociology and psychopathology can supply whereas it has been the peculiar triumph of tragic art in the past to affirm
the wonder of man. For ages, tragedy has been a high mystery by means of
which defeat has been transformed into victory for the human spirit. In this
mystery which converts despair over the human condition into reconciliation
with fate and leaves us exhilarated rather than dismayed, the protagonist is the
sacrifice; and the sacrifice must be worthy of the rite. With respect to both the
protagonist or sacrificial victim and the humanity which the rite redeems modern rationalistic inquiry is held to be altogether too disillusioning. But if the
modern viewpoint is too depressing, it is also too optimistic for tragedy, for modern liberalism has been inveterately melioristic. Denying that evil and suffering
are absolute and unalterable, the liberal viewpoint has proposed to remove or
moderate the very conditions that make tragedy possible and its ministrations
welcome, if not indeed imperative. The modern viewpoint, then, appears to be
both too hard and not hard enough for tragedy.

The critics of liberal modernism cannot, however, be completely represented by the above-given arguments, for they have set up their batteries not

only on the literary heights but on the summits of theological disputation. They have wondered, for example, how a modern writer of the liberal persuasion can expect to write tragedy while rejecting the doctrine of original sin, failing to make characters feel accountable to God, or depriving man of an inviolable ethos and of the solace of belief that his suffering has spiritual significance. And some critics have also become amateur anthropologists in emphasizing the ritualistic character of a tragic performance. They seem to believe that because tragedy developed out of religious ritual in Greece, the modern theatre, which is not at all pyramided upon any religious rites, is unable to engender tragic art. The error in this kind of reasoning is the familiar "genetic fallacy," which assumes that a thing must remain what it was at its inception. The proponents of this view are also inconsistent: they certify many Elizabethan and seventeenth-century plays as true tragedies, although neither the Elizabethan nor the neo-classic French theatre had any marked ritualistic basis or character.

The genetic fallacy, however, is not always conspicuously advanced. It is apt to be screened from view by the argument that a community of values (as best expressed in religion and ritual) is essential to the development of tragedy, and this is, on the surface, a reasonable belief. If the tragic experience demonstrates the calamitous results of a character's conduct, that conduct must obviously constitute a violation of a more or less accepted norm. In a community which sanctioned parricide and incest, for example, Oedipus would not be a tragic character. And if a tragically misguided character is to arrive at restorative perceptions or redeeming realizations in the course of his suffering, these must meet with agreement from the public. The emphasis upon the need for a community of values, however, becomes an argument against the possibility of writing tragedy today as soon as the critic implies that the agreement must be strict enough to disallow modern diversity and scepticism, if not strict enough indeed to constitute a religious or quasi-religious sanction. It is doubtful that such "communion" was ever absolute in the individualistic Athenian and Elizabethan periods, and it might be contended that communion is a religious experience that ought not to be confused with social conformity. History indeed supplies many examples of ancient despotisms and modern totalitarian societies that failed to produce tragic art. Conformity, however, does not seem to disturb contemporary neo-ritualists, provided the commonly held values are approvable; and they are apt to be approved if only they are pre-modern and traditional. The neo-conservative position, as laid down in previous decades by Hulme and T. S. Eliot, is indeed the final employment from which traditionalists offer resistance to the idea that playwrights whose thought has been contaminated by modern science or sociology can compose tragedy.

The position of the traditionalists on this issue tends to be inflexible. They rarely admit that any modern dramatist has written a true tragedy, and a play dealing "tragically" with a commoner's fate such as *Death of a Salesman* is treated as pretentious vulgarity. A more moderate position grants a few deviations into tragedy by Ibsen, O'Neill, and perhaps a few other writers. But the advanced and more persistent traditionalist view holds that realistic dramaturgy and prose are incompatible with tragedy, as are liberalism, meliorism, sympathy with ordinary persons, scepticism, and modern individualism. According to this view, the would-be tragedian, unless he renounces the ambience of modern thought and popular art, will end up only with melodrama, propaganda, pathology, pathos and sentimentality, or just plain nastiness and bathos. Tragic art, according to this view, has been achieved in the modern age by only two species of writers—the primitive and the ultra-sophisticated: by a Synge and Lorca, on the one hand, or a Cocteau, Yeats, and Eliot, on the other. The primitives have escaped modernity while the ultra-sophisticated have passed beyond it and returned to mystery, legend, ritual, and the racial unconscious.

II

That, in brief, is one side of the argument concerning tragedy in the modern theatre, and it is not difficult to understand why it should be punctuated with so much intellectual artillery. The fire is directed at the modern spirit, which presumably cannot have much worth if it does not produce tragic art—an assumption which would of course invalidate all but the three brief periods of human history which produced Attic, Elizabethan, and neo-classic French tragedy of the latter part of the seventeenth century.

But the other side of the argument, though less often maintained, has also been vigorously advanced. Implicit in the theatre's hopes and endeavors for the past three quarters of a century has been the conviction that tragedy could be revitalized by sinking its roots deeper in modern consciousness and by relating it more closely to the immediate life of the times. I do not know of any comprehensive statement that adequately presented this viewpoint until Herbert J. Muller published his vigorous book *The Spirit of Tragedy* late in 1956. Presentations of the modern liberal position have been scattered in a variety of prefaces, letters, diaries, and reviews; and liberal doctrine concerning tragedy has never been particularly impressive, even though such important writers as Hebbel, Zola, Strindberg, Galsworthy, and Arthur Miller have contributed to it. The real force of the argument must be sought in the works to which the theories were prefatory or supplementary; it resides in whatever realizations of modern tragedy can be found in the plays of Ibsen, Strindberg, Tolstoy, Curel, Hauptmann, O'Neill, Galsworthy, O'Casey, and other playwrights.

A fundamental premise has been the opinion that a great deal of the tragic art of the past, while excellent as far as it went, belongs to the past. The pagan beliefs that served Attic tragedy twenty-five centuries ago are no longer acceptable to modern man. Neither are the beliefs of the Elizabethan period and the age of Louis XIV. There is simply no single true philosophy of tragedy any more than there is a single inviolable tragic form. Tragic art is subject to evolutionary processes, and tragedy created in modern times must be modern. The fact that it will be different from tragedy written three, five, or twenty-five centuries ago does not mean that it will no longer be tragedy; it will merely be different. It will be as different from earlier tragic literature as *Hamlet*, let us say, is different from *Oedipus Rex* or as *Phaedra* is different from Euripides' *Hippolytus*. Aristotle himself did not presume to legislate on tragedy for all time, but spoke modestly about tragic art as he knew it from the works of a handful of Athenian playwrights. He spoke of tragedy as it had developed up to his time in Greece, rather than of an everlasting and invariable type of drama. In generalizing about tragic method he spoke of optimal approaches rather than of absolutes; in the *Poetics*, he even countenanced a turn of fortune from bad to good as a possible, though not as the most effective, pattern of a tragedy. It was apparent to him that the Greek plays differed in kind and degree of tragic artistry, whatever their external structural similarities. It could be apparent to us, too, if we did not invite the hobgoblin of consistency into literary theory and attributed to Greek tragedy a single form, quality, and effect. The leaders of the modern theatre after 1870 rejected esthetic absolutism. They envisaged not only the possibility of writing tragedy with modern minds, but of extending its range and enlarging its potentialities as a study of man and his world.

The modern view started, sensibly enough, with considerations of character and environment. Tragic art was allowed to focus on all, rather than on only class-privileged, representatives of the human race. By 1870, the destiny of nations was no longer being shaped exclusively or even predominantly by a dynasty or an aristocracy. It was virtually granted by then that a character's station in society was secondary in importance to his stature as a human being. Of first importance was his capacity to manifest desires and engage in actions that could reveal human nature and its strivings significantly. Ibsen and his successors did not intend to repeat the error of early writers of "bourgeois tragedy" such as Diderot and Lillo who made common characters commonplace in feeling, will, and destiny. Many writers proceeded to endow them with passion-charged personalities, as Ibsen proved himself capable of doing when he created Hedda Gabler and O'Neill when he created Christine and Lavinia, the modern Clytemnestra and Electra of his *Mourning Becomes Electra*. Moreover, even examples from the past favored latitude. It had been possible for Shakespeare to plumb human destiny with so hesitant and divided a character as Hamlet. It had even proved possible to create tragedy with essentially anti-heroic figures such as Richard II and Euripides' Orestes and Electra. If the modern playwright tended more and more to focus on characters of divided will and thwarted desire, he was under no necessity to renounce all intention of giving them tragic prominence. The generally non-heroic character could be revealed as heroic in some central aspect. Strindberg's mentally tormented Captain in *The Father*, for example, is a clinical case. Yet he could be fully analyzed without lessening the force of his defense of masculinity in an overfeminized society. His personality and experiences were too intensely realized by Strindberg to generate pity without also producing fear; he, the protagonist, fought too strenuously against his wife Laura, his antagonist, and he resisted his fate too forcefully to engender pathos rather than passion. Thus, too, the Willy Loman of *Death of a Salesman* could be tethered to the satchel of a traveling salesman, could be made to swallow the mental garbage of a materialistic society, could be drawn in all his littleness as a business failure, and yet be allowed to draw attention to the soaring part of his personality. His self-regard or ideal of himself wills him to assert his sense of worth against his own littleness and makes him rage like a caged lion in his suburban home—and suburban mind. According to liberal doctrine, indeed, modern dramatists could reveal more, rather than fewer, facets of humanity.

That communication with modern audiences was henceforth to be attained on the maximum levels of understanding available to modern consciousness was indeed the ruling conviction of Ibsen, Strindberg, Shaw, Hauptmann, Curel, and other pioneers of the late nineteenth-century theatre, to which our own is still very largely bound. In their view it was preposterous to compose tragedy according to histrionic notions of heroism, and they consequently broke with romanticism as firmly as romantic writers had broken with neo-classicism. The moderns, moreover, could admire Shakespeare without believing that the Elizabethan world-picture was correct or meaningful for the modern world; and they could find merit in classic tragedy or even employ its retrospective dramatic structure, as Ibsen did in *Ghosts*, without subscribing to Greek notions of Fate. It seemed sounder as well as more honest to attempt to translate ancient concerns into present ones and old concepts into new ones. Aeschylus and Euripides had not hesitated to do so, and there was no particular reason why Ibsen and Strindberg or O'Neill and Arthur Miller, after them, should.

The proponents of modern drama, moreover, could contend that they met the fundamental requirements of tragic art with considerable fidelity. They approached their subject with high seriousness, motivated human conduct, refrained from mere pathos by studying social and psychological causation, avoided melodrama, and made calamity a means for achieving significant revelations concerning the individual and his milieu. For them error, evil, and suffering were never ends in themselves, useless in providing the audience with a *frisson* and the playwright with an income. They knew that perception was a necessary element in the tragic experience and proposed to provide realization not by rote but by critical inquiry and by a realistic testing of the alternatives of action. Sometimes it was the main character who was led from passion to perception or from suffering to understanding; sometimes the final comprehension belonged to a group of secondary characters whose role was not radically different from that of a Greek chorus; sometimes it was the audience that was expected to understand what the characters could not express. The means might differ in respect to the situation and the intelligence of the character, but suffering was not allowed to be devoid of meaning. In one way or another, some means was to be found for compensating calamity with insight. And direct or indirect means were sought for supplying the tragic awareness that the protagonist of a modern play could not articulate because he could not be convincingly given the self-conscious intelligence of a Hamlet or the eloquence of persons in the more formal tragedies of the past.

Articulateness on the part of the characters was indeed very much the concern of the modernists, for, as critics impatient with prose in the theatre tend to forget, verse-drama had become quite decadent in the nineteenth century before it was abandoned. (Nor was it abandoned so absolutely that an Ibsen, Hauptmann, or Maxwell Anderson would not go back to verse.) Pioneers of the modern theatre found it necessary to reject verse and rhetorical prose not merely for the sake of "fourth-wall" verisimilitude, but for the sake of simple artistic integrity. They could not countenance the customary use of eloquence as a screen for hollow content and commonplace feeling and thought. The decision to write prose-drama was the result of clear deliberation on Ibsen's part. The author of *Brand* and *Peer Gynt* laid aside a considerable reputation as a poet and a hard-won success as a playwright when he entered upon the realistic and prose part of his career in his fiftieth year. That his prose in *A Doll's House* and the plays that followed became a very powerful instrument demonstrating the mental and emotional processes of his characters is evident even in translation. The planning of the dialogue, the verbal exchanges between the speakers, the innuendo or double-meaning of many a line, and the stress on key words and phrases do not indicate indifference to the role of language in the drama. The cumulative effect of his and other writers spare dialogue could provide the articulateness that had previously been allocated to the set speeches, harangues, and soliloquies of characters in the pre-realistic drama. Motivations could be found, moreover, for some distinctly infectious speeches when characters addressed an assembly or summarized a passionately held conviction. Ibsen's successors, among whom there were such masters of dialogue as Shaw and O'Casey, continued to prove that prose could be written for the theatre with compelling *brio*. Many a verse-drama of the past three centuries sounds exceedingly flat with its familiar tropes and metronomic regularity by comparison with the verbal explosions of modern realistic and expressionist plays. And to dramatic excitement could be added a variety of effects capable of lending nuance, poetic reverberation, and Chekhovian counterpoint. Peasant dialect, as in the plays of Synge, could be relied upon to yield a new music and a new imagery for the theatre, as could even the colloquialism of the city-streets. And symbolism could be imbedded in the soil of realism whenever a playwright was capable of composing a *Rosmersholm* and *The Master Builder*.

Nor does the search for a poetically charged prose exhaust the effort to ensure expressiveness on the modern stage. Developments in physical production and in the art of acting have contributed imaginativeness and power to the stage. We have supplemented the verbal element of the drama with the so-called *poésie de théatre*, ever since the turn of the century when Gordon Craig called for expressive stage design and Stanislavsky for *inner* realism in acting. The masters of this "poetry of the theatre" could give scenic atmosphere and visual symbolization to a tragic action. "A good scene design should not be a picture but an image," wrote Craig's American disciple Robert Edmond Jones, and it could create "an expectancy, a foreboding, a tension" in the theatre. That acting could add emotional depth and dramatic stature to a playwright's character was evident, of course, whenever a Duse or Nazimova played an Ibsen part.

Finally, we should not overlook the modern playwright's search for new dramatic form, especially in the turbulent expressionist mode which is marked by fantastic invention, explosive dialogue, and expressive distortion of scenes and characters. There have been expressionist attempts to write tragedy as well as realistic ones, ever since the turn of the century. Playwrights who gravitated toward expressionism tended to concern themselves with such contemporary themes as the Oedipus complex, the alienation of the individual in a cheapened world, and the crises of war and revolution. One could maintain indeed that the boundaries of tragic art were extended by the adoption of modern expressionist technique in such plays as *The Spook Sonata, The Hairy Ape*, and *Death of a Salesman*, as well as by naturalistic presentations of character and environment that closed a ring of inevitability around the dramatic action of the individual. If this argument does not at all prove that modern playwrights have written better tragedies than Sophocles and Shakespeare did (and the reverse is obviously the case), it does suggest that modernity may be relieved of the charge that it has extinguished the art of tragedy—which is one more charge added to the general indictment of our civilization or, rather, of the democratic and scientific spirit.

III

To mediate between the conflicting claims of the pro-modern and anti-modern factions is no easy matter. The value we place on specific works is the first and last consideration. There is no difficulty in claiming that the modern age can produce tragedy if we are prepared to qualify a considerable number of modern plays as "tragedies." And, conversely, it is easy enough to maintain that the modern spirit cannot support tragic writing once we disqualify them.

An agile disputant can easily sustain his aristocratic distaste for the world of the common man by invalidating almost any modern play. All he has to do is to insist on absolute standards of high tragedy derived from a few masterpieces of the past and prove that the modern work deviates from them. He can then protest, often with good reason, that the hero of some particular play written since *A Doll's House* lacks the magnitude of mind or spirit that could give him the "tragic stature" needed to dignify humanity even in the character's descent from grace and fall from good fortune. With respect to many a modern stage character from Ibsen's Oswald Alving to O'Neill's "Yank" and Miller's Willy Loman it has been possible for very intelligent critics to say, with Henry James, that "Our curiosity and our sympathy care comparatively little for what happens to the stupid, the coarse, and the blind." The critic may indeed multiply his strictures without ever being entirely wrong. The plays may impress him as depressing rather than exalting, and as topical rather than universal. They may also strike him as too prosaic, too intellectual or too unintellectual, too active or too passive, too optimistic or two pessimistic. Any one of these attributes can be easily identified, torn out of context, and used to invalidate the tragic status of such modern pieces as *Ghosts, Hedda Gabler, The Father, The Power of Darkness, The Lower Depths, The Hairy Ape, Desire Under the Elms, Mourning Becomes Electra, The Iceman Cometh*—and even *Saint Joan*. Advocates of a scrupulously restricted category of tragedy would probably certify only plays produced at some remove from the liberal-scientific spirit or deliberately set against it. They would certify peasant drama set in regions remote from our industrial civilization such as Synge's Aran Islands, off the west coast of Ireland, or Lorca's Spanish countryside. They would also qualify formally structured plays, preferably suggestive of ritual and rooted in theology or in myth: Among these would be Eliot's *Murder in the Cathedral* and *Family Reunion*, some short poetic pieces by Yeats patterned after medieval Japanese drama, and a few antirealistic French plays such as Giraudoux' *Electra* and Cocteau's *The Infernal Machine*, which one young American enthusiast recently recommended to us as *the* model for modern tragedy. To this, one may add a genre of neo-romantic verse-drama represented by Maxwell Anderson's Elizabethan trilogy, *Elizabeth the Queen, Mary of Scotland, Anne of the Thousand Days*, and his *Winterset*—plays well patterned after a conventional tragic blueprint.

A strenuous exponent of the realistic and more or less liberal persuasion, however, could, in turn, cut a good deal of the ground from under the literary opposition. Turning to specific works, he could show, for instance, that Anderson's achievement in the historical field, and similar achievements in other countries, are tragic only by rote, posture, and imitation. He could maintain, too, that *Winterset*, despite its powerful second act, was only factitiously tragic; that it consists of a forced marriage between poetic rhetoric and gangster melodrama, and that the playwright evades his Sacco and Vanzetti theme with rather transparent borrowings from *Hamlet* and *Romeo and Juliet*. These animadversions would probably win the endorsement of members of the literary élite of our day, since they have even less use than the liberal realists for popular romanticism. But the latter would promptly turn on their allies to remind them that literary formalism, too, has proved vain. On the one hand, we have had the example of so great a poet as Yeats withdrawing from the modern drama in order to compose tragic one-act plays intended for private performance, an admittedly thin harvest for the man who had helped to establish the Abbey Theatre and had discovered Synge and O'Casey for the Irish national stage. On the other hand, we have had the example of Cocteau and other French sophisticates leaning toward contrived tragicality and arriving at cleverness or virtuosity in the theatre much more conclusively than they have arrived at tragedy. And the argument would gravitate toward T. S. Eliot, the high priest of anti-modernism in our time, who abandoned the rigors of high tragedy with *The Cocktail Party* and edged closer to Noel Coward than Sophocles with drawing-room lines and scenes. This after having composed two tragedies with a marked ritualistic and theological basis, *Murder in the Cathedral* and *Family Reunion*, which owed a good deal to Shaw and Coward respectively in virtually all scenes in which the plays came to life as theatre. It will be apparent, then, that the uncertainties of tragic writing in the present world are not altogether on one side. And if the peril of trying to write tragedies under the modern liberal dispensation is an unliterary descent into *banality*, the peril of creating it under any other dispensation is a literary ascent into *futility*.

Which is the greater evil cannot be determined, I suppose, without bias. (My own is, on the whole, democratic, while that of some men of letters for whom I have entertained the greatest admiration is largely aristocratic.) Nevertheless the two factions are not fated to remain completely apart, and there are areas of agreement available to reasonable exponents of either viewpoint. The "liberals" can agree that variable degrees of inadequacy have attended the efforts of O'Neill, Ibsen, and the sociological playwrights to produce tragic literature, while "conservatives" have been known to concede some measure of tragic power to Ibsen, Strindberg, and O'Casey. It would certainly appear from the divergent enthusiasms of the partisans that, in one way or another, it has been possible to write tragic drama—that is, some clearly definable tragedies and many plays more or less tragic in feeling such as Chekhov's *The Three Sisters*.

Agreement could be reached especially if we first noted that there are degrees of tragic ascent today and that some are more favored than others. And this should not disturb us particularly, for there were, after all, degrees of tragic ascent even in the great ages of tragic literature—as we may observe, for instance, by comparing Sophocles' *Electra* with Euripides' *Electra* or *Macbeth* with *Richard II*. Modern playwriting is apt to fall into a category of "middle tragedy" or perhaps "low tragedy" instead of "high tragedy," a term suitable for some (and only for some) of the tragic pieces of the Attic, Elizabethan, and French neo-classic periods of the theatre. With agreement on this subject, we could then settle down to the essential business of encouraging and creating the plays, regardless of degree, that may best express the tragic and near-tragic understanding of which we are capable in our time and place.

We may also arrive at the conclusion that there is really no compelling reason for the modern stage to *strain* toward tragedy. There are other ways of responding to the human condition. There is, for one thing, the time-honored way of comedy. Shaw followed it so creditably in his so-called comedies of ideas that his plays have overshadowed the work of many a tragedian of modern, Victorian, or Elizabethan times. The writing of comedies is as serious a business as the writing of tragedies; comedy, too, constitutes a criticism of life, incorporates values, and affords a catharsis. The comic viewpoint is at least as relevant as the tragic to man's life in society and perhaps even more representative of human conduct. Nor does the comic playwright have to spare us glimpses into the abyss of human nature or encounters with what Nietzsche called "the terrible wisdom of Silenus." Comedy is an art of notable variety, and its complexion runs from light to dark and from sweet to bitter.

There is also the way of *drame*, of serious drama without tragic pretensions. Many provocative social and psychological dramas as diversified as *Awake and Sing* and *The Children's Hour*, as well as imaginative works such as *Our Town* and *The Skin of Our Teeth*, have filled a place in our theatre without conveniently fitting into pigeonholes of tragedy. Generally, indeed, our age has found its sensibility and mood most adequately expressed by amalgamations of grave and comic writing. We have been partial to a mixed genre represented at its best, perhaps, by several of Chekhov's masterpieces, although "mixed drama" is not at all exhausted by Chekhov's highly individual style. We can only conclude that if plays such as *The Cherry Orchard, Heartbreak House, Juno and the Paycock, The Glass Menagerie,* and *Six Characters in Search of an Author* have not conformed to any blueprints of tragedy (and there was no intention on their author's part to achieve such conformity), this has been no loss to the theatre of our century. It is the value of the specific work and not the *genre* that really and finally matters to the playgoer, and not to prefer a distinguished non-tragic composition to an undistinguished tragic one would be pedantry rather than responsible criticism.

Tragedies of one kind or another have been contributory to the interest and power of the modern theatre. But the creative spirit of an age should be allowed, and indeed expected, to engender its own dramatic forms or to modify existent ones. Overawed, it would seem, by premises and promises of tragic grandeur, playwrights from D'Annunzio to Maxwell Anderson (nor would I acquit O'Neill when he composed *Dynamo* and *Lazarus Laughed* or Miller when he wrote *A View from the Bridge*) have strained too much to produce standardized high tragedy with a contemporary fillip of interest. They would have been well advised to leave some tragic motifs and trappings alone, and they should have refrained from endeavoring to lift some of their characters and situations out of the non-tragic categories that would have suited them better. Critics and scholars have been prone to compound confusion for playwrights by harping on categories of drama, glorifying one of these above all others, and paying insufficient heed to the fact that tragedy has been infrequently produced throughout the ages and rarely in pure form. And since everybody has been infected at some time or other with the desire to see the modern drama live beyond its spiritual income, it may yet become necessary to stress the perils rather than the possibilities of tragedy.

A Rejection of Tragedy: Brecht*

Raymond Williams

The rejection of tragedy has many motives and takes many forms. In the case of Bertolt Brecht, we find at least two kinds of rejection, in different periods of his work, and we find also a series of experiments towards new dramatic forms. In this complicated development, the response to suffering is crucial. Brecht wrote in his poem, *An Die Nachgeborenen*:

> Indeed I live in the dark ages!
> A guileless word is an absurdity. A smooth forehead betokens
> A hard heart. He who laughs
> Has not yet heard
> The terrible tidings . . .
>
> I came to the cities in a time of disorder
> When hunger ruled.
> I came among men in a time of uprising
> And I revolted with them.
> So the time passed away
> Which on earth was given me.
>
> I ate my food between massacres.
> The shadow of murder lay upon my sleep.
> And when I loved, I loved with indifference.
> I looked upon nature with impatience.
> So the time passed away
> Which on earth was given me.
>
> In my time streets led to the quicksand.
> Speech betrayed me to the slaughterer.
> There was little I could do. But without me
> The rulers would have been more secure. This was my hope.

Here, clearly enough, is a consciousness of the weight of suffering, in the modern tragedy of Europe, which is not hyperbole but is precise and literal.

The variety of response to this weight, which we have all, though not equally, borne, is a key to our literature. Brecht lived at least two of its modes: here the identification of a political system as a main cause of suffering, and the find-

* Raymond Williams, *Modern Tragedy* (Stanford University Press; London: Chatto and Windus, 1966) pp. 190–204. Copyright © 1966 by Raymond Williams.

ing of hope in the fight against it. But it was not always so. In his early work, Brecht expressed, with characteristic power, one of the main alternative reactions: a cynical disillusion about the coexistence of public virtue and public murder, public morality and public poverty. In his work of the 1920s we find the characteristic sickness of a mind calloused by so established a coexistence. It is not the callousing of acquiescence, as it has been with a majority of men. It is rather the deliberate hardening against open sympathy, the sealing and covering of a too naked tenderness. If the substance of suffering enters, with its natural weight, the spectator will be broken, for he will become a participant. Yet as a participant, he can only condemn or comprehend the suffering by some active principle, and this he cannot find. Principle, it seems, is part of the world he rejects. An evil system is protected by a false morality. This balance is always delicate, and it can seem easier and clearer to turn, not against the system, but against the morality. Then the fact that the morality is part of the callousing leads to a bitter irony:

> You see, my business is trying to arouse human pity. There are a few things that'll move people to pity, a few, but the trouble is, when they've been used several times, they no longer work. Human beings have the horrid capacity of being able to make themselves heartless at will. So it happens, for instance, that a man who sees another man on the street corner with only a stump for an arm will be so shocked the first time that he'll give him sixpence. But the second time it'll be only a threepenny bit. And if he sees him a third time, he'll hand him over cold-bloodedly to the police. It's the same with these spiritual weapons.
>
> [*A large board is let down from the flies and on it is written: 'It is more blessed to give than to receive'.*]
>
> What's the use of the finest and most stirring sayings painted on the most enticing boards if they get used up so quickly? There are four or five sayings in the Bible that really touch the heart. But when they're used up, one's daily bread's just gone.

The operative irony, here, is that this is Peachum, in *The Threepenny Opera*, using pity as a trade, in his establishment for beggars. But the structural irony is deeper, and more easily overlooked. The assumption that human beings can and do 'make themselves heartless at will' is not only the complaint of the speculator who is exploiting pity. It is also the outraged but controlling assumption of the dramatist, and so the spring of his characteristic tone. Pity and suffering can deceive anyone, if men are like this. And if sympathy can exploit us, it is the last thing we must admit.

The perversion of values, by a false system, can go so deep only a new and bitter hardness seems relevant. Instead of sympathy, there must be direct shock. In Brecht's plays of the 1920s there is a raw chaotic resentment, a hurt so deep that it requires new hurting, a sense of outrage which demands that people be outraged. So deep is this that it is often expressed in the crudest physical imagery: a revulsion from spit and excrement which demands the exposure and the handling of both; a revulsion from false loving which leads straight to the whore. Many writers have used this simple exposure of dirt, this conscious turning to whores and criminals, as a way of expressing the tragic collapse of virtue. In Joyce, Mayakowsky and Brecht the same patterns of attraction and disgust are clear. In much *avant-garde* writing between the wars, and especially in the 1920s, the naming of filth and the open gesture of anti-morality were felt as creative. Brecht is more open than most, both in his gestures and in his marginal capacity for a different kind of response. *The Threepenny Opera*, for example, is offered or rationalised as a portrait of respectable bourgeois society. If all property is theft, and the institutions of property cold and false, then thieves and whores are the true if shocking portraits of a society trying to pass itself off as respectable. The shock of seeing this will penetrate the established false consciousness.

It does nothing of the kind, of course, and it is not difficult to see why. Nothing is more predictable, in a falsely respectable society, than the conscious enjoyment of a controlled and distanced low life. All such work reveals itself, finally, as a protection of conventional moral attitudes. The thieves and whores are the licensed types, on to whom a repressed immorality can very easily be projected, and through whom a repressed conscience can be safely controlled. There is no real shock, when respectable playgoers confront them, because they are seen, precisely, as a special class, a district. So we get, again and again, the consciously outrageous which nobody even pretends to be outraged by, but simply settles back to enjoy.

Brecht, in *The Threepenny Opera*, was caught in his own paradox. The more people sat back and enjoyed this kind of action, the safer their ordinary view of life was. When the play was published, he wrote:

> It is a sort of summary of what the spectator wishes to see of life. Since, however, he sees at the same time certain things that he does not wish to see and thus sees his wishes not only fulfilled but criticised . . . he is, in theory, able to give the theatre a new function[1]. . . . Complex seeing must be practised. . . . Thinking *above* the flow of the play is more important than thinking from *within* the flow of the play.

'In theory' is right. Brecht had found his theory, in the idea of complex seeing, but its practice was not there, in the actual play. He had considered that his 'epic style' would enforce 'thinking *above*', whereas the 'narrative style' of 'Aristotelian drama' (these terms make no historical or critical sense, but they are the manifesto terms of Brecht's own creative development) enforced 'thinking from *within*'. He had used distancing effects to push the spectator into 'the attitude of one who smokes at ease and watches'. But he was himself still confused, himself not distanced, and there was more ease than either watching or thinking. The play in fact fitted easily into 'what the spectator wishes to see': crime and coldness not structural in the society, but lived out in a romantic and theatrical district. Of course many speculators, accepted in their generation as writers and artists, have agencies in this district: making crime and vice theatrical, colourful, and in a simple way distanced, so that a false society can avoid having to look at itself. Brecht, I suppose, was never one of them, but he settled, for a time, in a neighbouring district, in which suffering also is masked. He settled for a conventionally dissident pattern of feeling, in which he still has company: the bitter-sweet professional who faced with an immoral society can display immorality as a kind of truth. People buy and sell each other, in *The Threepenny Opera* and on screens and pages beyond counting, with cold hearts and only occasionally

---

[1] Brecht, like nearly all important dramatists in the past hundred years, knew that a 'new function' for the theatre was *resisted* most strongly by 'the theatre itself': 'today we see the theatre being given absolute priority over the actual plays. The theatre apparatus's priority is a priority of means of production. This apparatus resists all conversion to other purposes, by taking any play which it encounters and immediately changing it so that it no longer represents a foreign body within the apparatus. The theatre can stage anything; it theatres it all down'.

covering sentiments, but always with colour, with wit, with the big musical number. And yes, of course, that's life; for who, while the number lasts, finds the nerve to say 'that shouldn't be life', 'that needn't be life'? When he does find the words, he's naive anyway, and a moraliser. But the actual moral is that we can all pretend to be livelier and brighter than we are, dispensing the cold-hearted muck about the warmhearted whores and engaging crooks who at least are *honest*, who have seen through hypocrisy, who have lived past the earnestness of the old quotations.

In ways like this, the writer who 'shocks', by his rejection of 'conventional morality', becomes rich and admired, and this is no paradox: he has done the State some service, even when he is disposed to deny it. Human wrong has been sealed off. Human suffering is a sick old joke. There is even a kind of moral stability, now that outrage itself is lapsed to a convention. Except that the callousing can become so general that a more openly vicious society can go on with its business of enforcing stability, of violent protection against change, unchallenged, since the moral reserve is deliberately played out.

Fascism, the ultimate protection of propertied society against radical change, fed on much of this bittersweet toughness. What had been imagined and conventionalised could now be done. But not, in the end, by Brecht. He was able to grow quite differently. He thought he had seen through the conventional establishment: that kind of seeing-through which is a parody of opposition and revolt. The society was false and the moralising hypocritical; so. But he came to realise that at this point you have really seen nothing, seen through nothing. For what you have seen is what the society wants you to see: 'eats first, morals after'. Brecht thought he was detaching himself from this by calling it bourgeois morality, but in *The Threepenny Opera* this is so external, so really casual, that it is in effect an indulgence. The displacement of feelings about modern capitalism on to a group of pseudo-eighteenth century thieves and whores is no more than an escape clause. The real detachment, the real distancing, required a new principle and a new start.

In the idea of 'complex seeing' Brecht had his new start, but under the pressure of danger he moved, for a time, in a different direction. He set himself to oppose false society by the idea of a true society, and in his first conscious acceptance of this principled opposition he simplified both his feelings and his plays. The linking work is *Saint Joan of the Stockyards*, where the charity of Joan Dark in the labour struggles of Chicago is not only shown as a false morality, covering crime and exploitation, but as a feeling to be consciously rejected and replaced by a new hardness:

> The ones that tell them they may be raised in spirit
> And still be stuck in the mud, they should have their heads
> Knocked on the pavement. No!
> Only force helps where force rules. . . .

For saying this, Joan is of course first suppressed and then canonised, in her former charitable innocence. Something of the later complexity is briefly present. But the new positive line soon takes over. In *Die Massnahme* Brecht offers what he takes to be a revolutionary morality: that the party worker who shows too much human sympathy (being moved by the presence of suffering to an attempt at alleviation and partial reform) endangers the revolutionary effort and must be killed. But this is not any dialectical transformation of goodness into its opposite.

It is a willing rejection of goodness as it is immediately known. We must say of this play what Orwell said of Auden's line in *Spain*:

> *The conscious acceptance of guilt in the necessary murder.* . . . It could only be written by a person to whom murder is at most a *word*.[1]

The complicated issues of revolutionary violence cannot be settled by a simple formula, either way. The weight of the choice of killing is, in experience, tragic. But its reduction to a hard formalised gesture is merely wilful. Indeed, the most important thing to be said about such a gesture is not political, but cultural. This brittle literary voice, which can set a tone towards killing that appears antiromantic, is simply the perverted romanticism of the earlier uncommitted decadence. As a literary line, it follows directly from the bittersweet amoralism, sharing with it a persuasive capacity to keep real experience at a distance. The literary revolutionary, with his tough talk of necessary killing, turns out in fact to be our former acquaintance: the honest criminal or the generous whore. This connection between the decadence and what was supposed to be a positive response to it has been widely and dangerously overlooked.

The extraordinary thing about Brecht is that he was able to grow through this position. Relapse from it is easy, as the later Auden has shown. The emphasis of love can look like growth, but is often a simple withdrawal from the human action in which love is being affirmed and fought for. Love is then defined and capitalised in separation from humanity. Brecht, however, learned to look beyond either formula, into the genuine complexity: the connections and contradictions between individual goodness and social action. It was this dimension of experience and perception which required his method of complex seeing. His first achievement, in this new kind, was *Mother Courage and her Children*, but it will be convenient, in describing the method, to look first at *The Good Woman of Sezuan*.

In this play Brecht invites us to look at what happens to a good person in a bad society: not by assertion, but by a dramatic demonstration. Shen Te is linked to some of his earlier figures in that she first appears as the conventional kindhearted prostitute (in an alienated society the most alienated person is good). But this is almost incidental to the main action. Brecht seeks to show, through Shen Te, how goodness is exploited, by gods and men. Where goodness cannot extend, but is merely used and abused, there is a split in consciousness. The only consistent way out is through sacrifice: an acceptance of sacrifice which can become redeeming, as in Christ. Brecht rejected any such acceptance, as he similarly rejected the idea that suffering can ennoble us. Christ, after all, was the son of God as well as the son of Man, and the significance of his action depends ultimately on a superhuman design. Rejecting the superhuman design, Brecht had the courage to reject sacrifice as a dramatic emotion. For even sacrifice is used, in the

---

[1] There are other things to say about Auden's line and Orwell's description of it. Murder is usually either a personal act or part of a specifically criminal pattern. There are, of course, political murders, but these are only one aspect of the general fact of political violence. Auden is simplifying, perhaps deliberately, to the norms of his own world, but so, in another way, is Orwell. It is interesting to imagine the line rewritten as 'the conscious acceptance of guilt in the necessary killing' and then ask how many people, in reality, dissent from this. Most people I know, and most humane liberals I have heard of, accept killing in this sense again and again: from Dresden to Hiroshima, and from Stanleyville to Da Nang. If Auden got his commitment too easily and cheaply, Orwell and others have got their humane dissent on much the same terms.

continuing human game (it had been used, he might have seen, in *Die Mass-nahme*). The ratifying fact about the martyr is that he is dead. Life can pass him by with a timeserving bob to his nobility. And just as it is a bad society that needs heroes, so it is a bad life that needs sacrifices. By a change of dramatic view-point, we have to look not only at the isolated experience of the martyr, but at the social process of his martyrdom. For this is where we live, we who are not martyrs. And at this point we reach the profoundly ambiguous question: is it not a sin against life to allow oneself to be destroyed by cruelty and indifference and greed?

Brecht's mature drama works continually around this question. In *The Good Woman of Sezuan* goodness, under pressure, turns into its opposite, and then back again, and then both coexist. For the individual person, the dilemma is beyond solution. And this is conveyed with simplicity and power in Shen Te's transformation of herself into her tough male cousin, Shui Ta, who is first a dis-guise but then in effect takes on an independent existence. Thus the experience is generalised within an individual. It is not the good person against the bad, but goodness and badness as alternative expressions of a single being. This is complex seeing, and it is deeply integrated with the dramatic form: the character who lives this way and then that, enacting choice and requiring decision. No resolu-tion is imposed. The tension is there to the end, and we are formally invited to consider it. The ordinary responses which we might use to cover the tension are clearly expressed by the other characters, so that we can discover their inade-quacy while the tension is still there to see. The methods of expressionist drama, which had normally been used to manifest this breaking tension within a single consciousness, are here extended to examination, where they normally stop short at exposure. Brecht has in fact transformed that method of special pleading which insists on the spectator seeing the world through the actions and tensions of a single mind. He achieves this transformation by deliberate generalisation and by the appeal to impersonal judgement. He grows through the ordinary decadence of the form (which had been rationalised in a theory of art as expo-sure, all other intentions being defined as impure), and grows through also the crude reply of didacticism. The play becomes, in its essential movement, a moral action.

Yet *The Good Woman of Sezuan* remains a minor play, because the sub-stance of this moral action is not so much created as given. It is in *Mother Cour-age and her Children* that he finds a new kind of dramatic action which creates a substance comparable in intensity with the moral inquiry. To call this action Shakespearean is not to put the praise too high. History and people come alive on the stage, leaping past the isolated and virtually static action that we have got used to in most modern theatre. The drama simultaneously occurs and is seen. It is not 'take the case of this woman' but 'see and consider what happens to these people'.

Criticism of the play has usually got off on the wrong track by starting with the question whether Mother Courage, as a person, is meant to be admired or despised. But the point is not what we feel about her hard lively opportunism; it is what we see, in the action, of its results. By enacting a genuine consequence, Brecht raises his central question to a new level, both dramatically and intellec-tually (though in the play there is no such separation). The question drives through the continuing action: what else can we do, here, where blind power is loose, but submit, chisel, try to play safe? And then by doing these things—either submitting and pretending to virtue, or submitting and cheating round the back—a family, see, is destroyed. The question is then no longer 'are they good people?' (the decision taken before or after the play). Nor is it, really, 'what should they have done?' It is, brilliantly, both 'what are they doing?' and 'what is this doing to them?'

All Brecht's dramatic skill is deployed to lead us to these essential questions. The contradictions in the characters—that they are sometimes hard, sometimes generous, and so on—are real, but they exist not only as personal qualities; they exist also in the play as a whole. The action is continually open, through the fact of these contradictions. It is not the inevitability of tragedy, as in the traditional tragic acceptance or the modern tragic resignation. The choices are made in a dimension that is always potential, and so the action is continually played and replayed. It could genuinely go either way, at any time. The action of consequence is intrinsically human, and in no way external:

So we shall all be torn in two if we let ourselves get too deep in this war.

But not torn once, torn again and again. Much of the speech is then the play speaking, drawing strength from its characters but also moving beyond them.

> CHAPLAIN: Mother Courage, I see how you got your name.
> MOTHER COURAGE: The poor need courage. They're lost, that's why. That they even get up in the morning is something, in *their* plight. Or that they plough a field, in wartime. Even their bringing children into the world shows they have courage, for they have no prospects. They have to hang each other one by one and slaughter each other in the lump, so if they want to look each other in the face once in a while, well, it takes courage.

At the level of direct comment, this is, in summary, the dramatic action. But at the same time the naming of courage, and of Mother Courage, extends its scope. We need this woman if we are to look ourselves, and her, in the face. The drama, with this character at its centre, is a way of looking at a continual action.

Mother Courage and her Children is a dramatisation of conflicting instincts, conflicting illusions, and commanding insights that are not, but might be, lived through. Its crisis is properly reached in the frantic drumming of the dumb girl: a desperate articulation of the blood, to protect the city. The final paradox is genuinely tragic: the dumb girl, speaking for life, and being killed; the living going on with a living that kills; the final song of the soldiers

> And though you may not long survive
> Get out of bed and look alive.

It is action illuminated by a tragic consciousness, in contrast with *The Life of Galileo*, where the consciousness is the action.

Galileo is fully conscious, and to that extent free, in ways that the pressed and the driven are not. In abstraction, the choice presented to him looks the same: accept our terms or be destroyed. But in detail the choice is quite different. Because he is conscious, he can not only foresee consequence and calculate it. He stands also for more than himself. In his own person, he is reason and liberation.

Once again, the question is not: 'should we admire or despise Galileo?'. Brecht is not asking this. He is asking what happens to consciousness when it is caught in the deadlock between individual and social morality. Galileo's submission can be rationalised and justified, at the individual level, as a way of gaining time to go on with his work. But the point this misses is what the work is for. If the purpose of science is that all men can learn to understand their world, Galileo's betrayal is fundamental. To detach the work from its human purpose is, Brecht sees, to betray others and so betray life. It is not, in the end, what we think of Galileo as a man, but what we think of this result.

The play brings this issue to consciousness, not as a problem, but as a living action. It is sometimes said that Brecht's Marxism was a handicap or at best an irrelevance to his drama. Yet it is just in this way of looking at the world that the dramatic action resides. We are used to martyrdom, and to the individual in conflict with his society. But we are not used to this radically different way of seeing an experience that is normally negotiated by these older conventions:

> Could we deny ourselves to the crowd and still remain scientists? The movements of the stars have become clearer; but to the mass of the people the movements of their masters are still incalculable. . . . With time you may discover all that is to be discovered, and your progress will only be a progression away from mankind. The gulf between you and them can one day become so great that your cry of jubilation over some new achievement may be answered by a universal cry of horror.

It is true that, trained to a different consciousness, we struggle to reduce the play to a different meaning, or, more plausibly, argue that this explicit conclusion is only there in this one speech and is not in the play as a whole. But of course we come to the story of Galileo with our own powerful image of the liberal martyr, and have real difficulty in seeing what is being actually presented. Certainly the play itself is explicit, through all its action. It is not only Galileo but the play that speaks. Thus Galileo's first speech sets the terms of the subsequent moral action:

> The most solemn truths are being tapped on the shoulder; what was never doubted is now in doubt. And because of that a great wind has arisen, lifting even the gold-embroidered coat-tails of princes and prelates, so that the fat legs and the thin legs underneath are seen; legs like our legs. . . . I predict that in our lifetimes astronomy will be talked about in the market-places. Even the sons of fishwives will go to school.

And then this is followed in the next scene, that of the presentation of the telescope, by this speech of the Curator of the Grand Arsenal of Venice:

> Once again a page of fame in the great book of the arts is embellished with Venetian characters. A scholar of world repute here presents to you, and to you alone, a highly saleable cylinder to manufacture and put on the market in any way you please. And has it occurred to you that in wartime by means of this instrument we shall be able to distinguish the build and number of an enemy's ships a full two hours earlier than he can descry ours?

The opposition is hardly too subtle to be seen. If we miss it, it is because we are resolutely interested in something else. The final scene, in which the manuscript of the *Discorsi* crosses the border, looks like a romantic liberation, unless we see also that the boys playing round the coach are still talking of witches.

The *coexistence* of these facts is always the point: the more moved we are by the one, the more ashamed we must be of the other. Galileo, committed to a universal and humanist view of science, has been trapped by another view: the imperatives of a different loyalty, to the ruling group that maintains him, to produce for the market and for war. It is not that as an individual he is a hypocrite. It is that under real pressures he embodies both a true consciousness and a false consciousness; the fact of their coexistence is what Brecht invites us to see. The movement of the play is from the ironic acceptance of false consciousness—what you say to get by, in an imperfect world—to the point where false consciousness becomes false action and is not irony but tragedy. It is like Mother Courage, who picked up her cart but to go on to the war.

In the end it is not only complex seeing. It is a very complex kind of feeling. Tragedy in some of its older senses is certainly rejected. There is nothing inevitable or ennobling about this kind of failure. It is a matter of human choice, and the choice is not once for all; it is a matter of continuing history. The major achievement of Brecht's mature work is this recovery of history as a dimension for tragedy. The sense of history becomes active through the discovery of methods of dramatic movement, so that the action is not single in space and time and certainly not 'permanent and timeless'. Struggling always with his own fixed consciousness, Brecht could only begin this transformation. But his epic theatre is at once a recovery of very early elements in the humanist drama of the Renaissance, where this capacity for historic action seemed at its full creative power, and a remaking of these elements in a modern mind. Continually limited by his own weaknesses, by his opportunism, which often comes through as dramatic cheating, and by his vestigial jeering and coarseness (the real dregs of his time and ours) he struggled towards a transformation and in part achieved it. Instead of trying to convert his work to the complacencies of our fashionable despair, or more easily to the grossness of our defensive cynicism, we should try to see what it means to drama when in recovering a sense of history and of the future a writer recovers the means of an action that is both complex and dynamic.

In most modern drama, the best conclusion is: yes, this is how it was. Only an occasional play goes further, with the specific excitement of recognition: yes, this is how it is. Brecht, at his best, reaches out to and touches the necessary next stage: yes, this is how it is, for these reasons, but the action is continually being replayed, and it could be otherwise.

The trap, at this last moment, is the wrong kind of emphasis on the undoubted fact that it could indeed be otherwise. To make it already otherwise, by selecting the facts and by subtly reducing the pressures, is to go over to propaganda or to advertising. We are committed to an actual process, and to seeing not only this movement but also that, so that not only this but also that must be said. We have to see not only that suffering is avoidable, but that it is not avoided. And not only that suffering breaks us, but that it need not break us. Brecht's own words are the precise expression of this new sense of tragedy:

> The sufferings of this man appal me, because they are unnecessary.

This feeling extends into a general position: the new tragic consciousness of all those who, appalled by the present, are *for this reason* firmly committed to a different future: to the struggle against suffering learned in suffering: a total exposure which is also a total involvement. Under the weight of failure, in tragedy that could have been avoided but was not avoided, this structure of feeling is now struggling to be formed. Against the fear of a general death, and against the loss of connection, a sense of life is affirmed, learned as closely in suffering as ever in joy, once the connections are made. The affirmation begins where Brecht ended, in his poem *An die Nachgeborenen*:

For we knew only too well:
Even the hatred of squalor
Makes the brow grow stern.
Even anger against injustice
Makes the voice grow harsh. Alas, we
Who wished to lay the foundations of kindness
Could not ourselves be kind.

In a continuing action—the word to posterity—such a recognition is absolute. It is the reality, in our time, of the struggle for happiness. But as a fixed position, in the manner of the early Brecht to which it is sometimes assimilated, it quickly degenerates, yet again, into a professional hardening: not the recognition but the acceptance of contradiction.

The recognition is a matter of history, the known harshness of the revolutionary struggle. But while this is seen as a process it can be lived through, resolved, changed. Whereas if it is seen, even briefly, as a fixed position—an abstract condition of man or of revolution—it becomes a new alienation, an exposure stopped short of involvement, a tragedy halted and generalised at the shock of catastrophe. In our own day, in a known complexity, it is the fixed harshness of a revolutionary regime which has turned to arrest the revolution itself, but which finds, facing its men turned to stone, the children of the struggle who because of the struggle live in new ways and with new feelings, and who, including the revolution in their ordinary living, answer death and suffering with a human voice.

Tragedy Now[*]

Walter Kerr

Twentieth-century man's continuing fear of the freedoms he has won for himself effectively prevents him not from pursuing those freedoms but from presenting himself on the stage or in any other art form as muscular champion of
the defiant advance. He labors steadily but speaks softly of himself, terrified lest
an excess of action betray a weakness he has not uncovered yet, rather inclined
to believe that the end of his researches will reveal him not a power in his own
right but the product of an ancestry and an unconscious that dominate him in a
manner more demonic than godlike.

How long this cringing posture that prohibits tragedy, this disbelief in a
boldly achieved mutation that may prove to be "good," will endure no one can
say. The ordinary materials of tragedy lie about us, but are untouched. Anyone
who has glanced, say, at Gene Smith's *When the Cheering Stopped* will recognize in it instantly the most conventional of all tragic outlines. Woodrow Wilson
has embarked with the best of intentions upon an entirely worthy course: the
evolution within our society of an instrument for outlawing war. His early successes, and the quality of his vision, have made him in many eyes something
close to a god. He nears his goal only to discover that he cannot have it on his
own terms. He must compromise, is denied his absolute. In his arrogance, which
is also dedication to an ideal, he refuses halfway measures. His refusal destroys
the possibility of the advance for which he has labored. The failure destroys him.
As he lies rejected and dying, there is an unexpected gathering in the streets.
Spontaneously, people come to cry and to pray for the defeated man who is taking on the contours of something like a "saint." In the end, after he has sacrificed himself, his vision catches hold and the evolutionary instrument he has
hoped to fashion comes into being in a new form.

In such an outline there is not only the traditional classroom formula for
tragedy: the great man who defeats himself by yielding to a flaw. There are
overtones of that larger tragic content we have been forced to take into consideration: self-assertion as an evolutionary sacrifice, followed by epiphany. But
though we are fully familiar with this action in all of its aspects, it does not occur
to us to place it upon the stage as tragedy. Literally, *it does not occur to us.* Our
habit of mind is otherwise. We do not see the narrative as a heroic exercise of
freedom, well or ill used. If we probe into its content at all, we probe for another
kind of knowledge. When, we ask, did Wilson suffer the first undetected stroke
that put him at the mercy of his arteries, that made a helpless victim of him? We

[*]Walter Kerr, "Tragedy Now," *Tragedy and Comedy* (Simon and Schuster, 1967) pp. 299–308.
Copyright © 1967 by Walter Kerr.

try to understand his arrogance as a pathological symptom, not as an intellectual conviction that he possessed the power to act absolutely. Perhaps we are quite right to do so, now that we are so much better informed about the human mechanism. But our present state of knowledge, and our acquired habits of mind, have controlled the beam of light we play over the narrative. We have specifically sought, and found, what was pathetic in it rather than what was tragic in it; we have looked for the conditioned act rather than the free act.

Are there any indications that our habits of mind are in process of being reversed? Perhaps. An impatient existentialism has forced man into the arena of free action again, through not yet in a fully tragic way. It might be better to say that existentialist philosophy has forced man to admit that he is in just such an arena, whether he knows it or not, whether he likes it or not. Man has no choice but to act, because it is only in acting that man can be said to have being. Plato had postulated being as a conceptual essence, as something prior to and independent of any individual man. First there was an idea of "man" and then there were men who corresponded to it, like so many samples. The existentialists reject this notion: existence precedes essence, and a "man" discovers who and what he is only through testing his otherwise unknown qualities in a succession of free choices. There is no matrix; there is only an experimental exploration of possibilities. Now this position in no sense relieves contemporary man of his blindness or of his fear of himself. Quite the contrary. He may be *anything*—only what he does will tell him what he is—and there are no helpful hints to guide him in earlier philosophical or religious systems; neither has he a prefabricated conscience or die-stamped instinct to supply him with information before he acts. Modern man must remain forlorn, Sartre says, "for he cannot find anything to depend upon either within or outside himself." He is alone in the universe without excuse, without given commands.

But, unpleasant as the situation may sound, there is for tragedy some small gain in this uncompromising vision. Tragedy cannot have its intended goal back: nothing is known about any "out there" to provoke a direct challenge. Certainly tragedy cannot here retrieve its sense of exerting godlike powers: in this view there is no available God to serve as a power model, and man himself is without defined resources. "For if indeed existence precedes essence, one will never be able to explain one's action by reference to a given and specific human nature," Sartre insists. Then he adds: "That is what I mean when I say that man is condemned to be free. Condemned, because he did not create himself, yet nevertheless at liberty, and from the moment that he is thrown into this world he is responsible for everything he does."

Freedom is, in this understanding, the whole of man's environment, the one and unavoidable atmosphere in which he must breathe and give himself a name. It is not presented as a precious right or as a tool to be used for intelligible advance. It is seen, rather, as a sentence to be served, as the hard labor meted out to man for the non-crime of having been born. Normally we think of the prison cell as a restraint upon freedom. Here we see the cell *as* freedom. Freedom unconfined becomes the one thing by which man is confined, the condition from which he can never escape. The pressure of infinitely open choices is immediately felt as a burden, as the same kind of nightmare and near-madness that formerly flooded in upon a man placed in solitary confinement. For the new state of awareness *is* solitary. Man is harrowingly alone, completely cut off from his equally solitary fellows, unaccountable to any structure outside himself and undefined by those limits—political or religious—which used to make him feel anchored in space by offering him a map of himself. Discovering himself mobile at the center of a void, man is not free to reject his own horrifying freedom. He must explore the void with a dizzying independence, eternally becoming himself.

The hallucinatory sensation which such a concept of freedom creates in man is readily seen in Camus' *Caligula*. Because there is no one thing which Caligula may not do, and because Caligula cannot become Caligula until he does what Caligula may do, Caligula presses his capacity for action to the extremes of his reach, deliberately and without either emotional or moral reserve. He violates the persons of others wantonly, blasphemes at will. "Before he is slain," Wallace Fowlie points out, "he experiences a nameless solitude . . ." The action has been coldly experimental in character. All possibility has been accepted. The void has been probed for boundaries without yielding any. When Caligula is destroyed, he is destroyed not by a shaped universe whose nature he has violated but by the independent action of other isolates exercising their own unlimited freedoms. When destruction comes, one senses that Caligula welcomes it. Only a vast and desperate weariness can come of never encountering a real obstacle. If we are in any way sickened by the spectacle of Caligula's excesses, he is much more sickened by the experience of exercising a freedom that can never find anything to resist it. If everything dissolves the moment a man puts a fist through it, man's only neighbor in the universe is dissolution itself.

Yet freedom is the area we have entered, and in entering it at all we have made some sort of beginning invasion of the tragic terrain. This emperor is driven mad by the discovery of the extent of his freedom; and existentialist thought is not yet prepared to make sanity of the madness by offering the tragic hero anything actual to contend with, or even to touch. In the circumstances, and by definition, the tragic hero, the play, and the experience of freedom itself must remain essentially shapeless. But to modern man, with his long-standing conviction that freedom is an illusion and his long-standing sensation of being helpless captive of a mechanical process, the very introduction of the notion must come as a reversal and a release. A tide is turning, without promising anything very pleasant; but it does say that swimming is permitted, even commanded.

Nor is the fact that this new insistence upon freedom is presented in terms of dizziness and pain in any way inimical to the promise of tragedy to come. Suffering has, of course, always been a part of the tragic scheme of things, so large a part that we have often mistaken it for the whole. But, as the tide turns, we begin to see suffering in something other than a dark and dispiriting light. As Philip Rahv says, suffering "is the price of freedom, and he who refuses to pay it can only dream of freedom without experiencing it, without substantiating it within the actual process of living." Mr. Rahv adds that this freshly sensed link between freedom and suffering is, in part at least, "close to existentialist thought."

And in his excellent introduction to the central themes of existentialist philosophy, *Irrational Man*, William Barrett makes it plain that the "condemned" man of Sartre's vision is by no means to regard himself as already executed. Rather, horror and hope are intermingled:

> Man is doomed to the radical insecurity and contingency of his being; for without it he would not be man but merely a thing and would not have the human capacity for transcendence of his given situation. There is a curious dialectical interplay here:

that which constitutes man's power and glory, that which lies at the very heart of his power to be lord over things, namely his capacity to transcend himself and his immediate situation, is at one and the same time that which causes the fragility, the wavering and flight, the anguish of our human lot.

The earlier tragic perception of the Greeks, of Shakespeare and of Racine, is not too far removed from this most contemporary sensation of doubleness, of a necessary effort at transcendence which can only be made through the surrender of all comforts, physical, emotional, and intellectual. The new need to seek identity itself which existentialism has affirmed and the emphasis placed upon free activity as the single guarantor of identity do something more than prod us toward the tragic arena of absolute action. They help man to begin to see himself as heroic once more by defining—or redefining—the essence of the heroic. In a way, we have spent three hundred years wanting to be comfortably heroic. That is to say, we have felt that we could not function as heroes unless we were coddled by a neighborly God, buoyed up by a clear pedigree, certified as clear thinkers by the possession of functioning minds that were plainly rational and not playing tricks on us. Given all, or any one, of these seals of prior approval, we might have been willing to do battle; but we did not quite see how we could issue challenges or explore absolutes without first having passed a fitness test. How could a man be a hero without a hero's license in his pocket?

What we are coming to understand is that heroism itself—any major invasion of the field of action—must be original, presumptive, exploratory, exacerbating, and possibly unrewarding. The hero is not the man who has safely survived and retired to his country estate; he is the man moving forward into a battle he may or may not survive. Heroism itself is a matter of the present tense. It is risk in action. This has always been true, of course—true of Prometheus, true of Oedipus, true of Lear—but, having seen too many monuments and watched too many triumphal parades, we forgot it. We confused the decorated survivor with the man striding blindly through mortar fire, and while our decorations were being stripped away we imagined that our capacities for entering the field were being diminished, too. We are beginning to look at free and forceful action from the point of view of the unproved, uncertain, unrecognized fledgling combatant again, and to see the battleground ahead as all menace but not beyond mastering by the man who exposes himself totally. Though the hero may be killed, he need not cringe; the hero's place is precisely where holocaust looms.

"We deal with a change in quantity," Lionel Trilling says. "It has always been true of some men that to pleasure they have preferred what the world called unpleasure. They imposed upon themselves difficult and painful tasks, they committed themselves to strange, 'unnatural' modes of life, they sought out distressing emotions, in order to know psychic energies which are not to be summoned up in felicity. These psychic energies, even when they are experienced in self-destruction, are a means of self-definition and self-affirmation." In the past the election of those freedoms which Mr. Trilling calls "unpleasure" has occurred rather rarely: "it is the choice of the hero, the saint and martyr, and, in some cultures, the artist." But "what was once a mode of experience of a few has now become an ideal of experience of many." Our awareness that pleasure, consolation, mere comfort is limiting grows rapidly. Freud noticed that vast numbers of men labored in some mysterious way to free themselves of the pleasure principle and to forge beyond it. But the conclusions he drew from the phenomenon were ambiguous when they were not by implication pessimistic: the impulse was fundamentally an impulse to self-destruction. Philosophic existentialism has, in effect, now altered this to read self-definition. And we are beginning to think—I would like to say hope—beyond existentialism's uncertain promise. "For Sartre," Mr. Barrett says, "the nothingness of the Self is the basis for the will to action. . . . Man's existence is absurd in the midst of a cosmos that knows him not; the only meaning he can give himself is through the free project that he launches out of his own nothingness."

But if he succeeds in giving himself a meaning he will have given himself somethingness. Our minds may be beginning to place the emphasis in this cruel activity upon the *meaning* it may arrive at, not upon the meaninglessness from which it is launched. Existentialism sees man as condemned to action, which is in itself a gain for tragedy. Postexistentialist thought dares to conceive of this action as potentially significant, as a means toward an end which may itself be a good. If we can simply alter our state of mind so that self-definition becomes a sought-after goal, if we can conceive of it as an absolute that might be wrested from a contest with the infinite, we shall be closer again to the temper that once set tragic man in motion. Mr. Trilling looks backward and forward to see this old-new impulse fumbling toward fresh awareness of its nature. Looking backward, he says, "if we consider the primitive forbidden ways of conduct which traditionally in tragedy lead to punishment by death, we think of them as being the path to reality and truth, to an ultimate self-realization. We have always wondered if tragedy itself may not have been saying just this in a deeply hidden way, drawing us to think of the hero's sin and death as somehow conferring justification, even salvation of a sort. . . ." And looking forward from our exhausted notions of comfort and pleasure which have ended only in ennui, we wonder if there is not developing in their place "an ideal of the experience of those psychic energies which are linked with unpleasure and which are directed toward self-definition and self-affirmation."

Our nerves grow somewhat steadier, even in the void, now that we have permitted ourselves to imagine activity in the void yielding a new and much firmer reality. Jung would even urge us to take our very oldest ideals of transcendence—our images of an archetypal God and of an immortality to be won—into the battle with us if we wish to, positing a superreality "out there" with which we are equipped to make contact. The fact that we must be less precise in describing beforehand the nature of the goals we seek to snatch need not inhibit us. Confidence is a matter of spirit, not of total information, and evolution will never tell us—as it never has told us—where our next suit of clothes is coming from. A man may, and probably must, shape in his mind the look of the things he thinks he is after, whether they bear him out or astound him when he at last has them in his grip. "If he believes in them, or greets them with some measure of credence," Jung reminds us, "he is being just as right or just as wrong as someone who does not believe in them. But while the man who despairs marches toward nothingness, the one who has placed his faith in the archetype follows the tracks of life and lives right into his death. Both, to be sure, remain in uncertainty, but the one lives against his instincts, the other with them. The difference is considerable, and gives the latter an advantage."

Tragedy may return to us, in this time of necessary action and enforced freedom, when man comes to feel once more that he does, or can, bring an advantage with him into the bruising fray. Tragedy, which is affirmation of the will at its fiercest, depends very largely upon the psychology of the historical moment. Doubt will not give it to us. Determination, however hotheaded, may. The philosophical outlook of recent years is in the process of creating a new psychology. Man is reevaluating himself, possibly readying himself for a test of strength that simply cannot be avoided. Certainly, if he is listening, he cannot help hearing the drumbeat of a new theme, a drumbeat which Mr. Barrett paraphrases from Heidegger in this way: "Man . . . is a creature of distance: he is perpetually beyond himself, his existence at every moment opening outward toward the future."

Or, to seize upon Karl Jaspers' formulation, "One can take courage to try to do that which passes beyond his strength from the fact that it is a human problem, and man is that creature which poses problems beyond its powers."

Such news may quite possibly, at some not too far distant time, alert the slumbering tragic hero, who is invariably eager to be the first man beyond himself.

IX
SOME CLASSICS
OF TRAGIC THEORY

From The Poetics*

Aristotle

A Tragedy, then, is an artistic imitation of an action that is serious, complete in itself, and of an adequate magnitude; so much for the object which is imitated. As for the medium, the imitation is produced in language embellished in more than one way, one kind of embellishment being introduced separately in one part, and another kind in another part of the whole. As for the manner, the imitation is itself in the form of an action directly presented, not narrated. And as for the proper function resulting from the imitation of such an object in such a medium and manner, it is to arouse the emotions of pity and fear in the audience; and to arouse this pity and fear in such a way as to effect that special purging off and relief (*catharsis*) of these two emotions which is the characteristic of Tragedy.

By 'language embellished in more than one way' is meant language which is simply rhythmical or metrical, language which is delivered in recitative, and language which is uttered in song. And by the separate introduction of one kind of embellished language in one part, and of another kind in another part, is meant that some portions of the tragedy (e.g., prologue and episode) are rendered in verse alone, without being sung or chanted, and other portions again (e.g., parode and stasimon) in the form of singing or chanting.

[The several elements in Aristotle's definition of tragedy are gathered from his previous remarks, as he says; save that hitherto the only possible reference to the function of tragedy, its effect upon the audience, or reader, is contained in the opening words of the treatise, where he promises to discuss the specific function of each kind of poetry. In the definition, he implies that other forms of art—we might instance comedy—have as their special end or pleasure the relief of others of the general class of disturbing emotions to which pity and fear belong.

The effect of tragedy upon the emotions is not merely something that took place in a former age, or among the Greeks alone; it may be observed at all times, and in virtually all persons, including the reader of this sentence. However much the malign influence of a narrowly intellectual education may check the native motions of the heart, few indeed must be they who are hopelessly bereft of all pleasure in the tragic *catharsis*. For generations, it is true, there has been a debate over the precise meaning one should attach to Aristotle's phrase—

*Aristotle, from *The Poetics* in *Aristotle on the Art of Poetry* [335–322 B.C.], Lane Cooper, tr. (Cornell University Press, 1947), pp. 17–31. [An amplified version with supplementary illustrations. Brackets enclose amplifications.]

a debate that frequently has turned upon the study of words apart from things, and on the whole has not been sufficiently concerned with the actual experience of audiences, or rather of specially qualified judges, during the presentation of good tragedy and immediately thereafter. But if the words of Aristotle describe an effect which really occurs, it must be that a person of intelligence and normal sympathies will undergo, and be able to mark, the experience, not only in witnessing the best tragedy, but even in reading it. The student of the *Poetics* might render his notion of the tragic *catharsis* more exact by an attempt to observe his own emotions when he reads, or re-reads, Sophocles' *Oedipus the King* or Shakespeare's *Othello*.

Furthermore, one might collect and examine the utterances of poets and other men of unusual sensibility on the feelings which tragic stories have aroused in them;—not primarily such conscious explanations of the Aristotelian *catharsis* as that of Milton in his preface to *Samson Agonistes*. This, though important, is a different kind of evidence from the lines in the first of Milton's Latin Elegies— thus translated by Cowper:

> I gaze, and grieve, still cherishing my grief;
> At times, e'en bitter tears yield sweet relief.

Similar spontaneous illustrations of the tragic pleasure have come from other English poets; for example, Wordsworth, in the Dedication preceding *The White Doe of Rylstone:*

> Pleasing was the smart,
> And the tear precious in compassion shed;

and Coleridge, in *Love:*

> She wept with pity and delight.

It is probable also that a study of emotional suspense and its relief in the audience, by an experimental psychologist, would throw light upon the passage in Aristotle. For the present, however, no explanation could prove more helpful to the general reader than a part of Bywater's note, his language being followed almost verbatim:

> In Greek physiology and pathology, *catharsis* is a very general term for a physical clearance or discharge, the removal by art or an effort of nature of some bodily product, which, if allowed to remain, would cause discomfort or harm. The *catharsis* of the soul as described in the *Politics* of Aristotle is a similar process in reference to certain emotions—the tacit assumption being apparently that the emotions in question are analogous to those peccant humors in the body which, according to the ancient humoral theory of medicine, have to be expelled from the system by the appropriate *catharsis*. With some adaptation of the statements and hints in *Politics* 8. 7, as thus interpreted, it is not difficult to recover the outlines at any rate of the Aristotelian theory of the cathartic effect of tragedy: Pity and fear are elements in human nature, and in some men they are present in a disquieting degree. With these latter the tragic excitement is a necessity; but it is also in a certain sense good for all. It serves as a sort of medicine, producing a *catharsis* to lighten and relieve the soul

of the accumulated emotion within it; and as the relief is wanted, there is always a harmless pleasure attending the process of relief.

It must be added that pleasure, to Aristotle, signifies, not a passive state of being, but a form of activity.

In his working definition he does not allude to the element of pleasure in the tragic relief. As he develops his thought, we become aware that the relief is itself a form of pleasure; so that the characteristic effect of tragedy may be referred to as either one or the other. We discover, too, that there are certain satisfactions contributory to the main effect; for example, the pleasure of discovery or recognition, when we learn the author of a deed or the upshot of an incident; the pleasure of astonishment, when the outcome of a series of events is unexpected, yet is seen to be inevitable; and the pleasure derived from 'embellished language,' that is, from the rhythm and music of tragedy. Furthermore, the pleasure is explained negatively: the play must not offend us with effects that are revolting, or with events that run counter to our sense of what is reasonable and likely.]

Advancing now from the synthetic definition of Tragedy, we proceed to analyze the elements that separately demand the attention of the tragic poet. Since there are *dramatis personae* who produce the author's imitation of an action, it necessarily follows that (1) everything pertaining to the appearance of the actors on the stage—including costume, scenery, and the like—will constitute an element in the technique of tragedy; and that (2) the composition of music ('Melody'), and (3) the composition in words ('Diction'), will constitute two further elements, as Melody and Diction represent the medium in which the action is imitated. By Diction is meant, in this connection, the fitting together of the words in metre; as for Melody (= 'Song'), the meaning is too obvious to need explanation.

But furthermore, the original object of the imitation is an action of men. In the performance, then, the imitation, which is also an action, must be carried on by agents, the *dramatis personae*. And these agents must necessarily be endowed by the poet with certain distinctive qualities both of (4) Moral Character (*ethos*) and (5) Intellect (*dianoia*)—one might say, of heart and head; for it is from a man's moral bent, and from the way in which he reasons, that we are led to ascribe goodness or badness; success or failure, to his acts. Thus, as there are two natural causes, moral bent and thought, of the particular deeds of men, so there are the same two natural causes of their success or failure in life. And the tragic poet must take cognizance of this.

Finally, the action which the poet imitates is represented in the tragedy by (6) the Fable or Plot. And according to our present distinction, Plot means that synthesis of the particular incidents which gives form or being to the tragedy as a whole; whereas Moral Bent is that which leads us to characterize the agents as morally right or wrong in what they do; and Intellect (or 'Thought') is that which shows itself whenever they prove a particular point, or, it may be, avouch some general truth.

In every tragedy, therefore, there are six constitutive elements, according to the quality of which we judge the excellence of the work as a whole: Plot (6); Moral Disposition (4); Diction (3); Intellect (5); Spectacle (1); Melody (2). Two of them, Melody and Diction, concern the medium of imitation; one, Spectacle, the manner; and three, Plot, Moral Disposition, and Intellect, the objects. There can be no other elements. These constitutive elements, accordingly, not a few of the tragic poets, so to speak, have duly employed [in spite of what adverse critics may assert]; for, indeed, every drama must contain certain things that are meant for the eye, as well as the elements of Moral Disposition, Plot, Diction, Melody, and Intellect.

[That element of a drama which is here called moral bent or disposition (*ethos*) is often rendered into English by the word 'character.' There is a danger, which Aristotle himself does not always avoid, of confusing character in this narrower sense with personality, and hence of identifying character with agent. From this confusion there often results a misunderstanding of Aristotle's subsequent remarks upon the relative importance of plot and moral bent (character in the narrower sense). In dealing with this point it is undesirable to refer to the *dramatis personae* as 'characters'; one would do well to use the word 'agents' instead, and to bear in mind that the personality of the agents is divided by Aristotle into two separate elements, corresponding to qualities of heart and head respectively. If at first we make the most of this distinction, we shall not go far astray in later passages where it is not so carefully preserved. What Aristotle next specifically maintains is that, among the six elements, plot or action is of greater importance than the moral bent of the agents; he might equally well have said it was of greater importance than their faculty of reason, i.e., than 'Thought.']

The most important of the constitutive elements is the Plot, that is, the organization of the incidents of the story; for Tragedy in its essence is an imitation, not of men as such, but of action and life, of happiness and misery. And happiness and misery are not states of being, but forms of activity; the end for which we live is some form of activity, not the realization of a moral quality. Men are better or worse, according to their moral bent; but they become happy or miserable in their actual deeds. In a play, consequently, the agents do not perform for the sake of representing their individual dispositions; rather, the display of moral character is included as subsidiary to the things that are done. So that the incidents of the action, and the structural ordering of these incidents, constitute the end and purpose of the tragedy. Here, as elsewhere, the final purpose is the main thing.

Such is the importance of this element that, we may add, whereas Tragedy cannot exist without action, it is possible to construct a tragedy in which the agents have no distinctive moral bent. In fact, the works of most of the modern tragic poets, from the time of Euripides on, are lacking in the element of character. Nor is the defect confined to tragic poets: it is common among poets in general. And there is a similar defect among the painters—in Zeuxis, for example, as contrasted with Polygnotus; for Polygnotus excels in the representation of the ethical element, whereas the pictures of Zeuxis are in this respect wholly deficient. [In the same way, one might compare the vigorous delineation of ethical qualities in Rembrandt with the absence of this power in Rubens. Among English poets of all sorts, Chaucer, Shakespeare, Milton, and Wordsworth serve to exemplify the presence of this quality; it is relatively lacking in Dryden, Shelley, and Byron.]

Again, one may string together a series of speeches in which the moral bent of the agents is delineated in excellent verse and diction, and with excellent order in the thoughts, and yet fail to produce the essential effect of Tragedy as already described. One is much more likely to produce this effect with a tragedy, however deficient in these respects, if it has a plot—that is, an artistic ordering of the incidents. In addition to all this, the most vital features of Tragedy, by which the interest and emotions of the audience are most powerfully aroused— that is, reversals of fortune, and discoveries of the identity of agents—are parts of the plot or action. It is significant, too, that beginners in the art become proficient in versification and in the delineation of personal traits before they are able to combine the incidents of the action into an effective whole. Herein the progress of the individual dramatist repeats the history of the art; for almost all the early poets succeeded better with these two elements than in the formation of plots.

(1) The Plot, then, is the First Principle, and as it were the very Soul of Tragedy.

(2) And the element of Character is second in importance.—There is a parallel in the art of painting: the most beautiful colors, laid on with no order, will not give as much pleasure as the simplest figure done in outline.—Tragedy is an imitation of an action: mainly on account of this action does it become, in the second place, an imitation of personal agents.

(3) Third in importance comes the Intellectual element. This corresponds to the power of the agent to say what can be said, or what is fitting to be said, in a given situation. It is that element in the speeches of a drama which is supplied by the study of Politics and the art of Rhetoric; for the older tragic poets [e.g., Sophocles] made their heroes express themselves like statesmen, whereas the modern [including Euripides] make theirs use the devices of the rhetoricians. This Intellectual element must be clearly distinguished from the Ethical element in the drama, for the latter includes only such things as reveal the moral bias of the agents—their tendency to choose or to avoid a certain line of action, in cases where the motive is not otherwise evident. And hence the poet has no call to employ the ethical element in speeches where the agent is neither choosing nor avoiding a line of action. The Intellectual element, on the other hand, is manifested in everything the agents say to prove or disprove a special point, and in every utterance they make by way of generalization.

(4) Next in importance among the four essential constituents comes the Diction. This, as has been explained, means the interpretation of the sentiments of the agents in the form of language, and is essentially the same thing whether the language is metrical or not.

(5) Of the two elements remaining, Melody is the more important, since it occupies the chief place among the accessory pleasures of Tragedy.

(6) The element of Spectacle, though is arouses the interest of the audience, is last in importance, since it demands the lowest order of artistic skill, and is least connected with the art of poetry as such. A tragedy can produce its effect independently of a stage-performance and actors—that is, when it is read; and besides, the business of preparing the stage and the actors is the affair of the costumer rather than of poets.

Having thus distinguished the six constitutive elements, we are now to discuss, as the first and most important consideration in the art of Tragedy, the proper organization of the incidents into a plot that will have the ideal tragic effect. According to the definition, a tragedy is an imitation of an action that is complete in itself, forming a whole of a sufficient magnitude or extent; for a thing may be a whole and yet wanting in magnitude.

Now a Whole is that which has (1) a Beginning, (2) a Middle, and (3) an End.

(1) A Beginning (= X) is that which does not itself come after anything else in a necessary sequence, but after which some other thing (= Y) does naturally exist or come to pass.

(3) An End (= Z), on the contrary, is that which naturally comes after something else (= Y) in either a necessary or a usual sequence, but has nothing else following it.

(2) A Middle (= Y) is that which naturally comes after something else (= X), and is followed by a third thing (= Z).

A well-constructed plot, therefore, can neither begin nor end where and when the poet happens to like. It must conform to the principles just enunciated.

And further, as to Magnitude: to be beautiful, a living organism, or any other individual thing made up of parts, must possess not only an orderly arrangement of these parts, but also a proper magnitude, for beauty depends upon these two qualities, size and order. Hence an extremely minute creature cannot be beautiful to us; for we see the whole in an almost infinitesimal moment of time, and lose the pleasure that comes from a distinct perception of order in the parts. Nor could a creature of vast dimensions be beautiful to us—a beast, say, one thousand miles in length; for in that case the eye could not take all of the object in at once—we should see the parts, but not the unity of the whole. In the same way, then, as an inanimate object made up of parts, or a living creature, must be of such a size that the parts and the whole may be easily taken in by the eye, just so must the plot of a tragedy have a proper length, so that the parts and the whole may be easily embraced by the memory. The artificial limits, of course, as these are determined by the conditions of stage-presentation, and by the power of attention in an audience, do not concern the art of poetry as such. If it were necessary to present one hundred tragedies in succession [an exaggerated illustration], they would doubtless have to be timed with water-clocks—as some say was formerly the custom. The artistic limit, set by the nature of the thing itself, is this: So long as the plot is perspicuous throughout, the greater the length of the story, the more beautiful will it be on account of its magnitude. But to define the matter in a general way, an adequate limit for the magnitude of the plot is this: Let the length be such that the story may pass from happiness to misfortune, or from misfortune to happiness, through a series of incidents linked together in a probable or inevitable sequence.

The Unity of a Plot does not consist, as some suppose, in having one man as subject; for the number of accidents that befall the individual man is endless, and some of them cannot be reduced to unity. So, too, during the life of any one man, he performs many deeds which cannot be brought together in the form of a unified action. . . . For, as in the other imitative arts, painting and the rest, so in poetry, the object of the imitation in each case is a unit; therefore in a epic or a tragedy, the plot, which is an imitation of a dramatic action, must represent an action that is organically unified, the structural order of the incidents being such that transposing or removing any one of them will dislocate and disorganize the whole. Every part must be necessary, and in its place; for a thing whose presence or absence makes no perceptible difference is not an organic part of the whole.

From **The Philosophy of Fine Art**[*]

Friedrich Hegel

The genuine content of tragic action subject to the *aims* which arrest tragic characters is supplied by the world of those forces which carry in themselves their own justification, and are realized substantively in the volitional activity of mankind. Such are the love of husband and wife, of parents, children, and kinsfolk. Such are, further, the life of communities, the patriotism of citizens, the will of those in supreme power. Such are the life of churches, not, however, if regarded as a piety which submits to act with resignation, or as a divine judicial declaration in the heart of mankind over what is good or the reverse in action; but, on the contrary, conceived as the active engagement with and demand for veritable interests and relations. It is of a soundness and thoroughness consonant with these that the really tragical *characters* consist. They are throughout that which the essential notion of their character enables them and compels them to be. They are not merely a varied totality laid out in the series of views of it proper to the epic manner; they are, while no doubt remaining also essentially vital and individual, still only the one power of the particular character in question, the force in which such a character, in virtue of his essential personality, has made himself inseparably coalesce with some particular aspect of the capital and substantive life-content we have indicated above, and deliberately commits himself to that. It is at some such elevation, where the mere accidents of unmediated individuality vanish altogether, that we find the tragic heroes of dramatic art, whether they be the living representatives of such spheres of concrete life or in any other way already so derive their greatness and stability from their own free self-reliance that they stand forth as works of sculpture, and thus the lofty tragic characters of the Greeks also interpret the essentially more abstract statues and figures of gods more completely than is possible for any other kind of elucidation or commentary.

Broadly speaking, we may, therefore, affirm that the true theme of primitive tragedy is the godlike. But by godlike we do not mean the Divine, as implied in the content of the religious consciousness simply as such, but rather as it enters into the world, into individual action, and enters in such a way that it does not forfeit its substantive character under this mode of realization, nor find itself converted into the contradiction of its own substance. In this form the spiritual substance of volition and accomplishment is ethical life. For what is ethical, if we grasp it, in its direct consistency—that is to say, not exclusively from the

[*] Friedrich Hegel, from *The Philosophy of Fine Art*, F. P. B. Osmaston, tr. (G. Bell & Sons, Ltd., 1920). [Footnotes in this selection have been renumbered.]

standpoint of personal reflection as formal morality—is the divine in its secular or world realization, the substantive as such, the particular no less than the essential features of which supply the changing content of truly human actions, and in such action itself render this their essence explicit and actual.

(b) These ethical forces, as also the characters of the action, are *distinctively defined* in respect to their content and their individual personality, in virtue of the principle of differentiation to which everything is subject, which forms part of the objective world of things. If, then, these particular forces, in the way presupposed by dramatic poetry, are attached to the external expression of human activity, and are realized as the determinate aim of a human pathos which passes into action, their concordancy is cancelled, and they are asserted *in contrast* to each other in interchangeable succession. Individual action will then, under given conditions, realize an object or character, which, under such a presupposed state, inevitably stimulates the presence of a pathos opposed to itself, because it occupies a position of unique isolation in virtue of its independently fixed definition, and, by doing so, brings in its train unavoidable conflicts. Primitive tragedy, then, consists in this, that within a collision of this kind both sides of the contradiction, if taken by themselves, are *justified;* yet, from a further point of view, they tend to carry into effect the true and positive content of their end and specific characterization merely as the negation and *violation* of the other equally legitimate power, and consequently in their ethical purport and relatively to this so far fall under *condemnation*.

I have already adverted to the general ground of the necessity of this conflict. The substance of ethical condition *is*, when viewed as concrete unity, a totality of *different* relations and forces, which, however, only under the inactive condition of the gods in their blessedness achieve the works of the Spirit in enjoyment of an undisturbed life. In contrast to this, however, there is no less certainly implied in the notion of this totality itself an impulse to move from its, in the first instance, still abstract ideality, and transplant itself in the real actuality of the phenomenal world. On account of the nature of this primitive obsession, it comes about that mere difference, if conceived on the basis of definite conditions of individual personalities, must inevitably associate with contradiction and collision. Only such a view can pretend to deal seriously with those gods which, though they endure in their tranquil repose and unity in the Olympus and heaven of imagination and religious conception, yet, in so far as they are actual, viewed at least as the energic in the definite pathos of a human personality, participate in concrete life, all other claims notwithstanding, and, in virtue of their specific singularity and their mutual opposition, render both blame and wrong inevitable.

(c) As a result of this, however, an unmediated contradiction is posited, which no doubt may assert itself in the Real, but, for all that, is unable to maintain itself as that which is wholly substantive and verily real therein; which rather discovers, and only discovers, its essential justification in the fact that it is able to *annul* itself as such contradiction. In other words, whatever may be the claim of the tragic final purpose and personality, whatever may be the necessity of the tragic collision, it is, as a consequence of our present view, no less a claim that is asserted—this is our *third* and last point—by the tragic resolution of this division. It is through *this* latter result that Eternal Justice is operative in such aims and individuals under a mode whereby it restores the ethical substance and unity in and along with the downfall of the individuality which disturbs its repose.

For, despite the fact that individual characters propose that which is itself essentially valid, yet they are only able to carry it out under the tragic demand in a manner that implies contradiction and with a one-sidedness which is injurious. What, however, is substantive in truth, and the function of which is to secure realization, is not the battle of particular unities, however much such a conflict is essentially involved in the notion of a real world and human action; rather it is the reconciliation in which definite ends and individuals unite in harmonious action without mutual violation and contradiction. That which is abrogated in the tragic issue is merely the *one-sided* particularity which was unable to accommodate itself to this harmony, and consequently in the tragic course of its action, through inability to disengage itself from itself and its designs, either is committed in its entire totality to destruction or at least finds itself compelled to fall back upon a state of resignation in the execution of its aim in so far as it can carry this out. We are reminded of the famous dictum of Aristotle that the true effect of tragedy is to excite and purify *fear* and *pity*. By this statement Aristotle did not mean merely the concordant or discordant feeling with anybody's private experience, a feeling simply of pleasure or the reverse, an attraction or a repulsion, that most superficial of all psychological states, which only in recent times theorists have sought to identify with the principle of assent or dissent as ordinarily expressed. For in a work of art the matter of exclusive importance should be the display of that which is conformable with the reason and truth of Spirit; and to discover the principle of this we have to direct our attention to wholly different points of view. And consequently we are not justified in restricting the application of this dictum of Aristotle merely to the emotion of fear and pity; but should relate it to the principle of the *content*, and appropriately artistic display of which ought to purify such feelings. Man may, on the one hand, entertain fear when confronted with that which is outside him and finite; but he may likewise shrink before the power of that which is the essential and absolute subsistency of social phenomena. That which mankind has therefore in truth to fear is not the external power and its oppression, but the ethical might which is self-defined in its own free rationality, and partakes further of the eternal and inviolable, the power a man summons against his own being when he turns his back upon it. And just as fear may have two objectives, so also may compassion. The first is just the ordinary sensibility—in other words, a sympathy with the misfortunes and sufferings of another, and one which is experienced as something finite and negative. Your countrified cousin is ready enough with compassion of this order. The man of nobility and greatness, however, has no wish to be smothered with this sort of pity. For just to the extent that it is merely the nugatory aspect, the negative of misfortune which is asserted, a real depreciation of misfortune is implied. True sympathy, on the contrary, is an accordant feeling with the ethical claim at the same time associated with the sufferer—that is, with what is necessarily implied in his condition as affirmative and substantive. Such a pity as this is not, of course, excited by ragamuffins and vagabonds. If the tragic character, therefore, just as he aroused our fear when contemplating the might of violated morality, is to awake a tragic sympathy in his misfortune, he must himself essentially possess real capacity and downright character. It is only that which has a genuine content which strikes the heart of a man of noble feeling, and rings through its depths. Consequently we ought by no means to identify our interest in the tragic *dénouement* with the simple satisfaction that a sad story, a misfortune merely as misfortune, should have a claim upon our sympathy. Feelings of lament of this type may well enough assail men on occasions of wholly external contingency and related circumstance, to which the individual does not contribute, nor for which he is responsible, such cases as illness, loss of property, death, and the like. The only real and absorbing interest in such cases ought to be an eager desire to afford immediate assistance. If this is impossible, such pictures of lamentation and misery merely rack the feelings. A veritable tragic suffering, on the contrary, is suspended over active characters entirely as the consequence of their own act, which as such not only asserts its claim upon us, but becomes subject to blame through the collision it involves, and in which such individuals identify themselves heart and soul.

Over and above mere fear and tragic sympathy we have therefore the feeling of *reconciliation*, which tragedy affords in virtue of its vision of eternal justice, a justice which exercises a paramount force of absolute constringency on account of the relative claim of all merely contracted aims and passions; and it can do this for the reason that it is unable to tolerate the victorious issue and continuance in the truth of the objective world of such a conflict with and opposition to those ethical powers which are fundamentally and essentially concordant. Inasmuch as then, in conformity with this principle, all that pertains to tragedy preeminently rests upon the contemplation of such a conflict and its resolution, dramatic poetry is—and its entire mode of presentation offers a proof of the fact—alone able to make and completely adapt the tragic, throughout its entire course and compass, to the principle of the art product. And this is the reason why I have only now found occasion to discuss the tragic mode of presentation, although it extends an effective force, if no doubt one of subordinate degree, in many ways over the other arts.

In the tragic drama we are now considering, the general basis or background for tragic action is supplied, as was also the case in the Epos, by that world-condition which I have already indicated as the *heroic*.[1] For only in heroic times, when the universal ethical forces have neither acquired the independent stability of definite political legislation or moral commands and obligations, can they be presented in their primitive jucundity as gods, who are either opposed to each other in their personal activities, or themselves appear as the animated content of a free and human individuality. If, however, what is intrinsically ethical is to appear throughout as the substantive foundation, the universal ground, shall we say, from which the growth of personal action arrests our attention with equal force in its disunion, and is no less brought back again from such divided movement into unity, we shall find that there are two distinct modes under which the ethical content of human action is asserted.

First, we have the simple consciousness, which, in so far as it wills its substantive content wholly as the unbroken identity of its particular aspects, remains in undisturbed, uncriticized, and neutral tranquillity on its own account and as related to others. This undivided and, we may add, purely formal state of mind in its veneration, its faith, and its happiness, however, is incapable of attaching itself to any definite action; it has a sort of dread before the disunion which is implied in such, although it does, while remaining itself incapable of action, esteem at the same time that spiritual courage which asserts itself resolutely and actively in a self-proposed object, as of nobler worth, yet is aware of

[1] See Chapter 11 [of *The Philosophy of Fine Art*].

its inability to undertake such enterprise, and consequently considers that it can do nothing further for such active personalities, whom it respects so highly, than contrast with the energy of their decision and conflict the object of its own wisdom, in other words, the substantive ideality of the ethical Powers.

The *second* mode under which this ethical content is asserted is that of the individual pathos, which urges the active characters with moral self-vindication into opposition to others, and brings them thereby into conflict. The individuals subject to this pathos are neither what, in the modern use of the term, we describe as characters, nor are they mere abstractions. They are rather placed in the vital midway sphere between both, standing there as figures of real stability, which are simply that which they are, without aught of collision in themselves, without any fluctuating recognition of some other pathos, and in so far—in this respect a contrast to our modern irony—elevated, absolutely determinate characters, whose definition, however, discovers its content and basis in a particular ethical power. Forasmuch as, then, the tragic situation first appears in the *antagonism* of individuals who are thus empowered to act, the same can only assert itself in the field of actual human life. It results from the specific character of this alone that a particular quality so affects the substantive content of a given individual, that the latter identifies himself with his entire interest and being in such a content, and penetrates it throughout with the glow of passion. In the blessed gods, however, it is the divine Nature, in its indifference, which is what is essential; in contrast to which we have the contradiction, which in the last instance is not treated seriously, rather is one which, as I have already noticed when discussing the Homeric Epos, becomes eventually a self-resolving irony. These two modes or aspects—of which the one is as important for the whole as the other—namely, the unsevered consciousness of the godlike, and the combating human action, asserted, however, in godlike power and deed, which determines and executes the ethical purpose—supply the two fundamental elements, the mediation of which is displayed by Greek tragedy in its artistic compositions under the form of *chorus* and *heroic figures* respectively.

In modern times, considerable discussion has been raised over the significance of the Greek chorus, and the question has been raised incidentally whether it can or ought to be introduced into modern tragedy. In fact, the need of some such substantial foundation has been experienced; but critics have found it difficult to prescribe the precise manner in which effect should be given to such a change, because they failed to grasp with sufficient penetration the nature of that in which true tragedy consists and the necessity of the chorus as an essential constituent of all that Greek tragedy implies. Critics have, no doubt, recognized the nature of the chorus to the extent of maintaining that in it we find an attitude of tranquil meditation over the whole, whereas the characters of the action remain within the limits of their particular objects and situations, and, in short, receive in the chorus and its observations a standard of valuation of their characters and actions in much the same way as the public discovers in it, and within the drama itself, an objective representative of its own judgment upon all that is thus represented. In this view we have to this extent the fact rightly conceived, that the chorus is, in truth, there as a substantive and more enlightened intelligence, which warns us from irrelevant oppositions, and reflects upon the genuine issue. But, granting this to be so, it is by no means, like the spectator, a wholly disinterested person, at leisure to entertain such thoughts and ethical judgments as it likes which, uninteresting and tedious on its own account, could

only be attached for the sake of such reflections. The chorus is the actual substance of the heroic life and action itself: it is, as contrasted with the particular
heroes, the common folk regarded as the fruitful earth, out of which individuals,
much as flowers and towering trees from their native soil, grow and whereby
they are conditioned in this life. Consequently, the chorus is peculiarly fitted to
a view of life in which the obligations of State legislation and settled religious
dogmas do not, as yet, act as a restrictive force in ethical and social development,
but where morality only exists in its primitive form of directly animated human
life, and it is merely the equilibrium of unmoved life which remains assured in
its stability against the fearful collisions which the antagonistic energies of individual action produces. We are made aware of the fact that an assured asylum of
this kind is also a part of our actual existence by the presence of the chorus. It
does not, therefore, practically co-operate with the action; it executes no right,
actively, as against the contending heroes; it merely expresses its judgment as a
matter of opinion; it warns, commiserates, or appeals to the divine law, and the
ideal forces imminent in the soul, which the imagination grasps in external guise
as the sphere of the gods that rule. In this self expression it is, as we have already
seen, lyrical; for it does not act and there are no events for it to narrate in epical
form. The content, however, retains at the same time the epic character of substantive universality; and its lyric movement is of such a nature that it can, and
in this respect in contrast to the form of the genuine ode, approach at times that
of the paean and the dithyramb. We must lay emphatic stress upon this position
of the chorus in Greek tragedy. Just as the theatre itself possesses its external
ground, its scene and environment, so, too, the chorus, that is the general community, is the spiritual scene; and we may compare it to the architectural temple
which surrounds the image of the god, which resembles the heroes in the action.
Among ourselves, statues are placed under the open sky without such a background, which also modern tragedy does not require, for the reason that its actions do not depend on this substantive basis, but on the personal volition and
personality, no less than the apparently external contingency of events and circumstances.

In this respect it is an entirely false view which regards the chorus as an accidental piece of residuary baggage, a mere remnant from the origins of Greek
drama. Of course, it is incontestable that its source is to be traced to the circumstance that, in the festivals of Bacchus, so far as the artistic aspect is concerned,
the choral song was of most importance until the introduction and interruption
of its course by one reciter, whose relation finally was transformed into and exalted by the real figures of dramatic action. In the blossoming season of tragedy,
however, the chorus was not by any means merely retained in honour of this
particular phase of the festival and ritual of the god Bacchus; rather it became
continuously more elaborate in its beauty and harmonious measures by reason of
the fact that its association with the dramatic action is essential and, indeed, so
indispensable to it that the decline of tragedy is intimately connected with the
degeneration of the choruses, which no longer remain an integral member of the
whole, but are degraded to a mere embellishment. In contrast to this, in romantic tragedy, the chorus is neither intrinsically appropriate nor does it appear to
have originated from choric songs. On the contrary, the content is here of a type
which defeats from the first any attempt to introduce choruses as understood by
Greek dramatists. For, even if we go back to the most primitive of those so-
called mysteries, morality plays, and farces of a similar character, from which

the romantic drama issued, we find that these present no action in that original Greek sense of the term, no outbreak, that is, of opposing forces from the undivided consciousness of life and the godlike. To as little extent is the chorus adapted to the conditions of chivalry and the dominion of kings, in so far as, in such cases, the attitude of the folk is one of mere obedience, or it is itself a party, involved together with the interest of its fortune or misfortune in the course of the action. And in general the chorus entirely fails to secure its true position where the main subject-matter consists of particular passions, ends, and characters, or where any considerable opportunity is admitted to intrigue.

In contrast to the chorus, the *second* fundamental feature of dramatic composition is that of the *individuals* who act in *conflict* with each other. In Greek tragedy it is not at all bad will, crime, worthlessness, or mere misfortune, stupidity, and the like, which act as an incentive to such collisions, but rather, as I have frequently urged, the ethical right to a definite course of action. Abstract evil neither possesses truth in itself, nor does it arouse interest. At the same time, when we attribute ethical traits of characterization to the individuals of the action, these ought not to appear merely as a matter of opinion. It is rather implied in their right or claim that they are actually there as essential on their own account. The hazards of crime, such as are present in modern drama, the useless, or quite as much the so-called noble criminal, with his empty talk about fate, we meet with in the tragedy of ancient literature, rarely, if at all, and for the good reason that the decision and deed depends on the wholly personal aspect of interest and character, upon lust for power, love, honour, or other similar passions, whose justification has its roots exclusively in the particular inclination and individuality. A resolve of this character, whose claim is based upon the content of its object, which it carries into execution in one restricted direction of particularization, violates, under certain circumstances, which are already essentially implied in the actual possibility of conflicts, a further and equally ethical sphere of human volition, which the character thus confronted adheres to, and, by his thus stimulated action, enforces, so that in this way the collision of powers and individuals equally entitled to the ethical claim is completely set up in its movement.

The sphere of this content, although capable of great variety of detail, is not in its essential features very extensive. The principal source of opposition, which Sophocles in particular, in this respect following the lead of Aeschylus, has accepted and worked out in the finest way, is that of the *body politic*, the opposition, that is, between ethical life in its social universality and the family as the natural ground of moral relations. These are the purest forces of tragic representation. It is, in short, the harmony of these spheres and the concordant action within the bounds of their realized content, which constitute the perfected reality of the moral life. In this respect I need only recall the "Seven before Thebes" of Aeschylus and, as a yet stronger illustration, the "Antigone" of Sophocles. Antigone reverences the ties of blood-relationship, the gods of the nether world. Creon alone recognizes Zeus, the paramount Power of public life and the commonwealth. We come across a similar conflict in the "Iphigenia in Aulis," as also in the "Agamemnon," the "Choephorae," and "Eumenides" of Aeschylus, and in the "Electra" of Sophocles. Agamemnon, as king and leader of his army, sacrifices his daughter in the interest of the Greek folk and the Trojan expedition. He shatters thereby the bond of love as between himself and his daughter and wife, which Clytemnestra retains in the depths of a mother's heart, and in revenge prepares an ignominious death for her husband on his return. Orestes, their son, respects his mother, but is bound to represent the right of his father, the king, and strikes dead the mother who bore him.

A content of this type retains its force through all times, and its presentation, despite all difference of nationality, vitally arrests our human and artistic sympathies.

Of a more formal type is that second kind of essential collision, an illustration of which in the tragic story of Oedipus the Greek tragedians especially favoured. Of this Sophocles has left us the most complete example in his "Oedipus Rex," and "Oedipus at Colonus." The problem here is concerned with the claim of alertness in our intelligence, with the nature of the obligation implied in that which a man carries out with a volition fully aware of its acts as contrasted with that which he has done in fact, but unconscious of and with no intention of doing what he has done under the directing providence of the gods. Oedipus slays his father, marries his mother, begets children in this incestuous alliance, and nevertheless is involved in these most terrible of crimes without active participation either in will or knowledge. The point of view of our profounder modern consciousness of right and wrong would be to recognize that crimes of this description, inasmuch as they were neither referable to a personal knowledge or volition, were not deeds for which the true personality of the perpetrator was responsible. The plastic nature of the Greek on the contrary adheres to the bare fact which an individual has achieved, and refuses to face the division implied by the purely ideal attitude of the soul in the self-conscious life on the one hand and the objective significance of the fact accomplished on the other.

For ourselves, to conclude this survey, other collisions, which either in general are related to the universally accepted association of personal action to the Greek conception of Destiny, or in some measure to more exceptional conditions, are comparatively speaking less important.

In all these tragic conflicts, however, we must above all place on one side the false notion of *guilt* or *innocence*. The heroes of tragedy are quite as much under one category as the other. If we accept the idea as valid that a man is guilty only in the case that a choice lay open to him, and he deliberately decided on the course of action which he carried out, then these plastic figures of ancient drama are guiltless. They act in accordance with a specific character, a specific pathos, for the simple reason that they are this character, this pathos. In such a case there is no lack of decision and no choice. The strength of great characters consists precisely in this that they do not choose, but are entirely and absolutely just that which they will and achieve. They are simply themselves, and never anything else, and their greatness consists in that fact. Weakness in action, in other words, wholly consists in the division of the personal self as such from its content, so that character, volition and final purpose do not appear as absolutely one unified growth; and inasmuch as no assured end lives in the soul as the very substance of the particular personality, as the pathos and might of the individual's entire will, he is still able to turn with indecision from this course to that, and his final decision is that of caprice. A wavering attitude of this description is alien to these plastic creations. The bond between the psychological state of mind and the content of the will is for them indissoluble. That which stirs them to action is this very pathos which implies an ethical justification and which, even in the pathetic aspects of the dialogue, is not enforced in and through the merely personal rhetoric of the heart and the sophistry of passion, but in the equally masculine and cultivated objective presence, in the profound possibilities, the harmony and vitally plastic beauty of which Sophocles was to a superlative degree master. At the same time, however, such a pathos, with its potential resources of collision, brings them to deeds that are both injurious and wrongful. They have no desire to avoid the blame that results therefrom. On the contrary, it is their fame to have done what they have done. One can in fact urge nothing more intolerable against a hero of this type than by saying that he has acted innocently. It is a point of honour with such great characters that they are guilty. They have no desire to excite pity or our sensibilities. For it is not the substantive, but rather the wholly personal deepening of the personality which stirs our individual pain. His securely strong character, however, coalesces entirely with his essential pathos, and this indivisible accord inspires wonder, not compassion. The drama of Euripides marks the transition to that.

The final result, then, of the development of tragedy conducts us to this issue and only this, namely, that the twofold vindication of the mutually conflicting aspects is no doubt retained, but the *one-sided* mode is cancelled, and the undisturbed ideal harmony brings back again that condition of the chorus, which attributes without reserve equal honour to all the gods. The true course of dramatic development consists in the annulment of *contradictions* viewed as such, in the reconciliation of the forces of human action, which alternately strive to negate each other in their conflict. Only so far is misfortune and suffering not the final issue, but rather the satisfaction of spirit, as for the first time, in virtue of such a conclusion, the necessity of all that particular individuals experience, is able to appear in complete accord with reason, and our emotional attitude is tranquillized on a true ethical basis; rudely shaken by the calamitous result to the heroes, but reconciled in the substantial facts. And it is only in so far as we retain such a view securely that we shall be in a position to understand ancient tragedy. We have to guard ourselves therefore from concluding that a *deñouement* of this type is merely a moral issue conformably to which evil is punished and virtue rewarded, as indicated by the proverb that "when crime turns to vomit, virtue sits down at table." We have nothing to do here with this wholly personal aspect of a self-reflecting personality and its conception of good and evil, but are concerned with the appearance of the affirmative reconciliation and the equal validity of both powers engaged in conflict, if the collision is complete. To as little extent is the necessity of the issue a blind destiny, or in other words a purely irrational, unintelligible fate, identified with the classical world by many; rather it is the rationality of destiny, albeit it does not as yet appear as self-conscious Providence, the divine final end of which in conjunction with the world and individuals appears on its own account and for others, depending as it does on just this fact that the highest Power paramount over particular gods and mankind cannot suffer this, namely, that the forces, which affirm their self-subsistence in modes that are abstract or incomplete, and thereby overstep the boundary of their warrant, no less than the conflicts which result from them, should retain their self-stability. Fate drives personality back upon its limits, and shatters it, when it has grown overweening. An irrational compulsion, however, an innocence of suffering would rather only excite indignation in the soul of the spectator than ethical tranquillity. From a further point of view, therefore, the reconciliation of *tragedy* is equally distinct from that of the *Epos*. If we look at either Achilles or Odysseus in this respect we observe that both attain their object, and it is right that they do so; but it is not a continuous happiness with which they are favoured; they have on the contrary to taste in its bitterness the feeling of finite condition, and are forced to fight wearily through difficulties, losses and sacrifices. It is in fact a universal demand of truth that in the course of life and all that takes place in the objective world the nugatory character of finite conditions should compel attention. So no doubt the anger of Achilles is reconciled; he obtains from Agamemnon that in respect of which he had suffered the sense of insult; he is revenged upon Hector; the funeral rites of Patroclus are consummated, and the character of Achilles is acknowledged in all its glory. But his wrath and its reconciliation have for all that cost him his dearest friend, the noble Patroclus; and, in order to avenge himself upon Hector for this loss, he finds himself compelled to disengage himself from his anger, to enter once more the battle against the Trojans, and in the very moment when his glory is acknowledged receives the prevision of his early death. In a similar way Odysseus reaches Ithaca at last, the goal of his desire; but he does so alone and in his sleep, having lost all his companions, all the war-booty from Ilium, after long years of endurance and fatigue. In this way both heroes have paid their toll to finite conditions and the claim of nemesis is evidenced in the destruction of Troy and the misfortunes of the Greek heroes. But this nemesis is simply justice as conceived of old, which merely humiliates what is everywhere too exalted, in order to establish once more the abstract balance of fortune by the instrumentality of misfortune, and which merely touches and affects finite existence without further ethical signification. And this is the justice of the Epic in the field of objective fact, the universal reconciliation of simple accommodation. The higher conception of reconciliation in tragedy is on the contrary related to the resolution of specific ethical and substantive facts from their contradiction into their true harmony. The way in which such an accord is established is asserted under very different modes; I propose therefore merely to direct attention to the fundamental features of the actual process herein involved.

First, we have particularly to emphasize the fact, that if it is the one-sidedness of the pathos which constitutes the real basis of collisions this merely amounts to the statement that it is asserted in the action of life, and therewith has become the unique pathos of a particular individual. If this one-sidedness is to be abrogated then it is this individual which, to the extent that his action is exclusively identified with this isolated pathos, must perforce be stripped and sacrificed. For the individual here is merely this single life, and, if this unity is not secured in its stability on its own account, the individual is shattered.

The most complete form of this development is possible when the individuals engaged in conflict relatively to their concrete or objective life appear in each case essentially involved in one whole, so that they stand fundamentally under the power of that against which they battle, and consequently infringe that, which, conformably to their own essential life, they ought to respect. Antigone, for example, lives under the political authority of Creon; she is herself the daughter of a king and the affianced of Haemon, so that her obedience to the royal prerogative is an obligation. But Creon also, who is on his part father and husband, is under obligation to respect the sacred ties of relationship, and only by breach of this can give an order that is in conflict with such a sense. In consequence of this we find immanent in the life of both that which each respectively combats, and they are seized and broken by that very bond which is rooted in the compass of their own social existence. Antigone is put to death before she can enjoy what she looks forward to as bride, and Creon too is punished in the fatal end of his son and wife, who commit suicide, the former on account of Antigone's death, and the latter owing to Haemon's. Among all the fine creations of the ancient and the modern world—and I am acquainted with pretty nearly everything in such a class, and one ought to know it, and it is quite possible—the "Antigone" of Sophocles is from this point of view in my judgment the most excellent and satisfying work of art.

The tragic issue does not, however, require in every case, as a means of removing both over-emphasized aspects and the equal honour which they respectively claim, the downfall of the contestant parties. The "Eumenides" ends, as we all know, not with the death of Orestes, or the destruction of the Eumenides, these avenging spirits of matricide and filial affection, as opposed to Apollo, who seeks to protect unimpaired the worth of and reverence for the family chief and king, who prompted Orestes to slay Clytemnestra, but with Orestes released from the punishment and honour bestowed on both divinities. At the same time we cannot fail to see in this adjusted conclusion the nature of the authority which the Greeks attached to their gods when they presented them as mere individuals contending with each other. They appear, in short, to the Athenian of everyday life merely as definite aspects of ethical experience which the principles of morality viewed in their complete and harmonious coherence bind together. The votes of the Areopagus are equal on either side. It is Athene, the goddess, the life of Athens, that is, imagined in its essential unity, who adds the white pebble, who frees Orestes, and at the same time promises altars and a cult to the Eumenides no less than Apollo. As a contrast to this type of objective reconciliation the settlement may be, *secondly*, of a more personal character. In other words, the individual concerned in the action may in the last instance surrender his one-sided point of view. In this betrayal by personality of its essential pathos, however, it cannot fail to appear destitute of character; and this contradicts the masculine integrity of such plastic figures. The individual, therefore, can only submit to a higher Power and its counsel or command, to the effect that while on his own account he adheres to such a pathos, the will is nevertheless broken in its bare obstinacy by a god's authority. In such a case the knot is not loosened, but, as in the case of Philoctetes, it is severed by a *deus ex machina*.

But as a *further* and final class, and one more beautiful than the above rather external mode of resolution, we have the reconciliation more properly of the soul itself, in which respect there is, in virtue of the personal significance, a real approach to our modern point of view. The most perfect example of this in ancient drama is to be found in the ever admirable "Oedipus at Colonos" of Sophocles. The protagonist here has unwittingly slain his father, secured the sceptre of Thebes, and the bridal bed of his own mother. He is not rendered unhappy by these unwitting crimes; but the power of divination he has of old possessed makes him realize, despite himself, the darkness of the experience that confronts him, and he becomes fearfully, if indistinctly, aware of what his position is. In this resolution of the riddle in himself he resembles Adam, losing his happiness when he obtains the knowledge of good and evil. What he then does, the seer, is to blind himself, then abdicate the throne and depart from Thebes, very much as Adam and Eve are driven from Paradise. From henceforward he wanders about a helpless old man. Finally a god calls the terribly afflicted man to himself, the man, that is, who refusing the request of his sons that he should return to Thebes, prefers to associate with the Erinyes; the man, in short, who extinguishes all the disruption in himself and who purifies himself in his own soul. His blind eyes are made clear and bright, his limbs are healed, and become a treasure of the city which received him as a free guest. And this illumination in death is for ourselves no less than for him the more truly visible reconciliation which is worked out both in and for himself as individual man, in and through, that is, his essential character. Critics have endeavoured to discover here the temper of the Christian life; we are told we have here the picture of a sinner, whom God receives into His grace; and the fateful misfortunes which expire in their finite condition are made good with the seal of blessedness in death. The reconciliation of the Christian religion, however, is an illumination of the soul, which, bathed in the everlasting waters of salvation, is raised above mortal life and its deeds. Here it is the heart itself, for in such a view the spiritual life can effect this, which buries that life and its deed in the grave of the heart itself, counting the recriminations of earthly guilt as part and parcel of its own earthly individuality; and which, in the full assuredness of the eternally pure and spiritual condition of blessedness, holds itself in itself calm and steadfast against such impeachment. The illumination of Oedipus, on the contrary, remains throughout, in consonance with ancient ideas, the restoration of conscious life from the strife of ethical powers and violations to the renewed and harmonious unity of this *ethical content itself*.

From The Birth of Tragedy*

Friedrich Nietzsche

We have tried to illustrate by this historical example how tragedy, being a product of the spirit of music, must surely perish by the destruction of that spirit. In order to moderate the strangeness of such an assertion and at the same time to demonstrate how we arrived at it, we must now frankly confront certain analogues of our own day. We must step resolutely into the thick of those struggles which are being waged right now between the insatiable thirst for knowledge and man's tragic dependency on art. I will not speak in this connection of those lesser destructive instincts which have at all times opposed art, and especially tragedy, and which in our own day seem to triumph to such an extent that of all the theatrical arts only the farce and the ballet can be said to thrive, with a luxuriance which not all find pleasing. I shall deal here only with the distinguished enemies of the tragic view, that is to say with the exponents of science, all dyed-in-the-wool optimists like their archetype, Socrates. And presently I shall name those forces which seem to promise a rebirth of tragedy and who knows what other fair hopes for the German genius.

Before rushing headlong into the fight let us put on the armor of such perceptions as we have already won. In opposition to all who would derive the arts from a single vital principle, I wish to keep before me those two artistic deities of the Greeks, Apollo and Dionysos. They represent to me, most vividly and concretely, two radically dissimilar realms of art. Apollo embodies the transcendent genius of the *principium individuationis;* through him alone is it possible to achieve redemption in illusion. The mystical jubilation of Dionysos, on the other hand, breaks the spell of individuation and opens a path to the maternal womb of being. Among the great thinkers there is only one who has fully realized the immense discrepancy between the plastic Apollonian art and the Dionysiac art of music. Independently of Greek religious symbols, Schopenhauer assigned to music a totally different character and origin from all the other arts, because it does not, like all the others, represent appearance, but the will directly. It is the metaphysical complement to everything that is physical in the world; the thing-in-itself where all else is appearance (*The World as Will and Idea, I*). Richard Wagner set his seal of approval on this key notion of all esthetics when he wrote in his book on Beethoven that music obeys esthetic principles quite unlike those governing the visual arts and that the category of beauty is altogether inapplica-

* Friedrich Nietzsche, from *The Birth of Tragedy and the Genealogy of Morals* [1870-1871], Francis Golffing, tr. (Doubleday, 1956). Copyright © 1956 by Doubleday & Company, Inc. Reprinted by permission of the publisher.

ble to it—although a wrongheaded esthetic based on a misguided and decadent art has attempted to make music answer to criteria of beauty proper only to the plastic arts, expecting it to generate *pleasure in beautiful forms*. Once I had become aware of this antinomy I felt strongly moved to explore the nature of Greek tragedy, the profoundest manifestation of Hellenic genius. For the first time I seemed to possess the key enabling me to inspect the problem of tragedy in terms that were no longer derived from conventional esthetics. I was given such a strange and unfamiliar glimpse into the essence of Hellenism that it seemed to me that our classical philology, for all its air of triumphant achievement, had only dealt with phantasmagorias and externals.

We might approach this fundamental problem by posing the following question: what esthetic effect is produced when the Apollonian and Dionysiac forces of art, usually separate, are made to work alongside each other? Or, to put it more succinctly, in what relation does music stand to image and concept? Schopenhauer, whose clarity and perspicuity on that point Wagner praises, has, in *The World as Will and Idea, I*, the following passage, which I shall quote entire: "According to all this, we may regard the phenomenal world, or nature, and music as two different expressions of the same thing, which is therefore itself the only medium of the analogy between these two expressions, so that a knowledge of this medium is required in order to understand that analogy. Music, therefore, if regarded as an expression of the world, is in the highest degree a universal language, which is related indeed to the universality of concepts, much as these are related to the particular things. Its universality, however, is by no means the empty universality of abstraction, but is of quite a different kind, and is united with thorough and distinct definiteness. In this respect it resembles geometrical figures and numbers, which are the universal forms of all possible objects of experience and applicable to them all *a priori*, and yet are not abstract but perceptible and thoroughly determinate. All possible efforts, excitements and manifestations of will, all that goes on in the heart of man and that reason includes in the wide, negative concept of feeling, may be expressed by the infinite number of possible melodies, but always in the universality of mere form, without the material; always according to the thing-in-itself, not the phenomenon—of which melodies reproduce the very soul and essence as it were, without the body. This deep relation which music bears to the true nature of all things also explains the fact that suitable music played to any event or surrounding seems to disclose to us its most secret meaning and appears as the most accurate and distinct commentary upon it; as also the fact that whoever gives himself up entirely to the impression of a symphony seems to see all the possible events of life and the world take place in himself. Nevertheless, upon reflection he can find no likeness between the music and the things that passed before his mind. For, as we have said, music is distinguished from all the other arts by the fact that it is not a copy of the phenomenon, or, more accurately, the adequate objectivity of the will, but is the direct copy of the will itself, and therefore represents the metaphysical of everything physical in the world, and the thing-in-itself of every phenomenon. We might, therefore, just as well call the world embodied music as embodied will: and this is the reason why music makes every picture, and indeed every scene of real life and of the world, at once appear with higher significance; all the more so, to be sure, in proportion as its melody is analogous to the inner spirit of the given phenomenon. It rests upon this that we are able to set a poem to music as a song, or a perceptible representation as a pantomime, or both as an opera. Such particular pictures of human life, set to the universal language of music, are never bound to it or correspond to it with stringent necessity, but stand to it only in the relation of an example chosen at will to a general concept. In the determinateness of the real they represent that which music expresses in the universality of mere form. For melodies are to a certain extent, like general concepts, an abstraction from the actual. This actual world, then, the world of particular things, affords the object of perception, the special and the individual, the particular case, both to the universality of concepts and to the universality of the melodies. But these two universalities are in a certain respect opposed to each other; for the concepts contain only the forms, which are first of all abstracted from perception—the separated outward shell of things, as it were—and hence they are, in the strictest sense of the term, *abstracta;* music, on the other hand, gives the inmost kernel which precedes all forms, or the heart of things. This relation may be very well expressed in the language of the schoolmen by saying: the concepts are the *universalia post rem,* but music gives the *universalia ante rem* and the real world the *universalia in re.* That a relation is generally possible between a composition and a perceptible representation rests, as we have said, upon the fact that both are simply different expressions of the same inner being of the world. When now, in the particular case, such a relation is actually given—that is to say, when the composer has been able to express in the universal language of music the emotions of will which constitute the heart of an event—then the melody of the song, the music of the opera, is expressive. But the analogy discovered by the composer between the two must have proceeded from the direct knowledge of the nature of the world unknown to his reason and must not be an imitation produced with conscious intention by means of conceptions; otherwise the music does not express the inner nature of the will itself, but merely gives an inadequate imitation of its phenomenon: all specially imitative music does this."

In accordance with Schopenhauer's doctrine, we interpret music as the immediate language of the will, and our imaginations are stimulated to embody that immaterial world, which speaks to us with lively motion and yet remains invisible. Image and concept, on the other hand, gain a heightened significance under the influence of truly appropriate music. Dionysiac art, then, affects the Apollonian talent in a twofold manner: first, music incites us to a symbolic intuition of the Dionysiac universality; second, it endows that symbolic image with supreme significance. From these facts, perfectly plausible once we have pondered them well, we deduce that music is capable of giving birth to myth, the most significant of similitudes; and above all, to the tragic myth, which is a parable of Dionysiac knowledge. When I spoke earlier of the lyric poet I demonstrated how, through him, music strives to account for its own essence in Apollonian images. Once we grant that music raised to its highest power must similarly try to find an adequate embodiment, it stands to reason that it will also succeed in discovering a symbolic expression for its proper Dionysiac wisdom. And where should we look for that expression if not in tragedy and the tragic spirit?

It is vain to try to deduce the tragic spirit from the commonly accepted categories of art: illusion and beauty. Music alone allows us to understand the delight felt at the annihilation of the individual. Each single instance of such annihilation will clarify for us the abiding phenomenon of Dionysiac art, which expresses the omnipotent will behind individuation, eternal life continuing beyond all appearance and in spite of destruction. The metaphysical delight in tragedy is a translation of instinctive Dionysiac wisdom into images. The hero, the highest manifestation of the will, is destroyed, and we assent, since he too is merely a phenomenon, and the eternal life of the will remains unaffected. Tragedy cries, "We believe that life is eternal!" and music is the direct expression of that life. The aims of plastic art are very different: here Apollo overcomes individual suffering by the glorious apotheosis of what is eternal in appearance: here beauty vanquishes the suffering that inheres in all existence, and pain is, in a certain sense, glossed away from nature's countenance. That same nature addresses us through Dionysiac art and its tragic symbolism, in a voice that rings authentic: "Be like me, the Original Mother, who, constantly creating, finds satisfaction in the turbulent flux of appearances!"

Dionysiac art, too, wishes to convince us of the eternal delight of existence, but it insists that we look for this delight not in the phenomena but behind them. It makes us realize that everything that is generated must be prepared to face its painful dissolution. It forces us to gaze into the horror of individual existence, yet without being turned to stone by the vision: a metaphysical solace momentarily lifts us above the whirl of shifting phenomena. For a brief moment we become, ourselves, the primal Being, and we experience its insatiable hunger for existence. Now we see the struggle, the pain, the destruction of appearances, as necessary, because of the constant proliferation of forms pushing into life, because of the extravagant fecundity of the world will. We feel the furious prodding of this travail in the very moment in which we become one with the immense lust for life and are made aware of the eternity and indestructibility of that lust. Pity and terror notwithstanding, we realize our great good fortune in having life— not as individuals, but as part of the life force with whose procreative lust we have become one.

Our study of the genesis of Greek tragedy has shown us clearly how that tragic art arose out of music, and we believe that our interpretation has for the first time done justice to the original and astounding meaning of the chorus. Yet we must admit that the significance of the tragic myth was never clearly conceptualized by the Greek poets, let alone philosophers. Their heroes seem to us always more superficial in their speeches than in their actions: the myth, we might say, never finds an adequate objective correlative in the spoken word. The structure of the scenes and the concrete images convey a deeper wisdom than the poet was able to put into words and concepts. (The same may be claimed for Shakespeare, whose Hamlet speaks more superficially than he acts, so that the interpretation of *Hamlet* given earlier had to be based on a deeper investigation of the whole texture of the play.) As for Greek tragedy, which we experience only through the printed word, I have already indicated that the incongruence between myth and word may lead us to think it more trivial than it actually is and to presume for it a more superficial effect than, according to the ancients, it must have had. It is so easy to forget that what the poet *qua* poet was unable to achieve, namely the supreme spiritualization of myth, might be achieved by him at any moment in his character of musician. . . .

Tragedy absorbs the highest orgiastic music and in so doing consummates music. But then it puts beside it the tragic myth and the tragic hero. Like a mighty titan, the tragic hero shoulders the whole Dionysiac world and removes the burden from us. At the same time, tragic myth, through the figure of the hero, delivers us from our avid thirst for earthly satisfaction and reminds us of another existence and a higher delight. For this delight the hero readies himself, not through his victories but through his undoing. Tragedy interposes a noble parable, *myth*, between the universality of its music and the Dionysiac disposition of the spectator and in so doing creates the illusion that music is but a supreme instrument for bringing to life the plastic world of myth. By virtue of this noble deception it is now able to move its limbs freely in dithyrambic dance and to yield without reserve to an orgiastic abandon, an indulgence which, without this deception, it could not permit itself. Myth shields us from music while at the same time giving music its maximum freedom. In exchange, music endows the tragic myth with a convincing metaphysical significance, which the unsupported word and image could never achieve, and, moreover, assures the spectator of a supreme delight—though the way passes through annihilation and negation, so that he is made to feel that the very womb of things speaks audibly to him.

Since, in this last passage, I have tentatively set forth a difficult notion, which may not be immediately clear to many, I would now invite my friends to consider a particular instance that is within our common experience and which may support my general thesis. I shall not address myself to those who use the scenic representation and the words and emotions of the actors to help them respond to the music. To none of these is music as a mother tongue, and, notwithstanding that help, they never penetrate beyond the vestibule of musical perception. Some, like Gervinus, do not even attain the vestibule by this means. I address myself only to those having immediate kinship with music, who communicate with things almost entirely through unconscious musical relations. To these genuine musicians I direct my question: 'how can anyone experience the third act of *Tristan and Isolde,* apart from either word or image, simply as the movement of a mighty symphony, without exhausting himself in the overstretching of his soul's pinions?' How is it possible for a man who has listened to the very heartbeat of the world-will and felt the unruly lust for life rush into all the veins of the world, now as a thundering torrent and now as a delicately foaming brook—how is it possible for him to remain unshattered? How can he bear, shut in the paltry glass bell of his individuality, to hear the echoes of innumerable cries of weal and woe sounding out of the "vast spaces of cosmic night," and not wish, amidst these pipings of metaphysical pastoral, to flee incontinent to his primordial home? And yet the reception of such a work does not shatter the recipient, the creation of it the creator. What are we to make of this contradiction?

It is at this point that the tragic myth and the tragic hero interpose between our highest musical excitement and the music, giving us a parable of those cosmic facts of which music alone can speak directly. And yet, if we reacted wholly as Dionysiac beings, the parable would fail entirely of effect, and not for a single moment would it distract our attention from the reverbations of the *universalia ante rem.* But now the Apollonian power, bent upon reconstituting the nearly shattered individual, asserts itself, proffering the balm of a delightful illusion. Suddenly we see only Tristan, lying motionless and torpid, and hear him ask, "Why does that familiar strain waken me?" And what before had seemed a hollow sigh echoing from the womb of things now says to us simply, "Waste and empty the sea." And where, before, we had felt ourselves about to expire in a violent paroxysm of feeling, held by a most tenuous bond to this our life, we now see only the hero, mortally wounded yet not dying, and hear his despairing cry: "To long, even in death, and be unable to die for longing!" And where, before, the jubilation of the horn after such an excess of feeling and such consuming pains would have cut us to the quick, as though it had been the crowning pain, now there stands between us and this absolute jubilation the rejoicing Kurwenal, turned toward the ship which brings Isolde. No matter how deeply pity moves us, that pity saves us from the radical "pity of things," even as the parable of myth saves us from the direct intuition of the cosmic idea, as idea and word save us from the undammed pouring forth of the unconscious will. It is through the workings of that marvelous Apollonian illusion that even the realm of sound takes plastic shape before us, as though it were only a question of the destinies of Tristan and Isolde, molded in the finest, most expressive material.

Thus the Apollonian spirit rescues us from the Dionysiac universality and makes us attend, delightedly, to individual forms. It focuses our pity on these forms and so satisfies our instinct for beauty, which longs for great and noble embodiments. It parades the images of life before us and incites us to seize their ideational essence. Through the massive impact of image, concept, ethical doctrine, and sympathy, the Apollonian spirit wrests man from his Dionysiac self-destruction and deceives him as to the universality of the Dionysiac event. It pretends that he sees only the particular image, e.g., Tristan and Isolde, and that the music serves only to make him see it more intensely. What could possibly be immune from the salutary Apollonian charm, if it is able to create in us the illusion that Dionysos may be an aid to Apollo and further enhance his effects? that music is at bottom a vehicle for Apollonian representations? In the pre-established harmony obtaining between the consummate drama and its music, that drama reaches an acme of visual power unobtainable to the drama of words merely. As we watch the rhythmically moving characters of the stage merge with the independently moving lines of melody into a single curving line of motion, we experience the most delicate harmony of sound and visual movement. The relationships of things thus become directly available to the senses, and we realize that in these relationships the essence of a character and of a melodic line are simultaneously made manifest. And as music forces us to see more, and more inwardly than usual, and spreads before us like a delicate tissue the curtain of the scene, our spiritualized vision beholds the world of the stage at once infinitely expanded and illuminated from within. What analogue could the verbal poet possibly furnish—he who tries to bring about that inward expansion of the visible stage world, its inner illumination, by much more indirect and imperfect means, namely word and concept? But, once musical tragedy has appropriated the word, it can at the same time present the birthplace and subsoil of the word and illuminate the genesis of the word from within. And yet it must be emphatically stated that the process I have described is only a marvelous illusion, by whose effects we are delivered from the Dionysiac extravagance and onrush. For, at bottom, music and drama stand in the opposite relation: music is the true idea of the cosmos, drama but a reflection of that idea. The identity between the melodic line and the dramatic character, between relations of harmony and character, obtains in an opposite sense from what we experience when we witness a musical tragedy. However concretely we move, enliven, and illuminate the characters from within, they will always remain mere appearance, from which there is no gateway leading to the true heart of reality. But music addresses us from that center; and though countless appearances were to file past that same music, they would never exhaust its nature but remain external replicas only. Nothing is gained for the understanding of either music or drama by resorting to that popular and utterly false pair of opposites, body and soul. Yet this contrast, crude and unphilosophical as it is, seems to have developed among our estheticians into an article of faith. About the contrast between the phenomenon and the thing-in-itself, on the other hand, they have never learned anything nor, for some obscure reason, wanted to learn.

If our analysis has shown that the Apollonian element in tragedy has utterly triumphed over the Dionysiac quintessence of music, bending the latter to its own purposes—which are to define the drama completely—still an important reservation must be made. At the point that matters most the Apollonian illusion has been broken through and destroyed. This drama which deploys before us, having all its movements and characters illumined from within by the aid of music—as though we witnessed the coming and going of the shuttle as it weaves the tissue—this drama achieves a total effect quite beyond the scope of any Apollonian artifice. In the final effect of tragedy the Dionysiac element triumphs once again: its closing sounds are such as were never heard in the Apollonian realm. The Apollonian illusion reveals its identity as the veil thrown over the Dionysiac meanings for the duration of the play, and yet the illusion is so potent that at its close the Apollonian drama is projected into a sphere where it begins to speak with Dionysiac wisdom, thereby denying itself and its Apollonian concreteness. The difficult relations between the two elements in tragedy may be symbolized by a fraternal union between the two deities: Dionysos speaks the language of Apollo, but Apollo, finally, the language of Dionysos; thereby the highest goal of tragedy and of art in general is reached.

The Ancient Tragical Motif as Reflected in the Modern*

Søren Kierkegaard

An Essay in the Fragmentary Read before a Meeting of the Symparanekromenoi

Should anyone feel called upon to say that the tragic always remains the tragic, I should in a sense have no objection to make, insofar as every historical evolution always remains within the sphere of the concept. Supposing, namely, that the word had a meaning, and that the two-fold repetition of the word tragic should not be regarded as constituting a meaningless parenthesis about a contentless nothing, then the meaning must be this, that the content of a concept does not dethrone the concept, but enriches it. On the other hand, it can scarcely have escaped the attention of any observer, and it is something that the reading and theater-going public already believes itself to be in lawful possession of, as its share dividend in the labors of the experts, that there is an essential difference between the ancient and modern tragedy. If one were again to emphasize this distinction absolutely, and by its aid, first stealthily, then perhaps forcibly, separate the conceptions of the ancient and modern tragical, his procedure would be no less absurd than that of the first, since he would forget that the foothold necessary for him was the tragic itself, and that this again was so far from being able to separate, that it really bound the ancient and modern together. And it must be regarded as a warning against every such prejudiced attempt to separate them, that aestheticians still constantly turn back to established Aristotelian determinations and requirements in connection with the tragical, as being exhaustive of the concept; and the warning is needed so much the more, as no one can escape a feeling of sadness in observing that however much the world has changed, the conception of the tragic is still essentially unchanged, just as weeping is still natural to all men alike.

Reassuring as this may seem to him who desires no such separation, least of all a breach, the same difficulty which has just been rejected reappears in an-

---

* Søren Kierkegaard, "The Ancient Tragical Motif as Reflected in the Modern," from *Either/Or; A Fragment of Life*, Vol. 1 [1843], David F. and Lillian M. Swenson, trs. (copyright 1944 © 1959 by Princeton University Press, Princeton Paperback 1971), pp. 111–113. Reprinted by permission of Princeton University Press.

other and almost more dangerous form. That we still constantly go back to the Aristotelian aesthetics, not merely from a dutiful sense of respect, or because of old habits, no one will deny who has any knowledge of modern aesthetics, and thus perceives how exactly this latter follows Aristotle in all the main points. But as soon as we view these a little more in detail, the difficulties immediately become evident. The qualifications are very general, and one may in one sense be quite in agreement with Aristotle, and in another sense wholly disagree with him. In order not to anticipate the following essay by mentioning at once the subject which will constitute its content, I prefer to illustrate my meaning by citing the corresponding observation with respect to comedy. If an old aesthetician had said that comedy presupposes character and situation, and has for its purpose the arousal of laughter, one might indeed turn back to this again and again; but when one reflects upon how widely different are the things which can make a human being laugh, then one soon becomes convinced of how tremendously inclusive this requirement was. Whoever has at any time made his own laughter and that of others the subject of his observation; whoever, as in this study, has had his eye not so much on the accidental as on the general; whoever has observed with psychological interest how different are the things which in each generation arouse laughter, will readily be convinced that the invariable requirement that comedy ought to arouse laughter contains a high degree of variability relative to the different conceptions of the ridiculous entertained in the world consciousness, without the variability becoming so diffuse that the corresponding somatic expression would be that the laughter expressed itself in tears. So also in relation to the tragic.

That which will here constitute the principal content of this little inquiry, is not so much the relation between ancient and modern tragedy, as it will be an attempt to show how the characteristic of ancient tragedy is embodied within the modern, so that the true tragedy appears therein. But however much I may endeavor to make this evident, I shall still refrain from every prophecy about this being what the age demands, so that its appearance becomes entirely without result, more especially so as the entire tendency of the age is in the direction of the comic. Existence is more or less undermined by doubt on the part of the subjects, isolation constantly gets more and more the upper hand, something one can best be convinced of by giving attention to the multitudinous social exertions. These movements show just as much about the isolated endeavors of the age that they seek to counteract, as they show that they are trying to counteract it in an irrational manner. The isolationist idea consists in one stressing oneself as number; when one will stress himself as one, then this is isolation; in this may all the friends of the Association grant me leave, even if unable or unwilling to see that there is quite the same isolation, if hundreds stress themselves exclusively as hundreds. The number is always a matter of indifference, whether it be one or a thousand, or the population of the whole world numerically determined. This spirit of the Association that stresses number, is, therefore, just as revolutionary as the spirit it would counteract. When David would rightly savor his power and glory, he took a census of the people; in our age, on the other hand, one might say that the people, in order to feel their importance in comparison with a higher power, count themselves. Hence, all these associations bearing the stamp of the arbitrary are most frequently created for some accidental purpose, naturally governed by the associations.

The many associations thus prove the disorganization of the age, and themselves contribute toward hastening that dissolution; they are the infusoria in the organism of the state, which indicate that it is disorganized. When was it that political clubs began to be general in Greece, if not at the very moment when the state was in process of dissolution? And has not our own age a remarkable similarity to that one, which not even Aristophanes could make more ludicrous than it actually was? Is not the invisible and spiritual bond which held the state together politically, lost; is not the power of religion which held fast to the invisible, weakened and annihilated; have not the statesmen and clergy this in common, that they, like the augurs of old, can scarcely look at one another without smiling? One characteristic our age certainly has to a greater degree than Greece, this namely, that it is more melancholy, and hence it is more profoundly in despair. Thus, our age is melancholy enough to realize that there is something which is called responsibility, and this indicates something significant. While, therefore, everyone wishes to rule, no one wishes to accept responsibility. There is even yet a story fresh in our memories, that a French statesman, when a portfolio was offered to him for a second time, declared that he would accept it, but only on the condition that the secretary of the council should become responsible. It is well known that the king of France is not responsible, while his ministers are; the minister does not wish to be responsible, but will be minister on condition that the secretary of state become responsible; it finally results naturally in the watchmen or street commissioners becoming responsible. Would not this story of shifted responsibility really be a proper subject for Aristophanes! And on the other hand, why are the government and rulers so afraid of accepting responsibility, unless because they fear an attack from an opposition, which equally seeks to evade responsibility? When, then, one considers these two powers in opposition to one another, but not able to come to grips with each other, because the one constantly vanishes from the other, the one only a duplicate of the other, then such a lay-out is certainly not without its comic effect. This is sufficient to show that the bond which essentially holds the state together is disorganized, but that it should thereby result in isolation is naturally comic, and the comic lies in trying to stress the *subjective as mere form.* Every isolated individual always becomes comic by stressing his own accidental individuality over against necessary development. It would undoubtedly be most deeply comic for some accidental individual to get the universal idea of wishing to be the savior of the world. On the other hand, the appearance of Christ is in a certain sense (in another sense it is infinitely more) the deepest tragedy, because Christ came in the fullness of time, and, what I must later particularly emphasize, He bore the sins of the world.

It is well known that Aristotle mentions two things, thought and character, as the source of action in tragedy, but he notes also that the main thing is the plot, and the individuals do not act in order to present characters, but the characters are included for the sake of the action. Here one readily notices a divergence from modern tragedy. The peculiarity of ancient tragedy is that the action is not only the result of the character, that the action is not reflected sufficiently into the subject, but that the action itself has a relative addition of suffering. Hence the ancient tragedy has not developed the dialogue to the point of exhaustive reflection, so that everything is absorbed in it; it has in the monologue and the chorus exactly the factors supplemental to the dialogue. Whether the chorus approaches nearer the epic substantiality or the lyric exaltation, it thus still indicates, as it were, the more which will not be absorbed in the individuality; the monologue again is more the lyric concentration and has the more which will not be absorbed in action and situation. In ancient tragedy the action itself has an epic moment in it, it is as much event as action. The reason for this naturally lies in the fact that the ancient world did not have the subjectivity reflected in it. Even if the individual moved freely, he still rested in the substantial categories of state, family, and destiny. This substantial category is exactly the fatalistic element in Greek tragedy, and its exact peculiarity. The hero's destruction is, therefore, not only a result of his own deeds, but is also a suffering, whereas in modern tragedy, the hero's destruction is really not suffering, but is action. In modern times, therefore, situation and character are really predominant. The tragic hero is subjectively reflected in himself, and this reflection has not only reflected him out of every immediate relation to state, race, and destiny, but has often even reflected him out of his own preceding life. We are interested in a certain definite moment of his life, considered as his own deed. Because of this the tragedy can be exhaustively represented in situation and dialogue, since nothing of the more immediate is left behind. Hence, modern tragedy has no epic foreground, no epic heritage. The hero stands and falls entirely on his own acts.

This brief but adequate analysis may be useful in illuminating the difference between ancient and modern tragedy, which I regard as having great significance, the difference, namely, in the nature of tragic guilt. It is well known that Aristotle requires the tragic hero to have guilt. But just as the action in Greek tragedy is intermediate between activity and passivity (action and suffering), so is also the hero's guilt, and therein lies the tragic collision. On the other hand, the more the subjectivity becomes reflected, the more one sees the individual left Pelagianally to himself, the more his guilt becomes ethical. The tragedy lies between these two extremes. If the individual is entirely without guilt, then is the tragic interest nullified, for the tragic collision is thereby enervated; if, on the other hand, he is absolutely guilty, then he can no longer interest us tragically. Hence, it is certainly a misunderstanding of the tragic, when our age strives to let the whole tragic destiny become transubstantiated in individuality and subjectivity. One would know nothing to say about the hero's past life, one would throw his whole life upon his own shoulders, as being the result of his own acts, would make him accountable for everything, but in so doing, one would also transform his aesthetic guilt into an ethical one. The tragic hero thus becomes bad, the evil becomes precisely the tragic subject, but evil has no aesthetic interest, and sin is not an aesthetic element. This mistaken endeavor certainly has its cause in the whole tendency of our age toward the comic. The comic lies exactly in isolation; when one would maintain the tragic within this isolation, then one gets evil in all its baseness, not the truly tragic guilt in its ambiguous innocence. It is not difficult when one looks about in modern literature, to find examples. Thus, the very ingenious work of Grabbe, *Faust and Don Juan*, is precisely constructed around this evil. However, in order not to argue from a single work, I prefer to show it in the whole general consciousness of the age. If one wished to represent an individual whom an unhappy childhood had influenced so disturbingly that this impression occasioned his downfall, such a defense would simply not appeal to the present age, and this naturally not because it was wrongly handled, for I have a right to assume that it would be handled with distinction, but because our age employs another standard. It would know nothing about such coddling; without knowing, it holds every individual responsible for his own life. Hence, if he goes to the dogs, it is not tragic, but it is bad. One might now believe that this must be a kingdom of the gods, this generation in which I have the honor to live. On the contrary, this is by no means the case; the energy, the courage, which would thus be the creator of its own destiny, aye, its own creator, is an illusion, and when the age loses the tragic, it gains despair. There lies a sadness and a healing power in the tragic which one truly should not despise, and when a man in the extraordinary manner our age affects, would gain himself, he loses himself and becomes comical. Every individual, however primitive he may be, is still a child of God, of his age, of his family and friends, herein lies its truth; if in this relativity he tries to be the absolute, then he becomes ridiculous.

One sometimes finds in the language a word which, because of its form, has been used so often in a certain case that at last it is used independently, like an adverb perhaps. Then for the experts such a word acquires an emphasis and a weakness that it never loses. If, in spite of this, it should attempt to change into a substantive and to be inflected in all five cases, it would be truly comic. And so it is, too, with the individual, when perhaps with great difficulty he issues from the womb of time, he will in this tremendous relativity be absolute. If, however, he renounces this claim of the absolute in order to become relative, then he has *eo ipso* the tragic, even if he was the happiest of individuals; indeed I might say that an individual does not become happy until he has the tragic. The tragic has in it an infinite gentleness; it is really in the aesthetic sense with regard to human life, what the divine love and mercy are; it is even milder, and hence I may say that it is like a mother's love, soothing and troubled. The ethical is strict and harsh. If a criminal should therefore plead before the judge that his mother had a propensity for stealing, especially at the time she was carrying him, then the judge might secure the opinion of the health commissioner about his mental condition, and decide that he was dealing with a thief, and not with a thief's mother. Since we are talking about a criminal, the sinner can hardly flee to the temple of aesthetics, but yet the aesthetic will provide an extenuating phrase for him. However, it would be wrong for him to resort to this, for his path leads him not to the aesthetic but to the religious. The aesthetic lies behind him, and it would be a new sin for him now to grasp at the aesthetic. The religious is the expression of a paternal love, since it contains the ethical, but it is softened, and so without being just the same, it gives mildness to the tragic through its continuity. But while the aesthetic gives this rest of continuity before the contrast of sin is stressed, the religious does not give it until this contrast is seen in all its frightfulness. Just at the moment when the sinner almost faints under the universal sin that he has taken upon himself, because he felt that only by becoming more guilty would the prospect of salvation be greater—in that same moment of terror, the consolation shows him that it is a universal sin which has also manifested itself in him. But this consolation is a religious consolation, and he who thinks to gain this in some other way, e.g., by aesthetic vaporings, has accepted this consolation in vain, and has not really gained it. In a certain sense, therefore, it is quite properly tactful of the age to hold the individual responsible for everything, but the unfortunate thing is that it does not do it deeply and intensively enough, and hence its vacillation. It is self-complacent enough to reject the tears of tragedy, but it is also self-complacent enough to dispense with the divine mercy. But what is human life when we take these two things away, what is the human race? Either the sadness of the tragic, or the profound sorrow and joy of the religious. Or is that not the characteristic of everything that proceeds from that happy people—a heaviness, a sadness, in its art, in its poetry, in its life, and in its joy?

In the preceding I have principally attempted to emphasize the difference between ancient and modern tragedy, insofar as this is illustrated in the guilt of the tragic hero. This is precisely the focus from which everything radiates in its peculiar difference. If the hero is unambiguously guilty, the monologue disappears and there is no destiny; the thought is transparent in the dialogue, and the action in the situation. The same thing may also be explained from another side, with regard to the mood which the tragedy evokes in the spectator. It may be remembered that Aristotle requires that tragedy should arouse fear and compassion in the spectator. I recall that Hegel in his *Aesthetics* adopted this view, and indulged in a double reflection about each of the points, which was not, however, particularly exhaustive. When Aristotle separates fear and compassion, then one might interpret fear as the mood which accompanies the individual idea, compassion as the mood which is the definitive impression. This latter mood is the one that appeals to me most, because it is the one which corresponds to the tragic guilt, and therefore, it has the same dialectic as the concept of guilt. Hegel observes that there are two kinds of sympathy, the ordinary kind which is concerned with the finite aspect of suffering, and the true tragic pity. This observation is indeed quite correct, but to me it is of less importance, since this common emotion is a misunderstanding which can just as well apply to ancient as to modern tragedy. True and powerful, however, is what Hegel adds regarding true compassion: "True compassion is, on the contrary, a synthesis of sympathy and the moral justification of the sufferer." While Hegel rather considers sympathy in general and its differences in the variations of the individualities, I prefer to emphasize the different kinds of sympathy in relation to the different kinds of tragic guilt. Before proceeding to indicate this immediately, I shall allow the word sympathy to split itself into the *suffering* (passion, *pathikos*), and add particularly the sympathetic which lies in the word *sym* and yet in such a manner that I do not seem to assert something about the spectator's mood, which might show his arbitrariness, but in such a way that when I explain the difference in his mood, I also express the difference of the tragic guilt.

In ancient tragedy the sorrow is deeper, the pain less; in modern, the pain is greater, the sorrow less. Sorrow always contains something more substantial than pain. Pain always implies a reflection over suffering which sorrow does not know. From a psychological standpoint it is always interesting to watch a child when it sees an older person suffer. The child is not reflective enough to feel grief, and yet its sorrow is infinitely deep. It is not reflective enough to have any conception about sin and guilt; when it sees an older person suffer, it does not occur to it to reflect upon it, and yet when the cause of the suffering is concealed from it, there is a dim suspicion about it in its sorrow. Such, but in complete and profound harmony, is the Greek sorrow, and therefore it is at one and the same time so gentle and so deep. When an older person sees a child suffer, his pain is greater, his sorrow less. The more clearly the conception of guilt stands out, the greater is the pain, the less profound the sorrow. If one now applies this to the relation between ancient and modern tragedy, then must one say: in the ancient tragedy, the sorrow is deeper, and in the consciousness which corresponds to this, the sorrow is deeper. It must in fact be constantly remembered that the sorrow does not lie in myself, but it lies in the tragedy, and that I, in order to understand

the deep sorrow of the Greek tragedy, must myself live in the Greek consciousness. Hence, it is certainly often only an affectation when so many profess to admire the Greek tragedies; for it is very evident that our age, at least, has little
sympathy for that which precisely constitutes Greek sorrow. The sorrow is deeper because the guilt has the aesthetic ambiguity. In modern times, the pain is
greater. It is a fearful thing to fall into the hands of the living God. One might
say this about Greek tragedy. The wrath of the gods is terrible, but the pain is
not so great as in modern tragedy where the hero bears the whole weight of his
guilt, is himself transparent in his suffering of his guilt. Here it is relevant in conformity with the tragic guilt, to show which sorrow is the true aesthetic sorrow,
and which the true aesthetic pain. The bitterest pain is manifestly remorse, but
remorse has ethical not aesthetic reality. It is the bitterest pain because it has the
total transparency of the entire guilt, but just because of this transparency, it
does not interest us aesthetically. Remorse has a sacredness which obscures the
aesthetic, it may not be seen, least of all by the spectator, and it requires quite a
different kind of self-activity. Modern comedy has sometimes presented remorse
on the stage, but this only shows a lack of judgment on the part of the author.
One may indeed be reminded of the psychological interest it can have to see remorse delineated on the stage, but again the psychological interest is not the aesthetic. This is part of the confusion which in our age asserts itself in so many
ways: we look for a thing where we ought not to look for it, and what is worse,
we find it where we ought not to find it; we wish to be edified in the theater,
aesthetically impressed in church, we would be converted by novels, get enjoyment out of books of devotion, we want philosophy in the pulpit, and the
preacher in the professorial chair. This pain of remorse is consequently not the
aesthetic pain, and yet it is apparently this which the modern age tends toward
as the highest tragic interest. This is also true with regard to the tragic guilt. Our
age has lost all the substantial categories of family, state, and race. It must leave
the individual entirely to himself, so that in a stricter sense he becomes his own
creator, his guilt is consequently sin, his pain remorse; but this nullifies the tragedy. Also, in a stricter sense, the tragedy of suffering has exactly lost its tragic interest, for the power from which the suffering comes has lost its significance, and
the spectators cry: "Help yourself, and heaven will help you!" or, in other words,
the spectator has lost his compassion, but compassion is in a subjective as well as
an objective sense, the precise expression for the tragic.

For the sake of clarity I shall now, before carrying this explanation farther,
define a little more carefully the true aesthetic sorrow. Sorrow has the opposite
movement from that which pain has; when one does not spoil this by means of a
wretched consistency—something I, too, shall avoid in another way—one may
say: the more innocent, the more profound the sorrow. If one insists on that, then
one destroys the tragic. An element of guilt always remains, but this element is
never really subjectively reflected; hence the sorrow in the Greek tragedy is so
deep. In order to prevent ill-timed consequences, I shall only note that all the exaggerations only succeed in carrying the matter over into another sphere. The
synthesis of absolute innocence and absolute guilt is not an aesthetic category,
but a metaphysical one. This is the real reason why one has always been
ashamed to call the life of Christ a tragedy, because one instinctively feels that
aesthetic categories do not exhaust the matter. Then, too, it shows in another
way, that Christ's life is something more than can be exhausted in aesthetic cate-

gories: that is, that these neutralize themselves in this phenomenon, and are hushed in indifference.

The tragic action always has an element of suffering in it, and the tragic suffering an element of action, the aesthetic lies in the relativity of these. The identity of an absolute action and an absolute suffering is beyond the powers of aesthetics, and belongs to metaphysics. This identity is exemplified in the life of Christ, for His suffering is absolute because the action is absolutely free, and his action is absolute suffering because it is absolute obedience. Hence the element of guilt which remains in the tragic consciousness is not subjectively reflected, and this makes the sorrow profound. The tragic guilt is something more than merely subjective guilt, it is an inherited guilt; but inherited guilt, like inherited sin, is a substantial category, and it is exactly this substantiality which makes the sorrow deeper. The ever admired tragic trilogy of Sophocles, *Oedipus Coloneus*, *Oedipus Rex* and *Antigone*, essentially centers about this true tragic interest. But inherited guilt contains the self-contradiction of being guilt, and yet not being guilt. The bond which makes the individual guilty is precisely piety, but the guilt which he thus draws down upon himself, has every possible aesthetic ambiguity. One might readily conclude that the people who developed profound tragedy must have been the Jews. Thus, when they say about Jehovah that He is a jealous God who visits the sins of the fathers upon the children unto the third and fourth generations, or when one hears those terrible imprecations in the Old Testament, then one might easily be tempted to seek here for tragic material. But Judaism is too ethically developed for this; Jehovah's curses are, even though terrible, still also righteous punishment. This was not the case in Greece; the wrath of the gods had no ethical character, but only aesthetic ambiguity.

In Greek tragedy a transition is found from sorrow to pain, and as an example of this I might mention *Philoctetes*. This, in the stricter sense, is a tragedy of suffering. But, too, a high degree of objectivity obtains here. The Greek hero rests in his fate, it is unchangeable, there is nothing farther to be said about it. This element furnishes the precise moment of sorrow in the pain. The first doubt with which pain really begins is this: why has this befallen me, why can it not be otherwise? There is, indeed, in Philoctetes a high degree of reflection, which has always seemed remarkable to me, and which essentially separates him from that immortal trilogy: there is the masterly depicting of the self-contradiction in his pain, which contains so deep a human truth, but there is still an objectivity which sustains the whole. Philoctetes' reflection is not absorbed in itself, and it is genuinely Greek when he complains that no one knows about his pain. There is an extraordinary truth in this, and there also appears here the precise difference between his pain and the precise reflective pain which always wants to be alone with its pain, which seeks a new pain in this solitude of pain.

The true tragic sorrow consequently requires an element of guilt, the true tragic pain an element of innocence; the true tragic sorrow requires an element of transparency, the true tragic pain an element of obscurity. This I believe best indicates the dialectic wherein there is a synthesis of the categories of sorrow and pain, as well as also the dialectic which lies in the concept of tragic guilt.

Since it is contrary to the spirit of our organization to produce closely coherent works or greater wholes, since it is not our purpose to labor upon a Tower of Babel, which God in His righteousness can descend upon and destroy, since we are conscious of the fact that this confusion of tongues happened justly, recognizing it as a characteristic of all human striving in its truth, that it is fragmentary, and that it is precisely this which separates it from Nature's infinite coherence; that the wealth of an individual consists precisely in the energy he shows in producing the fragmentary, and that that which brings enjoyment to the producing individual also brings enjoyment to the receiving individual, not the troublesome and meticulous execution, nor the tedious apprehension of this execution, but the production and enjoyment of the gleaming transitoriness, which for the producer contains something more than the thorough execution, since it is the appearance of the Idea, and for the recipient, it contains something more, since its fulguration awakens his own productivity—since, I say, all this is contrary to the purpose of our Association, moreover, since the period just read must be regarded as a serious attempt in the interjectory style, wherein the ideas break out without breaking through, which in our society has an official status: then I shall, after having called attention to the fact that my procedure still cannot be called rebellious, since the bonds which hold the sentence together are so loose that the intermediary clauses stand out aphoristically and arbitrarily enough, merely call to mind that my style has made an attempt apparently to be what it is not—revolutionary.

Our society needs in every way a renewal and rebirth, to the end that its inner activity may be renewed by a new description of its productivity. Let us then describe our purpose as an attempt in fragmentary pursuits, or in the art of writing posthumous papers. A completely finished work has no relation to the poetic personality; in the case of posthumous papers one constantly feels, because of the interruption, the desultoriness, a need to romance about the personality. Posthumous papers are like a ruin, and what haunted place could be more natural for the interred? The art, then, is artistically to produce the same effect, the same appearance of carelessness and the accidental, the same anacoluthonic flight of thought; it consists in producing an enjoyment which naturally never actually becomes present, but always has an element of the past in it, so that it is present in the past. This has already been expressed in the word: posthumous. In a certain sense, everything which a poet has produced is posthumous; but one would never think of calling a completed work posthumous, even though it has the accidental quality of not having been published in the poet's lifetime. Also, I assume that this is the true characteristic of all human productivity, as we have apprehended it, that it is a heritage, since men are not permitted to live eternally in the sight of the gods. Hence, I shall call the effects that are produced among us an artistic heritage; the negligence and the indolence, I shall call the genius we appreciate; the *vis inertia* the natural law that we worship. By this explanation I have now complied with our sacred customs and rules.

So draw nearer to me, dear brothers of Symparanekromenoi; close around me as I send my tragic heroine out into the world, as I give the daughter of sorrow a dowry of pain as a wedding gift. She is my creation, but still her outline is so vague, her form so nebulous, that each one of you is free to imagine her as you will, and each one of you can love her in your own way. She is my creation, her thoughts are my thoughts, and yet it is as if I had rested with her in a night of love, as if she had entrusted me with her deep secret, breathed it and her soul out in my embrace, and as if in the same moment she changed before me, vanished, so that her actuality could only be traced in the mood that remained, instead of the converse being true, that my mood brought her forth to a greater and greater actuality. I place the words in her mouth, and yet it is as if I abused her confidence; to me, it is as if she stood reproachfully behind me, and yet, conversely, it is in her mystery that she becomes ever more and more visible. She is my possession, my lawful possession, and yet sometimes it is as if I had slyly insinuated myself into her confidence, as if I must constantly see myself standing back of her; and yet, conversely, she lies constantly before me, she constantly comes into existence only as I bring her forth. She is called Antigone. This name I retain from the ancient tragedy, as I connect the whole development with that, although, from another point of view, everything is modern. First, however, a remark. I use a feminine figure because I firmly believe that a feminine nature will be most successful in showing the difference. As woman she will have substantiality enough to show sorrow, but as belonging in a reflective world, she will have reflection enough to feel pain. In order to experience sorrow, the tragic guilt must vacillate between guilt and innocence; that whereby the guilt passes over into her consciousness must always be a determination of substantiality. But since in order to experience sorrow, the tragic guilt must have this vagueness, so reflection must not be present in its infinitude, for then it would reflect her out of her guilt, in that the reflection in its infinite subjectivity cannot let the element of inherited guilt remain, which causes the sorrow. Since, however, her reflection is awake, it will not reflect her out of her sorrow, but into it, each moment transforming her sorrow into pain.

Labdakos' family is, then, the object of the indignation of the angry gods. Oedipus has slain the sphinx, liberated Thebes; he has murdered his father, married his mother, and Antigone is the daughter of this marriage. Thus goes the Greek tragedy. Here I diverge from the Greek. Everything is contained in mine, and yet everything is different. That he has slain the sphinx and liberated Thebes is known to everyone, and Oedipus lives honored and admired, happy in his marriage with Jocasta. The rest is concealed from the eyes of men, and no suspicion has ever called this horrible nightmare into actuality. Only Antigone knows it. How she has come to know it lies outside the tragic interest, and everyone is free to work out his own explanation in regard to it. At an early age, before she was fully developed, dim suspicions of this horrible secret had at times gripped her soul, until certainty with a single blow cast her into the arms of anxiety. Here we have at once a category of modern tragedy. Anxiety is, namely, a reflection, and insofar is essentially different from sorrow. Anxiety is the means by which the subject appropriates his sorrow and assimilates it. Anxiety is the energy of the movement by which sorrow burrows into one's heart. But the movement is not swift like the thrust of a dart, which is continuous, it is not once for all, but it is constantly continuing. As a passionate, erotic glance desires its object, so anxiety looks upon sorrow to desire it. As the quiet, incorruptible glance of love is preoccupied with the beloved object, so anxiety occupies itself with sorrow. But anxiety has another element in it which makes it cling even more strongly to its object, for it both loves and fears it. Anxiety has a two-fold function, partly it is the detective instinct which constantly touches, and by means of this key, discovers sorrow, as it goes round about the sorrow. Or anxiety is sudden, posits the whole sorrow in the present moment, yet so that this present moment instantly dissolves in succession. Anxiety is in this sense a truly tragic category, and the old saying: *quem deus vult pardere, primum dementat*, in truth rightfully applies here. The language itself proves that anxiety is a reflective determination; for I always say: my anxiety, about something in which I separate the anxiety from that for which I am anxious, and I can never use anxiety in an objective sense; whereas when I say: my sorrow, it can just as well express that which I sorrow over, as my sorrow over it. In addition, anxiety always contains a reflection in time, for I cannot be anxious about the present, but only about the past or the future; but the past and the future so resisting one another that the present vanishes, are reflective determinations. The Greek sorrow, on the contrary, like the whole of Greek life, is a present thing, and therefore, the sorrow is deeper, but the pain less. Anxiety therefore belongs essentially to the tragic. Hence, Hamlet is deeply tragic because he suspects his mother's guilt. Robert, the devil, asks how it could happen that he caused so much evil. Høgne, whom his mother had begotten by a troll, happens accidentally to see his image in the water, and asks his mother how his body had acquired such a shape.

The difference is now easily perceptible. In the Greek tragedy Antigone is not at all concerned about her father's unhappy destiny. This rests like an impenetrable sorrow over the whole family. Antigone lives as carefree as any other young Grecian maiden, indeed the chorus pities her, since her death is foreordained, because she must quit this life at so early an age, quit it without having tasted its most beautiful joys, evidently forgetting the family's own deep sorrow. However, it should by no means be said that it is thoughtlessness, or that the particular individual stands alone by himself, without worrying about his relationship to the family. But that is genuinely Greek. The life-relationships when once assigned to them are like the heaven under which they live. If this is dark and cloudy, it is also unchangeable. This furnishes the keynote of the Greek soul, and this is sorrow, not pain. In Antigone the tragic guilt concentrates itself about one definite point, that she had buried her brother in defiance of the king's prohibition. If this is seen as an isolated fact, as a collision between sisterly affection and piety and an arbitrary human prohibition, then *Antigone* would cease to be a Greek tragedy, it would be an entirely modern tragic subject. That which in the Greek sense affords the tragic interest, is that Oedipus' sorrowful destiny re-echoes in the brother's unhappy destiny, in the sister's collision with a simple human prohibition; the tragic fate of Oedipus is, as it were, the after effects which ramify from a single branch of his family. This is the totality which makes the sorrow of the spectator so infinitely deep. It is not an individual who goes down, it is a small world, it is the objective sorrow, which, released, now advances in its own terrible consistency, like a force of nature, and Antigone's unhappy fate is but an echo of her father's, an intensified sorrow. When, therefore, Antigone in defiance of the king's prohibition resolves to bury her brother, we do not see in this so much a free action on her part as a predestined necessity, which visits the father's crime upon the children. There is indeed enough freedom of action to make us love Antigone for her sisterly affection, but in the necessity of fate there is also, as it were, a higher refrain which not only includes Oedipus, but also his family.

While, then, the Greek Antigone lives so carefree that were it not for the disclosure of this new fact, we might imagine her life as very happy in its gradual unfolding, our Antigone's life, on the contrary, is essentially over. I have not endowed her stingily, and as we say that a good word is like apples of gold in pictures of silver, so I have placed the fruit of her sorrow in a cup of pain. Her dowry is not a vain magnificence which moth and rust can corrupt, it is an eternal treasure. Thieves cannot break in and steal it; she will herself be too vigilant for that. Her life does not unfold like that of the Greek Antigone, it is not turned outward but inward, the scene is not external but internal, it is an invisible scene.

Should it not make me happy, dear Symparanekromenoi, to arouse your interest in such a maiden, or shall I resort to a *captatio benevolentiae?* Then, too, she does not belong to the world she lives in; even though her life is flower-strewn and healthy, it is still really a secret life. Although she is living, she is in another sense dead; quiet is her life and secretive, the world does not even hear her sigh, for her sigh is buried in the depths of her soul. I do not need to remind you that she is by no means a weak and sickly woman, rather she is proud and vigorous. There is nothing, perhaps, which ennobles a human being so much as keeping a secret. It gives a man's whole life a meaning which it can have only for himself. It saves him from every vain consideration about his environment, self-contained he rests, blessed in his secret—that one could almost say even if his secret was most reprehensible.

Such was our Antigone. She is proud of her secret, proud that she has been selected in a peculiar manner to be the savior of her father's honor and renown, and of that of her family; and when the grateful people acclaim Oedipus with praise and gratitude, then she feels her own importance, and her secret sinks ever deeper into her soul, more inaccessible to every living being. She feels how much responsibility is placed in her hands, and this gives her a supernatural greatness, which is necessary if she is to engage our attention as a tragic personality. As an individual figure she must be able to interest us. She is more than a young girl in general, and yet she is a young girl; she is a bride, and yet she is all innocence and purity. As a bride, woman achieves her destiny, and hence a woman can ordinarily interest us only to the degree that she is brought into relation to her destiny. However, there is an analogy here. One says of a bride of God that she has the inward faith and spirit in which she rests. Our Antigone I should call a bride in a perhaps even more beautiful sense, indeed she is almost more, she is mother, she is in the purely aesthetic sense *virgo mater*, she carries her secret under her heart, hidden and concealed. She is silence, precisely because she is secretive, but this retrospection which lies in silence, gives her a supernatural bearing. She is proud of her sorrow, she is jealous for it, for her sorrow is her love. But still her sorrow is not a dead, immovable possession; it moves constantly, it gives birth to pain, and is born in pain. When a girl resolves to dedicate her life to an idea, when she stands there with the sacrificial wreath upon her brow, she stands as a bride, for the great inspiring idea transforms her, and the votive wreath is like a bridal garland. She knows not any man, and yet she is a bride; she does not even know the idea which inspires her, for that would be unwomanly, and yet she is a bride.

Such is our Antigone, the bride of sorrow. She dedicates her life to sorrow over her father's destiny, over her own. Such a misfortune as has overtaken her father calls for sorrow, and yet there is no one who can grieve over it, because there is no one who knows about it. And as the Greek Antigone cannot bear to have her brother's corpse flung away without the last honors, so she feels how hard it would have been if no man had known this; it worries her that no tears should be shed; she almost thanks the gods because she is selected as this instrument. So is Antigone great in her pain. Here again I can show a difference between Greek and modern tragedy. It is genuinely Greek for Philoctetes to complain that there is no one who knows what he suffers; it is a deep human need to wish that others should realize this; reflective grief, however, does not desire this. It does not occur to Antigone to wish that anyone should understand her grief, but on the other hand, in relation to her father, she feels it to be as aesthetically just that she should sorrow as that a man should suffer punishment when he has done wrong. While, therefore, the very conception that it is predestined that the living should be buried alive, wrings from Antigone in the Greek tragedy, the outburst of sorrow:

> O mockery of my woe!
> I go to the strong mound of yon strange tomb
> All hapless, having neither part nor room
> With those who live or those who die,

our Antigone can say it about her whole life. The difference is extraordinary; there is a factual truth in her assertion which makes the pain less. If our Antigone should say the same, then it would be unreal, but this unreality is the real pain. The Greeks do not express themselves precisely, just because the reflection which goes with this was not present in their lives. So when Philoctetes complains that he lives solitary and forsaken on a desert island, his assertion has in it an external truth; when, on the other hand, our Antigone feels pain in her solitude, then is the fact that she is alone figurative, but just because of this, her pain is real pain.

As far as tragic guilt is concerned, it consists partly in the fact that she buries her brother, partly in connection with her father's sorry fate, which was understood from the two preceding tragedies. Here again I come to the peculiar dialectic which posits the guilt of the family in relation to the individual. This is the hereditary guilt. If one generally considers dialectics fairly abstractly, one thinks more particularly of the logical movement. However, life will soon teach one that there are many kinds of dialectics, that almost every passion has its own. The dialectic, therefore, which posits the guilt of the race or the family in connection with a particular subject, so that he not only suffers under it—for this is a natural consequence against which one would vainly try to harden himself— but bears the guilt, participates in it, this dialectic is foreign to us, has nothing compelling for the modern mind. If a man, however, were to contemplate regeneration in terms of ancient tragedy, then must every individual contemplate his own regeneration, not merely in a spiritual sense, but in the finite sense of the rebirth of family and race. The dialectic which posits the individual in connection with family and race, is not a subjective dialectic, for this, on the contrary, raises the connection and the individual out of the continuity; it is an objective dialectic. It is essentially piety. To preserve this cannot be regarded as something injurious to the individual. In our age one permits something in a natural relation which he will not permit in a spiritual relation. Still, one would not wish to be so isolated, so unnatural, that one would not regard the family as a whole, of which one might say that when one member suffers, then all suffer. One does this involuntarily, otherwise why is a particular individual so afraid that another branch of the family may bring disgrace upon him, unless because he feels that he will suffer from it? This suffering the individual must obviously take with him, whether he will or not. But since the point of departure is the individual, not the family, this forced suffering becomes maximum; he feels that a man cannot become master over his own nature, but he desires this as far as possible. On the other hand, if the individual sees nature as a factor in his truth, this expresses itself in the spiritual world so that the individual becomes a participant in the guilt. This is a result many, perhaps, fail to understand, but then neither do they apprehend the tragic. If an individual is isolated, then he is either absolutely the creator of his own destiny, in which case nothing tragic remains, but only the evil—for it is not even tragic that an individual should be blindly engrossed in himself, it is his own fault—or the individuals are only modifications of the eternal substance of existence, and so again the tragic is lost.

With regard to the tragic guilt, the difference in the modern is readily apparent, after this has assimilated the ancient, for there something can really be said about this. The Greek Antigone participates with a filial piety in her father's guilt, as does also our modern one; but to the Greek Antigone her father's guilt and suffering is an external fact, a disquieting fact, which her sorrow does not alter (*quod non volvit in pectore*); and insofar as she herself personally, as a natural consequence, suffers under her father's guilt, this is again on the whole an external fact. It is otherwise with our Antigone. I assume that Oedipus is dead. Even while he lived Antigone had been aware of this secret, but she had not had courage to confide in her father. By his death she is deprived of the only way by which she could be freed from her secret. To confide it now to any living being would be to disgrace her father; her life acquires meaning for her, which she dedicates by her inviolable silence, daily almost hourly, in showing him the last honors. Of one thing, however, she is ignorant, whether her father himself had known this secret or not. In the modern tragedy this causes the unrest in her sorrow, the ambiguity in her pain. She loves her father with all her soul, and this love transports her out of herself and into her father's guilt; as the fruit of such a love, she feels herself alienated from mankind; she feels her own guilt the more she loves her father; only with him could she find rest, as equally guilty they would sorrow together. But while her father lived she had not been able to confide her sorrow to him, for she did not know whether he knew about it, and consequently there was a possibility of depressing him in a similar pain. And yet, was his guilt less if he had not known about it? The movement here is constantly relative. If Antigone had not known with certainty the actual relationship, then she would be insignificant, then she would have had nothing more than a suspicion to fight against, and that contains too little of the tragic to interest us. But she does know everything; yet even in this knowledge there is still an ignorance which can always keep sorrow in movement, always transform it into pain. Then, too, she is constantly at odds with her environment. Oedipus lives in the popular estimation as a fortunate king, honored and acclaimed; Antigone herself has admired as well as loved her father. She participates in every celebration and festival in his honor; she is more enthusiastic about him than any other young girl in the realm; her thoughts constantly turn back to him; she is praised throughout the kingdom as a model, loving daughter, and yet this enthusiasm is the only way in which she can give her sorrow any relief. Her father is always in her thoughts, but in what way is her painful secret. And yet she dares not give way to her sorrow, dares not grieve; she feels how much depends on her; she fears if anyone saw her suffering that people would begin to ask questions, and so, on this side too, she knows not sorrow but pain.

Considered in this way, I think that Antigone can really interest us; I think you will not reproach my extravagance nor my paternal partiality when I believe that she dares attempt this tragic subject, and dares appear in a tragedy. So far she is only an epic figure, and the tragic in her is only an epic interest.

It is not so difficult to discover a connection into which she might fit; in this respect we may readily be content with what the Greek tragedy gives. She has a sister living, who is, I assume, older than herself and married. Her mother might also be living. That these are naturally always subordinate characters is self-evident, as is the fact that the tragedy acquires an epic moment at all, such as the Greek has, without its needing to be so conspicuous; still, the monologue will here always play the principal role, even if it must be assisted by the situation. One must imagine everything united about this one chief interest which constitutes Antigone's life content, and when the whole is set in order, then the question arises as to how the dramatic interest is brought about.

Our heroine, as she has been presented in the foregoing, is on the point of passing over a moment of her life, she is about to become wholly spiritual, something nature does not tolerate. With the depth of soul she possesses, she must necessarily love with an extraordinary passion, if she does fall in love. Here, consequently, I encounter the dramatic interest—Antigone is in love, and I say it with pain. Antigone is head over heels in love. Here manifestly is the tragic collision. One ought generally to be a little more particular about what one calls a tragic collision. The more sympathetic the colliding forces are, the deeper but also the more homogeneous they are, the more important the collision. Hence she is in love, and he who is the object of her affections knows that she loves him. My Antigone is no ordinary woman, and consequently her dowry is unusual—it is her pain. She cannot belong to a man without this dowry, she feels that would be very hazardous; to conceal it from such an observer would be impossible, to wish to conceal it would be a betrayal of her love; but can she marry him with it? Dare she confide it to any human being, even to the beloved? Antigone has strength; the question is not whether for her own sake, to relieve her heart, she should reveal something of her pain, for she can indeed bear this without assistance; but the question is, can she justify this to the dead, even if she really suffers in a way by revealing her secret; for her own life, too, is sorrowfully interwoven with this. This, however, does not trouble her. The question is only concerning her father. Consequently the collision from this side is of a sympathetic nature. Her life which was formerly peaceful and quiet, now becomes violent and passionate, always of course within herself, and her speech here begins to be pathetic. She struggles with herself, she has been willing to sacrifice her life to her secret, but now she must sacrifice her love. She conquers, that is to say, the secret conquers, and she loses. Now comes the second collision, for in order that the tragic collision should really be profound, the colliding forces must be homogeneous. The collision just described had not this quality; for the collision is really between her love for her father and for herself, and not whether her own love is too great a sacrifice. The other colliding force is the sympathetic love for her beloved. He knows he is loved, and boldly risks his attack. Her reserve seems admirable to him; he notices that there must be quite peculiar difficulties, but he thinks they cannot be insurmountable to him. What is all important to him is to be able to convince her of how much he loves her, to persuade her that his life is over if he is obliged to relinquish her love. His passion at last becomes something almost unfair, but only the more ingenious because of her resistance. With every assurance of his love, he increases her pain, with every sigh he sinks the dart of sorrow deeper and deeper into her heart. He leaves no means untried to influence her. He knows, as did everyone, how deeply she had loved her father. He meets her at the grave of Oedipus, where she had gone to find relief for her emotion, where she surrenders herself to her longing for her father, even though this longing is mingled with pain because she does not know how she would meet him again, whether he was conscious of his own guilt or not. Her lover surprises her, and he adjures her by the love she bore her father; he notes that he makes an unusual impression upon her; he persists, he hopes for everything by this means, and he does not know that he has really worked against himself.

Consequently, the interest centers about his being able to wrest her secret from her. To allow her to become momentarily deranged and thus to betray her secret, would not help. The colliding forces are so evenly matched that action becomes impossible for the tragic individual. Her pain is now increased by her love, by her sympathetic suffering with him she loves. Only in death can she find peace; so her whole life is dedicated to sorrow, and she has, as it were, established a limit, a dam, for the evil destiny, which might perhaps fatally have transmitted itself to succeeding generations. Only in the moment of death can she admit the intensity of her love, only admit that she belongs to him in the moment that she does not belong to him. When Epaminondas was wounded in the battle of Mantinea, he left the arrow sticking in the wound until he heard that the battle was won, because he knew that the instant it was drawn out, he would die. So our Antigone bore her secret in her heart like an arrow, life constantly plunged it deeper and deeper within, without depriving her of life, for as long as it remained in her heart she could live, but in the moment it was drawn out, she must die. The beloved must constantly strive to wrest her secret from her, and yet this means her certain death. Who, then, is responsible for her death, the living or the dead? In a certain sense, the dead, and just as Hercules had predicted that he would not be slain by the living but by the dead, so this applies to her, insofar as the memory of her father is the cause of her death; in another sense it was caused by the living, insofar as her unhappy love is the occasion for her memory destroying her.

Selected Bibliography

There has been no attempt to make this bibliography as inclusive as possible. To do so would require a volume in itself. The books and articles listed here, in addition to the sources used for the text (listed elsewhere), constitute a basic working bibliography for all students interested in the subject of tragedy.

Abel, Lionel. *Metatheatre.* New York: Hill and Wang, 1963.

Abel, Lionel (ed.). *Moderns on Tragedy.* New York: Fawcett, 1967.

Adolf, Helen. "The Essence and Origin of Tragedy." *Journal of Aesthetics and Art Criticism,* vol. X, no. 2, December 1951.

Anderson, Maxwell. *The Essence of Tragedy.* Washington, D.C.: Anderson House, 1939.

Auden, W. A. *The Dyer's Hand.* New York: Random House, 1962.

Barrett, William. *Irrational Man.* New York: Doubleday, 1958.

Bentley, Eric. *The Playwright as Thinker.* New York: Harcourt Brace Jovanovich, 1957.

Berdyaev, Nicolas. *The Destiny of Man.* London: G. Bles, 1948.

Blau, Herbert. *The Impossible Theatre.* New York: Macmillan 1964.

Bodkin, Maud. *Archetypal Patterns in Poetry.* Oxford: Oxford University Press, 1963.

Bradley, A. C. *Shakespearean Tragedy.* London: Macmillan 1904.

Brereton, Geoffrey. *Principles of Tragedy.* Coral Gables, Fla.: University of Miami Press, 1968.

Brooks, Cleanth (ed.). *Tragic Themes in Western Literature.* New Haven, Conn.: Yale University Press, 1955.

Brooks, Cleanth, and Robert B. Heilman. *Understanding Drama.* New York: Holt, Rinehart and Winston, 1945.

Burke, Kenneth. *A Grammar of Motives.* Englewood Cliffs, N.J.: Prentice-Hall, 1945.

Caillois, Roger. *Man and the Sacred.* New York: The Free Press, 1960.

Calarco, N. Joseph. *Tragic Being: Apollo and Dionysus in Western Drama.* University of Minnesota Press, 1968.

Campbell, Joseph. *The Hero With a Thousand Faces.* New York: New American Library (Meridian Books), 1949.

Camus, Albert. "On the Future of Tragedy." *Lyrical and Critical Essays.* New York: Random House (Vintage Books), 1968.

Camus, Albert. *The Myth of Sisyphus and Other Essays.* New York: Random House (Vintage Books), 1955.

Camus, Albert. *The Rebel.* New York: Random House (Vintage Books), 1956.

Corrigan, Robert W. *The Theatre in Search of a Fix.* New York: Delacorte Press, 1963.

DeWitt, Norman J. "Tragedy and Personal Humanism," Introduction to *Renunciation as a Tragic Focus,* by E. H. Falk. Minneapolis: University of Minnesota Press, 1954.

Dodds, E. R. *The Greeks and the Irrational.* Berkeley, Ca.: University of California Press, 1951.

Downer, Alan. "The Life of Our Design." *Hudson Review*, vol. II, no. 2, March 1949.

Eberhart, Richard. "Tragedy as Limitation: Comedy as Control and Resolution." *Tulane Drama Review*. vol. VI, no. 4, June 1962.

Eliade, Mircea. *The Sacred and the Profane*. New York: Harcourt Brace Jovanovich (Harvest Books), 1961.

Else, Gerald F. *Aristotle's Poetics: The Argument*. Cambridge, Mass.: Harvard University Press, 1957.

Else, Gerald F. *The Origin and Early Form of Greek Tragedy*. Cambridge, Mass.: Harvard University Press, 1965.

Falk, Doris V. *Eugene O'Neill and the Tragic Tension*. New Brunswick, N.J.: Rutgers University Press, 1958.

Falk, Eugene H. *Renunciation as a Tragic Focus*. Minneapolis: University of Minnesota Press, 1954.

Farnham, Willard. *Shakespeare's Tragic Frontier*. Berkeley: University of California Press, 1950.

Fergusson, Francis. *The Human Image in Dramatic Literature*. New York: Doubleday (Anchor Books), 1957.

Fergusson, Francis. *The Idea of a Theater*. Princeton University Press, 1949.

Fergusson, Francis. "*Macbeth* as an Imitation of an Action." *English Institute Essays: 1951*. New York: Columbia University Press, 1952.

Frye, Prosser. *Romance and Tragedy*. Lincoln: University of Nebraska Press, 1961.

Gassner, John. *Theater at the Crossroads*. New York: Holt, Rinehart, and Winston, 1960.

Gassner, John. *The Theater in Our Times*. New York: Crown, 1954.

Girard, René. *Violence and the Sacred*. Baltimore: Johns Hopkins University Press, 1977.

Goheen, Robert F. "Aspects of Dramatic Symbolism: Three Studies of the *Oresteia*." *American Journal of Philology*, vol. LXXVI, no. 2, March 1955.

Goheen, Robert F. *The Imagery of Sophocles' Antigone*. Princeton University Press, 1951.

Goldman, Michael. *The Actor's Freedom: Toward a Theory of Drama*. New York: Viking Press, 1975.

Green, W. C. *Moira*. Cambridge, Mass.: Harvard University Press, 1944.

Grene, David. *Reality and the Heroic Pattern: Last Plays of Ibsen, Shakespeare, and Sophocles*. University of Chicago Press, 1967.

Hall, James W. *The Tragic Comedians*. Bloomington: Indiana University Press, 1962.

Hathorn, Richmond Y. *Tragedy, Myth, and Mystery*. Bloomington: Indiana University Press, 1962.

Heilman, Robert B. *The Iceman, The Arsonist, and The Troubled Agent: Tragedy and Melodrama on the Modern Stage*. Seattle: University of Washington Press, 1973.

Heilman, Robert B. *Tragedy and Melodrama: Versions of Experience*. Seattle: University of Washington Press, 1968.

Heller, Erich. *The Disinherited Mind*. New York: New American Library (Meridian Books), 1957.

Henn, T. R. *The Harvest of Tragedy*. London: Methuen, 1956.

Hoy, Cyrus. *The Hyacinth Room: An Investigation into the Nature of Comedy, Tragedy, and Tragicomedy*. New York: Knopf, 1964.

Jekels, Ludwig. "The Psychology of Pity." *Selected Papers*, New York: International Universities Press, 1952.

Jones, Ernest. *Hamlet and Oedipus*. New York: Doubleday (Anchor Books), 1949.

Kaufmann, Walter. *Tragedy and Philosophy*. New York: Doubleday, 1968.

Kermode, Frank. *The Sense of an Ending*. New York: Oxford University Press, 1967.

Kitto, H. D. F. *Form and Meaning in Drama*. London: Methuen, 1956.

Kitto, H. D. F. *Greek Tragedy: A Literary Study*. London: Methuen, 1939.

Klapp, Orrin E. *Heroes, Villains, and Fools*. Englewood Cliffs, N.J.: Prentice Hall, 1962.

Koestler, Arthur. *The Age of Longing*. New York: Macmillan, 1951.

Kott, Jan. *Shakespeare Our Contemporary*. New York: Doubleday, 1964.

Kott, Jan. *The Eating of the Gods*. New York: Random House, 1973.

Krook, Dorothea. *Elements of Tragedy*. New Haven, Conn.: Yale University Press, 1969.

Krutch, Joseph Wood. *"Modernism" in Modern Drama*. Ithaca, N.Y.: Cornell University Press, 1953.

Leavis, F. R. *The Common Pursuit*. New York: George W. Stewart, 1952.

Lenson, David. *Achilles' Choice*. Princeton University Press, 1975.

Maeterlinck, Maurice. *The Treasure of the Humble*. New York: Dodd, Mead, 1914.

Mandel, Oscar. *A Definition of Tragedy*. New York University Press, 1961.

McCollom, William. *Tragedy*. New York: Macmillan, 1957.

Michel, Laurence, and Sewall, Richard B. (eds.). *Tragedy: Modern Essays in Criticism*. Englewood Cliffs, N.J.: Prentice Hall, 1963.

Miller, Arthur. *The Theatre Essays of Arthur Miller*. New York: Viking Press, 1978.

Moravia, Alberto. "The Sterility of Suffering." *Yale Review*, vol. 47, no. 2, December 1957.

Muller, Herbert. *The Spirit of Tragedy*. New York: Knopf, 1956.

Niebuhr, Reinhold, *Beyond Tragedy*. New York: Scribners, 1938.

O'Connor, William Van. *Climates of Tragedy*. Baton Rouge: Louisiana University Press, 1943.

Olson, Elden. *Tragedy and the Theory of Drama*. Detroit: Wayne State University Press, 1961.

Pottle, F. A. "Catharsis." *Yale Review*, vol. 40, no. 4, June 1951.

Prior, Moody. *The Language of Tragedy*. New York: Columbia University Press, 1947.

Raglan, Lord. *The Hero*. London: Watts, 1949.

Rahv, Philip. *The Myth and the Powerhouse*. New York: Farrar, Straus, and Giroux, 1965.

Rank, Otto. *Myth and the Birth of the Hero*. New York: Johnson Reprints, 1970.

Ranson, J. C. *The World's Body*. Port Washington, N.Y.: Kennikat Press, 1938.

Raphael, D. D. *The Paradox of Tragedy*. Bloomington: Indiana University Press, 1960.

Roberts, Patrick. *The Psychology of Tragic Drama*. London: Routledge and Kegan Paul, 1975.

Rosenberg, James L. "Melodrama." From *The Context and Craft of Drama*, edited by Robert W. Corrigan and James C. Rosenberg. New York: Harper & Row, 1964.

Santayana, George. "Tragic Philosophy." *Scrutiny*, vol. 4, no. 4, March 1936.

Schwarz, Alfred. *From Büchner to Beckett: Dramatic Theory and the Modes of Tragic Drama*. Athens: Ohio University Press, 1978.

Scott, Nathan (ed.). *The Tragic Vision and the Christian Faith*. New York: Haddam House, 1957.

Snell, Bruno. *The Discovery of the Mind*. Cambridge, Mass.: Harvard University Press, 1953.

Steiner, George. *The Death of Tragedy*. New York: Knopf, 1961.

Terzakis, Angelos. *Homage to the Tragic Muse*. Boston: Houghton Mifflin, 1978.

Unamuno, Miguel de. *The Tragic Sense of Life*. New York: Dover, 1954.

Vinaver, Eugène. *Racine and Poetic Tragedy*. New York: Hill and Wang, 1959.

Warshow, Robert. "The Gangster as Tragic Hero." *The Immediate Experience*. New York: Doubleday, 1962.

Wasserman, E. H. "The Pleasures of Tragedy." *ELH*, vol. 14, no. 4, December 1947.

Weisinger, Herbert. *Tragedy and the Paradox of the Fortunate Fall.* East Lansing: Michigan State University Press, 1953.

Wheelwright, Philip. *The Burning Fountain.* Bloomington: Indiana University Press, 1954.

Whitman, Cedric. *Sophocles: A Study of Heroic Humanism.* Cambridge, Mass.: Harvard University Press, 1951.

Wilbur, Richard. "The Existential Hero." *Partisan Review*, vol. XXIX, no. 4, December 1962.

Yeats, W. B. *The Cutting of an Agate.* New York: Macmillan, 1912.